Patterns of American Jurisprudence

Patterns of American Jurisprudence

NEIL DUXBURY

CLARENDON PRESS · OXFORD

Oxford University Press, Great Clarendon Street, Oxford OX2 6DP
Oxford New York
Athens Auckland Bangkok Bogota Bombay
Buenos Aires Calcutta Cape Town Dar es Salaam
Delhi Florence Hong Kong Istanbul Karachi
Kuala Lumpur Madras Madrid Melbourne
Mexico City Nairobi Paris Singapore
Taipei Tokyo Toronto
and associated companies in
Berlin Ibadan

Oxford is a trade mark of Oxford University Press

Published in the United States
by Oxford University Press Inc., New York

First published 1995
First issued in paperback (with corrections) 1997

British Library Cataloguing in Publication Data
Data available

Library of Congress Cataloging in Publication Data
Data available
ISBN 0–19–825850–X
ISBN 0–19–826491–7 (Pbk)

Printed in Great Britain
on acid-free paper by
Bookcraft Ltd., Midsomer Norton, Avon

For Mary

Acknowledgements

This book represents an accumulation of debts, most of which I shall never extinguish. Various portions of the book have formed the basis of papers which I have delivered at a number of institutions. I should like to thank the organizers of and participants in staff seminars and workshops which I have presented at the universities of Belfast, Birmingham, Chicago, Edinburgh, Glasgow, Hull, Kent, Nottingham, Toronto, Virginia and Warwick, and at the University of California at Berkeley, the Benjamin N. Cardozo School of Law, New York, Carleton University, Ottawa, the Federal Judicial Center, Washington, DC, George Mason University, Virginia, Georgetown University Law Center, Washington, DC, Osgoode Hall Law School, Toronto, Queen Mary and Westfield College, London, the State University of New Jersey (Rutgers) at Camden and the State University of New York at Buffalo. I am also indebted to many individuals—Philip Allott, Jack Balkin, Ronald Coase, Sean Doran, Ronald Dworkin, Robert Ellickson, Richard Epstein, Bill Eskridge, Marie Fox, Walter Gellhorn, Andrew Griffiths, Rosalyn Higgins, Tony Honoré, Joseph Jaconelli, Tim Jones, Laura Kalman, Duncan Kennedy, Edmund Kitch, Craig Klafter, Nicola Lacey, Joe McCahery, Neil MacCormick, Myres McDougal, Henry Manne, Tim Murphy, Dennis Patterson, Edward Purcell, Dick Risk, the late Albert Sacks, Colin Scott, Nigel Simmonds, Robert Stevens, David Sugarman, Cass Sunstein, Peter Teachout, Mark Tushnet, the late Ronnie Warrington, Harry Wellington, Gillian White and Ted White—for comments on drafts and for other forms of assistance.

Certain people have been extremely helpful. The staff on the Inter-Library Loans counter at the John Rylands University Library, Manchester, ought to hide under their desks when they see me approaching. But they never do. Nor do they seem to know the meaning of the word, failure. My current dean, Rodney Brazier, has been unstinting in his support of my research. Besides being equally supportive, my previous dean, Anthony Ogus, has made me appreciate that law and economics is a subject deserving of serious study. While I have been working on this book, Peter Goodrich, Richard Posner, Jack Schlegel and William Twining have provided me with encouragement, criticism and all manner of assistance—more than I have deserved from any of them, given that I have not always treated their own works sympathetically. Finally my colleague, Martin Loughlin, has more than repaid any debt he might think he owes me. Without his criticisms, his generosity and his remarkable enthusiasm for the pursuit of ideas, I should have found writing this book a much less pleasurable experience.

Manchester, England
September 1994

Contents

Introduction
Jurisprudence as Intellectual History

What is jurisprudence? More or less anyone who has studied or taught the subject will have asked, or have been asked, this question, and they will know that it cannot satisfactorily be met with a stock answer. Many different types of intellectual endeavour go under the name of jurisprudence. A characterization of the subject which encompasses all these different types of endeavour will be so broad and so bland as to be worthless. The word jurisprudence is shorthand for a multitude of ideas; and there can be no universal consensus concerning what makes an idea 'jurisprudential'.

The term, 'American jurisprudence' is hardly less ambiguous. Not only does it denote different things for different people, but those who have attempted to explain and develop the subject have tended to rely on certain key concepts and themes in order to represent a variety of ideas about law. Terms like 'formalism' and 'realism' are rarely used in an homogeneous fashion: every expositor of American jurisprudence seems to have his or her own personal slant on what these and other terms signify. Lack of agreement over such terms—whether, for example, it is correct to characterize pre-realist jurisprudence as formalist, scientist, conceptualist, or whatever—and over what they might be taken to mean is something to which those engaged in American jurisprudence seem resigned. Like anyone faced with the task of explaining jurisprudence, those who concern themselves with American jurisprudence in particular recognize the necessity of thinking and writing in shorthand. A word like formalism will inevitably come to represent a variety of ideas about law, and disagreements are bound to arise over ways in which the word is understood.

There is plenty of shorthand to be found in this book; and there are many points at which particular interpretations and applications of this shorthand might be contested. For some readers, for example, the exposition of formalism presented in Chapter 1 is likely to provoke nothing if not disagreement. But the point of this book is not to suggest that there is a definite set of ideas about law which any particular jurisprudential concept or theme ought properly to denote. The premiss of the book, rather, is that the ways in which jurisprudential concepts and themes are interpreted and applied influence the manner in which ideas about law come to be understood historically. The primary objective of this book, in other words, is not to explore generally the problems that might arise from employing a handful of concepts and themes to explain a comparably large variety of ideas about law, but to try to demonstrate that our use of concepts and themes affects the way in which we represent the history of legal ideas.

The manner in which the interpretation and application of jurisprudential concepts and themes influences the history of legal ideas seems, in the United States, to be particularly significant and problematic. There runs, throughout this book, a distrust of what might be termed the 'pendulum swing' vision of American jurisprudential history. This vision, I believe, dominates American jurisprudential discourse; and its dominance seems to be attributable to the manner in which many of those engaged in American jurisprudence have conceptualized their subject matter. The problem, in essence, is that writers in American jurisprudence have tended to develop certain basic themes—in particular, the themes of legal formalism and legal realism—in an over-emphatic, sometimes over-dramatic, fashion. Formalism and realism have been made into more than mere shorthand. They have become theories, movements, schools of thought. As such, they are usually seen to cancel one another out. Thus it is that there exists a fairly conventional history of American jurisprudence since the 1870s: first there was formalism, epitomized by the Langdellian revolution; then came the realist revolt against formalism; after which came the renaissance of formalism, exemplified by both process jurisprudence and law and economics, which was superseded by the return to realism in the form of critical legal studies. The pendulum of history swings back and forth, accordingly, between formalism and realism. Sometimes the concepts are varied—formalism becomes scientism, realism becomes pragmatism, or whatever—but the basic pendulum-swing vision of American jurisprudential history remains more or less constant.

This book challenges that vision. The central thesis of the book is that American jurisprudence since 1870 is characterized not by the pendulum-swing view of history but by complex patterns of ideas. Jurisprudential ideas are rarely born; equally rarely do they die.[1] Indeed, even the event which is commonly considered to mark the birth of the modern American law school—the introduction of the case method of instruction at Harvard—was not really a birth; rather, it interconnected with and complemented certain other late nineteenth-century pedagogic developments aimed at raising the professional standards of the bar.[2] Ideas—along

[1] In the past, I have failed to recognize this. See e.g. Neil Duxbury, 'The Birth of Legal Realism and the Myth of Justice Holmes', *Anglo-American L. Rev.*, 20 (1991), 81–100.

[2] The introduction of the case method at Harvard was preceded, for example, by similar profession-enhancing educational initiatives at Columbia under the deanship of Theodore Dwight. See Chapter 1. Recently, it has been shown that although the pedagogic innovations at Harvard in the 1870s were intended to raise—and ultimately succeeded in raising—

with values, attitudes and beliefs—tend to emerge and decline, and sometimes they are revived and refined. But rarely do we see them born or die. History is not quite like that.

What does it mean to characterize American jurisprudence in terms of patterns of ideas? The pendulum swing vision of American jurisprudential history is premissed on a fairly simple pattern. Formalism and realism perpetually supersede one another: as one dies, the other is born or is reborn. The purpose of this book is to try to show that the history of American jurisprudence since 1870 does not conform to this pattern but displays a variety of patterns. Chapter 1 begins with a discussion of late nineteenth and early twentieth-century legal formalism in the United States. If one attempts to ascertain the jurisprudential significance of this theme at that time, two distinct formalist perspectives emerge. First of all, there evolved a species of formalism in the American law schools. While the Langdellian notion of legal science was not quite as inflexible as many commentators have assumed,[3] it was nonetheless premissed on the belief that law may and indeed ought to be conceived as a small body of formally-interrelated fundamental doctrinal principles—principles which are to be derived from upper-court (often old English) decisions. Secondly, there evolved a rather different species of formalism in the courts. In the late nineteenth and early twentieth-centuries, the United States Supreme Court in particular advanced a peculiarly Social Darwinist-inspired version of *laissez-faire*, arguing that real inequalities of bargaining power ought not to be the subject of regulatory legislation, because such inequalities are a natural and desirable consequence of a free market system which guarantees a formal equality of bargaining rights among citizens. It ought to be stressed that these two types of formalist thought are not taken to represent legal formalism *in toto*. Rather, it is argued that these two strands of thought epitomize legal formalism as it was understood at that time.

These two strands of thought also represent the formalism against which realist jurisprudence reacted. The elaboration of this point requires a good deal of caution. The second half of Chapter 1 represents an effort to demonstrate that there was never a 'revolt against formalism'. The movement away from formalist legal thinking was very slow and hesitant. In fact—and this is the basic point of Chapter 2—the endeavour to expose the shortcomings of formalism was far from successful: in some ways,

standards at the bar, practitioners within the American Bar Association were often very suspicious of the Harvard style of legal education. See William P. LaPiana, *Logic and Experience: The Origin of Modern American Legal Education* (New York: Oxford University Press, 1994), 132–147.

[3] See LaPiana, *Logic and Experience*, 122.

realist jurisprudence failed to progress significantly beyond formalist legal thought; and indeed, to a certain degree, it remained fixed in the clutches of such thought, in so far as the implications of certain realist arguments were demonstrably formalist. A more general purpose of Chapter 2 is to try to provide a sense of what realist jurisprudence was actually about. There was no realist movement. Realism was nothing more than an intellectual mood. Nor is it correct to regard realist jurisprudence as a celebration of uncertainty in law. When various so-called realists highlighted the existence of legal uncertainty, they were merely articulating—and, in some cases, lamenting—what they saw. The image of realism as a jurisprudence of tyranny, as an argument in favour of might equals right, is the fabrication of unsympathetic critics.[4] So-called realists recognized—but struggled to come to terms with the fact—that law is political.

Why should the proposition that law is political be considered in any sense troublesome? One particular outgrowth of realist jurisprudence, policy science, was premissed on the notion that, in the United States at least, the political nature of law ought not to be considered troublesome at all. Chapter 3 is devoted to the work of Harold Lasswell and Myres McDougal, the principal proponents of policy science. So long as lawyers subscribe to the right kind of politics, Lasswell and McDougal believed, the use of law to promote political objectives ought not to be discouraged. One of the primary purposes of policy science was to suggest how legal education might be reformed so that future lawyers could be better educated in the values of American democracy. By the end of the Second World War, McDougal in particular was beginning to develop policy science as a theory of international law. Not only should the law schools of the post-war era be concerned with promoting American democratic values within the national legal profession, he argued, but post-war scholars of international law in the United States ought to be promoting these values throughout the world. There rest, accordingly, two assumptions at the heart of the policy science perspective: first of all, that in the United States there is no reason to fear the political nature of law since American liberal democratic values are good values; and secondly, that if other countries could be persuaded to import these values into their own legal systems, the future of humanity would seem much less insecure.

Policy science turned out, for a variety of reasons, to be an unsuccessful jurisprudential venture. Part of the problem with policy science was that its credibility depended on acceptance of the proposition that a legal framework which promotes American or American-style democratic values is very likely to be a desirable one. In fact, any political system—

[4] See Neil Duxbury, 'The Reinvention of American Legal Realism', *Legal Studies*, 12 (1992), 137–77.

even the American system—is subject to change, and sometimes change will be welcomed, at other times it will be opposed. Given the inevitability of change—and given that change may be for better or for worse—should law always follow the vagaries of politics?

In the years following the Second World War, certain American lawyers were beginning to argue ever more forthrightly that, while political concerns inevitably feature in the legislative arena, they ought never to determine the course of adjudication. Judges, after all, are not elected; they cannot be voted out of office for reaching political decisions of which citizens and lawyers generally disapprove. Furthermore, political adjudication is attractive only when courts adjudicate in an enlightened fashion. Those who advocate such adjudication offer only a jurisprudence for good times.

But if judges ought not to decide cases politically, what should they do? The central message of the process tradition in American jurisprudence is that judges ought to place their faith not in politics but in reason; and this requires that they endeavour to base controversial decisions on apolitical principles—principles, that is, which are so broad and general that they will command the respect of both sides to a dispute. According to representatives of the process tradition, courts, unlike the other institutions which make up the legal process, are peculiarly competent at elaborating such principles. This turn towards principle in American jurisprudence is sometimes regarded as a response to the lessons of legal realism. Given that most so-called realists had little to say about how to restrain political adjudication—given, furthermore, that certain realists appeared not to want to restrain such adjudication—many post-realist lawyers became ever more preoccupied with the endeavour to promote the virtues of principled judicial decision-making. Chapter 4 is an attempt to demonstrate, however, that the quest for principle in American jurisprudence ought not to be regarded merely as a response to realism. The process tradition, it is argued, certainly developed alongside and may even have preceded realist jurisprudence. The pendulum swing version of American jurisprudential history—the image of one 'movement' dying and being replaced by another—fails to capture the intellectual development which actually occurred.

This argument is taken further in Chapter 5. Commentators on law and economics in America have tended to conceive of it as a jurisprudential sub-discipline which is somehow related to legal realism. For some commentators, law and economics ought to be understood as a continuation of the realist tradition. For others, it represents a rebellion against that tradition. In fact—and this is the premiss of Chapter 5—it is neither. Even during the New Deal period, most of the legal–economic analysis which was being undertaken in the United States had no connection with realist jurisprudence. Indeed, law and economics at this time was comprised of little more than various isolated lawyers and economists doing their own things. There was certainly no law and economics movement. When, eventually, a law and economics movement did emerge in the United States, it grew not out of the realist tradition, but out of developments in neo-classical price theory. Neo-classical economics first made its mark on antitrust and certain other patently 'market-based' areas of law, and was then gradually broadened out and applied to legal fields which had commonly been assumed to lack a significant economic dimension. The principal objective of Chapter 5 is to try to demonstrate that to understand properly the significance and the appeal of—not to mention the controversy generated by—the modern law and economics tradition in the United States, it must be conceived not against the backdrop of American jurisprudence, but in relation to developments in economics, primarily at the University of Chicago, since the 1930s.

Unlike law and economics, critical legal studies in the United States has clear connections with the realist jurisprudential tradition. Such connections, it is argued in Chapter 6, can be easily exaggerated: critical legal studies is not merely realism revived. It is also argued—and this is the one point in this study where the pendulum swing vision of jurisprudential history seems not entirely inappropriate—that critical legal studies is in large measure a reaction to what is termed a search for consensus in American jurisprudence. This search is epitomized by the process tradition and, to a lesser degree, by neo-classical law and economics. Critical legal studies, with its roots in New Left politics, represents both a critique of the consensus assumptions embodied in liberal legal thought and also an attempt to visualize and speculate on the possibility of establishing a different set of social and legal arrangements founded on a new, post-liberal consensus. Quite what this new consensus would be comprised of—that is, what the fundamental values shared by members of the post-liberal society would be—is far from clear in the literature of critical legal studies. Certain recent developments in American jurisprudence, in feminism and race theory in particular, reveal an essential distrust of the critical legal project. This distrust stems from the fact that critical legal scholars have generally failed to indicate how the consensual foundations of the post-liberal society would accommodate the values, experiences and concerns of women and minorities.

It would have been easy to conclude this book with a denouement, by declaring critical legal studies to be 'dead'. As intimated earlier, however, it is a central premiss of this book that intellectual historians ought to be wary of using words like birth and death. By studying the emergence and decline of ideas—by showing, for example, how the emergence or decline of one idea may be connected to the emergence or decline of another, or by demonstrating how, sometimes, apparently closely related ideas are in fact hardly connected at all—we are able to find our way to the heart of jurisprudence. Ideas have histories, and jurisprudence is a much more enlightening and engaging enterprise when it focuses on those histories. When we concern ourselves with the history of ideas about law, we are likely to appreciate not only how certain ideas come to be discredited, but also, equally importantly, why they were ever considered to be significant in the first place.

1
The Challenge of Formalism

During this century, American legal thought has frequently been categorized in terms of historical periods. The correct demarcation of these periods has often been a matter for debate, though there seems to be some consensus that the first period ran from the 1780s (the end of the War of American Independence) to the 1860s (the outbreak of the American Civil War). This period saw the evolution of a distinct legal profession in the United States, as well as the emergence of the first generation of legal treatise writers.[1] Furthermore, this was the period during which the common law courts, in an effort to shape social and economic development, gradually broke with their traditional practice of deciding cases purely on an *ad hoc* basis and began 'to frame general doctrines based on a self-conscious consideration of social and economic policies'.[2] After the Civil War, American law began to enter into a period of formalism. Eschewing the general policy-making role, the courts returned to a narrower, deductive approach to decision-making whereby legal relationships were treated as somehow subsumed under a small collection of fundamental legal principles.[3] This formalistic conception of the judicial process was reflected also in the scientific orientation of the modern law school, as promoted by the first dean of Harvard, Christopher Columbus Langdell. The period of legal formalism waned during the first three decades of this century and was gradually replaced by a third period, the period of American legal realism,[4] which emerged largely as a reaction to legal formalism both in the courts and at Harvard.

This chapter addresses the second period of American legal history, the period of legal formalism. Not surprisingly, formalism may be regarded as the antecedent of the third period of American legal history, realism; and it is by treating formalism thus that it is possible to set the scene for the emergence of realism in the 1920s and 1930s. The purpose of this chapter,

[1] See Perry Miller, *The Life of the Mind in America: From the Revolution to the Civil War* (New York: Harcourt, Brace & World, 1965), 99–265.

[2] Morton J. Horwitz, *The Transformation of American Law 1780–1860* (Cambridge, Mass.: Harvard University Press, 1977), 2.

[3] Duncan Kennedy, *The Rise and Fall of Classical Legal Thought 1850–1940* (Cambridge, Mass.: unpublished mimeograph [on file with author: copy supplied by Professor Kennedy], 1975), v, 10–13.

[4] See Grant Gilmore, *The Ages of American Law* (New Haven, Conn.: Yale University Press, 1977), 68–98.

however, is not simply to describe or to trace a particular course of events. While legal formalism constitutes the backdrop to legal realism, while it forms the intellectual tradition against which so-called legal realists 'rebelled', the nature of the rebellion was by no means as straightforward as some commentators have cared to suggest. Indeed 'rebellion', I shall try to show, is rather too strong a word to describe the intellectual progression which occurred.

The thesis of this chapter is that the commonly accepted idea of a 'revolt against formalism' in late nineteenth-century American intellectual life is, certainly so far as jurisprudence is concerned, a myth. The great proto-realist champions of anti-formalism—most notably Oliver Wendell Holmes, but also Benjamin Cardozo, John Chipman Gray and Roscoe Pound—were, on many jurisprudential issues, resolute formalists; just as many of the legal realists who followed in their footsteps seemed equally unable to rid themselves of similar formalist prejudices. In the first part of this chapter, I shall examine what, in the context of late nineteenth and early twentieth-century American jurisprudence, legal formalism might be taken to mean. In the second part, I shall consider how, before the advent of legal realism, American jurisprudence began, if only hesitantly, to question the premisses of formalist legal thinking.

LEGAL FORMALISM: THE LAW SCHOOL AND THE COURTS

During the late nineteenth century, legal formalism was but a fragment of a larger picture. Formalism—the endeavour to treat particular fields of knowledge as if governed by interrelated, fundamental and logically demonstrable principles of science—dictated most nineteenth-century intellectual pursuits. In particular, positivism, classical economics and evolutionary biology exemplified a general endeavour on the part of nineteenth-century intellectuals to elevate specific areas of investigation to the status of genuine sciences. The same trend was also to be detected in disciplines as diverse as history, political science, psychology, ethics and law. By the late nineteenth century, however, cracks were beginning to appear in the formalist edifice. In economics, the evolutionist premisses of the Spencerian classical approach were subjected to the criticisms of Thorstein Veblen who, in his development of an 'anthropological' economic perspective, set the scene for the emergence of institutional economics in the early twentieth century; in philosophy, positivism was challenged by pragmatism; and in history, the nineteenth-century framework of narrow scientific inquiry was superseded by a contextual or 'historicist' methodology.[5] From discipline to discipline, a distinct notion

[5] See Morton White, *Social Thought in America: The Revolt Against Formalism* (Oxford: Oxford University Press, 1976; orig. publ. 1949).

of anti-formalism began to prevail. The anti-formalist tendencies exhibited by the different branches of the social sciences bore 'a strong family resemblance, strong enough to produce a feeling of sympathy in all who opposed what they called formalism in their respective fields'.[6]

One might assume, from the above, that the so-called 'revolt against formalism' was a reaction against the idea of science. But such an assumption would be incorrect. While anti-formalists challenged particular formalist conceptions of science, especially social science, they did not wish to dispense with the scientific framework altogether. The historicist James Harvey Robinson, for example, attempted to demonstrate the scientific character of history, but at the same time to distinguish his own contextual approach from the narrow and uncritical scientific empiricism of formalist historians such as Leopold von Ranke.[7] Thorstein Veblen, similarly, criticized classical economics from the perspective of what he termed 'business science'.[8] Many legal realists, too, in their reaction against formalism, attempted effectively to displace one dominant conception of legal science by replacing it with a different conception.

But what was this dominant conception of legal science? There were, in fact, two broad formalist conceptions of science which dominated legal thought during the post-Civil War period in American legal history, although only one of these conceptions might properly be termed a specifically-legal science. There was, first of all, in the universities, the emergence of the Landgellian science of law; and secondly, in the courts, there was the entrenched faith in *laissez-faire*. These, together, constituted the basis of legal formalism. As such, they provided the impetus and inspiration for the jurisprudential tendency which, during the 1920s, became known as legal realism. Yet, realism criticized Langdellianism and *laissez-faire* quite severely, both traditions were ultimately to survive the attack. Let us consider each of these traditions in turn.

The Tradition of Langdell

The story of the beginnings of Langdellian legal science must, for any American lawyer, be an historical commonplace. By the 1820s, American law was well on the way to developing an identity of its own. In contrast with their previous convention of deciding each and every case by the straightforward application of the English common law, the courts of most states were, by this time, in the process of developing their own indigenous legal principles and precedents. While English cases remained the principal

6 White, *Social Thought*, 12.

7 See ibid. 28–29.

8 See Joseph Dorfman, *Thorstein Veblen and His America* (New York: Viking, 1934), 155–6.

authoritative source for the courts, the emergence of a uniquely American branch of legal doctrine prompted at least two significant and interrelated developments. First of all, the emergence of indigenous precedent and doctrine was accompanied by the evolution of a distinctly American legal literature. 'The decisions of American courts, state and federal, were being published. Books on American law were beginning to appear as well as American republications—with added local annotations—of English books and case collections.'[9] Secondly, the growth of American law was accompanied by a concomitant growth of the American legal profession. Grasp of the basic principles of English common law could no longer be considered a suitable criterion for admission to the bar. Accordingly, in order to keep pace with the initiatives of the courts, the American bar was forced to raise its professional standards. The task of raising standards, and thereby maintaining the professional status of the bar, fell on the law schools.[10]

The first significant effort to raise the professional standards of the bar took place at Columbia University. In 1857, Columbia had established a School of Jurisprudence and, in the year following, had appointed as its

[9] Gilmore, *supra* n. 4, 23; and see more generally William E. Nelson, *Americanization of the Common Law: The Impact of Legal Change on Massachusetts Society 1760–1830* (Cambridge, Mass.: Harvard University Press, 1975).

[10] Obviously my discussion here is highly generalized. For a detailed account, cf. Robert Stevens, *Law School: Legal Education in America from the 1850s to the 1980s* (Chapel Hill: University of North Carolina Press, 1983), 3–34. John Henry Schlegel has argued that Stevens's thesis—that the American law school emerged in response to the bar's desire to raise professional standards—is too narrow in its scope. Schlegel takes the view that the overlap between the emergence of Langdellian legal science and the raising of professional legal standards was purely adventitious. At least part of the reason for the emergence of the Langdellian tradition, he argues, was that legal education, in the hands of Langdell and his followers, was evolving in line with the development of the social sciences. That is, law, like the late nineteenth-century social sciences, was 'staking out part of the intellectual world as its "turf", adopting a particular way of looking at that turf, a method as it were, and moving to cut out the "amateurs" who formerly had a claim to that turf'. John Henry Schlegel, 'Between the Harvard Founders and the American Legal Realists: The Professionalization of the American Law Professor', *Jnl. Leg. Educ.*, 35 (1985), 311–25 at 314. To interpret the rise of the Langdellian tradition solely according to legal factors is, as Schlegel suggests, to rely on a rather narrow historical perspective. This does not mean, however, that his own historical analysis is particularly satisfactory. Schlegel seems to assume that Langdell and other late nineteenth-century legal educators would have been aware of what was happening in the social sciences. Yet American academic lawyers of this period—and in this matter Langdell was exemplary—appear to have been well-nigh impervious to developments in other disciplines. See Paul D. Carrington, 'Aftermath', in P. Cane and J. Stapleton (eds.), *Essays for Patrick Atiyah* (Oxford: Clarendon Press, 1991), 113–49 at 134. Langdell himself wished to raise the study of law to the level of a science—but not to the level of a social science. By the 1870s, moreover, social scientists were well on the way to having staked out their various areas of 'turf', and the debate among the social scientific disciplines was now ascending to a new plane: namely, how was that turf to be tended? By 1870, Langdell had still to stake out the legal turf. The question which Schlegel's analysis raises is: if Langdell and his epigoni had wished to map out their own intellectual terrain in a manner akin to the strategy of the general social sciences, why did they not follow late nineteenth-century social scientists wholeheartedly and adopt an anti-formalist perspective on law?

dean a municipal lawyer, Theodore William Dwight. Dwight was the first American academic lawyer explicitly to heed the bar's plea for the modernization of the legal profession through the law schools. 'He felt that it was his mission to supersede the obsolete methods of instruction and thereby to elevate the standards of the whole legal profession.'[11] In particular, he introduced two significant pedagogic innovations. First, he initiated the practice of teaching law by the Socratic method; secondly, he was the first dean openly to encourage the appointment of practitioners to lecture upon particular areas of the law. The latter innovation, while ostensibly intended to supplement instruction provided by full-time law teachers, served in fact to strengthen links between the Columbia School of Jurisprudence and the New York Bar. By fostering and encouraging such links, Dwight proved to be something of a pioneer, for he was the first academic to attempt to develop American legal education in accordance with the interests of the late nineteenth-century legal profession.[12]

Dwight's innovations at Columbia were overshadowed, however, by the rise of the Harvard Law School. In 1869, Harvard University appointed a new president, Charles William Eliot. Eliot was primarily a mathematician and a chemist, though he was also an excellent administrator with a passion for educational reform.[13] In the early 1860s, Eliot had moved to Europe to study continental methods of education. The perfect opportunity to put his learning into effect arose when, in 1865, he was offered a post at the Massachusetts Institute of Technology. It was there that he set about designing an industrial laboratory with a view to revolutionizing the teaching of chemistry. Eliot dispensed with the traditional lecture method of instruction and replaced it with a textbook-based, 'classroom laboratory method', whereby students attempted the experiments set out in their manuals not in an effort to imitate or repeat the observations to be found therein, but to deduce 'general principles from concrete cases'.[14] Believing that similar teaching methods could be exported to other disciplines, Eliot appointed a New York City lawyer named Christopher Columbus Langdell to the newly-created post of Dean of the Harvard Law School. With this appointment, modern American legal education began to evolve.

Eliot promoted his educational innovations throughout all of the

[11] William Nelson Cromwell Foundation, *A History of the School of Law: Columbia University* (New York: Columbia University Press, 1955), 43.

[12] See generally William Nelson Cromwell Foundation, *A History of the School of Law*, 33–132.

[13] See Hugh D. Hawkins, *Between Harvard and America: The Educational Leadership of Charles W. Eliot* (New York: Oxford University Press, 1972).

[14] Anthony Chase, 'The Birth of the Modern Law School', *Am. J. Leg. Hist.*, 23 (1979), 329–48 at 334–35; see also David S. Clark, 'Tracing the Roots of American Legal Education—A Nineteenth-Century German Connection', *Rabels Zeitschrift für ausländisches und internationales Privatrecht*, 51 (1987), 313–33 at 318–19, 326–7.

academic departments at Harvard, and it is not surprising that they should have been particularly well received by Dean Langdell. Besides being an eminent scientist, Eliot was also a teacher possessed of great experience, vision and ambition. Langdell, in comparison, was a tyro, a newly-appointed figure to a newly-created post. As a typical nineteenth-century American lawyer, he was accustomed to reasoning and acting on the basis of precedent. In his new post, however, there was no precedent. He was the *fons et origo*. Accordingly, just as American lawyers traditionally had looked to the English common law in search of legal authorities, Langdell similarly looked to Eliot's method of teaching to find the separate but compatible 'jurisdiction' which would provide him with the precedential authority and guidance that he needed. It was by looking to Eliot that Langdell found the case method.

Langdell himself did not, strictly speaking, initiate the use of the case method in law teaching,[15] nor was he responsible for popularizing it—this was the achievement of his successor, James Bar Ames. By following the example of Eliot, nevertheless, Langdell not only established the use of the case method as a pedagogical device, but also promoted the idea that the case method is necessary to the teaching of law as a science. It is the idea that law is a science, and the promotion of this idea by the use of the case method, which constitutes his sole yet fundamental contribution to American legal education. The following quotation encapsulates his views on the matter:

> Law, considered as a science, consists of certain principles or doctrines. To have such a mastery of these as to be able to apply them with constant facility and certainty to the ever-tangled skein of human affairs, is what constitutes a true lawyer; and hence to acquire that mastery should be the business of every earnest student of law. Each of these doctrines has arrived at its present state by slow degrees; in other words, it is a growth, extending in many cases through centuries. This growth is to be traced in the main through a series of cases; and much the shortest and best, if not the only way of mastering the doctrine effectually is by studying the cases in which it is embodied. But the cases which are useful and necessary for this purpose at the present day bear an exceedingly small proportion to all that have been reported. The vast majority are useless, and worse than useless, for any purpose of systematic study. Moreover the number of fundamental legal doctrines is much less than is commonly supposed; the many different guises in which the same doctrine is constantly making its appearance, and the great extent to which legal treatises are a repetition of each other, being the cause of much misapprehension. If these doctrines could be so classified and arranged that

[15] On the use of the case method prior to Langdell, see Stevens, *supra* n. 10, 66 n. 14. On coming to Harvard, Langdell, for at least one semester, taught by the traditional lecture method. See Thomas C. Grey, 'Langdell's Orthodoxy' *U. Pittsburgh L. Rev.*, 45 (1983), 1–53 at 1 fn. 2.

each should be found in its proper place, and nowhere else, they would cease to be formidable from their number.[16]

Langdellian legal science can be seen to consist of four interrelated elements. First, there is the intense respect for *stare decisis*. For Langdell, to be able to discern the precedential status of any case is to have found the key to the science of law. Secondly, anyone gifted with the ability to discern in this fashion will of necessity realize that most reported cases are in fact unhelpful repetitions of extant principles and precedents. Thirdly, anyone who has realized that only a handful of cases are truly relevant to the science of law must also recognize that the number of fundamental legal doctrines is similarly limited. Fourthly, the task of the legal scientist is to classify these fundamental doctrines so as to demonstrate their logical interconnection, as well as to dispel the myth of their formidable number.

The teaching of this legal science depended on two further elements. First of all, there was the necessity of devising appropriate teaching materials. If law students were to learn law as a science, then they would require texts which contained all the relevant adjudicated cases, classified in a fashion which both suggested the logical interrelationship of fundamental doctrines and facilitated the sieving out of authoritative legal principles. If law teachers were properly to promote such scientific learning, then part of their task was to produce such texts. To this end, Langdell argued, the law library constituted the foundation of legal science, for it is there that students and teachers alike may discover the sources of law which are necessary to their respective pursuits. 'We have . . . constantly inculcated the idea that the library is the proper workshop of professors and students alike; that it is to us all that the laboratories of the university are to the chemists and physicists, the museum of natural history to the zoologists, the botanical garden to the botanists.'[17] Langdell's legal science was an attempt to transpose Eliot's educational methods into a law school setting. As Eliot himself observed, 'Professor Langdell's method resembled the laboratory method of teaching physical science, although he believed that the only laboratory the Law School needed was a library of printed books.'[18]

[16] Christopher Columbus Langdell, *A Selection of Cases on the Law of Contracts* (Boston: Little, Brown & Co., 1871), viii.

[17] Christopher Columbus Langdell, 'Harvard Celebration Speeches', *Law Q. Rev.*, 3 (1887), 123–5 at 124.

[18] Charles W. Eliot, *A Late Harvest: Miscellaneous Papers Written Between Eighty and Ninety* (Boston: Atlantic Monthly Press, 1924), 54; and see also his 'Langdell and the Law School', *Harvard L. Rev.*, 33 (1920), 518–25; and Charles R. McManis, 'The History of First Century American Legal Education: A Revisionist Perspective', *Washington Univ. L.Q.*, 59 (1981), 597–659 at 646–8. Some of Eliot's ideas were, nonetheless, unacceptable to the Harvard Law School of Langdell's era. See Robert W. Gordon, 'Legal Thought and Legal Practice in the Age of American Enterprise', in G. L. Geison (ed.), *Professions and Professional Ideologies in America* (Chapel Hill: University of North Carolina Press, 1983), 70–110, 127–39 at 75.

But Langdell and Eliot did not share an educational method; indeed, the similarities between their pedagogic approaches are more apparent than real. While, like Eliot, Langdell adopted a method of teaching centred around the 'laboratory', the textbook and the deducing of general principles from specific cases, the two men could hardly have subscribed to more opposing notions of science. Eliot was very much a twentieth-century scientist. Langdell's vision of science, in contrast, was less nineteenth century than Baconian.[19] Furthermore, the Harvard method of legal education as devised initially by Langdell was premissed not only on inductivism, but also on an implicit belief in the survival of the fittest.

The Darwinian implications of Langdell's approach may be discerned from what he considered to be the second element essential to a properly scientific legal education: namely, the case method of teaching. Up until the time of Langdell, most teaching in American law schools took the form of lectures. The lecture method usually amounted to little more than a professor standing before a class and reading passages from a legal treatise. Students generally were required neither to participate nor to think for themselves.[20] Langdell's case method changed all this. Rather than simply handing down a set of rules taken from a legal treatise, the professor, employing the case method, encouraged students to discover legal principles for themselves. As one legal realist, writing in the 1930s, explained: 'the case method begins with a judgment already given by a court. The Langdellian Socrates may then proceed to determine the value of the judgment by slight or great variations in the facts, until he has got what is an apparently satisfactory general proposition which will cover this case and a great many others.'[21] Under Langdell's system, students would be required to read all the relevant decisions in a particular field of the law—which decisions would be set out in their case-books—so that the professor could then, through rigorous questioning, enable students to discover for themselves not only the 'true' principles of the law but also how, on occasions, some judges have deviated from those principles.

As a pathway to legal competence, Langdell's case method proved, for students, to be both narrow and perilous. The cases which students were required to read were more often than not old English cases; and they would always be appellate cases. By focusing solely on appellate decisions, the case method inevitably highlighted judge-made law while excluding from its ambit the study of legislation. One consequence of this was that

[19] See Paul H. Kocher, 'Francis Bacon on the Science of Jurisprudence', *Jnl. of the History of Ideas*, 18 (1957), 3–26; M. H. Hoeflich, 'Law and Geometry: Legal Science from Leibniz to Langdell', *Am. J. Leg. Hist.*, 30 (1986), 95–121 at 119–21; and Stevens, *supra* n. 10, 52–3.

[20] On the nineteenth-century lecture system and its shortcomings, cf. Christopher G. Tiedman, 'Methods of Legal Education', *Yale L. J.*, 1 (1892), 150–8.

[21] Max Radin, 'The Education of a Lawyer' *California L. Rev.*, 25 (1937), 676–91 at 679.

the growth of administrative law scholarship in the United States remained effectively stultified until the early decades of the twentieth century.[22] Furthermore, the case method was considered, even in Langdell's era, to be a rather repetitive form of instruction.[23] Owing to its narrowness of scope, it offered little opportunity for professors to use and develop their research ideas in the course of teaching.[24] Most significantly of all, it was not a fully-fledged science. Though the library was the lawyer's laboratory, and though law was 'discovered' by way of a process vaguely resembling scientific induction, Langdell's method of education omitted one important scientific ingredient: the practical experiment. Langdell's legal scientist lacked clinical experience.[25]

Narrowness of scope, however, mattered little to the late nineteenth-century Harvard law student. For him,[26] the case method was often a rebarbative exercise which generated as much ritual humiliation as Socratic enlightenment. In 1873, Langdell appointed to his faculty an assistant professor named James Barr Ames. As a student under Langdell, Ames had proved remarkably adept at the case method—more adept, in fact, than Langdell himself—and, as a professor, he transformed that method into a particularly demanding art. As one of Ames's students explained:

> This art or technique in general involves a discussion of the cases with different members of the class. It usually begins by one member of the class being asked to state the case. . . . The teacher . . . secures from the student a decided opinion upon the problem. Whatever it is, the instructor should be prepared to break him down . . . If the instructor can break the student expert down and force a reversal of his opinion and then start on him again and break him down a second time, so that he is forced to admit that his first opinion was right, the instructor will score a considerable success.[27]

This was legal education aimed at the survival of the fittest. While some students flourished, others inevitably floundered, and 'for those few students whose mental processes meshed perfectly with the demands of the case class—future law teachers, very often—the exhilaration experienced

[22] See William C. Chase, *The American Law School and the Rise of Administrative Government* (Madison: University of Wisconsin Press, 1982), 17, 20, 40–1; Grey, *supra* n. 15, 34. The view that Langdellian and Langdellian-inspired legal formalism has no part to play in the process of statutory interpretation is one which persists, in some quarters, to this day. See e.g. Richard A. Posner, 'Legal Formalism, Legal Realism, and the Interpretation of Statutes and the Constitution' *Case Western Reserve L. Rev.*, 37 (1986), 179–217.

[23] See Robert Stevens, 'Two Cheers for 1870: The American Law School' *Perspectives in American History*, 5 (1971), 403–548 at 442.

[24] See Josef Redlich, *The Common Law and the Case Method in American University Law Schools* (New York: Merrymount, 1914), 49–50.

[25] See Stevens, *supra* n. 23, 446.

[26] Harvard Law School did not admit women until 1950. See Stevens, *supra* n. 23, 84.

[27] Albert M. Kales, 'An Unsolicited Report on Legal Education' *Columbia L. Rev.*, 18 (1918), 21–42 at 22.

in being so clear-headed about what the teacher was driving at while all the rest of one's classmates foundered lasted for all their lives and confirmed their adherence to the Harvard Law School and its methods.'[28] Despite being a demanding teacher, Ames was nonetheless highly respected and popular among his students. For most of those who excelled under his instruction, the case method effectively became a faith. Many of his best graduates served as 'missionaries', taking that faith to the provincial law schools.[29] After some initial reservations on the part of the smaller law schools,[30] the case method spread like wildfire. Langdell, Ames and, indirectly, Eliot had pioneered a major reform of the law school curriculum. Today, most American law professors accept the case method as the primary mode of teaching.

Since the case method originally came to prominence at the top of the law school hierarchy, it was perhaps inevitable that schools less renowned than Harvard should have embraced its style of teaching. By the 1890s, the number of places at law schools—indeed, the number of law schools—was very much on the increase. Faced with a greater choice of institutions, the prospective student seeking product differentiation would tend to opt for a school which taught law *à la* Harvard. But the success of the case method cannot simply be put down to snobbery value. While it has met with far from unanimous approval, it is generally accepted that the advantages of the method far outweigh its disadvantages. Although, compared with the traditional system of lectures, the case method requires of professors that they prepare their teaching more thoroughly, their reward is the opportunity to bring their own personalities into the classroom. Whereas the pre-Langdellian law teacher had tended to be an automaton at a lectern, the case teacher was elevated to a leading—sometimes charismatic, sometimes fearsome—role in an invariably tense classroom drama. For both professor and student, the case method brought spice to law school life.[31]

[28] Chase, *supra* n. 22, 35. It has also been suggested by Marcia Speziale that Langdell's case method accorded more generally with the late nineteenth-century organicist conception of science: 'While there is no necessary connection between Langdell's method and organicism, the case method is akin to the idea that cases group together to form rules of law, with the patterns reformed by the addition of each new case'. Marcia Speziale, 'Langdell's Concept of Law as Science: The Beginning of Anti-Formalism in American Legal Theory', *Vermont L. Rev.*, 5 (1980), 1–37 at 19.

[29] Schlegel, *supra* n. 10, 314–15. Schlegel attributes the image of the Harvard-trained law teacher as missionary to John Henry Wigmore. While most provincial law schools introduced to the case method came gradually to accept it, they tended also to modify it so as to differentiate their own curricula from the Harvard model. See Chase, *supra* n. 22, 118.

[30] Reservations which certainly lingered until the first decade of this century: cf. Alfred S. Konefsky and John Henry Schlegel, 'Mirror, Mirror on the Wall: Histories of American Law Schools', *Harvard L. Rev.*, 95 (1982), 833–51 at 837.

[31] See Stevens, *supra* n. 10, 55–7, 63; and also Scott Turow, *One L: What They Really Teach You at Harvard Law School* (London: Sceptre, 1988; orig. publ. 1977), 36–38, and also 248 ('the peculiar privilege which Socratism grants a teacher to invade the security of every

For law professors more inclined to efficiency than to charisma, let alone university administrators, the primary merit of the case method is its low cost. By dispensing not only with traditional lectures but also with the ancillary recitation and 'quiz' classes, which were the stock in trade of pre-Langdellian legal education, early proponents of the case method were able both to reduce the number and to increase the size of their classes. Harvard Law School under Langdell operated on an approximate ratio of one professor to every seventy-five students. Legal education became cheaper and law schools, in turn, became increasingly self-supporting.[32]

The legal profession, furthermore, shared the academy's enthusiasm for the Langdellian initiative. American legal education before Langdell was effectively Blackstone imported. The fundamental principles of the English common law were handed down to students from old English cases and treatises. Langdell and Ames—like Pollock and Holland in England—continued in more or less the same tradition. That tradition was enlivened by the case method. The bar had looked to the law schools to raise professional standards, and the Langdellian revolution was seen to do just that. Both the library-based system of learning and the case method of instruction accommodated the indigenous body of American law which evolved after the Civil War. The new American case-book, while still markedly anglophone in orientation, was inevitably more up-to-date than the old English treatises, and had the additional advantage of facilitating periodic revisions to account for new legal developments.[33] At one level, the case method, too, complemented the growing dynamism of American law. Taught Socratically, the case method required students to take a Darwinian approach to legal reasoning, whereby only the 'best' interpretations of the law could survive, while weaker efforts would be expunged through natural selection in the form of professorial guidance and questioning. By emphasizing intellectual development rather than the capacity simply to memorize the law as a body of static facts, the proponents of the case method had, if only inadvertently, conjured up the ideal of a dynamic legal mind, a mind capable of evolving in pace with the law itself. Langdell's Harvard had served the bar well: it had found an answer to the problem of raising professional standards.[34]

student in the room means that in the wrong hands it can become an instrument of terror'). More generally cf. Russell L. Weaver, 'Some Reflections on the Case Method', *Legal Studies*, 11 (1991), 155–71.

[32] See Stevens, *supra* n. 10, 55–7; Turow, *supra* n. 31, 115.

[33] See, generally, Lawrence M. Friedman, *A History of American Law* (2nd edn. New York: Simon & Schuster, 1985), 631–2.

[34] For detailed accounts, see William P. LaPiana, *Logic and Experience: The Origin of Modern American Legal Education* (New York: Oxford University Press, 1994), 79–109; John Henry Schlegel, 'American Legal Theory and American Legal Education: A Snake Swallowing Its Tail?', in C. Joerges and D.M. Trubek (eds.), *Critical Legal Thought: An American-German Debate* (Baden-Baden: Nomos, 1989), 49–79 at 51–8; Jerold S. Auerbach,

This was not the sole professional accomplishment of Langdellian legal science. Before 1870—and, indeed, for at least three decades afterwards—American law schools were comprised predominantly of a small staff of practising and 'retired' lawyers and judges. Law teaching was not, in itself, a profession. From Langdell onwards, this began to change. To teach law scientifically 'required a faculty that would devote itself full-time to mining the library for the cases that would best illustrate that science'.[35] Langdell also insisted that the teaching of law as a science required an extended post-baccalaureate degree course. In 1871, owing to the initiatives of Langdell, Harvard lengthened the duration of its LL.B. course from eighteen months to two years; five years later, the Board of Overseers agreed to a regulation designed to encourage LL.B. students to extend their studies over three years; and, in 1899, the three year law degree—Langdell's dream—became mandatory. Other schools gradually followed suit.[36] In his endeavour to elevate law to the level of a science, Langdell had at the same time transformed the teaching of law into a distinct career. 'What qualifies a person . . . to teach law', he insisted, 'is not the experience in the work of a lawyer's office, nor experience in dealing with men, nor experience in the trial or argument of cases—not, in short, in using law, but experience in learning law.'[37]

It has been suggested that, by successfully promoting academic law as a profession in its own right, Langdell provided the basis for the emergence of legal realism.[38] While realism flourished in the Harvard-inspired 'professional' law schools (especially those with Ivy League status), however, not all of its proponents were to find their true vocations in those schools. Furthermore, some realists criticized vociferously Langdell's image of the professional law teacher. Prior to the emergence of realism, nevertheless, Langdellian legal science was to bask in its years of glory. Dean Langdell had been a reclusive, unworldly and uncharismatic scholar, a poor communicator who suffered from failing eyesight.[39] Leadership qualities were hardly his strong point. His fundamental contribution to legal education was to import a vaguely conceived scientific method into the study of law.[40] While his initiatives in this respect affected radically the

'Enmity and Amity: Law Teachers and Practitioners 1900–1922' *Perspectives in American History*, 5 (1971), 549–601; also Grey, *supra* n. 15, 36–7; Gordon, *supra* n. 18, 72–110; and Schlegel, 'Langdell's Legacy Or, The Case of the Empty Envelope', *Stanford L. Rev.*, 36 (1984), 1517–33 at 1521.

[35] Chase, *supra* n. 22, 33.

[36] See Stevens, *supra* n. 10, 36–7, 45 nn. 18–20.

[37] Langdell, *supra* n. 17, 124.

[38] See Edward A. Purcell, Jr., *The Crisis of Democratic Theory: Scientific Naturalism and the Problem of Value* (Lexington: University Press of Kentucky, 1973), 77–8.

[39] See Samuel Williston, *Life and Law* (Boston: Little, Brown & Co., 1940), 200.

[40] An amateur botanist, Langdell classified laws much as he did plants. See Laura Kalman, *Legal Realism at Yale: 1927–1960* (Chapel Hill: University of North Carolina Press, 1986), 11.

direction of American legal education and scholarship, he was neither a great innovator nor a great popularizer. These attributes may be ascribed more directly to his disciples. Ames, in particular, possessed the teaching and intercommunicative skills that Langdell lacked. The 'missionaries' who attempted to sell the case method to the provincial universities had in the main been inspired by the teaching of Ames, not Langdell.[41]

Not only was Langdell's legal science made more accessible and appealing in the hands of his disciples, it was also invested with a few new contours and subtleties. Whereas Langdell had argued that law—meaning always private law—should be reduced by legal scientists to a small group of logically categorized founding principles, at least some of those who followed in his wake recognized that legal science, thus conceived, failed so much as to acknowledge, let alone account for, an ever-burgeoning body of legal doctrine. Even those who subscribed to Langdell's brand of legal science generally found unacceptable his inordinate narrowness and selectivity in deciding what was and what was not worthy of scientific scrutiny. Samuel Williston suspected that Langdell had 'little interest [in] or sympathy with any development of law later than 1850'.[42] Williston's Harvard colleague, John Chipman Gray, writing at the end of the nineteenth century, observed that the body of the law has 'so enormously increased that its details cannot be known by any one man'.[43] Another Harvard contemporary, William Keener, suggested similarly that, owing to the increasing complexity of the law, Langdellian legal science must be redefined in order to accommodate a growing and potentially infinite variety of legal principles.[44] Keener added that the focus of the case ëthod must be altered accordingly so as to encourage students not to discover for themselves a small body of principles supposedly forming the basis of all legal rules, but to develop their own sense of the law as a specific type of

41 On Ames and the 'missionaries', cf. Konefsky and Schlegel, *supra* n. 30, 837. Langdell himself was never really a popular teacher. See Arthur E. Sutherland, *The Law at Harvard: A History of Ideas and Men 1817–1967* (Cambridge, Mass.: Belknap, 1967), 179–80.

42 Williston, *supra* n. 39, 72. Williston graduated from Harvard Law School in 1888, was appointed to the post of Assistant Professor there in 1890, and was promoted to full Professor in 1895.

43 John Chipman Gray, 'Cases and Treatises', *American L. Rev.*, 22 (1888), 756–64 at 759–60. Though one of the new breed of professional law teachers, Gray had not been one of Langdell's students; and though he was one of the first Harvardians to produce a case book, he was slow to adopt the case method of instruction. See below. On Gray's appointment to Harvard, cf. Sutherland, *supra* n. 41, 185.

44 See William A. Keener, *A Selection of Cases on the Law of Quasi Contracts* (two vols., Cambridge, Mass.: Sever, 1888–89), I, iii–iv. Keener graduated from Harvard Law School in 1877, was appointed to the post of Assistant Professor in 1883, and was promoted to Professor in 1888.

reasoning process.[45] The new objective behind the case method was to teach the student how to reason like a lawyer rather than how to discover 'the law'. 'Methodology rather than substance became the nub of the system.'[46] In 1907, Ames summarized this transition from substance to methodology thus:

> The object arrived at by us at Cambridge is the power of legal reasoning, and we think we can best get that by putting before the students the best models to be found in the history of English and American law, because we believe that men who are trained, by examining the opinions of the greatest judges the English Common Law System has produced, are in a better position to know what legal reasoning is and are more likely to possess the power of solving legal problems than they would be by taking up the study of the law of any particular state.[47]

For Ames and his colleagues, the shift of emphasis from legal doctrine to legal reasoning and process was but an attempt to modernize the case method and thereby take Langdellian legal science into the twentieth century. In historical perspective, however, the shift must be regarded as more than just an effort to revitalize Langdell's formalism, for its effects extended significantly beyond Langdell and his immediate successors. As Robert Stevens has observed, the lasting influence of the 'modernized' case method 'was to transfer the basis of American legal education from substance to procedure and to make the focus of American legal scholarship—or at least legal theory—increasingly one of process rather than doctrine'.[48]

Not all of Langdell's Harvard successors felt compelled to modernize his jurisprudence. In particular, Joseph Beale, a specialist in the conflicts of laws, subscribed to a conception of legal science which was every bit as reductionist as that which had been propounded by Langdell. The gist of Beale's thesis was that 'neither by legislative nor by judicial legislation can the basic system of law be changed',[49] for, at the foundation of both statute and common law, there exist certain essential, timeless principles which determine the nature of the legal system. Law 'is not a mere collection of

[45] It was, in fact, not Keener, but Ames who pioneered this switch in case method orientation at Harvard: 'His method became, at least for his pupils, the typical method of teaching cases: Keener followed it, and later Wambaugh, Williston, Beale, and their younger colleagues'. Harvard Law School Association, *Centennial History of the Harvard Law School 1817–1917* (Cambridge, Mass.: Harvard Law School Association, 1918), 81.

[46] Stevens, *supra* n. 10, 56.

[47] James Barr Ames, 'Discussion of Paper by A.M. Kales', *Reports of the American Bar Assoc.*, 31 (1907), 1012–27 at 1025.

[48] Stevens, *supra* n. 10, 56.

[49] Joseph H. Beale, *A Treatise on the Conflict of Laws* (1st edn. Cambridge, Mass.: Harvard University Press, 1916), 145. Beale graduated from Harvard Law School in 1887, was appointed to the post of Assistant Professor in 1892, and was promoted to Professor in 1897.

arbitrary rules, but a body of scientific principle',[50] and judicial decisions which conflict with this body of principle are of little concern to the legal scientist: 'Purity of doctrine may be lost through wrong decisions of courts, thus warping legal principle by bad precedent; but wrong decisions are after all uncommon, and the law is not seriously affected by them.'[51] Since legal systems are governed by principles, judges, according to Beale, do not make, but only find and apply law. '[T]he function of changing the law has never been committed by the sovereign to the judge, and consciously to make a change in the law would be a usurpation on the part of the judge.'[52] If, indeed, it were the case that 'the judge makes the law he declares', this would mean that 'the law did not exist at the commission of the alleged wrong with which he is dealing in the litigation. . . . This is contrary to all conceptions of justice.'[53] 'The decision and judgment of a court', quite simply, 'can in no sense be regarded as in itself law.'[54]

It is hardly surprising that Beale was to become a favourite *bête noire* for the realists. By depicting the legal system as a perfect, closed totality, built on a bedrock of scientifically-deducible principles, and by insisting that judges can only apply but cannot make law, he represented Langdellian jurisprudence at its most uncompromising and dogmatic. The primary purpose of legal science, for Langdell, was not to upgrade professional standards, but to establish the study of law as a pursuit befitting the modern university. For Beale, however, Langdell's conception of legal science was 'too academic'.[55] Beale was concerned more with using legal science to emphasize the professional prestige and expertise of lawyers: 'law is a traditional manner of thought about right behaviour',[56] the cultivation of which 'requires a scientific knowledge on the part of a legal caste, thus coming back to a characteristic of the most ancient times, where it was in the knowledge of a priestly caste'.[57] Put simply, 'lawyers and judges are experts'.[58] Trained in the science of law, they constitute a priesthood guarding over the secrets of a recondite craft.

Beale's attempt to develop a conception of legal science more attuned to the requirements of the profession coincided roughly with the emergence of the Restatement movement, for which he served as a reporter. As early as the 1880s, the American Bar Institute had passed a resolution supporting, in principle, the codification of the common law. Support at

[50] Ibid. 135. [51] Ibid. 135. [52] Ibid. 148.
[53] Ibid. 148. [54] Ibid. 153.
[55] Joseph H. Beale, 'Professor Langdell—His Later Teaching Days', *Harvard L. Rev.*, 20 (1906), 9–11 at 10.
[56] Joseph H. Beale, *A Treatise on the Conflict of Laws* (2nd edn. three vols. New York: Baker, Voorhis & Co. 1935), I, p. xiii.
[57] Warren J. Samuels, 'Joseph Henry Beale's Lectures on Jurisprudence, 1909', *U. Miami L. Rev.*, 29 (1975), 260–333 at 292.
[58] Beale, *supra* n. 56, xiii.

this time came also from Harvard professors such as Ames and Williston, both of whom, by the turn of the century, were involved in the drafting of various uniform acts.[59] In 1923, the élite of the bar formed the American Law Institute (ALI) for the purpose of preparing 'restatements' of the common law. The report of the first meeting of the ALI stated that the primary objectives of the restatements 'should not only be to help make certain much that is now uncertain and to simplify unnecessary complexities, but also to promote those changes which will tend better to adapt the laws to the needs of life. The character of the restatement which we have in mind can be best described by saying that it should be at once analytical, critical and constructive'.[60] Critics have tended to focus mainly on the first of the ALI's two objectives.[61] Alarmed by the increasing complexity and uncertainty which accompanied the relentless growth of an indigenous body of American law, the bar hoped that the restatement of the common law in a clear and logical fashion would eliminate 'unnecessary confusion about the true principles of the law'.[62] The bar's desire for simplicity over complexity, and for the demonstration of correct legal principles, betrayed an obviously Langdellian world-view—a fact which was confirmed by the ALI's selection of staff. The first four Restatement projects were assigned to Harvard professors: Williston was the reporter for the Restatement of contracts; Beale for conflicts of laws; Francis Bohlen for torts; and Warren Seavey for agency. Subsequently Austin Scott, another Harvard law professor, agreed to write the Restatement of the law of trusts. In the hands of these professors, legal science took its first decisive step outside the university. The ALI had bestowed professional credibility on the Langdellian idea that the basic principles of the law are simply there to be discovered by logical analysis and thereafter reported in a fashion which reflects their 'real'—meaning unambiguous—nature.

For the realists, the Restatement movement represented the high water-mark of Langdellian legal formalism. By the early 1920s, legal science had found a second home in the American Law Institute, although the hospitality previously extended to the methods of Langdell and his heirs was, certainly at some of the major law schools, beginning to wear rather thin, as intellectual emphasis shifted from the natural to the social

[59] See Nathan M. Crystal, 'Codification and the Rise of the Restatement Movement', *Washington L. Rev.*, 54 (1979), 239–73 at 243.

[60] 'American Law Institute Proceedings' (1923), in Henry M. Hart, Jr. and Albert M. Sacks, *The Legal Process: Basic Problems in the Making and Application of Law* (tentative edn. Cambridge, Mass: unpublished mimeograph [on file with author: copy supplied by Professor Sacks], 1958), 751.

[61] Not least because the ALI decided to abandon the second objective: cf. Kalman, *supra* n. 40, 14.

[62] Calvin W. Woodard, 'The Limits of Legal Realism: An Historical Perspective', *Virginia L. Rev.*, 54 (1968), 689–739 at 702.

sciences. This shift could be detected even at Harvard.[63] The flourishing of Langdellian legal science had depended on case-books, law journals and the classroom; these were the media by which its credo was spread. But by the turn of the century, law professors at some of the more élite institutions (along with the occasional judge) were beginning to use these very media to criticize rather than to promote Harvard's achievements. Inevitably, legal science suffered when academics began explicitly to rebel against the Langdellian world-view. The survival of this world-view depended, after all, on the existence of educators who were prepared to subscribe to it. Langdell's legal science had been devised precisely to boost the academic credentials of the law school. By the early decades of this century—the credentials of the major schools having been duly boosted—academic law had acquired the status of a profession, and, wishing to sustain their profession, law professors felt compelled to search out new horizons. While the case method remained a popular teaching device—and, indeed, remains so to this day—Langdell's style of legal science gradually became outmoded. By the 1920s, Harvard's empire was crumbling.

The Tradition of Laissez-Faire

There was, nevertheless, more to formalist legal science than the tradition of Langdell. The second strand of legal formalism with which I am concerned—the tradition of *laissez-faire*—was not a product of the academy; it was, rather, a product of the courts. Those legal realists who attacked *laissez-faire* were confronting not an academic but a judicial world-view. This side of legal realism has been all but ignored in Britain.[64] In the United States, in contrast, it is one of the intellectual bedrocks of modern critical legal studies (see Chapter 6).

[63] Thurman Arnold, who entered the Harvard Law School in 1911 after graduating from Princeton, remembered his student days thus: 'The professors at Harvard, compared with the Princeton faculty, seemed intellectual giants. The narrow logic of the law, the building of legal principle on the solid basis of a long line of precedents, and the analysis of cases in class by the Socratic method were fascinating. . . . But the world of the Harvard Law School was as much a world of eternal verities and absolute certainties as it had been at Princeton. The study of human society was divided into fields in which scholars could work without having to acquaint themselves with what people were doing in other fields. The principal fields were law and economics. Then there was another field called the social sciences, though real scholars were dubious about whether this field was truly a science. It was felt that only superficial scholars would be content to work in the field of sociology'. Thurman Arnold, *Fair Fights and Foul: A Dissenting Lawyer's Life* (New York: Harcourt, Brace & World, 1951), 20. During the 1930s, Arnold argued passionately in favour of—although he did little to develop—an inter-disciplinary approach to the study of law. That, in retrospect, he should have considered Harvard intellectually myopic and conservative is unsurprising. Yet his perspective, blurred by the experience of realism, betrays a lack of generosity. The social sciences, as Arnold rather begrudgingly concedes, had already found a place in the Harvard Law School by the early years of this century.

[64] With the exception of Hugh Collins, *The Law of Contract* (London: Weidenfeld & Nicolson, 1986; 2nd edn. 1993).

The tradition of *laissez-faire* which emerged during the nineteenth century was premissed on a fundamental belief in individualism as a moral and economic ideal. In the United States, as in England, the freedom of the market was essentially the freedom of the individual to strike, or indeed not to strike, private bargains.[65] This freedom formed the cornerstone of classical economics as it emerged on both sides of the Atlantic. The American classical economist and moral philosopher, Francis Wayland, writing in the mid-nineteenth century, observed that '[a] man's possessions are his talents, faculties, skill, and the wealth and reputation which these have enabled him to acquire; in other words, his industry and his capital. In order that industry be applied to capital with the greatest energy, it is necessary that every man be at liberty to use them both as he will; that is, that both of them be free.'[66] Liberty, thus conceived, denoted necessary absence of legislative constraint: 'Legislatures . . . are not wise enough, and never will be, to settle any of the great questions involved between capitalists and labourers . . . [E]ven to *try* to settle any such things . . . by legislation is an economic abomination.'[67] Likewise, 'any law or artificial obstacle that hinders two persons from trading who would otherwise trade, not only interferes with a sacred right, but destroys an inevitable gain that would otherwise accrue to two persons alike.'[68] For the American classical economists, the naturalness of economic freedom was supposedly not an ideology, but the foundation for a genuine science: any properly scientific theory of the production and distribution of wealth must be premissed on the model of free exchange.[69]

The endeavour of American classical economists to treat free exchange as a fundamental scientific principle went generally unnoticed—possibly because, for all their dogmatism, these writers said nothing that had not been stated already, with far more intellectual rigour and subtlety, by a generation of British classical economists stretching from Adam Smith to John Stuart Mill.[70] However, responsibility for the intellectual and

[65] See Patrick S. Atiyah, *The Rise and Fall of Freedom of Contract* (Oxford: Clarendon Press, 1979), 226-31. Atiyah's account focuses on England.

[66] Francis Wayland, *The Elements of Political Economy* (4th edn. Boston: Gould & Lincoln, 1851; orig. publ. 1837), 114.

[67] Arthur Latham Perry, *Political Economy* (18th edn. New York: Scribner, Armstrong & Co. 1883; orig. publ. 1865), 248.

[68] Ibid. 103.

[69] See generally Joseph Dorfman, *The Economic Mind in American Civilization, Volume III: 1865–1918* (New York: Viking, 1949), 49–82; also Archer Jones, 'Social Darwinism and Classical Economics: An Untested Hypothesis', *North Dakota Quarterly*, 46 (1978), 19–31.

[70] For an assessment of the American classical economists which is at once generous and critical, cf. Duncan Kennedy, 'The Role of Law in Economic Thought: Essays on the Fetishism of Commodities', *American Univ. L. Rev.*, 34 (1985), 939–1001 at 941–58. According to Kennedy (p. 942), '[t]he American classical economists were an undistinguished lot who differed among themselves on numerous particulars'.

political popularity of *laissez-faire* in mid-nineteenth to early twentieth-century America should not be laid squarely at the feet of British classical economics, for the conception of free exchange prevalent in American thought during this period was in fact inspired primarily by the Social Darwinism of the Victorian evolutionary theorist, Herbert Spencer.[71] While Spencer was not, strictly speaking, an economist, he wrote various books and essays which, among other things, defended the idea of *laissez-faire* in a forthright, unguarded and sometimes arrogant fashion—indeed, in precisely the fashion which British classical economists had been at pains, by and large, to avoid.[72] In his first book, *Social Statics*,[73] published in 1851, Spencer argued that it is necessary to the proper functioning of any economic system that individuals be allowed to pursue and realize their own private interests unimpeded by the mechanisms of the state. This requires that the state be precluded from intervening in the economy except occasionally to enforce contractual terms which have been breached. Generally, state regulation of the economy should be considered not only undesirable but unnecessary, for freedom of contract itself ensures that there exists among all individuals an equality of bargaining rights. Under an economic system which entails an absolute minimum of compulsion and constraint, everyone will share equally the unfettered right to engage, or to decline from engaging, in economic transactions: 'each is free to offer; each is free to accept; each is free to refuse. . . . But . . . no one may force another to part with his goods; no one may force another to take a specified price; for no one can do so without assuming more liberty of action than the man whom he thus treats.'[74] In short, *laissez-faire*, according to Spencer, promotes a natural economic equality.

But what sort of equality? Spencer insisted that although *laissez-faire* facilitates an equal right on the part of all economic agents to pursue and enter bargains, this does not mean that these agents enjoy an equality of bargaining power. While everyone will share an equal right to compete in the market under a system of *laissez-faire*, not everyone will in fact

[71] See generally Richard Hofstadter, *Social Darwinism in American Thought 1860–1915* (rev. edn. New York: Braziller, 1969).

[72] See generally Atiyah, *supra* n. 65, 294–323. For sketches of Spencer's influence on American law, see Arthur L. Harding, 'The Ghost of Herbert Spencer: A Darwinian Concept of Law', in A. L. Harding, *Origins of the Natural Law Tradition* (Dallas: Southern Methodist University Press, 1954), 69–93; Edward S. Corwin, 'The Impact of the Idea of Evolution on the American Political and Constitutional Tradition' in Stow Persons (ed.), *Evolutionary Thought in America* (New Haven, Conn.: Yale University Press, 1950), 182–99; Max Lerner, 'The Triumph of Laissez-Faire', in Arthur M. Slesinger, Jr. and Morton White (eds.), *Paths of American Thought* (Boston: Houghton Mifflin, 1963), 147–66, 549–50.

[73] Herbert Spencer, *Social Statics: or, the Conditions Essential to Human Happiness Specified, and the First of Them Developed* (London: Chapman, 1851).

[74] Ibid. 146–7.

compete equally. Some will compete more than others. Owing, furthermore, to natural inequalities of talent, initiative, and skill, some will compete more successfully than others. The economically fit will prosper while the economically weak flounder. *Laissez-faire*, in Spencer's hands, is thus coupled with the principle of natural selection.

While the American classical economists—in a typical nineteenth century bid to invest their discipline with 'scientific' respectability—simply elevated their belief in the desirability of free exchange to the level of an a priori principle, Spencer, in contrast, transformed *laissez-faire* into a genuine scientific paradigm. For him, *laissez-faire* is the key to understanding economics as an evolutionary science. The free market reflects a natural order of things, whereby every economic agent is equally at liberty to transact. Any attempt by the state to interfere with the market is likely to intrude on this liberty. As Spencer observed, 'the liberty which a citizen enjoys is to be measured, not by the nature of the governmental machinery he lives under, whether representative or other, but by the relative paucity of restraints it imposes on him'.[75] Governmental interference with the market frustrates natural competitiveness by enabling the economically weak to survive in the market longer than they would naturally do, thereby bolstering their bargaining position to the cost of the economically fittest.

In the United States, Spencer's Social Darwinism became economic credo not only for private entrepreneurs but also for senators, judges and other political figures. Such figures tended to share what Morton White has called a 'senatorial philosophy'—the philosophy, that is, of 'men of affairs' united in their opposition to all forms of state intervention.[76] Analysing this 'philosophy' as it emerged during the years following the Civil War, Charles Beard argues that those who subscribed to it 'believed in the widest possible extension of the principle of private property, and the narrowest possible restriction of state interference, except to aid private property to increase its gains'. Furthermore, '[t]hey supplemented their philosophy of property by a philosophy of law and politics, which looked upon state interference, except to preserve order, and aid railways and manufacturers in their enterprises, as an intrinsic evil to be resisted at

[75] Herbert Spencer, *The Man versus The State* (London and Edinburgh: Williams & Norgate, 1884), 15–16.

[76] White, *supra* n. 5, 37–8. It is both odd and ironic that, while Spencer's writings were never particularly well received in Britain, Americans (for whom Spencer had a decidedly low regard) received his work with open arms. Between 1860 and the beginning of the twentieth century, nearly 370,000 copies of Spencer's writings were sold in the USA. See Harold I. Sharlin, 'Herbert Spencer and Scientism', *Annals of Science*, 33 (1976), 457–65 at 464. Having stated this, nevertheless, there is no denying that many American social scientists read Spencer primarily to dispute his theses. See R. Jackson Wilson, *In Quest of Community: Social Philosophy in the United States, 1860–1920* (New York: Wiley, 1968), 155.

every point.'[77] Swayed by evolutionary economics, late nineteenth-century American public figures and policy-makers were on the whole convinced that the economy was fated to rise and fall at regular intervals in accordance with the natural laws of the market.[78]

Senatorial philosophy was certainly echoed in the courts. Supreme Court Justices in particular seemed, at times, to be attempting to write evolutionary economics into the Constitution. For example, defining the term 'liberty' for the purposes of the Fourteenth Amendment, Justice Peckham, speaking for the entire Court in the case of *Allgeyer* v. *Louisiana* in 1897, opined that:

> The 'liberty' mentioned in that amendment means, not only the right of the citizen to be free from the mere physical restraint of his person, as by incarceration, but the term is deemed to embrace the right of the citizen to be free in the employment of all his faculties; to be free to use them in all lawful ways; to live and work where he will; to earn his livelihood by any lawful calling; to pursue any livelihood or avocation; and for that purpose to enter into all contracts which may be proper, necessary, and essential to his carrying out to a successful conclusion the purposes above mentioned.[79]

This statement echoes Spencer. But it would be wrong to assume that the Supreme Court—or any other American court, for that matter—adopted an exclusively Social Darwinist conception of economic freedom. While the second half of the nineteenth century was the golden age of *laissez-faire* philosophy,[80] such a philosophy was hardly unknown to the courts in earlier years. Morton Horwitz has suggested that, following the American War of Independence, state and federal courts began gradually to develop a theory of contract which emphasized not the power of the courts to rewrite contractual terms, but the actual will of each contracting party.[81] '[O]nce conceived of as protective, regulative, paternalistic and, above all, a paramount expression of the moral sense of the community', contract law came gradually 'to be thought of as facilitative of individual desires and as

[77] Charles A. Beard, *Contemporary American History* (New York: Macmillan, 1914), 53. For examples of figures who subscribed to the so-called senatorial philosophy, see Michael Les Benedict, 'Laissez-Faire and Liberty: A Re-evaluation of the Meaning and Origins of Laissez-Faire Constitutionalism', *Law and History Rev.*, 3 (1985), 293–331 at 306.

[78] See, generally, Sidney Fine, *Laissez-faire and the General Welfare State: A Study of Conflict in American Thought 1865–1901* (Ann Arbor: University of Michigan Press, 1956).

[79] *Allgeyer* v. *Louisiana* (1897) 165 U.S. 578, 590. The *laissez-faire* interpretation of the Fourteenth Amendment in this case is one which persisted in the United States Supreme Court until the famous Court-packing crisis of 1937 and the decision in *West Coast Hotel Co.* v. *Parrish* (1937) 300 U.S. 379, in which the Supreme Court upheld state law establishing minimum wages for women. See, more generally, G. Edward White, 'The Path of American Jurisprudence', *U. Pennsylvania L. Rev.*, 124 (1976), 1212–59 at 1229–32.

[80] Friedman, *supra* n. 33, 178.

[81] Morton J. Horwitz, 'The Historical Foundations of Modern Contract Law', *Harvard L. Rev.*, 87 (1974), 917–56; *supra* n. 2, 160–210.

simply reflective of the existing organization of economic and political power.'[82] While Horwitz has been taken to task for oversimplifying and sometimes distorting his historical sources,[83] his thesis, when extended to private law generally, offers a convincing explanation of how, even before the Civil War, the courts increasingly developed private law doctrine as a purportedly neutral framework for facilitating voluntary market transactions and vindicating injuries to personal rights.[84] Even by the early nineteenth century, a judicial ideology of *laissez-faire*, congenial to the needs of a budding market economy, was beginning to emerge. Social Darwinism may have contributed significantly to this trend, but it did not precipitate it.

Having said this, nevertheless, the conception of *laissez-faire* which emerged in the late nineteenth-century American courts was of a distinctly Spencerian bent. This conception involved shifting the burden of regulation from the 'public' realm of the government to the 'private' realm of the market. The courts did not divest themselves of the responsibility of overseeing economic disputes, but simply insisted that the appropriate regulatory framework for settling such disputes was private rather than public law. 'When the subject of a contract is purely and exclusively private,' one state court claimed, 'there is no condition existing upon which the legislature can interfere for the purpose of prohibiting the contract or controlling the terms thereof.'[85] Private relations between economic actors were to be governed not by statutes, but by the contractual rights and duties accepted by those actors. By drawing a sharp distinction between public and private, and by opposing state regulation of private economic relations, the courts were effectively saying that the market governed itself.

Two early twentieth-century Supreme Court decisions exemplify the general judicial sanctification of *laissez-faire*. In the first of these cases, *Lochner* v. *New York* (1905),[86] the Court declared that a New York statute

[82] Morton J. Horwitz, 'The Rise of Legal Formalism', *Am. J. Leg. Hist.*, 19 (1975), 251–64 at 251, 259–60; *supra* n. 2, 253, 261–2.

[83] A. W. B. Simpson, 'The Horwitz Thesis and the History of Contracts', *U. Chicago L. Rev.*, 46 (1979), 533–601.

[84] See generally Horwitz, *supra* n. 2, *passim*.

[85] *Leep* v. *Railway Co.* (1894) 25 S.W. 75, 79. For other instances of the late nineteenth-century state courts striking down legislation deemed to interfere with the freedom to contract, cf. *State* v. *Goodwill* (1889) 10 S.E. 285; *Commonwealth* v. *Perry* (1891) 28 N.E. 1126; *San Antonio & A.P. Railway* v. *Wilson* (1892) 19 S.W. 910; and *Ritchie* v. *People* (1895) 40 N.E. 454.

[86] *Lochner* v. *New York* (1905) 198 U.S. 45. On the historical significance of this decision, see William E. Nelson, *The Fourteenth Amendment: From Political Principle to Judicial Doctrine* (Cambridge, Mass.: Harvard University Press, 1988), 197–200 and also 10–11: 'In the nearly century-long course of adjudication since *Lochner*, the Supreme Court has persistently identified fundamental rights with which states may not interfere, and the

setting a ten hour maximum work-day for bakers violated the stipulation in the Fourteenth Amendment that '[n]o State shall . . . deprive any person of life, liberty, or property, without due process of law.' In declaring the statute unconstitutional, the Court resorted to the language of freedom of contract. According to Justice Peckham:

The statute necessarily interferes with the right of contract between the employer and employees, concerning the number of hours in which the latter may labour in the bakery of the employer. The general right to make a contract in relation to his business is part of the liberty of the individual protected by the Fourteenth Amendment of the Federal Constitution. . . . The right to purchase and sell labour is part of the liberty protected by this Amendment, unless there are circumstances which exclude the right.[87]

The only circumstances in which the Court will limit freedom of contract, Peckham adds, 'relate to the safety, health, morals and general welfare of the public'.[88] If none of these is put at risk, then parties should be allowed to contract on whatever terms they like:

Statutes of the nature of that under review, limiting the hours in which grown and intelligent men may labour to earn their living, are mere meddlesome interferences with the rights of the individual, and they are not saved from condemnation by the claim that they are passed in the exercise of the police power and upon the subject of the health of the individual whose rights are interfered with, unless there be some fair ground, reasonable in and of itself, to say that there is material danger to the public health or to the health of the employees, if the hours of labour are not curtailed. If this be not clearly the case, the individuals, whose rights are thus made the subject of legislative interference, are under the protection of the Federal Constitution regarding their liberty of contract as well as of person; and the legislature of the State has no power to limit their right as proposed in this statute.[89]

Similarly the case of *Coppage* v. *Kansas* (1915).[90] Here, the Supreme Court declared that state legislation outlawing 'yellow dog' contracts—contracts requiring, as a condition of employment, that employees abstain from union activities—invaded the right of private parties freely to contract under the terms of the Fourteenth Amendment. The State of Kansas submitted that since these contracts were the result of coercion of the

Fourteenth Amendment has assumed a breadth that its proponents did not contemplate.' For a demonstration of the far-reaching legacy of *Lochner*, see Cass R. Sunstein, 'Lochner's Legacy', *Columbia L. Rev.*, 87 (1987), 873–919.

[87] *Lochner* v. *New York*, *supra* n. 86, 53.

[88] Ibid.

[89] Ibid. 61. For a subtle analysis of the 'formalism' of Justice Peckham's majority opinion in *Lochner*, see Frederick Schauer, 'Formalism', *Yale L.J.*, 97 (1988), 509–48 at 511–14.

[90] *Coppage* v. *Kansas* (1915) 236 U.S. 1. For a discussion of the (often misunderstood) significance of this case in the history of American law, see Kenneth M. Casebeer, 'Teaching an Old Dog Old Tricks: *Coppage* v. *Kansas* and At-Will Employment Revisited', *Cardozo L. Rev.*, 6 (1985), 765–97.

employee by the employer, the statute could not be deemed to impinge upon this freedom, for such freedom did not exist between the parties. The Court, nonetheless, held that the presence of economic coercion did not negate the principle of freedom of contract. In the words of Justice Pitney:

> The right of the employee to quit the service of the employer, for whatever reason, is the same as the right of the employer, for whatever reason, to dispense with the services of the employee . . . In all such particulars the employer and employee have equality of right, and any legislation that disturbs that equality is an arbitrary interference with the liberty of contract which no government can justify in a free land.[91]

Accordingly, all economic agents are assumed to share an equality of bargaining rights which they may exercise at their liberty. Like Spencer, however, Justice Pitney recognized that, while agents may share an equal freedom to bargain, they do not necessarily share an equality of bargaining power:

> A little reflection will show that wherever the right of private property and the right of free contract co-exist, each party when contracting is inevitably more or less influenced by the question whether he has much property, or little, or none; for the contract is made to the very end that each may gain something that he needs or desires more urgently than that which he proposes to give in exchange. And, since it is self-evident that, unless all things are held in common, some persons must have more property than others, it is from the nature of things impossible to uphold freedom of contract and the right of private property without at the same time recognizing as legitimate those inequalities of fortune that are the necessary result of those rights.[92]

Hence the necessity of inequality. An inequality of bargaining power is an inevitable consequence of an equality of rights, for different economic actors will exploit their liberty to strike bargains with differing degrees of success. In both *Lochner* and *Coppage*, the Court sanctified *laissez-faire* by declaring invalid statutes with the capacity to regulate 'voluntary' agreements between private parties. But in *Coppage* in particular, this sanctification had about it a distinctly Social Darwinist twist.

BETWEEN LEGAL FORMALISM AND LEGAL REALISM

Legal realism challenged Social Darwinism in the courts just as it challenged Langdellian legal science in the law schools. But realism did not just sprout up overnight. Even by the late nineteenth century, challenges to both *laissez-faire* and legal science were being made. This 'proto-realist'

[91] *Coppage* v. *Kansas*, *supra* n. 90, 10–11. [92] Ibid. 17.

critique of legal formalism tends to be associated most directly with the figure of Oliver Wendell Holmes, Jr.; and, indeed, there is good reason for this, for Holmes attacked the traditions of Langdell and *laissez-faire* in the courts. Despite this, however, Holmes was anything but an out-and-out anti-formalist. As with the other principal proto-realist jurists, Roscoe Pound and John Chipman Gray, both of whom we shall consider presently, there is a good deal of ambiguity, equivocation and contradiction underscoring Holmes's critique of formalism. Most realists tended to overlook these attributes in his writings and judgments, and yet their existence suggests that Holmes was as much an advocate of legal formalism as he was a forerunner to legal realism.

Holmes was not a professional academic in the same way as were Langdell and various of his epigoni. Though a passionate reader and dilettante, Holmes—like his great realist admirer, Jerome Frank—was attracted primarily to practice and the bench rather than to the law school. In 1870, while maintaining his legal practice in Boston, he accepted the post of part-time instructor in Constitutional Law at Harvard (from where he had graduated four years earlier); during the following year, he served as part-time lecturer in Jurisprudence.[93] However, ten years were to pass before Holmes accepted a full-time academic post. In 1882, he was appointed Professor of Law at Harvard—a position which he had accepted subject to various conditions, one of which was that, should he at any time be offered a judgeship, the Law School would not try to prevent him from taking it. Holmes began teaching at Harvard in September 1882. By the beginning of December, he had been appointed to the bench of the Supreme Judicial Court of Massachusetts, where he remained until his promotion to the United States Supreme Court in 1902. His professorial career had lasted three months.[94]

Holmes had been appointed as a professor at Harvard largely on the strength of a series of lectures which he had delivered at the Lowell Institute in Boston in November and December of 1880.[95] These lectures were, in part, revised versions of five articles written between 1876 and 1880 for the *American Law Review*. In March 1881, the lectures themselves were published as a volume entitled *The Common Law*.[96] Written while at

[93] See Mark deWolfe Howe, *Justice Oliver Wendell Holmes. vol. II: The Proving Years 1870–1882* (Cambridge, Mass.: Belknap, 1963), 26–9, 285.

[94] Much to the displeasure of his Harvard colleagues. For discussion, cf. Howe, ibid. 259–73; G. Edward White, 'The Integrity of Holmes' Jurisprudence', *Hofstra L. Rev.*, 10 (1982), 633–71 at 639–42; and Sheldon M. Novick, *Honorable Justice: The Life of Oliver Wendell Holmes* (Boston: Little, Brown & Co. 1989), 169. ('Holmes had taught his classes for just two months, and had resigned in the middle of the term. . . . The law school faculty were offended, not only because Holmes left so abruptly, but because he had not stopped to consult or even inform them. They learned about the appointment from the newspapers'.)

[95] Novick, *supra* n. 94, 259.

[96] Oliver Wendell Holmes, Jr., *The Common Law* (Boston: Little, Brown & Co. 1881).

the bar, Holmes's lectures proved a remarkable achievement. Never before in the history of American legal writing had any author produced such an intellectually-ambitious study of common law doctrine. The purpose of the collection was 'to give the rationale of the cardinal doctrines of the common law—using analysis only where that is sufficient, but resorting to history where the particular outline of a conception or a rule could not be explained without it'. Such an approach to the study of law was, Holmes insisted, well nigh unique: 'I do not understand any other science of the law than this and yet so far as I know my attempt stands almost alone.'[97]

Holmes was a highly-ambitious, self-regarding man who would not have thought twice about eschewing modesty,[98] and his insistence on the methodological uniqueness of *The Common Law* must be taken with a pinch of salt. Large portions of his book are clearly indebted to the nineteenth-century historical jurisprudence of Savigny and Maine. The themes of Holmes's lectures—Crimes, Torts, Possession, Contract and Succession—seem almost exactly to reflect equivalent chapters in Maine's *Ancient Law*.[99] Very much a polyglot, Holmes had also been influenced by the studies of Tylor, McLennan, Waitz, von Maurer, Laveley, and other historians of primitive culture and institutions, as well as by the Kantian- and Hegelian-inspired Germanic civil law treatises of Schuerl, Windschied and Keller. In fact, Holmes's historical approach was inspired by a fabulous miscellany of materials, spanning English legal history, German philosophy, civilian jurisprudence and nineteenth-century anthropology.[100] *The Common Law* was but the melting pot for his formidable erudition. Shelved alongside the many works that inspired his historical approach to doctrine, it ranks nevertheless as a rather derivative text—hardly the unique work of scholarship that Holmes would have us believe.

This is not, however, to underestimate its significant place in the history of American legal thought, nor is it to deny that there are elements of

[97] See generally Oliver Wendell Holmes, Jr. to Harold J. Laski, 1 February 1919, in Mark deWolfe Howe (ed.), *Holmes-Laski Letters: The Correspondence of Mr. Justice Holmes and Harold J. Laski 1916–1935* (two vols. Cambridge, Mass.: Harvard University Press, 1953), I, 182–4 esp. 184: 'Every book has the seeds of its own death in it, by provoking further investigation and clearer restatement, but it remains the original and I think it is already forgotten how far that is true of the *C[ommon] L[aw]*.'

[98] See Mark deWolfe Howe, *Justice Oliver Wendell Holmes. vol. I: The Shaping Years 1841–1870* (Cambridge, Mass.: Belknap, 1957), 282.

[99] Compare the chapter headings of *The Common Law* with those of Henry Sumner Maine, *Ancient Law: Its Connection With the Early History of Society and its Relation to Modern Ideas* (15th edn. London: Murray, 1894). I discuss Holmes *vis-à-vis* Savigny in Neil Duxbury, 'The Metaphysical Aspects of Law', in Hans Burkhardt and Barry Smith (eds.), *Handbook of Metaphysics and Ontology* (two vols. Munich: Philosophia, 1991), I, 443–46.

[100] See Howe, *supra* n. 93, 135–83.

Holmes's philosophy—as opposed to his history—which were truly revolutionary in jurisprudential terms. Holmes's philosophical predilections had in fact been shaped some years before the publication of *The Common Law*. His experiences as a soldier during the Civil War were far from enviable. He was wounded three times, and he wished for nothing more than for his three years' service to end so that he could return to his studies.[101] When, eventually, he returned to civilian life, he immersed himself in art, philosophy and poetry—in anything, basically, that contrasted with the brutality and ugliness of combat.[102] He shared this desire to pursue the cerebral and the aesthetic with other intellectuals eager to abandon their memories of the War. On returning to Massachusetts after being discharged from the army in 1864, Holmes would spend his evenings in intense intellectual debate: 'It was not only the law he desired to talk about. It was the cosmos itself, and all the problems of the universe. Wendell brought home young men studying law or medicine at Harvard, drew them upstairs to his room under the flaring gas lamp. William James . . . Charles Peirce . . . T. S. Perry, Chauncey Wright, John Ropes; John Gray when he came home on leave from the army. Men who were not embarrassed by the largest, angriest topics: the universe, the cosmos, all the *isms* from Kantian idealism to Comtian positivism.'[103] This meeting of kindred spirits continued throughout the 1860s and, by the end of that decade, 'The Metaphysical Club' was initiated.

The Metaphysical Club was comprised of a number of philosophers, scientists and lawyers—including, among others, William James, Charles Sanders Peirce and John Chipman Gray—all of whom were loosely united by 'an enthusiasm for the British tradition in philosophy, and a sense of the epoch-making importance of Darwin's *Origin of Species*'.[104] We shall see in due course that Holmes's own interpretation of Darwinism is crucial to a proper understanding of his jurisprudence. More commonly emphasized, however, is his indebtedness to the pragmatist philosophy of Peirce and, to a lesser extent, James. Various of the principal anti-formalist aspects of Holmes's legal thought appear in fact to be derived directly from the basic pragmatist outlook of these two philosophers. The prediction theory of law is the best place to start. Explaining the pragmatist conception of truth, William James observed that:

101 See Catherine D. Bowen, *Yankee from Olympus: Justice Holmes and His Family* (Boston: Little, Brown & Co. 1945), 185–90.

102 See Howe, *supra* n. 98, 201.

103 Bowen, *supra* n. 101, 210–11.

104 Max H. Fisch, 'Justice Holmes, the Prediction Theory of Law, and Pragmatism', *Jnl. of Philosophy*, 39 (1942), 85–97 at 88. On the Metaphysical Club—and particularly the place of Holmes and Peirce in this club—see Marcia J. Speziale, 'By Their Fruits You Shall Know Them: Pragmatism and the Prediction Theory of Law' *Manitoba L.J.*, 9 (1978), 29–51.

The truth of an idea is not a stagnant property inherent in it. Truth *happens* to an idea. It *becomes* true, is *made* true by events. Its verity *is* in fact an event, a process: the process namely of its verifying itself, its *veri-fication*. Its validity is the process of its valid-*ation*.[105]

According to pragmatist philosophy, then, truth 'happens' by way of a process of events. Events verify themselves and thereby 'become' true. Similarly, for Holmes, rights and duties amount to nothing more than a predictable process of events—namely, specific consequences that will ensue in the event of a breach of the law. Holmes explains:

The primary rights and duties with which jurisprudence busies itself . . . are nothing but prophecies. One of the many evil effects of the confusion between legal and moral ideas . . . is that theory is apt to get the cart before the horse, and to consider the right or the duty as something existing apart from and independent of the consequences of its breach, to which certain sanctions are added afterward . . . [A] legal duty so-called is nothing but a prediction that if a man does or omits certain things he will be made to suffer in this or that way by judgment of the court; and so of a legal right.[106]

While this is but one—and certainly not the most famous—passage among many to be found in Holmes's writings demonstrating the prediction theory of law, it is in fact extremely significant. Notice that Holmes, in this passage, is concerned not specifically with the purpose of law, but with jurisprudence. His conception of a predictivist jurisprudence constitutes a first, tentative step outside Langdell's laboratory. Jurisprudence, in Holmes's hands, is invested with an element of practicality. Whereas, for Langdell, everything about the law could be fitted between the covers of a book, Holmes introduced a totally new element into the jurisprudential framework: namely, people.

People want to know under what circumstances and how far they will run the risk of coming against what is so much stronger than themselves, and hence it becomes a business to find out when this danger is to be feared. The object of our study, then, is prediction, the prediction of the incidence of the public force through the instrumentality of the courts.[107]

Unlike Langdell, Holmes did not attempt to turn his jurisprudence into a teaching method. He was not, after all, a law teacher. Yet the pragmatism of his jurisprudence contrasted markedly with the formalism of Langdell's.

[105] William James, *Pragmatism: A New Name for Some Old Ways of Thinking* (New York: Longmans, Green & Co. 1910), 201; and cf. also Robert S. Summers, *Instrumentalism and American Legal Theory* (Ithaca, NY: Cornell University Press, 1982), 120–1.

[106] Oliver Wendell Holmes, Jr., 'The Path of the Law', *Harvard L. Rev.*, 10 (1897), 457–78 at 458.

[107] Ibid. 457. For other statements by Holmes in a similar vein, see the quotations collected and analysed by David H. Moskowitz, 'The Prediction Theory of Law', *Temple L.Q.*, 39 (1966), 413–31 at 413–16.

Holmes himself was not unaware of this, and it is significant that one of his most pointed aphorisms—'[t]he life of the law has not been logic: it has been experience'—was first coined in a review by Holmes of one of Langdell's contract textbooks.[108] One year after the publication of this review, the sentence appeared again on the first page of *The Common Law*. In his review, Holmes said of Langdell that '[h]e is, perhaps, the greatest living legal theologian . . . so entirely is he interested in the formal connection of things, or logic, as distinguished from the feelings which make the content of logic, and which have actually shaped the substance of the law'.[109] The description was not intended to flatter its subject.

The prediction theory of law was to become a cornerstone of realist jurisprudence. Even Jerome Frank—who, unlike other realists, did not accept the theory—was fundamentally indebted to Holmes's departure from the tenets of Langdell; for it was Holmes who, in formulating his theory, first suggested that jurisprudence should have something to say about the human element—the lawyers and the clients—behind the formal façade of the law. Frank himself believed that even legal realists, especially in their role as educators, placed too little emphasis on the life of the law. The law school, he argued, should teach students not only how to discover for themselves fundamental legal rules and principles; it should also instruct students in the application of those principles. The legal laboratory, he believed, should be transformed into the legal clinic. With the advent of realism, Holmes's insistence that law must be understood as a matter of experience rather than logic was to be put to the test.

Holmes himself, in criticizing Langdell from a pragmatist perspective, was simply echoing the sentiments of his philosophical *confrères*. And while the point about experience over logic was adopted as little short of a slogan by many realists, it should not be taken too far out of context. As a criticism of Langdell, it stands very much as an isolated comment. In his review of Langdell, Holmes also praised the Harvard dean for his 'ingenious and original thought',[110] just as, in the early 1870s, he had welcomed Langdell's pedagogical innovations.[111] It is interesting to note too that, in spite of his 'legal theologian' jibe, his appointment to the faculty of the Harvard Law School in 1882 met with no resistance from

[108] Oliver Wendell Holmes, Jr., review of C. C. Langdell, *Summary of the Law of Contracts* and W. R. Anson, *Principles of the Law of Contract*, *American L. Rev.*, 14 (1880), 233–35 at 234.

[109] Holmes, *supra* n. 108, 233.

[110] Ibid.

[111] See Joel Parker, *The Law School of Harvard College* (New York: Hurd & Houghton, 1871), 3–4; and Mathias W. Reiman, 'Holmes's *Common Law* and German Legal Science', in Robert W. Gordon (ed.), *The Legacy of Oliver Wendell Holmes, Jr.* (Edinburgh: Edinburgh University Press, 1992), 72–114 at 110: 'When [Holmes] attacked Langdell's logic as disastrous, he was condemning it as an approach to jurisprudence. But he recognized perfectly well its value as a teaching tool.'

Langdell. Most probably, Langdell would have welcomed the appointment.[112] Quite simply, to depict Holmes as a down-the-line anti-Langdellian would be a mistake. The ambiguity that can be discerned in Holmes's work emerges from the fact that, while he strived to achieve something unique[113]—while his writings are distinguishable from those of the Langdellian tradition—he was, nevertheless, remarkably respectful of that tradition. Realist writers took from Holmes what they considered to be his path-breaking anti-formalist iconoclasm, but they overlooked this crucial element of respect. Yet, without this element, any picture of Holmes is severely distorted.

This distortion of Holmes was recognized even by some of those on the periphery of realism. In 1931, Morris Cohen observed that the then blossoming realist tendency represented:

> a reaction by younger men against the *abuse* of abstract principles by an older generation that neglected the adequate factual analysis necessary to make principles properly applicable. It is natural, therefore, for the rebels to claim as their own one who for more than the time of one generation has valiantly stood for the need of more factual knowledge in the law. But no one group can claim Justice Holmes as its own unless it shares his respect for the complexity of the legal situation and exercises the same caution against hastily jumping from one extreme error to the opposite.[114]

This respect for the complexities of Holmesian jurisprudence was, Cohen argued, by and large lacking from realist legal thought. Realists tended falsely to ally Holmes's legal philosophy 'to some *ism* such as functionalism, behaviourism, institutionalism, or the like'.[115] Moreover, while realists would 'frequently support their case by his dictum that "experience not logic is the life of the law",' they would tend also 'to tear [this] passage out of its qualifying context' by using it to support the thesis that there is no place for logic in the study of law.[116] Although Holmes argued against the Langdellian desire to conceive of the law as a wholly logical, scientific system, he did not rule out the possibility of using logic for the purpose of studying particular branches of the law: that the law is not logical does not mean that there is no place for logic in legal study. Holmes made this point quite unequivocally in *The Common Law*: 'The business of the jurist is to

[112] See Howe, *supra* n. 93, 257.

[113] He once suggested, only half-flippantly, that if he was to accomplish anything in life he must do it before the age of 40: see Howe, *supra* n. 93, 135.

[114] Morris R. Cohen, 'Justice Holmes and the Nature of Law', *Columbia L. Rev.*, 31 (1931) 352–67 at 363.

[115] Ibid. 356.

[116] Ibid. For a further illustration of the realist tendency to latch on to Holmes's aphorisms while rather neglecting the surrounding detail, see Thomas C. Grey, 'Holmes and Legal Pragmatism', *Stanford L. Rev.*, 41 (1989), 787–870 at 818.

make known the content of the law; that is, to work upon it from within, or logically, arranging and distributing it, in order, from its *summum genus* to its *infima species*, so far as practicable.'[117] His critique of logic in the law is therefore rather weaker than it first appears. Though he rejected Langdellian legal science, Holmes in fact subscribed to a legal philosophy which is far from intolerant of legal logic. If one were to divest Holmes's writings of their famous, albeit usually isolated, coloratura passages denunciating legal formalism, one would most likely be left with a body of jurisprudential work every bit as formalistic as anything that came from the pen of Langdell. True to the Langdellian tradition, Holmes's ultimate ambition was 'to make the study of the law more scientific'.[118]

To understand how this was so, it is necessary, first of all, that we return to the pragmatist underpinnings of Holmes's work and, secondly, that we conceive of him not so much as a legal philosopher—this being very much a tag that legal realists pinned on him—as a doctrinal writer and judge. Commentators have tended to assume that Holmes's intellectual progression after the Civil War was strongly influenced by the pragmatist philosophy of Charles Sanders Peirce, a fellow patron of The Metaphysical Club. Yet, assumption is all that this is: Holmes and Peirce were little more than casual aquaintances; there is no record of Holmes having read any of Peirce's works before 1923; and since Holmes read so much and so widely, it is difficult to establish what might not have influenced him.[119] What is clear is that there is a striking similarity between the philosophy of Peirce and the jurisprudence of Holmes. Both men believed that external, public rather than internal, private standards constitute the correct basis for philosophical and legal judgement.[120] In Peirce's work, this philosophy was formulated primarily as a reaction against Cartesian philosophy of personal intuition. Descartes argued that we cannot know truth as a community, but only as individuals: that is, no matter how much we may collaborate with others in our quest for knowledge, the ultimate discovery of truth is a personal revelation to each and every one of us, the achievement of our own introspection.[121] To treat individual consciousness as the ultimate criterion

[117] Holmes, *supra* n. 96, 219. See further, on this point, E. Donald Elliott, 'Holmes and Evolution: Legal Process as Artificial Intelligence', *Jnl. Leg. Studs.*, 13 (1984), 113–46 at 116–17.

[118] G. Edward White, 'The Rise and Fall of Justice Holmes', *U. Chicago L. Rev.*, 39 (1971), 51–77 at 56.

[119] See Note [Rand Rosenblatt], 'Holmes, Peirce and Legal Pragmatism', *Yale L.J.*, 84 (1975), 1123–40 at 1125; Fisch, *supra* n. 104, 96.

[120] Peirce, it might be noted, embarked upon but never completed a book developing his own philosophy of law. See John M. Krois, 'Peirce's Speculative Rhetoric and the Problem of Natural Law', *Philosophy and Rhetoric*, 14 (1981), 16–30.

[121] See René Descartes, *Meditations of First Philosophy, With Selections from the Objections and Replies* (Eng. trans. J. Cottingham, Cambridge: Cambridge University Press, 1986), 44–5.

of truth, Peirce argues, is effectively to accord ontological priority to the beliefs of the individual rather than to those of the community, even though it is against the backdrop of generally held beliefs in the community that the intuitions of individual consciousness must be judged. Accordingly, 'to make single individuals absolute judges of truth is most pernicious'.[122] The discovery of truth is not a matter for the individual, but for the community: 'We individually cannot reasonably hope to attain the ultimate philosophy which we pursue; we can only seek it . . . for the *community* of philosophers.'[123]

According to the philosophy of Peirce, then, knowledge is essentially public and communal, acquired through shared, practical experience. In Holmes's writings, the distinction between public and private, while surfacing in a rather different way, is premissed on essentially the same philosophy.[124] On the first page of *The Common Law*, Holmes observes that the legal standards by which citizens are to be judged conform to '[t]he felt necessities of the time, the prevalent moral and political theories, intuitions of public policy, avowed or unconscious, even the prejudices which judges share with their fellow-men.'[125] Legal standards, in other words, are external, public, communal or objective standards. These are to be contrasted with internal or private standards of morality. In modern legal systems, Holmes argues, issues of legal liability, whether criminal, tortious or contractual, are to be decided by reference to rules which echo the general, shared standards of the community. 'The standards of the law are standards of general application. . . . The law considers, in other words, what would be blameworthy in the average man, the man of ordinary intelligence and prudence, and determines liability by that.'[126] Internal, moral standards cannot serve as a basis for determining legal liability; rather, such liability must be governed by external, communal criteria.[127]

[122] Charles Hartshorne, Paul Weiss and Arthur W. Burks (eds.), *Collected Papers of Charles Sanders Peirce* (eight vols. Cambridge, Mass.: Harvard University Press, 1931–58), V, 265.

[123] Ibid.

[124] See Rosenblatt, *supra* n. 119, 1132: 'For Holmes, extérnal standards govern imposition of liability in crime, tort, and contract. For Peirce, external rules govern the search for truth and the meaning of words.' Cf., however, Herbert Hovenkamp, 'Evolutionary Models in Jurisprudence', *Texas L. Rev.*, 64 (1985), 645–85 at 663–4 where the intellectual inspiration for Holmes's theory is traced (though without substantiation) to Edward Tylor's theory of cultural survivals.

[125] Holmes, *supra* n. 96, 1.

[126] Ibid. 108. For an excellent discussion of Holmes's theory of liability as presented in *The Common Law*, see Patrick S. Atiyah, 'The Legacy of Holmes Through English Eyes', *Boston Univ. L. Rev.*, 63 (1983), 341–82; and, on the Holmesian 'average man', cf. Jan Vetter, 'The Evolution of Holmes, Holmes and Evolution', *California L. Rev.*, 72 (1984), 343–68 at 366.

[127] Holmes applied his theory with some success during his years on the Massachusetts bench. See William A. Lundquist, 'Oliver Wendell Holmes and External Standards of

Holmes's subordination of personal moral culpability to external standards of liability was, certainly in American jurisprudence, without precedent.[128] This does not mean, however, that his theory offended against the tide of late nineteenth-century legal formalism. Indeed, if anything, the theory of external liability is resolutely formalist. It was Holmes's belief that external standards govern all modern principles of liability, whether criminal or civil, and that, because of this, such principles may be 'reduc[ed]' to 'a philosophically continuous series'.[129] In other words, external liability, for Holmes, constitutes a universal legal principle of Langdellian proportions. As Gilmore explains:

> Holmes's accomplishment was to make Langdellianism intellectually respectable. He provided an apparently convincing demonstration that it was possible, on a high level of intellectual discourse, to reduce all principles of liability to a single, philosophically continuous series and to construct a unitary theory which would explain all conceivable single instances and thus make it unnecessary to look with any particularity at what was actually going on in the real world.[130]

Thus we have here a picture of Holmes as a Langdellian legal unifier and logician. Logic prevails over experience. Peirce's philosophy of external knowledge is apparently transformed into a tool for demonstrating how prima facie distinct legal doctrines are of necessity interconnected by the same philosophical thread.

In promoting the external standard of liability, Holmes was again—as with his formulation of the prediction theory—engaging in pragmatist jurisprudence. For example, in tort law, the purpose of the external standard, he insisted, was to provide judges and juries with an objective criterion by which to ascertain whether or not a person should be liable for harms ensuing from his or her acts or omissions;[131] likewise, in contract law, its purpose was to facilitate the judicial settlement of disputed terms by reference to the outward sign of the parties' intentions.[132] Yet by setting up the idea of the external standard of liability as a universal template, as it were, Holmes was at least implicitly arguing that decisions

Criminal and Tort Liability: Application of Theory on the Massachusetts Bench', *Buffalo L. Rev.*, 28 (1979), 607–23; Patrick J. Kelley, 'A Critical Analysis of Holmes's Theory of Torts', *Washington Univ. L.Q.*, 61 (1983), 681–744; Robert L. Birmingham, 'Holmes on "Peerless": *Raffles* v. *Wichelhaus* and the Objective Theory of Contract', *U. Pittsburgh L. Rev.*, 47 (1985), 183–204; and, for a more critical and broad-ranging discussion, Mark V. Tushnet, 'The Logic of Experience: Oliver Wendell Holmes on the Supreme Judicial Court', *Virginia L. Rev.*, 63 (1977), 975–1052.

[128] See Grant Gilmore, *The Death of Contract* (Columbus: Ohio State University Press, 1974), 19–21; however, on the reception of the external liability theory in England, cf. Patrick S. Atiyah, 'Holmes and the Theory of Contract' in his *Essays on Contract* (Oxford: Clarendon Press, 1986), 57–72 at 59.

[129] Holmes, *supra* n. 96, 131.

[130] Gilmore, *supra* n. 4, 56.

[131] Holmes, *supra* n. 96, 77–129.

[132] Ibid. 289–307.

on issues of fault and breach of contract may be made mechanistically, as if courts are able to resolve disputes by applying a priori standards to particular fact-situations.[133] This sense of mechanistic application of purportedly universal, shared standards stands out particularly sharply in Holmes's discussion of the obligations of the jury:

> The theory or intention of the law is not that the feeling of approbation or blame which a particular twelve may entertain should be the criterion. They are supposed to leave their idiosyncrasies on one side, and to represent the feeling of the community. The ideal average prudent man, whose equivalent the jury is taken to be in many cases, and whose culpability or innocence is the supposed test, is a constant, and his conduct under given circumstances is theoretically always the same.[134]

The members of a jury, then, must apply not their own subjective standards, but those of a universal reasonable man. This is hardly the sort of sentiment that one commonly associates with the principal forebear of legal realism. The invocation of the reasonable man is in fact but one example of how Holmes presupposes the existence of certain objective, external criteria which, though they are supposed to represent the standards of the community at large, turn out to be the invention, and indeed betray the idiosyncracies, of Holmes himself. The following passage is illustrative:

> When men live in society, a certain average of conduct, a sacrifice of individual peculiarities going beyond a certain point, is necessary to the general welfare. If, for instance, a man is born hasty and awkward, is always having accidents and hurting himself or his neighbours, no doubt his congenital defects will be allowed for in the courts of Heaven, but his slips are no less troublesome to his neighbours than if they sprang from guilty neglect. His neighbours accordingly require him, at his proper peril, to come up to their standard, and the courts which they establish to take his personal equation into account.[135]

Holmes's vision is one of a community wholly unsympathetic to the weaker—in this case, the accident-prone—individual; a community which would make no distinction between presence and absence of intent but would rather condemn a person for their 'congenital defects'. Holmes's

[133] See Robert W. Gordon, 'Holmes' *Common Law* as Legal and Social Science' *Hofstra L. Rev.*, 10 (1982), 719–46 at 728–9: 'Holmes' standards for imposing liability were general inclusive standards applicable to everyone. The standards were expressed in a positivist form, suggesting that the enforcing court need only apply regularities observed in similar factual situations to determine the appropriate legal consequence of the facts in the present case. The aim of Holmes' scheme, like that of classical law generally, appears to be to maximize the sphere of autonomous freedom by giving individuals advised by lawyers reliable predictions of where the courts will limit their actions and the actions of others, and equalize the formal legal treatment of persons.'

[134] Holmes, *supra* n. 96, 111.

[135] Ibid. 108.

community is a community of the fittest. Like fellow members of The Metaphysical Club in the early 1870s, he discovered in Darwinism a philosophy which transformed the instinct of self-preservation—an instinct which he experienced vividly during the Civil War[136]—into the most fundamental condition of humanity.[137] As early as 1873, he wrote thus:

> In the last resort a man rightly prefers his own interest to that of his neighbours. And this is as true in legislation as in any other form of corporate action. All that can be expected from modern improvements is that legislation should easily and quickly, yet not too quickly, modify itself in accordance with the will of the *de facto* supreme power in the community, and that the spread of an educated sympathy should reduce the sacrifice of minorities to a minimum. But whatever body may possess the supreme power for the moment is certain to have interests inconsistent with others which have competed unsuccessfully. The more powerful interests must be more or less reflected in legislation; which, like every other device of man or beast, must tend in the long run to aid the survival of the fittest.[138]

Holmes's theme here—that statutory rights should serve not individuals but 'the will of the *de facto* supreme power in the community'—is one which has re-emerged in recent times on the left of American jurisprudence. One of the fundamental criticisms levelled at modern critical legal studies relates to the insistence by certain of its proponents that legal rights should be devised primarily to protect communities rather than individuals (see Chapter 6). Holmes's own argument, of course, was anything but leftist. The community, for Holmes, is not the community at large but rather a community of successful social competitors, of '[t]he more powerful interests' in society. Whereas the representatives of critical legal studies stand to the left of liberalism, Holmes, *qua* Social Darwinist,

136 See G. Edward White, *Justice Oliver Wendell Holmes: Law and the Inner Self* (New York: Oxford University Press, 1993), 49–86; Bowen, *supra* n. 101, 163–4; Edmund Wilson, *Patriotic Gore: Studies in the Literature of the American Civil War* (London: Deutsch, 1962), 743–96; Irving Bernstein, 'The Conservative Mr. Justice Holmes', *New England Quarterly*, 23 (1950), 435–52 at 440–42.

137 See Mark deWolfe Howe (ed.), *Holmes-Pollock Letters: The Correspondence of Mr. Justice Holmes and Sir Frederick Pollock 1874–1932* (two vols., Cambridge, Mass.: Harvard University Press, 1941), I, 58; C. H. S. Fifoot, *Judge and Jurist in the Reign of Victoria* (London: Stevens, 1959), 8–9; also text accompanying n. 104, *supra*. Howe suggests that Holmes did not read any of Darwin's work until as late as 1907. See Howe, *supra* n. 98, 156. In 1919, Holmes reminisced that, during his intellectually formative years, evolutionism 'was in the air, although perhaps only the few of my time felt it. [Charles Darwin's] *The Origin of Species* I think came out while I was in college—H[erbert] Spencer had announced his intention to put the universe into our pockets—I hadn't read either of them to be sure, but as I say it was in the air'. Oliver Wendell Holmes, Jr. to Morris R. Cohen, 5 February 1919, in Felix Cohen (ed.), 'The Holmes-Cohen Correspondence', *Jnl. of the History of Ideas*, 9 (1948), 3–52 at 14–15.

138 Oliver Wendell Holmes, Jr. (unsigned), 'Summary of Events: The Gas Stokers' Strike', *American L. Rev.* 7 (1873), 582–9 at 583.

stood markedly to the right. This much is clear from his rejection of utilitarianism:

Why should the greatest number be preferred? Why not the greatest good of the most intelligent and most highly developed? The greatest good of a minority of our generation may be the greatest good of the greatest number in the long run.[139]

It is possible to object that this classification of Holmes as a Social Darwinist offends against the grain of common wisdom. It was Holmes, after all, who, on the Massachusetts bench, dissociated himself from a majority ruling upholding an injunction prohibiting peaceful picketing: workers, he argued, enjoy the same economic freedoms as their employers and, to this end, should be considered to be perfectly at liberty to withhold their labour as a means of acquiring bargaining power.[140] It was Holmes too who, in the Supreme Court, demonstrated his toleration towards progressive legislation and, equally, his contempt for judges who used the provisions of the Constitution to further their own social and economic prejudices.[141] In *Lochner* v. *New York* he summarized his position in one short statement which, like his assertion regarding experience over logic, was to become a starting point for many legal realists. Dissenting, he observed that the majority Justices in *Lochner* had reached their decision on the basis of:

an economic theory which a large part of the country does not entertain. If it were a question whether I agreed with that theory, I should desire to study it further and long before making up my mind. But I do not conceive that to be my duty, because I strongly believe that my agreement or disagreement has nothing to do with the right of a majority to embody their opinions in law. . . . The Fourteenth Amendment does not enact Mr. Herbert Spencer's *Social Statics*. . . . Some . . . laws embody convictions or prejudices which judges are likely to share. Some may not. But a constitution is not intended to embody a particular economic theory, whether of paternalism and the organic relation of the citizen to the state or of

[139] Ibid. 584; though for some attempts to trace affinities between Holmes's legal thought and utilitarianism, cf. H. L. Pohlman, *Justice Oliver Wendell Holmes and Utilitarian Jurisprudence* (Cambridge, Mass.: Harvard University Press, 1984); *Justice Oliver Wendell Holmes: Free Speech and the Living Constitution* (New York: New York University Press, 1991), 20–52; Patrick J. Kelley, 'Oliver Wendell Holmes, Utilitarian Jurisprudence and the Positivism of John Stuart Mill', *Am. J. Jurisprudence*, 30 (1985), 189–219.

[140] *Vegelahn* v. *Gunter* (1896) 167 Mass. 92, 104; 44 N.E. 1077, 1079. (Holmes J. dissenting.) Holmes's dissent resulted, in some quarters, in his being branded as a pro-labour radical (cf. White, *supra* n. 118, 56), a characterization which did not please him: see Oliver Wendell Holmes, Jr. to Frederick Pollock, 23 February 1902, in Howe (ed.), *supra* n. 137, 106; Tushnet, *supra* n. 127, 1035–40; Gordon, *supra* n. 133, 736, fn. 118.

[141] See, as examples, Holmes's dissenting opinions in *Otis* v. *Parker* (1903) 187 U.S. 606; *Adair* v. *United States* (1908) 208 U.S. 161, 190; *Hammer* v. *Dagenhart* (1918) 247 U.S. 251, 277; *Truax* v. *Corrigan* (1921) 257 U.S. 312, 342; *Adkins* v. *Children's Hospital* (1923) 261 U.S. 525, 567.

laissez-faire. It is made for people of fundamentally differing views, and the accident of our finding certain opinions natural and familiar or novel and even shocking ought not to conclude our judgement upon the question whether statutes embodying them conflict with the Constitution of the United States.[142]

The middle sentence of this passage—'The Fourteenth Amendment does not enact Mr Herbert Spencer's *Social Statics*'—became a *locus classicus* in realist legal thought. On the basis of these few words, some legal realists constructed an image of Holmes as a progressive pitted against Social Darwinist ideology, and in particular against those Supreme Court Justices who devised a Spencerian interpretation of the Fourteenth Amendment in order to emasculate social legislation. As with his claim to favour experience over logic, however, it is important to keep this short quotation in perspective. As is clear from the passage above, Holmes rejected not only the judicial importation of Spencerian *laissez-faire* into the Fourteenth Amendment, but indeed the importation of any economic theory. While anti-formalist American jurisprudence after Holmes has upheld this quotation as a landmark rejection of Spencer, Holmes would equally, we might assume, have opposed an attempt to import, say, the institutionalist economics of Thorstein Veblen into the Constitution. Such an assumption is supported by the fact that, although there is clearly a Spencerian drift to the majority opinion in *Lochner*, Spencer does not—leaving aside Holmes's isolated reference to him—explicitly feature in the decision. Furthermore, '[n]owhere in the lengthy briefs submitted by the counsel for *Lochner* to either the New York Court of Appeals or the United States Supreme Court is there any reference which could be construed as having its source within Spencer's *Social Statics*, or any evidence that the attorneys were arguing for the survival of the fittest.'[143] It is tempting to conclude that Holmes introduced Spencer for the purpose of coining a pithy aphorism rather than to take a stand against Social Darwinism. Holmes in fact claimed to admire the work of Spencer as much as he did that of Darwin,[144] and even during his years as a Supreme Court Justice he continued to subscribe to an essentially Social Darwinist view of the world.[145] If he differed from Spencer, it was in so far as he believed

[142] *Lochner* v. *New York*, *supra* n. 86, 75–6. (Holmes J. dissenting). The passage has been hailed as 'perhaps the most famous put-down in American judicial history'. Mark G. Yudof, 'Equal Protection, Class Legislation, and Sex Discrimination: One Small Cheer for Mr. Herbert Spencer's *Social Statics*', *Michigan L. Rev.*, 88 (1990) 1366–408 at 1390.

[143] Joseph F. Wall, 'Social Darwinism and Constitutional Law with Special Reference to *Lochner* v. *New York*', *Annals of Science*, 33 (1976), 465–76 at 471; see also Benedict, *supra* n. 77, 305–8.

[144] Though he possibly remained reticent about *Social Statics*: see Howe, *supra* n. 98, 156.

[145] In 1915, he confessed to despair of those progressives 'who think that something particular has happened and that the universe is no longer predatory'. Oliver Wendell Holmes to John Henry Wigmore, 19 November 1915, in Howe, *supra* n. 98, 25. Generally, on Holmes's Darwinism, see Benjamin Kaplan, 'Encounters With O. W. Holmes, Jr.', *Harvard*

economic freedom to be as much a privilege of the working classes as it was of the middle classes. It was for precisely this reason that he objected to the judicial use of Social Darwinism to strike down legislation which served the cause of the employee.[146] Very crudely, Holmes was—in so far as there ever could be such a species—an egalitarian Social Darwinist. To his eyes, all economic agents, whatever their class or status, must be accorded the right to fight for their survival in the market-place. The point to be stressed is that, while legal realists celebrated Holmes's egalitarianism, they apparently failed to perceive his Social Darwinism—indeed, more generally, they failed to acknowledge the formalist predilections underscoring many facets of his legal philosophy.

Accordingly, while Holmes was certainly an important forerunner of American legal realism, it would be wrong to categorize him straightforwardly as an unequivocal anti-formalist. To chart, as some commentators have done,[147] a straight and uncluttered path from Holmes to the legal realists is to produce an oversimplified intellectual history; for there are arguments to be found in his work which stand antithetical to the basic philosophy of legal realism, arguments which realists tended to overlook or ignore. Various realists gleaned from Holmes all that corresponded with their particular versions of anti-formalism, and left behind them all that did not.

The merit of treating Holmes as the first great anti-formalist jurist is that such a treatment provides a convenient inroad for a study of legal realism. Without Holmes, it is difficult to locate, with anything approaching precision, the emergence of anti-formalist legal thinking. While our point here has been that Holmes's jurisprudence often offends against the spirit of anti-formalism, it must also be remembered that many of the famous passages to be found in his writings and decisions encapsulate precisely that

L. Rev., 96 (1983), 1828–52 at 1840; Richard A. Posner, 'Economics, Politics, and the Reading of Statutes and the Constitution', *U. Chicago L. Rev.*, 49 (1982), 263–91 at 267; E. Donald Elliott, 'The Evolutionary Tradition in Jurisprudence' *Columbia L. Rev.*, 85 (1985), 38–94 at 50–5; *supra* n. 117, *passim*; Hovenkamp, *supra* n. 124, 656–64; and Vetter, *supra* n. 126, 363–6.

[146] See Gordon, *supra* n. 133, 740.

[147] See Wilfrid E. Rumble, Jr., *American Legal Realism: Skepticism, Reform, and the Judicial Process* (Ithaca, NY: Cornell University Press, 1968), 38–44; Bernie R. Burrus, 'American Legal Realism', *Howard L.J.*, 6 (1962), 36–51 at 37–8; Ralph J. Savarese, 'American Legal Realism', *Houston L. Rev.*, 3 (1965), 180–200 at 186–7. Like these authors, William Twining too treats Holmes purely as an anti-formalist. See William Twining, *Karl Llewellyn and the Realist Movement* (rev. edn. London: Weidenfeld & Nicolson, 1985), 15–20. Twining nevertheless regards Holmesian anti-formalism as a failed project: 'The failure on the part of Holmes and his contemporaries to realize the full implications of the kind of perspective he was advocating in "The Path of the Law", together with the enormous practical difficulties of implementing an approach related to that perspective, must be counted among the most important reasons for the survival of the Langdellian system for many years' (19–20).

spirit. In his short book, *The Ages of American Law*, Grant Gilmore adopts a rather more radical stance than that taken here. Gilmore's Holmes betrays not so much as a hint of proto-realist progressivism. Even though 'the Langdellians . . . rejected, ignored, or perhaps simply misunderstood many aspects of Holmes's complex thought',[148] he must be seen, Gilmore argues, to fit squarely and exclusively within the tradition of Langdell.

If we treat Holmes simply as part of the tradition represented by Langdell's Harvard, where are we to take it that anti-formalist legal thinking began? Gilmore suggests the name of Benjamin Nathan Cardozo. In a series of lectures delivered at the Yale Law School in 1920 and published the following year under the title, *The Nature of the Judicial Process*, Cardozo—at that time a Judge on the New York Court of Appeals—reflected on the uncertain nature of the judicial function. These reflections were offered very much in the style of a personal confession. 'I own,' Cardozo remarked, 'that it is a good deal of a mystery to me how judges, of all persons in the world, should put their faith in dicta.'[149] Reminiscing on his early years on the bench, he recalled that:

> I was much troubled in spirit . . . to find how trackless was the ocean on which I had embarked. I sought for certainty. I was oppressed and disheartened when I found that the quest for it was futile. . . . As the years have gone by, and as I have reflected more and more upon the nature of the judicial process, I have become reconciled to the uncertainty, because I have grown to see it as inevitable.[150]

Elsewhere in his lectures, Cardozo adopts a markedly less anxious persona, treating the judicial function as purely a matter of mechanical application of established rules and principles to specific factual instances. Apart from 'in exceptional conditions', he remarks at one juncture, 'the work of deciding cases in accordance with precedents that plainly fit them . . . is a process of search, comparison, and little more.'[151] It is, however, Cardozo's *Sturm und Drang* which captures Gilmore's imagination. Cardozo, he believes, was 'a revolutionary *malgré lui*' whose 'hesitant confession that judges were, on rare occasions, more than simple automata' became 'widely regarded as a legal version of hard-core pornography'.[152] That this supposed figure of judicial self-abasement should have become, in 1932, a Justice of the Supreme Court rather suggests that Gilmore's image of Cardozo as a 'revolutionary' is very much an exaggeration. What is certainly clear is that Gilmore finds nothing in

[148] Gilmore, *supra* n. 4, 48.

[149] Benjamin N. Cardozo, *The Nature of the Judicial Process* (New Haven, Conn.: Yale University Press, 1921), 29.

[150] Ibid. 166.

[151] Ibid. and cf. also 18–19.

[152] Gilmore, *supra* n. 4, 77. For a critique of Gilmore's characterization, see Richard A. Posner, *Cardozo: A Study in Reputation* (Chicago: University of Chicago Press, 1990), 12–13.

Cardozo's lectures that could not already have been found in the writings of Holmes. Indeed, Cardozo's purportedly radical acceptance of the inevitability of judicial incertitude simply echoes a classic Holmesian aphorism: 'certainty generally is illusion, and repose is not the destiny of man'.[153] Likewise Cardozo's rather hesitant suggestion that, in the absence of statutory authority or applicable precedent, the judge 'must then fashion law for the litigants before him'.[154] According to Holmes:

> Ours is not a closed system of existing precedent. The law is not such a formal system at all. We [the United States Supreme Court] are not, as a court of last resort, absolutely bound by our own decisions. . . . We legitimately made the law in question and can legitimately change it. Courts must make law. Indeed courts are major policy makers in our system of government. We must be wary of petrifying the common law into a rigid system, utterly behind the times and totally at odds with the progress of science and social change.[155]

Holmes's argument here contrasts markedly with the equivocation to be found in Cardozo's lectures. The common law system, for Holmes, is not a 'brooding omnipresence in the sky'.[156] Judges can and do make law—though we shall see shortly that Holmes also, at least once, qualified this argument. The difficulty with treating Holmes as nothing more than a Langdellian legal formalist, as Gilmore does, is that one is obliged to overlook such outright anti-formalist statements. And to suggest that the reaction against Langdell began with Cardozo is to credit the latter with ideas which, as he himself would have conceded,[157] were in fact pioneered by Holmes.

Yet there is one argument offered by Cardozo—an argument not, ironically, addressed by Gilmore and, to my knowledge, never formulated explicitly by Holmes—which, during the decade following the publication of his lectures, was gradually shaped into one of the key theses of legal realism. In the fourth and last of the lectures which comprise *The Nature of the Judicial Process*, Cardozo turns his attention to the question of how judges reach decisions. Besides conscious consideration of fact and law, he argues, judges are swayed also by other factors: 'Deep below consciousness are other forces, the likes and the dislikes, the predilections and the prejudices, the complex of instincts and emotions and habits and convictions, which make the man, whether he be litigant or judge.'[158] This

[153] Holmes, *supra* n. 106, 460. On Cardozo and Holmes, see John T. Noonan, Jr., *Persons and Masks of the Law: Cardozo, Holmes, Jefferson, and Wythe as Makers of the Masks* (New York: Farrar, Straus and Giroux, 1976), 146–7; Bernard Weissman, 'Cardozo: "All-Time Greatest" American Judge', *Cumberland L. Rev.*, 19 (1988), 1–18 at 7–8.

[154] Cardozo, *supra* n. 149, 21, and cf. 10 for a bolder statement of this position. ('I take judge-made law as one of the existing realities of life.')

[155] *Southern Pacific Co.* v. *Jensen* (1917) 244 U.S. 205, 221 (Holmes J. dissenting.)

[156] Ibid. 222.

[157] Cardozo, *supra* n. 149, 32–3, 55, 79–82, 117–19.

[158] Ibid. 167.

argument, we shall see in the next chapter, was developed in a realist context primarily by one of Cardozo's sternest critics, Jerome Frank.[159] Cardozo himself, in presenting the idea that judges are swayed by their unconscious prejudices, was basically supplementing his observation that judges cannot always be taken straightforwardly to accept and operate on the basis of established precedents and statutes, but must at times be regarded as actual creators of law.

In treating the judge as an occasional creator of law, Cardozo was echoing rather faintly a theme originally broached by Holmes. It was, perhaps ironically, a figure from Langdell's Harvard who attempted to make this theme explicit. John Chipman Gray served on the Harvard law faculty as lecturer and professor from 1869 to 1913. Like Holmes, he was not only an immensely learned man but he was also neither straightforwardly a formalist nor a realist, and his position within the Langdellian scheme of things is somewhat ambivalent. Gray was slow to warm to the 'dogmatism' of the case method of teaching.[160] Furthermore, though he was one of the new breed of professional law teachers and the author of one of the most important late nineteenth-century case-books,[161] he continued to practise law throughout his academic career and professed a suspicion of 'school men'.[162] Not that Gray disliked intellectuals. He cultivated knowledge passionately. With Holmes, he was a casual attender of The Metaphysical Club,[163] and he 'possessed a natural and easygoing inclination towards scholarship'.[164] Unlike the majority of his Harvard

[159] Frank's primary criticism of Cardozo was that, as a legal writer, he conceived of the judicial process purely in terms of the appellate courts, paying little attention to the process of fact-finding in the trial courts. See Jerome Frank, 'Cardozo and the Upper Court Myth', *Law and Contemporary Problems*, 13 (1948), 369–90. On other occasions, Frank was more generous in his estimation of Cardozo. See Jerome Frank, *Law and the Modern Mind* (Gloucester, Mass.: Peter Smith, 1970; orig. publ. 1930), 7 n. 3, 164. For a general estimation of Frank's criticisms of Cardozo, see Paul Bricker, 'Justice Benjamin N. Cardozo: A Fresh Look at a Great Judge', *Ohio Northern Univ. L. Rev.* , 11 (1984), 1–36 at 14–24.

[160] See Williston, *supra* n. 39, 74; Sutherland, *supra* n. 41, 185. For Gray on the '*a priori* dogmatism' of the case method of teaching, see John Chipman Gray, 'Methods of Legal Education', *Yale L.J.*, 1 (1892), 159–161 at 161.

[161] John Chipman Gray, *Select Cases and Other Authorities on the Law of Property* (six vols. Cambridge, Mass.: Sever, 1888–92). On this case book, see Sutherland, *supra* n. 41, 152. Equally important was Gray's *The Rule Against Perpetuities* (Boston: Little, Brown & Co., 1886). On this book, see Friedman, *supra* n. 33, 422; and on Gray generally, see Roland Gray, 'Memoir', in R. Gray (ed.), *John Chipman Gray* (Boston: privately printed, 1917), 24–7.

[162] See Twining, *supra* n. 147, 20. Gray's links with practice apparently proved important to Harvard Law School in that, 'at the time when Langdell's [case] method was meeting with opposition among practitioners', it was Gray who 'was most valuable in convincing the bar of Boston that there must be something in the new fangled way of doing things'. *Centennial History of the Harvard Law School*, *supra* n. 45, 211.

[163] Apparently, Gray contributed very little at these meetings: see Fisch, *supra* n. 104, 88 fn. 8. On the friendship between Gray and Holmes, cf. Howe, *supra* n. 93, 276; *supra* n. 98, 251–52, 311 n. 25.

[164] Howe, *supra* n. 98, 252.

colleagues, however, the pursuit of scholarship did not take him down the path of Langdellian legal science. This much is clear from his outburst against Langdell in a letter to President Eliot:

> In the law the opinions of judges and lawyers as to what the law is, *are* the law, and it is in any true sense of the word as unscientific to turn from them, as Mr. Langdell does, with contempt because they are 'low and unscientific', as for a man to decline to take cognizance of oxygen or gravitation because it was low or unscientific . . . Langdell's intellectual arrogance and contempt is astounding. One may forgive it in him or Ames, but in an ordinary man it would be detestable. The idols of the cave which a school bred lawyer is sure to substitute for the facts, *may be much better material for intellectual gymnastics than the facts themselves and may call forth more enthusiasm in the pupils*, but a school where the majority of the professors shuns and despises the contact with actual facts, has got the seeds of ruin in it and will and ought to go to the devil.[165]

The style and the content of this passage—the excoriation of Langdell for his neglect of 'actual facts' in the pursuit of legal science—is not a million miles away from Holmes's prioritizing of experience over logic. But there is more here than a mere echoing of Holmes. In this passage, we find also the germ of Gray's own distinct jurisprudential perspective—a perspective which he developed in his last book, *The Nature and Sources of the Law*.[166] Up until the appearance of this book, published in his seventieth year, Gray had been regarded more or less solely as a property lawyer. Jurisprudence had hardly been his forte.[167] Holmes recalled in 1925 that, before the publication of *Nature and Sources*, he had never so much as suspected Gray of being a philosopher.[168] Yet the appearance of the book marked not only a new direction for its author, but also a partial reorientation of post-Langdellian jurisprudence.

Basically, Gray was unequivocal where Holmes and Cardozo were not. We have seen that Cardozo believed the creative role of the judge to be restricted to cases governed by 'exceptional conditions'.[169] Holmes, too,

[165] John Chipman Gray to Charles William Eliot, 8 January 1883, in Howe, ibid. 158.

[166] John Chipman Gray, *The Nature and Sources of the Law* (New York: Columbia University Press, 1916; orig. publ. 1909).

[167] Though *Nature and Sources* was not Gray's first incursion into jurisprudence: see John Chipman Gray, 'Some Definitions and Questions in Jurisprudence', *Harvard L. Rev.*, 6 (1892), 21–35.

[168] Oliver Wendell Holmes, Jr. to Harold J. Laski, 4 January 1925, in Howe (ed.), *supra* n. 97, 693.

[169] Cardozo in fact considered Gray's unequivocality to be unacceptable. See Cardozo, *supra* n. 149, 124. ('In thus recognizing, as I do, that the power to declare the law carries with it the power, and within limits the duty, to make law when none exists, I do not mean to range myself with the jurists who seem to hold that in reality there is no law except the decisions of the courts. I think the truth is midway between the extremes that are represented at the one end by Coke and Hale and Blackstone and at the other by such authors as Austin and Holland and Gray and Jethro Brown.)' See further ibid. 125–9; and cf. Frank, *supra* n. 159, 252–5 (on 'The Candor of Cardozo').

though he was rather more positive about the capacity of judges to make law, argued that they can in fact do so only 'interstitially'.[170] But Gray made no such qualifications. The basic thesis of *Nature and Sources* is the opposite of that which was presented by his Harvard colleague, Beale: namely, that judges always create law and, accordingly, that nothing is law until declared to be so by the courts. 'The Law of the State or of any organized body of men is composed of the rules which the courts, that is, the judicial organs of that body, lay down for the determination of legal rights and duties.'[171] Thus 'the Law is what the judges rule'.[172] By comparison, precedents and statutes—along with 'opinions of experts, customs, and principles of morality (using morality as including public policy)'[173]—merely constitute sources of law to which the courts give life.[174] 'As between the legislative and judicial organs of a society, it is the judicial which has the last say as to what is and what is not Law in a community.'[175] This argument, for Gray, applies not only to legislation but to all other sources of law.

With Gray, then, the judge is moved decisively from the wings to the centre-stage of American jurisprudence. But the candour of his argument should not be mistaken for radicalism. According to Gray, 'judges are but organs of the State; they have only such power as the organization of the State gives them; and what that organization is, is determined by the wills of the real rulers of the State.'[176] In other words, judges, though they create law, are also accountable in their actions to the 'real rulers' of society, and therefore may not exercise unfettered discretion. Gray adds to this that the question of '[w]ho are the rulers of a State, is a question of fact and not of form';[177] but elsewhere in his book he implicitly acknowledges the insufficiency of this remark:

> To determine who are the real rulers of a political society is well-nigh an impossible task,—for Jurisprudence a well-nigh insoluble problem. To estimate, even approximately, the power that a certain statesman or demagogue has or had in a political society is a problem whose elements are too conflicting and too obscure for human judgement.[178]

[170] Holmes, *supra* n. 155, 221. ('I recognize without hesitation that judges do and must legislate, but they can do so only interstitially.)' On Holmes's dislike of judicial creativity, see further Elliott, *supra* n. 117, 123, 129; and on the model of the interstitial legislator, see John Bell, *Policy Arguments in Judicial Decisions* (Oxford: Clarendon Press, 1983), 17–20, 226–46.

[171] See Gray, *supra* n. 166, 82. [172] Ibid. 91. [173] Ibid. 118.

[174] The metaphor of life-giving is Gray's. See ibid. 120. ('The courts put life into the dead words of the statute.') On the sources of the law generally, cf. ibid. 145–292.

[175] Ibid. 164. [176] Ibid. 116. [177] Ibid.

[178] Ibid. 76, and cf. also 77. ('The real rulers of political society are undiscoverable. They are the persons who dominate over the wills of their fellows.')

So the judge is the servant of these mysterious 'real rulers'.[179] Although Gray's insistence that judges make law has sometimes been interpreted as a foundation stone for legal realism,[180] such interpretations have tended to overlook the fact that his theory is one of both judicial creativity and judicial restraint. While, prima facie, he anticipates the realist thesis that judges are only human, he qualifies this thesis by arguing also that judges act in accordance with an objective plan, that is, in accordance with the 'will' of so-called real rulers. Why should Gray have argued thus? The reason may be found in the very first sentence of *The Nature and Sources of the Law*:

> Some fifty years ago I came across a copy of Austin's *Province of Jurisprudence Determined*, then little read in England, and all but unknown in this country; and since then, although my work has been mainly on other lines, the subject has seldom been for long wholly out of my mind.[181]

Gray's theory of judicial creativity is, in essence, a critique of Austin's theory of sovereignty. Austin's theory, Gray argues, has no relevance in a country such as the United States, where there is no equivalent of sovereign authority. In the United States, such authority is not, as Austin suggests, comprised by the collective powers of the governments of all States over individual citizens, for State powers over the individual are defined and limited by the Constitution.[182] Since the powers of the States as an aggregate body are restricted by constitutional safeguards, 'there may be no one sovereign in Austin's sense, with complete powers'.[183]

Gray did not, however, dismiss Austin's theory of sovereignty altogether. Despite its inapplicability to the law of the United States, Austin's theory, Gray believed, represented a pioneering rejection of metaphysics in jurisprudence:

> The great gain in its fundamental conceptions which jurisprudence made during the last century was the recognition of the truth that the Law of a State or other organized body is not an ideal, but something which actually exists. It is not that which is in accordance with religion, or nature, or morality; it is not that which ought to be, but that which is. To fix this definitely in the Jurisprudence of the Common Law, is the feat that Austin accomplished. He may have been wrong in

[179] For a critical analysis of this aspect of Gray's thesis, see Neil MacCormick, 'A Political Frontier of Jurisprudence: John Chipman Gray on the State', *Cornell L. Rev.*, 66 (1981), 973–85 at 979–80.

[180] See e.g. ibid. 973 ('it is surely neither injudicious nor unjust to see in [*The Nature and Sources of the Law*] a prototype for the "Realism" of the American law schools in their intellectual ferment of the 1920s and '30s'); Wilfrid Rumble, Jr., 'Law as the Effective Decisions of Officials: A "New Look" at Legal Realism', *Jnl. of Public Law*, 20 (1971), 215–71 at 236–7. Twining (*supra* n. 147, 22) observes that 'Gray's ideas presented no serious threat to the Langdellian orthodoxy', but he does not explain why this should have been the case.

[181] Gray, *supra* n. 166, vii.

[182] Ibid. 74.

[183] Ibid. 76.

> treating the Law of the State as being the command of the sovereign, but he was right in teaching that the rules for conduct laid down by the persons acting as judicial organs of the State, are the Law of the State, and that no rules not so laid down are the Law of the State.[184]

Gray's jurisprudence is, in effect, a continuation of the Austinian spirit of inquiry. Both authors insisted that there must exist a physical legal authority, distinct from religion, nature or morality; and where Austin invoked the Sovereign, Gray resorted to the judge. Though judges, unlike Austin's Sovereign, are not assumed to have unlimited powers, they are deemed by Gray to be the ultimate arbiters of legal rights and duties. 'Every State has judicial organs whose function it is, by aid of certain rules called the Law, to determine what interests are now entitled to be protected, and what acts and forbearances the State will now, on its own motion or on the motion of individuals, enforce.'[185] The judiciary, as an arm of the state, interprets sources of law in order to determine the legal rights and obligations of citizens. The judge is thus supposed, by Gray, to displace Austin's sovereign.

To distinguish law—namely, the decrees of judges—from the sources of the law leads to various ambiguities. This is most clear with regard to precedent. According to Gray, the rules laid down by courts when deciding cases are 'law'; yet, with regard to future cases, those rules, as precedents, are mere sources of law.[186] This is implicitly to suppose that there exists some miraculous cut-off point at which a legal decision suddenly expires as law, and becomes but a precedential source. Ambiguities such as this are not, however, our concern here. While Gray is commonly considered to be a forerunner of American legal realism, his jurisprudential perspective in fact fits far more squarely within the tradition of Austinian positivism. Considered thus, Gray, like Holmes, can be conceived equally to be an anti-formalist and a formalist. Certainly, he pre-dated legal realism by emphasizing the place of the courts in the law-making process; but equally he subscribed to an Austinian-cum-Langdellian view of the judicial role. As officials of the state, judges are empowered to make law; but the state requires that the process of making law be conceived as one of deducing principles from the available legal sources.[187] In *The Nature and Sources of the Law*, we discover a theory of judicial creativity with a catch.

Whether, in fact, Gray influenced many proponents of legal realism is somewhat doubtful.[188] Most legal realists were demonstrably more indebted intellectually to Holmes than to Gray, and only Jerome Frank,

[184] Ibid. 92.

[185] Ibid. 80–1.

[186] See Edwin W. Patterson, *Jurisprudence: Men and Ideas of the Law* (Brooklyn: Foundation Press, 1953), 210.

[187] See Gray, *supra* n. 166, 118–20.

[188] See Rumble, *supra* n. 180, 237.

among them, devoted significant critical attention to Gray's theory of the judicial role. As a professor at Harvard at the end of the nineteenth century, however, Gray proved to be a notable influence on one student who, in the coming decades, was to make as strong an impression on legal realism as did Holmes. Roscoe Pound entered the Harvard Law School as a student in September 1889 with no intention of staying there for longer than a year. Seventeen years later, he was to become Dean of the School. His conversion to the study of law—he had already acquired a doctorate in botany[189]—was inspired at least partially by the intellectual ambition of Gray.[190] Pound subscribed to Gray's thesis—albeit shorn of its Austinian baggage—that judges create law by interpreting the sources of law;[191] and there are themes and arguments in Pound's writings which seem clearly to anticipate and support the emergence of legal realism. Where, in the writings of Holmes and Gray, we have detected an implicit tension between formalism and anti-formalism, in the work of Pound this tension emerges writ large.

Pound's criticisms of legal formalism were considerably more acute than many of those put forward by legal realists. Like Holmes, furthermore, Pound criticized not only the tradition of Langdell, but also that of *laissez-faire*. Whereas it is possible to argue, however, that Holmes was in effect a formalist by default, Pound's espousal of legal formalism was explicit and often confrontational. Many of the arguments which he presented from the 1920s onwards were formulated precisely to challenge the tenets of legal realism. It is impossible here to do full justice to the many volumes of writing which comprise Pound's jurisprudence, or even to consider in any detail the conflicts of ideas and opinions to be found therein. Since our objective is to understand Pound in the context of the jurisprudential drift from formalism to realism, we shall offer only a core analysis of his allegiance to and divergence from both tendencies.

Pound's anti-formalist stance is encapsulated in two of his most famous articles, published within a year of one another, in which he criticizes the traditions of Langdell and of *laissez-faire*. In his article, 'Mechanical Jurisprudence', published in 1908, Langdell is not specifically mentioned though the tradition of Langdellian legal science is explicitly attacked.[192]

[189] Published in a revised form as Roscoe Pound and Frederic E. Clements, *Phytogeography of Nebraska* (Lincoln, Nebr.: North, 1898; 2nd edn. 1900).

[190] See David Wigdor, *Roscoe Pound: Philosopher of Law* (Westport: Greenwood, 1974), 39–43.

[191] See Roscoe Pound, *An Introduction to the Philosophy of Law* (rev. edn. New Haven, Conn.: Yale University Press, 1954), 49–50; also, more generally, 'The Theory of Judicial Decision', *Harvard L. Rev.*, 36 (1923), 641–62, 802–25, 940–59.

[192] Roscoe Pound, 'Mechanical Jurisprudence', *Columbia L. Rev.*, 8 (1908), 605–23.

Taking issue with 'the tendency of scientific law to become mechanical',[193] Pound argues that legal science must be conceived to have a purpose, namely:

> the administration of justice. . . . Law is scientific in order to eliminate so far as may be the personal equation in judicial administration to preclude corruption and to limit the dangerous possibilities of magisterial ignorance. Law is not scientific for the sake of science. Being scientific as a means towards an end, it must be judged by the results it achieves, not by the niceties of its internal structure; it must be valued by the extent to which it meets its end, not by the beauty of its logical processes or the strictness with which its rules proceed from the dogmas it takes for its foundation.[194]

Mechanical jurisprudence is thus 'the special tendency of the lawyer to regard artificiality in law as an end, to hold science something to be pursued for its own sake, to forget in this pursuit the purpose of law and hence of scientific law, and to judge rules and doctrines by their conformity to a supposed science and not by the results to which they lead.'[195] In truth, however, mechanical jurisprudence is not scientific at all, or at least not in the modern sense of the term, since, by the turn of the nineteenth century, '[t]he idea of science as a system of deductions ha[d] become obsolete'.[196] Science had acquired a distinctly pragmatic bent,[197] and the burden rested on modern jurisprudence to revise its outlook accordingly: 'We have, then, the same task in jurisprudence that has been achieved in philosophy, in the natural sciences and in politics. We have to rid ourselves of this sort of legality [*sc.* Langdellian legal science] and to attain a pragmatic, a sociological legal science.'[198]

The formalist principles of mechanical jurisprudence were to be displaced, accordingly, by the pragmatist principles of sociological jurisprudence. 'The sociological movement in jurisprudence is a movement for pragmatism as a philosophy of law; for the adjustment of principles and doctrines to the human conditions they are to govern rather than to assumed first principles; for putting the human factor in the central place and relegating logic to its true position as an instrument.'[199] Even Holmes had not sounded the clarion as clearly as this: Langdellian legal science had become an anachronism; the time had come, so far as Pound was

[193] Ibid. 607. [194] Ibid. 605. [195] Ibid. 607–8.

[196] Ibid. 608.

[197] Whereas, Pound argued, the nineteenth-century scientific disciplines 'conceived of a slow and ordered succession of events . . . whereby things perfected themselves by evolving to the limit of their idea,' pragmatism 'sees validity in actions . . . to the extent that they satisfy a maximum of human demands'. Roscoe Pound, *Interpretations of Legal History* (Cambridge: Cambridge University Press, 1923), 11. On Pound and pragmatism, see generally Note, 'Legal Theory and Legal Education', *Yale L.J.*, 79 (1970), 1153–78 at 1161–5.

[198] Pound, *supra* n. 192, 609. [199] Ibid. 610.

concerned, to call for a pragmatist-inspired, sociological jurisprudence—to call, in short, for an antidote to formalism.[200] This turn towards pragmatism was welcomed and echoed by an emerging generation of progressive lawyers.[201]

Pound's critique of legal formalism embraced not only the scientific pretensions of Langdell and his disciples, but also the Social Darwinist instincts of the American courts. 'The concept of liberty of contract, in particular,' he observed in 1908:

> has given rise to rules and decisions which, tested by their practical operation, defeat liberty. . . . The conception of freedom of contract is made the basis of a logical deduction. The court does not inquire what the effect of such a deduction will be, when applied to the actual situation. It does not observe that the result will be to produce a condition precisely the reverse of that which the conception originally contemplated.[202]

In the following year, in an article entitled 'Liberty of Contract',[203] Pound developed this argument at length. Inspired by, among other things, Holmes's dissent in *Lochner*—which Pound hailed as '[p]erhaps the best exposition' of 'the sociological movement in jurisprudence' to have emerged in the United States to that date[204]—he dismissed the notion of freedom of contract as a 'fallacy'.[205] The great majority of the courts' decisions on the subject, he insisted, 'are simply wrong, not only in constitutional law, but from the standpoint of the common law, and even from that of a sane individualism'.[206] Given that *de facto* equality does not exist among all citizens, why 'do courts persist in . . . forc[ing] upon legislation an academic theory of equality in the face of practical conditions of inequality? . . . Why is the legal conception of the relation of employer and employee so at variance with the common knowledge of mankind?'[207] Pound suggested a number of answers to these questions,[208] at least three of which are worth mentioning, given that they were later regenerated by various legal realists. His first answer was that there exists 'in juristic thought . . . an individualist conception of justice, which exaggerates the importance of property and of contract, exaggerates private right at the expense of public right, and is hostile to legislation, taking a minimum of law-making to be the ideal.'[209] A variation on this argument had, of

[200] See further Roscoe Pound, 'Law in Books and Law in Action', *American L. Rev.*, 44 (1910), 12–36; 'The Scope and Purpose of Sociological Jurisprudence', *Harvard L. Rev.*, 24 (1911), 591–619; *Harvard L. Rev.*, 25 (1911), 140–68; *Harvard L. Rev.*, 25 (1912), 489–516.

[201] See G. Edward White, 'From Sociological Jurisprudence to Realism: Jurisprudence and Social Change in Early Twentieth-Century America', *Virginia L. Rev.*, 58 (1972), 999–1028 at 1004–5.

[202] Pound, *supra* n. 192, 616.

[203] Roscoe Pound, 'Liberty of Contract', *Yale L.J.*, 18 (1909), 454–87.

[204] Ibid. 464.

[205] Ibid. 454.

[206] Ibid. 482.

[207] Ibid. 454.

[208] Ibid. 457–8.

[209] Ibid. 457.

course, already been offered by Holmes. The same is true of Pound's second answer—adverted to already in his article of the previous year—that the judicial philosophy of *laissez-faire* shares with mechanical jurisprudence an implicit faith in deductivism.[210] But his third answer, while again echoing Holmes, had a novel twist to it. The ideology of freedom of contract, he suggested, was at least partially attributable to 'the sharp line between law and fact in our legal system which requires constitutionality, as a legal question, to be tried by artificial criteria of general application and prevents effective judicial investigation or consideration of the situations of fact behind or bearing upon the statutes.'[211] These 'artificial criteria of general application' are invariably 'natural law notions'—for example, the supposed natural capacity among persons equally to contract.[212] Owing to their status as natural law concepts, Pound added, the interpretation and application of constitutional criteria by the courts tends to result in a distortion or neglect of the facts of any particular case. An appellate court, for example, preoccupied with the problem of constitutionality, is unlikely to concern itself all that deeply with issues of fact.

> In constitutional law . . . [i]t is felt that a law cannot be constitutional now if it would have been unconstitutional one hundred years ago. *In fact* it might have been an unreasonable deprivation of liberty as things were even 50 years ago, and yet be a reasonable regulation as things are now. But the question is not one of fact. Being for the court to decide, it must be decided upon some universal proposition, valid in all places and at all times. . . . As it is, in the ordinary case involving constitutionality, the court has no machinery for getting at the facts. It must decide on the basis of matters of general knowledge and on accepted principles of uniform application.[213]

In anticipating one strand of the nascent realist critique—the so-called 'higher law' background of American constitutional law[214]—Pound inadvertently anticipated another, namely, the divorce of the appellate courts from the process of fact-finding, and the consequent inappropriateness of limiting the study of cases, as Langdell had done, to an analysis of key upper-court decisions. Formalism in the courts, according to Pound, was not dissimilar to formalism in the law school. For an upper-court deciding on the constitutional meaning of freedom of contract, just as for a Langdellian law professor interpreting the decision of an upper-court, purportedly logical deductivism and an emphasis on principle rather than fact would be the order of the day. More than any of his predecessors,

[210] Ibid. [211] Ibid. 438. [212] Ibid. 465–6.
[213] Ibid. 469.
[214] See Edward S. Corwin, 'The "Higher Law" Background of American Constitutional Law', *Harvard L. Rev.*, 42 (1928–29), 149–85, 365–409.

Pound attempted to demonstrate how the formalist objectives of the Langdellians and of Social Darwinist judges intermeshed.

There is little in these early writings to suggest that Pound was anything but a realist *avant la lettre*. Despite an unfortunate penchant for laboured prose, he combined iconoclasm and reformist urgency. 'The attitude of many of our courts on the subject of liberty of contract,' he observed in 1909, 'is so certain to be misapprehended, is so out of the range of ordinary understanding, the decisions themselves are so academic and so artificial in their reasoning, that they cannot fail to engender [a growing distrust of the integrity of the courts].'[215] Sociological, as opposed to mechanical, jurisprudence was Pound's pathway to reform. Utilizing interdisciplinary research and empirical studies of law in action, the sociological jurist would first evaluate legal principles according to the goals which they achieved and the purposes for which they were originally framed, and then, if necessary, urge the adaptation or adjustment of those principles to accord more precisely with social ends. Sociological jurisprudence, in other words, required 'social engineering'—that is, it required 'such an adjustment of relations and ordering of conduct as will make the goods of existence, the means of satisfying human claims to have things, go round as far as possible with the least friction and waste.'[216] While the tone of much of the realist jurisprudence of the 1920s and 1930s was set by Holmes's Delphic aphorisms, Pound, by emphasizing pragmatism, a social scientific approach to law and the value of empirical research, provided many of its basic conceptual tools.[217] As Pound himself remarked in the late 1930s, many of the core themes of legal realism 'were anticipated by the sociological jurists of a generation ago'.[218]

While some legal realists regarded Pound's sociological jurisprudence as an admirable but failed aspiration,[219] Pound himself criticized legal realists when 'they appeared to be putting flesh on the bones of "social engineering" '.[220] However, the *dialogue des sourds* which emerged between sociological jurisprudence and American legal realism cannot be considered simply as a case of crossed wires. As with Holmes, Pound

[215] Pound, *supra* n. 203, 487.

[216] Roscoe Pound, *Social Control Through Law* (New Haven, Conn.: Yale University Press, 1942), 64–5; and see further William L. Grossman, 'The Legal Philosophy of Roscoe Pound' *Yale L.J.*, 44 (1935), 605–18 at 608–15.

[217] See Karl Llewellyn, *Jurisprudence: Realism in Theory and Practice* (Chicago: University of Chicago Press, 1962), 496; and, more generally, Rumble, *supra* n. 147, 9–16; Wigdor, *supra* n. 190, 260.

[218] Roscoe Pound, 'Fifty Years of Jurisprudence', *Harvard L. Rev.*, 50 (1937), 557–82; *Harvard L. Rev.*, 51 (1938), 444–72, 777–812 at pt. 3, 791.

[219] See e.g. Llewellyn, *supra* n. 217, 7 fn. 3; Felix Cohen, 'The Problems of a Functional Jurisprudence', *Mod. L. Rev.*, 1 (1937), 5–26 at 8–9.

[220] Stevens, *supra* n. 10, 136.

appeared to qualify quite significantly the anti-formalist implications of his own jurisprudential position. Even in 'Mechanical Jurisprudence', one of his earliest and most iconoclastic articles, Pound—like Holmes—was careful not to exclude logic entirely from his jurisprudential framework: logic, he argued, should not be eschewed, but merely 'relegated', so that it no longer dominates jurisprudential inquiry but instead forms one method among many in the endeavour to conceive of law instrumentally.[221] In later works, this qualification is stated with rather more force. Whereas, in 1909, he had prophesied that the subscription by the late nineteenth-century courts to the fallacy of *laissez-faire* would engender disbelief in their integrity, by 1923 he was arguing that many of the decisions of that period, while 'quite at variance with the facts', nevertheless represented 'an ideal of judicial decision to which for some purposes, and in some connections, the administration of justice ought to conform'.[222] More than this, he argued that where the law is basically uniform and static, the courts, equipped with 'fixed precepts of determined content', may legitimately reach their decisions by way of a 'mechanical ascertainment of whether the facts fit the rule' in any particular case.[223] Accordingly, in particular areas of the law, mechanical reasoning represented 'a distinct gain for the legal order'.[224] The mistake of Langdellians and proponents of *laissez-faire* was to assume that such reasoning could be applied to the legal system in its entirety. One of the primary purposes of sociological jurisprudence was to classify 'field[s] of the legal order' in terms of those fields which are sufficiently standardized to accommodate the mechanical application of rules to facts, and those which 'involv[e] unique situations, calling for standards and for individualized application'.[225] Pound classified fields of law rather as, in his doctoral dissertation, he had offered a taxonomy of Nebraskan plants.[226]

Pound's passion for classifying fields of law accorded well with the American Law Institute's Restatement project. From his earliest forays into sociological jurisprudence, he had insisted that one of the basic ambitions of 'the new juristic theory' was 'to lay sure foundations for the ultimate legislative restatement of law, from which judicial decision shall start afresh'.[227] Pound was involved in the foundation of the Restatement movement in 1923, and, at the ALI's behest, he prepared a paper on the

[221] See Pound, *supra* n. 192, 609–10.

[222] Pound, 'The Theory of Judicial Decision', *supra* n. 191, pt. 2 at 825.

[223] Ibid. pt. 3 at 947. [224] Ibid. pt. 2 at 825. [225] Ibid. pt. 3 at 958.

[226] On taxonomy in Pound's jurisprudence, see further Roger Cotterrell, *The Politics of Jurisprudence: A Critical Introduction to Legal Philosophy* (London and Edinburgh: Butterworths, 1989), 159–64; Edwin W. Patterson, 'Pound' s Theory of Social Interests' in P. Sayre (ed.), *Interpretations of Modern Legal Philosophies: Essays in Honor of Roscoe Pound* (Littleton: Rothman, 1981; orig. publ. 1947), 558–73.

[227] Pound, *supra* n. 192, 622.

classification of law.[228] To his eyes, the Restatements were not merely an effort to produce a national legal system; they were also a challenge to legal realism. As 'agents of the common law and allies of the courts,' the Restaters 'would ensure the dominance of judicial experience in the development of law by relying on "traditional conceptions and traditional categories"'.[229] This is a far cry from the progressivism of social engineering. Yet his promotion of formalism extended even beyond this. The dominance of judicial experience was important to Pound not simply as a means of preserving the continuity of traditional legal forms, but also as an indicator of the moral values of 'society at large'; for, like Holmes, he believed that the courts reached decisions—albeit 'seldom consciously'—on the basis of common moral values shared by the community.[230] Not only, then, did Pound support the formalist ambitions of the Restatement project; he also subscribed to an essentially Holmesian concept of external standards which, in his view, the Restatements promoted.

Clearly, like Holmes, Pound was both an anti-formalist and a formalist; but while Holmes was a hero to the realists, Pound 'ended up as the[ir] favourite whipping-boy'.[231] Why should this have been so? The answer to this question is not really all that difficult to discover. To the bewilderment of many who had welcomed the anti-formalist inclinations of sociological jurisprudence, Pound set himself up as an arch-enemy of realism. Legal realism grew in confidence as an intellectual tendency; and all the while Pound became an ever more vociferous critic of that tendency. Even in the early 1920s, when realism was in its nascency, Pound was criticizing 'the increasing group of those who seem to conceive of legal precepts as incapable of interdependence and logical connection'.[232] The realist attack on legal certainty, he claimed, obscured the high degree of stability and uniformity which characterized many fields of the law. 'Legal realism,' to his eyes, was 'misguided, misinformed, and a menace to the vital common law system.'[233]

Pound responded to this 'menace' by treating the common law—and especially property and commercial law—as for the most part comprised of fixed principles of certain application. Although, as a theory of law, Langdellian legal science left much to be desired, it was still far preferable to legal realism: 'of the two,' he declared, 'the old fashioned lawyer has the

[228] See Roscoe Pound, 'Classification of Law', *Harvard L. Rev.*, 37 (1924), 933–69.
[229] Wigdor, *supra* n. 190, 265.
[230] See White, *supra* n. 201, 1011–12.
[231] Gilmore, *supra* n. 4, 137. For some general reflections on the reasons for Holmes's popularity among realists, cf. Vetter, *supra* n. 126, 344–46, 361.
[232] Roscoe Pound, review of W. W. Cook, *Cases and Other Authorities on Equity*, *Harvard L. Rev.*, 37 (1923), 396–99 at 397.
[233] Wigdor, *supra* n. 190, 262.

more warrant'.[234] At least 'the mechanical theory had the public good in view', which is more than he would accord realism.[235] Yet by turning on legal realism, Pound was turning also on his own sociological jurisprudence. In his celebrated article on realism, published in 1931, Pound acknowledged the significance of the new jurisprudential tendency: 'realist jurisprudence', he observed, 'is an important movement in the science of law' which deserves to be assessed 'with some humility'.[236] Declaring that '[i]t is much more important to understand than to criticize', he insisted that he had 'been trying to understand how far [the new juristic realists] go in connection with how far they might go, rather than to suggest necessary shortcomings in not going further. It takes time for a new school to develop.'[237] With this humility and understanding he claimed also to combine a respect for pluralism: 'in the house of jurisprudence there are many mansions. There is more than enough room for all of us and more than enough work.'[238] Pound's generosity of spirit was, however, only a veneer: 'many of these realists seek to ignore the logical and rational element and the traditional technique of application, or art of the common-law lawyer's craft, which tends to stability and uniformity of judicial action';[239] indeed, '[r]adical or neo-realism seems to deny that there are rules or principles or conceptions or doctrines at all.'[240] While 'the realists'—Pound mentioned no names—were disrespectful of the common law, they tended to exaggerate the importance of the social sciences. The utilization by certain realists (Underhill Moore?) of empirical social science, for example, though doubtless important in demonstrating 'how justice is administered, and how and how far legal precepts are observed and enforced,' cannot 'show how justice must (in a psychological sense) be administered'.'[241] Likewise, those realists (Jerome Frank? Edward Robinson?) who attempted to construct a psychology of the judicial process were making a mockery of jurisprudence. 'We have problems enough of our own in the science of law without wasting our ammunition in broadsides at each other over our wrong choices of psychological parties.'[242]

By the mid-1930s, the interdisciplinary spirit of Pound's early writings seemed almost the product of a different man. More content to don the garb of a reactionary than embrace a jurisprudential tendency which eclipsed his own earlier initiatives, he assumed the role of legal philosopher

[234] Roscoe Pound, Address at Annual Dinner of the American Bar Association, *Report of the American Bar Association*, 55 (1930), 172–78 at 178.

[235] Pound, *supra* n. 216, 28–9.

[236] Roscoe Pound, 'The Call for a Realist Jurisprudence', *Harvard L. Rev.*, 44 (1931), 697–711 at 697.

[237] Ibid. 709.

[238] Ibid. 711.

[239] Ibid. 706.

[240] Ibid. 707.

[241] Ibid. 703.

[242] Ibid. 706.

engagé. His article criticizing 'the realists' did a good deal, ironically, to put legal realism on the jurisprudential map; in particular, it provoked a published response from Karl Llewellyn and Jerome Frank, in which the authors attempted to define legal realism as an intellectual movement.[243] Pound offered no formal rejoinder to this response. Rather, he continued, throughout the 1930s and beyond, to make isolated, often petty and invariably ill-conceived remarks accusing proponents of legal realism of political and moral bankruptcy. Realism, he alleged, 'is essentially an art that cultivates the ugly . . . in jurisprudence it is the cult of what we always supposed abnormal'[244]—the cult, that is, of might equals right. It 'eliminate[s] from its science of law all questions of what ought to be, all disputes as to canons of value, all system and principle and reason. Thus the realists bring us to an objective observation of what actually takes place judicially and administratively, assuming that it actually takes place as a series of independent actions, as a matter of individual courses of behaviour. To them law is whatever is done officially. The officials may do as they choose. What they choose to do, when they do it, becomes law.'[245]

By the mid-1940s, Pound was arguing that realism denied not only democracy but also constitutionalism, the separation of powers, limited government and the freedom of the individual.[246] In an effort to curb what he perceived to be both the popularity and the excesses of legal realism, he had not only shut the door once and for all on his own sociological jurisprudence; he had also lost his sense of critical proportion. The purported iniquities of 'the realists' had become an obsession. Besides the published remarks making clear his antipathy towards realism, certain of Pound's statements, actions and inactions, though not explicit criticisms of the legal realists, clearly offended against the basic progressive sentiments to which most if not all of them subscribed. As dean at Harvard, he was by and large opposed to making changes to the law school curriculum. He was content, apparently, to leave the structure of Langdell's LL.B. intact.[247] In 1915, he restricted his own jurisprudence course to postgraduate students, and by the end of his deanship—which ran until 1936—students were complaining about the the overall blandness of the curriculum.[248] Despite his avowed passion for sociological jurisprudence, Pound was strangely

[243] Karl N. Llewellyn, 'Some Realism about Realism—Responding to Dean Pound', *Harvard L. Rev.*, 44 (1931), 1222–64 at 1234.

[244] Roscoe Pound, 'Modern Administrative Law', *Reports of the Virginia State Bar Association*, 51 (1939), 372–88 at 385.

[245] Roscoe Pound, 'The Future of Law', *Yale L.J.*, 47 (1937), 1–13 at 6.

[246] See Roscoe Pound, 'The American Idea of Government', *American Bar Association Journal*, 30 (1944), 497–503.

[247] See Joel Seligman, *The High Citadel: The Influence of the Harvard Law School* (Boston: Houghton Mifflin, 1978), 62.

[248] Seligman, ibid. 64–7; Sutherland, *supra* n. 41, 284–5.

unwilling to take his ideas out of the books and the articles and into the classroom. Declining so much as to attempt to establish interdisciplinary study as more than just a minor segment of the Harvard curriculum, he further alienated those of his colleagues who did attempt as much. Autocratic, insensitive and generally unsupportive towards his faculty, Pound was disinclined to be drawn into the public debate over the *Sacco–Vanzetti* case in the late 1920s, even though he privately agreed with his colleague, Felix Frankfurter—who had at that time been accused of left-wing leanings in connection with the case—that the defendants had been unfairly condemned to execution.[249] And when A. Lawrence Lowell—the then President of Harvard and chairman of the committee which advised the Supreme Court of Massachusetts to refuse clemency to Sacco and Vanzetti—objected to the appointment of Jewish scholars to the Law School, Pound, despite faculty outrage, responded with timidity.[250]

When not tolerating Lowell, Pound was stooping to his level. In 1934, he remarked that the reports of Nazi violence throughout Europe were grossly exaggerated, and that Hitler was 'a man who can bring them [the Central Europeans] freedom from agitating "movements" '.[251] Though supportive of German political dominance in Europe, however, he became resistant towards the reception of continental legal ideas in the United States. Throughout his academic career, Pound, perhaps more than any other American legal academic, had been inspired by countless European philosophers and jurists. In 1914, he had bemoaned the parochialism of those who wished to erect 'a dead Chinese wall around the American legal intellect'.[252] Yet, by the early 1940s, he was proclaiming that American intellectuals 'do not . . . need any advice on law or politics from continental Europe'.[253] No one in the history of American jurisprudence underwent such a remarkable volte-face as did Pound. He set the scene for a new, progressive perspective in jurisprudence, and then systematically and quite fanatically set about denouncing that perspective.

[249] Wigdor, *supra* n. 190, 249–50. Wigdor is wrong, however, in his claim that Pound steadfastly refused to be drawn into the public debate about the *Sacco–Vanzetti* case. See N. E. H. Hull, 'Reconstructing the Origins of Realistic Jurisprudence: A Prequel to the Llewellyn–Pound Exchange Over Legal Realism', *Duke L.J.* [1989], 1302–34 at 1320–1. On Frankfurter's involvement in the case, see Felix Frankfurter, *The Case of Sacco and Vanzetti: A Critical Analysis of Lawyers and Laymen* (Boston: Little, Brown & Co., 1927); Twining, *supra* n. 147, 341–9. Cf. also Jerold S. Auerbach, *Unequal Justice: Lawyers and Social Change in Modern America* (New York: Oxford University Press, 1976), 147 where it is suggested (though without citation of a source) that Pound 'stood firmly by' Frankfurter.

[250] Wigdor, *supra* n. 190, 251; Hull, *supra* n. 249, 1325.

[251] Pound, cited in Wigdor, *supra* n. 190, 250.

[252] Roscoe Pound, 'Note to Fowler: "The New Philosophies of Law" ', *Harvard L. Rev.*, 27 (1914), 731–5 at 734.

[253] Pound, cited in Widgor, *supra* n. 190, 276.

CONCLUSION

There has been a tendency among commentators to assume that the discovery of cracks in the edifice of late nineteenth-century legal formalism led almost immediately to the birth of a new jurisprudence. This was not the case. There was never, in American jurisprudence, anything so extravagant as a 'revolt against formalism'.[254] There was, rather, only a gradual, somewhat hesitant development away from late nineteenth-century legal thinking. The great forerunners of American legal realism, Holmes and Pound, were not committed anti-formalists. Holmes was the master of ambiguity, while Pound was the master of recantation. And while some realists were intent on seeing the latter pay for his sins, with the former they had little quarrel.

The idea of a revolt against formalism implies the emergence of an explicit philosophy of anti-formalism; but between the eras of Langdell and Pound, no such legal philosophy emerged. Certain ideas and arguments at variance with the ideology of formalism came to fruition, for sure, but it was not until the emergence of legal realism that these ideas and arguments began to take the shape of a general jurisprudence. Even this interpretation of events requires qualification. Although realism was essentially opposed to legal formalism, not all realists shared the same anti-formalist outlook. Formalism meant different things for different realists. Some realists criticized primarily the tradition of Langdell, others the tradition of *laissez-faire*; and even among those realists criticizing the same tradition, there often existed discernible differences of perspective and emphasis. Who was, and what it meant to be, a realist is not entirely clear. All that is certain is that some so-called realists, despite their opposition to the tradition of legal formalism, did not, in their writings, extricate themselves once and for all from the clutches of that tradition. Legal realism, we might say, was not entirely anti-formalist; for legal formalism, often heavily disguised, persisted under the realist banner.

[254] For an example of a legal philosopher subscribing to the 'revolt against formalism' fallacy, see Martin P. Golding, 'Jurisprudence and Legal Philosophy in Twentieth-Century America—Major Themes and Developments', *Jnl. Leg. Educ.*, 36 (1986), 441–80 at 443.

2
The Evolution of a Mood

> When the clamour of partisan debate fades, scholars are presumably in a position to judge historical events more clearly and completely. Certainly distance is essential for any adequate evaluation of 'legal realism', that diffuse, exciting, infuriating, pretentious, perceptive, and incomplete 'movement' which was born at the turn of the century, matured in the twenties, dominated much of the thirties, and then . . . what? Perhaps even in the seventies our perspective is not yet quite long enough.[1]

American legal realism is one of the great paradoxes of modern jurisprudence. No other jurisprudential tendency of the twentieth century has exerted such a powerful influence on legal thinking while remaining so ambiguous, unsettled and undefined. More than anything else, this book is a testament to the intellectual impact of legal realism. Yet the distinctiveness of the mark which realism has made on modern legal thought is more than matched by the indeterminacy of its conceptual and thematic boundaries. With exasperation and flippancy in equal measure, John Henry Schlegel has suggested that legal realism 'is just a name. Like "chicken soup", it means what we choose to call it'.[2]

That a legal historian who has patiently and assiduously charted the emergence, the key figures and the accomplishments of legal realism should reach this conclusion is at once instructive and dispiriting. Realism, quite simply, remains as elusive as it has been influential. The quotation which opens this chapter is illustrative of the fact that academics have failed to grapple successfully with the idea of legal realism as a peculiar jurisprudential phenomenon. Fundamental to the approach taken here is the idea that realism forms but part of a broader intellectual and political history, and that it is important to try to understand not only what realism

[1] Edward A. Purcell, Jr., review of W. Twining, *Karl Llewellyn and the Realist Movement*, *Am. J. Leg. Hist.*, 29 (1975), 240–6 at 240.

[2] John Henry Schlegel, 'The Ten Thousand Dollar Question', *Stanford L. Rev.*, 41 (1989), 435–67 at 464; and see more generally William Twining, 'Talk about Realism', *New York Univ. L. Rev.*, 69 (1985), 329–84. According to Twining, most attempts at explaining the meaning of 'legal realism' ultimately re-emphasize the ambiguity and vagueness of the term.

was but, equally, what it bequeathed to modern jurisprudential culture. This demands an examination of the theoretical and political characteristics of realism, not simply to demonstrate how it failed to live up to its ambitions, but also to illustrate how certain of its messages have been neglected and suppressed.[3]

Perhaps it seems contradictory to suggest that realism has exerted a powerful influence over the direction of modern jurisprudence while simultaneously being neglected and suppressed. But there is no contradiction, for in different fields of jurisprudence realism has been treated differently. In one area of modern American jurisprudence, critical legal studies, realism has for the most part been treated in a fairly positive fashion, as the beginning of the so-called 'revolt' against legal formalism (a 'revolt' which proponents of critical legal studies have attempted to rekindle). In other areas, realism has proved influential precisely because it is perceived as the primary problem to be surmounted. Legal theorists have tended more generally to view realism as a rather barren wasteland, littered by various clichéd and largely discredited arguments and assertions.[4] 'The law is what judges do', 'judges are only human', 'stimuli and hunches, not rules, form the basis of judicial decision-making'—these and similar adages represent a common perception of legal realism: realism, that is, as the jurisprudence of legal incertitude and arbitrariness. To a certain degree, this outlook can be found in the literature of legal realism. But that is not all that there is to be found. There is much more besides, and it is important to try to excavate that which the caricature of realism leaves buried.

Not that there is no reason to take the caricature seriously. Hostility towards the view that legal rules play a limited, sometimes negligible role

[3] By far the best historical studies of legal realism are those of Laura Kalman and John Henry Schlegel. See Laura Kalman, *Legal Realism at Yale: 1927–1960* (Chapel Hill: University of North Carolina Press, 1986); John Henry Schlegel, 'American Legal Realism and Empirical Social Science: From the Yale Experience', *Buffalo L. Rev.*, 28 (1979), 459–586; 'American Legal Realism and Empirical Social Science: The Singular Case of Underhill Moore', *Buffalo L. Rev.*, 29 (1980), 195–323; *American Legal Realism and Empirical Social Science* (Chapel Hill: University of North Carolina Press, forthcoming 1995). For my own small-scale studies of particular realist figures and themes, see Neil Duxbury, 'Some Radicalism about Realism? Thurman Arnold and the Politics of Modern Jurisprudence', *Oxford J. Leg. Studs.*, 10 (1990), 11–41; 'Robert Hale and the Economy of Legal Force', *Mod. L. Rev.*, 53 (1990), 421–44; 'Jerome Frank and the Legacy of Legal Realism', *Jnl. Law and Society*, 18 (1991), 175–205; 'In the Twilight of Legal Realism: Fred Rodell and the Limits of Legal Critique', *Oxford J. Leg. Studs.*, 11 (1991), 354–95.

[4] See Robert W. Gordon, 'Introduction: J. Willard Hurst and the Common Law Tradition in American Legal Historiography', *Law and Society Rev.*, 10 (1975), 9–55 at 13 fn. 11. Gordon notes that commentators on legal realism have been inclined to treat proponents of the tendency 'as (rather inept) legal philosophers', thereby underplaying the considerable extent to which most realists were concerned with legal doctrine and procedure.

in the process of judicial decision-making contributed significantly to the demise of realism. From the 1930s onwards, realist jurisprudence suffered a series of increasingly penetrative body-blows as American legal philosophers, tormented by the spectre of Nazism, became ever more determined to discover democratic values, rational processes, neutral principles and, ultimately, integrity in the law. Realism suffered a form of caricature in British jurisprudence too, owing largely to the fact that, with the publication of H. L. A. Hart's *The Concept of Law* in 1961, rule-scepticism came gradually to be regarded by legal philosophers as little more than a convenient if somewhat feeble sparring partner for the philosophy of legal positivism.[5]

In recent times, and although based on certain fundamental differences, the American jurisprudential tradition of uncovering values, processes and principles in the law and the British positivist tradition of Hart and his successors have crossed paths. This first occurred when Hart and Lon Fuller debated the moral content of legal authority,[6] and it happened again when Ronald Dworkin rejected Hart's so-called rule of recognition in favour of the idea of principled decision-making.[7] There is no need here to re-tread what is, for most legal philosophers, familiar territory. But one crucial point should be noted. Although there has been more of an emphasis of differences than a meeting of minds between the supporters of and the detractors from legal positivism, supporters and detractors alike appear to be united on at least one matter: representatives of both sides of the debate either implicitly or explicitly distance their own particular perspectives from the caricatured version of legal realism. Placed in the context of modern positivist and positivist-inspired jurisprudence, realism, caricatured, appears to be wholly unenlightening, since it not only undermines the status of legal rules in the process of judicial decision-making, but also implicitly denies the credibility of any theory of objective or interpretive legal values. For the realist, according to the popular burlesque, the law is simply what legal officials—usually judges—do when settling disputes; and what judges do, being human, is settle disputes on the basis of their intuitions as to what is right or wrong, just or unjust—

[5] See H. L. A. Hart, *The Concept of Law* (Oxford: Clarendon Press, 1961), 134–5; also E. Hunter Taylor, Jr., 'H. L. A. Hart's Concept of Law in the Perspective of American Legal Realism', *Mod. L. Rev.*, 35 (1972), 606–20.

[6] See H. L. A. Hart, 'Positivism and the Separation of Law and Morals', *Harvard L. Rev.*, 71 (1958), 593–629; Lon L. Fuller, 'Positivism and Fidelity to Law—A Reply to Professor Hart', *Harvard L. Rev.*, 71 (1958), 630–72; *The Morality of Law* (New Haven, Conn.: Yale University Press, 1964), 187–242; H. L. A. Hart, review of L. L. Fuller, *The Morality of Law*, *Harvard L. Rev.*, 78 (1965), 1281–96; and, for a general discussion, David Lyons, *Ethics and the Rule of Law* (Cambridge: Cambridge University Press, 1984), 74–93.

[7] See Ronald Dworkin, *Taking Rights Seriously* (London: Duckworth, 1977), 14–130.

these intuitions being subject, of course, to the moods and whims of the particular judge. Hence, realism stands distanced both from positivism and from those critics of positivism who look beyond rules for other criteria of legal validity. Failing to contribute meaningfully to either side of the dialogue, refusing to connect the activity of judicial decision-making either to rules or to extra-legal criteria which might inform or supplement those rules, legal realism represents, for positivist and positivist-inspired jurisprudence, an antediluvian philosophy of legal validity, a perfect illustration, in short, of what jurisprudence used to be like, before legal philosophers became enlightened.

Thus caricature has led to suppression, to a cursory treatment of realism by modern legal philosophers as if it were a form of jurisprudence to be easily discredited. To attempt to undermine the essentially one-dimensional view of realism as a straightforward philosophy of legal incertitude, however, demands the recognition of a definitional trap from which there is no obvious escape. A detailed assessment of realism requires, inevitably, an explanation of what it means to attach to particular ideas, themes, arguments and individuals the label 'realist'. If realism is much more than its common caricature, what precisely is it? No attempt is made here either to present an exhaustive account of what realism is or to take stock of every figure who might, by one criterion or another, be categorized as a realist.[8] Emphasis is placed instead on what can only vaguely be described as the 'feel' of realism as an intellectual tendency—a tendency, that is, which evolved out of the period of academic and judicial formalism preceding it.

The treatment of realism here as nothing more than a tendency, without rigid intellectual boundaries, is as much a matter of accuracy as of convenience. Legal realists, one of their number once observed, 'do not constitute a "school" in any useful sense of that term, for they differ too much among themselves on too many matters'.[9] The most eminent proponent and promoter of legal realism, Karl Llewellyn, likewise hesitated to conceive of realism as a single school of thought. 'There is', he insisted, 'no school of realists. There is no likelihood that there will be such a school.'[10] Rather, he preferred to conceive of realism as 'a *movement* in thought and work about law'.[11] Others have followed Llewellyn's example,

[8] On the futility of trying to compile a precise list of realists, cf. Twining, *supra* n. 2, 341–2.

[9] Walter Wheeler Cook, review of J. H. Beale, *A Treatise on the Conflict of Laws*, *Columbia L. Rev.*, 35 (1935), 1154–62 at 1161. See also Max Radin, 'Legal Realism', *Columbia L. Rev.*, 31 (1931), 824–8 at 825: 'I have spoken of realists as a group, but I should properly speak only of one realist, that is, of myself, whose right to the designation to which I pretend may be challenged by others, the legal realists'.

[10] Karl N. Llewellyn, 'Some Realism about Realism—Responding to Dean Pound', *Harvard L. Rev.*, 44 (1931), 1222–64 at 1233.

[11] Ibid. 1234.

designating realism as a movement, even if sometimes putting that word in inverted commas.[12] Yet even 'movement' seems too strong a word in this context. Realism was more a mood than a movement. That mood was one of dissatisfaction with legal formalism, that is, with twentieth-century legal thought being dominated by a nineteenth-century legal world-view. 'Legal formalism' itself denoted different things for different realists; and different realists addressed their own particular conceptions of formalism in markedly different ways. So although a number of themes are singled out here as peculiarly 'realist' themes, this hardly masks the fact that realism was an intellectual phenomenon characterized as much by disparateness as by similarities among its proponents. Certainly to call realism a movement is to engage in terminological flattery; it is far more appropriate to describe it as an intellectual tendency.

Our terminological problems do not end here. The disparities which existed among so-called realists are exemplified by their disagreements over the term 'realism' itself. In 1934, Jerome Frank—rather curiously writing in the past tense (this was the period when realism was in full swing)—remarked that 'realistic jurisprudence was an unfortunate label, since the word "realism" has too many conflicting meanings'.[13] Hessel Yntema adopted a more appropriate attitude of retrospection when, in 1960, he wrote that, as an erstwhile realist, he had always disclaimed the term 'realism' for the reason that it was both inappropriate and obscure.[14] It is hardly surprising that various 'realists' should have raised such objections. American legal realism, after all, was nurtured under the wing of the social sciences, where 'realism' has traditionally been treated as something of a slippery concept.[15] This much can hardly have escaped the attention of those 'realists' who took seriously the idea of studying law in accordance with social–scientific methods. As a label, 'realism' was adopted most consistently by Llewellyn, although there is some ambiguity in his use of the term. For Llewellyn, '[a] realist is one who, no matter what

[12] William Twining, *Karl Llewellyn and the Realist Movement* (rev. edn. London: Weidenfeld & Nicolson, 1985), 26–7; Bernie R. Burrus, 'American Legal Realism', *Howard L.J.*, 8 (1962), 36–51 at 40–1; Martin P. Golding, 'Jurisprudence and Legal Philosophy in Twentieth-Century America—Major Themes and Developments', *Jnl. Leg. Educ.*, 36 (1986), 441–80 at 452.

[13] Jerome Frank, 'Experimental Jurisprudence and the New Deal', *Congressional Record*, 78 (1934), 12412–14 at 12412; and cf. also Llewellyn, *supra* n. 10, 1234 fn. 35.

[14] Hessel E. Yntema, 'American Legal Realism in Retrospect', *Vanderbilt L. Rev.*, 14 (1960), 317–30 at 320; and see also Leon Green, 'Innocent Misrepresentation', *Virginia L. Rev.*, 19 (1933), 242–52 at 247: 'If I am a "legal realist" I have been ignorant of the fact. At least I have never called myself one. I subscribe to no label. . . . As far as I recall I have never used the word "realism" in my writings, and while I have no prejudice against it, I do not know what it means'.

[15] For an illustration of this point, see David J. Levy, *Realism: An Essay in Interpretation and Social Reality* (Manchester: Carcanet, 1981).

his ideological or philosophical views, believes that it is important regularly to focus attention on the law in action at any given time and to try to describe as honestly as possible what is to be seen.'[16] There were, inevitably, realists who did not quite share this belief; just as there have been lawyers who, though not realists, have subscribed to this belief quite assiduously.[17] Logomachy over 'legal realism', it seems, is a cul-de-sac.[18]

In an inspired study of American legal theory, Robert Summers jettisoned the term 'legal realism' in an effort to introduce into jurisprudential discourse a comparably less vague nomenclature. Summers argues that it is more appropriate to conceive of a tradition of 'pragmatic instrumentalism' in American jurisprudence. This term, he claims, depicts accurately the philosophical premisses underpinning the early twentieth-century jurisprudential reaction against legal formalism. 'Legal realism', in contrast, lacks terminological precision.[19] In arguing as much, however, Summers concedes that he does not anticipate a straight terminological swap. The upshot of this is a thesis somewhat less persuasive than it first appears. While, within the specific context of his own study, Summers offers convincing arguments for dispensing with the term 'legal realism', these arguments rather lack validity when applied to the use of the term by others. The reason for this hinges upon his conception of pragmatic instrumentalism. For Summers, this term is of necessity defined by the ideas of those whom he considers to qualify for the title of pragmatic instrumentalist.[20] Yet, by his criteria, various figures commonly considered to be 'realists' would not in fact qualify for the title. Moreover, at least three of his so-called pragmatic instrumentalists—Oliver Wendell Holmes, John Chipman Gray and Roscoe Pound—are not usually described as realists, but as 'proto-realists'. While it is with some justification that Summers criticizes the term 'realism' as descriptively inapposite, his own conception of pragmatic instrumentalism denotes only a highly circumscribed group of realists and realist forebears. Some realists

[16] Twining, *supra* n. 12, 74.

[17] See e.g. Guido Calabresi, *A Common Law for the Age of Statutes* (Cambridge, Mass.: Harvard University Press, 1982), *passim* and esp. p. 180. (As a scholar, it is my job to look in dark places and try to describe, as precisely as I can, what I see'); and cf. also, in a similar vein, Guido Calabresi, letter to Paul D. Carrington, in ' "Of Law and the River", and of Nihilism and Academic Freedom', *Jnl. Leg. Educ.*, 35 (1985), 1–26 at 23–4.

[18] Wilfrid E. Rumble, Jr., *American Legal Realism: Skepticism, Reform, and the Judicial Process* (Ithaca, NY: Cornell University Press, 1968), 45.

[19] Robert S. Summers, *Instrumentalism and American Legal Theory* (Ithaca, NY: Cornell University Press, 1982), 36–7. For a similar reservation concerning 'pragmatic instrumentalism', see Twining, *supra* n. 2, 339–40 fn. 24.

[20] Summers, *supra* n. 19, 23. Summers lists eleven pragmatic instrumentalists: John Chipman Gray, Oliver Wendell Holmes, Jr., John Dewey, Roscoe Pound, Walter Wheeler Cook, Joseph Bingham, Underhill Moore, Herman Oliphant, Jerome Frank, Karl Llewellyn and Felix Cohen. This list, Summers adds, is not intended to be exhaustive.

were not pragmatic instrumentalists, just as some pragmatic instrumentalists were not realists. And whereas 'legal realism' can be criticized as a hopelessly broad catch-all category, 'pragmatic instrumentalism', when removed from the specific confines of Summers's own project, proves rather too limiting and idiosyncratic for common usage.

So, where does this leave us? The term 'legal realism' is retained here for two specific reasons. First, despite the criticisms of Summers and others, it may be argued that the merit of the term 'realism' lies precisely in its generality. 'Realism' describes accurately what was possibly the single unifying ambition of so-called realists: namely, the commitment to candour, to telling it—whatever 'it' happened to be—as it is.[21] Certainly this commitment to candour is neither the sole province nor feature of realist jurisprudence—if this were all that realism was, we would indeed all be realists now. But although candour *per se* hardly serves as a criterion for demarcating realism as a discrete intellectual tendency, its thematic importance rests in the fact that there emerged, during the early decades of this century, a peculiar 'style' of candour—one which, though it has since been emulated, did not exist in the United States prior to the advent of realist jurisprudence.

The second reason for retaining the term 'realism' is little more than a confession of resignation. For better or worse, and despite the reservations of some so-called realists, the term 'realism' stuck; and it seems, now, that it is here to stay. In his despair over the ambiguity of the term 'literature', Terry Eagleton once suggested that it should, in his writings, be considered placed under an invisible crossing-out mark, as if to indicate that while the term will not really do, we apparently have nothing better with which to replace it.[22] Perhaps there is good reason to do the same with 'realism'. Yet one should not blow this matter out of proportion. Our purpose here is to analyse an intellectual tendency. Whether or not that tendency was given the correct name—whatever that could mean—seems hardly of crucial importance.

COMPOUNDING A CONTROVERSY

That legal realism 'happened' seems now—if, indeed, it did not always seem—an inevitability. The claim that formalism is not working became, for many early twentieth-century American lawyers, something of a

[21] Or, in the words of Pound, the commitment to the 'accurate recording of things as they are'. Roscoe Pound, 'The Call for a Realist Jurisprudence', *Harvard L. Rev.*, 44 (1931), 697–711 at 697. See also Edward S. Robinson, 'Law—An Unscientific Science', *Yale L.J.*, 44 (1934), 235–67 at 257.

[22] Terry Eagleton, *Literary Theory: An Introduction* (Oxford: Blackwell, 1983), 11.

truism. However, the question of precisely how—or, more importantly, what it means to say that—realism 'happened' has never been answered satisfactorily. Realism did not simply come about overnight; its evolution was, rather, a hesitant one. Yet, there has been a tendency to try to conceive of the evolution of legal realism in terms of some triggering event, without which—so the assumption seems to be—'the realists' would never have come into being. The fault with this argument is that it is premissed on a name-tag approach to the history of ideas, as if the gradual movement away from legal formalism would have been an inconsequence—as if it could not properly be said to have occurred—if someone had not coined a name for it.

That 'someone' who came up with the label of realism is commonly considered to be Karl Llewellyn;[23] and indeed, in the endeavour to locate a point at which legal realism began, there has been a tendency for commentators to hone in on the famous Llewellyn–Pound *controverse* of the early 1930s. The story is something of a commonplace. Having, in early 1931,[24] accused an unnamed body of 'realists' of demonstrating an exaggerated faith in empiricism and social science while simultaneously neglecting—if not, at times, denying—the legal significance of rules, doctrines and principles, Pound quickly found himself at loggerheads with those who had made the most effort to popularize anti-formalist jurisprudence. At this point in time, the realist centre-stage was already dominated by Llewellyn and Jerome Frank. Both had just written books which were to become landmarks in the literature of realism,[25] and both felt that Pound had caricatured their ideas.[26] Llewellyn felt particularly dispirited, given that Pound had previously accepted his academic criticisms with good grace.[27] Thus it was that Llewellyn and Frank set about composing a rejoinder to Pound, eventually published in Llewellyn's name alone, in which 'twenty men and ninety-odd titles' were put forward as 'representative'[28] of 'the new ferment'[29] in jurisprudence.

Llewellyn and Frank's response is as much an exercise in legal realism as it is an idiosyncratic description of it. 'Ferment', Llewellyn begins, 'is abroad in the law. . . . It spreads. It is no mere talk.'[30] Those involved in this ferment 'are folk of modest ideals. They want law to deal, they

[23] See Twining, *supra* n. 2, 363: 'Karl Llewellyn is generally regarded as the leading internal interpreter of the Realist Movement. He neither coined the term nor founded the movement, but he is acknowledged as its first labeller and publicist.'

[24] See Pound, *supra* n. 21, *passim*.

[25] Karl N. Llewellyn, *The Bramble Bush: On Our Law and Its Study* (New York: Oceana, 1951; repr. of orig. student edn. 1930); Jerome Frank, *Law and the Modern Mind* (Gloucester, Mass.: Peter Smith, 1970; orig. publ. 1930).

[26] See Twining, *supra* n. 12, 72–3.

[27] Ibid. 71.

[28] Llewellyn, *supra* n. 10, 1227.

[29] Ibid. 1225.

[30] Ibid. 1223.

themselves want to deal, with things, with people, with tangibles . . . not with words alone. . . . They view rules, they view law, as means to ends.'[31] While sharing 'certain points of departure',[32] these so-called realists 'are not a group'.[33] 'They differ among themselves well-nigh as much as any of them differs from, say, Langdell.'[34] Among the realists, individualism is the order of the day: 'the justification for grouping these men together lies not in that they are *alike* in belief or work, but in that from certain common points of departure they have branched into lines of work which seem to be building themselves into a whole, a whole planned by none, foreseen by none, and (it may well be) not yet adequately grasped by any.'[35] A collection of somewhat disparate legal academics, the realists were, according to Llewellyn, united only by their apparent—sometimes inadvertent—acceptance of certain shared premisses.

The list of twenty realists which Llewellyn and Frank offer in response to Pound is but a selection and by no means intended to be exhaustive. They 'had hoped to be more precise . . . There are doubtless twenty more. But half is a fair sample.'[36] Certainly, as a sample, it was sufficient to stymie the unsubstantiated allegations made by Pound. In structuring his critique of Pound around the names on the list, furthermore, Llewellyn invoked two exemplary realist motifs: the imagery of trial court fact-finding procedure and the methodology of empiricism. Pound, according to Llewellyn, was to be tried by fact.[37] The question was: were any of Pound's allegations substantiated by anything which any of the listed realists had ever claimed? The 'evidence' discovered in Pound's favour turned out to be scant.[38] But what was most significant about Llewellyn and Frank's retort to Pound—what, equally, has by and large been overlooked—was not so much the wholly predictable conclusion that they reached, but the manner in which they purported to reach it.

Llewellyn and Frank's counter-critique of Pound is period-piece realist social science. In compiling their list, they 'selected such writings as seemed to speak most directly to points of legal theory, or most likely to contain evidence on any of [Pound's] allegations'.[39] They also '[w]rote to the men, requesting from each his suggestion as to where he had expressed himself' along lines which Pound was insisting typified realism.[40] Pound's observations were then compared with the sample material which Llewellyn and Frank had compiled, and 'the results of the test'[41]—as if arrived at in a laboratory—were put forward as a 'scientific' refutation of Pound's critique. By detailed use of what was—when all is said and done—

[31] Llewellyn, *supra* n. 10, 1223.
[32] Ibid. 1234.
[33] Ibid. 1256.
[34] Ibid. 1234.
[35] Ibid. 1235.
[36] Ibid. 1226–7.
[37] Ibid. 1225.
[38] Ibid. 1233.
[39] Ibid. 1227.
[40] Llewellyn, *supra* n. 10.
[41] Ibid. 1228.

an idiosyncratically concocted sample of legal academics and their writings, Llewellyn and Frank had not simply responded to a response, but had done so with an air of apparent objectivity. Their article—as the title makes clear—purported to offer 'some realism about realism'.

In contrast with their refutation of Pound's critique, Llewellyn and Frank were consciously less objective in presenting their own opinions on realism. 'What we here further say of realists,' Llewellyn states, having finished with Pound, is 'to be read as giving a vague and very fallible impression.'[42] Realism was not a new phenomenon, but an 'attitude' which had been around at least since 1914;[43] the response to Pound was in part a 'descriptive' endeavour[44]—descriptive, that is, of something which had been in existence for some time. For all that the Llewellyn–Pound exchange may have instilled a fragmented group of academics with a sense of unity under the banner of legal realism,[45] the tendency was certainly not born with that exchange. It was, at best, baptized by it.[46] With the Llewellyn–Pound controversy, the mood of realism, of the challenge to formalism, somehow gelled. But it was not a new mood. And it would be wrong, accordingly, to assume that realism emerged in the aftermath of the controversy. The realist mood of discontentment preceded its label.

Like all good stories, the Llewellyn–Pound exchange is not without a sub-plot. The underbelly of legal realism is to be discovered in the archives of the major American law schools. It is here, in the marginalia, the letters and the unpublished manuscripts, that there can be found many a genuine revelation, and it would have been surprising if consultation of archive sources had not shed fresh light on the Llewellyn–Pound dispute. In her archival research into Llewellyn and Pound, Natalie Hull has dug beneath the surface of their exchange as it appears in the pages of the *Harvard Law Review* and offered some 'newly uncovered' evidence on the affair.[47] Pound's article of 1931 attacking realism, she argues, may be interpreted as a response, in part, to criticisms of his work which Llewellyn had made both in print and in private correspondence between the two men dating back to 1927. She also traces the history behind Llewellyn and Frank's rejoinder, revealing, in the process, that their famous 'sample' of realists had originally extended to over double its published number, and also that, prior to the publication of their article, Pound had accused Frank—unfairly, it seems—of having mis-quoted his views. 'If there was any feud

[42] Llewellyn, *supra* n. 10, 1233. [43] Ibid. 1227. [44] Ibid. 1234.

[45] See Robert Stevens, *Law School: Legal Education in America from the 1850s to the 1980s* (Chapel Hill: University of North Carolina Press, 1983), 155.

[46] See Yntema, *supra* n. 14, 317.

[47] N. E. H. Hull, 'Some Realism about the Llewellyn–Pound Exchange over Realism: The Newly Uncovered Private Correspondence, 1927–1931', *Wisconsin L. Rev.*, [1987], 921–69.

among the principals of the controversy, it was between Pound and Frank, not between Pound and Llewellyn.'[48]

The archival sources in fact reveal Pound, certainly during the first two decades of this century, to be very much a realist *malgré lui*, a man, indeed, whom Llewellyn regarded more as a kindred spirit than as an intellectual adversary. In 1925, Llewellyn wrote an unpublished essay in which he acknowledged Pound's considerable influence on the development of realist thinking in American law. 'Llewellyn's view of Realistic Jurisprudence', at this point in time, 'almost totally coincided with Pound's description of Sociological Jurisprudence.'[49] It was only later, in 1931, that 'Llewellyn deliberately rewrote the public version of the intellectual history of the [Realist] movement to conceal Pound's vital role in it'.[50] 'During the six years between Llewellyn's acknowledgment of Pound's inspiration of the Realist movement and the *Harvard Law Review* debate, Llewellyn completely reconceptualized the intellectual pedigree of "Realistic Jurisprudence", banishing Pound from the central place in its development.'[51]

The question to which Hull seeks an answer is that of why Llewellyn's estimation of Pound changed so radically. At one level, her answer is quite straightforward: Llewellyn 'simply adored the parry and thrust of an intellectual duel for its own sake'.[52] Pound had dropped the gauntlet, and Llewellyn was only too happy to pick it up. A consequence of this was that he adopted a rather less generous, or at least explicitly generous, view of his adversary than that which he had previously held: formal respect became the first casualty of rigorous critique. Hull, however, in developing her answer, digs rather deeper than this, and in doing so she points to two specific incidents. The first was the *Sacco–Vanzetti* affair. Llewellyn not only campaigned vigorously against the execution of Sacco and Vanzetti but also, more generally, wrote about the affair as an exemplary illustration of certain grave shortcomings in the American system of justice. For Llewellyn, the case was something of a crusade.[53] Pound, on the other hand, for all that he may privately have shared some of Llewellyn's sentiments, did his utmost to treat the affair with an attitude of 'calculated neutrality'.[54] Hull suggests that this aloofness on Pound's part probably led Llewellyn to regard him suspiciously. Yet no evidence is adduced, nor does any appear to exist, which so much as hints that Llewellyn and Pound's differing approaches to *Sacco–Vanzetti* contributed decisively to their intellectual estrangement in the early 1930s.

[48] Ibid. 948–9.

[49] N. E. H. Hull, 'Reconstructing the Origins of Realistic Jurisprudence: A Prequel to the Llewellyn–Pound Exchange over Legal Realism', *Duke L.J.*, [1989], 1302–34 at 1314.

[50] Ibid. 1306.

[51] Ibid. 1317.

[52] Hull, *supra* n. 47, 942.

[53] See Twining, *supra* n. 12, 344–49.

[54] Hull, *supra* n. 49, 1323.

The second incident on which Hull focuses to explain this estrangement proves similarly inconclusive. At the beginning of the 1930s, there emerged a possibility of Llewellyn and Pound collaborating on an article on the law of contract. Owing, basically, to crossed wires—and perhaps also to the fact that Pound seemed not particularly keen on the idea—the project never got off the ground, and eventually each published his research independently. According to Hull, this abortive venture appears to be indicative if not indeed the cause of a general falling out between Llewellyn and Pound. Again, however, there exists no evidence to support such a conclusion. Llewellyn was disappointed that the collaboration had not worked out, and was rather bewildered as to why this had been the case.[55] But to suggest, as Hull does, that Pound's failure to carry through the collaborative venture was a 'betrayal' which 'enraged' Llewellyn[56] is not only to embellish the account with an emotive gloss, but also to impute a convenient yet unsubstantiated motive for Llewellyn's decision to revise his estimation of Pound's intellectual significance *vis-à-vis* realism. The trek through the archives proves, here, to be fruitless. The reason for Llewellyn's change of mind, rather like the case of Nietzsche's forgotten umbrella,[57] remains a mystery.

The importance of Hull's research rests in the fact that it serves indirectly as a warning against interpreting legal realism primarily through the initiatives of Karl Llewellyn. Whatever Llewellyn's motives happened to be in his endeavour to put realism on the map as a distinct jurisprudential movement, it seems clear that he wished to initiate a

[55] Karl N. Llewellyn to Arthur L. Corbin, 6 April 1931, in Karl N. Llewellyn Papers, University of Chicago Law Library, A.II, 65(b), cited in Hull, ibid. 1333: 'I still can't understand how he [Pound] could write the article.'

[56] Hull, *supra*, n. 49, 1333.

[57] On the case, and the significance, of Nietzsche's forgotten umbrella, see Jacques Derrida, *Spurs: Nietzsche's Styles* (Eng. tr. B. Harlow, Chicago: University of Chicago Press, 1979), 123: (' "I have forgotten my umbrella". These words were found, isolated in quotation marks, among Nietzsche's unpublished manuscripts. . . . We will never know *for sure* what Nietzsche wanted to say or do when he noted these words, nor even that he actually *wanted* anything.') According to Hull, '[t]he historian who attempts to reconstruct the reality of what the jurisprudents themselves were doing at the time that they created the public discourse, penetrates to a second deeper level of discourse, a private level. This private discourse consists in correspondence and informal discussion among academic jurisprudents. The student of the private discourse reconstructs the reality of these intellectual exchanges, revealing the authors' intended meaning of words used in the public discourse. . . . We historians must rediscover the private discourse and use it to reinterpret the public discourse.' N. E. H. Hull, 'Networks and *Bricolage*: A Prolegomenon to a History of Twentieth-Century American Academic Jurisprudence', *Am. J. Leg. Hist.*, 35 (1991), 307–22 at 309–10. In other words, by resorting to the archival and the unpublished, we can reconstruct private discourse, and by reconstructing private discourse we can discover real authorial intentions. For a constrasting—and, to my mind, more convincing—view, see Dominick LaCapra, *Rethinking Intellectual History: Texts, Contexts, Language* (Ithaca, NY: Cornell University Press, 1983), 36–7.

definitive break with the past. Realist jurisprudence, for Llewellyn, was distinct not only from the tradition of legal formalism but also from the proto-realist initiatives of Holmes, Cardozo, Gray and, of course, Pound. None of these 'pre-realists' featured in either the published or unpublished versions of Llewellyn and Frank's sample lists.[58] None, indeed, was conceived to be part of the new ferment. Precisely why not remains a mystery. The suggestion—intimated, in fact, by Pound[59]—that the difference between the pre-realists and the realists was to some degree a generational one is rather refuted by the fact that certain of the realists named by Llewellyn and Frank were almost as old as Pound himself.[60] It is odd, too, that Llewellyn and Frank should have neglected the pre-realists while including in their sample lists—particularly the unpublished version—academics who were almost as obscure in 1931 as they are today.[61] Some of those listed were only 'realists' by virtue of their association with Llewellyn.[62] Most of those listed would not have applied the label to themselves.[63] In short, the sample of realists was a wholly arbitrary affair, the concoction of which appears to have served primarily to banish the past from the present; to ensure that there existed a cut-off point, however fabricated, between the pre-realists and the realists.

Once we move beyond this cut-off point, the task of understanding legal realism as an intellectual phenomenon seems rather more conceivable. It becomes clear that there are no good historical or conceptual reasons for demarcating the pre-realists from the realists, and that realism should, accordingly, be regarded as the continuation of a particular trend—namely, the growing dissatisfaction with legal formalism—rather than as the beginning of something substantively new. Even Llewellyn acknowledged that, by the early 1930s, the realist spirit had been in the air for well over a decade. His basic failing was that, while he recognized that the pre-realists shared in this spirit, he regarded their ideas as somehow removed from the new scene. They were inspirational—in Holmes's case, crucially inspirational—but ultimately distant voices.

Those commentators who resist according especial significance to the Llewellyn–Pound exchange have attempted generally to conceive of realism in rather broader terms than have those who treat the exchange as somehow foundational or indispensable to any proper discussion of the subject. Grant Gilmore, who had no taste at all for the Llewellyn–Pound

[58] Hull, *supra* n. 47, 967–9.

[59] Pound, *supra* n. 21, 697 (characterizing legal realists as certain of 'our younger teachers of law').

[60] See Hull, *supra* n. 47, 954; Twining, *supra* n. 12, 76, 410 fn. 25.

[61] See, in particular, the people discussed briefly by Hull, *supra* n. 47, 961.

[62] Hull, ibid. 961–2.

[63] Ibid. 957.

dispute,[64] once suggested that 'realism was the academic formulation of a crisis through which our legal system passed during the first half of this century'.[65] Realism was not, in fact, an exclusively academic affair. It was, nevertheless, very much a response to a 'crisis', even if that crisis was rather more complex than the one which Gilmore describes.

According to Gilmore, the crisis was fairly straightforward. With the initiation of the National Reporter system in the 1870s, the West Publishing Company undertook to publish all federal appellate and some trial court opinions, as well as higher state court decisions, throughout the United States. By the end of the nineteenth century, the reporting and printing of cases had reached nightmarish proportions. The avalanche of reported decisions not only made it impossible for lawyers ever to be fully informed but also resulted in the discovery, with increasing frequency, of inconsistencies and contradictions among the precedents upon which the profession relied.[66] This, Gilmore argues, was the crisis to which realism attempted to respond. Yet a more obvious response to this crisis came from a different, distinctly Langdellian-inspired, source. From its inception in 1923, a primary goal of the largely Harvard-staffed Restatement of the Law project was to eradicate unnecessary complexities in legal doctrine. It was an initiative devised precisely to meet the 'crisis' represented by the flood of reported precedents. Realism, in contrast, represented not so much a response to this crisis as a somewhat resigned acknowledgement that it existed. Indeed, if anything, legal realists tended to treat the ever-burgeoning body of published cases as less of a cause for alarm than the Restatement project itself.

The 'crisis' to which realism responded was much broader than that which Gilmore describes. Very simply, the crisis may be characterized as the persistence, into the twentieth century, of legal formalism in both of its guises. The ways in which legal formalism represented a crisis, and the ways in which so-called realists responded to this crisis, were diverse, and to make any sense of legal realism and its intellectual legacy it is necessary to attempt to untangle that diversity. This requires not the search for a key event which may have started the realist ball rolling, but rather an examination of various factors which appear to have contributed to the evolution of realism as an intellectual mood. The most general and important factor to be taken into account is the manner in which, from the earliest years of this century, the insights and the methods of the social sciences began to find their way into the American law schools. Social

[64] See Grant Gilmore, *The Ages of American Law* (New Haven, Conn.: Yale University Press, 1977), 78, 136–7 n. 25.

[65] Grant Gilmore, 'Legal Realism: Its Cause and Cure', *Yale L.J.*, 70 (1961), 1037–48 at 1037.

[66] Ibid. 1041.

science formed a crucial backdrop to legal realism, though the manner in which it did so is far from straightforward.

MAKING WAY FOR THE SOCIAL SCIENCES

Formalism left a void in American legal scholarship. The Langdellian legal scientist had a clear objective: to reduce legal doctrines to their core elements and thereby remove from the law all unnecessary complexity. But what if that objective were to be achieved: what then, beyond teaching, would be the *raison d'être* of the American academic lawyer? John Henry Schlegel has suggested that the Langdellian task of systematization had in fact been realized by around the time of the First World War; that, by then, '[t]here really wasn't much more to do'.[67] In one sense, this is a curious assertion. American law, both common law and statute, continued to proliferate and become ever more complex through-out and beyond the War—to the extent, indeed, that by the 1920s the American Law Institute had turned its attention to the matter of restatement. Clearly the task of systematization was not accomplished. Yet in another sense, Schlegel's remark rings true, for by the early decades of this century legal scholarship in the Langdellian mould had become somewhat stale. The fundamental legacy of Langdellian formalism was a decidedly monolithic conception of legal scholarship; indeed, the criterion of good scholarship—painstaking arrangement of principles with a view to demonstrating the scientific underpinnings of legal doctrine—had been established by Langdell himself. The only significant choice open to the academic lawyer in the Langdellian tradition rested in the matter of which area of law to reduce to its basics.

The mood of legal realism evolved out of this academic malaise.[68] Realism signified discontentment not just with formalism as a distinct jurisprudence but, still more fundamentally, with the fact that formalism in its Langdellian guise rather limited the range of intellectual activities that the academic lawyer could legitimately pursue. Realism represented the feeling that it was time to inject into legal research at least a semblance of the *frisson* that the case method had already brought to teaching. For all that realism constituted a general sense of unease concerning legal formalism, however, it could not be described as an outright distaste for scientific methods. Many so-called realists were happy, in principle, to embrace the

[67] John Henry Schlegel, 'Langdell's Legacy Or, The Case of the Empty Envelope', *Stanford L. Rev.*, 36 (1984), 1517–33 at 1529.

[68] Ibid. 1530–1.

idea of science as a good thing. Just as Pound had argued as early as 1908 that mechanical jurisprudence was premissed on the outmoded scientific model of deductivism,[69] so too, during the following decades, various so-called realists sought after a new 'paradigm' on which to base their own juristic inquiries. The physical sciences, Walter Wheeler Cook observed in 1924, are moving from a deductive to an inductive paradigm, a paradigm which betrays an emerging scientific faith in experimentation, in trial and error, in the observation of physical phenomena and the collection and study of data with a view to 'formulating general statements which will describe [that which has been observed] as accurately and simply as possible' and to 'predict[ing] future observations'.[70] Realism was following precisely this path. 'For we as lawyers, like the physical scientists, are engaged in the study of objective physical phenomena. Instead of the behaviour of electrons, atoms, or planets, however, we are dealing with the behaviour of human beings. As lawyers we are interested in knowing how certain officials of society—judges, legislators, and others—have behaved in the past, in order that we may make a prediction of their probable behaviour in the future.'[71] Whereas Langdellian legal formalism had been scientific only in name, Cook and certain other realists aspired towards a 'truly scientific study of law', a '[s]ystematized study, deliberately focused towards getting an adequate knowledge of the entire social structure as a functioning and changing but coherent mechanism'.[72] Realism, thus described, was an attempt to turn jurisprudence into 'an applied science'.[73]

There are, almost inevitably, voices of dissent to be found. The general desire for scientific method in legal research is occasionally offset in some realist writings by a professed impatience with theory.[74] Others, moreover,

[69] Roscoe Pound, 'Mechanical Jurisprudence', *Columbia L. Rev.*, 8 (1908), 605–23 at 608.

[70] Walter Wheeler Cook, 'The Logical and Legal Bases of the Conflict of Laws', *Yale L.J.*, 33 (1924), 457–88 at 458.

[71] Ibid. 475.

[72] Herman Oliphant, 'A Return to Stare Decisis', *Am. Bar Assoc. Jnl.*, 14 (1928), 71–6, 107, 159–62 at 159.

[73] Hessel E. Yntema, 'The Hornbook Method and the Conflict of Laws', *Yale L.J.*, 37 (1928) 468–83 at 481; 'Jurisprudence and Metaphysics—A Triangular Correspondence', *Yale L.J.*, 59 (1950), 273–90 at 273. See also Simon N. Verdun-Jones, 'Cook, Oliphant and Yntema: The Scientific Wing of American Legal Realism', *Dalhousie L.J.*, 5 (1979), 3–44, 249–80; Anthony Kronman, 'Jurisprudential Responses to Legal Realism', *Cornell L. Rev.*, 73 (1988), 335–40 at 338. ('[T]he scientific branch of realism sought to realize Langdell's vision of law, but by abandoning the idea of law as an autonomous or independent discipline.') Realism did not represent the first attempt to turn American jurisprudence into an applied science. For an earlier attempt, see the collection of essays, *Centralization and the Law. Scientific Legal Education: An Illustration* (with an introduction by Melville M. Bigelow, Boston: Little, Brown & Co. 1906).

[74] See e.g. Herman Oliphant, 'Facts, Opinions, and Value-Judgments', *Texas L. Rev.*, 10 (1932), 127–39 at 127 fn. 1. ('Must we wait in libraries more centuries until [those who live by

viewed the prospect of bringing scientific methods to jurisprudence with extreme caution. 'When it comes to exploration and tentative development of . . . jurisprudence as a true (naturalistic) science,' Llewellyn observed, 'I find myself differing even while I agree.'[75] 'Knowledge does not have to be scientific, in order to be on the way towards Science. . . . What we need is knowledge moving carefully and cannily *towards* the scientific pole, accompanied by some indication of its present latitude. *That* is the scientific road *towards* Science.'[76] The apparent gist of this argument—that legal knowledge is not scientific, even though it appears gradually to aspire towards scientific status—is captured rather more precisely in the work of the Yale realist and psychologist, Edward Stevens Robinson. Law, according to Robinson, is 'an unscientific science'—unscientific in the sense that lawyers prefer to follow in the footsteps of, and occasionally borrow ideas from, scientists rather than attempt to innovate in a scientific fashion for themselves.[77] Thus it is that lawyers suffer from what he terms 'cultural lag',[78] in so far as the scientific insights on which they rely are usually at least twice removed from their source: ideas percolate down from the natural to the social sciences and then, eventually, to law. The problem, from a realist point of view, is that a good deal gets lost in the process of percolation. Lawyers, furthermore, tend to fail to appreciate the importance of the scientific innovations which ultimately reach them. As 'a profession of *social* engineers,' they 'are specialists in social arrangements'.[79] But the modern lawyer hardly thinks like a modern engineer. 'Typically frightened by social innovation' and generally 'content to justify social changes after they have happened,' the modern lawyer fails generally to recognize how 'the experimental, fact-dominated, forward-looking view of natural science is relevant to the process of social adjustment.'[80]

> The most important distinction between the man of law and the man of natural science is that the jurist is philosophically lost. . . . The intellectual embarrassments pervading the law today are not due simply to the antiquity of the conceptions of jurisprudence. The difficulty arises rather out of the fact that, living in a world in which the power of scientific ways of thinking is constantly growing, the man of law simply cannot keep clear of psychological and sociological ideas. On the other hand, he is stubborn about accepting those ideas as more than tools to be used when convenient. He feels that his fundamental aims can still be satisfactorily

philosophy] agree on a theory of knowledge?'); also Wesley A. Sturges and Samuel O. Clark, 'Legal Theory and Real Property Mortgages', *Yale L.J.*, 37 (1928), 691–715 at 704.

75 Karl N. Llewellyn, 'The Theory of Legal "Science" ', *North Carolina L. Rev.*, 20 (1941), 1–23 at 3.

76 Ibid. 22.

77 Robinson, *supra* n. 21, 235.

78 Robinson, *supra* n. 21, 235.

79 Ibid. 237.

80 Ibid. 238–9.

dictated by philosophical conceptions that somehow stand above or apart from the conceptions of natural science.[81]

The task of the modern lawyer is to engage in a 'continuous constructive effort to solve legal problems by the use of the method and viewpoint of natural science'; indeed, 'the established natural sciences must be scoured for facts and concepts applicable to law'.[82] Only thus might lawyers 'become leaders in social thinking instead of guardians of outworn ideas'.[83] Yet the import of Robinson's assertions is not entirely clear. This is not straightforwardly an appeal for a return to source, for lawyers to become initiated in the ways of natural scientists. It is, rather, an appeal for lawyers to become familiar with the methods of the natural sciences specifically through the methods of the social sciences. At core, Robinson's argument—an argument which harks back explicitly to Pound—is that lawyers should become adept at general social scientific method. 'There is greatly needed a social engineer who will apply that method over a wide front and in the practical solution of urgent social problems. There is greatly needed a social engineer who, through the application of the best available knowledge, will teach men new and better ways of meeting their problems—of settling their disputes. There is no doubt of the opportunity. There is simply a question as to whether the lawmen will grasp it or whether the opportunity will, itself, create a new type of public servant—a real social engineer.'[84]

Semi-prophetic allusions of this nature landed Robinson and others in hot water with those critics who suspected that the realists' social servant of the future would be a ruthless, undemocratic technocrat. At another, more obvious level, however, Robinson's argument is decidedly less controversial. The appeal to science was an appeal not to natural science but to social science—for the use, that is, of scientific methods in the study of law in society. While the likes of Cook, Oliphant, Yntema and Robinson were prone to drawing affinities between legal realism and the methods of natural science, it was to the social sciences that they in fact looked for inspiration. The realist appeal to and identification with natural science has about it a distinct air of credibility-seeking. Legal realism as applied science was, in fact, jurisprudence conceived as social science.

SOCIAL SCIENCE AND THE LAW SCHOOLS

Yet even this claim must be subjected to critical scrutiny. There has been a tendency for commentators simply to assert rather than to explain the

[81] Robinson, *supra* n. 21, 245–6. [82] Ibid. 248. [83] Ibid. 266–7.
[84] Ibid. 267.

interaction between realism and social science.[85] It is beyond doubt that a good majority of those writers who came to be associated with realism during the 1920s and 1930s were attracted in one way or another to the social sciences. This much is clear from the emergence, during those decades, of Columbia and Yale as the two great bastions of realist thought. Two years after his appointment as a professor at Columbia Law School in 1921, Herman Oliphant wrote formally to the president of the University, outlining a proposal for the reorganization of the School curriculum—a reorganization which would demand of the faculty 'a great deal of concentrated research on the interrelation of law to the other social sciences'.[86] The proposal marked the beginning of a power struggle between those who, with Oliphant, believed that the Columbia faculty should devote its energies exclusively to the task of turning the School into a major centre for research into law as an aspect of social organization, and those who believed that, instead of emphasizing only research, the faculty should devote equal energy to the task of turning the School into the leading institution for training people for public service in the law.

Oliphant and his supporters ultimately 'failed' in their quest. The struggle between the pro- and anti-Oliphant factions culminated in 1928 with the appointment of Young B. Smith in preference to Oliphant as dean of the faculty.[87] While Smith himself accepted, within certain limits,[88] the desirability of a social scientific approach to the study of law,[89] he 'was unacceptable to those who thought the Law School should devote itself exclusively to research'.[90] Yet although the initiatives of Oliphant and his supporters had made only marginal ground at Columbia, an important and lasting precedent, an alternative to the conventional law school curriculum of the time, had emerged. Columbia of the 1920s represented a tentative departure from the Langdellian world-view: law could be studied not merely as a collection of logically classifiable, interconnected principles, but as a means of social control.

The fundamental thesis which emerged was this: Since law is a means of social control, it ought to be studied as such. . . . Columbia proceeded at once to put this

[85] For examples, see Thomas W. Bechtler, 'American Legal Realism Revaluated', in T. W. Bechtler (ed.), *Law in a Social Context: Liber Amicorum Honouring Professor Lon L. Fuller* (Dordrecht: Kluwer, 1978), 1–48 at 9; Ralph J. Savarese, 'American Legal Realism', *Houston L. Rev.*, 3 (1965), 180–200 at 181; Wolfgang Friedmann, *Legal Theory* (5th edn. London: Stevens & Sons, 1967), 299.

[86] William Nelson Cromwell Foundation, *A History of the School of Law: Columbia University* (New York: Columbia University Press, 1955), 299.

[87] For an account of the events, see Twining, *supra* n. 12, 41–55.

[88] On Smith's markedly qualified enthusiasm for a social scientific approach to the study of law, see Stevens, *supra* n. 45, 139–40; Twining, *supra* n. 12, 46.

[89] Cromwell Foundation, *supra* n. 86, 300.

[90] Ibid. 304.

programme into practice reorganizing courses along functional lines, reinforcing the faculty by the appointment of specialists in philosophy, business, and political science, and plunging with prodigious industry into reoriented research and the preparation of new course materials.[91]

The study of law in terms of its social functioning rather than its purported inner logic resulted in a heavy emphasis both on constitutional law and on economics in law. Typical of the latter trend was Robert Hale's course on legal economics, which ran from the early 1920s to the mid-1950s.[92] Other courses at Columbia in the 1920s, dealing with industrial relations and trade regulation, were similarly slanted towards economic analysis.[93] More generally, by looking to other disciplines for their inspiration, the social science sympathizers on the Columbia faculty began to see the American law school tradition in a fresh light. By the mid-1920s, moves were under way at Columbia to produce an entirely new law school curriculum. The report, penned by Oliphant, which resulted from this initiative stressed the recognition by the faculty that:

> the time has come for at least one school to become a 'community of scholars', devoting itself to the non-professional study of law, in order that the function of law may be comprehended, its results evaluated, and its development kept more nearly in step with the complex developments of modern life. This means not merely a broadening of the content of the legal curriculum, and not merely a graduate school in law added to the regular course; it means an entirely different approach to the law. It involves critical, constructive, creative work by both faculty and students rather than a regime devoted primarily to the acquisition of information.[94]

To this day, Oliphant's report stands as one of the most important and challenging documents to have been produced in the history of American legal education.[95] For all that, however, it failed, as a statement of purpose, to reflect the real sentiments of the Columbia faculty. While the majority was happy, in principle, to move towards the study of law as a social science, there remained a strong feeling that even a social scientific approach should place an especial emphasis on professional training. The

[91] Brainerd Currie, 'The Materials of Law Study, Parts I and II', *Jnl. Leg. Educ.*, 3 (1951), 331–87 at 334–7.

[92] See Duxbury, 'Robert Hale and the Economy of Legal Force', *supra* n. 3, 423.

[93] See Brainerd Currie, 'The Materials of Law Study, Part III', *Jnl. Leg. Educ.*, 8 (1955), 1–78 at 3. The industrial relations course was run by Noel T. Dowling, while the trade regulation course was run by Herman Oliphant.

[94] Herman Oliphant (ed.), *Summary of the Studies on Legal Education by the Faculty of Law of Columbia University* (New York: Faculty of Law of Columbia University, 1928), 20–1. Earlier in the 1920s, Oliphant had been concerned with broadening the law school curriculum specifically for the purpose of improving professional legal standards. See Herman Oliphant and Percy B. Bordwell, 'Legal Research in Law Schools', *American Law School Rev.*, 5 (1924), 293–9 at 293–7.

[95] See Stevens, *supra* n. 45, 138; Twining, *supra* n. 12, 50; Currie, *supra* n. 91, 332–41.

'entirely different approach to the law' which Oliphant was proposing was, for some of his colleagues, rather too different. His report was welcomed by the faculty, but few of its recommendations were ever implemented.[96]

The eventual choice of Smith over Oliphant for the deanship—a choice which was made by the President of the University rather than by the faculty itself—led to the resignation of certain faculty members who had supported Oliphant's candidacy and who had promoted the 'non-professional', social scientific approach to legal study at Columbia throughout the 1920s. William O. Douglas and, in 1930, Underhill Moore departed to Yale; and Hessel Yntema, Oliphant himself and a visiting professor, Leon C. Marshall, left to accept posts at Walter Wheeler Cook's newly founded Institute for the Study of Law at Johns Hopkins University.[97] Having spearheaded the social scientific approach to the study of law throughout the 1920s, the Columbia Law School, by the end of that decade, had lost some of its most innovative scholars. While, throughout Smith's deanship and beyond, the School continued to recruit talented lawyers sympathetic to the methods of the social sciences,[98] by the beginning of the 1930s, Yale and, to a lesser extent, Johns Hopkins, had emerged as the institutional centres for the social scientific approach to law. According to one commentator, the Columbia project had been 'revolutionary', it had been 'historic', but it had not been 'epoch-making'.[99]

The departure of Yntema, Oliphant and Marshall to Johns Hopkins should have marked the beginning of a marriage made in heaven. The Institute of Law offered precisely what Columbia did not: the opportunity to pursue research free from teaching commitments. For Cook, too, having spent some years prior to the founding of the Institute flitting restlessly between Columbia and Yale, here was the chance to settle with a group of talented and largely like-minded colleagues. The Johns Hopkins Board of Trustees required the Institute to develop a programme of legal research which complemented the more general, established tradition of applied science at the University. That broad remit apart, the Institute was given a free rein to pursue its goals however it wished.[100]

96 Stevens, *supra* n. 45, 138.

97 Cromwell Foundation, *supra* n. 86, 305. Technically, Marshall, an economist with no legal training, did not resign. His temporary appointment came to an end at the time of Smith's elevation to the deanship and, possibly as a protest, he passed over the opportunity to secure an extended contract.

98 See generally Currie, *supra* n. 93, 22–64; Twining, *supra* n. 12, 58–9.

99 Currie, *supra* n. 91, 337.

100 See generally Anon., 'The Johns Hopkins Institute for the Study of Law', *American Law School Rev.*, 6 (1928), 336–8; Leon C. Marshall, 'The Institute of Law, Johns Hopkins University', *American Scholar*, 2 (1933), 115.

Given such freedom, the Columbia emigrés each began their careers at Johns Hopkins by setting about completing the various projects upon which they had embarked at their previous institution. Only once this was done did the research programme of the Institute begin to acquire an identity of its own. During the years 1931 to 1933, the members of the Institute produced a series of detailed, mainly statistics-based studies of judicial administration and civil litigation, focusing on selected state courts in New York, Maryland, and Ohio.[101] The prodigious output and careful co-ordination of research during this period was nothing short of remarkable. Without the burden of having to run a traditional law school, the members of the Institute were able to devote almost all of their energies to the pursuit of scholarship in the form of empirical social science. The bubble, however, was soon to burst. Without either students or alumni, and without the backing of a major foundation, the Institute was forced to rely on just about any organization—usually law firms—willing to play the role of benefactor. The cost of this dependence was a frequent pressure to produce research with an immediate 'practical value'. Academic integrity was, accordingly, rather compromised at times by the need for hard cash. And it was precisely this need which ultimately brought about the death of the Institute. As the Depression years rolled on, funds quickly dried up, and by the early 1930s the Institute was forced to close.[102]

Yale, however, was a different story. The appointment of Robert Maynard Hutchins as dean of the Yale Law School in 1927 marked the beginning of a new chapter in the School's history. Having been generally disaffected with teaching at the School while a student, Hutchins—still only in his late twenties when he accepted the deanship—set about breaking with the traditions of the School's rather conservative past by promoting novel methods of teaching, establishing new programmes for research and, most importantly of all, securing a number of controversial appointments to the faculty. Columbia, throughout the 1920s, had built up a strong faculty of social science-inspired lawyers; and even though the original vitality of the Law School was diminished with the resignations of 1928, Dean Smith was quick to replace lost talent.[103] Throughout this decade, Harvard too enjoyed a period of revitalization as Langdellianism found a home at the American Law Institute. Hutchins's primary ambition was to bring to New Haven a standard of academic distinction comparable with that which had been established at both Columbia and Harvard—a

[101] For a discussion of the publications of the Johns Hopkins Institute, see John W. Johnson, *American Legal Culture, 1908–1940* (Westport, Conn. : Greenwood Press, 1981), 101–2.

[102] See Stevens, *supra* n. 45, 140.

[103] See Cromwell Foundation, *supra* n. 86, 310–11.

standard which, he believed, Yale had at least glimpsed in the work of one of its earlier professors, Wesley Newcomb Hohfeld.[104] His strategy was to set about creating a faculty which—for all its distinctness—would essentially be an extension of the Columbia model.

'If you run over their articles and book reviews, in the bound volumes of the old law journals, you can still catch an authentic whiff of cordite.'[105] Thus wrote Eugene Rostow, dean of the Yale Law School from 1955 to 1965. The cause for Rostow's reminiscence, the Yale realists of the 1930s, is one of the most famous sagas in the history of American jurisprudence. Reduced to its essence, it is a story about the efforts of a group of men, professing a common distrust of the doctrinal orthodoxies of the time, who were prepared to articulate their sense of distrust with an unprecedented, iconoclastic fervour. The story has been told many—perhaps too many[106]—times, and there will be no attempt here to recount it again. Worth considering briefly, nonetheless, is the inspirational but short-lived deanship of Hutchins, for it is possible to discern, in his contribution to the development of the Yale faculty, an equally short-lived enthusiasm for the 'scientific' ethos—an enthusiasm which exemplified the difficulties underlying the endeavour to introduce social scientific methods into law.

That Hutchins played a crucial role—indeed, the crucial role—in setting the scene for the emergence of realism at Yale during the 1930s is, in a sense, ironic, for by the time that decade arrived, he was already part of the School's history, having departed to the University of Chicago in 1929. During his short deanship, he had achieved a great deal. Recruiting heavily so as to double the size of the faculty which he inherited from the outgoing dean, Thomas W. Swan, Hutchins at the same time reduced student intake so that, between 1927 and 1928, the number of students at the School fell from 422 to 318. 'The stated purpose of the reduction', according to his biographer, 'was to free his interdisciplinary faculty from routine instruction so that the Law School could be converted into a research institution

[104] See Schlegel, 'From the Yale Experience', *supra* n. 3, 477. Hohfeld came from Stanford to Yale in 1914. He died in 1918. He is best remembered for his quasi-scientific theory of 'jural correlatives' and 'jural opposites' which, he argued, constitute the lowest common denominators of the law. See generally the posthumous collection of essays: Wesley N. Hohfeld, *Fundamental Legal Conceptions as Applied in Judicial Reasoning* (ed. A.L. Corbin, New Haven. Conn.: Yale University Press, 1964) esp. 63–4.

[105] Eugene V. Rostow, 'American Legal Realism and the Sense of the Profession', *Rocky Mountain L. Rev.*, 34 (1962), 123–49 at 129. See also his 'The Realist Tradition in American Law' in A.M. Schlesinger, Jr. and M. White eds., *Paths of American Thought* (Boston: Houghton Mifflin, 1963), 203–18, 556–9 at 209.

[106] Much of the general literature on legal realism produces the impression that the story of realism is little more than the story of the Yale Law School of the early 1930s. The works by Kalman and Schlegel, *supra* n. 3, are singularly important in that they resist such a characterization.

that gave selected students an appreciation of the underlying principles of jurisprudence as well as an understanding of how the law actually worked.'[107] While he could not provide the paradise of a pure research institution as was on offer at Johns Hopkins, Hutchins was determined to provide the next best thing; and it was to this end that, in 1929, in collaboration with the then dean of the Yale Medical School, Milton C. Winternitz, with the support of the president of the University, James Rowland Angell, and with the assistance of a substantial endowment from the Rockefeller Foundation, he set about establishing the Institute of Human Relations, a joint Law School-Medical School venture, devoted to 'the development of co-operative research in all fields relating to man'.[108]

The Institute was the crowning glory of Hutchins's short deanship. 'When the Yale Law School discovered that law was a social science,' he observed, 'it found that it needed the help of people trained in the social sciences.'[109] The Institute—dedicated to 'break[ing] down departmental barriers, bringing together men of common tastes and inclinations, placing at the disposal of each the resources of the other'[110]—was intended to provide the Law School with just that help. The Columbia refugees, Douglas and Moore, along with Hutchins and his former teacher and successor to the deanship, Charles E. Clark, were some of the first to embark on research under the auspices of the Institute. Hutchins also secured the appointment of Donald Slesinger, a psychologist whom he had originally brought to the law faculty to collaborate with him on a scientific analysis of the rules of evidence,[111] as executive secretary of the Institute. While the Law School and the Institute remained administratively and financially separate, an important academic link had been made which provided the faculty with the perfect opportunity for the social scientific study of law; and although Dean Clark would adopt a rather less positive view of the Institute during the 1930s, its continuation in tandem with the faculty was integral to the growth of realism at Yale.[112] It is hardly

[107] Harry S. Ashmore, *Unseasonable Truths: The Life of Robert Maynard Hutchins* (Boston: Little, Brown & Co., 1989), 55.

[108] Robert M. Hutchins, 'An Institute of Human Relations', *American Journal of Sociology*, 35 (1929), 187–93 at 192.

[109] Ibid. 190.

[110] Ibid. 191.

[111] See Robert M. Hutchins and Donald Slesinger, 'Some Observations on the Law of Evidence', *Columbia L. Rev.*, 28 (1928), 432–40; 'Some Observations on the Law of Evidence—the Competency of Witnesses', *Yale L.J.*, 37 (1928), 1017–28; 'Some Observations on the Law of Evidence—Memory', *Harvard L. Rev.*, 41 (1928), 860–73; 'Some Observations on the Law of Evidence: State of Mind in Issue', *Columbia L. Rev.*, 29 (1929), 147–57.

[112] See Charles E. Clark, 'The Educational and Scientific Objectives of the Yale School of Law', *Annals of the American Academy of Political and Social Sciences*, 167 (1933), 165–72; Dorothy Swaine Thomas, 'Some Aspects of Socio-Legal Research at Yale', *American Journal of Sociology*, 37 (1931), 213–21.

surprising to find an ebullient Hutchins claiming, in his final annual report to the faculty, that '[t]he conclusion of the year 1928-9 finds the Yale School of Law in the best condition in its history'.[113] Inspirational appointments had been made, student numbers reduced, staff complement enlarged, new honours courses established, teaching and research revitalized; in short, Yale had acquired the academic identity which Hutchins had sought for it—and the *belle époque* of realism had still to come.

Yet, even before Clark succeeded Hutchins as dean, even before realism at Yale had hit full swing, something was amiss. Rather like the precocious football talent who constantly wants the ball but is uncertain of what to do with it once in possession, Hutchins's Yale was fast and furious but ultimately lacked vision. Every bit equal to the faculty's demand for innovation was a basic absence of strategy, an inability, on Hutchins's part, to marshal its formidable talent.

> In considering Hutchins' career at the law school one can almost hear him yell, 'Do Something!' And his style reflects that command. The pace was frenetic as he constantly pushed, jostled, and probed both law in general and legal education in particular for ways to make them better, more sensible, more reputably a subject for academic inquiry . . . [T]he style put a premium on starting and little on following through, on creating opportunities but not on working with the opportunities created, on coming up with ideas but not on working them through.[114]

This style was one which 'many of the Realists shared'.[115] While they appeared to break decisively from the Langdellian past, most realists had, in fact, little notion of what they were looking for in the law schools of the future. There was simply a widespread assumption that the social sciences would provide all the necessary answers. As early as 1931, Morris Cohen—having previously welcomed Pound's interdisciplinary initiatives in attempting to undermine the dominance of mechanical jurisprudence[116]—warned that 'the gravest peril perhaps is that in reacting violently against our former isolation of law we shall neglect the results of centuries of legal scholarship and slavishly imitate other social sciences or borrow from them methods and results that are not suitable to our subject. Let us not forget that some of the social sciences are very young, and are as yet in large part only vocabularies of generous aspiration.'[117] It is a warning which, by and large, fell on deaf ears.

[113] Robert M. Hutchins, 'Dean's Report to the Faculty, Yale Law School, 1928–1929', 117; quoted in Kalman, *supra* n. 3, 115; Ashmore, *supra* n. 107, 55.

[114] Schlegel, 'From the Yale Experience', *supra* n. 3, 489–90.

[115] Ibid. 490.

[116] Morris R. Cohen, 'Jurisprudence as a Philosophical Discipline', *Journal of Philosophy, Psychology and Scientific Methods*, 10 (1913), 225–32.

[117] Morris R. Cohen, 'Justice Holmes and the Nature of Law', *Columbia L. Rev.*, 31 (1931), 352–67 at 364–5.

The 'scientific' goals of the Langdellian law school had at least been fairly obvious. What were the 'scientific' goals of the post-Langdellian law school to be? The appeal to the methods of the social sciences suggested that the realists, if no one else, had a good idea of what they were looking for. But once the general spirit of the 1920s and 1930s had dwindled, various of those who had been in the midst of the ferment acknowledged that their initiatives had tended to lack direction.[118] By and large, the so-called realists—whether they feigned or truly believed otherwise—had clung to the precipice of legal formalism, preferring, for all their admirable critical sensibilities, to remain rooted in the past rather than take a decisive leap towards the future. Thus it is that the revolt against formalism which supposedly culminated with the coming of legal realism never quite occurred. The turn to the social sciences promised far more than ever was delivered.

Hutchins was perhaps the first to concede as much. Soon after leaving Yale, he became, as one commentator has put it, 'an apostate realist'.[119] Though, by 1934, realism at Yale was at its peak, Hutchins, now president of the University of Chicago, was conceiving of the social scientific approach to law as a phenomenon of the past:

> In attempting to decide which rule worked better we had to assume a social order and the aims thereof, and then try to determine which rule did more to achieve the aims we favoured. What made this difficult was that we didn't know much about the social order. . . . Suddenly we discovered that there were people who knew all these things, people who could tell us how the law worked and why. They were the social scientists. We had every reason to resort to them. The courts were social agencies; their conclusions must be conditioned by society. The social scientists could help us to predict what the courts would do. The psychologists would help us understand the behaviour of judges . . . Hand in hand with these other scientists we could become scientific.[120]

Alas, the quest for an interdisciplinary legal science proved futile. So far as the study of law was concerned, the insights to be gained from

[118] See e.g. William O. Douglas, *Go East, Young Man: The Early Years* (New York: Random House, 1974), 170; Karl N. Llewellyn, 'On What Makes Legal Research Worthwhile?', *Jnl. Leg. Educ.*, 8 (1956), 399–421 at 400–3.

[119] Edward A. Purcell, Jr., *The Crisis of Democratic Theory: Scientific Naturalism and the Problem of Value* (Lexington: University Press of Kentucky, 1973), 152; though cf. Johnson, *supra* n. 101, 138. ('Hutchins took many of the realists' ideas with him to the University of Chicago, where he was instrumental in inaugurating a four-year curriculum in the Law School that included courses in psychology, English constitutional history, economic theory, and ethics.')

[120] Robert M. Hutchins, 'The Autobiography of an Ex-Law Student', *U. Chicago L. Rev.*, 1 (1934), 511–8 at 512.

collaboration between lawyers and social scientists were, for Hutchins, negligible:

Imagine our confusion . . . when we discovered that from their disciplines as such the social scientists added little or nothing. . . . The fact was that though the social scientists seemed to have a great deal of information, we could not see and they could not tell us how to use it. It did not seem to show us what the courts would do or whether what they had done was right. . . . We did not know what facts to look for, or why we wanted them, or what to do with them after we got them. We were simply after facts. These facts did not help us to understand the law, the social order, or the relation between the two.[121]

Given Hutchins's account, it may seem unsurprising that fact-research at the Yale Law School began to wane almost as soon as it had become established.[122] Yet, in one sense, his account is slightly misleading, in so far as concern at Yale during the early 1930s with the empirical study of law did not disappear altogether. At the time that Hutchins was writing of the passing of the social scientific approach at Yale, Underhill Moore—probably the most committed legal empiricist American has ever seen—had only just embarked on his protracted study of driving offences in the light of New Haven's traffic and parking ordinances.[123] While Moore's work has attracted a good deal of knee-jerk ridicule,[124] including from Hutchins himself,[125] it represents a unique if rather solitary testament to the persistence at Yale during the 1930s of a quantitative social science approach to the study of law. Initiated at the end of 1933, Moore's project lasted until 1937, and would no doubt have continued for longer had funding not dried up.[126]

[121] Ibid. 512–13; and cf. also Currie, *supra* n. 93, 75–76; Arthur Nussbaum, 'Fact Research in Law', *Columbia L. Rev.*, 40 (1940), 189–219 at 199.

[122] See Kalman, *supra* n. 3, 35. ('Empiricism was disappearing from the law by 1932'); also Peter H. Schuck, 'Why Don't Law Professors Do More Empirical Research?', *Jnl. Leg. Educ.*, 39 (1989), 323–36 at 329. ('[T]he "golden age" of empiricism in law never really dawned—even on Morningside Heights or in Baltimore or New Haven during the heydey [*sic*] of the realists.') For all this, the empiricist strand of legal realism was not uninfluential as regards the subsequent development of American legal scholarship. See Arthur Nussbaum, 'Some Aspects of American "Legal Realism" ', *Jnl. Leg. Educ.*, 12 (1959), 182–92 at 185–9.

[123] For a detailed account, see Schlegel, 'The Singular Case of Underhill Moore', *supra* n. 3, 264–303.

[124] For a critique of the criticisms that have been levelled at Moore, see Schlegel, *supra* n. 3, 292–3.

[125] It is most likely that Hutchins had Moore in mind when he referred disparagingly to the degeneration of quantitative social science at Yale Law School into an exercise in 'counting telephone poles'. See Ashmore, *supra* n. 107, 154.

[126] See John P. Dawson, 'Legal Realism and Legal Scholarship', *Jnl. Leg. Educ.*, 33 (1983), 406–11 at 407. The main fruit of Moore's labour was a massive article, written in collaboration with Charles Callahan, a researcher at the Institute of Human Relations: see Underhill Moore and Charles Callahan, 'Law and Learning Theory: A Study in Legal

In another sense, Hutchins's observations are rather more telling, in that they point to an obvious yet highly significant question: namely what, precisely, were social scientific studies of law supposed to achieve? What, of value, could social scientists give to lawyers that lawyers did not have already? By resorting to the social sciences, so-called realists were attempting to engage in much more than a reaction against legal formalism. They were attempting also to carve out a future, a life after Langdellianism, for the modern American law school. Paradoxically, realism both failed and succeeded in this task. It failed in that, as Hutchins detects, the realists were by and large content to espouse, in the abstract, the virtues of the social sciences rather than demonstrate specifically how those virtues might have a special significance and validity for the study of law. But it succeeded in that the realists' affair with the social sciences set the agenda for American jurisprudence of the future. Even the jurisprudential tendencies which were to emerge as reactions against realism would not be shy of the social sciences. Realism made the interdisciplinary study of law respectable, even among its opponents.

A reactionary few have regarded this as the most pernicious legacy of legal realism. With the advent of realism, so the argument goes, American legal culture lost its innocence; law could never again be conceived as a purely autonomous body of principles and doctrines.[127] More common, though, is the failure of post-realist legal academics to recognize just how fundamental a transformation the mood of realism brought to American jurisprudence. In his survey of modern legal philosophies, for example, Richard Posner announces from the outset his intention to 'pass over the realists' for the reason that he has 'difficulty in understanding what is original in [legal realism]'.[128] The originality of legal realism was that it set the scene for the emergence of jurisprudential sub-disciplines of the 'law and' variety.[129] Realism marked the marriage of social science and law.

Control', *Yale L.J.*, 53 (1943), 1–136. For an appreciative assessment of Moore's jurisprudence, cf. Simon N. Verdun-Jones and F. Douglas Cousineau, 'The Voice Crying in the Wilderness: Underhill Moore as a Pioneer in the Establishment of an Interdisciplinary Jurisprudence', *Int. Jnl. Law and Psychiatry*, 1 (1978), 375–94; and for a less sympathetic estimation, see David H. Moskowitz, 'The American Legal Realists and an Empirical Science of Law', *Villanova L. Rev.*, 11 (1966), 480–524 at 490–7, 509–13.

[127] The most unequivocal proponent of this view is Charles Fried, 'Jurisprudential Responses to Legal Realism', *Cornell L. Rev.*, 73 (1988), 331–4.

[128] Richard A. Posner, *The Problems of Jurisprudence* (Cambridge, Mass.: Harvard University Press, 1990), 19–20. For a discussion of Posner's neglect of legal realism, see Neil Duxbury, 'Pragmatism Without Politics', *Mod. L. Rev.*, 55 (1992), 594–610 at 609–10.

[129] Mark Tushnet, 'Post-Realist Legal Scholarship', *Jnl. of the Society of Public Teachers of Law*, 15 (1980), 20–32 at 23; Arthur Allen Leff, 'Law and', *Yale L.J.*, 87 (1978), 989–1011 at 1005–11; John Brigham and Christine B. Harrington, 'Realism and its Consequences: An Inquiry into Contemporary Sociological Research', *Int. Jnl. Sociology of Law*, 17 (1989), 41–62. This is not to claim, however, that realism was responsible for the rise of law and economics. On this matter, see the introduction to ch. 5.

Yet it is Hutchins's contention, in raising the question of what 'social science' meant for the realists, that this marriage was basically one of convenience. The point is of fundamental importance. The rather hesitant and ingenuous manner in which most legal realists brought the social sciences into the legal arena established a crucial precedent for future generations of legal scholars. Not only did so-called realists never properly come to grips with the social sciences but, more importantly, post-realist social science-oriented legal scholarship generally took its cue from their promotion of a 'new', post-Langdellian scientific ethos. After realism, American academic lawyers more or less stopped asking questions about what it meant to use the social sciences in the study of law. Such questions, it was assumed, had been raised by the legal realists; and while the realists themselves might not have been particularly adept social scientists, they had demonstrated, in principle, that interdisciplinary legal study was a virtue beyond doubt.

Thus it was that realism, ironically, brought to American legal scholarship a peculiar element of complacency. It is, indeed, doubly ironic that, in the aftermath of 1930s Yale, among the minority of voices dissenting from the view that a social scientific approach to law is an enlightened approach to law were certain of the later, second-generation realists themselves.[130] One of the fundamental failures of modern American jurisprudence has been the general unwillingness of its proponents to consider—except in the most rudimentary of terms—the question of what, for the legal realists, 'social science' actually meant. The question is not straightforwardly an institutional one—a question of who was doing what at Columbia, Johns Hopkins, Yale and elsewhere in the 1920s and 1930s—but a question concerning, first of all, how social science was coupled with the spirit of realism and, secondly, what social science meant generally for early twentieth-century American social scientists.

SOCIAL SCIENCE AND REALISM

'Realism' is an established piece of twentieth century Western intellectual currency. The term is far more prevalent in philosophy, art, literature, politics and history than ever it has been in law; and indeed, in those fields, it has come to denote ideas and beliefs which at times rather contrast with the notion of 'realism' in jurisprudence. Even in jurisprudence, 'realism' is not an exclusively American preserve;[131] and in philosophy, the term has

130 See e.g. Fred Rodell, 'Legal Realists, Legal Fundamentalists, Lawyer Schools, and Policy Science—Or How Not to Teach Law', *Vanderbilt L. Rev.*, 1 (1947), 5–7.

131 For an illustration of this point, see Karl Olivecrona, *Law as Fact* (2nd edn. , London: Stevens & Sons, 1971), 168–85; and also, from another perspective, Gaston Gavet, 'Individualism and Realism', *Yale L.J.*, 29 (1920), 523–38, 643–53.

attracted a meaning which most legal realists would probably have considered wholly at odds with their own ideas about the world.[132] Yet, for all that 'realism' means different things for different people, it is a term which, perhaps better than any other, captures what can only be vaguely described as a peculiarly North American, early twentieth-century 'collective unconscious'.[133] During the first three decades of this century, 'realism', in competition with 'modernism', represented a primary mode of cultural expression, especially in the cinema and the art gallery.[134] Realism was part of the cultural climate; it was 'in the air'.

In the American social sciences, a distinct ethos of 'realism' developed as early as the 1870s, parallel with Langdellianism in the law schools. Early realist social thought was inspired by the experience of the Civil War and the powerful nationalist sentiments which it aroused, and also by escalating industrialism and subsequent economic depression during the post-war years.[135] Social scientists of the 1870s were very much aware of the extent to which, after the Civil War, American culture and social experience had changed, and the ethos of realism was very much a consequence of this new awareness.[136] For the first time in American history, cultural traditions of the past were not inevitably or directly related to the here and now. The problem of understanding post-War social consciousness was to be solved not, primarily, by looking to history, but by focusing on 'contemporary reality'. Thus it was that, for example, in late nineteenth and early twentieth-century American literature, 'realism' became 'the aesthetic of disinheritance', the prioritization of the present by way of response to the sense of dislocation from the past.[137] Likewise in the social sciences. In his inaugural lecture in 1872, the American sociologist, William Graham Sumner, declared that 'the traditions and usages of past ages are broken,

[132] Philosophical realism might be defined very basically 'as the belief that statements . . . possess an objective truth-value, independently of our means of knowing it: they are true or false in virtue of a reality existing independently of us.' Michael Dummett, *Truth and Other Enigmas* (Cambridge, Mass.: Harvard University Press, 1978), 146; and see also Richard Rorty, *Objectivity, Relativism, and Truth: Philosophical Papers, Volume I* (Cambridge: Cambridge University Press, 1991), 2–12. A classic example of 'realist' jurisprudence in this philosophical sense is the phenomenological legal philosophy of Adolf Reinach, on which see Neil Duxbury, 'The Legal Philosophy of Adolf Reinach', *Archiv für Rechts- und Sozialphilosophie*, 77 (1991), 314–47, 466–92. On the incompatibility of philosophical realism and American legal realism, see Summers, *supra* n. 19, 36–7.

[133] The term is a Jungian one, though I use it here in a non-technical manner, following David Mamet, *Some Freaks* (London: Faber & Faber, 1989), 70.

[134] See generally Douglas Tallack, *Twentieth-Century America: The Intellectual and Cultural Context* (London: Longman, 1991), 37–113.

[135] On the effect of the Civil War on American social thought, see George M. Frederickson, *The Inner Civil War* (New York: Harper & Row, 1965).

[136] See generally Raymond J. Seidelman, *Disenchanted Realists: Political Science and the American Crisis, 1884–1984* (Albany, NY: State University of New York Press, 1985).

[137] Roger B. Salomon, 'Realism as Disinheritance: Twain, Howells, and James', *American Quarterly*, 16 (1964), 531–44 at 533.

or at least discredited. New conditions require new institutions and we turn away from tradition and prescription to reexamine the data from which we learn what principles of the social order are *true*, that is are conformed to human nature and to the conditions of human society.'[138] In the social sciences, 'realism emerged as a way of coping with the new industrial world'.[139]

Indeed, by the turn of the nineteenth century and the onset of the era of progressivism, the social-scientific idea of realism—the search for 'facts' to depict 'contemporary reality'—had become an established method of producing authoritative knowledge about modern industrial America. 'The new concentrations of economic power, the teeming, polyglot cities, and the expansion of urban, state, and federal governance created new worlds that required detailed knowledge. The great preponderance of social scientists' publications during these years were empirical studies of the concrete operation of business, government, and social life.'[140] Typical of the social-scientific evolution towards realist empiricism was the development of late nineteenth and early twentieth-century political science. By the beginning of this century, American political scientists were distinguishing between formalist and realist styles of social inquiry. A study of 'political conditions as they now exist in the United States', wrote Frank Goodnow in 1900, reveals 'that the formal governmental system as set forth in the law is not always the same as the actual system'.[141] Three years earlier, in his study of municipal problems, the same author had asserted that to understand 'what the city really is,' it is necessary 'to treat the city rather as part of the governmental system than as an isolated phenomenon'.[142] Goodnow's preference for 'realist' political inquiry is typical of a more general endeavour by his contemporaries 'to get beneath the traditional structure of constitutional principle and examine how party politics, city government, and administration actually functioned in American political life'.[143]

It is precisely this desire for realism which made its way into the law schools; and it was the general idea of social science that was seen by most

[138] William Graham Sumner, *The Challenge of Facts and Other Essays* (ed. A. G. Keller, New Haven: Yale University Press, 1914), 394–5; and, on Sumner's sense of the break with the past after the Civil War, see further Robert C. Bannister, Jr., 'William Graham Sumner's Social Darwinism: A Reconsideration', *History of Political Economy*, 5 (1973), 89–109 at 93–4.

[139] Dorothy Ross, *The Origins of American Social Science* (Cambridge: Cambridge University Press, 1991), 64.

[140] Ibid. 156.

[141] Frank J. Goodnow, *Politics and Administration* (New York: Macmillan, 1900), v.

[142] Frank J. Goodnow, *Municipal Problems* (New York: Macmillan, 1897), v.

[143] Ross, *supra* n. 139, 297–8; and see more generally Martin Landau, 'The Myth of Hyperfactualism in the Study of American Politics', *Political Science Quarterly*, 83 (1968), 378–99.

legal realists to provide the requisite key to reality.[144] In an introduction to a text entitled *From the Physical to the Social Sciences*, published under the auspices of the Johns Hopkins Institute for the Study of Law, Herman Oliphant lamented in 1929 that:

> [m]ost of the literature of the law, whether found in judicial decisions or in academic writings, is devoted to erecting, defending, or attacking elaborate structures of autonomous thought. . . . There has been such a complete absence of effort methodically to develop the empirical side of law and such an over-elaboration of its rational side that scholarship in law tends more and more to neglect how courts actually decide cases and more and more to consider what they say about why they decide as they do, which, after all, is stating the same thing in another way.[145]

By embracing the inductive paradigm of the modern social sciences, Oliphant argues, lawyers will discover the futility of assuming law to be 'a system of fundamental and changeless "principles" existing apart from cases decided in the past,'[146] and will learn instead to treat 'the reality' of law as 'the actual decisions of cases by courts'.[147] The argument is, in one sense, rather banal, illustrative as it is of the commonplace realist faith in the indiscriminate application of social scientific methods to the study of law. In another sense, however, the argument is instructive, for it suggests how the 'realist' element of legal realism rested precisely in the appeal to the social sciences. By looking to the social sciences, particularly to those of an empirical bent, legal realists saw a means of developing on the insights of Pound and—more particularly—Holmes, of prioritizing law in action over law in books, legal experience over legal logic. The social sciences appeared to provide a method for telling it—namely, 'law'—as it is; for demonstrating how 'the concepts which the courts are using can be broken down and translated into the varying factual combinations which are found';[148] for getting almost 'as near to a case as the judge who decides it'.[149] The realist reaction against legal formalism was not straightforwardly a reaction against the idea of legal certainty, but rather a reaction against the particular certainties which formalism promoted. Legal realism

[144] See David M. Trubek, 'Back to the Future: The Short, Happy Life of the Law and Society Movement', *University of Wisconsin Law School Institute for Legal Studies Working Papers*, series 4, 1990, 28–9.

[145] Herman Oliphant and Abram Hewitt, 'Introduction', in Jacques Rueff, *From the Physical to the Social Sciences: Introduction to a Study of Economic and Ethical Theory* (Eng. tr. H. Green, Baltimore: The Johns Hopkins Press, 1929), ix–xxxii at xxvi–xxviii. Hewitt, a former student of the Columbia Law School, was Oliphant's research assistant at Johns Hopkins.

[146] Ibid. xviii.

[147] Ibid. xxvi.

[148] William O. Douglas and Carrol M. Shanks, 'Insulation from Liability Through Subsidiary Corporations', *Yale L.J.*, 39 (1929), 193–218 at 210.

[149] Oliphant, *supra* n. 72, 160.

sought a qualitatively different type of certainty—certainty, that is, in the form of a purported juridical authenticity; and this it did by looking to the social sciences. For most legal realists, social science was realism.

Law and Economics

The early intersections between law and economics provide a clear illustration of this point. Late nineteenth-century economic developments in the United States supported the move towards social-scientific realism. Though economic hardship was prevalent during the last three decades of the nineteenth century, organized industrial action generally rubbed against the grain of largely conservative public opinion and led to concerted anti-labour campaigns.[150] The ideological conflict between pro- and anti-labour supporters was reflected in an academic context primarily by late nineteenth-century developments in economics. Inspired principally by the growth of state-oriented, historical economics in Germany, an emerging group of American economists—including the likes of John Bates Clark, Henry Carter Adams, Richard T. Ely and E. R. A. Seligman—challenged the classical conception of the American political economy by questioning the 'scientific' status which classical economists accredited to the idea of free exchange.[151] The fundamental failing of *laissez-faire*, according to the new generation of economists, rested in its inability to provide a credible remedy for the problems of unemployment and working-class poverty. However, this did not amount to an outright rejection of the classical economic model. The brand of economic interventionism which this new generation of economists promoted was decidedly restrained. 'Adams, Ely, and particularly Clark continued to value the individual independence and moral strength that competitive exertion in the capitalist economy could create. Wherever genuine competition could be made to work, they hoped to retain it. By the same token, state action would be used only where necessary: to raise the plane

[150] See generally David Montgomery, *Beyond Equality: Labor and the Radical Republicans, 1862–1872* (New York: Knopf, 1967); J. H. M. Laslett, *Labor and the Left: A Study of Socialist and Radical Influences in the American Labor Movement, 1881–1924* (New York: Basic Books, 1970); Leon Fink, *Workingmen's Democracy: The Knights of Labor and American Politics* (Urbana: University of Illinois Press, 1983).

[151] For discussion in general, see Mary Furner, *Advocacy and Objectivity: A Crisis in the Professionalization of American Social Science, 1865–1905* (Lexington: University Press of Kentucky, 1975), 49–57; Dorothy Ross, 'Socialism and American Liberalism: Academic Social Thought in the 1880s', *Perspectives in American History*, 11 (1977–78), 5–79 at 15–22, 69–70; A. W. Coats, 'Henry Carter Adams: A Case Study in the Emergence of the Social Sciences in the United States, 1850–1900', *Jnl. of American Studies*, 2 (1968), 179–85; Benjamin G. Rader, *The Academic Mind and Reform: The Influence of Richard T. Ely in American Life* (Lexington: University Press of Kentucky, 1966), 1–7.

of competition, regulate monopoly, or enforce the rights of labour as workingmen increasingly gained control of industry.'[152] Retaining a basic faith in the moral legitimacy of the free market, the new generation of economists argued for 'social justice without socialism',[153] for a philosophy which fell somewhere in between interventionism and *laissez-faire*. Qualified interventionism was the flavour of the day.

It was with the advent of the philosophy of qualified interventionism that modern economics began to accommodate the ethos of social-scientific realism. While resorting primarily to formal economic laws in order to try to understand change and facilitate prediction, the new generation of economists recognized also that a persuasive method by which to demonstrate the shortcomings of free market philosophy would be to situate and test it empirically. Yet it was really only with the advent of post-classical economics proper—that is, with the emergence of the so-called 'institutionalist' economic perspective during the first two decades of this century—that economists began to regard empirical research and the gathering of quantitative facts as a peculiarly 'scientific' means of eradicating subjectivism and irrationalism from economic analysis.[154] One of the earliest proponents of institutionalism, Wesley Clair Mitchell, remarked in 1915 that 'proof means usually an appeal to the facts—facts recorded in the best cases and in statistical form. To write books of assertion or shrewd observation, won't convince people who have been in the habit of asserting other things or seeing things in a different perspective . . . [T]he only real answer lies in doing a lot of work with statistics.'[155]

Much of Mitchell's own work epitomized the style of statistics-based research into actual economic processes and activities which he believed was the proper purpose of institutionalism.[156] However, for all that they were prepared, in principle, to attest to the worthiness of such tasks, some institutionalists were reluctant, in practice, to devote much energy to the collection of data and compilation of statistics. In contrast with their often platitudinous espousals of quantitative research, a more important intellectual bond among the majority of institutional economists was their indebtedness to the work of Thorstein Veblen. In his endeavour to develop

[152] Ross, *supra* n. 139, 108–9.

[153] John Bates Clark, *Social Justice Without Socialism* (Boston: Houghton Mifflin, 1914).

[154] On institutionalist economics as part of the so-called 'revolt against formalism', see Ben B. Seligman, *Main Currents in Modern Economics: Economic Thought Since 1870* (New York: Free Press, 1962), 129–253.

[155] Wesley Clair Mitchell, 'Social Progress and Social Science', unpublished manuscript, 6 September 1915, in Wesley Clair Mitchell Papers, Rare Book and Manuscript Division, Butler Library, Columbia University.

[156] See e.g. Wesley Clair Mitchell, 'The Rationality of Economic Activity', *Jnl. of Political Economy*, 18 (1910), 197–216.

a theory of economics which was both critical and scientific, Veblen looked to late nineteenth-century evolutionary anthropology, from which he derived not only a theory of evolution but also a specific notion of objectivity, epitomized by the standpoint of the hypothetical 'alien observer'.[157] In turning to anthropology, Veblen attempted to develop an evolutionary theory of economics which countered the classicists' tendency to accord paradigmatic status to the idea of free exchange. Economics, he insisted, must be transformed into a genuine evolutionary science, into a study not of *laissez-faire* supported by the principle of natural selection, but of the American political economy as an evolving cultural process. It is not in the abstract paradigm of free exchange, but 'in the human material that the continuity of development is to be looked for; and it is here . . . that the motor forces of the process of economic development must be studied if they are to be studied in action at all. Economic action must be the subject-matter of the science if the science is to fall into line as an evolutionary science.'[158] Basically, 'an evolutionary economics must be the theory of a process of cultural growth as determined by the economic interest, a theory of a cumulative sequence of economic institutions stated in terms of the process itself'.[159] For Veblen, evolutionary science teaches that, in economics as elsewhere, historical study must focus on culture rather than causality.

It was thus that Veblen contributed to the emergence of institutionalism in economics. By re-casting economics as an evolutionary science, rather than merely as an ideology backed up by the scientific gloss of Social Darwinism, he 'showed how economists could accept history and legitimate change, even radical change, while assuming a stance of scientific objectivity; how they could undermine convention, yet speak in the name of universal truth'.[160] After Veblen, economic theory premissed on the validity of market intervention—intervention, as Veblen would have it, for the sake of 'cultural growth'—could be just as 'scientific', in an evolutionary sense, as competing, classical theories founded on the primacy of free exchange. Evolutionism provided a theoretical grounding for both pro- and anti-economic interventionists. 'Science' was no longer the preserve of economic inquiry in the classical tradition.

Building on the initiatives of Veblen, the economists who came to typify the institutionalist perspective during the early decades of this century by and large adopted as their primary focus of critique not the espousal by classical economists of free market virtues, but the neo-classicist faith in

[157] See Ross, *supra* n. 139, 154.

[158] Thorstein Veblen, 'Why is Economics Not an Evolutionary Science?', *Quarterly Journal of Economics*, 12 (1898), 373–97 at 388.

[159] Ibid. 393.

[160] Ross, *supra* n. 139, 215.

qualified interventionism. 'What fueled the institutionalist ambition was an overflow of realism and new liberal idealism that could not be contained by neoclassical practice. Impatient with the incapacity of economic theory to lead the way to real social democracy, the institutionalists gathered up the hopes and discontents of the [First World] war years into a call for a new kind of economic science.'[161] True to the Veblenian spirit, the new 'science' for which institutionalists appealed was a science of economic interventionism.

But it was not the language of economic interventionism which the institutionalists employed in putting forward their plans for the reorganization of the market in the interests of general social welfare and democracy. Rather, it was the language of the broader social sciences to which they resorted. Institutionalists concerned themselves not, specifically, with the notion of economic intervention but, more generally, with the use of economics to facilitate 'social control'. In what is, perhaps, the exemplary institutionalist text, John Maurice Clark conceives of social control as an insidious economic phenomenon:

> 'Control' means, primarily, coercion: orders backed by irresistible power. . . . But there are other less obvious ways of exercising control. In a broad sense, you can control me if you can make me do what you want, no matter what motive you use. . . . Suppose a labourer canvasses the field and finds no one offering a satisfactory living wage for his grade of work. He is 'compelled' to accept less; but whence comes the compulsion? Does it come from the employer who last discharged him, or from an informal control of the market by the employers in general, or from the customs and habits of business, or from the 'impersonal and immutable laws' of supply and demand? If he is actually getting the benefit of active competition, he will have chances to get approximately as much as some typical employer can afford to pay him, so that if he is still underpaid it is due to the forces of supply and demand, and not to deliberate oppression. But this occurs chiefly at times of business depression, which is coming to be regarded as a remediable disease of industry, so that society has some responsibility for the compulsions of supply and demand, to the extent that it has power to alleviate them. And this impersonal machinery of private industry evidently has penalties at its disposal which often carry more material hardship than a jail sentence. Yet a jail sentence is coercion such as only the state can employ; while the loss of one's job is merely an incident of 'free bargaining'.[162]

The casual disparaging of classical economics here,[163] and the optimistic belief that the 'new' economics would herald a remedy to the Depression,

[161] Ross, *supra* n. 139, 411.

[162] John Maurice Clark, *Social Control of Business* (Chicago: University of Chicago Press, 1926), 6; and, in a similar institutionalist vein, see Rexford G. Tugwell, 'The Economic Basis for Business Regulation', *American Economic Rev.*, 11 (1921), 643–58.

[163] Clark was to some extent an exception among the institutional economists in so far as his criticisms of the neo-classical tradition were, for the most part, decidedly restrained. This

betray a peculiar institutionalist naivety. With the approach of the 1930s, institutionalism began to appear every bit as ineffectual in pragmatic terms as the tradition of non-interventionism to which it supposedly offered a challenge[164]—so much so, indeed, that President Hoover eventually sought a Keynesian remedy to the economic downturn.[165] While rejecting the argument that the economic slump would right itself with a minimum of market intervention, institutionalist economists were nonetheless unable to procure a better understanding of, or propose a more convincing remedy for, the Depression than had their neo-classical precursors: for all that they were convinced of the shortcomings of neo-classicism, they were unable convincingly to improve upon those shortcomings. Part of the problem was the general institutionalist preoccupation with critique at the expense of pragmatic proposals for economic reform. Indeed, rather ironically, institutionalist economists generally devoted little energy to the study of institutions, preferring instead to draw upon the insights of the likes of Veblen, Marx, and Sydney and Beatrice Webb. A greater problem, however, rested in the fact that, having acquired prominence very much on the back of the Depression, most institutionalists simply turned away from the problem on realizing that, beyond the rhetoric of social control, they had little idea as to how to deal with it. When, for example, Wesley Clair Mitchell was proved wrong by time in his prediction that the sharp economic downturn following the Crash would remedy itself within a year or two, he retreated from the problem by turning his attention exclusively to empirical research into economic planning.[166]

While institutionalism was something of a pragmatic failure, however, its broader intellectual legacy was more enduring and impressive. This much is clear from the manner in which institutionalist sentiments gradually permeated progressive legal thinking. Given their general preoccupation with the nature of social control, it is unsuprising that most institutionalist economists should have been concerned in one way or another with the

may have been because his father, John Bates Clark, was a prime exponent of neo-classicist economics. For an illustration of Maurice Clark's cautious critique of neo-classicism, see John Maurice Clark, 'Soundings in Non-Euclidean Economics', *Papers and Proceedings of the American Economic Association*, 11 (1921), 132–43; and, for an illustration of his respect for the intellectual achievements of his father, his review of A. C. Pigou, *Wealth and Welfare*, *American Economic Rev.*, 3 (1913), 623–5 at 624.

164 Although institutionalism never died out once and for all, as is clear from its continuing if somewhat marginal impact on American legal scholarship. For a discussion, see Neil Duxbury, 'Is There a Dissenting Tradition in Law and Economics?', *Mod. L. Rev.*, 54 (1991), 300–11.

165 See John Kenneth Galbraith, *The Great Crash 1929* (Harmondsworth: Penguin, 1962; orig. publ. 1954), 156–7; and also Seligman, *supra* n. 154, 730–47.

166 It was to this end that he accepted a post as a visiting professor at the University of Oxford for the academic year 1931–2. See generally Joseph Dorfman, *The Economic Mind in American Civilization, Volume V: 1918–1933* (New York: Viking, 1949), 666–9.

legal system as regulatory apparatus; so too is it unsurprising that, as progressive lawyers became drawn ever more to the methods of the social sciences, institutionalist economics should have proved a peculiarly attractive proposition. One of Hutchins's earliest initiatives at the Yale Law School was to secure the appointment of Walton Hale Hamilton, an institutionalist economist without any formal legal training. Yet it was at Columbia, where John Maurice Clark held a chair in economics, that institutionalism made its most profound impact on legal thinking.

According to Clark, the fundamental failure of classical economics rests in its misapprehension of interventionism as a purely public-regulatory affair. Analysis of the concept of social control, he insists, reveals that 'external' regulation of economic activities is essentially a private rather than a public phenomenon. '[W]hen the state acts . . . it is always some individual official who is really acting . . . [F]or all practical purposes, he is the state.'[167] The same point is made with equal force by Clark's institutionalist *confrère*, John Commons:

> The state is what its officials do. . . . The state is not 'the people,' nor 'the public,' it is the working rules of the discretionary officials of the past and present who have had and now have the legal power to put their will into effect within the limits set by other officials, past and present, and through the instrumentality of other officials or employees, present and future.[168]

As a source of social control, the state is inevitably instrumental in the shaping of economic liberties. 'An economic liberty', Commons suggests, 'exists only through official behaviour designed to permit and authorize it.'[169] However, the limits, as opposed to the existence, of any particular economic liberty is not exclusively a matter for the state. Indeed, according to Clark, so far as the social control of business is concerned, the state, even under a system of interventionism, plays only a minimal governmental role, since liberty is primarily at the mercy of internal market forces:

> The substance of liberty . . . has an economic basis. It depends, in the first instance, on knowledge, especially (in the economic field) knowledge of the market and knowledge of how to produce something with a marketable value and how to dispose of it at a fair market price. A person who does not have a job or any other source of income, and who does not know where to get one and how to go about canvassing the market effectively, does not possess the substance of liberty. That person is in a position to be exploited and to be forced to make contracts which are essentially made under duress.[170]

[167] Clark, *supra* n. 162, 9.

[168] John R. Commons, *Legal Foundations of Capitalism* (New York: Macmillan, 1924), 122, 149. Commons was a professor of economics at the University of Wisconsin.

[169] Ibid. 127.

[170] Clark, *supra* n. 162, 110.

Thus it is that the possession of a liberty is by no means tantamount to the possession of a right. 'Has a labourer a right to work? He clearly has a liberty to work . . . but so long as no one has a duty to furnish him a job, getting a chance to work is not a right in the strict sense.'[171] Equally, '[t]he freedom to make a million dollars is not worth a cent to one who is out of work. Nor is the freedom to starve, or to work for wages less than the minimum of subsistence, one that any rational being can prize—whatever learned courts may say to the contrary'.[172] Hence the institutionalist objection to the classical idea of free exchange. The liberty which the classical economists extolled was an insubstantial, unprotected liberty: freedom as mere absence of restraint. Real liberty—liberty backed by rights—could only be achieved through the simultaneous promotion and facilitation of economic equality:

> If all individuals were exactly equal in physical, economic and persuasive powers, then there would be no reasonable purpose in placing any limits on their liberties, since no one could harm or mislead another anyhow. But, since the real fact is one of astounding inequalities, limits are placed somewhat on the liberties of the more powerful under the name of duties, such that a more reasonable degree of equality may be maintained. These duties create correlative rights on behalf of the inferiors which are equivalent to reducing the exposure of the weaker parties by reducing the liberty of the stronger. Conversely, a reduction of duties on the part of inferiors increases their liberty while reducing the rights and enlarging the exposures of the stronger. According to the degree to which these determinations are carried is there constructed a reciprocal exposure of each to the liberty of the other and a reciprocity of rights and duties.[173]

While more directly indebted to Hohfeld's theory of jural relations than to the writings of any particular proto-realist jurist,[174] the institutionalist critique of economic liberty bolstered the spirit of dissent against liberty of contract which had found its original, if somewhat tentative, expression in the various anti-*laissez-faire* statements of Holmes and Pound. It is hardly surprising, accordingly, that certain realists, in reacting against legal formalism, should have latched on to the institutionalist position. Yet those realists who looked to institutionalism found more than just intellectual inspiration and affinity. That, after all, they had already found in the writings of Holmes and Pound. What institutionalism gave to some realists was a sense of external approval. Here was a number of lawyers who were taking their first, hesitant steps into the realm of the social

[171] Ibid. 100.

[172] Morris R. Cohen, 'The Basis of Contract', *Harvard L. Rev.*, 46 (1933), 553–92 at 560.

[173] Commons, *supra* n. 168, 129–30.

[174] See Commons, ibid. 91–100; 'Law and Economics', *Yale L.J.*, 34 (1925), 371–82 at 375; 'The Problem of Correlating Law, Economics and Ethics', *Wisconsin L. Rev.*, 8 (1932), 3–26 at 14–18.

sciences. That they were to discover a group of social scientists reaching essentially the same conclusions as themselves about the idea of free exchange can only have strengthened their resolve to take further steps in the same direction.

Institutionalist economists, too, were happy to build bridges with so-called realists. Karl Llewellyn, who joined the Columbia law faculty as a visiting lecturer in May 1924, is acknowledged by John Maurice Clark in the preface to *Social Control of Business* for having, at the author's invitation, read and commented on an earlier draft of the book.[175] Clark also expressed his approval of Llewellyn's own ideas on the relationship between law and economics,[176] which ideas were developed by Llewellyn in a paper delivered to the American Economic Association in December 1924. Adopting the terminology then prevalent among economists and other social scientists, Llewellyn suggests in his paper that the institutionalist preoccupation with social control is mirrored in jurisprudence by the Poundian concept of social engineering.[177] '[T]he legal feature of this age', he argues, is 'the emergence of diverse and specialized groups with a need for specialized control.'[178] As agencies of control, '[l]egal institutions provide a general atmosphere of security from personal aggression without which economic life could hardly be expected to unfold.'[179] Accordingly, as important as the question of what economic theory may offer for the understanding of law is the question, 'what may law have to contribute to economic theory?'[180] By regulating competition, distribution and production, for example, 'legal institutions fix and guarantee the presuppositions on which the economic order rests'.[181] Of all the institutionalist-inspired realists, Llewellyn was unique in that he was concerned more with the impact of law on economics than with economics on law.

Llewellyn did, nevertheless, acknowledge that institutionalism highlights some novel legal insights. Having recognized, as early as 1924, the 'striking contribution of Professor Commons' to the economic analysis of law,[182]

[175] See Clark, *supra* n. 162, xv.

[176] Ibid. 187 fn. 1.

[177] Karl N. Llewellyn, 'The Effect of Legal Institutions Upon Economics', *American Economic Rev.*, 15 (1925), 665–83 at 666. More generally, on the concept of social control in modern American jurisprudence and law and economics, see Robert C. Ellickson, 'A Critique of Economic and Sociological Theories of Social Control', *Jnl. Leg. Studs.*, 16 (1987), 67–99.

[178] Llewellyn, *supra* n. 177, 669.

[179] Ibid. 668.

[180] Ibid.

[181] Ibid. In a similar vein, see H.W. Robinson, 'Law and Economics', *Mod. L. Rev.*, 2 (1938), 257–65 at 260–1.

[182] Llewellyn, *supra* n. 177, 680. For a similarly appreciative assessment of Commons's contribution to the economic analysis of law, see generally Raymond J. Heilman, 'The Correlation Between the Sciences of Law and Economics', *California L. Rev.*, 20 (1932), 379–95.

Llewellyn, throughout his writings of the 1920s, came to question with increasing vigour the formalist picture of law without a human element. Just as Commons had asserted that the state is what its officials do, Llewellyn, by 1929—though ultimately he would retract the statement—was telling his students at Columbia that '[w]hat [legal] officials do about disputes is . . . the law itself'.[183] Perhaps more importantly, he also recognized that while the development of economics was in various ways parasitic on the functioning of legal institutions, the regulatory threshold of those institutions could, in one vital sense, be illustrated through economic theory, since, from an institutionalist perspective,

> it may be queried whether any sane public regulation of economic activity in the public interest—whatever that may be—is not largely accidental. The way of growth seems to be along whatever balance results from the pull and prodding of this and the other private interest.[184]

This one short quotation rather captures the institutionalist contribution to realist legal thought. To resist the public regulation of economic activities out of a respect for market freedom is to fail, unwittingly or otherwise, to see how the market itself is an oppressive rather than a liberating force. This is precisely the argument which various realists adopted in their attempts to discredit the tradition of *laissez-faire* in the courts. Llewellyn himself, writing in 1931, drew attention to the subtle regulatory function of the 'lop-sided' contract, that is, the contract where 'skill and power enter on one side only'.[185] 'It is', he insists, 'a form of contract which, in the measure of the importance of the particular deal in the other party's life, amounts to the exercise of unofficial government of some by others, via private law.'[186] For all that such bargains can sometimes 'press to the point where contract may mean rather fierce control,' the courts have nonetheless 'been slow to see what was needed, or to find means to fill the need. Beneath the surface of the opinions one feels a persistent doubt—one feels it even while interference proceeds—as to the wisdom of any interference with men's bargains.'[187] Essentially the same argument is offered by Morris Cohen. In their subscription to 'the classical economic optimism that there is a sort of pre-established harmony between the good of all and the pursuit by each of his own selfish economic gain,' the American courts had come under the spell of the 'cult of freedom'.[188] Supreme Court decisions such as *Lochner* v. *New York*[189] and *Coppage* v. *Kansas*[190] had the effect of

183 Llewellyn, *supra* n. 25, 3; and for Llewellyn's retraction, see ibid. ix–xi; and Twining, *supra* n. 12, 149–52.

184 Llewellyn, *supra* n. 177, 672.

185 Karl N. Llewellyn, 'What Price Contract?—An Essay in Perspective', *Yale L.J.*, 40 (1931), 704–51 at 731.

186 Ibid.

187 Ibid. 732.

188 Cohen, *supra* n. 172, 558–9.

189 *Lochner* v. *New York* (1905) 198 U.S. 45.

190 *Coppage* v. *Kansas* (1915) 236 U.S. 1.

legitimizing 'the fiction of the so-called labour contract as a free bargain', when 'not only is there actually little freedom to bargain on the part of the steel worker or miner who needs a job, but in some cases the medieval subject had as much power to bargain when he accepted the sovereignty of his lord.'[191] 'There is, in fact, no real bargaining between the modern large employer . . . and its individual employees. The working-man has no real power to negotiate or confer with the corporation as to the terms under which he will agree to work. He either decides to work under the conditions and schedule of wages fixed by the employer or else he is out of a job.'[192]

Thus it is that legal realism, following in the path of the institutionalist economists, came to challenge legal formalism in the courts.[193] For all that it had been cherished by the Supreme Court, the free market was not a natural phenomenon, guided by the invisible hand of natural selection; rather, it was a social construct, an ideology. Economic freedom—the freedom to choose—conceals economic duress; coercion is an integral feature of the free market. The advent of realism marked the demise—if only temporary—of a pervasive legal-economic myth: the myth, that is, of unimpeded voluntary action, of the free economic agent situated in a realm of pure choice and motivated by competitive Darwinist instinct. By the late 1930s and 1940s, as the Supreme Court—beginning with *West Coast Hotel*

[191] Morris R. Cohen, 'Property and Sovereignty', *Cornell L.Q.*, 13 (1927), 8–30 at 12.

[192] Cohen, *supra* n. 172, 569; and see also Cohen, *supra* n. 117, 353–5; Felix S. Cohen, 'Transcendental Nonsense and the Functional Approach', *Columbia L. Rev.*, 35 (1935), 809–49 at 816–17.

[193] Although my thesis here is that legal realists, in so far as they adopted economic arguments, tended to apply institutionalist insights to doctrinal problems, it should be noted that there was one specific strain of realist legal analysis—namely, the study of tort doctrine—which drew on economics in a rather different manner. Leon Green, Dean of the Northwestern University School of Law from 1929 through to the mid-1940s, exemplified this tendency. According to G. Edward White, 'Green was the most influential Realist tort theoretician of the early twentieth century.' G. Edward White, *Tort Law in America: An Intellectual History* (New York: Oxford University Press, 1980), 76. A good deal of Green's work addressed issues relating to the role of judges and juries in tort cases; and he insisted, in his analysis of these issues, that a primary consideration for judges and juries is the allocation of economic risk. See Wilfrid Rumble, Jr., 'Law as the Effective Decisions of Officials: A "New Look" at Legal Realism', *Jnl. of Public Law*, 20 (1971), 215–71 at 265. According to one commentator, 'Green would use the term ["risk"] in a way that . . . has economic significance as well as moral and personal injury connotations . . . Green has opened the door in negligence law to such a comprehensive value approach.' Walter Probert, 'Causation in the Negligence Jargon: A Plea for Balanced "Realism" ', *U. Florida L. Rev.*, 18 (1965), 369–97 at 392; and see also David W. Robertson, 'The Legal Philosophy of Leon Green', *Texas L. Rev.*, 56 (1978), 393–437 at 422–4. Green was not, in fact, the first American lawyer to attempt an economic interpretation of the law of torts: in this matter, he had been foreshadowed by his academic rival, Francis Bohlen. See Francis Bohlen, *The Basis of Affirmative Obligations in the Law of Tort* (Philadelphia: Department of Law of the University of Pennsylvania, 1905). See also Green, *supra* n. 14, 245–51; and Roscoe Pound, 'The Economic Interpretation and the Law of Torts', *Harvard L. Rev.*, 53 (1940), 365–85.

Co. v. *Parrish*[194]—gradually outgrew the formalism of *Lochner* and *Coppage*, realist-inspired doctrinal lawyers began to wonder how any court could ever have taken seriously the late nineteenth-century liberty of contract model.[195] By the late 1970s and 1980s, proponents of critical legal studies in the United States had adopted the realist attack on the tradition of *laissez-faire* as part of their own jurisprudential agenda.[196]

Of all the realists who challenged the tradition of *laissez-faire*, none was more inspirational to future generations of American academic lawyers than Robert Hale. Trained in both law and economics, Hale was appointed as a full-time professor at the Columbia Law School in 1928 as part of Dean Smith's drive to replenish a somewhat depleted faculty following the resignations over the deanship controversy. Through his training, Hale was able to recognize clearly the manner in which late nineteenth and early twentieth-century legal and economic ideas were following parallel paths. Beginning with *Lochner*, the classic dissenting opinions of Justice Holmes marked, for Hale, the demise of Spencerian economic austerity in the courts. He cited as a 'literary masterpiece'[197] Holmes's dissent in *Tyson & Bro.* v. *Banton*, in which the majority of the Supreme Court declared unconstitutional a New York statute limiting the resale price of theatre tickets to fifty cents in excess of the box office price.[198] In that case, Holmes took the view that 'the legislature may forbid or restrict any

[194] *West Coast Hotel Co.* v. *Parrish* (1937) 300 U.S. 379, overruling *Adkins* v. *Children's Hospital* (1923) 261 U.S. 525. Compare also *Hebe* v. *Shaw* (1919) 248 U.S. 297 (early indication of the Supreme Court moving away from *Lochner*); and see, generally, Samuel Herman, 'Economic Predilection and the Law', *American Political Science Rev.*, 31 (1937), 821–41 at 823–6; David P. Currie, 'The Constitution in the Supreme Court: The New Deal, 1931–1940', *U. Chicago L. Rev.*, 54 (1987), 504–55 at 541–53.

[195] See John P. Dawson, 'Economic Duress and the Fair Exchange in French and German Law', *Tulane L. Rev.*, 11 (1937), 345–76 at 345; 'Economic Duress—An Essay in Perspective', *Michigan L. Rev.*, 45 (1947), 253–90 esp. 266–7; John Dalzell, 'Duress by Economic Pressure', *North Carolina L. Rev.*, 20 (1942), 237–77, 341–86.

[196] The proponent of critical legal studies who has championed the realist assault on *laissez-faire* most vigorously is Joseph W. Singer, 'Legal Realism Now', *California L. Rev.*, 76 (1988), 465–544, though this is not to overlook the efforts of so-called 'first-generation' critical legal scholars such as Karl Klare, Duncan Kennedy and especially Morton Horwitz. See e.g. Karl E. Klare, 'Judicial Deradicalization of the Wagner Act and the Origins of Modern Legal Consciousness, 1937–1941', *Minnesota L. Rev.*, 62 (1978), 265–339 at 296–310; Duncan Kennedy, 'The Role of Law in Economic Thought: Essays on the Fetishism of Commodities', *American University L. Rev.*, 34 (1985), 939–1001 at 951–2; and Morton J. Horwitz, 'The History of the Public/Private Distinction', *U. Pennsylvania L. Rev.*, 130 (1982), 1423–8 at 1426; *The Transformation of American Law 1870–1960: The Crisis of Legal Orthodoxy* (New York: Oxford University Press, 1992), 169–246. Nor should one overlook the fact that the realist analysis of the concept of coercion has been influential outside critical legal circles. See e.g. Summers, *supra* n. 19, 224–35.

[197] Robert L. Hale, 'The Constitution and the Price System: Some Reflections on *Nebbia* v. *New York*', *Columbia L. Rev.*, 34 (1934), 401–25 at 415.

[198] *Tyson & Bro.* v. *Banton* (1927) 273 U.S. 418.

business when it has a sufficient force of public opinion behind it.'[199] Hale also lauded Holmes's recognition that, in an economic transaction, choice and duress are by no means mutually exclusive.[200]

More clearly than any other realist, Hale saw too that Holmes's ostensibly anti-Spencerian remarks were but tentative allusions to a broader anti-classical economic tradition. By drawing on this tradition—the emerging tradition of institutionalism—it would be possible, Hale believed, to put forward a detailed legal-economic critique of *laissez-faire*; a critique far more carefully and constructively worked out than anything to be gleaned from the random, often qualified, invariably contextually specific remarks which peppered Holmes's Supreme Court opinions. Hale took it upon himself to formulate this critique, and his starting point was, perhaps inevitably, Thorstein Veblen. Published one year prior to the decision in *Lochner*, and very much a natural progression from his earlier work castigating the failure of late nineteenth-century economists to embrace the insights of evolutionary science, Veblen's *The Theory of Business Enterprise* had become established as a classic proto-institutionalist critique of the notion of economic liberty. By the end of the nineteenth century, Veblen argues in that book, the idea of natural economic liberty had 'taken the firmest hold on the legal mind',[201] owing primarily to the judicial imperative that 'the principle of free contract be left intact in so far as the circumstances of the case permit'.[202] '[T]hrough gradual change of the economic situation, this conventional principle of unmitigated and inalienable freedom of contract began to grow obsolete,' Veblen concludes, 'from about the time when it was fairly installed; obsolescent, of course, not in point of law, but in point of fact.'[203]

This is, in effect, the argument which was adopted by Hale. Even though the principle of natural liberty 'may perhaps be derived by intuition from some highly respectable source—the Fourteenth Amendment, or the genius of our institutions, or Herbert Spencer . . . it is incapable of

[199] Ibid. 446.

[200] See *Union Pacific Railway* v. *Public Service Commission of Missouri* (1918), 246 U.S. 67, 70 (Holmes J. dissenting); and *The Eliza Lines* (1905) 199 U.S. 119, 130–1, (Holmes J. dissenting); also Robert L. Hale, 'Force and the State: A Comparison of "Political" and "Economic" Compulsion', *Columbia L. Rev.*, 35 (1935), 149–201 at 150 *et seq.*; 'Unconstitutional Conditions and Constitutional Rights', *Columbia L. Rev.*, 35 (1935), 321–59 at 339 *et seq.* A detailed study of Hale's own brand of law and economics is scheduled to appear in 1995: Barbara H. Fried, *Robert Hale and Progressive Legal Economics* (Cambridge, Mass.: Harvard University Press, forthcoming).

[201] Thorstein Veblen, *The Theory of Business Enterprise* (New York: Mentor, 1958; orig. publ. 1904), 130.

[202] Ibid. 131.

[203] Ibid.

application',[204] since 'the systems advocated by professed upholders of *laissez-faire* are in reality permeated with coercive restrictions of individual freedom and with restrictions, moreover, out of conformity with any formula of "equal opportunity" or of "preserving the equal rights of others". Some sort of coercive restriction is absolutely unavoidable, and cannot be made to conform to any Spencerian formula.'[205] By turning coercion into the nub of the economic apparatus, Hale inspired as much as he followed other institutionalists. He preceded both Commons and Clark in his insistence that, since 'economy' connotes regulation and management, the notion of a 'free economy' is an oxymoron.[206] Indeed, in this respect, he was very much an institutionalist *sui generis*. 'Every price, like every tax,' he insisted 'is in some measure regulatory and to some extent interposes an economic impediment to the use of the article for which the price is charged.'[207] Coercion thus lies at the heart of every bargain, since the extent of our 'freedom' as economic agents is relative to the level of our individual bargaining power, our ability to afford the requisite price. Greater bargaining power entails a capacity to require those with comparably less bargaining power to accept one's economic terms; it entails also a comparably greater capacity to reject or modify the contractual terms set by others. Very simply, the more bargaining power I have, the less susceptible I am to the economic coercion of others, and vice versa.

That Hale recognized this was important enough. The free market ethos of the late nineteenth and early twentieth-century Supreme Court had been exposed as a myth. Economic freedom was economic compulsion. More important yet, however, was Hale's transformation of this insight into a specific theory of regulation. The use of economic wealth to facilitate both freedom and coercion, he argued, demonstrates that government is a private as well as a public phenomenon. Formalism persisted in the American courts owing precisely to a general judicial inability or unwillingness to face this fact. In its interpretation of the due process clause of the Fourteenth Amendment, for example, the Supreme Court of the *Lochner* era emphasized the constitutional impropriety of state interference with agreements between private citizens. 'No State shall . . . deprive any person of life, liberty, or property, without due process of law'

204 Robert L. Hale, 'Rate Making and the Revision of the Property Concept', *Columbia L. Rev.*, 22 (1922), 209–16 at 212.

205 Robert L. Hale, 'Coercion and Distribution in a Supposedly Non-coercive State', *Political Science Quarterly*, 38 (1923), 470–94 at 470.

206 Robert L. Hale, 'Law Making by Unofficial Minorities', *Columbia L. Rev.*, 20 (1920), 451–6 at 455.

207 Robert L. Hale, 'Our Equivocal Constitutional Guaranties', *Columbia L. Rev.*, 39 (1939), 563–94 at 566.

was taken to mean, *inter alia*, that states have no business attempting to regulate private economic relations. Such relations were a matter for the market, to be governed only by the contractual terms freely accepted by economic agents. Public (state) government, in other words, has no right to interfere with private economic freedom. For Hale, however, there is no such thing as economic freedom. The 'free market' is every bit as much a regulatory apparatus as is the state. Accordingly, the constitutional protection of freedom of contract from state intervention is premissed on a fictional differentiation between public and private, on an assumption, that is, that the potential to regulate economic affairs is solely a characteristic of the public domain.

> A man's liberty is thought to need no constitutional protection against private individuals, for the ordinary law protects him against any violent interference practised by others. If others induce him to refrain from exercising any of his constitutional rights, by refusing otherwise to deal with him, his renunciation is looked upon as a voluntary one, made in the course of a process known as 'freedom of contract', in which all the participants have equal rights. It is the federal and state governments, and their subordinate branches, which are alone thought capable of forcibly interfering with this liberty, and it is against these governments that his constitutional rights are for the most part protected.[208]

The constitutional protection of the individual's right to contract is, accordingly, a protection of the individual against the state. But it is not a protection against interference by other individuals—individuals, that is, who, owing to their superior bargaining power, are possessed of the ability to influence, if not to control, the contractual choices of their economic subordinates. This ability to exert economic influence and control over others with comparably less bargaining power is the essence of what Hale terms private government. 'Various private groups to which a man belongs may govern him quite as effectively as do organs of the official government', indeed, 'both in scope and in efficiency many exertions of what is called economic power are indistinguishable from many exertions of what is recognized as political power.'[209] For Hale, legal formalism in the late nineteenth and early twentieth-century American courts consisted of more than just the sanctification of *laissez-faire*; it was defined also by a separation of the public and the private which was as strict as it was artificial. Only the state could unreasonably interfere with private economic transactions. The possibility of the entrepreneurial abuse of private government—of monopoly, unfair competition, economic duress and the like—was overlooked. Yet, ironically, only public government—in

[208] Ibid. 564.

[209] Robert Lee Hale Papers, Rare Book and Manuscript Division, Butler Library, Columbia University, folder 56, item 1, p. 17; and folder 80, item 8, p. 7.

the form of state legislation or constitutional protection—could ever realistically keep such abuse in check. 'The individual liberty of the governed often demands some sort of protection against abuses of private governing power, analogous to the safeguards which our constitutional system furnishes against the abuse of official government. Such safeguards only the official government itself can furnish.'[210] Through their reluctance to acknowledge that economic coercion has its private as well as its public dimension, the late nineteenth and early twentieth-century American courts failed to appreciate that the major obstacle preventing a flourishing free market economy was not the threat of public control over private economic affairs, but the nature of the market itself.

In recent times, the task of collapsing the public/private distinction has been revived by certain proponents of critical legal studies.[211] Hale, in his writings on the nature of economic coercion, was the first American academic lawyer to bring this task to light. The modern critique of the public/private dichotomy can, accordingly, be said to have its origins in the early twentieth-century intermeshing of institutionalist economics and realist juristic sensibilities. If only inadvertently and indirectly, realism, in its appeal to institutionalism, set the scene for a good deal of modern American jurisprudential debate.

Realism, History and the Constitution

Whereas Hale's theory of economic coercion was of an unmistakably institutionalist bent, other realist affinities with institutionalism—while no less significant so far as the intellectual history of realism is concerned—were of a distinctly broader variety. Some realists, while not especially indebted to institutionalist insights, seemed to have a passion for imitating Veblenian polemic. In his famous tirade against the leisure class, first published in 1899, Veblen claimed that the progression from feudalism to modernity was distinguished by subtle changes in the nature of control and consumption on the part of the dominant class. Fraud, first of all, had supplanted brute force as the primary method of dominance and exploitation. The modern entrepreneurial élite, in its successful utilization of fraudulent techniques, was aided and abetted by the profession of lawyers. 'The lawyer is exclusively occupied with the details of predatory fraud, either in achieving or checkmating chicanery, and success in the

[210] Hale Papers, ibid. folder 57, item 9, p. 10.

[211] See Kenneth M. Casebeer, 'Toward a Critical Jurisprudence—A First Step by Way of the Public-Private Distinction in Constitutional Law', *U. Miami L. Rev.*, 37 (1983), 379–431; Alan Freeman and Elizabeth Mensch, 'The Public–Private Distinction in American Law and Life', *Buffalo L. Rev.*, 36 (1987), 237–57; and cf. also the 'Symposium on the Public/Private Distinction', *U. Pennsylvania L. Rev.*, 130 (1982), 1289–609.

profession is therefore accepted as marking a large endowment of that barbarian astuteness which has always commanded men's respect and fear.'[212] Secondly, whereas the feudal aristocrat had been happy to cultivate to a high art a conspicuous personal disdain for work and utility, the modern captain of industry, being concerned above all with economic productivity, has come to conceive of leisure in a rather more subtle fashion, namely, as the celebration of such productivity, as consumption. The modern aristocracy, for Veblen, is a leisure class, a class of conspicuous consumers, held under the sway of mass advertising.

This style of broad-brush polemic is mirrored in the writings of 'radical' realists such as Fred Rodell and Thurman Arnold. The opening lines of Rodell's *succès de scandale* in denunciation of the legal profession are a perfect illustration of Veblenian bombast:

> In tribal times, there were the medicine men. In the Middle Ages, there were the priests. Today there are the lawyers. For every age, a group of bright boys, learned in their trades and jealous of their learning, who blend technical competence with plain and fancy hocus-pocus to make themselves masters of their fellow men. For every age, a pseudo-intellectual autocracy, guarding the tricks of its trade from the uninitiated, and running, after its own pattern, the civilization of its day.[213]

Rodell's modern lawyer, like Veblen's modern entrepreneur, is the successor to an earlier dominant class. Law is a fraud, a scam, 'a high-class racket';[214] its practice is but the manipulation of the laity by an élite. Veblen's work provided Rodell and other realists with an attractive, if flagrantly overgeneralized historical perspective. By resorting to Veblenian rhetoric, the ills of modern North America, or certainly of modern North American law, could conveniently be diagnosed as the outcome of the pernicious process of evolution from medieval brute force to modern predatory fraud. Thus it was that the tradition of institutionalism in the American social sciences gave some legal realists a taste not so much for economic analysis as for historical generalization about the law.

It is perhaps unsurprising that those realists who looked to institutionalism should have found history rather than economics. Most institutionalist writings were highly technical and focused on specific problems such as overhead costs and business cycles—the sorts of problems which would have made little sense to, or held little appeal for, realists without any economic training. Veblen's romantic, conspiratorial *grands récits*, in

[212] Thorstein Veblen, *The Theory of the Leisure Class: An Economic Study of Institutions* (New York: Mentor, 1953; orig. publ. 1899), 156. For an excellent, general discussion of the Veblenian position, see Theodor W. Adorno, *Prisms* (Eng. trans. S. and S. Weber, Cambridge, Mass.: MIT Press, 1981), 75–94.

[213] Fred Rodell, *Woe Unto You, Lawyers!* (New York: Berkeley, 1980; orig. publ. 1939), 1.

[214] Ibid. 10.

contrast, were as readable as good fiction—and in some ways were best treated as such. However, there was a tendency for legal realists to treat Veblen quite literally, primarily because they found in his work an 'indictment of classical economic theory' which could 'be applied word for word to classical jurisprudence',[215] but also because they discovered there a potted history of modern America which rather confirmed their own intuitions about the legal world. It is not insignificant that historically-oriented legal scholarship was never particularly prevalent among so-called realists. A possible reason for this is that, in their various attempts to use—or at least to toy with—the methods of the social sciences, these realists discovered—ready-formulated, as it were—various hypotheses, including historical hypotheses, which amply supported their own arguments. Given that, by the late 1920s, the basic historical path which some realists might have cared to tread had already been covered by Veblen and other social scientists with institutionalist leanings, there seemed little point for any legal realist to retrace those steps again.

This is not to assert, as Grant Gilmore does, that legal realism was totally ahistorical.[216] Realists such as Karl Llewellyn, Walton Hale Hamilton, Walter Nelles and Max Radin produced excellent historical studies in their own areas of specialization.[217] Such studies, however, were the exception rather than the rule.[218] The literature of legal realism is, for the most part, distinguished not only by a paucity of original historical scholarship, but also by a general lack of appreciation for history in its own right. The conception of history to be found in most realist literature conforms with what Laura Kalman has termed 'presentist' history—the idea, that is, that the only worthwhile reason for studying the past is to cast light on the problems of the present.[219] Presentism was very much a *fil*

215 Cohen, *supra* n. 192, 832; and cf. also Kalman, *supra* n. 3, 19.

216 See Gilmore, *supra* n. 64, 103. ('In the law schools, until some time after World War II, the study of any field of law from a historical point of view was almost unheard of. Indeed, the Realists (with the exception of Karl Llewellyn) were no more interested in the past than the Langdellian formalists had been.')

217 See e.g. Karl N. Llewellyn, 'On Warranty of Quality and Society', *Columbia L. Rev.*, 36 (1936), 699–744; *Columbia L. Rev.*, 37 (1937), 341–409; 'Across Sales on Horseback', *Harvard L. Rev.*, 52 (1939), 725–46; 'The First Struggle to Unhorse Sales', *Harvard L. Rev.*, 52 (1939), 874–904; Walton H. Hamilton, 'The Ancient Maxim *Caveat Emptor*', *Yale L.J.*, 40 (1931), 1133–87; Walter Nelles, '*Commonwealth* v. *Hunt*', *Columbia L. Rev.*, 32 (1932), 1128–69; 'Towards Legal Understanding', *Columbia L. Rev.*, 34 (1934), 862–89, 1041–75; Max Radin, 'The Right to a Public Trial', *Temple L.Q.*, 6 (1932), 381–98.

218 See Gordon, *supra* n. 4, 28–29 fn. 61. On the dearth of historical scholarship in the American law schools generally, see Daniel J. Boorstin, *The Americans: The National Experience* (London: Cardinal, 1988; orig. publ. 1965), 444.

219 Kalman, *supra* n. 3, 37. Presentism is also a feature of Holmesian jurisprudence. See Oliver Wendell Holmes, Jr., 'The Path of the Law', *Harvard L. Rev.*, 10 (1897), 457–78 at 474. ('We must beware of the pitfall of antiquarianism, and must remember that for our purposes our only interest in the past is for the light it throws upon the present.')

conducteur in Veblen's writings. Those realists who adopted a presentist perspective on legal history, however, did so not simply out of admiration for Veblen's polemical initiatives; they did so because of their similarly high regard for the works of various largely Veblen-inspired early twentieth-century political scientists and constitutional scholars.

Principal among these was Charles Beard. As early as 1907, Beard had declared his intention to 'subordinate[] the past to the present'.[220] The past—more specifically, the period leading up to 1787—holds the key, he insisted, to the political conservatism of early twentieth-century interpretations of the Constitution. The politics of the 1780s had been 'dominated by a deep-seated conflict between a popular party based on paper money and agrarian interests, and a conservative party centred in the towns and resting on financial, mercantile, and personalty interests.'[221] Hampered by a Confederation government, and unable to achieve substantial reform through formal congressional channels, the conservatives effectively bypassed the existing legal framework by adopting the Constitution of 1787; in doing this, they acted not, primarily, out of respect for constitutional principles, but out of concern for economic interests. For the conservatives, the successful promotion of economic interests demanded the creation of a national government. 'Only by locating the source of authority and political obligation in the "nation" itself could the constitutional order adapt to the changing realities of social and economic power.'[222] Accordingly, the purpose of the Constitution was not, as had originally been anticipated, to support a fragmented system of government, but instead to provide a federal mechanism for the control of the national economy. Modern constitutional arrangements, for Beard, must be seen to be premissed upon and motivated by powerful economic considerations and pressures.[223]

Other political scientists, particularly during the Progressive era, shared Beard's presentist outlook. Charles Merriam, Herbert Croly, Charles Groves Haines and other constitutional scholars of this period took the view that the Constitution must be treated primarily as a contemporary

[220] James Robinson and Charles Beard, *The Development of Modern Europe* (two vols. Boston: Ginn & Co. 1907), I, ix.

[221] Herman Belz, 'The Realist Critique of Constitutionalism in the Era of Reform', *Am. J. Leg. Hist.*, 15 (1971), 288–306 at 292.

[222] Andrew W. Fraser, *The Spirit of the Laws: Republicanism and the Unfinished Project of Modernity* (Toronto: University of Toronto Press, 1990), 92.

[223] See Charles A. Beard, *An Economic Interpretation of the Constitution of the United States* (1st edn. New York: Macmillan, 1913); and, for a careful analysis of Beard's thesis, cf. also Pope McCorkle, 'The Historian as Intellectual: Charles Beard and the Constitution Reconsidered', *Am. J. Leg. Hist.*, 28 (1984), 314–63.

governmental institution rather than just as a code of law behind which, historically, there exists some mystical 'original intent' of the Framers.[224] 'The constitution', wrote Arthur Bentley in 1908, 'is always what is.'[225] Less cryptically, Howard McBain observed that '[t]he constitution of the United States was not handed down on Mount Sinai by the Lord God of Hosts. It is not revealed law. . . . It is human means. The system of government which it provides can scarcely be read at all in the stately procession of its simple clauses.'[226] Basically, political scientists of the Progressive era were fast coming round to the view that 'the constitution means what the courts say it means'.[227]

In this sense, the notion of rule scepticism—so strong an undercurrent of realist legal thinking—was paralleled if not prefigured by a belief, common among early twentieth-century political scientists, that judicial review of legislation was a far from objective affair. During the second and third decades of this century, the Supreme Court, under the respective Chief Justiceships of Edward Douglass White and William Howard Taft, interpreted key amendments to the Constitution in an increasingly erratic fashion. On the one hand, for example, the Court used liberty of contract—a principle nowhere mentioned in the Constitution—to declare invalid governmental restrictions on the disposal of private property, while on the other it distorted the language of the First Amendment by upholding governmental interference with certain kinds of speech.[228] Such doublethink was recognized not only by so-called legal realists. Progressive intellectuals and politicians in general believed that the search for objectivity and principled consistency in Supreme Court decision-making was a rather futile exercise. 'Progressives scoffed at the idea that as soon as an individual donned black judicial robes he gained the wisdom of King Solomon. . . . They contended that jurists were conscious moulders of policy rather than impersonal vehicles of revealed truth.'[229]

[224] See Belz, *supra* n. 221, *passim*; Kalman, *supra* n. 3, 39.

[225] Arthur F. Bentley, *The Process of Government: A Study of Social Pressures* (Evanston: Principia, 1949; orig. publ., 1908), 295.

[226] Howard L. McBain, *The Living Constitution: A Consideration of the Realities and Legends of Our Fundamental Law* (New York: Workers Education Bureau Press, 1927), 3–5, 272.

[227] Charles Evans Hughes, Speech at Elmira, New York, 3 May 1907, quoted in Kalman, *supra* n. 3, 40.

[228] For general doctrinal analysis and commentary, see David P. Currie, 'The Constitution in the Supreme Court: 1910–1921', *Duke L.J.*, [1985], 1111–62; 'The Constitution in the Supreme Court: 1921–1930', *Duke L.J.*, [1986], 65–144; and also Howard Owen Hunter, 'Problems in Search of Principles: The First Amendment in the Supreme Court From 1791–1930', *Emory L.J.*, 35 (1986), 59–137 at 90–127.

[229] Steven F. Lawson, 'Progressives and the Supreme Court: A Case for Judicial Reform in the 1920s', *The Historian*, 42 (1979–80), 419–36 at 429–30.

Parallels between progressivism and legal realism should nonetheless be drawn with a measure of circumspection. In its broadest sense, progressivism denoted the general late nineteenth and early twentieth-century idea of a search for order, of a basic social scientific endeavour to 'professionalize' knowledge by situating it within specific disciplinary categories.[230] In this sense, even Langdellian legal formalism could be conceived to be vaguely progressive. Langdellianism, after all, while it lacked input from the social sciences, represented an attempt to elevate law to the status of an epistemologically discrete entity through the compartmentalization of legal doctrine. In a more specific sense, progressivism denoted the quest to rationalize the American political economy by reorienting social thought away from the inequities of nineteenth century *laissez-faire* liberalism. In this sense, legal realism was progressive in a manner that Langdellian formalism most definitely was not. Yet this is not to assert that political progressivism and legal realism were ideologically indistinguishable. Political scientists of the 1920s 'tended to be liberals, who, unlike the lawyers of the era, worried that judicial review was antidemocratic and that the openness with which the Supreme Court manipulated law made the end of judicial review inevitable'.[231] 'Suspicious of judicial activism, they contended that restraint had to be imposed upon the justices from outside the court and legal profession. . . . Seeking to limit the institutional power of the Supreme Court, progressives refused to budge from their blanket condemnation of judicial review. In the following decade, their solutions lost appeal to New Deal liberals who eventually discerned that judicial power could also serve as an instrument for promoting social reform and civil rights.'[232]

It would be incorrect, accordingly, to argue that realist interpretations of the Constitution were but jurisprudential exercises in political progressivism. That some realists were indebted to progressive political science is certainly beyond doubt. Karl Llewellyn, for example, in his disparaging of theories of original intent in favour of an 'institutionalist' study of the Constitution in its contemporary political setting, takes his cue from progressives such as Veblen, McBain and, especially, Bentley.[233] Fred

[230] See Robert H. Wiebe, *The Search for Order, 1877–1920* (Westport, Conn.: Greenwood Press, 1980; orig. publ. 1967), 111–95; and also Furner, *supra* n. 151, *passim*; Thomas L. Haskell, *The Emergence of Professional Social Science: The American Social Science Association and the Nineteenth Century Crisis of Authority* (Urbana: University of Illinois Press, 1977); Peter Novick, *That Noble Dream: The 'Objectivity Question' and the American Historical Profession* (Cambridge: Cambridge University Press, 1988), *passim* esp. 47–60.

[231] Kalman, *supra* n. 3, 40.

[232] Lawson, *supra* n. 229, 435.

[233] Karl N. Llewellyn, 'The Constitution as an Institution', *Columbia L. Rev.*, 34 (1934), 1–40. For criticisms of Llewellyn's position, see Max Ascoli, 'Realism versus the Constitution', *Social Research*, 1 (1934), 169–84; Giovanni Tarello, *Il realismo giuridico Americano* (Milan: Giuffrè, 1962), 98–104.

Rodell, too, followed squarely in the presentist path of Beard when, as late as 1955, he asserted that '[t]he origins of Supreme Court power are of little real import today,' given that 'that power indubitably exists.'[234] 'Those who see the past through the rosy glow of fable,' he concluded, 'too readily misapprehend the present.'[235] In contrast, however, the critique of the so-called 'higher law' background to constitutional law—the idea that the text of the Constitution itself is but the secularization of specific (primarily Lockean) natural rights[236]—remained very much an initiative of political scientists rather than lawyers.[237] While progressives of the 1920s insisted that the Constitution must be understood first and foremost to be a contemporary political institution, furthermore, legal realists of the 1930s were generally intent on stressing its totemic function. This shift in emphasis was as fundamental as it was subtle. Progressive political scientists were concerned not so much with the symbolic importance of the Constitution as with its use in the process of judicial review to secure apparently contradictory ends—for example, the Supreme Court's curbing one form of freedom while promoting another. Gradually, however, with the progression of the 1930s, the symbolic function of the Constitution became as much a matter for concern as its judicial interpretation; for it was with the authority of the Constitution that the Supreme Court—showing scant regard for the principle that statutes should, if possible, be construed so as to preserve their constitutionality—effectively swept aside major New Deal legislative initiatives.[238] Legal realists—some of whom were, by this stage, active New Dealers—tended to be surprised less by the heavy-handed authoritarianism of the Supreme Court than they were by the willingness of the American public to accept the Court's decisions. The explanation for this general acceptance seemed to rest in the symbolic value that ordinary Americans were prepared to attach to their Constitution. On this point, Thurman Arnold, the Yale realist turned New Dealer, wrote with unmatched candour:

[234] Fred Rodell, *Nine Men: A Political History of the Supreme Court From 1790 to 1955* (New York: Random House, 1955), 34. For Rodell's indebtedness to Beard, see Fred Rodell, *Fifty Five Men* (Harrisburg: The Telegraph Press, 1936), 7–8.

[235] Rodell, *Nine Men*, 35.

[236] For discussion, see Steven M. Dworetz, *The Unvarnished Doctrine: Locke, Liberalism, and the American Revolution* (Durham, NC: Duke University Press, 1990); David A. J. Richards, *Foundations of American Constitutionalism* (New York: Oxford University Press, 1989), 150–53.

[237] The classic illustration here being the work of the Princeton constitutional scholar, Edward S. Corwin, 'The "Higher Law" Background of American Constitutional Law', *Harvard L. Rev.*, 42 (1928–29), 149–85, 365–409.

[238] See e.g. *Panama Refining Co.* v. *Ryan* (1935) 93 U.S. 388; *Schechter Poultry Corp* v. *United States* (1935) 295 U.S. 495; and *Carter* v. *Carter Coal Co.* (1936) 298 U.S. 238.

The Constitution is praised in general as the great bulwark, even though there could be no possible agreement in the group which was praising it as to how that Constitution should reconcile their conflicting interests. The Supreme Court hovers over the whole picture, and it is to it that prayers are addressed. However, they are fearful prayers, because the group knows that there is never any certainty as to what the next decision will be. Yet in times of confusion and fear, there is nothing that so comforts the heart [*sic*] of timid men as a combination of prayer and denunciation. For this purpose the Constitution becomes for most conservatives the symbol of security in which all conflicting hopes and fears are somehow resolved.[239]

Writing in 1933, Llewellyn observed that 'popular loyalty' to the Constitution, 'though real, is blind'.[240] Yet Arnold insisted that while faith in the Constitution as an irrefragable symbol of security may be blind faith, it is an understandable faith, for such reverence is fostered and maintained both by the courts and by a 'scholargarchy' of jurists.[241] Academic and practising lawyers alike take it to be 'essential to constitutionalism as a vital creed that [the Constitution] be capable of being used . . . on both sides of any question, because it must be the creed of all groups in order to function as a unifying symbol'.[242] For all that debates may rage as to the proper interpretation of constitutional provisions and amendments, what is not open to debate is the legitimacy of the Constitution itself. 'Arguments may occur within the terms of the constitution, but to attack the constitution itself is heresy.'[243] During the 1930s, other writers with inclinations towards realism were quick to adopt Arnold's tack. Max Lerner observed in 1937 that the 'Constitution and Supreme Court are symbols of an ancient sureness and a comforting stability'.[244] 'Constitution worship'[245] on the part of the American people, he insisted, owes more to emotion than to reason: 'Men are notably more sensitive to images than to ideas, more responsive to stereotypes than to logic. . . . Men possess thoughts, but symbols possess men.'[246] Essentially the same point had been made by Edward Corwin only one year earlier: 'American constitutional symbolism looks . . . to the past and links hands with conceptions which long antedate the rise of science and its belief in a predictable, manageable causation. Its consecration of an *already established order of things* harks back to primitive man's terror of a chaotic universe, and his struggle towards

[239] Thurman W. Arnold, *The Symbols of Government* (New York: Harcourt, Brace & World, 1962; orig. publ. 1935), 230–1.

[240] Llewellyn, *supra* n. 233, 24.

[241] Thurman W. Arnold, *The Folklore of Capitalism* (New Haven, Conn.: Yale University Press, 1937), 67.

[242] Ibid. 29.

[243] Ibid. 28.

[244] Max Lerner, 'Constitution and Court as Symbols', *Yale L.J.*, 46 (1937), 1290–319 at 1291.

[245] Ibid. 1295.

[246] Ibid. 1293.

security and significance behind a slowly erected barrier of custom, magic, fetish, tabu.'[247]

The Modern Legal Mind

The emphasis placed on symbolism by legal realists in their analyses of the Constitution was by no means casual. The power of symbolism over humanity, as certain of their number recognized, was a Holmesian theme.[248] More than this, the fascination with symbolism was yet another facet of the general realist inclination towards the methods, ideas and indeed trends to be found in the early twentieth-century social sciences. As early as 1922, a political commentator, Walter Lippmann, had suggested that successful governmental control of public opinion depended on the political manipulation of symbols of democracy.[249] In the following year, the theme of symbolism was popularized still further with the publication of Charles Ogden and Ivor Richards's classic study, *The Meaning of Meaning*. 'From the earliest times,' the authors asserted, 'the Symbols which men have used to aid the process of thinking and to record their achievements have been a continuous source of wonder and illusion. The whole human race has been so impressed by the properties of words as instruments for the control of objects, that in every age it has attributed to them occult powers. . . . Unless we fully realize the profound influence of superstitions concerning words, we shall not understand the fixity of certain widespread linguistic habits which still vitiate even the most careful thinking.'[250] Some legal realists were quick to heed this message, or at least to adapt it to their own ends. The basic realist disdain for 'abstract magniloquence'[251] in the law—the respect for the Holmesian injunction 'to keep to the real and the true'[252]—became, in the wake of Ogden and

[247] Edward S. Corwin, 'The Constitution as Instrument and as Symbol', *American Political Science Rev.*, 30 (1936), 1071–85 at 1072. See also Edward Stevens Robinson, *Law and the Lawyers* (New York: Macmillan, 1935), 53.

[248] Oliver Wendell Holmes, Jr., *Collected Legal Papers* (New York: Harcourt, Brace & Howe, 1920), 270; and see also Cohen, *supra* n. 117, 355; Lerner, *supra* n. 244, 1290.

[249] Walter Lippmann, *Public Opinion* (New York: Harcourt, Brace & Co., 1922); and see also Purcell, *supra* n. 119, 104–8.

[250] C. K. Ogden and I. A. Richards, *The Meaning of Meaning: A Study of the Influence of Language upon Thought and the Science of Symbolism* (London: Ark, 1985; orig. publ. 1923), 24.

[251] Max Radin, 'The Theory of Judicial Decision: Or How Judges Think', *Am. Bar Assoc. Jnl.*, 11 (1925), 357–62 at 360.

[252] 'We must think things not in words, or at least we must constantly translate our words into the facts for which they stand, if we are to keep to the real and the true.' Oliver Wendell Holmes, Jr., 'Law in Science and Science in Law', *Harvard L. Rev.*, 12 (1899), 443–63 at 460.

Richards, something rather more grandiose. Lawyers were no longer just verbose; rather, they practised 'word magic'.[253] 'Word magic', Charles Clark wrote, 'is the bane and life of the law.'[254] 'Word ritual under one guise or another has always been one of the primary methods of law administration. . . . We can scarcely realize the part which sacred words, taboo words, magic words, continue to play in our law.'[255]

Throughout the literature of legal realism, the spirit of Ogden and Richards is nowhere more at large than it is in the work of Jerome Frank. Just as *The Meaning of Meaning* was comprised largely of miscellaneous insights taken from psychoanalysis, behaviourism, philosophy, ethnology and aesthetics (to mention but some of the disciplines from which the authors drew); Frank's *Law and the Modern Mind* was a similar piece of unrestrained eclecticism. 'Legal Absolutism', Frank argues in that book, is a form of 'word-worship'.[256] The legal formalist of the Langdellian tradition, whom he labels as 'the Bealist',[257]

> dematerializes the facts he purports to describe; the vagueness of his vocabulary aids him to avoid recognizing contradictions and absurdities which his assertions involve . . . Such dematerialized but sonorous terms as Uniformity, Continuity, Universality, when applied to law by the legal Absolutist, have the same capacity for emotional satisfaction that terms like Oneness, Eternity, or The True, have when applied by the metaphysician to the Absolute. Although the Bealist's arguments may be full of contradictions . . . they acquire, by means of the emotive value of his words, a compensatory significance.[258]

The use of 'compensatory verbiage'[259] enables Frank's Bealist to neglect the reality of law as an activity and to concentrate instead on law as an abstract ideal, that is, as a determinate system of formally interrelated rules and principles. This concentration on the abstract ideal, Frank argues, 'tends to breed nihilistic scepticism' within the legal profession:

> Bealism, which is the verbal expression of excessive optimism, is sure to breed excessive cynicism. To many a young Bealish-trained lawyer the judges seem to be traitors to the true law; when the promised juristic parade turns out to be a fairy story, the whole juristic world seems drab and dull; or worse—intellectually or perhaps even morally dishonest.[260]

[253] Ogden and Richards, *supra* n. 250, 40.
[254] Charles E. Clark, 'The Restatement of the Law of Contracts', *Yale L.J.*, 42 (1933), 643–67 at 647.
[255] Leon Green, 'The Duty Problem in Negligence Cases', *Columbia L. Rev.*, 28 (1928), 1014–45; *Columbia L. Rev.*, 29 (1929), 255–84 at pt. I, 1016; and see also Sturges and Clark, *supra* n. 74, 714–15.
[256] Frank, *supra* n. 25, 63.
[257] Or sometimes (and no less vaguely), 'Beale & Co.' See Frank, ibid. 66–7.
[258] Frank *supra* n. 25, 67.
[259] Ibid. 68.
[260] Ibid. 68–9.

It is interesting that Frank criticizes the Langdellian world-view for what he considers to be its implicit nihilism. In some quarters, during the 1940s and 1950s, he himself was branded a nihilist precisely because of his denunciation of that world-view.[261] Still more interesting is Frank's suggestion that even the disillusioned lawyer trained in the Langdellian tradition will have some conception of 'the true law'. For it is commonly assumed that a defining characteristic of legal realism is apostasy, in so far as those who, willingly or otherwise, came to be branded as realists were united at least in their endeavour to break from the formalist belief that some sort of 'truth' resides in the law. Such an assumption, however—and Frank's work implicitly bears testament to this—is not quite correct. Rather than abandon the idea of truth in law, most legal realists replaced what they perceived to be the formalist version of truth with their own.

Traditionally, Frank argues, scientific logic and legal logic have shared the same sin: both are 'inveterately verbalistic'.[262] However, whereas ' "scholasticism" and verbalizing have survived in lawyerdom . . . they have become obsolescent (if not obsolete) in the natural sciences'.[263] Having offered this unsubstantiated assumption as if it were an indubitable fact, Frank sets about outlining the problem which he intends to solve: namely, why have lawyers continued to keep faith in word magic and, *a fortiori*, in the formalistic ideal of the complete certainty of law? The core of his answer to this question—and here we have the centre-piece of Frank's jurisprudence—is that lawyers and ordinary citizens alike subscribe to a basic legal myth—the myth, that is, that legal rules are certain and that their application to specific cases is essentially a mechanical task to be performed by the courts. The reason we subscribe to this myth, the reason we believe in absolute legal certainty, is essentially psychological: law, for the adult, is a father substitute. As the father is the controlling force in childhood, so the law serves precisely the same function in adulthood:

> To the child the father is the Infallible Judge, the Maker of definite rules of conduct. He knows precisely what is right and what is wrong and, as head of the family, sits in judgement and punishes misdeeds. The Law—a body of rules apparently devised for infallibly determining what is right and what is wrong and for deciding who should be punished for misdeeds—inevitably becomes a partial substitute for the Father-as-Infallible-Judge.[264]

261 See, in particular, Edward F. Barrett, 'Confession and Avoidance?—Reflections on Rereading Judge Frank's *Law and the Modern Mind*', *Notre Dame Lawyer*, 24 (1949), 447–59; John T. Schuett, 'A Study of the Legal Philosophy of Jerome N. Frank', *U. Detroit L.J.*, 35 (1957), 28–69.

262 Frank, *supra* n. 25, 73.

263 Ibid. 74.

264 Ibid. 19.

To look for certainty in the law, accordingly, is to nurture a faith in authority which has its origins in childhood. Through their acceptance of the basic legal myth, most lawyers fail to appreciate the true complexity of the American legal system. In seeking a surrogate paternal authority in the law, the psychologically immature adult will accept at face value the censoriousness, the certainty and the apparent irrefragability of the American system of justice while having little or no regard for the ethical or political criteria which that system promotes. The time has come, Frank insisted, not only for the lawyers but also for the citizens of America to develop a 'modern mind', to shake off their childish emotions and attachments and grow up.

Apart, however, from asserting that the writings and judicial opinions of Oliver Wendell Holmes provide 'an indispensable aid and an inspiration'[265] for the post-formalist lawyer, Frank, in his early works, offered little by way of suggestion as to how the modern mind might be cultivated. He himself, rather ironically, seemed to treat Holmes as something of a father figure.[266] Furthermore, he had a tendency to suggest that the basic legal myth is not just a feature of the American psyche but also foundational to and pervasive throughout Western religion and culture.[267] Given the supposedly all-encompassing nature of this myth, his own reticence with regard to the matter of how it might successfully be exposed and outstripped is perhaps unsurprising. But even in so far as Frank explains the basic legal myth as an essentially psychological phenomenon, there seems to be a fundamental fault with his reasoning, since it seems impossible, on his terms, ever to define adulthood. If a defining characteristic of the adult mind is the childhood craving for patriarchal order and security, how, psychologically, are we to distinguish between the adult and the child? Adults are assumed to have more or less the same basic emotions as children. Thus it is that Frank, in developing the idea of the basic legal myth, makes no provision for rites of passage.

In this sense, his argument seems to be essentially self-defeating. It might nevertheless be claimed that his rather half-hearted attempt at grappling with psychoanalytical ideas hardly frustrates his basic realist sentiment, which is that we must stop conceiving of law as a fairly strict system of rules. In essence, Frank was adding social scientific gloss to an argument which had, he believed, originated in the proto-realist writings of

[265] Frank, *supra* n. 25, 270.

[266] See ibid. 270–7; and Jan Vetter, 'The Evolution of Holmes, Holmes and Evolution', *California L. Rev.*, 72 (1984), 343–68 at 359–60 fn. 90.

[267] Frank, *supra* n. 25, 281–2.

Holmes, Cardozo and Gray,[268] and which he regarded as having been developed further by certain of his realist *confrères*. 'Judges, we know, are people,' Max Radin had asserted in 1924. 'They eat the same foods, seem moved by the same emotions, and laugh at the same jokes.'[269] 'The control of judges', according to Leon Green, 'is not to be found in rules, but in the fact that they are men nourished on the same thoughts and other life-giving forces as the rest of us, and are subject to be influenced by the same factors in making their judgements as those which influence their fellows generally.'[270] 'If, therefore, in a controversy in which we are engaged, we could rid ourselves of the personal interest in it, we might shrewdly guess that a great many judges would like to see the same person win who appeals to us.'[271] Whereas Langdellian legal science was founded on the assumption that the normative scope of legal rules is a matter of 'formal certitude',[272] the realist assumption, by which it was gradually superseded, was that judges—stimulated, primarily, by the facts before them rather than by the rules to which those facts might be fitted[273]—work backwards, 'from a desirable conclusion to one or another of a stock of logical premises'.[274] To put the matter at its simplest, judges are not inhibited by rules but liberated by them. It is by resorting to legal rules, after all, that judges are able retroactively to furnish their instincts with authority. Precisely this point had been made in the early 1920s by the pragmatist philosopher, John Dewey. Human beings, according to Dewey, 'act not upon deliberation but from routine, instinct, the direct pressure of appetite, or a blind "hunch" '.[275] Successful lawyering entails the tailoring of a conclusion to fit the particular hunch.[276] One judge, by the late 1920s, had the candour to confess that the Deweyan—or, as he saw it, Rabelaisian—notion of lawyering by hunch seemed to capture the decision-making process to a T.[277] Indeed, it was this 'discovery'—the revelation of the 'hunch' as the primary factor in the decision-making process—which fuelled Frank's scepticism with regard to the nature and

[268] Ibid. 39, 131–3, 252–5, 270–7.

[269] Radin, *supra* n. 251, 359.

[270] Green, *supra* n. 255, pt. I, p. 1021.

[271] Radin, *supra* n. 251, 359.

[272] Yntema, 'The Hornbook Method and the Conflict of Laws', *supra* n. 73, 468.

[273] See Oliphant, *supra* n. 72, 161; also *supra* n. 74, 132–3.

[274] Radin, *supra* n. 251, 359.

[275] John Dewey, 'Logical Method and Law', *Cornell L.Q.*, 10 (1924), 17–27 at 17. With regard to this article, see Golding, *supra* n. 12, 467–9.

[276] Dewey, *supra* n. 275, 23; and see also John Dewey, *Experience and Nature* (New York: Dover, 1958), 272–3.

[277] Joseph C. Hutcheson, Jr., 'The Judgment Intuitive: The Function of the "Hunch" in Judicial Decision', *Cornell L.Q.*, 14 (1929), 274–88. Hutcheson apparently later qualified his position. See Karl N. Llewellyn, 'On Reading and Using the Newer Jurisprudence', *Columbia L. Rev.*, 40 (1940), 581–614 at 604.

function of legal rules. 'Whatever produces the judge's hunches,' he insisted, 'makes the law.'[278]

Frank's embracing of the hunch-thesis epitomizes the realist rejection of Langdellian formalism. Langdell himself, Frank believed, had been a 'neurotic escapist character'[279] possessed by 'an obsessive and almost exclusive interest in books',[280] a man with regard solely for the life of the law as logic rather than as human experience and action. 'The lawyer–client relation, the numerous non-rational factors involved in a trial, the face-to-face appeals to the emotions of juries, the elements that go to make up the "atmosphere" of a case—everything that is undisclosed in upper-court opinions—was virtually unknown (and was therefore all but meaningless) to Langdell.'[281] All these factors which Langdell ignored, Frank was to stress. After the exhilarating if ultimately unconstructive polemic of *Law and the Modern Mind*, he began to develop an increasingly hortatory style of anti-formalist critique. Whereas, during the early 1930s, he had exploited the idea of the modern mind to bemoan the conservatism of the psychologically immature, certainty-craving, ethically non-committed lawyer, the spectre of Nazism forced him to recognize that this so-called mind—were it to be more than a handy rhetorical tool—would have to represent the basic *Zeitgeist* of a post-fascist democracy.[282] Throughout the 1930s, Frank had barraged 'Bealism' so frequently and unequivocally that his own peculiar anti-formalist perspective had become something of a saturated ploy. Gradually, he came to regard his task not simply to be one of uncovering the ills of the American legal system and the Langdellian pedagogic framework by which it was supported, but of suggesting how that system might be transformed into an institutional reflection of his postulated modern mind.

Frank approached this task from a variety of angles, some of which are unique to his own work, others of which are but instances of a more general realist world-view. Having originally treated legal formalism as, at core, a psychological problem—the problem of the basic legal myth—he subsequently considered the possibility that psychology might also provide a partial cure as well as a diagnosis. 'Lawyers and judges', he came to

[278] Frank, *supra* n. 25, 112.

[279] Jerome Frank, *Courts on Trial: Myth and Reality in American Justice* (Princeton, NJ: Princeton University Press, 1973; orig. publ. 1949), 227.

[280] Ibid. 225.

[281] Ibid. 225–26; and see also Calvin Woodard, 'The Limits of Legal Realism: An Historical Perspective', *Virginia L. Rev.*, 54 (1969), 689–739 at 716.

[282] Frank's most eloquent expression of this belief came near the end of his life. See Jerome Frank, 'Some Reflections on Judge Learned Hand', *U. Chicago L. Rev.*, 24 (1957), 666–705 at 686–87.

believe—as had the political scientist, Harold Lasswell, before him[283]—'must constantly act as psychologists or psychiatrists' so as to become aware of and, so far as possible, to overcome their own limitations as social agents.[284] Like Lasswell, Frank assumed that, by resorting to the methods of psychoanalysis, judges would not only discover their prejudices but would also, in consequence, set about ridding themselves of those prejudices. The judge who is periodically subjected to psychoanalysis, furthermore, would be likely not only to remedy his or her own biases but also to understand better the behaviour of witnesses in any particular case.[285]

Psychology, Pragmatism and Predictivism

While Frank espoused the virtues of psychology and psychoanalysis in his own distinct way, he was not the only or even the first legal realist to resort to such ideas.[286] Psychology began its rise to prominence as a social scientific discipline in the United States as early as the 1890s, and within a few years legal theorists were trying to learn from its insights and methods.[287] The popularity of psychology, among social scientists and legal realists alike, may be attributed to the fact that it not only accommodated but appeared actually to cast new light on many of the most pressing social-scientific themes of the day. Premissed on the idea that the human mind has an infinite capacity for adaptation and creative rationality, late nineteenth-century functional psychology accorded well with the spirit of evolutionism which bore such a strong influence over the development of anthropology and other social sciences. By the turn of the nineteenth century, behaviourist psychology was beginning to make a still stronger impact on American social thought, as social scientists turned their attentions increasingly to the problem of how modern societies control the conduct of their citizens. 'Psychology as the behaviourist views it,' one early twentieth-century psychologist explained, 'is a purely objective

283 See Harold D. Lasswell, 'Self-analysis and Judicial Thinking', *Int. Jnl. of Ethics*, 40 (1930), 354–62.

284 Jerome Frank, 'Judicial Fact-Finding and Psychology', *Ohio State L.J.*, 14 (1953), 183–9 at 183. Compare, however, Frank's concurring opinion, written only a few months before his death, in *United States* v. *Flores–Rodriguez*, 237 F.2d 405, 412 (2nd Cir. 1956): 'I think it is a mistake for my colleagues needlessly to embark . . . on an amateur's voyage on the fog-enshrouded sea of psychiatry.'

285 On Frank's own experience of therapy, see Duxbury, 'Jerome Frank and the Legacy of Legal Realism', *supra* n. 3, 199 n. 9.

286 For a general discussion of the impact of psychoanalysis on mid-twentieth-century American jurisprudence, see Edwin W. Patterson, *Jurisprudence: Men and Ideas of the Law* (Brooklyn: Foundation Press, 1953), 548–52.

287 See, in particular, Theodore Schroeder, 'The Psychologic Study of Judicial Opinions', *California L. Rev.*, 6 (1918), 89–113.

experimental branch of natural science. Its theoretical goal is the prediction and control of behaviour.'[288] Behaviourism thus offered the prospect of the scientific study of social control. 'Behaviourism promised the scientific control of life to a generation who felt their lives increasingly out of control.'[289]

It was through behaviourism, accordingly, that social control became part of the common currency of the early twentieth-century social sciences. Owing to its emphasis on the concept of social control, furthermore, behaviourism became a distinct social scientific facet of legal realism. Concerned 'with law conceived as human *behaviour* instead of the traditional body of rules and concepts',[290] behaviourist-inspired realists argued that rules are essentially stimuli for prompting particular kinds of human response.[291] This argument is epitomized by Underhill Moore's so-called 'learning theory', which he developed in his study of New Haven parking offences. The motorist's behaviour is determined, according to Moore, 'by the relation between four factors—drive, cue, response, and reward—which relation he has learned, or is learning. In order to learn one must be driven to make a response in the presence of a cue, and that response must be rewarded.'[292] The necessary 'drive' of which he writes is prompted by legal rules, for it is such rules which—for example, with regard to the regulation of traffic—provide the 'reward' (that is, the omission of sanction) for the individual motorist's compliance in learning the appropriate responses to the relevant ordinances.

Moore apart, however, legal realists generally were disinclined to apply the methods of behavioural science to the study of law with any real rigour.[293] Indeed, in so far as behaviourism made any significant mark on American legal theory, that mark had been made some years before the emergence of legal realism—with the publication, to be precise, of Joseph Bingham's article, 'What is the Law?' in 1912. In that article, Bingham

[288] John B. Watson, 'Psychology as a Behaviourist Views It', *Psychological Rev.*, 20 (1913), 158–77 at 158.

[289] Ross, *supra* n. 139, 312.

[290] Yntema, *supra* n. 14, 318.

[291] See e.g. Underhill Moore, 'Rational Basis of Legal Institutions', *Columbia L. Rev.*, 23 (1923), 609–17 at 610; Oliphant, *supra* n. 74, 137; and cf. also Rumble, *supra* n. 18, 159–61; Summers, *supra* n. 19, 88–9; G. Edward White, 'From Sociological Jurisprudence to Realism: Jurisprudence and Social Change in Early Twentieth-Century America', *Virginia L. Rev.*, 58 (1972), 999–1028 at 1015–16.

[292] Moore and Callahan, *supra* n. 126, 61. For critical estimations of this theory, see Clark L. Hull, 'Moore and Callahan's "Law and Learning Theory": A Psychologist's Impressions', *Yale L.J.*, 53 (1944), 330–337; Hessel E. Yntema, ' "Law and Learning Theory" through the Looking Glass of Legal Theory', *Yale L.J.*, 53 (1944), 338–47.

[293] See Kalman, *supra* n. 3, 18–19; David E. Ingersoll, 'Karl Llewellyn, American Legal Realism, and Contemporary Legal Behaviouralism', *Ethics*, 76 (1966), 253–66 at 263; also, for a critique of behaviourism as applied to law, cf. Cohen, *supra* n. 117, 357–60.

developed what was to become the trademark realist view that the formalist notion of law as 'a system of rules and principles enforced by political authority . . . is fundamentally erroneous and . . . a bar to a scientific understanding of our law'.[294] Properly understood, rules and principles are but 'mental tools'—ideas held subjectively by those who think about law—to be used to explain human responses to authoritative governmental control.[295] Law, accordingly, is 'dependent on the existence of authoritative government',[296] and '[t]he practical interest of lawyers and of laymen lies in the concrete operations and effects of governmental machinery and not in generalizations excepting insofar as they cause, explain, or indicate such phenomena.'[297]

The scientific study of law, then, according to Bingham, consists of analysing the operation of judicial machinery with a view to predicting future decisions: 'cases past and potential are the essential substance in the field of law. Past cases are experimental guides to prognostications of future decisions.'[298] By 'observation, report, inductive and deductive reasoning and the other methods of scientific investigation', the concrete phenomena of authoritative government 'may be generalized into rules and principles'[299]—rules and principles deduced not by way of Langdellian speculation, but by treating law as a practical activity. Bingham was, in essence, attempting to take the proto-realist insights of Pound and Holmes one step further by appropriating the already established idea of science in law and putting it to a more progressive use. No longer, he was arguing, need science be the preserve of mechanical jurisprudence, for the foundations of legal science could be re-cast in order to serve predictivist ends. While Bingham's argument hinted at behaviourism—not to mention the predictivist rhetoric of Holmes[300]—it was, more directly, the broader philosophy of pragmatism to which he seemed to appeal.

Pragmatism brought to late nineteenth and early twentieth-century American social thought the idea that science could be put to the service of

294 Joseph W. Bingham, 'What is the Law?', *Michigan L. Rev.*, 11 (1912), 1–25, 109–121 at 3. For a discussion of Bingham *vis-à-vis* legal realism, see Françoise Michaut, *L'École de la 'Sociological Jurisprudence' et le Mouvement Realiste Americain: Le Rôle du Juge et la Théorie du Droit* (Doctoral dissertation, Université de Paris X, Nanterre, année universitaire 1984–5), 118–23.

295 Bingham, *supra* n. 294. 9–11.

296 Ibid. 10.

297 Joseph W. Bingham, 'Science and the Law', *Green Bag*, 25 (1913), 162–7 at 164–5.

298 Bingham, *supra* n. 294, 17.

299 Ibid. 9.

300 Compare Bingham, *supra* n. 297, 164–5 with Oliver Wendell Holmes, Jr., 'The Path of the Law', *Harvard L. Rev.*, 10 (1897), 457–78 at 457.

understanding social change.[301] William James, in 1910, wrote in defence of pragmatism that it could 'remain religious like the rationalisms, but at the same time, like the empiricisms, it can preserve the richest intimacy with the facts'.[302] This was precisely the claim which Bingham made with regard to jurisprudence. If grounded in predictivism, jurisprudence could maintain the scientific pretensions beloved of Langdellian formalism while outstripping the limitations of such formalism by establishing an intimacy with the facts of law. The key to achieving this near-paradigm shift was for jurists to conceive of law not as a static body of rules and principles, but as a phenomenon in flux. According to John Dewey, writing in the same year as James, pragmatism required philosophers to transfer their attention 'from the permanent to the changing' and, rather than seek to establish universal certainties, treat their discipline as 'a method of moral and political diagnosis and prognosis'.[303] While the value of prediction had, of course, found early juristic recognition in the writings of Holmes, it was through the pragmatism of James and Dewey that the activity of prognosis was elevated to the status of a science. Holmes bequeathed to legal realism an implicitly anti-Langdellian notion of prediction as a legal activity. But it was a fairly modest, pragmatically specific activity—the activity, primarily, of gauging just how far individuals might be able to tread before becoming legally accountable for their actions. Pragmatist philosophers, ironically, treated the activity of prediction as a less specifically pragmatic affair.

This much is clear from the manner in which early twentieth-century social theorists looked to the philosophy of pragmatism for scientific inspiration. In its emphasis on prognosis and prediction as peculiarly scientific means of understanding social change, the philosophy of pragmatism fitted well with the then prevalent spirit of social-scientific realism. The capacity to predict—especially to predict 'scientifically'—was, after all, but another facet of the broader ethos of social control. But predictivism, for social scientists, was more than just another tool for understanding social change. Its acceptance as such marked an important shift in social-scientific outlook:

> The realistic search for concrete experience continued as a new reality continually presented itself for observation. . . . Yet even realism began to change under the

[301] See David Hollinger, 'The Problem of Pragmatism in American History', *Jnl. of American History*, 67 (1980), 88–107.

[302] William James, *Pragmatism: A New Name for Some Old Ways of Thinking* (New York: Longmans, Green & Co. 1910), 33.

[303] John Dewey, 'The Influence of Darwin on Philosophy', in John Dewey, *The Middle Works, 1899–1924* (15 vols. ed. J. A. Boydston, Carbondale: Southern Illinois University Press, 1976–83), IV, 13.

impact of modernism. As the social scientists began to see facts as process, the concrete reality they sought to grasp receded into flux. . . . A science of natural process tended to drive beneath the level of concrete facts to causal process.[304]

Social-scientific realism, then, was supplemented by a predictivist-inspired emphasis on causality. The upshot of this was that realism, in a social scientific context, no longer meant the discovery and analysis of the facts which constitute reality. Rather, it denoted analysis of the processes by which those facts come into existence—analysis with a view, furthermore, to predicting how, and indeed what manner of, further facts will come into existence in the future.

For all that legal realists rarely utilized it with much conviction, this scientifically premissed, pragmatist concept of predictivism became, for many of them, almost as basic to their thinking as the juridically specific prediction theory of Holmes. One possible reason for this is that the pragmatist inclination towards analyses of processes complemented the general realist concern with judicial procedure—that is, with process—over and above legal doctrine.[305] Karl Llewellyn, for example, took the view that 'almost the only way to get deeply under the skin of a pre-science about behaviour in matters legal is by way of the detailed *processes* which lead to the larger phenomena—watching the men, within the institution, under the impact of fresh stimuli'.[306] A more likely reason for the general realist turn towards pragmatism rests in the fact that the philosophy had already been applied to law with some success by Pound. Indeed, the concept of social engineering rather epitomized the pragmatist ethos that scientific knowledge about law could be made useful.[307] Those legal realists who looked to pragmatism to give scientific credibility to their claims about the legal world were looking to a philosophy which they regarded as juridically tried and tested.[308] Their use of that philosophy to turn the process of legal prediction into a purportedly scientific task hardly constituted a radical step forward either from Poundian proto-realism or even Langdellian legal formalism.

This much becomes especially clear if one considers the question of what purpose legal prediction was supposed to serve. The immediate answer to the question is the answer which was offered up by certain realists: predictivism provides the key to the study of law as a modern social

[304] Ross, *supra* n. 139, 318–19.

[305] See Rumble, *supra* n. 193, 250; Kalman, *supra* n. 3, 20; Stevens, *supra* n. 45, 56; Grant Gilmore, 'Law, Logic and Experience', *Howard L.J.*, 3 (1957), 26–41 at 38.

[306] Llewellyn, *supra* n. 75, 10–11.

[307] See Note [Rand Rosenblatt], 'Legal Theory and Legal Education', *Yale L.J.*, 79 (1970), 1153–78 at 1157–65.

[308] See Yntema, *supra* n. 14, 322; Woodard, *supra* n. 281, 703–4.

science. 'Surely progress in the science of law', Walter Wheeler Cook claimed, 'consists in continually reformulating our generalizations so as to make them bring out more clearly just what the past phenomena described really are and just what we predict will happen in the future.'[309] Similarly, for Herman Oliphant, '[t]he predictable element' in the judicial decision 'will be the dominant subject matter of any truly scientific study of law.'[310] But such an answer simply raises the same question afresh. Even if it is granted that predictivism provides a key to the understanding of law as a social science, why should anyone wish to conceive of law as such a science? What, precisely, might the appeal to social science achieve?

Throughout the literature of legal realism there runs a distinct caginess with respect to this last question. Conspicuously little effort was made by any of the so-called realists to explain why, exactly, the integration of law with the broader social sciences should prove to be such an enlightened initiative. By the early 1940s, Karl Llewellyn, for one, was willing to concede that realist attempts at such integration had not been a success;[311] and, indeed, from the mid-1930s onwards, realism suffered a gradual institutional and intellectual demise as its proponents became ever more indifferent and even hostile to 'the clumsy jargon of the so-called social sciences'.[312] Disillusionment with the social sciences was, of course, only part of the reason for this general demise. The cause of the disillusionment itself is crucial to any detailed assessment of legal realism. In appealing to the social sciences, and to pragmatism in particular, various legal realists discovered what they considered to be a vital conceptual apparatus for articulating the essential 'realism' of their particular perspectives: the social sciences provided a pathway to the legal facts, to the reality of law. This social science-induced realism turned out, however, to entail its own brand of formalism. And while it would be hyperbole to assert that so-called realists were 'Langdellians *malgré eux*',[313] it is important nonetheless to recognize the formalist elements implicit in realist thought.

The essential purpose behind the realist stress on predictivism was the promotion of certainty in law. Prediction entails focusing not only on legal rules, but also on other factors which might effect the outcome of a

[309] Cook, *supra* n. 70, 485.
[310] Oliphant, *supra* n. 72, 159.
[311] See Karl N. Llewellyn and E. Adamson Hoebel, *The Cheyenne Way: Conflict and Case Law in Primitive Jurisprudence* (Norman: University of Oklahoma Press, 1941), 41. ('Effort after effort at synthesis of the social disciplines over the past ten years has made worthwhile headway in all phases, except that of integrating law-stuff with the rest.') The language is unmistakably Llewellyn's, a fact which is confirmed by E. Adamson Hoebel, 'Karl Llewellyn: Anthropological Jurisprude', *Rutgers L. Rev.*, 18 (1964), 735–44 at 740 fn. 23.
[312] Rodell, *supra* n. 130, 6; and see also Kalman, *supra* n. 3, 42.
[313] Gilmore, *supra* n. 64, 78.

decision—factors such as the known predilections and background of the judge. Such factors are likely to be important for the purposes of ensuring consistently accurate prediction.[314] But what might this be taken to imply? The implication seems to be that judicial decisions 'could and should become more predictable'.[315] But just how predictable? Are we to assume that an ideal legal system would be one in which all future legal decisions could be predicted? Certainly no legal realist was so naive as to treat such an aspiration as a real possibility. However—and this is the important point—the realist notion of predictivism as a science is founded on the idea that the aspiration is a worthy one. That is, predictivist-inspired realism treats as notionally desirable the facilitation of a formally certain, 'prediction-friendly' system of law. At the same time, the general predictivist quest for legal certainty betrays an implicit fear of judicial discretion and incertitude. And it is thus that realism, certainly in its predictivist guise, appears to attempt to discredit one formalist conception of law only to replace it with another. This much is clear from Max Radin's analysis of the nature of judicial decision-making. Having expressed his dismay over the Langdellian tendency to treat the legal dispute 'like a nickel in a slot machine',[316] whereby the correct result is reached as if automatically by the judicial application of the appropriate precedent, Radin argues that the business of legal realism—as a reaction to Langdellian formalism—is prophecy, through which 'we can come fairly near certainty'.[317] This, it seems, is to denounce mechanical jurisprudence in one breath while reinstating it in the next. The assumption that it may be possible to predict future legal decisions with considerable, if not quite total, accuracy is hardly less formalist—is hardly less supportive of so-called slot machine justice—than the basic Langdellian belief that legal doctrine is reducible to a handful of common law principles which may be applied uncontroversially to future legal disputes.

This is not to claim that the formalism of legal realism was intentional. Rather, formalism persisted *faute de mieux*. Legal realists had been fairly successful in adopting social scientific methods and insights to criticize the

[314] Oliphant, *supra* n. 74, 130–32; and see also Summers, *supra* n. 19, 143–4.

[315] Rumble, *supra* n. 18, 140.

[316] Radin, *supra* n. 251, 358.

[317] Radin, ibid. 362; and cf. further, for a detailed pronouncement of this position, Karl N. Llewellyn, *The Common Law Tradition: Deciding Appeals* (Boston: Little, Brown & Co., 1960), 302–3; *The Case Law System in America* (P. Gewirtz ed., Eng. trans. M. Ansaldi, Chicago: University of Chicago Press, 1989; orig. German publ. 1933), 76–89; Max Radin, 'Case Law and Stare Decisis: Concerning *Präjudizienrecht in Amerika*', *Columbia L. Rev.*, 33 (1933), 199–212 at 212; Lon L. Fuller, 'American Legal Realism', *U. Pennsylvania L. Rev.*, 82 (1934), 429–62 at 431–4. On the realist quest for certainty, see generally Charles E. Clark and David M. Trubek, 'The Creative Role of the Judge: Restraint and Freedom in the Common Law Tradition', *Yale L.J.*, 71 (1961), 255–76 at 267–76.

laissez-faire formalism of the courts. It is significant, indeed, that those legal realists who attempted this task—Robert Hale was exemplary—tended to be academics with a more than casual interest in interdisciplinary study. Owing, however, to a mixture of reluctance and inability on the part of most legal realists to pay little more than lip service to the methods of the social sciences, the utilization of interdisciplinary perspectives to criticize Langdellian formalism fared comparably poorly. That certain realists turned the predictivist element of pragmatist philosophy into an implicitly formalist method is indicative of as much.

The same is illustrated, too, by the manner in which some realists embraced the concept of functionalism. For such realists, functionalism, as Felix Cohen observed, tended to be little more than a synonym for pragmatism.[318] In fact, the use of the term 'functionalism' by certain realists was usually but an intimation of their desire to demonstrate a peculiar form of legal certainty—of their intention, that is, to dig beneath the conceptual façade of law and tell it as it really is.[319] William O. Douglas, for example, declared that a 'functional' approach to the law of business associations demands 'a consideration of the phenomena observed in the organization and operation of a business' rather than an examination 'of the mere form itself of business'.[320] Such an approach 'would result in observations of the things men attempt to do and are found doing when engaging in business'.[321] For Cohen, the problem with approaches such as that adopted by Douglas is that they are not, in any specific sense, functionalist. Indeed, those realists who attempted to appropriate the concept of functionalism by and large lacked the inclination or the imagination to develop and apply it in a legal setting. 'Unfortunately,' Cohen lamented, 'certain advocates of realistic jurisprudence, after using the functional method to break down rules and concepts into atomic decisions, refuse to go any further with the analytic process.'[322]

318 Cohen, *supra* n. 192, 821–2.

319 See Kalman, *supra* n. 3, 8–10, 30–1.

320 William O. Douglas, 'A Functional Approach to the Law of Business Associations', *Illinois L. Rev.*, 23 (1929), 673–82 at 675.

321 Ibid.

322 Cohen, *supra* n. 192, 843. Cohen himself suggests that a functional approach to law would not be entirely hostile to the tenets of Langdellian formalism: 'The functionalist must have recourse to the logical instruments that analytical jurisprudence furnishes. Analytical jurisprudence, in turn, may develop more fruitful modes of analysis with a better understanding of the law-in-action.' Felix S. Cohen, 'The Problems of a Functional Jurisprudence', *Mod. L. Rev.*, 1 (1937), 5–26 at 7. For a critical analysis of Cohen's own application of the functional method to law, see Martin P. Golding, 'Realism and Functionalism in the Legal Thought of Felix S. Cohen', *Cornell L. Rev.*, 66 (1981), 1032–57 at 1051–7; and cf. also, more generally, 'Jurisprudential Symposium in Memory of Felix S. Cohen', *Rutgers L. Rev.*, 9 (1954), 343–475.

It should be recognized that Jerome Frank—with whom, originally, we were dealing—regarded neither functionalism nor predictivism as a useful legal tool. Indeed, with regard to predictivism he could be particularly disparaging. Since the outcome of any particular legal decision will depend on the variable instincts of the judge or the feelings of the jury, the quest for accurate prediction must be 'doomed to failure'.[323] Psychology demonstrates precisely this fact.[324] The concept of behaviourist psychology with which certain realists had dabbled during the 1920s was premissed on the idea that the human mind responds rationally to given stimuli. It is the essential rationality of human thought and action, indeed, which, for the behaviourist, allows for the possibility of scientific prediction. However, as Freudianism began to make its mark on American social thought during the 1920s and 1930s, legal realists—and Frank is exemplary here—began to conceive of psychology in a somewhat different fashion.[325] To put the matter simplistically, rationalism in psychology was supplanted by irrationalism.[326] Edward S. Robinson wrote in the mid-1930s that '[i]t is especially important that the student of jurisprudence should be aware of the nature of the psychology written by Freud and his followers',[327] since Freudianism demonstrates 'the possibility of viewing human nature with a new honesty and a new detachment; it has shown us how to look behind the rationalizations that men give of their own conduct and to view candidly any motive whatever that may be discovered there'; indeed, 'it is just this new psychological detachment that is needed as a basis for a natural science of the law. In no field of human endeavour is it more precarious to take human nature at its own face value than in the field of social regulation'.[328] Frank, though he approached psychoanalysis in a markedly more casual fashion than did Robinson, similarly adopted the view that psychology generally provides a strong theoretical basis for criticizing the idea of legal rationality.[329] That is why he was keen to see psychoanalysis established as part of the judicial craft; and it is also why he rejected the more general realist view that there is an implicit rationality

323 Frank, *supra* n. 25, 399.

324 Ibid. 126 fn. 13.

325 On the impact of Freudian psychoanalysis in the United States, see Nathan G. Hale, Jr., *Freud and the Americans: The Beginnings of Psychoanalysis in the United States, 1876–1917* (New York: Oxford University Press, 1971); Harold D. Lasswell, 'The Impact of Psychoanalytic Thinking on the Social Sciences', in L.D. White ed., *The State of the Social Sciences* (Chicago: University of Chicago Press, 1956), 84–115. On Freudianism and legal realism, see Radin, *supra* n. 9, 827–8; Savarese, *supra* n. 85, 181–2, 194–5; Duxbury, 'Jerome Frank and the Legacy of Legal Realism', *supra* n. 3, 180–1.

326 See Kalman, *supra* n. 3, 6, 20; Purcell, *supra* n. 119, 99.

327 Robinson, *supra* n. 247, 108.

328 Ibid. 61.

329 See generally Anthony Chase, 'Jerome Frank and American Psychoanalytic Jurisprudence', *Int. Jnl. Law and Psychiatry*, 2 (1979), 29–54.

about the legal process which allows for the possibility of predicting future decisions with a fair degree of accuracy. The ingenuity of Frank was that he recognized how predictivist rhetoric, for all its appeal to the 'reality' of law, was actually little other than a variant on the more traditional, 'Bealist' version of legal formalism.[330]

Yet despite this, Frank himself was unable to escape the grip of formalist jurisprudence. This much is especially clear from his critique of the jury system. Throughout his writings, Frank was consistent in professing 'to disbelieve thoroughly'[331] in the use of juries. As a collection of twelve legally uneducated lay-persons, the jury, he insisted, is an incompetent fact-finding body. Happily he would have seen their use seriously curtailed, if not eradicated altogether. His main work on the subject, written with his daughter and published posthumously, is essentially a chronicle of the cases of thirty-six men who, owing primarily to the errors of juries, were found guilty only later to be discovered innocent.[332] While obviously the jury system is not about to fall into disuse, there is no reason, he argued, that juries should not be made more accountable to judges. That he should have adopted this line of argument, however, is curious. Given that judges supposedly act primarily on instincts rather than on rules, why should we place any more faith in the judge than we do in the jury? Frank's answer is revealing:

> To comprehend the meaning of many a legal rule requires special training. It is inconceivable that a body of twelve ordinary men, casually gathered together for a few days, could, merely from listening to the instructions of the judge, gain the knowledge necessary to grasp the true import of the judge's words. For these words have often acquired their meaning as a result of hundreds of years of professional disputation in the courts.[333]

Thus it is that, in condemning the jury system, Frank elevates the judge to a status not obviously compatible with his original realist thesis. No longer straightforwardly a human being, the judge has been transformed into the saviour and the oracle of the law, into the repository and guardian of an artificial reason which the untrained plebeian should neither pretend, nor be expected, to understand. The implication is clear: law is, of necessity, the preserve of a legal priesthood. Such an argument is distinctly more

[330] See Frank, *supra* n. 25, 127.

[331] Jerome Frank, 'Are Judges Human?', *U. Pennsylvania L. Rev.*, 80 (1931), 17–53, 233–67 at 27.

[332] Jerome Frank and Barbara Frank, *Not Guilty* (New York: Doubleday, 1957); and for further discussion of Frank's dislike of the jury system, see Duxbury, 'Jerome Frank and the Legacy of Legal Realism', *supra* n. 3, 188–9.

[333] Frank, *supra* n. 279, 116.

Bealist than realist,[334] and it is odd that Frank should have offered it, given that he claimed more generally to reject the notion of expertise as elitist and undemocratic.[335] Fifteen years after his initial denunciation of childish legal thought-ways, he lamented that 'perhaps . . . despite my years, I have not yet fully matured'.[336] *Law and the Modern Mind* had fallen 'like a bomb on the legal world';[337] and yet, as with many a *succès de scandale*, it ultimately demanded more of its author than it did of anyone else. In rejecting the jury system, Frank had implicitly celebrated the verities of legal certainty and tradition. And it was precisely thus that he trapped himself within his own realist critique.

LEGAL REALISM AND LEGAL EDUCATION

Frank himself seemed to be blissfully unaware of this fact. Almost two decades on from the first publication of *Law and the Modern Mind*, and nearly eighty years after Langdell's appointment as dean at Harvard, he was still vilifying the legacy of Langdellian formalism *con brio*, even if his peculiar style of disparagement had, over the years, acquired something of a constructive edge. Whereas, in his early writings, the poverty and the popularity of the Langdellian legal world-view was attributed to the widespread if implicit acceptance of the basic legal myth, in his writings from the late 1940s onwards he began to stress the pervasive effect of 'the myth that upper courts are at the heart of court-house government. This myth induces the false belief that it is of no importance whether or not trial judges are well-trained for their job, fair-minded, conscientious in listening to testimony, and honest. In considerable part, this belief arises from the fallacious notion that the legal rules, supervised by the upper courts, control decisions.'[338]

Although Frank was not the first legal realist to draw attention to this so-called upper-court myth,[339] he was the only one of their number to accord it especial juridical significance. As with the basic legal myth, the upper-court myth was very much a part of the Langdellian scheme of things. Langdell himself had founded the case method on old English appeal

[334] See Warren J. Samuels, 'Joseph Henry Beale's Lectures on Jurisprudence, 1909', *U. Miami L. Rev.*, 29 (1975), 260–333 at 292; Duxbury, 'Some Radicalism about Realism?', *supra* n. 3, 29.

[335] Jerome Frank, 'The Place of the Expert in a Democratic Society', *Philosophy of Science*, 16 (1949), 3–24 at 23.

[336] *United States* v. *Rubenstein*, 151 F.2d. 915, 923 (2nd Cir. 1945), (Frank J., dissenting).

[337] Charles E. Clark, 'Jerome N. Frank', *Yale L.J.*, 66 (1957), 817–18 at 817.

[338] Frank, *supra* n. 279, 222.

[339] See e.g. Green, *supra* n. 255, pt. I, 1037.

cases, and had paid almost no attention to the decisions of lower courts. Even Cardozo 'completely by-passed the operations of the trial courts'.[340] A truly post-Langdellian jurisprudence, in contrast, would focus not primarily on the upper court interpretations and applications of legal rules and principles, but on the lower court process of fact-finding upon which upper court decision-making depends. Not that Frank believed facts to be any more determinate than rules. 'The trial court's facts are not "data", not something that is "given"; they are not waiting somewhere, ready made, for the court to discover, to "find" '.[341] Facts are simply testimonies about past events, and, as such, are eminently susceptible to distortion through human fallibility. Yet for all this, they are crucial to realist legal thought. Since most decisions are not appealed, fact-finding at first instance determines the outcome of a majority of cases. Even when a case is appealed, the upper court will tend to accept as final the trial court's finding of facts. For whereas the trial court hears witnesses' oral testimonies, and is able to scrutinize the demeanour of witnesses presenting their testimonies, the upper court has before it only a transcript of the trial court's findings, thus putting it in a poor position to review issues of fact. Accordingly, only by focusing on facts might jurisprudence become more reform-oriented. Through careful and critical study of fact-finding procedure we may be able to identify and eradicate distortions in human testimonies, and, more than this, we may come to understand, and eventually to remedy, more general procedural and administrative faults inherent in the adjudicative process itself.

Whereas the basic legal myth seemed so psychologically pervasive as to be well-nigh insurmountable, the upper-court myth, Frank believed, posed a problem which could be remedied. This myth had been created in the law school; it could be destroyed there also. The law schools of the Langdellian tradition, Frank argued, 'are upper-court law schools',[342] engaged in a form of 'ersatz teaching'[343] which stresses the written reports of upper-court decisions without ever considering the reality of the relationship between those who represent and those who have dealings with the legal process. To combat the upper-court myth, these 'library law schools' must liberate themselves from the case-book tradition and become 'lawyer schools'.[344] This new lawyer school would be staffed mainly by teachers with at least five years' experience practising law; the 'book law teacher' would not be eliminated entirely from the new régime, but would occupy

[340] Jerome Frank, 'Cardozo and the Upper Court Myth', *Law and Contemporary Problems*, 13 (1948), 369–90 at 373.

[341] Frank, *supra* n. 279, 23.

[342] Jerome Frank, 'A Plea for Lawyer Schools', *Yale L.J.*, 56 (1947), 1303–44 at 1306.

[344] Jerome Frank, 'Both Ends Against the Middle', *U. Pennsylvania L. Rev.*, 100 (1951), 20–47 at 28.

[344] Frank, *supra* n. 342, 1312–13.

only a subordinate role (for example, instructing students on how to write briefs for the appellate courts); the student would complete his or her entire course of upper-court decision reading in around six months; and the rest of the degree course would be devoted to a clinical legal education.[345]

The legal clinic is at the heart of Frank's proposals for reform. Under the guidance of their teachers, students would be required to spend a period of their time at law school working in the clinic—which would operate very much along the lines of the local legal aid clinic—providing legal services either free or for a small fee. In this way, law students, like medical students, would be required actually to practise various elements of their discipline before they could complete their formal legal education. The ultimate benefit of such a system would be that law would be brought down from the clouds of rules, principles and upper-court decisions, so that students would experience it as a human phenomenon rather than merely as a set of concepts to be encountered in the textbooks.[346]

Although Frank was not the first American lawyer to propose a clinical model of legal education,[347] there is a striking irony in the fact that he devised any sort of blueprint for pedagogic reform given that he was never, at any stage throughout his career, a full-time member of an academic institution. While his proposals had a fairly limited impact on the way in which clinical programmes ultimately developed in the American law schools,[348] they represented nonetheless a classic—perhaps the classic—realist attempt to move beyond the confines of the Langdellian library–laboratory. The clinical model provided the vital element of practical experiment which had been absent from its Langdellian counterpart. Furthermore, the idea of clinical experience as the inculcation of the practitioner's craft seemed to demonstrate that, for all the various appeals to the methods of the social sciences, the roots of realism were in fact profoundly professional.[349] Perhaps, after all, it was both fitting and typical that the prime realist advocate of the clinical model should have been an erstwhile Wall Street corporate specialist; for the clinical lawyer school was intended, more than anything else, to be the training ground for the hard-boiled legal technician.

[345] See Jerome Frank, 'What Constitutes a Good Legal Education?', *American Law School Rev.*, 7 (1933), 894–902.

[346] See Jerome Frank, 'Why Not a Clinical Lawyer School?', *U. Pennsylvania L. Rev.*, 81 (1933), 907–23 at 914–23.

[347] See Stevens, *supra* n. 45, 165 n. 14; John M. Lindsey, 'John Saeger Bradway—the Tireless Pioneer of Clinical Education', *Oklahoma City Univ. L. Rev.*, 4 (1979), 1–16.

[348] See Robert Stevens, 'Two Cheers for 1870: The American Law School', *Perspectives in American History*, 5 (1971), 403–548 at 491–2; *supra* n. 45, 162, 215–16.

[349] See Angèle Auburtin, 'Amerikanische Rechtsauffassung und die neueren amerikanischen Theorien der Rechtssoziologie und des Rechtsrealismus', *Zeitschrift für ausländisches öffentliches Recht und Völkerrecht*, 3 (1933), 529–67 at 557–8; Kalman, *supra* n. 3, 17, 21; Bechtler, *supra* n. 85, 19.

Since Frank's proposals were as divorced from the opinions of most realists as they were from the tradition of Langdell, it was perhaps typical also that, during the 1930s, the lawyer school blueprint should generally have fallen on fallow ground. Apart from the occasional, vague aside to the effect that the introduction of snippets of 'the humanities' into the clinical curriculum might enable law students to identify with the feelings and grievances of their clients,[350] Frank's suggestions seemed almost entirely to neglect that which most realists cherished above all: namely, the teaching of and research into law as a social science. Hardly surprising was it that Llewellyn declared, in 1935, that 'I do not believe, as Frank seems to, in the substitution of practice or clinic for theoretical instruction.'[351] For legal realists to take the lawyer school route would have involved massive sacrifices, given especially the fundamental changes in curricular content and structure, in personnel, and the vast expenditure of energy and resources that the implementation of the clinical model would have demanded.

It was not until the 1960s that the clinical model—and even then, not Frank's model—began to flourish in the American law schools.[352] In the early 1930s, when Frank held a post as a research associate at Yale, the faculty had 'welcomed him warmly and his ideas with reservations'.[353] The occasional vocationally oriented course had been added to the curriculum; but by and large clinical education failed to take root. Frank seemed genuinely frustrated by this fact. In an address to the Yale Law School in 1941, he chided his erstwhile realist colleagues for their quiescence: 'You folks here at New Haven take a programme for having law students act like lawyers—and you talk about it. Gosh, if you're going to spank—or woo—our Lady of the Law, go and do it. Don't become mere Yodellers—or, for that matter, Rodellers.'[354] The pun is not without significance. Fred Rodell spent much of his academic energy vilifying the Harvard Law School and insisting on the intellectual superiority of Yale[355]—complaining about the ills of modern legal education, in other words, rather than trying to remedy them. It was precisely this words-over-action world-view of which Frank became disenamoured. And yet, ironically, Frank hardly hesitated to join

[350] See Frank, *supra* n. 343, 38–40, 46–7.

[351] Karl N. Llewellyn, 'On What is Wrong With So-Called Legal Education', *Columbia L. Rev.*, 35 (1935), 651–78 at 675. For general critical discussion of Frank's clinical law school model, see George K. Gardner, 'Why Not a Clinical Lawyer-School?—Some Reflections', *U. Pennsylvania L. Rev.*, 82 (1934), 785–804; Leon T. David, 'The Clinical Lawyer School: The Clinic', *U. Pennsylvania L. Rev.*, 83 (1934), 1–22.

[352] Stevens, *supra* n. 45, 157, 215–16.

[353] Kalman, *supra* n. 3, 172.

[354] Jerome Frank, 'Yodellers and Rodellers', talk before the Judge's Gavel, Yale Law School, 15 February 1941, in Jerome N. Frank Papers, Yale University, Sterling Memorial Library, Manuscripts and Archives Division, box 169, folder 628 at 16.

[355] See Duxbury, 'In the Twilight of Legal Realism', *supra* n. 3, 385–90.

in the same game. 'Where the Langdellian atmosphere is thickest,' he wrote in 1933, 'teaching is weakest; where that atmosphere is thinnest, teaching is strongest.'[356] Almost fifteen years later, he remained steadfast to his belief 'that, as a whole, Yale Law School . . . comes closer to grips with lawyers' realities than Harvard'.[357] Very simply, Frank was a Harvard-baiter just as was Rodell.

Indeed, Harvard-baiting—or certainly disenchantment with the academic and professional prestige which the Harvard Law School enjoyed—was at the core of a good deal of realist pedagogic critique. Viewed in rather crude terms, realism was very much an Ivy League law school phenomenon, a controversy between Harvard on the one hand, and Columbia and Yale on the other. When, in 1935, Karl Llewellyn offered his reflections on the state of American legal education, he prefaced his comments with the warning that he was concerned only with ' "legal education" as practised at Columbia, Harvard, and Yale'.[358] While, furthermore, neither Llewellyn nor any other so-called realist was willing to indulge Harvard-phobia as shamelessly as did Rodell, there was a widespread recognition of the problem which the latter liked to dramatize. Edmund M. Morgan, for example, a Harvard Law School graduate and professor there from 1925 onwards, professed no sympathy at all for Rodell's anti-Harvard histrionics;[359] yet he was prepared privately to acknowledge that the School faced something of a problem during the 1930s in so far as it was 'regarded as entirely too much satisfied with itself, and as having a supercilious, if not a hostile, attitude towards experiments in legal education and new methods of attack upon legal problems which originate elsewhere'.[360]

Naturally, during the the 1930s, there were those in Cambridge—not least Felix Frankfurter—who insisted that allegations of Harvardian academic aloofness and condescension were unfair and unfounded.[361] Yet

[356] Frank, *supra* n. 345, 898.

[357] Frank, *supra* n. 342, 1342.

[358] Llewellyn, *supra* n. 351, 652. In the 1920s, Harvard, Yale, Columbia and possibly a half-dozen other law schools were distinct in so far as they conceived themselves to be national institutions, without any special obligation to prepare students to pass the bar examinations of any particular state. Other schools, in contrast, were rather more concerned with preparing students for provincial legal practice. See Bruce A. Ackerman, '*Law and the Modern Mind* by Jerome Frank', *Daedalus*, 103 (1974), 119–130 at 126 n. 2.

[359] See Edmund M. Morgan to Guy W. Ross, 8 March 1961, in Edmund M. Morgan Papers, Vanderbilt University, Heard Library, Special Collections Department, box 3 ('You are entirely right in thinking that I have a low opinion of Fred Rodell. . . . He would rather make smart sentences than tell the truth'); also Felix Frankfurter to Edmund M. Morgan, 10 November 1947, in Edmund M. Morgan Papers, Harvard Law School Library, Manuscripts Division, box 11, folder 16.

[360] Edmund M. Morgan to Karl N. Llewellyn, 28 March 1931, in Karl N. Llewellyn Papers, University of Chicago Law Library, A.65(b), cited in Hull, *supra* n. 47, 952.

[361] See Kalman, *supra* n. 3, 174.

even Frankfurter could not but have recognized how such allegations would have got off the ground. Harvard was, among other things, the birthplace of the modern law school, the home of the case method and the academic arm of the Restatement project. This, too, during the Depression period, when many lesser schools were struggling to find funds, let alone establish solid links with the profession. Harvard enjoyed academic and professional kudos which even its Ivy League rivals could not match; to say that the School had a good deal going for it would be rather gross understatement.

Realism, accordingly, emerged at Columbia and Yale largely as an endeavour to supplant, or at least genuinely to compete with, Harvard's professional and academic dominance. Purely at the level of legal education, the endeavour involved four fundamental, interrelated strategies, all of which revolved around the debunking of Langdellianism.

First of all, and most generally, there was the basic realist desire to conceive of legal education in non-Langdellian terms. For many legal realists, this meant looking to the methods of the social sciences for an alternative to Harvard-style formalism. The strategy of others was to play down the Langdellian tradition while venerating the achievements of proto-realists such as—indeed, especially—Holmes. Some adopted both of these strategies. Some also looked to their past teachers for inspiration. For example, at Yale, Hohfeld and the great contracts scholar, Arthur L. Corbin, were elevated by some to a quasi-Langdellian status, the latter in particular being treated as something of a realist *éminence grise*. This was primarily because of Corbin's redoubtable influence as a teacher—Llewellyn, for instance, regarded him as a father-figure[362]—though it was also because of his penchant for making realist-style pronouncements on the nature of legal evolution, on judicial creativity, and on the importance of facts as well as rules in the decision-making process.[363] These, after all, were precisely the themes to which Corbin's realist successors resorted in developing their second anti-Langdellian strategy: namely, the critique of *stare decisis* as a foundational pedagogic principle.

The classic illustration of the realist critique of *stare decisis* is commonly considered to be Herman Oliphant's presidential address to the Association of American Law Schools in 1927. In truth, Oliphant was markedly less outspoken on the matter of *stare decisis* than commentators have tended to assume. Indeed, rather than reject the doctrine, he lamented its erosion. '*Stare decisis*', he argued, 'has been sapped of much of the spirit of

362 See Hull, *supra* n. 49, 1327.

363 On Corbin's realist predilections, see Kalman, *supra* n. 3, 98–107; Twining, *supra* n. 12, 27–34; and E. Donald Elliott, 'The Evolutionary Tradition in Jurisprudence', *Columbia L. Rev.*, 85 (1985), 38–94 at 55–9.

the common law,'[364] owing to the fact that Langdellianism precipitated a 'general retreat in legal thinking towards supergeneralized and outworn abstractions'.[365] For all its simplicity, the argument was an ingenious one. Langdellian legal science, so received wisdom had it, was premissed upon an intense respect for *stare decisis*. Yet here was Oliphant, suggesting that Langdellianism did not nurture but rather suffocated the doctrine. How could this be so? Oliphant's answer was that Langdellian formalists tended to conceive of *stare decisis* in an inordinately narrow fashion, that is, as the following of principles—*stare dictis*—rather than as the following of decisions. Langdellian legal science, accordingly, required the student only to seek the general 'doctrine' or 'principle' of a case without any consideration of the peculiar facts upon which the decision itself was founded. In sacrificing particularism in the pursuit of generalized abstractions, Langdellianism had mistaken *stare dictis* for *stare decisis*. '[T]here has', Oliphant summarized, 'been such a shift in our work on cases from particularity to generality of treatment and such a shift of life from the grooves of our present long-standing abstractions, that our scholarship becomes loose and unreal. . . . Our categories of thought have become unreal by life having left them behind and no alert sense of actuality checks our reveries in theory.'[366] The fundamental task facing legal realists, he concluded, is one of securing a return to *stare decisis* proper: 'Because our law students are to be the scholars, advocates, counselors, and judges of tomorrow, their training is the area of supreme strategic importance in this whole situation. That is our opportunity and responsibility. Regaining the values lost to judicial government by the retreat from *stare decisis* and making law more a science of realities and less a theology of doctrines require a radical reorganization of legal education.'[367]

While Oliphant took the view that the formalist conception of *stare decisis* was not the genuine article, other realists were willing to accept Langdellianism at face value and criticize it for its slavish adherence to precedent. 'A decision of a case is no more law than the light from last night's lamp is electricity,' wrote Leon Green.[368] The general tenor of the realist argument was that, in so far as precedents existed, conflict could invariably be found among them, and it was precisely that conflict which allowed—indeed, required—judges to make law.[369] The fundamental failure of the Langdellian reliance on *stare decisis* rested in the unquestioned assumption that precedents bred legal certainty. In truth, so the realist argument went, precedents tend to breed uncertainty.

It was the recognition of this fact which inspired the third realist

[364] Oliphant, *supra* n. 72, 160.
[365] Ibid. 75.
[366] Ibid. 76.
[367] Ibid. 159.
[368] Green, *supra* n. 255, pt. I, 1015.
[369] See generally Kalman, *supra* n. 3, 21–2.

pedagogic strategy: namely, the critique of the case method. At the beginning of the 1950s, Thurman Arnold wrote of the case method that '[n]o more time-wasting system of studying law has ever been devised. . . . Yet a blind faith in the case-by-case system still persists in the great majority of American law schools.'[370] Much the same point had been made by Llewellyn in the 1930s when he denounced the case method as a 'pseudo-Socratic monologue'.[371] Yet, as Arnold pointed out, the case method did indeed survive. Why should this have been so? Legal realism itself seems largely to have been responsible for the longevity of the case method; for, the comments of Arnold and Llewellyn aside, it is possible to discern in the literature of realism a marked reluctance to abandon case method teaching. This is hardly surprising. The qualities of the case method as an efficient and engaging teaching style were appreciated by most American academic lawyers by the early decades of this century.[372] And even realists recognized a good thing when they saw one—even, indeed, when that good thing had Langdellian pedigree. While, moreover, no legal realist would have wished to use the case method as Langdell and his successors had used it, they saw nevertheless that it provided a superb means of encouraging a broadly sceptical approach to the study of law.[373] Thus it was that realists such as Max Radin and Herman Oliphant, though opposed to Langdellian legal science, considered the case method to be a perfect vehicle for demonstrating the shortcomings of that so-called science.[374] The case method could be employed to demonstrate to students that the principles to be found in cases sometimes conflict, that legal doctrine often conceals uncertainties and contradictions, and that judges frequently rely on instinct rather than on precedent.

Legal realism, then, entailed the reorienting rather than the jettisoning of the case method. A similar, if slightly more ruthless strategy was adopted with regard to the traditional case-book. Brian Simpson has suggested that realism contributed significantly to the demise of the treatise-writing tradition in the United States.[375] Possibly it did. Wesley Sturges's 'severely analytical'[376] article, 'Legal Theory and Real Property

[370] Thurman Arnold, *Fair Fights and Foul: A Dissenting Lawyer's Life* (New York: Harcourt, Brace & World, 1951), 263.

[371] Llewellyn, *supra* n. 351, 677, also 653, 666.

[372] See Stevens, *supra* n. 45, 122–3.

[373] See Jerold S. Auerbach, *Unequal Justice: Lawyers and Social Change in Modern America* (New York: Oxford University Press, 1976), 78.

[374] See Max Radin, 'The Education of a Lawyer', *California L. Rev.*, 25 (1937), 676–91; Oliphant, *supra* n. 72, 161.

[375] A. W. B. Simpson, 'The Rise and Fall of the Legal Treatise: Legal Principles and the Forms of Legal Literature', *U. Chicago L. Rev.*, 48 (1981), 632–79 at 677–9.

[376] Grant Gilmore, 'For Wesley Sturges: On the Teaching and Study of Law', *Yale L.J.*, 72 (1963), 646–54 at 651.

Mortgages', is an obvious if unique illustration of realist hostility towards the genre of conventional treatise-writing. Written in collaboration with a third-year student, Samuel O. Clark, Sturges's article is an examination of how 'an American law student'[377] might be expected to conceive of mortgages, in both law and equity, from reading the classic treatises on the subject. By way of a series of rhetorical questions, Sturges demonstrates that any student who cared to examine critically the legal language of the treatises would discover that, certainly as regards mortgages, the relationship between law and equity is defined by inconsistency, uncertainty and conflict. The legal treatises, he insisted, glossed over doctrinal incoherence in the 'fruitless quest'[378] to depict law as a well-nigh flawless body of logically interlocking concepts.

Similar remarks were made by Hessel Yntema with regard to the 'hornbook method' of studying the conflict of laws. According to Yntema, both Joseph Beale and Herbert Goodrich—the prime advocates of this method—used it to promote a brand of 'juristic theology' which confined legal study to 'the squirrel-cage of conceptualism', without any concern whatsoever for 'the realities of judicial administration'.[379] Yet the major contribution of realism to the development of legal writing rested not in the occasional outburst against the legal treatise or the hornbook, but in the more general rejection of the Langdellian-style case-book in favour of a new type of legal text, the 'cases and materials' text.

In one sense, the emergence of this new style of text may be regarded as an academic response to the initiatives of the National Reporter system. An ever-burgeoning body of case material quickly rendered impossible the concept of a 'pure' case-book offering a complete, systematically ordered body of decisions.[380] In a broader sense, however, the evolution of the cases and materials text was part and parcel of the realist disappointment with Langdellian educational goals. Originating at Columbia in the early 1920s,[381] the new case-books, or rather their authors, tended to utilize a variety of 'materials'—statutes, doctrinal commentary, the methods of the social sciences, among other things—in an endeavour to offer to students an idea of how legal doctrines function in a social context. Sometimes, furthermore, these new texts would be structured around novel doctrinal, often comparativist-oriented categories: so that, for example, whereas the old, Langdellian-style case-book would offer *A Selection of Cases on the Law of Contracts*, the new-style text might be comprised of *Cases and*

377 Sturges and Clark, *supra* n. 74, 701.

378 Ibid. 704.

379 Yntema, 'The Hornbook Method', *supra* n. 73, 481.

380 See Albert Ehrenzweig, 'The American Casebook: "Cases and Materials" ', *Georgetown L.J.*, 32 (1944), 224–47 at 225–6.

381 Herman Oliphant's *Cases and Materials on the Law of Trade Regulation* (St. Paul, Minn.: West Publishing Co. 1923) set the ball rolling. See Kalman, *supra* n. 3, 78; also Currie, *supra* n. 91, 337.

Materials on the Law of Corporate Reorganization.[382] Throughout the 1930s, cases and materials texts proliferated to such a degree—a dozen such texts emanated from Yale in 1931 alone—that, by the following decade, they were unquestionably an integral part of the American law school curriculum; indeed, by the early 1950s, the literal case-law instructor had become more or less extinct.[383]

Certain of the cases and materials texts hardly departed radically in substance from the old case-books. But others rather encapsulated the realist disaffection with Langdellianism. Most commonly singled out for its originality is Llewellyn's *Cases and Materials on the Law of Sales* of 1930,[384] a text which, besides having been hailed as 'the first major work of the realist movement',[385] constitutes a germinal expression of some of the ideas which, in later years, would find their way into Llewellyn's drafts of article 2 of the Uniform Commercial Code.[386] Llewellyn's approach to the editing, classification and arrangement of cases and materials was unprecedented. In order to compile a text containing far more legal material than had previously been reproduced in a case-book on sales, he took the bold step of summarizing a good many decisions, thereby 'violating the classic principle' that cases be reproduced in their entirety.[387] He also made extensive use of digests of cases. In both structure and content, the resulting text was a far cry from more conventional, Langdellian-inspired offerings.[388]

Cases and Materials on the Law of Sales also entailed a novel approach to legal doctrine. Rather than simply anchor his discussion on the case law relating to sales, Llewellyn addressed specific matters of economics and business practice—matters which, in his view, shaped the expectations and behaviour of commercial buyers, sellers and middlemen. The opening lines of the first chapter, for example, highlight the function of price: 'Price is the heart of the sales contract; and peculiarly so in sales to a dealer. Ours is a money economy, a price system; business centres on profit; profit centres

[382] See Stevens, *supra* n. 45, 158; *supra* n. 348, 483–4.

[383] See Stevens, *supra* n. 348, 483–4; Woodard, *supra* n. 281, 723; and Albert J. Harno, *Legal Education in the United States: A Report Prepared for the Survey of the Legal Profession* (San Francisco: Bancroft-Whitney, 1953), 69.

[384] Karl N. Llewellyn, *Cases and Materials on the Law of Sales* (Chicago: Callaghan, 1930).

[385] William Twining, 'Two Works of Karl Llewellyn', *Mod. L. Rev.*, 30 (1967), 514–30; *Mod. L. Rev.*, 31 (1968), 165–82 pt. I, 517.

[386] See Twining, *supra* n. 12, 139; and Zipporah Batshaw Wiseman, 'The Limits of Vision: Karl Llewellyn and the Merchant Rules', *Harvard L. Rev.*, 100 (1987), 465–545 at 476. More generally, cf. Eugene F. Mooney, 'Old Kontract Principles and Karl's New Kode: An Essay on the Jurisprudence of Our New Commercial Law', *Villanova L. Rev.*, 11 (1966), 213–258.

[387] Ehrenzweig, *supra* n. 380, 235.

[388] By Llewellyn's estimation, *Cases and Materials on the Law of Sales* was 33% cases, 36% digests, 28% annotations and 3% statutes. See Kalman, *supra* n. 3, 79.

on price.'[389] Unlike earlier writers on the subject, furthermore, Llewellyn emphasized the contractual rather than the proprietary dimension of the law of sales, on the basis that 'the contract for future delivery . . . is far more important to the lawyer in practice and more typical of business transactions in a credit economy'.[390] Students, he insisted, must eschew generalized legal concepts and categories in favour of an essentially pragmatic, particularistic approach to legal doctrine. A classic piece of realist revisionism, and 'a major step forward in the development of teaching tools in American law schools',[391] Llewellyn's case-book refuted the Langdellian conception of doctrine every bit as vigorously as Langdellians themselves had promoted it.

Yet while Llewellyn's case-book epitomized a particular realist achievement—the gradual discrediting of the Langdellian case-book tradition—it also, in another sense, exemplified failure. In the Preface to his work, Llewellyn professed his intention to utilize the findings of experimental logic, social psychology, anthropology and sociology; yet, for the most part, his presentation of the law of sales unfolds without any resort whatsoever to social scientific methods or materials. Generally, those legal realists who produced case-books tended neither to make effective use of the social sciences nor to raise matters of social policy over which such sciences could have cast light.[392] Indeed, for all that it became established in the mainstream of American university law teaching, the cases and materials text stands as a testament to the failure of legal realists to develop a social scientific approach to the study of law beyond the planning stage. Critique of Langdellian assumptions was easy compared with implementing a programme of legal education; and while realists tended to excel at the former task, they fared comparably poorly at the latter. As stated earlier, ideas proliferated; but little emphasis was placed on following through. Quotations from the letters of two Yale law students of the early 1940s illustrate the point. On the one hand, Irving Clark viewed Yale of the 1930s with bright-eyed awe. Under Hutchins's deanship, he claimed, 'Yale shot to the front rank—precisely because it acquired a faculty equipped as no other in the country to present every philosophy of the law, to relate the law to all the other social sciences; a faculty, in short, whose catalytic influence has leavened the thought of lawyers everywhere from Wall Street to Washington.'[393] Grant Gilmore, on the other hand,

389 Llewellyn, *supra* n. 384, 1.

390 Twining, *supra* n. 385, pt. I, 524.

391 Ibid. pt. I, 526.

392 See Kalman, *supra* n. 3, 88–94.

393 Irving Clark, Jr. to Charles Seymour, 26 July 1943, in Charles Seymour Papers, Yale University, Sterling Memorial Library, Manuscripts and Archives Division, box 94, folder 807.

reflecting on his own education in the 1940s, took a less sanguine view of Yale's achievements:

What has most puzzled me over the years in thinking about the instruction we received in the early 1940s is how extremely conventional or traditional it was. . . . Of course the prime movers and shakers (Hutchins, Clark, Douglas, Arnold) had long since left New Haven. However, Underhill Moore, Walton Hamilton, Wesley Sturges, and Harry Shulman (not to mention Arthur Corbin) were still on the faculty—and indeed I took courses with each of them. Without exception, the courses they taught were entirely standard exercises in case law (or, occasionally, statutory) analysis, which would not have been out of place at Harvard. Not a word from any of them about history, jurisprudence, the scientific approach, empirical research—except that Corbin gave a preliminary lecture in the first-year Contracts course on Hohfeldian analysis (after which no more was heard of Hohfeld). . . . If there is anything in the Great Teacher idea, these men were Great Teachers—certainly the greatest I ever studied under. But, by 1940, despite their own deep involvement in the ferment of Legal Realism, they had all evidently decided to exclude from their teaching any reference to the ideas which had concerned, indeed obsessed them, during the 1920s and 1930s.[394]

The intellectual ferment of legal realism, as Karl Llewellyn called it, failed to make much of an impact on the bulk of the American law schools.[395] Even at the schools where it had come to prominence, realism was more an endeavour to relate legal study to legal practice than to make use of the social sciences. The appeal to the social sciences, it turned out, had been but an appeal to 'otherness'. Lawyers had become frustrated with, even jealous of, other lawyers. Harvard seemed to be holding all the best cards, and the social sciences offered law professors—mainly, though by no means exclusively, at other Ivy League universities—a good opportunity for bluff-calling. Here, it was claimed, was a collection of disciplines which would at once expose Langdellianism as antediluvian and inject new life into the study of law. And who, in the 1920s and early 1930s, was to say that these disciplines could not deliver the goods? Only as the 1930s progressed did it become increasingly clear that most legal realists were either unable or unwilling to use social scientific methods to facilitate a genuinely non-Langdellian approach to the teaching of law. Rather than becoming the norm, the interdisciplinary approach developed, or rather disintegrated, into an *ad hoc* affair,[396] to be adopted by particular academics rather than throughout the law school system. Legal realism

[394] Grant Gilmore to John Henry Schlegel, 18 June 1980 (letter supplied to author by Professor J. H. Schlegel).

[395] Stevens, *supra* n. 45, 172.

[396] See Dawson, *supra* n. 126, 408: 'Many of us concluded that what we needed and wanted to know from other disciplines, we would have to learn all by ourselves, with occasional help from friends in other specialties after we had learned enough to ask them questions.'

certainly inspired the future flourishing of interdisciplinary legal research and education. Yet inspiration was basically all that it achieved.

To the four anti-Langdellian, realist pedagogic initiatives outlined above, there may be added a fifth strategy: namely, the critique of the Restatement movement. While this critique was not straightforwardly a rejection of the methods of the Langdellian law school, it was very much a part of the realist assault on legal formalism. Not that every realist viewed the Restatement project with disdain. Herman Oliphant, for example, apparently without irony, lauded the project as 'truly impressive'.[397] But generally, legal realists considered the Restatements to represent 'the high-water mark of conceptual jurisprudence'.[398]

The fundamental ambition of the restaters was not to codify the common law, but, in true Langdellian fashion, to reduce its principles to a simpler and more systematic form. This entailed stripping the major common law fields—contracts, trusts, property, torts, agency, business corporations, conflict of laws—of their doctrinal complexity and leaving only the bare bones of black-letter rules and principles.[399] The first Restatement, of contracts, was completed in 1932; and the task of restating—and re-restating—continues to this day. The longevity of the project is something of a miracle, not least because, during its formative years, it was subjected to sustained and fairly ferocious critical onslaught. Indeed, the Restatements inspired some of the most carefully conceived realist doctrinal critique of the 1930s.[400] They also inspired an equal amount of unashamedly negative polemic. 'The undertaking to restate the rules and principles developed by the English and American courts finds in the field of torts a most hopeless task,' wrote Leon Green in 1928.[401] For Charles Clark, the Restatement of the Law of Contracts possessed 'the rigidity of a code . . .

[397] Oliphant, *supra* n. 72, 71.

[398] Lawrence M. Friedman, *A History of American Law* (2nd edn. New York: Simon & Schuster, 1985), 676.

[399] On the emergence of the Restatement project, see Nathan M. Crystal, 'Codification and the Rise of the Restatement Movement', *Washington L. Rev.*, 54 (1979), 239–73; N. E. H. Hull, 'Restatement and Reform: A New Perspective on the Origins of the American Law Institute', *Law and History Rev.*, 8 (1990), 55–96.

[400] See, in particular, Arthur L. Corbin, 'The Restatement of the Law of Contracts', *Am. Bar Assoc. Jnl.*, 14 (1928), 602–5, 652–6; 'The Restatement of the Common Law by the American Law Institute', *Iowa L. Rev.*, 15 (1929), 19–41; Thurman W. Arnold, 'The Restatement of the Law of Trusts', *Columbia L. Rev.*, 31 (1931), 800–23; Clark, *supra* n. 254, *passim*; Leon Green, 'The Torts Restatement', *Illinois L. Rev.*, 29 (1935), 582–607; Ernest G. Lorenzen and Raymond J. Heilman, 'The Restatement of the Conflict of Laws', *U. Pennsylvania L. Rev.*, 83 (1935), 555–89; Hessel E. Yntema, 'The Restatement of the Law of Conflict of Laws', *Columbia L. Rev.*, 36 (1936), 183–223; William R. Vance, 'The Restatement of the Law of Property', *U. Pennsylvania L. Rev.*, 86 (1937), 173–88.

[401] Green, *supra* n. 255, pt. I, 1014.

without the opportunity for reform and advance which a code affords'.[402] Even William Reynolds Vance, one of the most conservative legal scholars at Yale during the 1930s, was prepared to denounce the Restatement of the Law of Property as a series of 'solemn declarations . . . so obvious that they are rather ludicrous. . . . The judge who would base his decision of any question of law upon these black letter declarations would be worse than lazy; he would be incredibly stupid.'[403]

Possibly the most outspoken critic of the Restatement project was Edward Robinson. '[T]he American Law Institute', he observed, 'has thought that it can help simple-minded lawyers by giving an artificial and arbitrary picture of the principles in terms of which human disputes are supposed to be settled.'[404] However, 'the result thus far secured is hideously difficult. There is some reason to believe that it would be easier and more satisfactory to learn law by random sampling of the cases with all their contradictions and complexities than by reading the abstract propositions in the volumes issued by the Institute.'[405] Indeed, he concluded, '[w]hen one considers these "restatements" of the common law and how they are being formulated, one remembers how the expert theologians got together in the Council of Nicaea and decided by a vote the nature of the Trinity.'[406]

One collaborator in the Restatement project, Dean Herbert Goodrich of the University of Pennsylvania Law School, took offence at Robinson's remarks, condemning them as 'fighting words, clearly passing the limit of fair comment' and 'bitterly resent[ed]' by 'all of us who have put in a share of the sweat and tears which have gone into the effort thus far'.[407] Robinson's Yale *confrère*, Thurman Arnold, offered a purportedly semi-placatory rejoinder. 'Dean Goodrich', Arnold asserted, 'completely misunderstands what Professor Robinson is trying to say, and interprets [his remarks] out of context, as a personal attack on himself and his collaborators.'[408] Whereas Goodrich 'is a disciple of a science *of* law,' Robinson 'is talking in terms of a science *about* law'.[409] And while, '[f]rom the point of view of a science *of* law, the Restatement by the American Law Institute is as near perfection as human beings can make it', from the perspective 'of a science *about* law, the picture is entirely different. To understand the problem as an observer of human affairs . . . it is necessary to describe the great post-war legal inflation of cases and concepts which

[402] Clark, *supra* n. 254, 650.

[403] Vance, *supra* n. 400, 187–88.

[404] Robinson, *supra* n. 21, 260.

[405] Robinson, *supra* n. 247, 36.

[406] Robinson, *supra* n. 21, 261.

[407] Herbert Goodrich, 'Institute Bards and Yale Reviewers', *U. Pennsylvania L. Rev.*, 84 (1936), 449–66 at 452.

[408] Thurman Arnold, 'Institute Priests and Yale Observers—A Reply to Dean Goodrich', *U. Pennsylvania L. Rev.*, 84 (1936), 811–24 at 812.

[409] Ibid. 814.

has not yet reached its peak.'[410] The ever-inflating body of published cases and legal materials, Arnold insisted, 'is beginning to be a great burden. . . . And the only thing that can stop it is a complete change of attitude which will produce a different and simpler type of legal literature.'[411] The Restatements, he concluded, were not the solution to the problem.

But then, what was the solution to the problem? By Arnold's own admission, a science about law—whatever that might entail—would provide only a means of understanding the problem. He himself, rather than suggest a method for coping with the crisis of an ever-ballooning legal literature, simply evades the issue: 'The writer suggests no new formula because at present it is only too evident that no new formula will be accepted.'[412] Again, as with the treatment of Langdellian legal education generally, one finds in the literature of realism a reluctance to develop critique of the Restatements into solid proposals for reform. Possibly this reluctance stemmed from the fact that, for all the formalist underpinnings of the Restatement movement, one of its primary goals—the simplification of the common law—rather echoed the general realist disdain for legal verbosity and word magic. Fred Rodell, for example, wondered why legal documents lack the plainness of language of cook-books, almanacs or columns of classified advertisements: surely, he reasoned, it must be possible 'to cut through those layers upon layers of verbal varnish and bare the true grain that lies beneath'.[413] Such a sentiment would not have been out of place at the Harvard Law School, which he so despised. The restaters too, after all, were trying to uncover the true grain of the law.

REALISM AND THE REGULATORY STATE

The changes which certain legal realists were busy trying to procure in the law schools seem minor when compared with those of a more general nature that were taking place in American law and society. By the early decades of this century, the process of 'statutorification' had been set in motion.[414] Nineteenth century legislative activity, most of which had taken place in commercial law, had largely been a matter of re-casting existing

[410] Ibid. 817. [411] Ibid. 822. [412] Ibid. 813.

[413] Rodell, *supra* n. 213, 123; 'Judicial Activists, Judicial Self-Deniers, Judicial Review and the First Amendment—Or, How to Hide the Melody of What You Mean Behind the Words of What You Say', *Georgetown L.J.*, 47 (1959), 483–90 at 484.

[414] Calabresi, *A Common Law for the Age of Statutes*, *supra* n. 17, 1. The classic exposition of this point is to be found in James McCauley Landis, 'Statutes and the Sources of Law', in R. Pound (ed.), *Harvard Legal Essays Written in Honor of and Presented to Joseph Henry Beale and Samuel Williston* (Cambridge, Mass.: Harvard University Press, 1934), 213–246.

common law principles.[415] By the 1930s, the significance of statute-making had altered radically. Following the Wall Street Crash of 1929, the United States national income dropped from 81 billion dollars to 41 billion dollars in 1932. During this same period, 85,000 businesses went into dissolution, 5,761 banks failed and 9 million savings accounts disappeared. Between 1932 and 1933, somewhere in the region of 13 to 16 million—roughly a quarter of the labour force of the time—were unemployed.[416] On the continent, furthermore, the emergence of Stalinism and fascism was highlighting both the importance and the political precariousness of government by democracy. Still clinging to the coat-tails of the *Lochner* era, the American courts proved slow to respond to social change. Statute-making, in contrast, offered the possibility of efficient and effective social planning. Through the creation of statutes, institutional constraints could be placed upon economic freedom and the foundations could be laid for the development of a democratic welfare state. In short, statute-making offered the key to curbing the worst effects of the Depression while promoting the credo of Rooseveltian welfare liberalism. Within the famous first 'Hundred Days' of the New Deal, the statutorification of American law had arrived with a vengeance.

The coming of statutorification meant more than just Roosevelt working in tandem with Congress to produce an unprecedented outpouring of legislation. For the passing of legislation itself often necessitated the founding of new federal government bureaus and independent administrative agencies, charged with the task of monitoring specific social concerns and empowered to apply laws and issue rulings. The dramatic increase in legislation signalled an equally dramatic boost in administrative activity. When statutorification arrived, the regulatory state arrived with it.

Early twentieth century American administrative lawyers—what few of them there were—were hardly surprised by this development. As early as 1915, the pioneer of modern American administrative law, Ernst Freund, had advocated an increase in delegative legislation. 'Legislative power can', he argued, 'be exercised more effectually and more in accordance with the spirit of the Constitution through delegation [to administrative commissions] than directly.'[417] As the century progressed, administrative scholars, Freund included, began to reject this notion of delegation, on the basis that the promotion of responsible administrative decision-making

[415] See Grant Gilmore, 'On Statutory Obsolescence', *U. Colorado L. Rev.*, 39 (1967), 461–77 at 466.

[416] It almost goes without saying that the literature on the Depression period in United States history is voluminous. For a reliable account of the period, see Lester V. Chandler, *America's Greatest Depression* (New York: Harper & Row, 1970).

[417] Ernst Freund, *Standards of American Legislation* (Chicago: University of Chicago Press, 1965; orig. publ. 1917), 302. The book was written originally as a series of lectures for delivery at Johns Hopkins University in 1915.

demands of the legislature not that it authorizes widespread delegation, but that it endeavours to constrain the discretionary exercise of legislative power by issuing precise directives detailing the scope and purpose of particular administrative initiatives.[418] Yet for all that administrative law developed gradually towards a doctrine of non-delegation,[419] the basic philosophy of regulation remained constant. The advantage of delegating powers to administrative agencies, Freund had argued in 1915, is that such bodies 'are likely to be better trained and informed and more professional in their attitude than legislative bodies'.[420] More or less the same sentiment emerged again in James Landis's Storrs Lecture to the Yale Law School in 1938. 'Efficiency in the process of governmental regulation is best served by the creation of more rather than less agencies', Landis insisted.[421] 'With the rise of regulation, the need for expertness became dominant; for the art of regulating an industry requires knowledge of the details of its operation.'[422] Such 'expertness' was not to be found in the American courts, for judges, trained in the common law tradition, were 'jacks-of-all-trades and masters of none'.[423] The proliferation of administrative agencies during the New Deal era 'sprang from a distrust of the ability of the judicial process to make the necessary adjustments in the development of both law and regulatory methods as they related to particular industrial problems'.[424] Specialization was the key to successful regulation; and the agencies, unlike the courts, were staffed by specialists.

Yet these were specialists who, for all their expertise, enjoyed a great deal of discretion. It would be intolerably inefficient, Landis argued, to require administrators to follow rigid judicial procedures.[425] Others, however, were not convinced. In some quarters, not least in the Supreme Court, the delegation of broad discretion to administrators was considered

[418] See Ernst Freund, *Administrative Powers over Persons and Property* (Chicago: University of Chicago Press, 1928), 582–3.

[419] On which see Richard B. Stewart, 'The Reformation of American Administrative Law', *Harvard L. Rev.*, 88 (1975), 1667–813 at 1672–97.

[420] Freund, *supra* n. 417, 301.

[421] James M. Landis, *The Administrative Process* (New Haven, Conn.: Yale University Press, 1938), 24.

[422] Ibid. 23.

[423] Ibid. 31. According to Mitchell Franklin, writing in 1934, '[t]he very existence of the administrative body indicates that in some measure the common law procedure has failed.' Mitchell Franklin, 'Administrative Law in the United States', *Tulane L. Rev.*, 8 (1934), 483–506 at 498.

[424] Landis, *supra* n. 421, 30. For a discussion of Landis's position, see Thomas K. McCraw, *Prophets of Regulation: Charles Francis Adams, Louis D. Brandeis, James M. Landis, Alfred E. Kahn* (Cambridge, Mass.: Belknap Press, 1984), 212–16.

[425] Landis, *supra* n. 421, 10–24, 46, 91–100.

inimical to the principles of separation of powers and formal justice.[426] Indeed, one of the Court's primary reasons for striking down certain New Deal statutes during the mid-1930s was that legislative delegation, under the terms of those statutes, appeared to be running riot.[427] By the middle of the next decade, judicial power to review administrative action was supplemented by statutory control in the form of the Administrative Procedure Act of 1946. Certainly the political developments abroad which culminated in the War had convinced many American lawyers that bureaucracy must be kept firmly in check. But, for some, the experience of the New Deal had proved equally persuasive. By the late 1930s, Roscoe Pound, once keen for the expansion of administrative powers,[428] was rallying against what he termed the recrudescence of administrative absolutism.[429] Like Friedrich Hayek, he took the view that administrative action, being premissed generally on the prioritization of collectivist planning rather than on the maintenance of individualized justice, could lead only to the erosion of the Rule of Law ideal.[430] Certainly as Pound expressed it, the view seemed rather exaggerated, if not hysterical.[431] It was a view with a peculiar political context, set, as it was, not only against the backdrop of political tyranny abroad, but also against Roosevelt's endeavour to enlarge the composition of the Supreme Court from nine to fifteen Justices in a bid to create a judiciary more sympathetic to New Deal legislative programmes.[432]

[426] See e.g. John Dickinson, 'Legal Change and the Rule of Law', *Dickinson L. Rev.*, 44 (1940), 149–161 at 158–9; and also Stewart, *supra* n. 419, 1678–9. For the origins of the American distrust of delegated authority, see Alexander Hamilton, 'Federalist Papers, LXXVIII: A View of the Constitution of the Judicial Department in Relation to the Tenure of Good Behaviour' in James Madison, Alexander Hamilton and John Jay, *The Federalist Papers* (ed. I. Kramnick, Harmondsworth: Penguin, 1987; orig. publ. 1788), 436–42 at 438 ('every act of a delegated authority, contrary to the tenor of the commission under which it is exercised, is void').

[427] See cases cited *supra* n. 238; and also Currie *supra* n. 194, 517–23.

[428] See Roscoe Pound, 'The Growth of Administrative Justice', *Wisconsin L. Rev.*, 2 (1924), 321–39 at 330–1.

[429] See Roscoe Pound, Walter F. Dodd, James R. Garfield, O. R. McGuire and Robert F. McGuire, 'Report of the Special Committee on Administrative Law', *American Bar Assoc. Reports*, 63 (1938), 331–68 at 342–54; Roscoe Pound, 'The Recrudescence of Absolutism', *Sewanee Review*, 47 (1939), 18–28 at 26; 'Individualization of Justice', *Fordham L. Rev.*, 7 (1938), 153–66 at 160–5.

[430] See Roscoe Pound, 'The Future of Law', *Yale L.J.*, 47 (1937), 1–13 at 12; 'Modern Administrative Law', *Reports of the Virginia State Bar Association*, 51 (1939), 372–88; *Social Control Through Law* (New Haven, Conn.: Yale University Press, 1942), 27. Cf. also Friedrich A. von Hayek, *The Road to Serfdom* (London: Routledge & Kegan Paul, 1944), 54–65.

[431] See David Wigdor, *Roscoe Pound: Philosopher of Law* (Westport, Conn. : Greenwood Press, 1974), 271.

[432] For discussion of Roosevelt's court-packing plan and its genesis, see William E. Leuchtenburg, *Franklin D. Roosevelt and the New Deal, 1932–1940* (New York: Harper & Row, 1963), 231–8; and Kermit L. Hall, William M. Wiecek and Paul Finkelman, *American Legal History: Cases and Materials* (New York: Oxford University Press, 1991), 483–6.

Pound's intellectual development—from the supremely confident and iconoclastic critic of mechanical jurisprudence to the rather reactionary opponent of the New Deal administrative agencies—highlights the manner of development of early twentieth-century American jurisprudence itself. By the late 1930s, Pound was faced with a totally different jurisprudential ball-game from that which he had first confronted three decades earlier.[433] With the arrival of statutorification and the regulatory state had come the danger—or the possibility, depending on how one viewed it—of widespread political manipulation of law. It was precisely such manipulation to which Pound was objecting. Despite the faults of the common law system as enshrined in the Langdellian tradition, he seemed to be arguing, it had at least eschewed the tendency towards overt politicization which was so much a feature of the modern regulatory apparatus. Statutorification had changed the entire complexion of American law. With the coming of the New Deal, lawyers trained in common law techniques were suddenly expected to speak a new and different language, the language of the administrative state.[434] Legal realism, Pound insisted, was instrumental in creating that language: 'realist doctrine . . . may be seen in action in administrative absolutism'.[435]

This assumption—that realist jurisprudence was New Deal jurisprudence—is something of a commonplace. Yet it needs to be questioned very seriously. Certainly some legal realists became active participants in Roosevelt's New Deal programmes. But quite what bearing realist legal thought had on the New Deal administration—or vice versa—is difficult to ascertain. In 1934, Jerome Frank, having recently been appointed by Roosevelt as General Counsel for the Agricultural Adjustment Administration, argued that realist jurisprudence and New Deal politics share a basic faith in experimentalism: both treat legal institutions 'as human contrivances to be judged by their everyday human consequences'.[436] Indeed that, he suggested, is why many legal realists were eager for a piece of the political action: they were 'stimulated by the opportunity to help contrive new governmental agencies to be used experimentally as means for achieving better results in agriculture, industry, labour conditions, taxation, corporate reorganization, municipal finance, unemployment relief, and a multitude of other subjects'.[437] While certain legal realists did

433 As Pound himself recognized. See Roscoe Pound, 'The Ideal and the Actual in Law—Forty Years After', *George Washington L. Rev.*, 1 (1933), 431–47 at 443.

434 See Bruce A. Ackerman, *Reconstructing American Law* (Cambridge, Mass.: Harvard University Press, 1984), 6–11; and cf. Leon Green, 'Must the Legal Profession Undergo a Spiritual Rebirth?', *Indiana L.J.*, 16 (1940), 15–30 at 23–4.

435 Roscoe Pound, *Contemporary Juristic Theory* (Claremont, CA: Ward Ritchie, 1940), 20.

436 Frank, *supra* n. 13, 12414; and cf. Robinson, *supra* n. 21, 239.

437 Frank, *supra* n. 13, 12414.

indeed rise to the challenge of the New Deal, this is hardly proof that realist jurisprudence was wrapped up in Rooseveltian politics.

The case of Thurman Arnold is illustrative. In 1937, Arnold ridiculed the essentially symbolic, toothless nature of American antitrust regulation. 'The antitrust laws,' he asserted, 'being a preaching device, naturally performed only the functions of preaching.'[438] In the following year, Roosevelt appointed Arnold to succeed Robert Jackson as head of the Antitrust Division of the Justice Department. Suddenly, Arnold was vested with the responsibility of administering the very laws which he had debunked only a year earlier. How could he be expected to do this with conviction?

Arnold's answer to those who viewed with scepticism his ability to enforce the antitrust laws was simple: as a writer, he had attempted merely to observe how these laws were used—or rather, not used—throughout the Depression period; once in office, however, he regarded his task to be one of enforcing these laws and ensuring that New Deal antitrust policy was implemented and administered efficiently.[439] Those who doubted the sincerity of his resolve were to be proved wrong. By the time he left the Justice Department in 1943, he had expanded significantly both the budget and the staff of his Division; fiscal appropriations had almost quadrupled during his five years of office; and he had filed, and won, more antitrust cases than the Justice Department had initiated in its entire previous history.[440] More importantly, Arnold revived the idea that antitrust laws could form a basis for public policy. Particularly significant was the emphasis which he placed on the symbolic function of the Sherman Antitrust Act of 1890. This Act, he insisted, represents the American ideal of free competition; and while earlier interpretations had concealed and encouraged business consolidation—owing primarily to the fact that the terminology of the Act was so vague as to permit the concentration of corporate wealth in the absence of vigorous enforcement policies—it could, if interpreted differently, be applied more efficiently as a means of protecting consumers' interests. Basically, what mattered was the manner in which the Act was conceived and promoted as a political symbol. Arnold's tactic was to promote it as 'a symbol of our traditional ideals'—that is, not only as a symbol of free enterprise, but as a symbol of democracy itself.[441]

[438] Arnold, *supra* n. 241, 211–12.

[439] See Arnold, *supra* n. 370, 136.

[440] See generally Corwin D. Edwards, 'Thurman Arnold and the Antitrust Laws', *Political Science Quarterly*, 58 (1943), 338–55.

[441] See Thurman Arnold, *The Bottlenecks of Business* (New York: Reynal & Hitchcock, 1940), 92; *Democracy and Free Enterprise* (Norman: University of Oklahoma Press, 1942),

What is particularly interesting about Arnold's trust-busting activities is the manner in which he was willing to separate theory and practice. In his writings of the mid-1930s, he had insisted that, to be effective, institutions must escape from their ideals. Yet, as head of the Antitrust Division, his primary assertion was that business institutions could not be effective if they failed to promote the ideal of free competition as embodied in the Sherman Act. While, as a legal writer, Arnold had denounced the enshrining of the *laissez-faire* ideal in symbolic legislation, as a New Dealer, he was more than happy to embrace this ideal, legislation and all, if it served a desired political goal.[442] Thurman Arnold the legal realist was a rather different beast than Thurman Arnold the New Dealer.

The point for emphasis is simple: while legal realists such as Arnold, Frank, Oliphant, Clark, William O. Douglas and Felix Cohen may have flocked to Washington to work under Roosevelt, they did not necessarily take their realist ideas with them. Certainly, at a very generalized level, realist jurisprudence and New Deal politics intermeshed. This is hardly surprising. Whereas a basic tenet of realism was that the abstract concepts of legal formalism must be brought down from the clouds and shown for what they are—that is, limited, pliable, often flawed tools for dealing with disputes and social problems—an equally basic requirement of the New Deal agencies (especially during the first New Deal programme, when administrative experimentation was considered a necessity) was a legal staff trained to treat law as a tool for shaping social policy. This explained, Karl Llewellyn believed, why students educated in the values of legal realism tended to make good New Deal lawyers.[443] There has been a tendency, however, too readily to assume that the New Deal lawyer put realism into political practice. In fact, as G. Edward White has remarked, '[g]raduates of law schools in the 1930s . . . did not necessarily join the New Deal because they had been imbued with realist messages, nor did the existence of New Deal programmes necessarily provide a stimulus for the articulation of Realist jurisprudential theories.'[444] Apart from the institutionalist-realist critique of *laissez-faire*, the tenor of which re-emerged in a good measure of New Deal legislation, realist jurisprudence made a fairly limited impact on American politics in the 1930s.

46; and cf. more generally Alan Brinkley, 'The New Deal and the Idea of the State', in S. Fraser and G. Gerstle (eds.), *The Rise and Fall of the New Deal Order, 1930–1980* (Princeton, NJ: Princeton University Press, 1989), 85–121.

442 See generally Duxbury, 'Some Radicalism about Realism?' *supra* n. 3, 34–5; and also Douglas Ayer, 'In Quest of Efficiency: The Ideological Journey of Thurman Arnold in the Interwar Period', *Stanford L. Rev.*, 23 (1971), 1049–86.

443 See Llewellyn, *supra* n. 351, 662.

444 G. Edward White, 'Recapturing New Deal Lawyers', *Harvard L. Rev.*, 102 (1988), 489–521 at 514.

The reasons for this may be many. But if one reason stands out above others, it is that realism never truly evolved into a jurisprudence of legislation and administrative regulation. First-year courses in administrative law began to appear at many law schools in the 1930s. But these courses tended to be court-centred, focusing primarily on judicial review of administrative action. It would be another decade before there was widespread academic recognition that the activities of administrative agencies themselves were an appropriate subject for legal study.[445] Furthermore, if any school deserves to be described as pioneering in the administrative law field, it is Harvard.[446] Purely as regards the recruitment of lawyers to the New Deal administrative agencies, it was Felix Frankfurter—a Harvardian, and a man whom Llewellyn declined to label a realist[447]—who served as Roosevelt's principal talent scout.[448] Certain of Frankfurter's students—figures such as James Landis, Louis Jaffe and Charles Wyzanski—not only acted as consultants to the Roosevelt government on questions of administrative law and practice but also wrote on and taught the subject.[449] If anything bound these and other Harvard-educated administrative lawyers together, aside from their indebtedness to Frankfurter, it was a general feeling that, just as the courts of the 1930s, in exercising judicial review, often failed to appreciate the nature and objectives of administrative decision-making, so too studies of law from an essentially court-centred perspective tended to misconceive or neglect the legislative basis of modern administrative regulation.[450]

By no means, then, did administrative law find its first foothold in the realist law schools. Indeed, it has been suggested that realism stultified rather than fostered the development of administrative law as an academic discipline. According to William Chase, for Columbia and Yale, '[b]reaking with "Harvard" had meant replacing, a little sooner than Harvard did, an older conception of the nature of judge-made law with a newer one, or using a little earlier social science materials to supplement the study of cases. But the experience of the case class remained the balance wheel of

[445] See Stevens, *supra* n. 45, 160; *supra* n. 348, 487.

[446] See William C. Chase, *The American Law School and the Rise of Administrative Government* (Madison: University of Wisconsin Press, 1982), x.

[447] See Llewellyn, *supra* n. 10, 1227. Fred Rodell's view of Frankfurter as an anti-realist bordered on paranoia. See Duxbury, 'In the Twilight of Legal Realism', *supra* n. 3, 386.

[448] See Johnson, *supra* n. 101, 139; Leuchtenburg, *supra* n. 432, 64; and also G. Edward White, 'Felix Frankfurter, the Old Boy Network, and the New Deal: The Placement of Elite Lawyers in Public Service in the 1930s', in his *Intervention and Detachment: Essays in Legal History and Jurisprudence* (New York: Oxford University Press, 1994), 149–74.

[449] See H. N. Hirsch, *The Enigma of Felix Frankfurter* (New York: Basic Books, 1981), 99–111.

[450] See Chase, *supra* n. 446, 141–2; also Robert M. Cooper, 'Administrative Justice and the Role of Discretion', *Yale L.J.*, 47 (1938), 577–602 at 596–7.

the professional law teacher's existence, determining for him what was "strictly legal" and what he should be about in his scholarship.'[451] While legal realists were hardly hostile to the growth of legislation[452]—and indeed occasionally encouraged such growth in certain areas of private law[453]—they were nonetheless concerned mainly with adjudication rather than with administration or the interpretation of statutes. When, in 1930, Max Radin offered a realist perspective on statutory interpretation, concluding that the intent of the legislature is irrelevant because generally undiscoverable,[454] James Landis pronounced his arguments to be a mixture of the uninformed and the unintelligible.[455] Ignoring 'not only theoretical but practical considerations of Anglo-American government',[456] Landis asserted, Radin seemed unaware of the fact that '[l]egislative history . . . affords in many instances accurate and compelling guides to legislative meaning.'[457] For example, '[t]he voting down of an amendment or its acceptance . . . may disclose real evidence of intent.'[458] Legal realism had emerged primarily as an endeavour to discredit nineteenth-century formalist notions about private law doctrine; and for all that certain so-called realists became eminent New Deal administrators, realist jurisprudence itself, lacking a distinct public law dimension, failed to develop a critical literature devoted either to administrative regulation or to statutory interpretation. The conservatism of legal realism rested ultimately in the fact that it remained a private law jurisprudence in a

[451] Chase, *supra* n. 446, 116.

[452] See Yntema, *supra* n. 14, 325–6; Hans A. Linde, 'Judges, Critics, and the Realist Tradition', *Yale L.J.*, 82 (1972), 227–56 at 227–8; Julius Cohen, 'Towards Realism in Legisprudence', *Yale L.J.*, 59 (1950), 886–97 (attempting to extend realist insights beyond judge-made law to legislation). Nor were realist insights relevant only to common law jurisdictions. See Fritz Morstein Marx, 'Juristischer Realismus in den Vereinigten Staaten von Amerika', *Revue internationale de la théorie du droit*, 10 (1936), 28–38 at 31; though cf. Fuller, *supra* n. 317, 438.

[453] Llewellyn's work on the Uniform Commercial Code is exemplary here—on which, see Wiseman, *supra* n. 386, *passim*.

[454] Max Radin, 'Statutory Interpretation', *Harvard L. Rev.*, 43 (1930), 863–85.

[455] James M. Landis, 'A Note on "Statutory Interpretation" ', *Harvard L. Rev.*, 43 (1930), 886–93 at 887. See also, generally, Frederick J. de Sloovère, 'The Functions of Judge and Jury in the Interpretation of Statutes, *Harvard L. Rev.*, 46 (1933), 1086–110.

[456] Landis, ibid.

[457] Landis, ibid. 889. More generally, on Radin and Landis, see Patrick O. Gudridge, 'Legislation in Legal Imagination: Introductory Exercises', *U. Miami L. Rev.*, 37 (1983), 493–572; and William N. Eskridge, Jr., *Dynamic Statutory Interpretation* (unpublished mimeograph, Georgetown University Law Center, Washington, DC, n.d. [on file with author: copy supplied by Professor Eskridge]), ch. 7 ('A Jurisprudential History of Extrinsic Sources in Statutory Interpretation').

[458] Landis, *supra* n. 455, 889. Radin continued, nevertheless, to develop a realist perspective on statutory interpretation. See further Max Radin, 'Solving Problems by Statute', *Oregon L. Rev.*, 14 (1934), 90–107; and compare his 'A Short Way With Statutes', *Harvard L. Rev.*, 56 (1942), 388–426.

public law world. The problems of modern administrative government never supplemented its original critical agenda.[459]

CONCLUSION

There are, to this day, lawyers here and there who claim to be 'legal realists'.[460] They are, however, a very rare breed. The common view is that realism is something which modern lawyers outgrew once they had assimilated its primary messages.[461] But what were those messages?

The fact is that 'realism' was a complex array of messages, some of which seemed rather feeble once placed in an institutional context. Legal realists made a good deal of fuss about bringing social sciences to the law schools. But they did disappointingly little with such sciences once they had got them there. Legal realists rallied against the Langdellian pedagogic framework. But they failed to devise a convincing alternative framework of their own. By shining a harsh spotlight on the system of *stare decisis*, legal realists cleared the way for the growth of legislation. But they proved themselves rather prudish once the 'orgy of statute making' was set in motion.[462] Some legal realists were drawn to New Deal politics. But the overlap between jurisprudence and politics turned out to be largely adventitious.

Such a catalogue of missed opportunities rather suggests that legal realists generally lost their nerve when faced with the implications of their own jurisprudential constructions.[463] Realism evolved as a broad critique of the formalist assumptions at the basis of late nineteenth and early twentieth-century private law doctrine and teaching. Beyond this critique, however, there remained little but a marked absence of vision. Rather than emerge as the jurisprudence of the New Deal, realism was outstripped by political and legal developments, and when various realists left their faculties to head for Washington they did so not out of a desire to put experimental jurisprudence into practice, but in search of promising career prospects. The development of administrative law as an academic subject, further-

[459] Bruce Ackerman argues that 'it was only by assimilating large chunks of Realist wisdom' that the legal profession of the 1930s 'managed to preserve so much of its traditional common law discourse'. Ackerman, *supra* n. 434, 13.

[460] See e.g. John E. Nowak, 'Resurrecting Realist Jurisprudence: The Political Bias of Burger Court Justices', *Suffolk Univ. L. Rev.*, 17 (1983), 549–620; 'Realism, Nihilism, and the Supreme Court: Do the Emperors Have Nothing but Robes?', *Washburn L.J.*, 22 (1983), 246–67.

[461] See e.g. Twining, *supra* n. 2, 381–3.

[462] The metaphor belongs to Gilmore, *supra* n. 64, 95.

[463] See Schlegel, 'From the Yale Experience', *supra* n. 3, 460; 'The Singular Case of Underhill Moore', *supra*, n. 3, 196.

more, remained principally in the hands of the Harvard Law School, where the study of the activities of legislatures and administrative agencies as well as of courts was gradually broadened to cover the entire legal process (see Chapter 4). With the entrenchment of the regulatory state, realism had conceded defeat.

Realism had made a fairly profound impact, nevertheless, on American jurisprudential culture. Even in the late 1930s, the critique of legal formalism continued in certain quarters to touch some particularly sensitive nerves. Indeed, there existed a feeling that realism, especially in its anti-Langdellian guise, had violated a basic sense of legal integrity which needed to be restored. Massive political upheavals both at home and abroad had convinced many American lawyers that legal systems ought to promote not *ad hoc* justice, but political values and moral principles founded on genuine social consensus. In the eyes of certain detractors, realist scepticism seemed to deny the possibility of such consensus.[464] As legal realism slowly faded from view, American academic lawyers began to acquire a sense that there was a good deal of jurisprudential rebuilding to be done.

464 See, generally, Neil Duxbury, 'The Reinvention of American Legal Realism', *Legal Studies*, 12 (1992), 137–77.

3

Lawyers for the Future

We saw, in the previous chapter, that no sooner had the mood of realism emerged in certain of the American law schools than it became the subject of fairly intense critical reaction. From the 1930s onwards, various legal writers began to detect in the writings of Oliver Wendell Holmes and his intellectual successors arguments which seemed not simply to fly in the face of conventional democratic wisdom but implicitly to support ethical relativism and political tyranny. The consequence of this perception was that legal realism came to be conceived in markedly narrow terms. Rather than being treated as the diverse assortment of professional and educational initiatives which have been identified, it was taken to stand for something much less complex: for the sceptical—or, as some detractors would have it, nihilistic—insistence that neither morals nor rules necessarily guide or even influence legal policy and decision-making. At its crudest, the anti-realist critique entailed reading into the literature of legal realism an essentially anti-democratic ideology to which no so-called realist would consciously have subscribed. Caricatured as communistic and totalitarian jurisprudence',[1] with its roots in the faith that might equals right, realism was branded 'unacceptable to those who look for justice, liberty, and the democratic way of life, under law'.[2] It was in this way that, during the middle period of this century, realism came to be accorded an historico-political identity which bore little relation to the professional, pedagogic and general sociological concerns which motivated realist legal thought.[3]

Despite being rooted in caricature, the anti-realist critique was significant, for it epitomized a general mid-twentieth-century sense of anxiety over the threat which totalitarianism seemed to pose for the future survival of American democratic theory and policy.[4] Fascism and communism had alerted many American lawyers to the importance of treating law not

[1] Francis E. Lucey, 'Jurisprudence and the Future of Social Order', *Social Science*, 16 (1941), 211–17 at 213.

[2] Miriam T. Rooney, 'Law and the New Logic', *Proceedings of the American Catholic Philosophical Association*, 16 (1940), 192–222 at 217.

[3] For a development of this argument, see Neil Duxbury, 'The Reinvention of American Legal Realism', *Legal Studies*, 12 (1992), 137–77.

[4] For an analysis of this anxiety, see Edward A. Purcell, Jr., *The Crisis of Democratic Theory: Scientific Naturalism and the Problem of Value* (Lexington: University Press of Kentucky, 1973); Robert A. Skotheim, *Totalitarianism and American Social Thought* (New York: Holt, Rinehart and Winston, 1971), 38–67.

merely as a system of social control, but also as a system for promoting and maintaining the social values of a liberal democracy. Academic lawyers in particular were beginning to consider the teaching of 'correct' political values to be a legitimate feature of the modern law school. 'For decent politics,' Karl Llewellyn had asked as early as 1935, 'what training do our law schools offer? A course in Constitutional Law, perhaps a sketchy course in Legislation. Trade Regulation may be added, or some new venture say on federal legislation. But what of *sustained* work, *throughout* the course, on the wherewithal for judging and *shaping* policy intelligently?'[5]

Llewellyn's highlighting of the problem of bringing policy considerations into legal education was, in part, a comment on the failure of the American law schools—especially the Ivy League law schools[6]—adequately to train lawyers for the New Deal. While the New Deal cast light on the shortcomings of the modern law school, however, it equally pointed the way towards pedagogic change. As we saw at the end of the previous chapter, there emerged during the 1930s the first coterie of American legal experts, entrusted to oversee the administrative process. Lawyers drafted New Deal statutes, served in the administrative agencies and shaped the common law of regulation which emerged from agency decisions. In so far as the major law schools devised various piecemeal initiatives—particularly in the form of courses along the lines of those suggested by Llewellyn in the quotation above—with a view to training law students for the Roosevelt administration, it is fair to say that American legal education responded to the New Deal by producing an élite of well qualified, highly skilled, dynamic legal professionals versed to at least some degree in the language of the modern regulatory state.[7] But the challenge posed by the New Deal to the modern American law school did not end there. A legal career in government was a sign of talent, and administrative experience quickly became a marketable professional commodity. In particular, New Deal lawyers trained in commercial areas such as antitrust, securities and trade agreements were able to move easily from government service to corporate practice. Professional training 'in the public interest' became a means of enhancing legal career prospects.[8] The New Deal had, in effect, promoted

[5] Karl N. Llewellyn, 'On What is Wrong With So-Called Legal Education', *Columbia L. Rev.*, 35 (1935), 651–78 at 656. On the politics of Llewellyn's own jurisprudence, see Kenneth M. Casebeer, 'Escape From Liberalism: Fact and Value in Karl Llewellyn', *Duke L.J.*, [1977], 671–703.

[6] See Llewellyn, *supra* n. 5, 652.

[7] On the development of this language, see Bruce A. Ackerman, *Reconstructing American Law* (Cambridge, Mass.: Harvard University Press, 1984), 6–22.

[8] See Jerold S. Auerbach, *Unequal Justice: Lawyers and Social Change in Modern America* (New York: Oxford University Press, 1976), 224–30. The notion of 'public interest' law has, in the United States, a long and detailed history encompassing the work of the ACLU, the

an image of the major law school graduate as somehow blessed with a special form of expertise—an expertise as suited to the efficient handling and running of, say, a large corporate law firm as it was to the enforcement of the New Deal regulatory apparatus. It seemed almost inevitable—as Llewellyn had recognized as early as 1935—that, in the future, the major American law schools at least would be expected to produce graduates in conformity with this image.

While the New Deal marked the emergence of the modern American lawyer as policy maker, however, the type of lawyer-cum-policy-maker envisaged during the Roosevelt era quickly became an anachronism. The economic problems which had essentially dictated the nature of policy development throughout the New Deal years rapidly evaporated as it became clear that the United States would be going to war. Military and industrial mobilization heralded the rehabilitation of big business, and the Roosevelt administration was able, at last, to put an end to the economic depression which had blighted it in peace-time. By the early 1940s, New Deal policies had been superseded by wartime policies, and the idea that law schools should instil in their students what Llewellyn had termed 'decent politics' had come to mean something rather different from what it had meant in 1935. Policy no longer revolved around the Rooseveltian goal of securing prosperity in peace-time. Rather, policy revolved around the affirmation and promotion of democratic sensibilities both at home and abroad. Faith in such sensibilities intensified as the Second World War came to an end. In a world witnessing the emergence of communism as a dominant international ideology, '[o]nly the United States had the power to engage fully in international counterrevolution and sustain the forces of conservatism for long periods of time, and it was this militant intervention into the affairs of literally every area of the world that set the pattern for postwar world politics. By 1945, Washington's decision to undertake that role was an unquestioned postulate in America's plans for the future of its power in the world.'[9] At the foundation of post-war American foreign policy rested the belief that the individualist values of a liberal-democratic society are indispensable to a peaceful and prosperous world order.

The changing face of American politics between the New Deal years and the post-war years is at the heart of this chapter. Part of the failure of realist jurisprudence, we have seen, was that it was unable significantly to shape New Deal policy-making. During the Second World War, there

NAACP and people such as Brandeis, Chaffee and Frankfurter. In this chapter, the term 'public interest' is used in a narrow sense, relating specifically to the policy science perspective in American jurisprudence.

[9] Gabriel Kolko, *The Politics of War: The World and United States Foreign Policy, 1943–1945* (New York: Random House, 1968), 622.

emerged at the Yale Law School a peculiar form of realist-inspired jurisprudence which purported to accord far more significance to the matter of policy formation than so-called legal realists had ever done. This new jurisprudence—the jurisprudence of Harold Dwight Lasswell and Myres Smith McDougal—was concerned not with New Deal policies but with emerging wartime policies.[10] Indeed, after the war, Lasswell and McDougal began to focus less on the intellectual impoverishment of the North American law schools—this having provided the initial spur for their collaboration—and more on the problem of how to establish a post-war world order in accordance with American democratic values. Guided by post-war American foreign policy, Lasswell and McDougal gradually transformed their own conception of post-realist jurisprudence into a theory of international law.

The basic purpose of this chapter is to develop a critical intellectual history of the jurisprudence of Lasswell and McDougal. Originating as an endeavour to move beyond and yet remain essentially sympathetic to certain of the tenets of realist jurisprudence, Lasswell and McDougal's project came ultimately to be regarded as a failed neo-realist initiative. Yet their efforts did—owing, especially, to the work of McDougal—make a fairly significant impact on international law. By tracing Lasswell and McDougal's work from its roots in legal realism through to its impact on modern international law scholarship, I hope here to be able to produce more than just a straightforward intellectual history. My basic thesis is that the jurisprudence of Lasswell and McDougal marks the first American attempt to conceive of what might broadly be termed lawyering—legal teaching, research, practice and decision-making—as an overtly political endeavour. Realist jurisprudence itself was not, by and large, explicitly political. Rather, political meanings were read into it. That is precisely what happened from the 1930s onwards, as detractors began to detect in the literature of legal realism an affirmation of ethical relativism and an implicit disdain for traditional democratic values. In contrast, Lasswell and McDougal, by offering an explicitly pro-democratic approach to the development of legal policy, ensured that their own jurisprudential perspective could not suffer from the same misinterpretation.[11] Yet the legal theory which they produced—despite its emphasis on the careful articulation of policy perspectives—was, in its own way, every bit as ideologically manipulable as realism had been; for it was a theory which

[10] This is a point which Llewellyn apparently failed to recognize when he complained that the type of policy which Lasswell and McDougal championed was already in evidence in his own writings. See Karl Llewellyn, 'McDougal and Lasswell Plan for Legal Education', *Columbia L. Rev.*, 43 (1943), 476–85 at 484.

[11] See John Norton Moore, 'Prolegomenon to the Jurisprudence of Myres S. McDougal and Harold Lasswell', *Virginia L. Rev.*, 54 (1968), 662–88 at 687.

could be used to promote North American democratic policies as if, in every political instance, their rectitude was a matter beyond doubt. It was a theory, furthermore, which, despite its foundations in realism, turned out to be peculiarly anti-pragmatic.

FROM LEGAL REALISM TO POLICY SCIENCE

One of the most illustrious courses to run at the Yale Law School during the 1930s was the series of graduate seminars—instigated in the fall of 1932 and taught initially by Thurman Arnold, George Dession, Jerome Frank and Edward Robinson—on 'The Judicial Process from the Point of View of Social Psychology'. Eventually taken over by Arnold and Robinson alone, these seminars—illustrative, as they were, of realist legal education at its most critical and uncompromising[12]—became known disparagingly among students as 'The Cave of the Winds'.[13] The seminars ran until the end of the academic year 1938–39, although their demise had already been signalled by the abrupt death of Robinson in the fall of 1937 and Arnold's permanent departure to Washington in the following spring.[14] 'As a younger member of the Faculty', Myres McDougal was, in 1937, 'drafted to replace Robinson' as Arnold's co-teacher.[15] A former Rhodes scholar at the University of Oxford, McDougal acquired his J.S.D. from Yale Law School in 1931,[16] and was subsequently 'farmed out for retooling at the University of Illinois',[17] where he spent his time teaching credit transactions and 'acquainting himself with the vast and improving literature of the social sciences'.[18] Returning to Yale as a visiting associate professor in 1934, he quickly established a reputation as a Young Turk, owing largely to

[12] The flavour of the seminar series may be discerned from the two books which it spawned: Thurman W. Arnold, *The Symbols of Government* (New York: Harcourt, Brace & World, 1962; orig. publ. 1935); and Edward S. Robinson, *Law and the Lawyers* (New York: Macmillan, 1935).

[13] Myres S. McDougal, letter to author, 13 March 1990. See also John Henry Schlegel, 'American Legal Realism and Empirical Social Science: From the Yale Experience', *Buffalo L. Rev.*, 28 (1979), 459–586 at 512 fn. 263; Laura Kalman, *Legal Realism at Yale, 1927–1960* (Chapel Hill: University of North Carolina Press, 1986), 254 n. 28.

[14] Robinson was struck and killed by a bicycle on his way from the Yale Graduate School. McDougal, *supra* n. 13. Arnold, already on leave at the Department of Justice, decided to stay on to administer the Antitrust Division. See Neil Duxbury, 'Some Radicalism about Realism? Thurman Arnold and the Politics of Modern Jurisprudence', *Oxford Jnl. Leg. Studs.*, 10 (1990), 11–41 at 34.

[15] McDougal, *supra* n. 13.

[16] Myres S. McDougal, *Collateral Mistake in Contractual Relations* (unpublished J.S.D. diss., Yale Law School, New Haven, Conn., 1931). McDougal's dissertation was supervised by Arthur L. Corbin.

[17] Myres S. McDougal, letter to author, 14 February 1990.

[18] Frederick Samson Tipson, 'The Lasswell-McDougal Enterprise: Toward a World Public Order of Human Dignity', *Virginia Jnl. of International Law*, 14 (1974), 535–85 at 552.

his vigorous denunciation of the American Law Institute's attempt to restate the law of property.[19] McDougal's broadly realist sentiments and his leanings towards the social sciences—along with his remarkably high estimation of Arnold's intellectual abilities[20]—made him a rather obvious successor to the 'Judicial Process' seminars on Robinson's death.

Only a few weeks after Robinson's death, Arnold took a leave of absence from Yale to serve in the Tax Division of the Department of Justice. McDougal was left, as it were, holding the baby. Faced with the daunting challenge of organizing and preparing a graduate seminar series which had previously provided work for two professors, he searched around for a collaborator and found Harold Lasswell. McDougal had first met Lasswell while serving as a visiting professor at the University of Chicago in the summer of 1935. A specialist in propaganda techniques, Lasswell had a reputation at Chicago for being generally unintelligible. His book, *World Politics and Personal Insecurity*,[21] for example, first published in 1935, 'was met with a kind of pop-eyed disbelief and dismay in many quarters'.[22] Possibly 'the great majority of political scientists, unable or unwilling to master Lasswell's special vocabulary, has never understood what he was writing about.'[23] McDougal, nevertheless, was impressed by him.[24] Trained in the Chicago tradition of sociology, Lasswell was an avid cross-disciplinary scholar who made no secret of his eagerness to collaborate with lawyers and other social scientists.[25] On one occasion, he even went

[19] For McDougal's earliest rally against the Restatements, see Myres S. McDougal, review of Restatement of the Law of Property, vols. 1–2 *Illinois L. Rev.*, 32 (1937), 509–15. For later statements in the same vein, cf. Myres S. McDougal and Charles Runyon, review of Restatement of the Law of Torts, vol. 4, div. 10, ch. 41 [natural rights of property holders] *Yale L.J.*, 49 (1940), 1502–7; Myres S. McDougal, 'Future Interests Restated: Tradition versus Clarification and Reform', *Harvard L. Rev.*, 55 (1942), 1077–115.

[20] 'Thurman Arnold was one of [realism's] most brilliant, articulate, and productive proponents.' McDougal, *supra* n. 17. McDougal's high regard for Arnold did not, however, develop immediately. Indeed, as a student, he had been unimpressed by the man. McDougal, *supra* n. 13: 'In 1930, Arnold's first year on this Faculty, we Graduate Fellows thought Arnold was a little wild, even chaotic, and undisciplined. Frankly, we were a little surprised that Yale had kept him. In 1934 when I returned as a member of this Faculty, I was astonished to find that Arnold was a dominant, perhaps the dominant, intellectual leader of the [realist] group. Only Sturges could whip him in person to person combat.' See also Kalman, *supra* n. 13, 137–8.

[21] Harold D. Lasswell, *World Politics and Personal Insecurity* (New York: McGraw-Hill, 1935).

[22] Bruce Lannes Smith, 'The Mystifying Intellectual History of Harold D. Lasswell', in A. A. Rogow (eds.), *Politics, Personality, and Social Science in the Twentieth Century: Essays in Honor of Harold D. Lasswell* (Chicago: University of Chicago Press, 1969), 41–105 at 71.

[23] Arnold A. Rogow, 'Toward a Psychiatry of Politics', in Rogow (ed.), *supra* n. 22, 123–45 at 123.

[24] Kalman, *supra* n. 13, 177–8.

[25] On Lasswell's intellectual indebtedness to the cross-disciplinary ethos of the Chicago School, see Harold D. Lasswell, 'The Cross Disciplinary Manifold: The Chicago Prototype', in A. Lepawsky, E. H. Buehrig and H. D. Lasswell (eds.), *The Search for World Order: Studies by Students and Colleagues of Quincy Wright* (New York: Appleton-Century-Crofts, 1971),

so far as to compile a list of 'personal policy objectives' which he circulated among colleagues in the hope of attracting collaborative research proposals.[26] Sharing the young McDougal's realist sentiments—one of Lasswell's earliest essays proposed the use of the psychoanalytical method of 'free-phantasy' in the analysis of judicial behaviour[27]—he first suggested that they collaborate in 1935.[28] It was, in fact, another three years before the collaboration got off the ground. Despairing of his career prospects at Chicago, Lasswell resigned his associate professorship in 1938 and moved to Washington, DC, whereupon he accepted a post at the Washington School of Psychiatry, as well as a Visiting Lectureship in Social Science at the Yale Law School.[29]

By the time of Lasswell's appointment to the Yale Law School, McDougal had become involved in the Arnold–Robinson graduate seminar course, which, in line with his research interests, he had begun to revise under the title of 'Property in a Crisis Society'.[30] The arrival of Lasswell, and his desire to participate in the teaching of the course, led to its content being broadened and a further change of rubric: the course now became 'Law in a Crisis Society'.[31] After the Second World War, the title was changed to 'Law, Science, and Policy', with a sub-title, 'The Jurisprudence of a Free Society'.[32] 'We came together', Lasswell wrote of his collaboration with McDougal, 'at a moment when we were in search of complementary associates. In my case the desire to work with a legal scholar was acute . . . McDougal . . . was dissatisfied with traditional jurisprudence' and he had become 'disenchanted with American legal realists.'[33]

The collaboration was, at the outset, probably of less importance to

416–28; and on the Chicago School generally, see Martin Bulmer, *The Chicago School of Sociology: Institutionalization, Diversity, and the Rise of Sociological Research* (Chicago: University of Chicago Press, 1984); Alain Coulon, *L'école de Chicago* (Paris: Presses Universitaires de France, 1992).

[26] Rodney Muth, 'Harold Dwight Lasswell: A Biographical Profile', in R. Muth, M. M. Finley and M. F. Muth, *Harold D. Lasswell: An Annotated Bibliography* (Dordrecht: Kluwer, 1990), 1–48 at 17–18.

[27] Harold D. Lasswell, 'Self-analysis and Judicial Thinking', *International Jnl. of Ethics*, 40 (1930), 354–62.

[28] Kalman, *supra* n. 13, 177.

[29] See Muth, *supra* n. 26, 13–14. At Chicago, Robert Hutchins, then President of the University, did not consider Lasswell's writing to be of sufficient quality to justify his promotion to a full professorship.

[30] See Tipson, *supra* n. 18, 553.

[31] See Muth, *supra* n. 26, 15 fn. 74.

[32] See Robert Shimane and Robert Rich, *Works of Myres S. McDougal* (Asa V. Call Law Library Bibliography Series no. 97, Los Angeles: University of Southern California Law Center, 1980), 2; also Tipson, *supra* n. 18, 558. A revised version of the materials from this course has now been published: Harold D. Lasswell and Myres S. McDougal, *Jurisprudence For a Free Society: Studies in Law, Science and Policy* (Dordrecht: Kluwer, 1992).

[33] Harold D. Lasswell, 'In Collaboration with McDougal', *Denver Jnl. of International Law and Policy*, 1 (1971), 17–19 at 17.

McDougal than it was to Lasswell, coming, as it did, at something of a crisis point in the latter's career. After resigning from Chicago, Lasswell was unable to find a permanent university post; moreover, his removal van had crashed in the move to Washington and most of his notes and research materials were destroyed by fire.[34] Wishing to improve his academic profile and refocus his intellectual pursuits, Lasswell found, in McDougal, a perfect associate. Throughout the 1930s, Lasswell had devoted a good deal of his energies to developing the framework for what he termed a 'science of democracy'—a social scientific theory, that is, geared towards the 'achievement of democratic ideals'.[35] Between the two world wars, he argued, social theory had 'failed to connect with the policy-forming process of governmental and private organizations'.[36] It was now imperative, he believed, that consideration of policy goals be made an explicit feature of the social sciences.[37] Lasswell's own policy-oriented, social-scientific perspective—'policy science', as he came to label it—'held that the scientific aspirations of social scientists at least were frustrated by their failure to think contextually and to apply a comprehensive problem-oriented methodology to the study of man.'[38] Collaboration with McDougal presented the perfect opportunity to expand the policy science thesis to the field of law. Lasswell could take care of the social theory, while McDougal possessed the 'technical know-how'[39] which, in Lasswell's view, was necessary for the successful application of policy science to legal problems. It was this desire to introduce policy science into the study of law which provided the initial inspiration for the Lasswell and McDougal graduate seminars. Lasswell was delighted at the opportunity to promote his ideas in a legal setting. '[T]he Yale seminar group is more interesting than any [others] I have found up there,' he wrote to his parents in 1940, 'and I believe that we will succeed in getting work accomplished along the lines that have long been planned.'[40]

Such enthusiasm was scarcely to be encountered among Yale law

[34] Leo Rosten, 'Harold Lasswell: A Memoir', in Rogow (ed.), *supra* n. 22, 1–13 at 10.

[35] Harold D. Lasswell, 'The Developing Science of Democracy', in L. D. White (ed.), *The Future of Government in the United States: Essays in Honor of Charles E. Merriam* (Chicago: University of Chicago Press, 1942), 25–48; reprinted in Harold D. Lasswell, *The Analysis of Political Behaviour: An Empirical Approach* (New York: Oxford University Press, 1948), 1–12 at 1. See also Ithiel de Sola Pool, 'Content Analysis and the Intelligence Function', in Rogow (ed.), *supra* n. 22, 197–223 at 199.

[36] Harold D. Lasswell, 'The Significance of Vicos for the Emerging Policy Sciences', in H. F. Dobyns, P. H. Doughty and H. D. Lasswell (eds.), *Peasants, Power, and Applied Social Change: Vicos as a Model* (Beverly Hills: Sage, 1971), 179–93 at 180.

[37] See Harold D. Lasswell, 'The Relation of Ideological Intelligence to Public Policy', *Ethics*, 53 (1942), 25–34.

[38] Lasswell, *supra* n. 36, 182.

[39] Lasswell, *supra* n. 33, 17; and see also Tipson, *supra* n. 18, 553–4; Smith, *supra* n. 22, 42.

[40] Harold D. Lasswell to Anna P. and Linden Lasswell, 7 October 1940, in Harold D. Lasswell Papers, Yale University, Manuscripts and Archives Division, Sterling Memorial Library, New Haven, Conn.

students. If Arnold and Robinson's seminars had been the Cave of Winds, the Lasswell and McDougal collaboration signalled the arrival of a gale. From the policy science perspective, the successful teaching of law demanded of students that they endeavour to cultivate the very methodological skills which, according to Lasswell, were in short supply among trained social scientists. This was, to say the least, rather a tall order, and it is hardly remarkable that students should have proved resistant. 'My classmates seemed, in general, to have a negative reaction', one student commented of McDougal's classes in particular. 'By seeming to force his ideas on them, they tended to resent the ideas themselves.'[41]

Yet, for all that Lasswell and McDougal's teaching seemed to invite student resentment, their first attempt at turning that teaching into research produced a landmark in modern American jurisprudence. Their article, 'Legal Education and Public Policy', first published in March 1943,[42] has been typically hailed as 'mark[ing] the clear beginning of the post-realist period' in American legal scholarship.[43] Whether the article in fact constitutes such an unequivocal break from the past is questionable, for the proposals which it contains are as much a continuation of realist legal thinking as they are a reaction against it. What is clear, nevertheless, is that Lasswell and McDougal intended the article to signal a definitive break with the past. 'Heroic, but random, efforts to integrate "law" and "the other social sciences"', they wrote, 'fail through lack of clarity about *what* is being integrated, and *how*, and *for what purposes*. . . . The relevance of "non-legal" materials to effective "law" teaching is recognized but efficient techniques for the investigation, collection and presentation of such materials are not devised.'[44] Since realism, in particular, failed successfully to utilize social scientific methods and thereby develop into a 'positive systematic theory' about law,[45] it remained but a 'preliminary'

41 Anon., 'Reactions of One Member of June '48 Class to His Course and Instructors', in Dean's Papers, box 66, folder 86, Yale University, Manuscripts and Archives Division. In 1948, the Dean of the Yale Law School was Wesley Sturges. One student who apparently did appreciate McDougal's classes was the now retired Supreme Court Justice, Byron White. See Jeffrey Rosen, 'The Next Chief Justice', *The New Republic*, 12 April 1993, 21, 24–6 at 24 col. 2.

42 Harold D. Lasswell and Myres S. McDougal, 'Legal Education and Public Policy: Professional Training in the Public Interest', *Yale L.J.*, 52 (1943), 203–95. For references to subsequent reprints of this article, see Muth, Finley and Muth, *supra* n. 26, 100-1.

43 Robert Stevens, 'Two Cheers for 1870: The American Law School', *Perspectives in American History*, 5 (1971), 403–548 at 530. On the impact of the article, see further Fred R. Shapiro, 'The Most-Cited Articles From *The Yale Law Journal*', *Yale L.J.*, 100 (1991), 1449–514 at 1506–7.

44 Lasswell and McDougal, *supra* n. 42, 263.

45 Myres S. McDougal, Harold D. Lasswell and W. Michael Reisman, 'Theories about International Law: Prologue to a Configurative Jurisprudence', *Virginia Jnl. of International Law*, 8 (1968), 188–299 at 261.

inquiry into the 'affirmative problems of jurisprudence'.[46] By failing, moreover, to recognize that '[i]nfluential decisions are not restricted to judges'[47]—by failing, that is, to consider how the judicial decision is itself 'guided by and related to preferred community policies'[48]—so-called realists conceived of the legal system in an inordinately narrow fashion: they 'did not extend their insights to new or comprehensive conceptions of constitutive process. They were content to work with largely conventional categorizations both of the phases of decision process and of the different types of decisions.'[49] In short, Lasswell and McDougal concluded, the 'attitudes and methods' of legal realism 'are not adequate to the opportunities and obligations of our time.'[50]

Lasswell and McDougal thus set out to move American jurisprudence onwards from legal realism. In endeavouring to take jurisprudence into some sort of new phase, however, they rather underplayed the legacies of the past. That 'preferred community policies' may influence the development of legal principles, for example, was hardly an insight unique to themselves; the claim has its origins in the external standards jurisprudence of Holmes.[51] Nor did Lasswell and McDougal accord much attention to realist endeavours to bring social-scientific methods and insights to the study of law; they were content, rather, simply to proclaim that such endeavours had proved fruitless. Yet although their desire to break with the past led them to overlook or underestimate certain earlier jurisprudential ideas and initiatives, their approach to the social sciences was, in historical terms, both original and significant.

We saw, in the previous chapter, that by the early 1940s, American academic lawyers, having witnessed the mood of realism flourish and fade in the law schools, began to cast doubt on the possibility of successfully integrating law with the social sciences. The demise of realism convinced some academics—even academics who were sympathetic to attempts at integration—that the development of interdisciplinary legal study was a

[46] Harold D. Lasswell and Myres S. McDougal, 'Criteria for a Theory about Law', *Southern California L. Rev.*, 44 (1971), 362–94 at 373.

[47] Lasswell and McDougal, *supra* n. 42, 263.

[48] Myres S. McDougal, 'Jurisprudence for a Free Society', *Georgia L. Rev.*, 1 (1966), 1–19 at 9.

[49] Harold D. Lasswell and Myres S. McDougal, 'Trends in Theories about Law: Comprehensiveness in Conceptions of Constitutive Process', *George Washington L. Rev.*, 41 (1972), 1–22 at 19.

[50] Myres S. McDougal, 'The Law School of the Future: From Legal Realism to Policy Science in the World Community', *Yale L.J.*, 56 (1947), 1345–55 at 1355.

[51] See Oliver Wendell Holmes, Jr., 'The Path of the Law', *Harvard L. Rev.*, 10 (1897), 457–78 at 459; and also Mark DeWolfe Howe, 'The Positivism of Mr Justice Holmes', *Harvard L. Rev.*, 64 (1951), 529–46 at 541.

risky business which could involve as many drawbacks as benefits.[52] Judged by the mood of the time, Lasswell and McDougal seemed unusually optimistic about the future of the social sciences in the American law schools. In 1941, writing in response to Lon Fuller's natural law-inspired critique of legal realism,[53] McDougal asserted that the most effective way 'to encourage a creative legal scholarship in this country today . . . is . . . by seeking the organization and endowment of better law schools',

> that is, of law schools adequately staffed with all of the skills of modern social science and with resources ample for the exercise of these skills in both investigation and teaching. In such schools it might eventually come to pass that the principal policy makers and executors of our society and their teachers could be trained as such, and not as priests in outworn and meaningless faiths.[54]

McDougal argued for the introduction of social-scientific techniques into the law schools almost as if he was the first ever to have done so—as if realism had never happened. The reason for this is that he was indeed arguing for something new, because the conception of social science to which Lasswell had introduced him was vastly different from that to which certain so-called realists had been committed. Legal realists, Lasswell and McDougal felt, looked to the social sciences without any real idea of what they were looking for: the social sciences were simply something exotic, outside the framework of the law, and thus a source of inspiration—though inspiration for what, it was not at all clear. If so-called realists were looking to the social sciences for anything, it was in the hope of finding a conceptual apparatus which would enable them convincingly—that is, 'scientifically'—to articulate their disenchantment with the persistence of formalism in the law schools and the courts. Lasswell and McDougal, however, did not view realism this way. Although they applauded realist jurisprudence for the fact that it represented, in general, a pioneering attempt to integrate law with the social sciences,[55] they dismissed all particular realist attempts at integration as lacking clear, articulated

[52] See especially in this context, David Reisman, Jr., 'Law and Social Science: A Report on Michael and Wechsler's Classbook on Criminal Law and Administration', *Yale L.J.*, 50 (1941), 636–53.

[53] See Lon L. Fuller, *The Law in Quest of Itself* (Chicago: The Foundation Press, 1940), 48–65.

[54] Myres S. McDougal, 'Fuller v. The American Legal Realists: An Intervention', *Yale L.J.*, 50 (1941), 827–40. Almost fifty years onwards from this article, McDougal remained committed to this point: *supra* n. 17 (arguing that the reason that legal education has failed to progress along policy science lines in the United States is not that 'the content of our attack is too intellectualized but rather because adequate resources have never been put into hard reform').

[55] See Harold D. Lasswell and Myres S. McDougal, 'The Relation of Law to Social Process: Trends in Theories about Law', *U. Pittsburgh L. Rev.*, 37 (1976), 465–85 at 467.

objectives. If an interdisciplinary approach to legal research and law teaching was to serve a useful purpose, they insisted, then that purpose was not simply to give the impression that legal critique may be 'scientifically' informed but, more importantly, to demonstrate to legal decision-makers, present and future, that the social sciences may be an invaluable source of normative guidance.[56]

Lasswell and McDougal not only took the view that legal realists had failed to appreciate the fundamental reason for developing a social-scientific approach to the study of law. They also felt that so-called realists were committed to a view of social science which was essentially outdated. Indeed, the reason that Lasswell and McDougal remained enthusiastic about integrating law and the social sciences when others were beginning to lose hope was that they conceived of social-scientific inquiry in a distinctly novel fashion. Karl Llewellyn wrote disparagingly of their 'indiscriminate swallowing' of 'large quantities of published half-sense or non-sense'[57]—an observation which, given some of Lasswell and McDougal's more recondite claims,[58] seems not entirely unfair. Whereas Llewellyn, in writing about realism, had professed to identify what he termed a ferment in legal scholarship,[59] Lasswell and McDougal, in developing their own approach to the study of law, were in effect highlighting the existence of a more general ferment within the social sciences themselves. That ferment centred around the question of what was intended by the notion of policy science.

Laurence Tribe has argued that the systematic development of policy science as a form of social inquiry after the Second World War marked the birth of a peculiarly modern faith in what he terms 'objectivist' methodology. As purportedly objectivist, the basic purpose of policy science, according to Tribe, has been 'to enlarge the role of explicit, logical reasoning, of empirical knowledge, and of consensual discourse in realms of decision-making otherwise dominated by supposedly less trustworthy sources of choice'.[60] Yet the policy scientist's faith in objectivism has been misplaced, since the 'elusive ideal of wholly objective, impersonal, and detached instrumental analysis . . . is not only unattainable but destructive—in that the very act of striving for it tends to warp the perspective of policy analyst and decision-maker alike.'[61] For Tribe, 'the supposedly

[56] See Anthony Kronman, 'Jurisprudential Responses to Legal Realism', *Cornell L. Rev.*, 73 (1988), 335–40 at 337–89.

[57] Llewellyn, *supra* n. 10, 483, 482.

[58] See e.g. Lasswell and McDougal, *supra* n. 42, 268 ('we are indulging in *pragmatics*, as distinguished from *semologics*').

[59] See Karl N. Llewellyn, 'Some Realism about Realism—Responding to Dean Pound', *Harvard L. Rev.*, 44 (1931), 1222–64.

[60] Laurence H. Tribe, 'Policy Science: Analysis or Ideology?', *Philosophy and Public Affairs*, 2 (1972), 66–110 at 78.

[61] Ibid. 108.

"expert" views of any adviser, policy analyst or otherwise', must be treated as always and ineluctably *personal*'.[62]

Tribe does not discuss directly the work of Lasswell and McDougal. But his criticism that policy science assumes the attainability of an unrealistic state of detachment is one which might be levelled at their own methodological assumptions. In particular, Lasswell and McDougal insist that the academic lawyer may profitably assume a detached, observational standpoint when engaging in any form of legal inquiry. Whereas 'authoritative decisionmakers' are ultimately interested 'in power, in the making of effective choices', the primary concern of the 'scholarly observer' is for 'enlightenment'[63]—enlightenment, that is, 'about the aggregate interrelationships of authoritative decision and other aspects of community process'.[64] Accordingly, Lasswell and McDougal argue, borrowing a classic realist distinction:

> what the scholarly observer requires is a theory *about* law, designed to facilitate performance of pertinent tasks in inquiry about decision, as distinguished from the theories of law which are employed by decision-makers and others for obtaining and justifying outcomes within the decision process and are, thus, among the variables about which the scholar seeks enlightenment.[65]

In order to develop a theory about law, 'the scholar must distinguish himself and his purposes and procedures from the events which he has under observation, including the purposes and procedures of the participants in those events.'[66] 'If the scholarly observer does not assume perspectives different from those of the community member making claims or of the authoritative decision-maker who responds to such claims, he can have no criteria for appraising the rationality in terms of common interest of either the claims or decision.'[67]

Thus it is that the legal scholar, for Lasswell and McDougal, ought to assume an observational perspective. However, this perspective, though purportedly 'detached', is not intended to be an objective one. While the academic lawyer is supposed to stand back from the decision-making process and analyse it in relief, as it were, he or she cannot, Lasswell and McDougal concede, become disengaged from the value preferences which

[62] Ibid.

[63] Harold D. Lasswell and Myres S. McDougal, 'Trends in Theories about Law: Maintaining Observational Standpoint and Delimiting the Focus of Inquiry', *U. Toledo L. Rev.*, 8 (1976), 1–50 at 1.

[64] Lasswell and McDougal, *supra* n. 46, 376.

[65] Ibid. The distinction first surfaces in the writings of Edward Robinson and was subsequently used by Thurman Arnold. See Duxbury, *supra* n. 14, 21–2; also Myres S. McDougal, 'Some Basic Theoretical Concepts about International Law: A Policy-Oriented Framework of Inquiry', *Jnl. of Conflict Resolution*, 4 (1960), 337–54 at 350–3.

[66] Lasswell and McDougal, *supra* n. 46, 378.

[67] McDougal, *supra* n. 48, 8.

inform that process. 'The scholarly observer is . . . inextricably a part of community process; he, like other community members, is incurably affected by preferences about value distribution.'[68] In other words, the Lasswell and McDougal version of policy science implies a distinction between institutional and ideological commitment: while the legal scholar is supposedly able to view the mechanics of the legal process in a wholly dispassionate light—such detachment being the key to constructive legal critique—he or she cannot assume detachment from, and therefore cannot regard objectively, the social culture and values upon which the legal process is founded.

Precisely how Lasswell and McDougal's scholarly observer is supposed to achieve this strange state of semi-detachment is not clear. Nor is it obvious that ascension to the observational standpoint would produce new insights on the working of the legal process. But these matters need hardly detain us. The point to be stressed, for the purpose of tracing the intellectual history of post-realist jurisprudence, is that Lasswell and McDougal's conception of policy science is derived from a more general conception of social science as a value-laden form of inquiry. This point is important, for it represents the fundamental methodological break between legal realism and the policy science approach to law. Those so-called realists who resorted to the methods of the social sciences tended to do so in order to create the impression that their critical reactions to legal formalism were more than just subjective expressions of disenchantment with a perceived juridical order of things—to create the impression, that is, that their criticisms were somehow grounded in value-free social inquiry. The policy science perspective of Lasswell and McDougal, in contrast, far from being 'premissed on an assumption of a value-free social science',[69] is in fact 'assertoric rather than didactic. . . . It is unashamedly and intentionally value-laden.'[70] Since the scholar can never be detached from social culture and values, social-scientific inquiry must always be ideologically informed.

In arguing as much, Lasswell and McDougal were, it has been suggested, 'emphasizing the importance of value questions and policy-oriented perspectives during a period when these views were out of fashion in the social sciences'.[71] Such perspectives had perhaps never been in fashion in the social sciences. It would be the 1950s before the idea of a value-free social science was treated by American social theorists to anything

[68] Lasswell and McDougal, *supra* n. 46, 378.
[69] Stevens, *supra* n. 43, 531.
[70] Philip Allott, 'Language, Method and the Nature of International Law', *British Yearbook of International Law*, 45 (1971), 79–135 at 123.
[71] Oran R. Young, 'International Law and Social Science: The Contributions of Myres S. McDougal', *American Jnl. of International Law*, 66 (1972), 60–76 at 75.

approaching unequivocal scepticism.[72] Lasswell, nevertheless—as his arguments, during the 1930s, for a science of democracy testify—was sceptical of the notion of value-freedom even in his Chicago days. Indeed, it was at Chicago that, as a student, he had come under the spell of the utopian scientism of his teacher, Charles Merriam.[73] The social sciences, Merriam observed in 1925, are pointing the way towards 'a new world, with new social conditions and with new modes of thought and inquiry'.[74] 'We are rapidly approaching a time', he insisted, 'when it may be necessary and possible to decide not merely what types of law we wish to enact, but what types of person we wish to develop.'[75] Merriam's strategy in extending this line of argument was to preach the message of the eugenics movement. In a 'new world order made over by modern science',[76] he claimed that selective breeding would prove to be an important factor in determining 'what sorts of creatures are to be born'.[77] Lasswell, for his part, steered clear of the language of eugenics, but he remained faithful to Merriam's basic utopian vision—to the image, that is, of a new world order in which social policy is generated, primarily, by social science.

It is precisely this image which rests at the heart of the policy science perspective on law. Far from providing some sort of value-free framework, Lasswell and McDougal insist, the social sciences constitute a collection of conceptual tools to which decision-makers of the future will be able to resort in order to make legal values explicit. Enlightened by the social sciences, lawyers of the future will recognize themselves to be dealing not only with law but also with policy. It must be remembered that Lasswell's vision for the social sciences themselves is that they be made to serve the ideals of democracy. The purpose of the social sciences, as conceived by him, is to demonstrate that liberal-democratic values are essentially correct values, that in an ideal world they would be universally shared values.[78] The purpose of introducing policy science into the study of law is to demonstrate to lawyers that the legal values of a liberal democracy may be scientifically approved—approved, that is, by pro-democratic, scientific methodology. American lawyers, in other words, are urged to look beyond the law for normative guidance not so that they might discover any old values, but so that they might affirm explicitly the values to which they are already committed, the individualistic values of American democracy. Thus it is that the jurisprudence of Lasswell and McDougal turns out to be

[72] See, in particular, C. Wright Mills, *The Sociological Imagination* (Harmondsworth: Penguin, 1970; orig. publ. 1959), 91–6.

[73] See Dorothy Ross, *The Origins of American Social Science* (Cambridge: Cambridge University Press, 1991), 455–7.

[74] Charles E. Merriam, *New Aspects of Politics* (Chicago: University of Chicago Press, 1925), 19. [75] Ibid. 2. [76] Ibid. 21–2. [77] Ibid. 155.

[78] See e.g. Harold D. Lasswell, 'The Function of the Propagandist', *International Jnl. of Ethics*, 38 (1928), 258–68; *Democracy Through Public Opinion* (Menasha, WI: Banta, 1941).

quintessentially American: while policy science is a type of social science, social science itself is an ideology; and by looking at law through the lens of policy science, the American lawyer will not only find that ideology articulated 'scientifically', but will be reassured to discover that it is an ideology to which he or she already subscribes.

JURISPRUDENCE, POLITICS AND PROPAGANDA

The ideological nature of policy science has, perhaps unsurprisingly, been a favourite theme among Lasswell and McDougal's detractors. Yet criticism has tended to take the form of labelling, so that policy science been variously described as concealing a natural law ideology,[79] a utilitarian ideology,[80] a neo-Langdellian ideology,[81] and so on.[82] While descriptions along these lines may be justified at one level or another, none of them reveals anything about policy science as an ideology *sui generis*.

The distinctiveness of policy science as an ideology is in fact obvious from Lasswell and McDougal's earliest collaborative excursion into jurisprudence. 'Legal Education and Public Policy' was written during the Second World War, a time when—given that the American law schools were relatively quiet—suggestions for curricular change might have been expected to meet with less than normal resistance from rank-and-file law professors. Certainly this is what Lasswell and McDougal hoped: 'War is the time to retool our educational processes in the hope of making them fit instruments for their future job.'[83] It was precisely this matter of the future purpose of the educational process which concerned them most specifically. In spite of the initiatives of the legal realists, as well as certain of their

[79] See Edgar Bodenheimer, *Jurisprudence: The Philosophy and Method of the Law* (Cambridge, Mass.: Harvard University Press, 1962), 141; Grant Gilmore, *Ages of American Law* (New Haven, Conn.: Yale University press, 1977), 90; Kalman, *supra* n. 13, 183 (citing Jerome Frank). Lasswell and McDougal attempted, on occasion, to distance themselves from natural law jurisprudence: see for example, *supra* n. 46, 365.

[80] See William Twining, 'Pericles and the Plumber', *Law Quarterly Review*, 83 (1967), 396–426 at 412–14; Roger Cotterrell, *The Politics of Jurisprudence: A Critical Introduction to Legal Philosophy* (London: Butterworths, 1989), 207; Allott, *supra* n. 70, 126 (on 'McDougal's international utilitarianism'). Again, Lasswell and McDougal attempted to distance themselves from utilitarianism: see e.g. *supra* n. 55, 471. Nevertheless, there are passages in their writings which betray a distinctly utilitarian outlook e.g. *supra* n. 46, 375 ('a legal system is to be appraised in terms of the values to be maximized in the total context of public order'). See also Myres S. McDougal, review of C. W. Everett, *The Education of Jeremy Bentham*, *Illinois L. Rev.*, 27 (1933), 580–1.

[81] See Llewellyn, *supra* n. 10, 481; Gilmore, *supra* n. 79, 90.

[82] See further Mark Tushnet, 'Post-Realist Legal Scholarship', *Jnl. of the Society of Public Teachers of Law*, 15 (1980), 20–32 at 22–3.

[83] Lasswell and McDougal, *supra* n. 42, 211.

forebears,[84] American jurisprudence remained conspicuously inarticulate on the matter of how to relate 'legal structures, doctrines, and procedures . . . clearly and consistently to the major problems of a society struggling to achieve democratic values.'[85] The spread of despotism throughout Europe provided a sharp reminder that the acceptance of democracy can never be taken for granted; and it was in recognition of precisely this fact that Lasswell and McDougal began to develop their thesis that the fundamental goal of post-realist jurisprudence should be the better promotion of democratic values.[86]

> We submit this basic proposition: if legal education in the contemporary world is adequately to serve the needs of a free and productive commonwealth, it must be conscious, efficient, and systematic *training for policy making*. The proper function of our law schools is, in short, to contribute to the training of policy-makers for the ever more complete achievement of the democratic values that constitute the professed ends of American polity.[87]

Accordingly, 'a legitimate aim of education is to seek to promote the major values of a democratic society and to reduce the number of moral mavericks who do not share democratic preferences.'[88] While, in a democracy, there can be no 'complete consensus' as to what constitute preferred values, 'unless some such values are chosen, carefully defined, explicitly made the organizing focii of the law school curriculum, and kept so constantly at the student's focus of attention that he automatically applies them to every conceivable practical and theoretical situation, all talk of integrating "law" and "social science", or of making law a more effective instrument of social control, is twaddling futility.'[89] In other words, the only conceivable purpose for developing an interdisciplinary approach to legal education is to use the social sciences as a medium through which to immerse the law student in certain values which are deemed to be representative of the values of democracy. 'The student may be allowed to reject the morals of democracy and embrace those of despotism; but his education should be such that, if he does so, he does it by deliberate choice, with awareness of the consequences for himself and others, and not by sluggish self-deception.'[90] That is, the rejection of democracy must itself be recognized to be a democratic privilege—a privilege accorded only in societies which respect the freedom of the individual to make choices. While there may be no precise consensus

[84] Especially Wesley Newcomb Hohfeld: see ibid. 203 fn. 1; Myres S. McDougal, 'Law as a Process of Decision: A Policy-Oriented Approach to Legal Study', *Natural Law Forum*, 1 (1956), 53–72 at 61; and also Tipson, *supra* n. 18, 549.

[85] Lasswell and McDougal, *supra* n. 42, 205.

[86] Ibid. 264.

[87] Ibid. 206.

[88] Ibid. 212.

[89] Ibid. 244.

[90] Ibid. 212.

regarding what constitute preferred democratic values, and while there may exist a maverick few who claim to reject such values, the purpose of the social sciences is to demonstrate that democracy is in fact an unquestionable, a priori virtue—to demonstrate that, without democracy, differences of perspective and minority opinions would not be tolerated. The purpose of the social sciences, in short, is to guide students towards a pro-democratic consensus. That is why the social sciences may perform an invaluable role in the law schools.

But what will be the nature of this consensus? That is, which specific values should be chosen to form what Lasswell and McDougal term 'the organizing focii of the law school curriculum'? The pivotal value to be stressed, they assert, 'is the dignity and worth of the individual', for it is only through respect for this value that students may come to recognize that 'a democratic society is a commonwealth of mutual deference—a commonwealth where there is full opportunity to mature talent into socially creative skill, free from discrimination on grounds of religion, culture or class.'[91] Aside from their basic respect for the distinctness of the individual, students will also recognize other 'general values in which they participate as members of a free society'.[92] These values are the shared values of 'power, respect, knowledge, income, and safety (including health)'.[93] In later writings, this list was expanded, so as to include the additional values of 'morality'—later changed to 'rectitude'—and 'affection', and also amended, so that 'knowledge' was replaced by the separate categories of 'enlightenment' and 'skill', 'income' was broadened to 'wealth', and 'safety' to 'well-being'.[94] For Lasswell and McDougal, these values are 'the basic values of human dignity'[95] and, as such, their worth is a matter beyond political or moral debate—they exist, as it were, 'beyond ethics'.[96]

The purpose of jurisprudence developed along policy science lines is to demonstrate to law students that their recognition of these values as essential and self-evident is of fundamental importance for the maintenance and furtherance of a properly democratic legal order. 'In our view', Lasswell and McDougal observe, 'the democratic values of our society can

[91] Ibid., and see also Hardy Cross Dillard, 'The Policy-Oriented Approach to Law', *Virginia Quarterly Rev.*, 40 (1964) at 629–30.

[92] Lasswell and McDougal, *supra* n. 42, 246.

[93] Ibid. 217.

[94] See McDougal, *supra* n. 50, 1347; *supra* n. 84, 56. The list was, in fact, devised by Lasswell (see Young, *supra* n. 71, 67). It receives its most comprehensive exposition in Harold D. Lasswell and Abraham Kaplan, *Power and Society: A Framework for Political Inquiry* (New Haven, Conn.: Yale University Press, 1950), 87.

[95] McDougal, *supra* n. 48, 15.

[96] Myres S. McDougal, 'The Ethics of Applying Systems of Authority: The Balanced Opposites of a Legal System', in Harold D. Lasswell and Harlan Cleveland (eds.), *The Ethic of Power: The Interplay of Religion, Philosophy, and Politics* (New York: Harper & Bros., 1962), 221–41 at 230.

only be effectively fulfilled if all who have an opportunity to participate significantly in the forming of policy share certain ways of thinking, observing and managing.'[97] Since lawyers are 'especially skilled expert[s] in the use of authoritative language and authoritative procedures for affecting or influencing decisions',[98] the education process to which they are subjected must aim to ensure that they leave law school fully and collectively aware and prepared 'to make full use of the enormous potentialities of the fundamental ideological doctrine of a free society'.[99] This requires the reorientation of 'every phase of law school curricula and skill training towards the achievement of clearly defined democratic values in all the areas of social life where lawyers have or can assert responsibility'.[100] By educating lawyers in the basic values of human dignity, the law school of the future may play its part in maintaining and strengthening American democracy. Policy science is intended to guide the American law school along precisely this route.

REINVENTING THE AMERICAN LAW SCHOOL

So, how was policy science supposed to work? The answer to this question, for Lasswell and McDougal, was as easy to assert as it would be difficult to implement: law schools must be urged to set about organizing their curricula around the basic values of human dignity. Langdellian educators, so-called realists recognized, had removed legal doctrine from its 'total context'.[101] More specifically, Lasswell and McDougal argue, Langdellian legal science stripped doctrine of its policy context. Inspired by Thurman Arnold,[102] they contend that, by de-contextualizing doctrine, proponents of Langdellian legal education were able to sustain the impression that law is, in essence, a closed body of formally interlocking symbols—symbols, that is:

> of identification that are available for use in referring to parties who invoke hierarchies of normative statements purporting to specify which relations ought to obtain among such parties when certain factual statements can be assumed to be true and can be subsumed under certain other legal definitions and doctrines. What is commonly called 'the law' can, thus, be defined as a syntactic system of propositions composed of terms that are supposedly defined, plus some admittedly indefinable terms, whose modes of combination are governed by certain postulates and rules. In venerable fiction this system, like that of a science or a theology, is

97 Lasswell and McDougal, *supra* n. 42, 291.
98 McDougal, *supra* n. 84, 53.
99 Lasswell and McDougal, *supra* n. 42, 289.
100 Ibid. 207.
101 McDougal, *supra* n. 84, 71.
102 See Lasswell and McDougal, *supra* n. 42, 221, 246; McDougal, *supra* n. 84, 64–5.

internally consistent and complete in its reference; from its central terms, definitions and rules, all possible relations can be deduced.[103]

Ironically, Arnold himself claimed that he failed to understand what it was that Lasswell and McDougal were trying to do.[104] What they were in fact trying to do was to use his own critique of formalist jurisprudence as a basis for reformist proposals. Arnold had attempted to expose the poverty of the Langdellian approach to legal education. The first goal of policy science was to produce a plausible alternative to that approach. While the teaching of black-letter legal doctrine was, without doubt, an important function of the law school, it was not, as most Langdellians seemed to believe, the only function. Equally, however, the emphasis placed by certain realists on the teaching of particular legal techniques—such as prediction—would not inspire the creation of a curriculum suitable for 'training lawyers to put democratic values into policy'.[105] What was needed, beyond the teaching of doctrine and technique, was a system of legal training devised to 'aid the developing lawyer to acquire certain skills of thought: goal-thinking, trend-thinking, and scientific-thinking. The student needs to clarify his moral values (preferred events, social goals); he needs to orient himself in past trends and future probabilities; finally, he needs to acquire the scientific knowledge and skills necessary to implement objectives within the context of contemporary trends.'[106] Not only must the law school of the future offer these skills of thought; it must also develop courses which suit 'the needs of selected, influential *policy-makers*, such as business managers, government officials, and labour leaders'.[107] By teaching 'general policy skills'[108] within a curriculum structured around the particular interests and needs of policy-makers—and by teaching those skills from a 'pro-democratic'[109] perspective—the law school of the future will, Lasswell and McDougal claim, both provide 'a realistic and comprehensive picture of the structure and functions of society' and will also be 'oriented towards the implementing of a consistent and explicit set of democratic values'.[110] Accordingly, not only will the lawyer of the future be trained, as certain realists had envisaged,[111] to be a 'social technician'; he, or she, will be trained to be a social technician of explicitly liberal-democratic persuasion.

The creation of a new breed of lawyer depends itself on the creation of a

[103] Lasswell and McDougal, *supra* n. 42, 235.

[104] Thurman Arnold to Sergius M. Boikan, 22 June 1960, in Gene M. Gressley (ed.), *Voltaire and the Cowboy: The Letters of Thurman Arnold* (Boulder, Colo.: Colorado Associated University Press, 1977), 436–7 at 436.

[105] Lasswell and McDougal, *supra* n. 42, 243. [106] Ibid. 245. [107] Ibid.

[108] Ibid. 264. [109] Ibid. 275. [110] Ibid. 248.

[111] Primarily, those who adopted Pound's notion of social engineering. See, in particular, Robinson, *supra* n. 12, *passim*; and also Frederick K. Beutel, 'Some Implications of Experimental Jurisprudence', *Harvard L. Rev.*, 48 (1934), 169–97.

new breed of law teacher. New courses must be devised, and traditional ones reoriented along policy science lines. All curricular revision ought to be guided by one basic criterion: namely, whether current doctrines and practices in particular areas of law serve to promote or to retard basic democratic values.[112] The promotion of these values matters more than anything else: 'the heart of the matter is not the re-christening of courses but the changing of aim and emphasis'.[113] Among other things, the new law teacher must 'make plain to the student not only that there are different ways of settling disputes but many ways of getting results other than by disputation'.[114] In so far as law is conceived to be a process of dispute settlement, the law teacher must emphasize to students that such settlements ought properly to be assessed in terms of whether or not they accord with the democratic objectives of 'authoritative community policy'.[115] In attempting to guide students towards the realization of basic democratic values, law teachers must themselves demonstrate a scholarly commitment to self-enlightenment; for it is only through analysis, clarification and exposure of their own values and prejudices that they might 'diminish their own danger to students'.[116]

Such a commitment to self-enlightenment entails also a commitment to self-improvement, since '[t]he well-qualified student will want to have first-hand acquaintance with the most authoritative expositions of major ideologies'.[117] In order to ensure that the student may become so acquainted, the law teacher ought to provide, along with more conventional course materials, a periodically revised 'guide and companion to many of the skills valuable to the law student. . . . Such a volume would contain reprints, original articles by experts, and unpublished research; it would give "who's who" information on authors.'[118] Students might also be provided with what Lasswell and McDougal term a 'Trend Book', that is, a volume which 'brings together information about how people spend their time in production and about the volume and efficiency of output, the level of consumption, the degrees of depletion of potential resources, and the intensity of inventiveness in relation to the exploitation of natural advantages'.[119] By using these materials in conjunction with classroom instruction, the law teacher will be able to educate students in the skills vital to effective policy-making—that is, not only in conventional skills such as mastering legal jargon and syntax and analysing court-room dynamics, but also in less conventional ones such as diplomacy, data

112 Lasswell and McDougal, *supra* n. 42, 248–62.
113 Ibid. 265.
114 Ibid. 263.
115 McDougal, *supra* n. 84, 57; and see also Tipson, *supra* n. 18, 554.
116 Lasswell and McDougal, *supra* n. 42, 284.
117 Ibid. 275.
118 Ibid. 269.
119 Ibid. 273.

collection, analysis of public opinion, cost–benefit analysis, management of public relations and effective use of propaganda.[120]

Just as the law teacher must be reincarnated, so too must the law school. A primary goal of modern legal training, Lasswell and McDougal assert, must be 'to project the student into situations that resemble as closely as possible the circumstances of his future career'.[121] One strategy is to ensure that students participate in moot trials. Such participation may be assessed by audio-visual recording: 'Through proper testing facilities, unsuspected aptitudes may be revealed and the source of many inhibitions on effective expression may be exposed, understood and eliminated.'[122] Students should also be provided with 'opportunities . . . for direct contact with courts, administrative agencies and other parts of our social process'.[123] These recommendations differed little from those which had been made by certain legal realists.[124] Lasswell and McDougal did set themselves apart from the majority of legal realists, nevertheless, by casting doubt on the pedagogic effectiveness of the case method as the primary form of legal instruction. At the very least, they argued, large, Langdellian-inspired classes should be complemented by seminars, that is, by 'comparatively small group[s] of professors and students engaged in creative analysis and research on problems'.[125] The seminar should be conducted by more than one professor—the objective being to bring students into contact with scholars 'who share not only quite general values but specific concern with the achievement of rather restricted objectives'.[126] Apart from acquiring skills 'in the organization and presentation of material', participating students should be directed towards 'the discovery of new problems'—problems, that is, not raised in the classroom—'and to the patient exploration of new sources and even new skills marginal to the central apparatus of legal technicality.'[127] Seminars should facilitate not only 'the mastery of legal doctrine and procedure'—this being something which can, by and large, be developed in the classroom—but also 'the acquisition of general policy skills'.[128]

THE FRUSTRATION OF THE FUTURE

It is perhaps ironic—given Lasswell and McDougal's professed enthusiasm for legal instruction by seminars—that McDougal should have admitted to a preference for teaching large classes *à la* Langdell. 'I prefer a [class of a]

[120] Lasswell and McDougal, *supra* n. 42, 269, 286, 280–1, 276, 255, 277, 275–6.

[121] Ibid. 290.

[122] Ibid. 291

[123] Ibid.

[124] One thinks, in particular, of Jerome Frank's proposals for the development of clinical legal education. See ch. 2.

[125] Lasswell and McDougal, *supra* n. 42, 289.

[126] Ibid. 290.

[127] Ibid. 289.

[128] Ibid.

hundred', he is reported to have said. 'I will work for a hundred and put on a good show; I'll go to sleep with ten or twelve.'[129] The comment is significant, for it highlights what is perhaps the fundamental stumbling-block of Lasswell and McDougal's jurisprudence: namely, that their policy-oriented law school of the future was but a vaguely formulated ideal bearing little resemblance to anything that either students or teachers actually wanted from legal education. Jerome Frank wrote, in 1947, that 'I thoroughly agree with those who, like Professors Lasswell and McDougal, urge that law schools should emphasize democratic values, and should stimulate future lawyers to think of themselves in the role of makers of policies which will implement such values.'[130] While he approved of their pro-democratic rhetoric, however, he had no time for their specific proposals. The initiative to reform the law schools along policy science lines was, he felt, a non-starter.[131] It was a feeling shared by many.

Lasswell and McDougal's proposals are open to two broad types of objection, which might be termed intellectual and institutional. The most basic intellectual objection concerns their conception of democratic values. The values to which they point—power, enlightenment, wealth, well-being, skill, affection, respect and rectitude—are treated as if they subsist a priori whereas, in fact, they are peculiarly western, indeed, North American values. One of the most frequent criticisms of the policy science perspective on law concerns the manner in which liberal-democratic value-preferences are treated as if they are not preferences at all, that is, as if they are fundamental truths with which the world must come to terms if the future of civilization is to be secured. Since, Lasswell and McDougal suggest, the core purpose of policy science is the promotion of democracy, critique of the American legal system is a valid exercise only in so far as it points the way towards the improvement or reinforcement of that system: critique is to be in the interests of furthering democracy rather than directed against democracy itself.[132] Indeed, the very reason for developing the law school along policy science lines is to transform the lawyer into a guardian of democracy, willing and able to play a vital part in ensuring that America never becomes—to use Lasswell's phrase—a garrison state.[133]

Aside from their belief that American liberal-democratic values deserve to be treated as somehow omnipotent, Lasswell and McDougal commit

[129] Myres S. McDougal, cited in Martin Mayer, *The Lawyers* (New York: Harper & Row, 1966), 83.

[130] Jerome Frank, 'A Plea for Lawyer Schools', *Yale L.J.*, 56 (1947), 1301–44 at 1323.

[131] See Kalman, *supra* n. 13, 183.

[132] See McDougal, *supra* n. 84, 59, 64; Moore, *supra* n. 11, 676.

[133] Lasswell and McDougal, *supra* n. 42, 208. See also Harold D. Lasswell, 'The Garrison State', *American Jnl. of Sociology*, 46 (1941), 455–68; and, for a critique, Raymond Aron, 'Remarks on Lasswell's "The Garrison State" ', *Armed Forces and Society*, 5 (1979), 347–59.

themselves to other assumptions which give rise to further intellectual objections. In view of their insistence that legal decision-making accord with authoritative community policy,[134] it may be argued, from one modern liberal perspective, that Lasswell and McDougal prove themselves to be peculiarly anti-liberal, since they demand, in effect, that collective goals be given precedence over individual rights—that considerations of policy, that is, be accorded priority over considerations of principle.[135] From another liberal perspective, policy science may be criticized for its crude utilitarian leanings: Lasswell and McDougal simply advocate the maximum attainment of democratic goals[136]—goals, that is, which accord with their own conception of democratic values—without providing any criteria for choosing among competing values or for judging the acceptability of trade-off between one value and another.[137]

The broad commitment to democratic values entails also, for Lasswell and McDougal, commitment to an idealized vision of absolute freedom. Their aim is to develop 'a jurisprudence which would serve the purposes of a free society'.[138] But what is a 'free' society? Lasswell and McDougal take freedom to mean absence of coercion when exercising choice. As we saw when we considered the work of Robert Hale, however, there can be no such thing as freedom in this sense, for such a conception of freedom requires a system of social arrangements in which there exist no relations of power. McDougal and Lasswell certainly recognize the existence of power relations; but they insist that such relations are primarily a source of freedom rather than coercion.[139] According to McDougal, 'power is most usefully conceived . . . as a coercive relation between human beings in which some are able . . . to make, and enforce, for others choices affecting a distribution of values'.[140] In other words, power entails a coercive relationship whereby the empowered are able to determine the range of choices available to all: power is to be exercised in the name of choice. But such exercise of power is hardly determinative of free choice. To take an example: as persons suitably empowered, law teachers are normally able to determine the range of choices available to students within the law school curriculum; and, within this narrow frame, students may be said to be able to exercise freedom of choice. But it is hardly 'real' freedom of choice. The courses on offer may not suit all student preferences; certain listed courses

[134] See, in particular, Lasswell and McDougal, *supra* n. 46, 374.

[135] See Ronald Dworkin, *Taking Rights Seriously* (London: Duckworth, 1977).

[136] See David Little, 'Toward Clarifying the Grounds of Value-Clarification: A Reaction to the Policy-Oriented Jurisprudence of Lasswell and McDougal', *Virginia Jnl. of International Law*, 14 (1974), 451–61 at 454.

[137] See John Rawls, *A Theory of Justice* (Oxford: Oxford University Press, 1972), 34–40.

[138] See, in particular, Lasswell and McDougal, *supra* n. 46, 374.

[139] See, in particular, Lasswell and Kaplan, *supra* n. 94, 74–102.

[140] McDougal, *supra* n. 84, 66.

may not actually be running; students may be precluded from opting, say, for two courses which involve a degree of substantive overlap; and of course, while students may opt for certain courses, they are unlikely to be able to choose the content of those courses. In the context of the law school, we may say, power is not so much the facilitation of freedom of choice as its denial and constraint: freedom exists only minimally, within a framework of coercion, a framework which is itself to be determined by a body of 'experts'. And this captures precisely one of the fundamental problems of policy science: the determination of the limits of freedom is treated as an unquestionable prerogative of the policy maker. 'Lasswell and McDougal . . . seem prepared to have the "experts" tell us that we cannot have some range of choices, and to tell us this in the name of democratic values.'[141]

The idea of the 'expert' is itself problematic. Policy-oriented education seems to require law students to cultivate so many different skills that it would be impossible for any of those skills to be developed satisfactorily. The lawyer of the future would be not so much an expert as a jack-of-all-trades.[142] Yet this is not what Lasswell and McDougal envisaged.

> The lawyer . . . is a member of a learned profession. . . . For nurturing him in the necessary skills and information society offers him a peculiarly long period of training and incubation; and, if that period is filled with the proper experiences, he can—our whole educational system is based on the premise—be trained for responsible leadership.[143]

The lawyer of the future, then, will be not just a lawyer but—potentially, at least—a national leader. Such an expectation is élitist, even by the standards of an Ivy League law school such as Yale.[144] 'It may be', Robert Stevens has written,'that at a few élite schools, a number of students may expect a career which will take them in and out of influential positions in private life and government, but such students are atypical even for the graduates of these schools.'[145] Lasswell and McDougal appeared, in fact, to be setting their sights on the atypical student: 'a law student', they insisted, 'easily conceives of himself as a legal adviser to a huge corporation or to one of the most important departments or agencies of government.'[146] One suspects that this highly ambitious, vocationally motivated model student would hardly welcome, or feel at home with, a style of legal education

[141] Stewart Macaulay, 'Law Schools and the World Outside their Doors: Notes on the Margins of "Professional Training in the Public Interest" ', *Virginia L. Rev.*, 54 (1968), 617–36 at 629.

[142] See Llewellyn, *supra* n. 10, 480; and Richard E. Speidel, 'A Matter of Mission', *Virginia L. Rev.*, 54 (1968), 606–16 at 610–11.

[143] Lasswell and McDougal, *supra* n. 42, 211.

[144] See Twining, *supra* n. 80, 413–14.

[145] Stevens, *supra* n. 43, 534.

[146] Lasswell and McDougal, *supra* n. 42, 247.

which placed minimal emphasis on technique and doctrine and stressed instead the value of the social sciences as a framework for policy-training. Again, however, Lasswell and McDougal envisaged otherwise. Students, they believed, would recognize and welcome policy science as a truly scholarly approach to legal study and teaching; as an attempt to raise professional standards both by promoting the development of legal and extra-legal skills and by emphasizing the importance of value-clarification and general self-enlightenment.[147]

Students in fact recognized and welcomed nothing of the sort. For all that American law professors may appeal periodically for what one of their number has termed 'the academizing of legal training',[148] the fact is that—whatever that phrase is taken to mean—most students are not interested.[149] Even if students were interested, it is doubtful that many of them would be inspired by the particular proposals which Lasswell and McDougal put forward; for they are proposals which require the student to achieve the well-nigh impossible.

This much is clear from the emphasis which Lasswell and McDougal place on value-clarification and self-enlightenment within the context of a policy-oriented legal education. According to McDougal, 'policy-oriented study must . . . postulate and clarify values.'[150] That is, a fundamental purpose of legal education developed along policy-science lines is to ensure that lawyers of the future, as policy-makers, are able and willing to make explicit the values which inform their decisions. But what are these values? Lasswell and McDougal express their hope that any lawyer who has gone through the process of policy-oriented legal education will become committed, if they are not already, to the so-called basic values of human dignity.[151] One of the primary objectives of policy-oriented legal education is to ensure that students who purport not to accept these values become aware of their own prejudices and, by becoming so aware, attempt to come to terms with and eliminate them. This, however, is to take a highly simplistic view of human nature. To recognize and to understand one's failings is by no means necessarily to rid oneself of those failings: diagnosis is not cure. Just as Jerome Frank appeared to believe that the revelation of the basic legal myth would lead to its elimination, Lasswell and McDougal seem similarly to assume that 'enlightenment' will lead their law student of the future to the recognition that prejudices must be abandoned in favour

[147] See e.g., ibid. 252–54.

[148] Thomas S. Bergin, 'The Law Teacher: A Man Divided Against Himself', *Virginia L. Rev.*, 54 (1968), 637–57 at 642; and see also Edward L. Rubin, 'The Practice and Discourse of Legal Scholarship', *Michigan L. Rev.*, 86 (1988), 1835–905 at 1904.

[149] See Stevens, *supra* n. 43, 536–7.

[150] McDougal, *supra* n. 84, 67.

[151] See Harold D. Lasswell and Myres S. McDougal, 'Jurisprudence in Policy-Oriented Perspective', *U. Florida L. Rev.*, 19 (1966–7), 486–513 at 508.

of the basic values of human dignity.[152] Properly to understand oneself, for them, is to understand oneself to be a democratic animal.

Since the basic values of human dignity are the values which are most likely to influence the lawyer's policy-making activities, they must not remain 'vague and implicit assumptions' but should be brought 'to a clear focus' so as to allow 'examination and appraisal' by anyone who should wish to take issue with a particular matter of public policy.[153] Clarification of value-preferences, Lasswell and McDougal argue, is the first fundamental step towards integrity and openness in policy-making. The style of clarification which they recommend, however, is as likely to breed subterfuge as it is to encourage accountability. Given that policy-makers are expected to be committed collectively to the same broadly formulated democratic values, policy-making itself might be conceived to be an essentially monolithic enterprise, whereby the justification of any official action is simply a matter of demonstrating, in a clear fashion, how that action may be said to have its roots in the basic values of human dignity. It is perhaps not utterly cynical to suggest that policy science is intended as an exercise in teaching potential future policy-makers how to use the rhetoric of value-clarification in order to embellish even the most questionable official activities with the gloss of democratic accountability and rectitude.

Such cynicism is rather compounded by the fact that Lasswell and McDougal emphasize the precise use of language as a vital feature of value-clarification. Trained as a policy scientist, the lawyer of the future will, they insist, be able 'to locate his position in the total context of communication, and [will be able] deliberately to choose whether to employ particular terms in a sense that is conventional within a given legal system, or according to definitions that are chosen to perform the distinctive functions of jurisprudence'.[154] Lasswell and McDougal's own work is an attempt to demonstrate how conventional legal discourse may usefully be supplemented by social-scientific concepts devised to facilitate the clear articulation of policy objectives. But it can hardly be deemed a success in this respect. One former Harvard Law School dean put the point diplomatically when he suggested that their initiatives for reform were 'impaired by a certain tendency towards grandiloquence'.[155] Fred Rodell, true to character, eschewed any such tact: 'like Prof. McDougal,' he observed 'I make and express "value judgements" and care deeply about "policy goals", though you'll never catch me talking that kind of language.'[156]

152 See McDougal, Lasswell and Reisman, *supra* n. 45, 199.

153 McDougal, *supra* n. 48, 8.

154 Lasswell and McDougal, *supra* n. 151, 487.

155 Erwin N. Griswold, 'Intellect and Spirit', *Harvard L. Rev.*, 81 (1967), 292–307 at 297.

156 Fred Rodell, 'Legal Realists, Legal Fundamentalists, Lawyer Schools, and Policy Science—Or How Not to Teach Law', *Vanderbilt L. Rev.*, 1 (1947), 5–7 at 7. Lasswell in particular was criticized for verbosity even by social scientists. See Rosten, *supra* n. 34, 3.

Others expressed the same view.[157] Whatever the merits or otherwise of reorienting legal education along policy-science lines, the dense prose and idiosyncratic jargon favoured by Lasswell and McDougal made their proposals seem rather ridiculous: here were two academics, writing in a fashion which few lawyers could comprehend, insisting that lawyers must be trained to express themselves more effectively. Certain of those lawyers who professed themselves able to understand Lasswell and McDougal's jargon detected a further anomaly in their jurisprudence: namely, its leanings towards legal formalism. The purpose of introducing policy science into the law schools seemed, in a sense, to be eminently Langdellian. 'Why,' Rodell asked, 'in the name of the ghost of Langdell—that first and worst standardizer of law-teaching technique—must [Lasswell and McDougal] try to cram their highly personalized approaches down the craws of other law teachers?'[158] Not only did the desire for standardization seem Langdellian; so too did the quest for certainty. The modern lawyer, by turning to policy science, would supposedly be 'never at a loss for a conceptual outline or agenda to guide him through the stages of his work. For those who have mastered the complexities of the apparatus . . . it offers a genuine sense of certainty and security.'[159] Yet that certainty and security could be procured only by conceiving of policy-making as an activity governed by a rigid conceptual framework.[160] Whereas Langdell had been determined to find certainty in legal doctrine, Lasswell and McDougal seemed intent on discovering a comparable certainty in the conceptual apparatus of policy science; it was for precisely this reason that Rodell mocked what he termed their 'earnest search for certainty in the substitution of one logomachy for another'.[161]

The verbosity and conceptual outlandishness which characterized Lasswell and McDougal's agenda for pedagogic reform prompted the bulk of the institutional objections to it. Teaching law students to be future policy-makers depended on law professors becoming adept in the strange language of Lasswellian policy science. Only by learning this language could those professors secure a radical reorientation of the American law school. However, not only were most law professors decidedly reluctant to learn a new language; they were generally uninterested in radical reform.[162] Lasswell and McDougal expected that the law student of the future would be trained not only as a social scientist, but as a social scientist with a mission. Since legal realism had failed to inspire law professors to

[157] See e.g. Yehezkel Dror, review of R. Arens and H. D. Lasswell, *In Defense of Public Order: The Emerging Field of Sanction Law*, *Yale L.J.*, 71 (1962), 797–800 at 800. For a dissenting view, however, see Moore, *supra* n. 11, 665, 674, 680.

[158] Rodell, *supra* n. 156, 7.

[159] Young, *supra* n. 71, 68.

[160] Ibid. 69.

[161] Rodell, *supra* n. 156, 6.

[162] See Macaulay, *supra* n. 141, 619 *et seq.*

achieve even the first half of this task, there seemed little reason that Lasswell and McDougal should have fared any better.

Indeed, if it were possible, they were likely to fare rather worse. The policy science perspective on law constitutes nothing more than a blueprint for the future direction of legal education. As Lon Fuller observed, no effort is made by Lasswell and McDougal to explain how practical reform along policy-science lines might be secured; nor do they pause to consider the possibility that their proposals might not yield the desired results.[163] In fact, if anything, their proposals seem almost as if designed to irritate American academic lawyers of the period, premissed as they are on the belief that, prior to 1940, legal education in the United States was basically devoid of valuable intellectual content.

Harvard Law School took particular umbrage at Lasswell and McDougal's proposals. Along with Griswold and Fuller, W. Barton Leach represented the main thrust of the Harvardian reaction against policy science. For Leach, the jurisprudence of Lasswell and McDougal was a barely concealed vilification of the Langdellian tradition; indeed, he insisted, the 'evangelical aspects' of their jurisprudence 'are accompanied by saturation bombing of strategic targets in the Cambridge area'.[164] Yet, Leach's own views regarding the future development of legal education in the United States were not all that far removed from those of Lasswell and McDougal. One of the primary objectives of modern property law teaching, Leach argued, should be that of 'adapting training to professional tasks'.[165] More generally, he appeared, like Lasswell and McDougal, to be of the opinion that the law schools should aim 'to train a large proportion of future national leaders'.[166] Leach and other Harvardians were by no means reluctant to see law schools become more policy-oriented. Where they differed from Lasswell and McDougal was over the matter of policy science. Bringing policy considerations into the classroom seemed, to Leach and others, to be an admirable initiative. But using jargon and grand theory to do so appeared pointless and even counter-productive. While Lasswell and McDougal criticized the inordinate narrowness (as they saw it) of post-war, process-oriented education at the Harvard Law School,[167] professors at that institution regarded themselves to be leading by

163 See Lon L. Fuller, 'American Legal Philosophy at Mid-Century', *Jnl. Leg. Educ.*, 6 (1954), 457–85 at 479; Macaulay, *supra* n. 141, 624.

164 W. Barton Leach, 'Property Law Taught in Two Packages', *Jnl. Leg. Educ.*, 1 (1948), 28–63 at 33.

165 Ibid. 28.

166 Ronnie Warrington, 'Land Law and Legal Education: Is There any Justice or Morality in Blackacre?', *Law Teacher*, 18 (1984), 77–94 at 83; and see, more generally, Kenneth E. Gray, 'What We Do to Law Students—Or The Judicial Philosophy of W. Barton Leach', *Duquesne L. Rev.*, 17 (1978–9), 381–418.

167 See Lasswell and McDougal, *supra* n. 46, 385. The process tradition in American jurisprudence is examined in ch. 4.

example—producing policy-makers, that is, without resorting to the high-falutin strategies of policy science.[168]

Whereas Ivy League institutions would have seen no need to develop along policy-science lines, smaller law schools would have been unable to do so even had it been their desire. To the average provincial law school professor, Lasswell and McDougal's proposals must have seemed not only self-indulgent and élitist but, perhaps even more crucially, impossible to finance. 'Only too often in the past,' Lasswell and McDougal wrote, 'brave new worlds of integrated law and social science have been proposed; but a short time afterwards it has been painfully apparent that the high aspirations of the founding fathers had come to little because of the practical difficulties of providing adequate financial and honorific inducements to enable people to "take the long chance" of cultivating marginal problems and skills.'[169] It is nothing short of bizarre that they could not recognize that their own ambitious proposals were destined to suffer the same fate. Even had they wanted to, most law schools were financially incapable of restructuring the syllabus in anything other than a piecemeal fashion; and money was certainly not available—even in the best schools—to introduce a general system of seminar teaching.[170] Furthermore, American law schools are guided, by and large, by a profession which demands not that students be trained as policy-makers, but that they satisfy the requirements of the bar. It is these requirements 'which determine the length of every law school programme—even the most prestigious—just as they determine the length of the terms, the form of the examination period, and through the examination process with its compulsory subjects on bar exams and recommended courses, it is they which control and influence, directly and indirectly, much of the content of legal education.'[171] Rather curiously—not to mention ironically—in offering detailed proposals for the improvement of professional training in the law schools, Lasswell and McDougal neglected to consider the preferences and the needs of the legal profession itself.

Policy science, it is generally agreed, failed to make any significant impact on the American law schools. Even Yale proved resistant.[172] Lasswell and McDougal's proposals were considered to be too élitist and costly, their conceptual apparatus too recondite, their normative premises too idiosyncratic.[173] That their proposed reforms were doomed to failure is obvious from the very assumption on which their entire jurisprudence is

[168] See Kalman, *supra* n. 13, 185–6.
[169] Lasswell and McDougal, *supra* n. 42, 290.
[170] See Stevens, *supra* n. 43, 534–5.
[171] Ibid. 537.
[172] See Bergin, *supra* n. 148, 642.
[173] See Kalman, *supra* n. 13, 184; Young, *supra* n. 71, 75; Stevens, *supra* n. 43 530–1; Tipson, *supra* n. 18, 556; Mayer, *supra* n. 129, 89–91; Macaulay, *supra* n. 141, 618.

founded. If lawyers really are as socially important as Lasswell and McDougal consider them to be, if they really are natural leaders of the community, it is unlikely that, as a professional group, they will feel much compulsion to become versed in the language and methods of the social sciences, or to learn skills which—from the general perspective of that group—seem surplus to requirement. Policy science was intended as an exercise in bringing prestige to a profession which already enjoyed prestige. For students, teachers, and practitioners of law alike, the only real difference between policy science and traditional doctrinal education is that the latter aims to provide professional kudos at considerably less cost.

It is not surprising, then, that the policy-science approach to law should have been adjudged a failure. However, if it was straightforwardly a failure, it would hardly deserve the attention that it has been accorded here. One professor at the Yale Law School has recently argued that Lasswell and McDougal's proposals for the reform of legal education have been tragically neglected. According to Anthony Kronman, their classic article on legal education and public policy 'defines more clearly than any other document the spirit of American legal scholarship today'.[174] In that article, he argues, it is possible to discover the seeds of both law and economics and critical legal studies.[175] The estimation of policy science offered in this chapter is decidedly less charitable. It would be a mistake, nevertheless, summarily to dismiss policy science as a project without a legacy. Accordingly, the remainder of this chapter will be devoted to two basic arguments. The first is that, while policy science may have foundered in the field of legal education, it was readapted with slightly more success in the field of international law. The second argument is that policy science is historically significant because—for all that Lasswell and McDougal may have intended otherwise—it represents a suppression rather than a continuation of the realist faith in pragmatism.

WHEN JURISPRUDENCE BECOMES INTERNATIONAL LAW

During the First World War, the maintenance of international order was a matter which seemed barely to trouble the minds of American lawyers. '[T]he present war', wrote Philip Marshall Brown in 1918, 'is in no way evidence of what some cynics have chosen to regard as the breakdown of either civilization, of Christianity, or of international law. On the contrary,

174 Anthony T. Kronman, *The Lost Lawyer: Failing Ideals of the Legal Profession* (Cambridge, Mass.: Belknap Press, 1993), 202.

175 Ibid. 201–9, 249, 253–4. I address law and economics and critical legal studies in chs. 5 and 6.

the union of twenty and more nations against one outlaw nation with its dupes and accomplices is striking evidence of the vigour of law and of the respect with which it is held. . . . This is truly a war in defence of law.'[176] The Second World War, however, was a different matter. Developments in military technology since the First World War had left the United States at least potentially vulnerable to foreign attack—a fear which would be confirmed, in 1941, by the Japanese raid on Pearl Harbor. The United States was forced to come to terms not only with the rise of fascism, but with the possibility that fascism might make its mark on American soil. It was for this reason that American lawyers began to adopt a rather less complacent attitude towards the security of the international legal order than that which they had adopted during the First World War. By 1938, Philip Marshall Brown was preaching a rather different message than that which he had preached two decades earlier:

> That international law is seriously discredited and on the defensive is all too evident. . . . The blatant demands of national egoism are producing inevitably another epoch of lawlessness. . . . National sovereignty, as expressed by authoritarian, totalitarian, corporative, or communist states, has become the stumbling-block of international jurisprudence. . . . The time has come for juriconsults frankly to acknowledge this desperate state of affairs and to undertake the renovation of international law or the creation of an entirely new system of law adequate to the demands of a new social order. It is futile to denounce the violations of international law or reaffirm principles now being derisively ignored or brazenly repudiated. Something much more constructive and even revolutionary is required.[177]

If something more revolutionary is to be attempted, Brown concluded, then its 'main object' ought to be 'the protection of the individual in his eternal struggle for freedom of personality . . . wherever he may be and whatever his national or racial allegiance'.[178] The rise of fascism, in short, had persuaded American lawyers of the need to revitalize international law.[179] Policy science became a feature of this move towards revitalization.

The Second World War took both Lasswell and McDougal to Washington. Lasswell was engaged in the War Communications Research Project at the Library of Congress, where he worked with others on the development of military intelligence through 'content analysis'—analysis, that is, of the political language of foreign states with a view to improving

[176] Philip Marshall Brown, 'War and Law', *American Jnl. of International Law*, 12 (1918), 162–5 at 164.

[177] Philip Marshall Brown, 'International Lawlessness', *American Jnl. of International Law*, 32 (1938), 775–8 at 776–7.

[178] Ibid. 777.

[179] See e.g. Ellery C. Stowell, 'The Juridical Significance of World War II', *American Jnl. of International Law*, 38 (1944), 106–8.

the possibility of anticipating enemy aggression.[180] The project complemented Lasswell's more general efforts to orient the social sciences towards the promotion and protection of democratic values.[181] McDougal began his wartime service as a legal adviser to various federal agencies. Subsequently, he was appointed General Counsel to the Office of Foreign Relief and Rehabilitation (later to become the United Nations Relief and Rehabilitation Administration), and it was in this capacity that he developed an interest in international law.

McDougal studied international law first at the University of Mississippi in 1923 and then later as a B.C.L. student at Oxford. Whereas, at Mississippi, international law had been taught by the University football coach—he 'wanted to be a scholar and that was all they would let him teach'[182]—at Oxford it was a highly regarded academic course. Indeed, at Oxford, McDougal studied under James Brierly, a leading exponent of the positivist school of international law. Brierly took the view that international law is constituted essentially by a body of rules; that is, there exists 'a body of rules and principles of action which are binding upon civilized states in their relations with one another'.[183] It is precisely this positivist view of the legal world which McDougal—once caught by the sway of legal realism at Yale—came to reject. However, it was neither the influence of realism nor his education at Oxford which first took him into the arena of international law scholarship, but his developing awareness of United States foreign policy.

McDougal's knowledge of American policy on foreign relief and rehabilitation led him to anticipate, before the Second World War had ended, that Congress would be reluctant to ratify the United States' membership of the post-war international organizations. In a lengthy article which marked his return to academic life, he attempted to demonstrate that the President could in fact join such organizations by executive agreement. The article marked McDougal's first foray into international law scholarship. There is 'an increasing consciousness' on the part of the people of the United States, he argued, 'that the world is

[180] For essays drawn from this research, see Harold D. Lasswell, Nathan Leites *et al.*, *Language of Politics: Studies in Quantitative Semantics* (New York: George Stewart, 1949).

[181] See de Sola Pool, *supra* n. 35, 199–200.

[182] Myres S. McDougal, 'Remarks by Myres S. McDougal', *Proceedings of the American Society of International Law*, 67 (1973), 292–6 at 294.

[183] J. L. Brierly, *The Law of Nations: An Introduction to the International Law of Peace* (6th edn. ed. H. Waldock, Oxford: Clarendon Press, 1963), 1. Note also Myres S. McDougal, letter to author, 17 February 1992. ('I went to Oxford as a Rhodes Scholar from the University of Mississippi from 1927 to 1930, taking a "double first" in the Honours School of Jurisprudence and the B.C.L. examination. Sir William Holdsworth, the Vinerian Professor who had been tutor at St. Johns, volunteered to be my tutor and was superb. James Brierly also gave me special tutelage in International Law, as did the older Jolowicz in Roman Law. There was no way I could escape an academic career after having had such tutors.')

shrinking every more rapidly, irrevocably, and imperiously into . . . "One World" '.[184]

> The judgement of the American people that their interests can no longer be protected by nineteenth-century neutrality, isolation, and inaction is based upon a realistic appraisal of the pervasive interdependence of all peoples. This basic condition of interdependence, the profound weakness of the world's present system of organization, and, conversely, the strong power position of the United States in the world society make it imperative that the United States not only participate, but take a leading part, in establishing a new order of political, economic, and cultural relationships and institutions, both in direct association with other nations, great and small, and through international organizations.[185]

In their seminal article on legal education and public policy, Lasswell and McDougal had raised the question of how it may be possible to develop 'a world state'.[186] The question had been raised purely *en passant*. McDougal, however, on returning to Yale after the Second World War, began to consider the question not only to be of immense political importance, but, still more significantly, to be one which could be answered by resorting to the methods of policy science. Thus began his involvement in international law.[187]

The development of international law along policy-science lines demanded, first of all, the rejection of the positivist model. In international law as elsewhere, McDougal argued, legal rules 'are but shorthand expressions of community expectations, and as instruments of communication, have the same inadequacies as any shorthand'.[188] Just as rules can provide only minimal legal guidance, general doctrines, too, must be regarded as sources of indeterminacy. Within any legal system, though especially under a system of international law, doctrines 'have the habit of travelling in pairs of complementary opposites'—for example, *pacta sunt servanda* (treaties must be respected) as compared with *rebus sic stantibus* (changed conditions may warrant revision)—'the terms of which are framed at such high levels of abstraction, or in such ambiguity, that they admit of many differing, alternative applications in particular instances'.[189]

184 Myres S. McDougal and Asher Lans, 'Treaties and Congressional-Executive or Presidential Agreements: Interchangeable Instruments of National Policy', *Yale L.J.*, 54 (1945), 181–351, 534–615 at pt. I, 183.

185 Ibid. 185.

186 Lasswell and McDougal, *supra* n. 42, 256.

187 See Gilmore, *supra* n. 79, 142.

188 McDougal, *supra* n. 48, 2.

189 McDougal, *supra* n. 96, 221–2. McDougal's argument here echoes—or rather, anticipates—the indeterminacy thesis as it has been developed by certain representatives of the critical legal studies movement (see ch. 6). However, neither policy science nor critical legal studies can be said to have embraced one another. See e.g. James Boyle, 'Ideals and Things: International Legal Scholarship and the Prison-house of Language', *Harvard International L.J.*, 26 (1985), 327–59 at 343. ('To claim that one can inject a universal value ("human dignity") into an avowedly means-end technique is a contradiction in terms. For this to become one of the dominant approaches to international law is a travesty'); also McDougal, *supra* n. 17. (We seek more emphasis upon the deliberate creation and

Since neither rules nor doctrines can be said fully to capture the reality of international law, the move towards the codification of such rules and doctrines—very much a going concern among international lawyers in the United States during the early decades of this century[190]—was to be treated with equal scepticism. If the American Society of International Law spends its energies 'repeating the follies of the American restatements in private law', McDougal commented in 1947, 'it will bring great discredit upon what can be done by the application of intelligence to the problems of international law and the world community'.[191]

Rather than conceive of international law simply as a collection of rules and doctrines to be codified, McDougal insists, it should be regarded more broadly as a constantly evolving process of authoritative decision-making.[192] International law is a process of decision-making which, first of all, has the backing of the international community—hence it is authoritative rather than merely effective—and, secondly, concerns and affects the promotion of values within that community.[193] Since international law is concerned with the promotion of values, the philosophy of international law, McDougal argues, ought to focus on the question of which values might best be supported by the authoritative decision-making process. Hardly surprisingly, the values which he himself favours for the international community are precisely the ones which he favours for the law school. 'The great challenge to students of international law today,' he wrote in 1953, is that of determining which approach to the subject 'is best designed to promote a free world society'.[194] His own rather inevitable conclusion is that one ought to settle on 'a "policy-oriented" approach'.[195]

The horizons of policy science as a jurisprudential perspective were accordingly broadened. The basic values of human dignity were no longer to be promoted simply within the context of the North American law schools. Rather, policy science had become the enterprise of promoting 'a world public order of human dignity', of developing a jurisprudential

appreciation of policy than most prior framers of jurisprudence and we recognize the need for a comprehensive, integrated set of values to achieve this emphasis. It is here that we differ from the Critical Legal Studies people . . . [W]e try to be constructive as well as destructive.')

190 The American Law Institute—in collaboration, primarily, with the Harvard Law School—had begun to campaign for the codification of international law as early as 1927. Their initiatives culminated in a series of draft codes, published in 1935: see *American Jnl. of International Law*, (Suppt.) 29 (1935), 40–64 at 48.

191 Myres S. McDougal, remark made in 'Development and Codification of International Law', *Proceedings of the American Society of International Law*, 41 (1947), 40–64 at 48.

192 See McDougal, *supra* n. 48, 2–7; *supra* n. 84, 58; Dillard, *supra* n. 91, 629.

193 See Moore, *supra* n. 11, 667; Young, *supra* n. 71, 61.

194 Myres S. McDougal, 'International Law, Power and Policy: A Contemporary Conception', *Recueil des Cours*, 82 (1953), 137–258 at 140.

195 Ibid.

framework in accordance with which the entire world might be transformed into a rationally organized, democratically governed 'free society' encompassing all peoples and offering the greatest enjoyment of human values for the largest number of individuals.[196] McDougal had invested policy science with a global dimension. Not surprisingly, Lasswell was similarly eager to develop policy science in this fashion. By the late 1950s, he too had turned his attention to international law.[197] Together, and with the assistance of numerous associates, Lasswell and McDougal—or rather, 'McDougal and Lasswell', a change which seemed to signal that the former had become the driving force behind the collaboration[198]—developed in great detail a policy-oriented approach to international law, premissed on their so-called basic values of human dignity, which not only came to be recognized as a 'school' of jurisprudence in its own right,[199] but which, to this day, continues to occupy a place within the field of international legal scholarship.[200] Policy-oriented jurisprudence may have failed to revolutionize the law schools, but it has not been a total failure.

It appears, in retrospect, almost inevitable that policy science should have been reoriented in this fashion. 'America's attempt since World War II to lay the foundations for a new system of international peace', Eugene Rostow wrote in 1968, 'has been primarily an attempt to persuade all nations and all peoples to accept certain fundamental ideas as to the nature of international society and the permissible limits of rivalry within it.'[201] Developed as a theory of international law, policy science could hardly have lent itself better to this general strategy of persuasion. According to McDougal, 'a world public order' is one 'in which values are shaped and

[196] See generally Myres S. McDougal and Florentino P. Feliciano, *Law and Minimum World Public Order: The Legal Regulation of International Coercion* (New Haven, Conn.: Yale University Press, 1961).

[197] See Myres S. McDougal and Harold D. Lasswell, 'The Identification and Appraisal of Diverse Systems of Public Order', *American Jnl. of International Law*, 53 (1959), 1–29. After having come to the subject through McDougal, Lasswell went on to produce international law scholarship in his own right. See e.g. Harold D. Lasswell, 'The Impact of Crowd Psychology Upon International Law', *Philippine International L.J.*, 1 (1962), 293–309; 'The Relevance of International Law to the Development Process', *Proceedings of the American Society of International Law*, 60 (1966), 1–8.

[198] A view certainly held by most international lawyers. See, for example, Richard A. Falk, 'Myres S. McDougal: Pioneer for the Year 2010', *Denver Jnl. of International Law and Policy*, 1 (1971), 13–16.

[199] See, for example, Gidon Gottlieb, 'The Conceptual World of the Yale School of International Law', *World Politics*, 21 (1968), 108–32; Eisuke Suzuki, 'The New Haven School of International Law: An Invitation to a Policy-Oriented Jurisprudence', *Yale Studies in World Public Order*, 1 (1974), 1–48.

[200] For a fairly recent example, see Lung-chu Chen, *An Introduction to Contemporary International Law: A Policy-Oriented Perspective* (New Haven, Conn.: Yale University Press, 1989).

[201] Eugene V. Rostow, *Law, Power, and the Pursuit of Peace* (Lincoln, NB: University of Nebraska Press, 1968), xv.

shared more by persuasion than by coercion, and which seeks to promote the greatest production and the widest possible sharing . . . of all values among all human beings'.[202] Yet, 'all values' is to be taken, in this context, to mean all American, liberal-democratic values; for policy science is premissed on the development, in the future, of a single international community, a world public order, within which there exist certain common political interests—interests which, though supposedly divorced from national interests, turn out to be the embodiment of post-war American foreign policy.[203] The promotion of this policy throughout the world entails not merely the acceptance of American democratic values, but also the rejection of all competing ideologies. The policy science approach to international law thus turns out to be an exercise not so much in persuasion and policy promotion as in propaganda and ideological aggression.[204] This much is clear from the manner in which, from the Truman era onwards, policy science became a cloak for Cold War chauvinism. The following quotation is illustrative:

> The prospect of the possible use of the hydrogen bomb against human beings is almost too horrible to contemplate. It appears probable that each half of the world will shortly have the capacity quickly to destroy the other: the common analogy of two death-dealing scorpions enclosed in a small bottle has become all too apt. . . . We do not, however, regard it as a rational response for the free world unilaterally to disarm itself. . . . Until a reasonably secure world public order can be established, the free half of the world has no alternative but to make certain that it remains a scorpion and does not invite transformation into inanimate radioactive dust.[205]

[202] Myres S. McDougal, 'Perspectives for an International Law of Human Dignity', *Proceedings of the American Society of International Law*, 53 (1959), 107–32 at 107.

[203] See Myres S. McDougal, 'The Impact of International Law upon National Law: A Policy-Oriented Perspective', *South Dakota L. Rev.*, 4 (1959), 25–92; also Boyle, *supra* n. 189, 349 *et seq*.

[204] On the problem of distinguishing policy promotion from ideological propaganda, see Rosalyn Higgins, 'Policy and Impartiality: The Uneasy Relationship in International Law', *International Organization*, 23 (1969), 914–31.

[205] Myres S. McDougal and Norbert A. Schlei, 'The Hydrogen Bomb Tests in Perspective: Lawful Measures for Security', *Yale L.J.*. 64 (1955), 648–710 at 709. In a similar vein, see Myres S. McDougal, 'The Soviet-Cuban Quarantine and Self-Defense', *American Jnl. of International Law*, 57 (1963), 597–604; Myres S. McDougal and Richard M. Goodman, 'Chinese Participation in the United Nations: The Legal Imperatives of a Negotiated Solution', *American Jnl. of International Law*, 60 (1966), 671–727; Myres S. McDougal and W. Michael Reisman, 'Rhodesia and the United Nations: The Unlawfulness of International Concern', *American Jnl. of International Law*, 62 (1968), 1–19. Lasswell, ironically, was hounded during the McCarthy era because of his interest in communism. See Muth, *supra* n. 26, 14. The experience, if anything, turned him more towards the ideology of the Cold War. See e.g. Harold D. Lasswell, 'The Universal Peril: Perpetual Crisis and the Garrison-Prison State', in L. Bryson, L. Finkelstein and R. M. MacIver (eds.), *Perspectives on a Troubled Decade. Science, Philosophy and Religion, 1939–1949: Tenth Symposium* (New York: Harper, 1950), 323–8; 'The Strategy of Soviet Propaganda', *Proceedings of the Academy of Political Science*, 24 (1951), 214–26; ' "Inevitable" War: A Problem in the Control of Long-Range Expectations', *World Politics*, 2 (1949), 1–39.

Policy science became, accordingly, a mission not merely to promote democratic ideals but to save the free world. Essential differences among political systems were to be sacrificed for the purpose of creating a globally legitimate international order founded upon the basic values of human dignity. McDougal and Lasswell even suggested that, should extra-terrestrials ever land on this planet, they too might be urged to recognize the fundamental desirability and rectitude of these values.[206] Such is the imperialistic, colonizing, thrust of policy science. It is a classic example of a theory which calls for an end to history.[207]

Despite its rootedness in a distinctly North American liberal democratic value-system, policy science, as an approach to international law, has been influential in countries other than the United States.[208] This is not entirely surprising, for the policy science perspective represents a serious and sustained attempt to move beyond the positivist tradition which dominated international law scholarship throughout the late nineteenth and early twentieth centuries.[209] However, the jurisprudential framework which McDougal and Lasswell devised, like the positivist framework which it was intended to supersede, failed fully to capture the reality of international legal relations. This much was made clear by the Vietnam War.[210] By the

[206] See Myres S. McDougal, Harold D. Lasswell and Ivan A. Vlasic, 'Potential Interactions with Advanced Forms of Non-Earth Life', *Egyptian Review of International Law*, 18 (1962), 53–101; reprinted in M. S. McDougal, H. D. Lasswell and I. A. Vlasic, *Law and Public Order in Space* (New Haven, Conn.: Yale University Press, 1963), 947–1021.

[207] On 'the end of history', see Francis Fukuyama, 'The End of History?', *The National Interest*, 16 (1989), 3–18 (arguing that liberal democracy is the only legitimate ideology remaining in the world). A rather more subtle presentation of the 'end of history' thesis is now to be found in Francis Fukuyama, *The End of History and the Last Man* (London: Hamish Hamilton, 1992). According to Fukuyama, there appears to be 'a fundamental process at work that dictates a common evolutionary pattern for *all* human societies—in short, something like a Universal History of mankind in the direction of liberal democracy' (ibid. 48). 'It is possible,' Fukuyama concludes, 'that if events continue to unfold as they have done over the past few decades, that the idea of a universal and directional history leading up to liberal democracy may become more plausible to people, and that the relativist impasse of modern thought will in a sense solve itself.' (ibid. 338.)

[208] See e.g. Rosalyn Higgins, *The Development of International Law Through the Political Organs of the United Nations* (Oxford: Oxford University Press, 1963); Manual M. Ortega, 'La Concepción del Derecho International de Myres S. McDougal', *Revista Juridica de la Universidad de Puerto Rica*, 36 (1967), 1–39; Bent Rosenthal, *Étude de Myres Smith McDougal en Matière de Droit International Public* (Paris: Librairie Générale de Droit et de Jurisprudence, 1970); and also Rosalyn Higgins, review of Rosenthal, *American Jnl. of International Law*, 66 (1972), 646–8 at 648 fn. 1; Frederick S. Tipson, Bibliography of Works by and Relating to Myres S. McDougal', in W. Michael Reisman and Burns H. Weston (eds.), *Toward World Order and Human Dignity: Essays in Honor of Myres S. McDougal* (New York: Free Press, 1976), 578–93 at 591–3.

[209] See Chen, *supra* n. 200, 11.

[210] See Richard A. Falk, *The Status of Law in International Society* (Princeton, NJ: Princeton University Press, 1970), 570–90.

end of the war, communist governments remained in control of Vietnam, Cambodia and Laos, and none of the goals which the United States had used to justify military intervention had been achieved.[211] If the Vietnam War had done anything, it had served as a powerful illustration that other nations could not simply be remodelled in accordance with American liberal-democratic ideals. Contrary to what McDougal and Lasswell believed, the world was not ready to be remade in the image of the United States.

It is for this reason that, nowadays, many if not most international lawyers are fairly quick to dismiss policy science. Possibly its demise reflects a cooling of interest, in the American law schools, in the discipline of international law itself.[212] It may well be that the world would be a better place if governed by an international legal order founded on McDougal and Lasswell's basic values of human dignity; certainly the collapse of various communist régimes in recent years has made their ideal world seem like less of a pipe-dream. To assume that this world is just around the corner, however, 'serves only to reinforce the perception of international law as naive, utopian, and unconnected with the real world'.[213] International lawyers have hardly been insensitive to this image of their subject. Indeed, their sensitivity has led certain of them to attempt to develop new, 'post-policy science' theories of international law.[214] By the end of the Vietnam War, one of their number has observed, 'it was just no longer possible to speak of an American-inspired world democracy'.[215] Policy science had been undermined by the progress of history, and international law—the subject which McDougal in particular had worked so hard to revolutionize—had acquired the appearance of 'a discipline which had lost its way and kept its jobs'.[216] The very theory which had been adapted in order to revitalize and reorient international law scholarship in accordance with the major problems of the modern world served, ironically, to expose the basic vulnerability of the discipline.

[211] See, generally, George C. Herring, *America's Longest War: The United States and Vietnam, 1950–1975* (2nd edn. Philadelphia: Temple University Press, 1986).

[212] See John King Gamble, Jr. and Natalie S. Shields, 'International Legal Scholarship: A Perspective on Teaching and Publishing', *Jnl. Leg. Educ.*, 39 (1989), 39–46.

[213] Phillip R. Trimble, 'International Law, World Order, and Critical Legal Studies', *Stanford L. Rev.*, 42 (1990), 811–45 at 816.

[214] See, for example, David Kennedy, *International Legal Structures* (Baden-Baden: Nomos, 1987); Guyora Binder, *Treaty Conflict and Political Consideration: The Dialectic of Duplicity* (New York: Greenwood, 1988); Marrti Koskenniemi, *From Apology to Utopia: The Structure of International Legal Argument* (Stockholm: Almqvist & Wiksell, 1989).

[215] David Kennedy, 'A New Stream of International Law Scholarship', *Wisconsin International L.J.*, 7 (1988), 1–49 at 6.

[216] Ibid.

CONCLUSION: STALLING OVER REALISM

International law held little appeal for so-called legal realists;[217] and by turning their attention to the subject and conceiving of it in terms of policy science, Lasswell and McDougal set themselves apart from their jurisprudential forebears. But one hardly needs to look to international law in order to detect the differences between policy science and realism. Both 'law' and 'social science' have different meanings in a policy-science context than they do in any realist context. Furthermore, while realist jurisprudence was only half-heartedly aligned with the politics of the New Deal, policy science gave American jurisprudence an overtly political face by insisting that law students be trained as servants of democracy. Whereas legal realism remained a private law jurisprudence in a public law world, moreover, the policy-science approach to legal education was an exercise in training lawyers as public lawyers—as lawyers equipped to interpret and create public policy. In these and other ways, the policy-oriented approach to jurisprudence may be said to constitute a fundamental step onwards from legal realism.

From an historical point of view, however, it is not sufficient merely to describe policy science as an attempt to move American jurisprudence onwards from realism. Policy science did not straightforwardly build upon realist insights; rather, it entailed a methodology, for want of a better word, which seemed to counter the basic faith in pragmatism inherent in realist legal thinking. This is, without doubt, a strange claim to make, for policy science is purportedly a pragmatic theory. 'The policy sciences', Lasswell observed, 'are a contemporary adaption of the general approach to public policy that was recommended by John Dewey and his colleagues in the development of pragmatism.'[218] Certainly the purpose of jurisprudence conceived as policy science seems eminently pragmatic, since it must, according to Lasswell and McDougal, be oriented towards improving the problem-solving and policy-making skills of the would-be lawyer. While, however, policy science may have been intended as a pragmatic perspective on law, this is not the case in reality.

The explanation for this is traceable to the manner in which policy science draws upon the work of Dewey. There are to be found in the literature of policy science two discernibly-Deweyan themes. First, there is the emphasis on democracy. Dewey prefigured Lasswell and McDougal in arguing that democracy is not merely a form of government but a set of

[217] See Tipson, *supra* n. 18, 558.

[218] Harold D. Lasswell, *A Pre-View of Policy Sciences* (New York: American Elsevier, 1971), xiii–xiv.

basic human ideals, and that the optimum realization of these ideals throughout society demands the existence of institutions which reflect and promote them.[219] Secondly, there is the emphasis on intellectual tasks. The 'reconstruction' of philosophy, according to Dewey, 'can be nothing less than the work of developing, of forming, of producing . . . the intellectual instrumentalities which will progressively direct inquiry into the deeply and inclusively human—that is to say, moral—facts of the present scene and situation.'[220] Reconstruction requires, accordingly, the development of 'an apparatus for conducting investigation, and for recording and interpreting (organizing) its results'.[221] Policy-science, as a form of jurisprudence, is an attempt to reconstruct legal education along more or less the same lines. 'A viable jurisprudence must', McDougal argues, 'provide a theory and specify goal procedures for the systematic, disciplined, and contextual performance of a comprehensive range of policy and relevant intellectual tasks.'[222] The reconstruction of jurisprudence demands, therefore, the cultivation of the same sorts of skills—analysis of policy, clarification of values, systematization of goals and the like—as are emphasized within the Deweyan philosophical framework.[223]

That policy science follows a Deweyan line in emphasizing democracy and the cultivation of particular skills does not, however, make it a pragmatic theory. For policy science is too preoccupied with the development of a methodology and too little concerned with the matter of how that methodology may prove in some way to be useful. If policy-makers are to map out the future of American society, Lasswell argued, they must first of all have an overview of the entire social processes and institutions with which they are concerned. Such an overview can only be developed, he insisted, by establishing a system of education equipped to provide policy-makers with skills in evaluation, self-appraisal, problem-solving and the like.[224] Only by creating an appropriately skilled, democratically enlightened cadre of experts might society progress. But in what way is society supposed to progress? Indeed, what does it mean, to progress? Policy science does not answer these questions. Rather, it simply stresses that the progression of society is dependent on the creation of enlightened policy-makers.

219 See, generally, Robert B. Westbrook, *John Dewey and American Democracy* (Ithaca, NY: Cornell University Press, 1991).

220 John Dewey, *Reconstruction in Philosophy* (enl. ed. Boston: Beacon, 1948; orig. publ. 1920), xxvii.

221 John Dewey, *The Public and its Problems* (New York: Holt & Co., 1927), 203.

222 McDougal, *supra* n. 48, 9–10.

223 For further comparison, see Tipson, *supra* n. 18, 540.

224 The argument is to be found throughout Lasswell's writings. For a succinct statement, see Chris Argyris, Joseph Goldsen and Harold Lasswell, 'Looking for a Decent Future', *Yale Reports*, 527 (1969), 1–7.

This captures the fundamental problem with policy science as a form of jurisprudence. At best, it is groundwork; interpreted less charitably, it is the use of theory to encourage procrastination over matters practical. 'A jurisprudence which would effectively serve the needs of both scholars and specialists in decision', Lasswell and McDougal claim, 'must achieve clarity in distinguishing the observational standpoints of the scholar and the decision-maker . . . must establish a focus of attention both comprehensive and selective . . . must identify the whole range of intellectual tasks relevant to problem-solving . . . [and] must make explicit . . . the values which are postulated, or assumed, to be at stake in decision and inquiry.'[225] The policy-oriented approach to law transpires in this way to be but an inventory of broad objectives and things-to-get-clarified. We saw, in the previous chapter, that the Yale Law School under Robert Hutchins's deanship was marked—indeed, ultimately blighted—by a basic philosophy of 'Do Something!' In contrast, Lasswell and McDougal's philosophy was one of: 'before anything is done, let us talk about it; let us determine what the problems are; let us specify, systematize and operationalize what we consider to be our tasks; let us figure out, and then clarify, what our values, policies and objectives are. Only once goals such as these have been achieved should we think about "doing something".' Policy science advocated a step backwards from social institutions in order to achieve a better view of their shortcomings. That, however, is all that it purported to do: to provide a better view. It was simply assumed that, by doing this, social and institutional change would occur inevitably.

Thus it was that, apart from the impact that it made on international law scholarship in the United States, the jurisprudence of Lasswell and McDougal met with rejection. The policy science project was deemed to be too idiosyncratic, élitist, jargon-laden and utopian: it projected a hazy vision of law in a future society without any real indication of how lawyers were supposed to turn that vision into reality. The idea that they might achieve as much by becoming versed in the language and methods of policy science demanded too great a leap of faith. It demanded also, certainly of American academic lawyers, too radical a reorientation of perspective. Whereas Poundian and realist jurisprudence had been criticized for emphasizing social engineering and pragmatism without specifying or even considering the types of moral and political values and objectives that the American legal system ought to embody and promote, the jurisprudence of Lasswell and McDougal veered too much to the other extreme by over-emphasizing preliminary, policy-oriented skills such as value- and goal-clarification. In their later collaborative writings, Lasswell and McDougal appeared to despair over the fact that post-realist American legal theorists

[225] Lasswell and McDougal, *supra* n. 46. 375.

seemed generally disinclined to make much use of policy science.[226] That they considered this to be a cause for despair illustrates the degree to which they misread the mood of the American law schools in the aftermath of the Second World War. Those academic lawyers who were looking for a post-realist perspective on law certainly did not wish to take jurisprudence along the policy-science route. Something much less maverick, much more middle-ground, was required. What was being sought after was an approach which eschewed both the perceived rashness of realism and the theoretical excess of policy science. Given this, it is not at all surprising that the approach which emerged came not out of Yale, the home of legal realism and Lasswell and McDougal, but out of Harvard, the well-spring of Langdellianism. With the flourishing of the 'process' perspective on law in the 1950s, the Harvard Law School began again to mark out the future of American jurisprudence.

226 See e.g. Lasswell and McDougal, *supra* n. 55, 483.

4

Finding Faith in Reason

Legal realism, we have seen, constituted a rather half-hearted, largely unsuccessful attack on legal formalism. The 'radical' impetus which commentators have tended to find in the literature of realism was, in fact, neither as pronounced nor as sincere as is commonly believed. This chapter represents an effort to dispel another common misconception about American jurisprudence. It is frequently remarked that that field of American legal thought which is traditionally labelled 'process' jurisprudence emerged as a post-war response to legal realism. Such an assumption, I shall try to show, is incorrect. Certainly process jurisprudence began to flourish once the mood of realism began to wane. But that did not mark the birth of the process perspective. Historically, the process-oriented approach to the study of law parallels if not precedes legal realism itself.

In this chapter, locating process jurisprudence historically forms only a minor part of my agenda. My primary aim is to try to make sense of process jurisprudence. What was process jurisprudence about? What was it for? The simple answer to these questions is that process jurisprudence exemplifies the emergence of *reason* as the dominant ideological and theoretical motif in American legal thought. Process jurisprudence, that is, marks the beginning of American lawyers' attempting to explain legal decision-making not in terms of deductive logic or the intuitions of officials, but in terms of reason which is embodied in the fabric of the law itself. By finding faith in reason, it has been remarked, process jurisprudence illustrates how post-war American legal theorists turned their attention 'to the task of finding an objective basis for legal decision-making'.[1]

The problem with such a statement is that it conveys the impression that the jurisprudence of process is the jurisprudence of reason, end of story. In fact, within the process tradition, reason has not remained a static concept. As process thinking has developed, the language of reason has changed. Key themes such as principle, purpose, integrity and prudence have, in different ways and at different times, been employed and refined by process writers to articulate and promote the idea of reason immanent in

[1] James Boyle, 'The Politics of Reason: Critical Legal Theory and Local Social Thought', *U. Pennsylvania L. Rev.*, 133 (1985), 685–780 at 703.

law. Understanding the process tradition demands an appreciation of how the significance and the import of such themes changes over time. For it is only by treating process jurisprudence as an evolving body of thought that we might recognize its significance in the context of American law.

Charting the historical evolution of process jurisprudence proves difficult. Retrospective rationalization of the subject has stripped it of its nuances. Such rationalization is perhaps a necessary consequence of writing history.[2] Yet, even if this is so, it is surely the case that the past can be rationalized with differing degrees of subtlety and care. With process jurisprudence, such qualities have often been in rather short supply. Commentators have been content to lump names and works and themes together and hold them up as representative of some vaguely-conceived process 'school'.[3] They have tended, furthermore, both to give that 'school' a date of birth and also to write its obituary.[4] At one level, such initiatives are not unwelcome, for they facilitate the focusing of thought. At another level, however, they are highly problematic, since they gloss over the complexity of that which is being studied. Certain themes are seen to recur throughout the literature of process jurisprudence, and from this it is concluded that these themes must be regarded as dominant and definitive within the process tradition. This is a fair and sensible conclusion to reach. But it is a conclusion which can be pushed further. That certain themes recur is only half of the story. In the process of recurrence, those themes may take on a new dimension, or even a new life.

It would not be entirely inappropriate to characterize the process tradition with a phrase—by no means unproblematic, as we shall see in due course—borrowed from one of its most notable proponents: as an example, that is, of 'the maturing of collective thought'.[5] Process jurisprudence was never packaged as a discrete theory. Rather, it evolved

[2] See Paul Veyne, *Writing History: Essay on Epistemology* (Eng. trans. M. Moore-Rinvolucri, Manchester: Manchester University Press, 1984), 44–6, 110–11; Michael Oakeshott, 'The Activity of being an Historian', in his *Rationalism in Politics and Other Essays* (London: Methuen, 1962), 137–67.

[3] The most renowned, and indeed useful, example is Bruce A. Ackerman, '*Law and the Modern Mind* by Jerome Frank', *Daedalus*, 103 (1974), 119–30 at 128–9 n. 26. The writer who first suggested the existence of a process school has since retracted that claim. See G. Edward White, *The American Judicial Tradition: Profiles of Leading American Judges* (New York: Oxford University Press, 1976), 404 n. 1; and compare G. Edward White, 'The Evolution of Reasoned Elaboration: Jurisprudential Criticism and Social Change', *Virginia L. Rev.*, 59 (1973), 279–302, repr. in G. Edward White, *Patterns of American Legal Thought* (Indianapolis: Bobbs-Merrill, 1978), 136–63.

[4] See e.g. Mark V. Tushnet, 'Metaprocedure?', *Southern California L. Rev.*, 63 (1989), 161–79 at 178. ('The legal process school flourished in the 1950s and 1960s, but its intellectual vitality was sapped thereafter, as the disorders of the late 1960s and early 1970s showed that one could not presume that fundamental social agreement existed.')

[5] Henry M. Hart, Jr., The Supreme Court, 1958 Term—Foreword: The Time Chart of the Justices', *Harvard L. Rev.*, 73 (1959), 84–125 at 100.

slowly, through subtle and gradual refinement. It is instructive, in this regard, to compare process jurisprudence with policy science. While policy science was very much a manufactured affair—a conscious effort by Harold Lasswell and Myres McDougal to develop a pedagogic framework which would move American legal thought onwards from realism—process jurisprudence just came about and caught on. There was no grand, initiating text.[6] Indeed, when, in the 1950s, the classic work of the process tradition—Henry Hart and Albert Sacks's *The Legal Process*[7]—appeared, process-oriented legal thought was already fairly well established in the United States. To claim that *The Legal Process* 'appeared' is actually something of an overstatement. Although widely circulated and used as teaching materials in many American law schools, Hart and Sacks's manuscript was never published—indeed, it was never completed.

A fact which conceals an immense irony. The difference between policy science and process jurisprudence is akin to the difference between the person who is too eager to be liked and the person who exudes natural charm. Lasswell and McDougal worked hard, published widely and were ultimately unsuccessful in promoting their master-plan for the post-realist law school. Process jurisprudence, in contrast, was founded on attitude rather than on strategy. It was a fairly low-key attitude, an attitude which tended to bobble to the surface of, rather than to dominate, the works of those who shared it. Yet it was an attitude which lent itself perfectly to the tackling of legal problems. Those who adopted the process attitude were concerned not so much with developing a distinct theory as with cultivating their attitude in order to cast light on what they considered to be the principal problems in the creation and application of law. It was through such cultivation that this general attitude came ever so gradually to be refined, and it is because process jurisprudence was premissed on nothing more specific or substantial than an attitude that it proves to be remarkably difficult to pin down.

It may seem odd to conceive of a major area of American legal thought in this way. I would insist, nevertheless, that if we are to understand the process tradition, it is the only way. To trace the history and significance of process jurisprudence is to trace the development of a particular attitude towards law. It is an attitude about the point and the value of law, about the social role of the lawyer and the law school, and about the purpose of

[6] Quite the opposite with policy science. See Harold D. Lasswell and Myres S. McDougal, 'Legal Education and Public Policy: Professional Training in the Public Interest', *Yale L.J.* , 52 (1943), 203–95.

[7] Henry M. Hart, Jr. and Albert M. Sacks, *The Legal Process: Basic Problems in the Making and Application of Law* (tentative edn. Cambridge, Mass.: unpublished mimeograph [on file with author: copy supplied by Professor Sacks], 1958). Hereinafter cited as *The Legal Process*. All citations are to the 1958 edition.

legal scholarship. It is an attitude premissed in every instance on the belief that those who respect and exercise the faculty of reason will be rewarded with the discovery of a priori criteria which give sense and legitimacy to their legal activities. Different exponents of process jurisprudence adopt and express this attitude in different ways, and some are more explicit than are others in so doing. The point to be stressed is that the attitude exists and that it is embedded in modern American jurisprudential discourse. Understanding the process tradition demands not just that we pinpoint the key figures, themes and texts of that tradition, but that we identify and chart the development of the attitude on which the tradition is founded. It requires, in other words, that we see the process perspective not as a legal school, but as a peculiar facet of American legal culture.

To conceive of the process tradition in this manner is, of course, to create problems. It would be much easier to write a history of process jurisprudence beginning with its emergence in response to realism and ending with the inability of its proponents to come to terms with the judicial activism of the Warren Court. This history has already been written, and indeed written well.[8] The problem with such a history is that it fails either to convince or to do justice to its subject matter. For if process jurisprudence is the expression of a particular attitude about law which is embedded in American legal culture, then we cannot simply give it a beginning, a middle, and an end. One of the most important questions to be addressed is that of how, if at all, this attitude continues to feature in contemporary legal thought. To write a history of the process tradition is not necessarily to confine its relevance to the past.

There is one final introductory point to be made about process jurisprudence conceived as a cultural attitude. American legal realism has been the subject of controversy ever since it was first identified as a distinct intellectual phenomenon. Yet it would be to court no controversy at all to suggest that realism illustrates some of the earliest efforts of American lawyers to forge explicit links between law and the social sciences. Nothing so definite can be asserted about the process tradition. At the heart of process jurisprudence generally there seems to rest the assumption that the social sciences will normally prove enlightening when adopted for the purposes of studying law.[9] Whereas, for many so-called legal realists, the effort to utilize social-scientific methods was regarded as something of an issue in itself, proponents of process jurisprudence tended—and still tend—to undertake such an effort in a rather less self-conscious fashion. For legal realists, the appeal to the social sciences had, if nothing else, novelty value. But for those writing in the wake of realism, the novelty had generally worn off. Although, by the 1940s, many lawyers remained

[8] See White, 'The Evolution of Reasoned Elaboration', *supra* n. 3, *passim*.
[9] See e.g. Hart and Sacks, *The Legal Process*, 116.

convinced that the adoption of interdisciplinary perspectives on law might generate fresh insights into its machinery and operation, simply to profess to adopt such a perspective—a common strategy of the so-called realist—no longer caused any great shakes. Linking law with social science was no longer tantamount to breaking new jurisprudential ground.

It is for this reason that the literature of the process tradition is characterized by, among other things, a decidedly casual attitude towards the social sciences. One of the basic sentiments behind process thinking is that, although profitable connections might be made between law and social science, the fact that the connections are there to be forged is hardly deserving of fuss. A consequence of this sentiment is that, in process literature, social-scientific perspectives rarely if ever take centre-stage and an interdisciplinary ethos features in only a very informal and unobtrusive manner. Proponents of process jurisprudence have been occasionally inspired rather than significantly guided by non-legal scholarship. That is, whereas so-called realists would often structure their analyses around specific branches of the social sciences such as psychology or institutional economics, process writers have tended to borrow ideas *ad hoc* from particular philosophical and social-scientific movements and texts. To put the matter simply, process writers have made no special effort to be 'social scientific': while respect for the social sciences is a feature of their basic attitude, no general attempt has been made to use the social sciences to develop an overall process strategy.

The most significant consequence of this absence of strategy, from an historical point of view, is that the intellectual foundations of process jurisprudence are difficult to locate with any degree of precision. For all that legal realism seems to defy definition, it is at least possible to develop some sense of where most so-called realists were coming from, for the simple reason that they tended to parade their particular social-scientific predilections. Given that exponents of the process tradition have for the most part avoided linking their jurisprudential inquiries with broader social-scientific initiatives, it is very difficult to conceive of that tradition in a general intellectual as opposed to a specifically legal context. The connections which might be made between process-orientation in law and process-orientation in other disciplines are largely speculative. That process writers themselves have tended not to make these connections could be for the reason that they do not believe them to exist, or because it seems unnecessary to make them explicit. Yet, for the purposes of historical analysis, it is important to identify these potential connections. Only by so doing might we appreciate that the process tradition is the reflection of a general intellectual tendency; that, in the United States during this century, jurisprudence has not been alone in developing a distinctively rationalist vocabulary of process.

THE STIRRING OF PROCESS

It might be argued that, in American jurisprudence, this vocabulary of process was already emerging during Langdell's era. Certain of those who were responsible for popularizing the case method—James Barr Ames and William Keener at Harvard are signal in this respect[10]—promoted it as a technique by which to demonstrate not simply the existence of essential legal principles but, more fundamentally, that such principles are integral to a general process of legal reasoning (see Chapter 1). Teaching the case method in this fashion demanded that law students not only be able to identify the substantive legal rules and principles at the heart of a particular case, but that they be able to determine the importance of those rules and principles to the reasoning of that case. Conceived in this way, the study of law became the study of a procedure by which judges, rather than simply apply doctrine in a mechanical fashion, use doctrine in the process of reasoning towards a decision.[11]

This 'modernized' version of the case method survived into the realist era, and indeed seems to have borne some influence on realist legal thought. Writing in 1937, Max Radin observed that 'the "case system", as it was devised and applied by the masters of that method, was not meant merely as an orderly arrangement of propositions, ticketed with case-names, each proposition being recorded in the student's mind as the "rule" that the case "stands for" '.[12] '[T]he method as a mnemonic device for legal propositions is one thing and the method as a training in the technique of a lawyer is another. It may serve both purposes.'[13] Working from the proposition that '[t]he only technique that can be taught in law schools is that of dialectic',[14] Radin explores the possibility of adapting the case method, as a 'method of dialectic',[15] to the 'goal of making a large and coherent system of many of the classes and sub-classes of the law'.[16] The case method, he insists, 'is in part an excellent device' for fulfilling 'this larger purpose' behind legal study 'if it is really used as it professes to be'.[17] While all forms of dialectical training and technique will probably always remain inadequate to the task of teaching justice,[18] the case method, suitably modified, may assist students in cultivating their skills of reasoning and argument, and provide 'the kind of general training that

[10] See Harvard Law School Association, *Centennial History of the Harvard Law School, 1817–1917* (Cambridge, Mass.: Harvard Law School Association, 1918), 81.

[11] See further Robert Stevens, *Law School: Legal Education in America from the 1850s to the 1980s* (Chapel Hill: University of North Carolina Press, 1983), 56.

[12] Max Radin, 'The Education of a Lawyer', *California L. Rev.*, 25 (1937), 676–91 at 679.

[13] Ibid. 680.

[14] Ibid. 681.

[15] Ibid.

[16] Ibid. 682.

[17] Ibid.

[18] Ibid. 690.

enables them to speak the language and understand the ideas of those who guide and control the community, the kind of education that a few generations ago was called the education of a gentleman'.[19]

Thus it is that the case method was promoted by Radin as a pathway to legal integrity. Although dialectical training may never satisfactorily impart the meaning of justice, immersion in such training compels the law student to respect and to develop the ability to reason like a lawyer. Cultivating such ability is not only essential to professional legal competence; it also demands recognition of 'the fact that the lawyer's task is ultimately concerned with justice'.[20] For it is in the hope of securing justice that lawyers engage in legal reasoning. This, for Radin, is the reality of law. It is for this very reason, he insists, that 'any legal teaching that ignores justice has missed most of its point. . . . "Realists" who ignore this fact should abandon the pretence that they are realists.'[21]

It is not clear why Radin believed that dialectical teaching cannot impart a sense of justice. Nor is it a necessary reality of law that the interests of justice will be served by legal reasoning. Yet, for all that his argument is problematic, it must, for two reasons, be treated as significant. First of all, in offering such an argument, Radin to some extent undermines the popular mid-century caricature of realism as a legal philosophy unconcerned with justice.[22] Secondly, as will become clear in due course, his argument—particularly in so far as it links reason both with justice and with professional legal competence—anticipates certain themes which would come to feature prominently in process thinking. More generally, it might be observed that Radin and other realists anticipated the move towards process thinking by conceiving of law primarily in procedural as opposed to substantive terms. 'There is a sense', Radin remarked, 'in which procedure is the essence of the law.'[23] 'Everything that you know of procedure,' Karl Llewellyn told his students at Columbia, 'you must carry into *every* substantive course. You must read every substantive course, so to speak, through the spectacles of procedure. For what substantive law says should be means nothing except in terms of what procedure says that

[19] Ibid. 691.

[20] Ibid. 688. On the historical connection between professionalism and justice in American law, see Samuel Haber, *The Quest for Authority and Honor in the American Professions, 1750–1900* (Chicago: University of Chicago Press, 1991), 206–39.

[21] Radin, *supra* n. 12, 688.

[22] For an analysis of this caricature, see Neil Duxbury, 'The Reinvention of American Legal Realism', *Legal Studies*, 12 (1992), 137–77. Of course, not all mid-century legal philosophers subscribed to the caricature. See e.g. Edwin N. Garlan, *Legal Realism and Justice* (New York: Columbia University Press, 1941).

[23] Max Radin, 'The Achievements of the American Bar Association: A Sixty Year Record', *American Bar Assoc. Jnl.*, 26 (1940), 19–26 at 23.

you can make real.'[24] That so-called realists could be found voicing such sentiments is hardly surprising, since process-orientation rests at the foundations of realist legal thought. Holmes's classic predictivist view of law, for example, entails conceiving of right and duty as 'the hypostasis', as he would have it,[25] of a process whereby people are adjudged to be legally entitled or responsible by reference to their actions and omissions.[26] Realism was anything but divorced from the trend towards process-orientation in early twentieth century American legal thought.[27]

Yet, if this is so, why is legal realism not commonly treated as 'process jurisprudence'? Why, indeed, is the move towards process thinking regarded generally as a response to the failure of realism? The short answer to these questions is that, in process jurisprudence, 'process' is a distinctly more sophisticated idea than ever it was either in the literature of legal realism or in the teachings of Langdellian innovators such as Ames and Keener. Throughout both the Langdellian and realist periods of American legal thought, furthermore, the notion of process was incidental rather than central to jurisprudential initiatives. An important implication attaches to these assertions. To claim that, between the Langdellian and realist periods, there emerged a somewhat casual tendency in American jurisprudence to conceive of law as a 'process' is not to claim that there emerged at this time a distinct jurisprudence of process. Rather, it is to claim that, in the context of American law, process thinking preceded the development of a specific process jurisprudence. Although neither Langdellianism nor legal realism is illustrative of this jurisprudence, they represent what we might call the stirring of process thought. The theme of process had, as it were, been put into play.

The question remains, however, as to how this theme came to characterize a distinct approach to jurisprudence. To answer this question demands, first of all, that we identify the emergence of another basic concept in American legal thought: the concept of principle.

THE ANIMATION OF PRINCIPLE

In an address delivered to the New York State Bar Association in January 1937, almost a decade after his appointment as Dean of the Yale Law

[24] Karl N. Llewellyn, *The Bramble Bush: On Our Law and its Study* (New York: Oceana, 1951; repr. of orig. student edn. 1930), 9; and see further his *The Case Law System in America* (P. Gewirtz (ed.), Eng. trans. M. Ansaldi, Chicago: University of Chicago Press, 1989; orig. German publ. 1933), 45.

[25] Oliver Wendell Holmes, Jr., 'Natural Law', *Harvard L. Rev.*, 32 (1918), 40–4 at 42.

[26] See Oliver Wendell Holmes, Jr., 'The Path of the Law', *Harvard L. Rev.*, 10 (1897), 457–78 at 458.

[27] See Laura Kalman, *Legal Realism at Yale, 1927-1960* (Chapel Hill: University of North Carolina Press, 1986), 20.

School, Robert Maynard Hutchins, by now President of the University of Chicago, reflected on the failure of that broad jurisprudential initiative which he was largely responsible for nurturing throughout his two years in New Haven. Legal realism, he observed, had proved to be 'a realism in name only,'[28] having 'produce[d] a descriptive type of education, in which no effort is made to communicate principles'.[29] The formulation and promotion of principles had, during the 1930s, become something of a pet obsession for Hutchins. In his controversial monograph, *The Higher Learning in America*, first published in 1936, he lamented the emergence in the United States of the 'anti-intellectual university',[30] the university bereft of an 'ordering principle'.[31] The time had come, he believed, for universities to turn their attention again to the study of first principles and the general pursuit of truth. Whereas, in the medieval university, theology was the discipline around which such pursuit was ordered, in modern America, as in ancient Greece, the pursuit was to be rooted in metaphysics.

> In metaphysics we are seeking the causes of the things that are. It is the highest science, the first science, and as first, universal. It considers being as being, both what it is and the attributes that belong to it as being. The aim of higher education is wisdom. Wisdom is the knowledge of principles and causes. Metaphysics deals with the highest principles and causes. Therefore metaphysics is the highest wisdom.[32]

Metaphysics points the way towards first principles, and the demonstration of such principles, Hutchins believed, must be a process of rational demonstration, of convincing all rational persons that these principles are truly universal, a priori principles.[33] Just as the search for principles could enrich American higher education generally, so it could do the same for legal education in particular. For it is through the discovery and articulation of principles that American jurisprudence might become invested with a rational dimension which had been absent throughout the realist era. According to Hutchins, it is the 'duty of the legal scholar' to formulate and develop legal principles 'in the light of the rational sciences

[28] Robert Maynard Hutchins, 'Legal Education', *U. Chicago L. Rev.*, 4 (1937), 357–68 at 364.

[29] Ibid. 362.

[30] Robert Maynard Hutchins, *The Higher Learning in America* (New Haven, Conn.: Yale University Press, 1962; orig. publ. 1936), 27. On the controversy surrounding this book, see Harry S. Ashmore, *Unseasonable Truths: The Life of Robert Maynard Hutchins* (Boston: Little, Brown & Co., 1989), 161–4.

[31] Hutchins, *supra* n. 30, 94.

[32] Ibid. 87.

[33] See Edward A. Purcell, Jr., *The Crisis of Democratic Theory: Scientific Naturalism and the Problem of Value* (Lexington: University Press of Kentucky, 1973), 149; and also John Henry Schlegel and David M. Trubek, 'Charles E. Clark and the Reform of Legal Education', in P. Petruck (ed.), *Judge Charles Edward Clark* (New York: Oceana, 1992), 81–113 at 82–3.

of ethics and politics'.[34] While his own efforts at formulating and developing such principles proved (as at least one legal realist intimated[35]) to be rather bland,[36] the fact that he should have made such an effort—that he should have regarded principles as the key to understanding 'man as a rational animal engaged in making and administering laws'[37]—is significant. For it shows Hutchins not only turning his back on realism but also proposing a task which would, in time, become central to process jurisprudence—that task being the development of principles in order to demonstrate the pivotal place of reason in law.

Hutchins's turn to principles is hardly surprising. Edward Purcell has told the story of how, in the United States prior to the Second World War, the spectre of totalitarianism prompted 'a passionate reaffirmation of traditional political principles,'[38] of principles, that is, embodying the conviction 'that democracy [is] both rationally and morally the best possible form of government'.[39] The discovery of rationality through the formulation and development of principles was very much an intellectual strategy of the period; and few adopted the strategy in a more forthright fashion than did Hutchins.[40] What is remarkable about the manner in which Hutchins developed this strategy is that, certainly as regards American jurisprudence, he seemed wholly inattentive to precedent: that is, he failed—or at least appeared to fail—to notice that the discovery of rationality in law through the articulation and development of principles was by no means anything new.

Whereas legal realists had been essentially unconcerned with principles, Langdellian law professors, Hutchins argued, had been content simply to encourage the discovery of core doctrinal principles without so much as attempting to demonstrate how they might be 'intimately and inextricably connected with moral principles'.[41] Thus it was that Langdellianism and realism alike suppressed 'the intellectual content and the intellectual tradition of the law'.[42] In asserting as much, Hutchins seemed to be assuming that the entirety of late nineteenth and early twentieth century jurisprudence could be clustered under the banners of Langdellianism and realism. Yet this is not so. Certain early twentieth-century jurists

[34] Robert Maynard Hutchins, *No Friendly Voice* (Chicago: University of Chicago Press, 1936), 48.

[35] See Radin, *supra* n. 12, 688.

[36] See Hutchins, *supra* n. 28, where he offers examples of principles such as 'that law is work of practical reason in the regulation of social conduct' (p. 365) and 'that the law is a body of rules promulgated and enforced by those who are vested with the political authority to do so' (p. 366). While Hutchins presents such statements as 'basic principles in the philosophy of law' (p. 364), it is not at all obvious that they are principles. Rather, they seem simply to be characterizations of law as an activity.

[37] Hutchins, ibid. 367.

[38] Purcell, *supra* n. 33, 138.

[39] Ibid. 5.

[40] See generally Purcell, ibid. 139–58; Ashmore, *supra* n. 30, 165–75.

[41] Hutchins, *supra* n. 28, 368.

[42] Ibid. 360.

developed what can only vaguely be termed a middle-ground between Langdellianism and realism. One of the general characteristics of this middle-ground was the idea that principles often play an important role within the legal—especially the judicial—process. Indeed, it is in the works of certain of these middle-ground jurists, as we might call them, that we find the first signs of a distinct jurisprudence of process emerging in American legal thought.

The notion of principles underscoring the law makes one of its earliest appearances in the work of John Chipman Gray. In *The Nature and Sources of the Law*, a text which seems to have influenced more process writers than it did legal realists, Gray argues that judges will be compelled to seek out 'sound ethical principles'[43] where the sources of the law are silent. 'When a case comes before a court for decision,' he observes, 'there may be no statute, no judicial precedent, no professional opinion, no custom, bearing on the question involved, and yet the court must decide the case somehow.'[44] In such an instance, the judge 'must find out for himself; he must determine what the law ought to be; he must have recourse to the principle of morality.'[45] It is thus that moral principles form, as it were, an extra source, or sub-source of the law. As Gray puts it, 'a source of the law, not the only source, but a source and a main source, is found in the principles of ethics. These principles, therefore, are legitimately a part of Jurisprudence.'[46]

Gray, here, is formulating in a rather tentative fashion an idea which, in due course, would acquire an especial significance in process jurisprudence: the idea, that is, that 'principles' provide solutions to hard cases. Where, owing to the absence of an applicable rule, reprehensible conduct appears not to be legally punishable, judges, Gray argues, must reach a decision by considering the consequences of that conduct.[47] Consideration of consequences will require that the judge base his or her decision on a principle, But '[w]hat is the import of this word "principle" '?[48] Gray raises but does not answer the question. Rather, he commits himself to a circular argument: resort to principle demands that the judge considers the consequences of relevant conduct; but assessment of consequences demands the invocation of principle. Consequences determine principle, in other words, and principle defines consequences.

The theme of principle takes on a little more shape in the writings of Roscoe Pound. On various occasions, and especially in his earlier work, Pound observed that, throughout history, the growth and direction of legal systems has been influenced by moral principles concerning what is

43 John Chipman Gray, *The Nature and Sources of the Law* (New York: Columbia University Press, 1916; orig. publ. 1909), 286. 44 Ibid. 285. 45 Ibid.
46 Ibid. 292. 47 Ibid. 271. 48 Ibid.

considered to be fair and just.[49] In his later writings, this observation is offered more often as a comment on the present rather than on the past. 'By principles,' Pound wrote in 1941, 'I mean authoritative starting points for legal reasoning. . . . They furnish a basis for reasoning when a situation not governed by a precise rule comes up for consideration as to what should be made for it.'[50] Principles, in other words, become active in hard cases—precisely the point which had been made by Gray. Pound, however, pushes the analysis slightly further. 'You cannot frame a principle with any assurance on the basis of a single case,' he maintains, for, within the judicial process,

> [w]e have continually competing starting points, sometimes a number of them. All these starting points for legal reasoning are equally authoritative, and the court must choose from among them, but as it chooses from among them and develops one, and if it does its job properly, it does develop such starting points, we get gradually a line of decisions which work out a principle applicable over a very considerable field of law . . . and when that principle has become worked out in that way, established in that way, there is something that has authority.[51]

Encapsulated in this statement is the recognition that principles may conflict. Pound's point is that it is for the courts to eradicate any such conflict by deciding which principles should apply to which areas of legal doctrine. Such decisions are unlikely to be made within any one case or by any one judge, for only as judicial thought matures over time does it become clear which principles should be included and which excluded from any particular area of doctrine. Once judicial thought begins to mature on the matter of which principles are appropriate where, reason begins to surface in the law. 'When a principle has been worked out through this process of judicial inclusion and exclusion, as you look back over the course of development, you can see every case in that line would be decided exactly as it was by the principle finally formulated.'[52] To cultivate legal principles, in other words, is to uncover reason in the law.

Pound sees principles as performing a rather more ambitious role in the law than did Gray. And yet, like Gray, he only tells us what principles are by outlining what they do: principles fill in the gaps where the positive law is found wanting. 'These principles, like rules, conceptions and standards, are instrumentalities by which we are able to achieve justice in the

[49] See e.g. Roscoe Pound, 'The Limits of Effective Legal Action', *American Bar Assoc. Jnl.*, 3 (1917), 55–70 at 61; *Law and Morals* (2nd edn. Chapel Hill: University of North Carolina Press, 1926; 1st edn. 1924), 56–7.

[50] Roscoe Pound, 'Roscoe Pound', in Julius Rosenthal Foundation, *My Philosophy of Law: Credos of Sixteen American Scholars* (Boston: Boston Law Book Co. 1941), 249–62 at 257.

[51] Roscoe Pound, 'Survey of the Conference Problems', *U. Cincinnati L. Rev.*, 14 (1940), 324–42 at 330.

[52] Ibid. 331.

adjustment of relations, in the ordering of conduct.'[53] No indication is given as to what a principle actually is. Pound leaves the concept, as it were, unanimated.

Others seemed more intent on injecting life into the concept. In his classic, much-underestimated volume of lectures, *The Nature of the Judicial Process*,[54] Benjamin Cardozo proposed a jurisprudence of realism tempered by principle. 'I take judge-made law as one of the existing realities of life,' he claimed.[55] 'There, before us, is the brew.'[56] Yet '*[s]ome* principle, however unavowed and inarticulate and subconscious, has regulated the infusion.'[57] For '[t]he judge, even when he is free, is still not wholly free. He is not to innovate at pleasure.'[58] Rather, '[h]e is to draw his inspiration from consecrated principles.'[59]

Anticipating Pound, Cardozo argues that these principles emerge through the maturing of judicial thought. 'Cases do not unfold their principles for the asking. They yield up their kernel slowly and painfully.'[60] Within the judicial process, 'principles themselves are continually re-tested';[61] and when earlier decisions or lines of decisions appear wrong, they may be reformulated.[62] When a principle is reformulated, it 'becomes a datum, a point of departure, from which new lines will be run, from which new courses will be measured'.[63] And, over time, this principle will be tested further and perhaps even reformulated again. Such is the nature of the judicial process: 'principles that have served their day expire, and new principles are born'.[64] It is through the testing and reformulation of principles that judicial reasoning evolves.

Principles are not merely the key to understanding how judicial reasoning evolves. They may also explain the different directions in which it evolves. For this reason it is important, Cardozo argues, to appreciate '[t]he directive force of a principle'.[65] Again anticipating Pound, he concedes that principles may conflict and that, where they do, judges may be forced to make a choice.[66] Unlike Pound, however, he does not let the matter rest there. It is of fundamental importance, Cardozo insists, to try to understand precisely how judges make that choice. That is, what gives one principle more directive force than another? In endeavouring to answer this question, Cardozo turns his attention to a case which would eventually become one of the classic heuristic tools of process jurisprudence: *Riggs* v. *Palmer*.

[53] Ibid. 340.

[54] Benjamin N. Cardozo, *The Nature of the Judicial Process* (New Haven, Conn.: Yale University Press, 1921). For an explanation of the proposition that the text is both a classic and underestimated, see Richard A. Posner, *Cardozo: A Study in Reputation* (Chicago: University of Chicago Press, 1990), 20–32.

[55] Cardozo, *supra* n. 54, 10.

[56] Ibid. 10–11.

[57] Ibid. 11.

[58] Ibid. 141.

[59] Ibid.

[60] Ibid. 29.

[61] Ibid. 23.

[62] Ibid. 24–5.

[63] Ibid. 48.

[64] Ibid. 167.

[65] Ibid. 30.

[66] Ibid. 31.

In *Riggs* v. *Palmer*, the Court of Appeals of New York was faced with the question of whether an heir named in the will of his grandfather could inherit under that will, even though he had murdered his grandfather to do so. Although '[i]t is quite true that statutes regulating the making, proof and effect of wills, and the devolution of property, if literally construed . . . give this property to the murderer,'[67] Justice Earl observed:

> all laws . . . may be controlled in their operation and effect by general, fundamental maxims of the common law. No one shall be permitted to profit by his own fraud, or to take advantage of his own wrong, or to found any claim upon his own iniquity, or to acquire property by his own crime. These maxims are dictated by public policy, have their foundation in universal law administered in all civilized countries, and have nowhere been superseded by statutes.[68]

Since '[t]hese maxims, without any statute giving them force or operation, frequently control the effect and nullify the language of wills,'[69] the murderer in this case, it was decided, could not inherit.

For Cardozo, the decision illustrates the directive force of principle. At least two other principles, which would have upheld the title of the murderer, could conceivably have been chosen by the Court. First, '[t]here was the principle of the binding force of a will disposing of the estate of a testator in conformity with law.'[70] Secondly, '[t]here was the principle that civil courts may not add to the pains and penalties of crimes.'[71] Why were neither of these principles chosen? That is, why did the Court opt for the principle that people should not be permitted to profit from their own wrongs? The simple answer, for Cardozo, is that this principle was chosen because it 'led to justice'.[72]

> [I]n the end, the principle that was thought to be most fundamental, to represent the larger and deeper social interests, put its competitors to flight. . . . The murderer lost the legacy for which the murder was committed because the social interest served by refusing to permit the criminal to profit by his crime is greater than that served by the preservation and enforcement of legal rights of ownership.[73]

For his own part, Cardozo, in turning to the decision, had advanced the concept of principle significantly within jurisprudence. Whereas Gray had argued that principles may be invoked where sources of law remain silent,

[67] *Riggs* v. *Palmer* (N.Y., 1889) 22 N.E. 188, 188; and cf. Hart and Sacks, *The Legal Process*, 89–110 esp. 101–2; Ronald Dworkin, *Taking Rights Seriously* (3rd impr. London: Duckworth, 1981; orig. publ. 1977), 23-45. See also Posner, *supra* n. 54, 29 (claiming that 'Cardozo is a precursor of Ronald Dworkin').

[68] *Riggs* v. *Palmer*, *supra* n. 67, 188–90.

[69] Hart and Sacks, *The Legal Process,* 91.

[70] Cardozo, *supra* n. 54, 41.

[71] Ibid.

[72] Ibid.

[73] Ibid. 42–3.

Cardozo demonstrated that they may prove decisive where such sources are not silent but simply unable to resolve the problem in hand. While Pound argued no more than that judges must choose among competing principles, Cardozo made at least a rudimentary attempt to explain how this choice comes about. Finally, Cardozo, by framing his explanation around *Riggs* v. *Palmer*, had brought the concept of principle to life. Principles were no longer mysterious jurisprudential abstractions. Rather, they could be seen to be encapsulated in some of the classic maxims of common law and equity.

In advancing the concept of principle thus, Cardozo in fact raised more questions than he answered. Clearly the decision in *Riggs* v. *Palmer* accorded with the notion that people should not be allowed to profit from their own wrongdoing. But was this a legal principle? A moral principle? Both? Indeed, was it a principle? The Court in *Riggs* treated the unjust enrichment maxim as a fundamental maxim of the common law, dictated by public policy. So, was the refusal to sanction unjust enrichment a legal policy rather than a moral principle? What is the difference between a policy and a principle anyway?

The policy–principle distinction had not yet acquired any significance for American jurists—although it was only a matter of time before it would. The reason that it would eventually become significant is implicit in Cardozo's own analysis. Cardozo conceived his task to be one of explaining the 'principled' nature of the judicial process: judges, he insisted, never make law purely by instinct, for there is always some principle underscoring their decisions. However, he also argued that judges, in reaching decisions, choose principles which will lead to justice being done. But how is this choice to be made? That is, by what criteria are judges to choose which principles will best facilitate justice? Is the choice of principle itself a matter of principle? Cardozo's answer is nothing if not hesitant: 'History or custom or social utility or some other compelling sentiment of justice or sometimes perhaps a semi-intuitive apprehension of the pervading spirit of our law, must come to the rescue of the anxious judge, and tell him where to go.'[74] It is in this way that Cardozo undermines his own argument. Judicial decisions cannot be based entirely on instinct because they will always be founded on principle. However, the choice of principle will itself be a matter of judicial instinct—a matter, that is, of how any particular judge conceives of justice. Cardozo equates principles with justice, and justice with individual sentiment, so that principles cannot be said to be neutral. Since principles cannot be said to be neutral, 'principled' decisions, in Cardozo's terms, cannot be objective decisions.

Much of the significance of Cardozo's jurisprudence rests in what he did

[74] Ibid. 43.

not do. If he had conceived of justice as founded in reason rather than in sentiment, his conception of principle would have had an entirely different complexion. As it stands, his jurisprudence entails a view of principles as tools which enable judges to give effect to their own versions of justice. Conceived in this way, principles actually reinforce rather than temper a particular realist legal world-view. Of course, if principles could be shown to be founded in reason, they would serve to invalidate that world-view. Possibly this explains why critics of realism such as Pound and Hutchins adverted to a link between principle and reason in law. But whereas Pound and Hutchins did little more than sketch this link, other critics of realism attempted actually to cultivate it.

Without doubt, the most important critic of realism to do so was Lon Fuller. Before turning to Fuller, however, it is important to take account of the jurisprudential initiatives of John Dickinson. Apart from his doctoral dissertation—a study of administrative law, written under the joint supervision of Pound and one of the key figures of the process tradition, Felix Frankfurter[75]—Dickinson's major academic work was a series of articles which he produced during the late 1920s and early 1930s.[76] Running throughout these articles there is to be discerned a basic anti-realist thrust. Legal realists, Dickinson argued, underestimated the significance of rules while overestimating the importance of prediction in law.[77] More generally, and like many other lawyers of this period, he regarded realism to be a 'nihilistic theory', according to which 'law is simply whatever government does'.[78] Dickinson seems at least implicity to have set himself the very task which, in his view, legal realism dismissed as pointless: the task, that is, of demonstrating the existence of determinate legal foundations.

Identifying such foundations, Dickinson argues, is no easy feat. Commonly, custom has been 'thought to supply the basis of most new rules of law'.[79] Yet such a conclusion ought to be resisted, for the vitality of a custom usually means that it is in no need of legal enforcement. 'It is only when a custom is breaking down, and thus either meeting with resistence [*sic*]

[75] See John Dickinson, *Administrative Justice and the Supremacy of Law in the United States* (Cambridge, Mass.: Harvard University Press, 1927); also William C. Chase, *The American Law School and the Rise of Administrative Government* (Madison: University of Wisconsin Press, 1982), 171.

[76] Dickinson's academic career was fairly short-lived. See George L. Haskins, 'John Dickinson, 1894–1952', *U. Pennsylvania L. Rev*, 101 (1952), 1–25.

[77] See John Dickinson, 'Legal Rules: Their Function in the Process of Decision', *U. Pennsylvania L. Rev.*, 79 (1931), 833–68; 'Legal Rules: Their Application and Elaboration', *U. Pennsylvania L. Rev.*, 79 (1931), 1052–96. I discuss Dickinson's criticisms of legal realism in my 'The Reinvention of American Legal Realism', *supra* n. 29, 140–4.

[78] John Dickinson, 'John Dickinson', in *My Philosophy of Law*, *supra* n. 50, 91–106 at 98.

[79] John Dickinson, 'The Law Behind Law', *Columbia L. Rev.* 29 (1929), 113–46, 285–319 at pt. II, 296 fn. 25, and cf. also pt. I, 138–41.

or is coming into conflict with other customs that the need arises for its enforcement by adjudication.'[80] Thus it is that we must look elsewhere if we are to discover a primary generative source of the law. This source, Dickinson believes, is in fact constituted by certain core legal principles. 'Out of the seething welter of human interests and desires,' he observes, the law:

> seems to have selected certain great fundamental ones for recognition and protection—the interest of bodily security, the interest of reputation, the interest of private property, the interest of being able to rely on the good faith of others. The fact that the law sanctions these fundamental interests and places its authority behind them is expressed in its broadest and most basic principles—the principles that the right to life and property will be protected, that contracts will be enforced, and the like.[81]

Whereas Cardozo characterized principles simply in terms of certain classic legal maxims, Dickinson conceives of them in a slightly more precise fashion: as legal stipulations of basic moral beliefs. Like both Cardozo and Pound, he concedes that principles may conflict. But the choosing of one principle over another or others cannot be explained by Cardozo's notion of directive force. Two competing principles may appear to be equally fundamental to the same legal dispute—for example, where freedom of expression violates privacy—and, in the case of disputes for which the law presently provides no answer, 'difficulties develop because competing interests have an unexpected habit of expressing their conflict precisely in the form of an apparent conflict between . . . accepted fundamental principles of the law'.[82] The fact is, Dickinson argues, that '[t]he broad general principles of the law have a significant habit of travelling in pairs of opposites'.[83] In such instances, neither principle can be said to possess directional force. 'Each is a general expression of the fact that the law will protect a certain kind of human interest; but, the conditions of human life and association being what they are, every such interest if carried beyond a certain point is bound to come into conflict with some other interest or interests of a kind which the law also protects—and will thus come into conflict with a competing principle of equal validity.'[84]

Since principles are indeterminate, Dickinson argues, they cannot be laws. They are, however, in a very specific manner, the foundations from which laws emerge. The judicial formulation of a legal rule entails striking a balance between two competing principles, that is, 'drawing a line somewhere between two opposing general principles and saying that each shall be valid only up to the line and that beyond it the other shall prevail'.[85] The matter of where the line is to be drawn will be determined

80 Ibid. pt. II, 296–97 fn.25.
81 Ibid. pt. II, 296.
82 Ibid.
83 Ibid. pt. II, 298.
84 Ibid.
85 Ibid. pt. II, 299.

by considerations of policy',[86] and such considerations will themselves be arbitrary, for there is no coherent system of policy underlying the rules of the common law.[87] Indeed, often it will be the case 'that the scheme of policy followed by one judge or generation of judges was not the same as that of all other contemporary judges or other generations of judges. Each adds new views, new appreciations, new values. These are drawn not from within the law but from without.'[88]

In presenting this argument, Dickinson, like Cardozo, appears unwittingly to commit himself to a realist conception of judicial creativity: judges, when forced to strike a balance between fundamental principles, do so by considering issues of policy, and these considerations reflect their general attitudes, values and beliefs. But Dickinson tries to hold back from reaching quite this conclusion. Judges, 'in bringing new law into existence,' do not 'create law out of nothing.'[89] Rather, 'they are generally concerned, when devising a new rule, to frame one which can be made by some process of reasoning, facile or tortuous, to appear as a necessary logical deduction from some already established rule.'[90] The process of balancing principles, in other words, is not simply a matter of resorting to policy but also a matter of respecting legal reason and tradition. It is precisely this, Dickinson argues, that explains the 'superiority of much judge-made law over that of the statutory variety', since respect for precedent 'is a necessity from which legislatures are of course free'.[91] Indeed, it is for the courts, through the mechanism of judicial review, to 'bring[] legislative rules within the confines of some rational order and mak[e] them accountable to general principles which can reasonably be anticipated and acted upon'.[92] Whereas legislatures create law on the basis of policies, courts create law on the basis of principles—principles which, though weighed in accordance with policies, generate reason and consistency in law.

Gray, Cardozo and Pound regarded principles to be foundational to the legal process: rules emerge from principles; and in the hard case scenario, where no applicable precedent exists, it is by resorting to principles that judges are able to develop new rules. Dickinson accepts the broad outline of this thesis, but also qualifies it substantially. It is in the process of qualifying it that he anticipates certain further features of process thinking as it would emerge from the 1940s onwards. Not all rules, according to Dickinson, emerge from principle. Only common law rules do so. Legislation, in contrast, emerges from policy. Thus it is that we encounter for the first time in American jurisprudence the distinction between policy and principle. The distinction, for Dickinson, is significant, since law

[86] John Dickinson, 'The Law Behind Law', pt. II, 302.
[87] Ibid. pt. II, 303.
[88] Ibid. pt. II, 304.
[89] Ibid. pt. II, 308.
[90] Ibid. pt. II, 315.
[91] Ibid.
[92] Dickinson, *supra* n. 78, 104.

founded on policy is deemed to be somehow 'inferior' to law founded on principle. The court, he argues, is the forum of principle and, by extension, the forum of reason. It is through the process of judicial review that law founded on policy is subjected to principled—that is, 'rational'—scrutiny.

With Dickinson, certain of the basic themes and premisses of process jurisprudence began to take shape. In particular, the theme of principle itself—conceived to be peculiar to judicial reasoning and distinct from policy—was accorded a more precise juridical role than had been attributed to it in the writings of Gray, Cardozo and Pound. Despite this, however, the significance of principle as a jurisprudential theme still remained somewhat unclear. Like Pound, Dickinson had connected principle with reason in only the most casual fashion: the fact that the same principle may form a *fil conducteur* linking a line of cases, it was assumed, demonstrates reason at the core of common law doctrine. This assumption remained unelaborated. Whereas, in later decades, process jurists would attempt to connect reason and principle with more precision, Dickinson and Pound, and to a lesser extent Hutchins also, seemed to make the connection in order to distance themselves from legal realism. Once this distance had been established, there was no need to develop the connection any further. For these writers, the resort to principle was essentially a strategy of avoidance rather than an attempt to develop a new jurisprudence. Accordingly, the connection between principle and reason was not especially significant to them. Only with the development of a new jurisprudence in which the theme of principle featured centrally would the connection acquire significance. That new jurisprudence—process jurisprudence—would eventually be initiated by Lon Fuller.

PRINCIPLE, PURPOSE AND PROCESS

Fuller was both a critic and an advocate of realist legal thought. As a perspective on law focusing primarily on judicial behaviour, he argued, realism was peculiarly unrealistic, since '[t]here is no such thing as a field which consists simply of judicial behaviour; it is in fact a greater phantom than Austin's sovereign, which at least had the merit of corresponding to something in the ordinary man's thinking about law.'[93] Nevertheless, he insisted, realism had 'done an immense service to American legal science in inculcating in it a healthy fear of such very real demons as Reified Abstractions, Omnibus Concepts, and Metaphors Masquerading as Facts'.[94] Fuller's own realist sentiments are most evident from his work on

93 Lon L. Fuller, *The Law in Quest of Itself* (Chicago: The Foundation Press, 1940), 59.

94 Lon L. Fuller, 'American Legal Realism', *U. Pennsylvania L. Rev*, 82 (1934), 429–62 at 443.

contract law. In his seminal, co-authored article of 1936, on 'The Reliance Interest in Contract Damages', he sought to demonstrate that remedies, rather than being determined by pre-existing legal rights—the traditional Langdellian view—in fact determine rights.[95] In his contracts case-book of the following decade, Fuller consolidated this thesis by presenting remedies before formation and consideration[96]—an arrangement which suggested 'that he had accepted, if only in part, the realists' critique of the late nineteenth and early twentieth century doctrinal universe'.[97]

More important than the fact that Fuller saw both problems and merits in legal realism is the fact that he avoided developing his own jurisprudence in its shadow. In his Rosenthal Lectures, delivered at Northwestern University in April 1940, only months after securing a permanent post at the Harvard Law School, Fuller outlined his own basic philosophical perspective on law. Realism, or, as he would have it, the basic error of realism, clearly inspired that perspective—but only partially. Legal positivism, of which realism is but one example, was his main object of criticism. The problem with legal positivism generally, Fuller argued, rests in 'its objective of some clear-cut distinction between law and morality'.[98] By failing 'sufficiently to realize that . . . in the moving world of law, the *is* and the *ought* are inseparably linked,'[99] legal positivists, realists included, denied the moral quality, and hence the reality, of law. '[T]o distinguish sharply between the rule as it is, and the rule as it ought to be, is to resort to an abstraction foreign to the raw data which experience offers us.'[100] In truth, '[t]he facts most relevant to legal study will generally be found to be what may be called moral facts.'[101] The primary task of jurisprudence is to account for this moral dimension of the law, to try to make sense of law 'in its ethical context'.[102] This demands that 'is' and 'ought' be seen to melt into one another. It demands, in short, 'a revival of natural law'.[103]

Fuller's natural law theory, as is well known, is a secular theory, premissed on the key concepts of reason, morality and purpose rather than on the notion of an absolute author of the law.[104] In the early 1940s, and particularly in his Rosenthal Lectures, Fuller was more concerned with

[95] Lon L. Fuller and William Perdue, Jr., 'The Reliance Interest in Contract Damages', *Yale L.J.*, 46 (1936–7), 52–96, 373–420.

[96] Lon J. Fuller, *Basic Contract Law* (St. Paul, Minn.: West Publishing Co.,1947); and cf. also Karl Klare, 'Contracts Jurisprudence and the First-Year Casebook', *New York Univ. L. Rev.*, 54 (1979), 876–99 at 882–3.

[97] Alfred S. Konefsky, Elizabeth B. Mensch and John Henry Schlegel, 'In Memoriam: The Intellectual Legacy of Lon Fuller', *Buffalo L. Rev.*, 30 (1981), 263–4; though cf. Robert S. Summers, *Lon L. Fuller* (London: Arnold, 1984), 131.

[98] Fuller, *supra*, n. 93, 85. [99] Ibid. 64. [100] Ibid. 10.

[101] Ibid. 65. [102] Ibid. 60. [103] Ibid. 116.

[104] See Summers, *supra* n. 97, 151.

demonstrating why it is important to develop—as distinct from actually developing—such a theory. The call for a natural law revival came not simply because positivism was the dominant jurisprudential perspective in the United States and Europe, but because, in Fuller's view, the political implications of legal positivism were unacceptable. 'We live', he observed,

in a period when major readjustments in our economic and social order have become necessary. . . . Since many of these necessary changes have to be brought about by legislative and administrative decree, the power of governmental fiat is being stretched to the utmost. . . . It would seem that the present is a time when our social structure requires to be held together by a cement firmer than that supplied by the abstract principle of respect for law as such.[105]

The gist of Fuller's argument is that, by failing to account for the moral dimension of law, by conceiving the reality of law to be nothing more than the authorized exercise of power, positivist jurisprudence equates law with fiat. And if law is simply fiat, any coercive order—be it within a system of democracy or within a system of tyranny—is a valid legal order. Hence, positivism accommodates *dirigisme*, and even despotism.

Abandoning positivism in favour of natural law would mean not only reorienting jurisprudence but also recognizing and revising the politics of jurisprudence. For there would be no point in calling for a revival of natural law theory if that theory turned out to embody the same political implications as legal positivism. Cultivating a jurisprudence which embraces morality, Fuller believed, entails the recognition that legal institutions ought to be founded upon the values of individual freedom and democracy; and the recognition of these values requires, in turn, the recognition of reason at the heart of the law.

In my opinion, democracy must be founded . . . on a faith that in the long run ideas are more important than the men who form them. . . . [I] is only in a democratic and constitutionally organized state that ideas have a chance to make their influence felt. . . . In a dictatorship, on the other hand, the chief requisite for the success of an idea is that it serve the interests of those who have enough power to make it effective. . . . It is my belief that our society will not survive unless . . . we can reattain an atmosphere in which a man can gain a respectful audience for his views on the institution of private property in spite of the fact that he happens to own a house and lot. This atmosphere will only be regained when we have again come to believe that reason can have something to say concerning legal and social institutions. Some minimum faith in ideas is necessary to give practical significance to the doctrine of free speech and free thought.[106]

105 Fuller, *supra* n. 93, 115–16.

106 Ibid. 122–3, 126; and cf. also Lon L. Fuller, 'Lon L. Fuller', in *My Philosophy of Law*, *supra* n. 50, 113–25 at 124–5.

Reason is thus a fundamental—possibly the fundamental[107]—legal value. It is antithetical to tyranny. It goes hand in hand with liberal democracy. Through reason, human tolerance flourishes. To revive natural law is to abandon the positivist vision of law as pure fiat and to rediscover faith in reason. In law, there must be room for both fiat and reason.

As the 1940s progressed, Fuller elaborated this thesis. 'When we deal with the law,' he wrote in 1946, 'we inevitably see that it is compounded of reason and fiat, of order discovered and order imposed, and that to attempt to eliminate either of these aspects of the law is to denature and falsify it.'[108] Jurisprudence must concern itself with 'the whole view of law'[109]—of law as both reason and fiat—despite the tendency of legal philosophers of the past 'to hold exclusively to one branch of the antinomy'.[110] For all that he champions what he terms the whole view, however, Fuller, possibly because of his own predisposition towards natural law, seems generally more inclined to the analysis of reason rather than fiat. Judicial activity, he argues, is predicated on reason;[111] it 'cannot be predicted, or even talked about meaningfully, except in terms of reasons that give rise to it'.[112] In producing a reasoned decision, moreover, the judge, instead of acting on 'personal predilections', is attempting 'to discover the natural principles underlying group life, so that his decisions might conform to them'.[113] To appeal to such principles is to invoke 'external criteria, found in the conditions required for successful group living, that furnish some standard against which the rightness of [the judge's] decisions should be measured'.[114] Thus it is 'that the basic problem of the judicial process remains that of discovering and applying those principles that will best promote the ends men seek to attain by collective action'.[115]

For Fuller, then, the themes of reason and principle are interconnected. In a moment, we shall see that his recognition of this interconnection took him down a specific jurisprudential path. Before we develop this point, however, a more general observation might be made. Fuller believed that the values of clarity, candour and integrity should reign supreme in legal scholarship.[116] These values are extolled throughout his writings. This in

[107] See Robert S. Summers, 'Professor Fuller's Jurisprudence and America's Dominant Philosophy of Law', *Harvard L. Rev.*, 92 (1978), 433–49 at 437.

[108] Lon L. Fuller, 'Reason and Fiat in Case Law', *Harvard L. Rev.*, 59 (1946), 376–95 at 382. A version of this paper was first delivered to The Association of the Bar of the City of New York in October 1942.

[109] Ibid. 395.

[110] Ibid. 391.

[111] Ibid. 384.

[112] Ibid. 386.

[113] Ibid. 378.

[114] Ibid. 379.

[115] Ibid. 380.

[116] Almost any of his works could be cited in support of this assertion. See e.g. Lon L. Fuller, 'Positivism and Fidelity to Law—A Reply to Professor Hart', *Harvard L. Rev.*, 71 (1958), 630–72 at 631, 635.

itself is hardly remarkable. What is remarkable, however, is the manner in which these values surface and are realized in his writings.

Fuller realizes these values by developing a technique which previously had been scarcely used in American jurisprudence: the technique of reasoning by analogy and allegory. By using this technique throughout his jurisprudential writings, Fuller is able gradually to unfold his ideas rather than simply to offer them neatly packaged. The plight of King Rex—the story which Fuller presents to demonstrate his famous notion of the internal morality of law[117]—exemplifies his use of this technique. So too does his article, 'The Case of the Speluncean Explorers'.[118] In that article, Fuller presents an imaginary case in which a group of explorers, having become trapped in a cave, cast dice to decide which of their number should be killed in order to provide food for their survival. Once rescued, the survivors, on the basis of a statute which provides that '[w]hoever shall willfully take the life of another shall be punished by death', are sentenced to hang. Fuller presents us with the opinions of a fictional Supreme Court which considers whether or not this sentence should be upheld or set aside. One Justice concludes that it should be set aside, but does not elaborate any reasons for his conclusion. Another concludes that the sentence should be set aside because that would reflect the wishes of public opinion. Yet another concludes that the sentence should be affirmed since it accords with the law of the land. And still another is unable to reach a conclusion, and withdraws from the case. Fuller's fifth judge, Justice Foster, argues that the sentence ought to be set aside because reason shows it to be wrong. Fidelity to law, Justice Foster argues, demands not slavish, but intelligent fidelity: '[e]very proposition of positive law, whether contained in a statute or a judicial precedent, is to be interpreted reasonably, in the light of its evident purpose.'[119] Interpreting the statute in this case in terms of its purpose rather than its literal wording, Foster concludes, forces the recognition that it permits of exceptions such as self-defence.

'The Case of the Speluncean Explorers' illustrates how, for Fuller, jurisprudence entails not simply formulating ideas about law, but ensuring that those ideas unfold within a process of reasoning. The implication is that jurisprudence must be founded on reason if it is to promote reason. Given this view, it is hardly surprising to find that Fuller himself subscribed to the position which he ascribes to his fictional Justice Foster. Purposes, he

[117] See Lon L. Fuller, *The Morality of Law* (rev. edn. New Haven, Conn.: Yale University Press, 1969; orig. publ. 1964), 33–94. Guido Calabresi is another great exponent of this technique. See e.g. Guido Calabresi, *Ideals, Beliefs, Attitudes and the Law: Private Law Perspectives on a Public Law Problem* (Syracuse: Syracuse University Press, 1985).

[118] Lon L. Fuller, 'The Case of the Speluncean Explorers', *Harvard L. Rev.*, 62 (1949), 616–45.

[119] Ibid. 624.

argues, are a defining feature of human nature.[120] Most human actions of any complexity are purposive actions; understanding them requires that they be interpreted in terms of their underlying purposes.[121] This is as true of law as it is of any form of human activity. The creation and application of law is a purposeful enterprise.[122] Legal rules and institutions characteristically serve a multiplicity of purposes.[123] If we are properly to understand law, we must interpret it by reference to those purposes.[124] For we can only know what a law means if we appreciate what it is supposed to be for. We are back to Fuller's basic thesis: the 'is' and the 'ought' are not separate entities. Facts cannot be divorced from values:

> [I]n a sufficiently homogeneous society certain 'values' will develop automatically and without anyone intending or directing their development. In such a society it is assumed that the legal rules developed and enforced by courts will reflect these prevailing 'values' . . . [A] court is not an inert mirror reflecting current mores but an active participant in the enterprise of articulating the implications of shared purposes.[125]

Judges, then, must engage in the purposive interpretation of legal rules. Such an argument was by no means novel to Fuller. Learned Hand, for one, had been advocating the purposive interpretation of law since the mid-1940s.[126] And by the end of that decade, affirmation of the purposive perspective had become quite common in American legal literature.[127] The principal reason for this rests in the significance of the perspective in relation to legislation. Felix Frankfurter saw this more clearly than did anyone else, Fuller included. As early as 1930, Frankfurter had written that '[t]he *Index to State Legislation* recently published by the Congressional Library reads like an inventory of all man's secular needs and the means for their fulfilment.'[128] Like his Harvard colleague of that period, James Landis, he recognized that the legal profession and the law schools alike remained, as Landis put it, committed to 'the traditional method of

[120] See Lon L. Fuller, 'American Legal Philosophy at Mid-Century', *Jnl. Leg. Educ.*, 6 (1954), 457–85 at 472.

[121] Lon L. Fuller, 'Human Purpose and Natural Law', *Jnl. of Philosophy*, 53 (1956), 697–705.

[122] Fuller, *supra* n. 117, 145.

[123] Lon L. Fuller, *The Anatomy of Law* (Harmondsworth: Penguin, 1971; orig. publ. 1968), 54–8.

[124] Fuller, *supra* n. 116, 662.

[125] Lon L. Fuller, 'The Forms and Limits of Adjudication', *Harvard L. Rev.*, 92 (1978), 353–409 at 378.

[126] See e.g. *Borella* v. *Borden Co.* (2d. Cir., 1945) 145 F.2d 63, 64–5.

[127] See e.g. Edward H. Levi, *An Introduction to Legal Reasoning* (Chicago: University of Chicago Press, 1949), 104; Karl N. Llewellyn, 'Remarks on the Theory of Appellate Decision and the Rules or Canons About How Statutes Are to be Constructed', *Vanderbilt L. Rev.*, 3 (1950), 395–406 at 400; Charles P. Curtis, 'A Better Theory of Legal Interpretation', *Vanderbilt L. Rev.*, 3 (1950), 407–37 at 411, 413–14.

[128] Felix Frankfurter, *The Public and Its Government* (New Haven, Conn.: Yale University Press, 1930), 29.

developing law purely from earlier judicial precedents', even though legislation was 'assuming both a volume and a creative aspect of purpose that makes it impossible to ignore'.[129] Landis in particular bemoaned the 'cavalier treatment of legislation'[130] within the American legal tradition. 'Legislation is presumed immune to "principle"; its judgements' are taken to 'represent merely the political pressure of a special class.'[131] The truth of the matter, Landis insisted, is that statutes may be founded on both policy and principle.[132]

Frankfurter offered a similar argument but adopted a slightly different tack. Writing in 1947, he suggested that the rapid growth of statutes in modern times requires that judges become more accomplished in the art of interpretation. Looking over the opinions of Holmes, Brandeis and Cardozo, he remarked, one finds that 'the statutes presented for their interpretation became increasingly complex'.[133] One finds also in their opinions the recognition 'that laws are not abstract propositions' but 'expressions of policy arising out of specific situations and addressed to the attainment of particular ends'.[134] For these three Justices, 'a statute was expressive of purpose and policy'.[135] So too for Frankfurter:

> Legislation has an aim; it seeks to obviate some mischief, to supply an inadequacy, to effect a change in policy, to formulate a plan of government. That aim, that policy is not drawn, like nitrogen, out of the air; it is evinced in the language of the statute, as read in the light of other external manifestations of purpose. That is what the court must seek and effectuate . . . [T]he purpose which a court must effectuate is not that which Congress should have enacted, or would have. It is that which it did enact, however inaptly, because it may fairly be said to be imbedded in the statute, even if a specific manifestation was not thought of, as is often the very reason for casting a statute in very general terms.[136]

Interpretation of a statute, then, demands an estimation of its purpose. Since that purpose is unlikely to be 'directly displayed in the particular enactment',[137] however, judges must be wary of importing into the statute—for example, through the '[s]purious use of legislative history'[138]—an incongruous or bogus purpose. '[O]ne is admonished to listen attentively to what a statute says. One must also listen carefully to what it does not say.'[139] Thus it is that, for Frankfurter, the purposive interpretation of statutes is part and parcel of a more general philosophy

[129] James McCauley Landis, 'Statutes and the Sources of Law', in R. Pound (ed.), *Harvard Legal Essays Written in Honor of and Presented to Joseph Henry Beale and Samuel Williston* (Cambridge, Mass.: Harvard University Press, 1934), 213–46 at 219.

[130] Ibid. 233. [131] Ibid. 222. [132] Ibid. 215, 223, 229, 230.

[133] Felix Frankfurter, 'Some Reflections on the Reading of Statutes', *Columbia L. Rev.*, 47 (1947), 527–46 at 530. [134] Ibid. 533. [135] Ibid. 532.

[136] Ibid. 538–9. [137] Ibid. 539. [138] Ibid. 543. [139] Ibid. 536.

of judicial restraint.[140] Rather than facilitating unfettered judicial discretion, the search for purpose demands that the judge acts with integrity and circumspection. '[L]aws have ends to be achieved,'[141] and the judge must strive to remain faithful to those ends. 'Perhaps the most delicate aspect of statutory construction', Frankfurter suggests, 'is not to find more residues than are implicit nor purposes beyond the bounds of hints.'[142] '[C]onstruction must eschew interpolation and evisceration.'[143] And '[f]or judges at least it is important to remember that continuity with the past is not only a necessity but even a duty.'[144] To put the point simply, the purposive approach constrains rather than liberates: 'the courts . . . are confined by the nature and scope of the judicial function in its particular exercise in the field of interpretation.'[145]

Fuller, unlike Frankfurter, did not develop the purposive perspective to support the philosophy of judicial restraint. For him, the purposive interpretation of statutes—indeed, of laws generally—is simply a feature of adjudication which had commonly been overlooked by jurists working in the positivist tradition. '[A]djudication is a form of social ordering institutionally committed to "rational" decision',[146] Fuller claims, and a judge cannot be committed to rational decision-making if he or she interprets law literally rather than purposively. There is, nevertheless, more to adjudication than just purposive interpretation. Indeed, according to Fuller, there is a peculiar 'integrity' about adjudication as a form of social ordering;[147] and the demonstration of this integrity demands that adjudication be seen not, primarily, in terms of purposive interpretation, but in terms of institutional competence, reason and principle.

[140] For a statement of this philosophy, see Felix Frankfurter, 'John Marshall and the Judicial Function' in A. E. Sutherland (ed.), *Government Under Law* (Cambridge, Mass.: Harvard University Press, 1956), 6–31 at 20–1:'Only for those who have not the responsibility of decision can it be easy to decide the grave and complex problems they raise, especially in controversies that excite public interest. This is so because they too often present legal issues inextricably and deeply bound up in emotional reactions to sharply conflicting economic, social and political views. It is not the duty of judges to express their personal attitudes on such issues, deep as their individual convictions may be. The opposite is the truth; it is their duty not to act on merely personal views. . . . Of course, individual judgement and feeling cannot be wholly shut out of the judicial process. But if they dominate, the judicial process becomes a dangerous sham.' See also Erwin N. Griswold, 'Felix Frankfurter—Teacher of the Law', *Harvard L. Rev.*, 76 (1962), 7–13 at 11–12: '[Frankfurter's] teaching has been of the integrity of the judicial process, of the essential importance of sound procedure, of judicial self-restraint, and of the intellectual humility of the judge. . . . [T]he integrity of the judicial process requires a deep awareness on the part of the judge of the limitations on his own power of decision, and of the necessity, except within narrow and ultimate limits, of seeking to avoid decision on grounds of personal belief, or even of personal convictions.'

[141] Frankfurter, *supra* n. 133, 538. [142] Ibid. 535. [143] Ibid. 533.

[144] Ibid. 535. [145] Ibid. 533. [146] Fuller, *supra* n. 125, 380.

[147] Ibid. 364. See also Lon L. Fuller and John D. Randall, 'Professional Responsibility: Report of the Joint Conference', *American Bar Assoc. Jnl.*, 44 (1958), 1159–62, 1216–17 at 1160.

This is a thesis which Fuller develops in his article, 'The Forms and Limits of Adjudication'. Although published in 1978, shortly after his death, Fuller had circulated a first draft of this article among members of the Legal Philosophy Discussion Group at Harvard as early as 1957.[148] Along with reciprocity and organization by common aims, Fuller argues in this article, adjudication is a basic form of social ordering. While rationality inheres in all social ordering,[149] its presence in adjudication is peculiar. '[T]he distinguishing characteristic of adjudication lies in the fact that it confers on the affected party a peculiar form of participation in the decision, that of presenting proofs and reasoned arguments for a decision in his favour.'[150] Furthermore, as a specifically legal activity—as opposed, say, to refereeing a sport or judging a competition—adjudication requires that decisions be reached within an institutional framework that is intended to assure to the disputants an opportunity for the presentation of proofs and reasoned arguments'.[151] In short, adjudication, as a legal phenomenon, demands a particular institutional context which supports a particular type of rationality:

> Adjudication is . . . a device which gives formal and institutional expression to the influence of reasoned argument in human affairs. As such it assumes a burden of rationality not borne by any other form of social ordering. A decision which is the product of reasoned argument must be prepared itself to meet the test of reason.[152]

Having highlighted rationality as an integral feature of adjudication, Fuller returns again to the interconnection between reason and principle which had occupied him during the 1940s. Since adjudication is 'a process of decision in which the affected party's participation consists in an opportunity to present proofs and reasoned arguments',[153] that party, 'if his participation is to be meaningful', must assert some principle or principles by which his arguments are sound and his proofs relevant'.[154] Principles are fundamental to the adjudicative process, for it is only by resorting to principles that disputing parties are able convincingly to assert their rights within its peculiar institutional framework. Fuller demonstrates this point by resorting to his favourite method of reasoning—the imaginary scenario:

> We may see this process . . . in the case of an employee who desires an increase in pay. If he asks his boss for a raise, he may, of course, claim 'a right' to the raise. He may argue the fairness of the principle of equal treatment and call attention to the fact that Joe, who is no better than he, recently got a raise. But he does not have to rest his plea on any ground of this sort. He may merely beg for generosity, urging the needs of his family. Or he may propose an exchange, offering to take on extra

148 Fuller, *supra* n. 125, 353. 149 Ibid. 360. 150 Ibid. 364.
151 Ibid. 365. 152 Ibid. 366–7. 153 Ibid. 365. 154 Ibid. 369.

> duties if he gets the raise. If, however, he takes his case to an arbitrator he cannot, explicitly at least, support his case by an appeal to charity or by proposing a bargain. He will have to support his demand by a principle of some kind, and a demand supported by principle is the same thing as a claim of right.[155]

Within the peculiar institutional framework of the adjudicative process, then, principles are foundational to legal reasoning, for they mark the distinction between arbitrary demands and legal rights. 'A right is a demand founded on a principle.'[156] Thus it is that 'adjudication is institutionally committed to a "reasoned" decision, to a decision based on "principle" '.[157]

It is in Fuller's writings that we can see a distinct 'process' perspective on law beginning to gel. By emphasizing reason as well as fiat in law, by demonstrating the essential irrationality of non-purposive legal interpretation, by reinforcing the interconnection of reason and principle and, most importantly of all, by arguing that adjudication is an institutionally-discrete, rationalistic, rights-oriented and hence principle-based process of decision-making, Fuller contributed significantly to the construction of a distinctive post-realist 'process jurisprudence'. He 'put a strong intellectual mark on the Harvard Law School', wrote Fuller's erstwhile student and colleague, Albert Sacks, in 1978.[158] '[H]is impact on me and others . . . lay in convincing [us] that his questions were right—that they had to be faced and that they deserved careful thought.'[159]

THE BROADER SCENE

It is important, however, to appreciate that although Fuller's contribution to the development of process thinking was highly significant, it was not altogether unique. As we have already seen, he was not the first American jurist to conceive of the interconnection between principle and reason; rather, he simply brought that interconnection into sharper focus. Likewise, we have seen that Fuller was not alone in advocating a purposive

[155] Fuller, *supra* n. 125, 369.

[156] Ibid. 404. It is tempting here to draw comparisons between Fuller's position and that held by Ronald Dworkin. We shall consider Dworkin in relation to the process tradition in due course. At this point, it is worth noting that Robert Summers (*supra* n. 97, 51) claims that 'Fuller does not specifically address himself to what Dworkin calls legal principles'. For an examination of how Fuller is echoed by Dworkin, see Charles Covell, *The Defence of Natural Law: A Study of the Ideas of Law and Justice in the Writings of Lon L. Fuller, Michael Oakeshot [sic], F. A. Hayek, Ronald Dworkin and John Finnis* (Basingstoke: St Martin's Press, 1992), xvi, 43, 60–1, 63, 180.

[157] Fuller, *supra* n. 125, 372.

[158] Albert M. Sacks, 'Lon Luvois Fuller', *Harvard L. Rev.*, 92 (1978), 349–50 at 349.

[159] Ibid. 350.

approach to legal interpretation. We shall see in due course that the image of adjudication as a legal activity governed by peculiar criteria of rationality and integrity was illustrative of a more general belief, shared by many law professors of the 1950s, that judicial and legislative functions may and indeed ought to be treated as institutionally distinct. Fuller, in short, was not the first to sound the major themes of process thinking. His achievement was to show how those themes fit together, how they comprise a distinct jurisprudence.

Such was the modesty of Fuller that he would have been quick to dissociate himself from any claims to the effect that he had pioneered a 'process' perspective on law.[160] Indeed, just as Albert Sacks paid tribute to Fuller's inspirational role at Harvard, Fuller, as early as 1940, acknowledged his intellectual indebtedness to Sacks's academic collaborator, Henry Hart.[161] Certainly, between Fuller and Hart, intellectual inspiration seems to have cut both ways. Fuller's voice can be heard throughout the *Legal Process* materials,[162] and is most dominant where Hart and Sacks reproduce excerpts from the 1957 draft of 'The Forms and Limits of Adjudication' and 'draw heavily upon Professor Fuller's analysis'.[163] Fuller, for his own part, was eager to stress the path-breaking significance of *The Legal Process*. It was in those materials, he insisted, that institutional competence was first raised as a distinct legal problem. 'Instead of asking, "What is the rule?" or even, "What is the best rule?" ' Fuller observed, Hart and Sacks raised, in an unprecedented fashion, the question: 'What is the nature of the basic problem and how shall we choose among the various procedures of social ordering that might be applied to it?'[164] For Fuller, Hart and Sacks—and Hart in particular—demonstrated that the question of 'who should do what?'—that is, 'which institution within the legal process might be considered best equipped to deal with which problems?'—ought to be treated as a fundamental question of modern jurisprudence.[165]

Fuller was certainly right to emphasize the importance of Henry Hart's work. For it is in that work that the notion of 'process' itself begins to take shape. Whereas, in Fuller's writings, process jurisprudence takes the form of analytical legal philosophy, in Hart's writings it emerges as doctrinal critique premissed on a specific conception of what the legal process is and how it ought to function. A pro-New Deal lawyer who, in 1937, had

[160] On Fuller's modesty, see Erwin N. Griswold, 'Lon Luvois Fuller—1902–1978', *Harvard L. Rev.*, 92 (1978), 351–2 at 352.

[161] See Summers, *supra* n. 97, 6.

[162] See e.g. Hart and Sacks, *The Legal Process*, 98, 111, 121, 206, 447–8.

[163] Ibid. 421–6, 686.

[164] Lon L. Fuller, 'Mediation—Its Forms and Functions', *Southern California L. Rev.*, 44 (1971), 345–39 at 307.

[165] See Fuller, *supra* n. 97, 180.

supported F. D. Roosevelt's Court Packing plan on the assumption that a larger Supreme Court would be a more 'enlightened' Court,[166] Hart co-authored a series of articles with Felix Frankfurter in the mid-1930s which warned against the erosion of the very legal ideal which conservatives believed the Court Packing plan was intended to undermine: the ideal, that is, of the separation of powers.[167] Legislation and adjudication, Frankfurter and Hart argued, are institutionally distinct activities, and must remain so.

> A Court the scope of whose activities lies as close to the more sensitive areas of politics as does that of the Supreme Court must constantly be on the alert against undue suction into the avoidable polemic of politics. Especially at a time when the appeal from legislation to adjudication is more frequent and its results more far-reaching, laxity in assuming jurisdiction adds gratuitous friction to the difficulties of government. . . . Inevitably, fulfilment of the Supreme Court's traditional function in passing judgment upon legislation, especially that of Congress, occasions the reaffirmation of old procedural safeguards and the assertion of new ones against subtle or daring attempts at procedural blockade-running.[168]

'The volume of litigation of which the Court now disposes at a single term', Frankfurter and Hart observed, 'would startle the shades of Marshall and Taney even as they would have hampered the eloquence of Clay and Webster'.[169] 'It is not enough, however, for a court to dispose of a huge volume of litigation with despatch'.[170] For the Supreme Court has a more fundamental duty not to overstep its mark by assuming the power to make policy. The fulfilment of this duty demands judicial restraint:

> As governmental problems become more and not less complicated, as the dislocating impact of technological advances becomes more powerful and less imperceptible, as the forces of economic interdependence demand more and more determination and ingenuity for the maintenance of a simpler but perhaps socially more satisfying society, the deep wisdom of the Court's self-restraint against undue or premature intervention, in what are ultimately political controversies, becomes the deepest wisdom for our times.[171]

Thus it is that, as early as the mid-1930s, one of the fundamental messages of process jurisprudence was being voiced. The message is simple to summarize: adjudication is a peculiar type of institutional activity which

[166] See G. Edward White, 'Closing the Cycle', *Jnl. Leg. Educ.*, 33 (1983), 449–52 at 450. On Hart and the New Deal, see also Karl E. Klare, 'Judicial Deradicalization of the Wagner Act and the Origins of Modern Legal Consciousness, 1937–1941', *Minnesota L. Rev.*, 62 (1978), 265–339 at 322.

[167] See Felix Frankfurter and Henry M. Hart, Jr., 'The Business of the Supreme Court at October Term, 1932', *Harvard L. Rev.*, 47 (1933), 245–97; 'The Business of the Supreme Court at October Term, 1933', *Harvard L. Rev.*, 48 (1934), 238–81; 'The Business of the Supreme Court at October Term, 1934', *Harvard L. Rev.*, 49 (1935), 68–107.

[168] Frankfurter and Hart, 'The Business of the Supreme Court at October Term, 1934', Ibid. 90–1.

[169] Ibid. 107.

[170] Ibid. 69.

[171] Ibid. 107.

does not embrace policy-making; and if the integrity of adjudication is to be preserved, judicial self-restraint must dominate the courts. The first half of this message is to be found in Fuller's reflections on adjudication. The message in its entirety was heard and accepted by many post-realist law professors.

Most, though by no means all, of those responsible for promoting this message were professors at the Harvard Law School. Various commentators have remarked that when Erwin Griswold succeeded James Landis as Dean of the School in July 1946, the Harvard faculty became committed increasingly to the teaching of law as a 'craft'.[172] Quite what such a comment might mean is far from clear, not least because it implies that the Langdellian approach to teaching was somehow 'craftless'. What is clear, however, is that the remark is rarely intended as a compliment. By teaching law as a craft, Ralph Nader has written, the Harvard Law School under Griswold's deanship cultivated 'a process of engineering the law student into corridor thinking and largely non-normative evaluation'.[173] 'This process', according to Jerold Auerbach, 'entailed a highly stylized mode of intellectual activity that rewarded inductive reasoning, analytical precision, and verbal felicity.'[174] Above all, teaching law as a craft meant training students to think like lawyers.[175]

Certainly process jurisprudence, as it evolved at Harvard, would have contributed to such training. For it is premissed on the idea that law involves special techniques to be mastered. Mastery of these techniques, according to Frankfurter, demands both natural and artificial reason.[176] '[T]he only sure safeguard against crossing the line between adjudication and legislation', he insisted, 'is an alert recognition of the necessity not to cross it and instinctive, as well as trained, reluctance to do so.'[177] More generally, by emphasizing the question of which institution is best equipped to deal with which legal problems, process jurisprudence requires of students that they recognize and appreciate the place and the role of each and every institution within the legal process. As Henry Hart and Herbert Wechsler wrote in the preface to their case-book of 1953, *The*

[172] See e.g. Kalman, *supra* n. 27, 219; Joel Seligman, *The High Citadel: The Influence of Harvard Law School* (Boston: Houghton Mifflin, 1978), 78.

[173] Ralph Nader, 'Law Schools and Law Firms', *Case and Comment*, 75 (1970), 30–7 at 30. For a criticism of Nader on this point, cf. Carl A. Auerbach, 'Some Comments on Mr. Nader's Views', *Case and Comment*, 75 (1970), 39–41 at 39.

[174] Jerold S. Auerbach, *Unequal Justice: Lawyers and Social Change in Modern America* (New York: Oxford University Press, 1976), 276.

[175] See Nader, *supra* n. 173, 31; Auerbach, *supra* n. 174, 276.

[176] On natural and artificial reasons, cf. *Prohibitions Del Roy* (1907) 77 *Eng. Rep.* 1342 at 1343 (per Coke C.J.); and see, more generally, John Underwood Lewis, 'Sir Edward Coke (1552–1633): His Theory of "Artificial Reason" as a Context for Modern Basic Legal Theory', *Law Quarterly Rev.*, 84 (1968), 330–42.

[177] Frankfurter, *supra* n. 133, 535.

Federal Courts and the Federal System, 'we pose the issue of what courts are good for—and are not good for—seeking thus to open up the whole range of questions as to the appropriate relationship between the federal courts and other organs of federal and state government.'[178] This does not mean, however, that process jurisprudence is simply a descriptive or taxonomic exercise. It is equally an exercise in legal critique.

The style of critique to be found in process jurisprudence is very distinctive. Different organs have different tasks to perform within the legal process; and it is for students and scholars not only to identify those tasks but also to ascertain whether or not they are being performed properly. Jurisprudence, in other words, conceived as quality control. From the late 1940s through to the 1960s, process jurisprudence flourished as many academic lawyers took it upon themselves to act as quality assessors. The product of the Supreme Court was subjected to especial scrutiny. This was something different from legal realism. To say that judges make law, the Harvard professor, Paul Freund, remarked in 1949, 'is not the end but only the beginning of sophistication'.[179] Post-realist jurisprudence must depart from the truism that judges make law and begin instead with the question of how they make law. Freund's view was that judges must cultivate 'morality of mind—by understanding self-restraint, and the even-handed application of principle'.[180] Writing in the same year, Edward Levi of the University of Chicago Law School suggested that judges, in making law, ought to furnish their decisions with reasons.[181] From a contemporary perspective, such a suggestion might seem no less bland than the proposition that judges make law. In the late 1940s, however, at the time when process jurisprudence was beginning to find its feet, the suggestion could hardly have been more insightful or significant. For it was not at all obvious that judges did endeavour consistently to furnish their decisions with reasons.

For those who were preoccupied with quality control, the initiatives of the Supreme Court were the primary cause for concern. Indeed, the development of process jurisprudence from the 1950s onwards can be charted in large measure by looking to the series of Forewords, initiated by the *Harvard Law Review* in 1951, in which leading—usually Harvard-based—legal scholars of the period would analyse the work of the Supreme Court during the preceding term. In the first of these Forewords, the Harvard law professor, Louis Jaffe, suggested that the Court needed to

[178] Paul M. Bator, Paul J. Mishkin, David L. Shapiro and Herbert Wechsler, *Hart and Wechsler's The Federal Courts and the Federal System* (2nd edn. Mineola, NY: The Foundation Press, 1973; 1st edn. 1953), xx (preface to 1st edn.). On the same theme, see Henry M. Hart, Jr., 'The Power of Congress to Limit the Jurisdiction of Federal Courts: An Exercise in Dialectic', *Harvard L. Rev.*, 66 (1953), 1362–402.

[179] Paul A. Freund, *On Understanding the Supreme Court* (Westport, Conn.: Greenwood Press, 1977; orig. publ. 1949), 3.

[180] Ibid. 75.

[181] See Levi, *supra* n. 127, 53.

break decisively from its immediate past. 'The Roosevelt Court in which the Black-Murphy-Douglas-Rutledge bloc held a pivotal position' had manipulated 'constitutional doctrines and statutory interpretation to forward its programme of social reform.'[182] During this era, 'the Court's work was not law but politics'.[183] While, under Chief Justice Vinson, the Court had moved away from this work, Jaffe argued, it was still not entirely cured of the bad habits which it had acquired during the New Deal era.[184] In particular, the Court paid too little attention to 'the stating of reasons' while displaying 'an excess of passion for immediate results, a naive expectation that if only institutions were correctly devised and men were of good will, all things could be quickly put right.'[185] Jaffe's assessment was basically diagnostic and descriptive. As the 1950s progressed, the *Harvard Law Review* Forewords would become increasingly more critical.

There was a reason for this. It is well known that the appointment of Earl Warren as the successor to Chief Justice Vinson in September 1953 marked the beginning of a new period of judicial activism in the United States Supreme Court. In due course, we shall have cause to consider the activism of the so-called Warren Court. For the moment, however, it is sufficient simply to note that, during the 1950s, process jurisprudence evolved largely as a critical analysis of specific Warren Court initiatives. Whereas the Vinson Court had been criticized in certain quarters for taking too few cases,[186] many writers associated with the process tradition felt that the Warren Court emphasized judicial expediency at the expense of reason. In the first Foreword of the Warren era, Albert Sacks criticized the Court for its extensive use of the summary opinion. Justices were too eager, he complained, to hand down '*per curiam* opinions in which the reasons for the decision are either omitted or set forth in a few sentences'.[187] 'Since', in such opinions, 'the Court's reasoning processes are not fully set forth, the observing critic can never be wholly confident that he has taken into account all possible reasons for the Court's choice of a summary statement.'[188] 'The difficulty is not in the result reached, but in the absence of explanation of what was decided.'[189] The problem of putting

[182] Louis L. Jaffe, 'The Supreme Court, 1950 Term—Foreword', *Harvard L. Rev.*, 65 (1951), 107–14 at 107. [183] Ibid. [184] Ibid. 114. [185] Ibid. 110.

[186] See e.g. Fowler V. Harper and Alan S. Rosenthal, 'What the Supreme Court Did Not Do in the 1949 Term—An Appraisal of Certiorari', *U. Pennsylvania L. Rev.*, 99 (1950), 293–325; Fowler V. Harper and Edwin D. Etherington, 'What the Supreme Court Did Not Do During the 1950 Term', *U. Pennsylvania L. Rev.*, 100 (1951), 354–409; Fowler V. Harper and George C. Pratt, 'What the Supreme Court Did Not Do During the 1951 Term', *U. Pennsylvania L. Rev.*, 101 (1953), 439–79; Fowler V. Harper and Arnold Leibowitz, 'What the Supreme Court Did Not Do in the 1952 Term', *U. Pennsylvania L. Rev.*, 102 (1954), 427–63.

[187] Albert M. Sacks, 'The Supreme Court, 1953 Term—Foreword', *Harvard L. Rev.*, 68 (1954), 96–103 at 99. [188] Ibid. 99–100. [189] Ibid. 103.

expediency above reason was readdressed by Sacks's colleague, Ernest Brown, in his Foreword to the 1957 term. Brown lamented 'the Court's increasingly frequent practice of granting certiorari and simultaneously reversing the decision of a federal court of appeals or a state supreme court without briefs or arguments upon the merits'.[190] The quality of the Court's work, he insisted, is dependent on the quality of its procedures.

By the latter half of the 1950s, quality control was being preached at Yale as well as at Harvard. 'The Court's product has shown an increasing incidence of the sweeping dogmatic statement,' wrote the Yale law professors, Alexander Bickel and Harry Wellington, in 1957.[191] '[O]pinions have, of late, often said very little and have carried an air of assertion, as opposed to one of deliberation and rational choice.'[192] While 'decision by assertion'[193] may make for swift and efficient adjudication, it undermines 'the Court's real strength',[194] its ability to engage in reasoned elaboration. Not only is 'the elaboration of reasons'[195] a judicial strength; more importantly, it ought to be treated as a judicial duty. For if an organ such as the Supreme Court is free from any duty to give reasons, if it need 'not attempt to gain reasoned acceptance for [its] result[s]', it can hardly be said to 'make law in the sense which the term "law" must have in a democratic society.'[196] If a court feels compelled to articulate reasons supporting the law which it creates, then it will not create law arbitrarily. In short, reason fosters accountability and restraint.

Having promoted the virtue of reasoned elaboration, Bickel and Wellington failed, ironically, to develop their own argument in a sufficiently elaborate fashion. A court may provide detailed reasons for its decisions and yet still make bad law; for even detailed reasons may prove to be inadequate reasons. Precisely what sort of reasons, then, ought any court to produce? '[T]he right reasons,'[197] according to Bickel and Wellington. But what are 'right reasons'? This was a question process jurisprudence had yet to answer. Bickel and Wellington turned their attention instead to a problem which other process writers had already tackled with confidence: the problem of statutory interpretation. As with the articulation of reasons, they argued, the purposive interpretation of statutes fosters judicial restraint. For such interpretation allows not the importation of any old purpose into the words of a statute, but only 'a purpose which may reasonably be imputed to "those who uttered the words" '.[198] The same point was advanced, albeit from a different angle, by Louis Jaffe. Judicial discretion in the interpretation of statutes, he

[190] Ernest J. Brown, 'The Supreme Court, 1957 Term—Foreword: Process of Law', *Harvard L. Rev.*, 72 (1958), 77–95 at 77.

[191] Alexander M. Bickel and Harry H. Wellington, 'Legislative Purpose and the Judicial Process: The Lincoln Mills Case', *Harvard L. Rev.*, 71 (1957), 1–39 at 3.

[192] Ibid. [193] Ibid. 14. [194] Ibid. 4. [195] Ibid. 5.

[196] Ibid. [197] Ibid. 38. [198] Ibid. 17.

argued, should be exercised only in those instances where the court is uncertain of the clear purpose of the statute.[199] Where courts fail to heed this injunction, they undermine 'the integrity of the legal system'.[200]

Although Bickel and Wellington each contributed further to the development of process jurisprudence during the 1960s and 1970s, it is, for two reasons, worth reflecting at this point on their collaboration in the 1950s. First of all, it seems ironic that what would become the classic phrase of process jurisprudence, 'reasoned elaboration', was first put into circulation not at Harvard, as one would expect, but by two Yale law professors. Not that Bickel and Wellington were typical of the Yale faculty. Both were Harvard law graduates. Bickel had clerked for Justice Frankfurter during the 1952 Term. Wellington had clerked for him during the 1955 Term. Only after Frankfurter had failed in his efforts to secure for him a permanent position on the Harvard faculty did Bickel accept his post at Yale.[201] For Fred Rodell, ever the conspiracy theorist, Bickel and Wellington were living proof of Frankfurter's efforts to 'Harvardize' the Yale Law School in the post-war years.[202] While Rodell's view betrays more about him than it does about post-war Yale, it is nevertheless true that Bickel and Wellington were displaced Harvardians, developing 'Harvard-style' jurisprudence in New Haven rather than in Cambridge.

The second point to consider is Bickel and Wellington's emphasis on the link between reason and democracy. By stressing this link, they advanced a line of thought which was already being developed by other process writers. In the early 1950s, Herbert Wechsler of the Columbia Law School had argued that the American federal system is uniquely suited to the preservation of democracy.[203] Since, however, federal intervention into state affairs is primarily a matter for congressional determination, the Supreme Court must be seen to play an essentially subordinate role in settling the balances of federalism.[204] Where the Supreme Court does break free from congressional control, Wechsler noted, is in the area of civil liberties, where the Court must determine the scope of those constitutional restraints which serve to protect individuals from the interventions of federal and state government.[205] It was in this area, many

199 Louis L. Jaffe, 'Judicial Review: Question of Law', *Harvard L. Rev.*, 69 (1955), 239–76 at 261.

200 Ibid. 274.

201 See Edward A. Purcell, Jr., 'Alexander M. Bickel and the Post-Realist Constitution', *Harvard Civil Rights-Civil Liberties L. Rev.*, 11 (1976), 521–64 at 528. On Bickel's intellectual indebtedness to Frankfurter, cf. Alfred S. Konefsky, 'Men of Great and Little Faith: Generations of Constitutional Scholars', *Buffalo L. Rev.*, 30 (1981), 365–384 at 377–81.

202 For an account of Rodell's Harvard-phobia, see Neil Duxbury, 'In the Twilight of Legal Realism: Fred Rodell and the Limits of Legal Critique', *Oxf. Jnl. Leg. Studs.*, 11 (1991), 354–95 at 385–7.

203 Herbert Wechsler, 'The Political Safeguards of Federalism: The Role of the States in the Composition and Selection of National Government', *Columbia L. Rev.*, 54 (1954), 543–60.

204 Ibid. 559–60

205 Ibid. 560 fn. 59.

process writers felt, that the Warren Court fared particularly poorly in articulating reasons for its decisions. Bickel and Wellington were among the first to argue that, no matter how laudable certain of the Court's decisions might seem, where it fails to articulate reasons it neglects the requirements of democracy.

Unfortunately, as we have already seen, although Bickel and Wellington argued that reason ought to be regarded as essential to adjudication in a democracy, they failed to explain what reason might mean. Clearly there was a gap here which needed to be filled. Filling this gap required no new substantive developments in process jurisprudence. It demanded simply a return to the interconnection of reason and principle. By the end of the 1950s, Henry Hart had grasped the connection which needed to be made: adjudication in a democracy must be founded on reasons, and it is in the character of reasons that they involve an appeal to principle. In his Foreword to the 1958 Term, he commented that 'too many of the Court's opinions are about what one would expect could be written in twenty-four hours . . . [F]ew of the Court's opinions, far too few, genuinely illumine the area of law with which they deal. . . . Issues are ducked which in good lawyership and good conscience ought not to be ducked. Technical mistakes are made which ought not be made in the decisions of the Supreme Court of the United States.'[206] The Court was doing too much and doing it badly. Concerned more with expediency than with the maturing of their collective thought, the Justices of the Warren era were producing:

> [o]pinions which . . . lack the underpinning of principle which is necessary to illumine large areas of the law and thus to discharge the function which has to be discharged by the highest judicial tribunal of a nation dedicated to exemplifying the rule of law not only to itself but to the whole world. Only opinions which are grounded in reason and not on mere fiat or precedent can do the job which the Supreme Court of the United States has to do. . . . [T]he Court is destined in the long run . . . to be a voice of reason, charged with the creative function of discerning afresh and of articulating and developing impersonal and durable principles of constitutional law and impersonal and durable principles for the interpretation of statutes and the resolution of difficult issues of decisional law.[207]

Neither logic, nor experience, but 'reason is the life of the law'.[208] Reason demands the articulation and development of those principles which maintain the integrity and the workability of the legal system as a whole.[209] Never before had the process perspective been expounded in such a strident fashion. Thurman Arnold dismissed Hart's Foreword as complacent, Ivory Tower bunkum, a collection of 'pompous generalizations

[206] Hart, *supra* n. 5, 100. [207] Ibid. 99. [208] Ibid. 125.

[209] Henry M. Hart, Jr., 'The Aims of the Criminal Law', *Law and Contemporary Problems*, 3 (1958), 401–41 at 402.

dropped on the Court from the heights of Olympus'.[210] There can be no such thing as a maturing of collective judicial thought, Arnold insisted, because judges of necessity differ in their thoughts.[211] To assume otherwise is to demonstrate 'an ignorance of the rules of elementary psychology'.[212] Dean Griswold was quick to jump to his colleague's defence: 'many times,' he confessed, 'clearly held views of mine have been radically changed by discussions with associates or colleagues. . . . To me "the maturing of collective thought" is a profound reality.'[213] This assertion in fact supported rather than refuted Arnold's point, for Griswold had identified not the maturing of collective thought, but the maturing of his own thought.

The question of whether or not thought can ever be said to mature collectively was a fairly trivial one. There were other, more fundamental problems which needed to be resolved. The meaning and the import of 'principle' within the process tradition remained ambiguous, as also did the concept of 'process' itself. Certain process writers focused on 'the legal process', arguing, for example, that within that process, 'each agency of decision ought to make those decisions which its position in the institutional structure best fits it to make.'[214] Others were concerned not with the general theme of institutional competence, but specifically with the idea that a Supreme Court decision ought, in a democracy, to be based on a 'process of reasoning'.[215] Thus it was that, within the process tradition as it evolved in the 1950s, the term 'process' acquired a dual meaning. This in itself ensured that the ideology of process jurisprudence remained indistinct. Certainly, process jurisprudence was 'pro-democratic'. The work of Bickel and Wellington had demonstrated that much. Since, however, 'process' was an imprecise, protean concept, it seemed difficult if not actually impossible to demonstrate how 'process' jurisprudence was rooted in democratic thought. Elaborating the democratic character of process jurisprudence demanded a more considered analysis of the concept of process. That analysis came, in the late 1950s, in the form of Hart and Sacks's *The Legal Process*, a text which deserves careful analysis. Before we turn our attention to that text, however, it is worth considering the manner in which, in American political science during the middle period of this century, 'process' became a central theme of democratic theory.

210 Thurman Arnold, 'Professor Hart's Theology', *Harvard L. Rev.*, 73 (1960), 1298–317 at 1299.
211 Ibid. 1312.
212 Ibid. 1313.

213 Erwin N. Griswold, 'The Supreme Court, 1959 Term—Foreword: Of Time and Attitudes—Professor Hart and Judge Arnold', *Harvard L. Rev.*, 74 (1960), 81–94 at 85.

214 Hart, *supra* n. 209, 426; and see, more generally, Robert S. Summers, 'Evaluating and Improving Legal Processes—A Plea for "Process Values" ', *Cornell L. Rev.*, 60 (1974), 1–52 at 13–14.

215 Bickel and Wellington, *supra* n. 191, 18.

PROCESS AND POLITICAL SCIENCE

It is often said that, in the years following the United States' entry into the Second World War, American social thought underwent a profound transformation. By the late 1930s, the reality of liberal democracy clearly contradicted the expectations of liberal-democratic theory.[216] The time was ripe for the emergence of a new type of theory, one which would at once affirm the status quo and revive confidence in liberal democratic values. Faith in rational consensus was a primary feature of this new type of theory. Generally resistant to calls for widespread economic and social change, social theorists of the post-war era placed little emphasis on economic and social inequalities and highlighted instead the democratic values of freedom, toleration and, above all, the idea that, where social conflict surfaces, the institutional framework of American society will always accommodate a 'reasonable' compromise.[217]

This 'rhetoric of reasonableness', as one commentator has called it,[218] reinforced an image of the United States which, in truth, belonged to the previous century. 'I do not think that it is as easy as is supposed', Tocqueville wrote in 1839, 'to uproot the prejudices of a democratic people, to change its belief, to supersede principles once established by new principles in religion, politics, and morals.'[219] American democracy, he observed, demands shared experience, received wisdoms and 'a settled order of things'.[220] Many mid-twentieth century social theorists were offering essentially the same observation: despite differences of opinion on particulars, there existed a broad agreement that post-war America

[216] See generally Purcell, *supra* n. 33, 235–66. A good illustration of the mid-century crisis of democratic thought is to be found in a series of articles, stressing the need for a more credible theory of democracy, written by successive presidents of the American Political Science Association. See Clarence Dykstra, 'The Quest for Responsibility', *American Political Science Rev.*, 33 (1939), 1–25; Robert Brooks, 'Reflections on the "World Revolution" of 1940', *American Political Science Rev.*, 35 (1941), 1–28; Frederick Ogg, 'American Democracy—After War', *American Political Science Rev.*, 36 (1942), 1–15; William Anderson, 'The Role of Political Science', *American Political Science Rev.*, 37 (1943), 1–17; Robert Cushman, 'Civil Liberty After the War', *American Political Science Rev.*, 38 (1944), 1–20.

[217] See Purcell, *supra* n. 216, 254–55.

[218] Michael Paul Rogin, *The Intellectuals and McCarthy: The Radical Specter* (Cambridge, Mass.: MIT Press, 1967), 278. ('To argue that discussion can resolve all differences, in an apparent spirit of tolerance and democracy, implies that no legitimate conflict of interest or opinion exists. Those who seek to organize and exert pressure in opposition to those with power then become illegitimate. . . . The rhetoric of reasonableness, whether employed by group leaders, national politicians, or liberal intellectuals, can too easily be turned against thoroughgoing political opposition.')

[219] Alexis de Tocqueville, *Democracy in America* (2 vols. New York: Vintage, 1990; 1st vol. orig. publ. 1835, 2nd vol. 1840), II, 257–8.

[220] Ibid. II, p. 262.

enjoyed social stability owing to widespread political and cultural consensus. These social theorists, Edward Purcell has explained, 'viewed the consensus as morally good. If Americans did enjoy such cultural agreement and if it was the basis of the nation's democratic tradition, then its rejection courted destruction of democracy. Political action that was to be both rational and effective had to be carried out within the terms of that cultural agreement.'[221] Not only, then, did post-war social theory emphasize consensus; it suggested also that any opposition to that consensus must be unreasonable and thus politically illegitimate.[222] In essence, faith in rational consensus entailed a commitment to liberal democracy as the only viable political ideal.[223]

The vocabulary of process featured significantly in the development of the rational consensus perspective. Not that process had previously been a concept alien to American social thought. As early as 1908, in *The Process of Government*, Arthur Bentley wrote that:

> In government we have to do [*sic*] with powerful group pressures which may perhaps at times adjust themselves through differentiated reasoning processes, but which adjust themselves likewise through many other processes, and which, through whatever processes they are working, form the very flesh and blood of all that is happening. It is these group pressures, indeed, that not only make but also maintain in value the very standards of justice, truth, or what not that reason may claim to use as its guides.[224]

For Bentley, group pressure, rather than processes of reasoning, is the key to understanding political reality. To chart the role of group pressure within the governmental process is to demonstrate that politics is founded on power rather than on reason. 'When the groups are adequately stated, everything is stated.'[225] Reason, in contrast, is but 'soul stuff',[226] and as such is impossible to study empirically. This rejection of reason as the touchstone of political reality impressed many political scientists of the Progressive era.[227] By the 1940s, however, it was becoming clear that the Bentley-inspired approach to the study of political power was seriously inadequate. By denying the validity of reason within politics, Bentley and

[221] Purcell, *supra* n. 33, 256.

[222] Purcell, ibid. 257; Rogin, *supra* n. 218, 278.

[223] See Purcell, *supra* n. 222. ('Rationality meant that all "ideologies" were mythical and had to be abandoned.')

[224] Arthur F. Bentley, *The Process of Government: A Study of Social Pressures* (Evanston: Principia, 1949; orig. publ. 1908), 447.

[225] Ibid. 208.

[226] Ibid. 176.

[227] See e.g. Charles Beard, *An Economic Interpretation of the Constitution of the United States* (New York: Macmillan, 1913); Walter Lippmann, *The Phantom Public* (New York: Macmillan, 1925); and Dewey, *The Public and Its Problems* (New York: Holt, 1927). For a general discussion, cf. Raymond Siedelman, *Disenchanted Realists: Political Science and the American Crisis, 1884–1984* (Albany, NY: State University of New York Press, 1985), 60–100.

those who followed in his footsteps were, in effect, suggesting that the governmental process may legitimately be influenced by groups pressing for the implementation of 'irrational', anti-democratic policies. The equation of political reality with group power, furthermore, implied that the governmental process is open to legitimate domination by one group, or by a collection of groups which share the same political perspective. Bentley's account of the American governmental process had failed to capture its essentially democratic nature. The question of how political power is exerted within a system of democracy remained, in effect, unanswered.

In attempting to answer this question, political scientists of the 1940s gradually moved away from the group pressure perspective as advocated by Bentley and his followers. They nevertheless kept faith with the idea that the struggle to exert power is at the heart of the political process. This did not mark an immediate reinstatement of reason in political science. In *Politics, Parties, and Pressure Groups*, first published in 1942, V. O. Key argued that the function of the major political parties in the United States is not primarily to provide voters with a choice at the polls, but to mediate between the claims of competing interest groups within the political system. Governmental action, he insisted, is determined by pressure group power, not by popular will; indeed, the electorate does little more than determine who should fill a particular office.[228] Stated thus, this vision of the American governmental process seems no less bleak than that presented by Bentley. Unlike Bentley, however, Key regarded the American governmental process as the embodiment of democratic norms and values. While the impact of elections on governmental activity may be minimal, he argued, 'these occasional interventions of the electorate into the direction of government are in a sense the characteristic that differentiates democracies from other forms of government.'[229] Within a democracy, citizens at least have the right to choose their government, even if they cannot determine governmental policy.

This argument was developed rather more emphatically by the Harvard professor of economics, Joseph Schumpeter. In *Capitalism, Socialism and Democracy*, another political science text which appeared in 1942, Schumpeter argued that '[t]he principle of democracy . . . merely means that the reins of government should be handed to those who command more support than any of the competing individuals or teams.'[230] 'The

[228] See V. O. Key, Jr., *Politics, Parties, and Pressure Groups* (New York: Thomas Crowell Co., 1942), 256.

[229] V. O. Key, Jr., *Politics, Parties, and Pressure Groups* (2nd edn. New York: Thomas Crowell Co., 1947), 637.

[230] Joseph A. Schumpeter, *Capitalism, Socialism and Democracy* (New York: Harper & Bros., 1942), 273.

democratic method', he insisted, 'is that institutional arrangement for arriving at political decisions in which individuals acquire the power to decide by means of a competitive struggle for the people's vote.'[231] Although a democracy cannot function satisfactorily unless the bulk of the population agrees on the fundamentals of the existing institutional structure, it is nonetheless incorrect to assume that democratic government must reflect some abstract, 'rational will' of the people.[232] The simple fact is that there is no such rational will: political opinions are formed not rationally, but by advertising, sloganeering and other manipulative techniques.[233] It is for this reason that the political system of a democratic society resembles a free-enterprise system, in which pressure groups compete to manipulate political opinion by promoting their own causes and advancing the interests of their supporters.[234] For Schumpeter, the absence of rationality from the governmental process does not undermine but rather affirms its democratic character, for it ensures that élites must compete for power within the electoral framework.[235]

By the following decade, political scientists were beginning to build on Schumpeter's theory of the democratic political process. In doing so, however, certain of them promoted the very interconnection of reason and politics which Schumpeter himself had eschewed. In *The Governmental Process*, published in 1951, David Truman, a professor of government at Columbia University, cited Bentley rather than Schumpeter as his principal inspiration.[236] Like Bentley, he considered the role of interest groups to be the key to understanding governmental activity. Yet there is a sense in which his work could hardly have been further distanced from Bentley's. For Truman, the key to understanding the governmental process rests in the interaction among interest groups. Such groups tend to regulate one another because their memberships often overlap, and also because they subscribe to the same basic democratic standards, attitudes and beliefs—what Truman terms the 'rules of the game'.[237]

[231] Ibid. 269. [232] Ibid. 301. [233] Ibid. 250–64.

[234] See Ibid. 282; and cf., more generally, David M. Ricci, 'Democracy Attenuated: Schumpeter, the Process Theory, and American Democratic Thought', *Jnl. of Politics*, 32 (1970), 239–67 at 256–8.

[235] On this point, see generally Gottfried Haberler, 'Schumpeter's *Capitalism, Socialism and Democracy* after Forty Years', in A. Heertje (ed.), *Schumpeter's Vision: Capitalism, Socialism and Democracy after Forty Years* (Eastbourne: Praeger, 1981), 69–94.

[236] David B. Truman, *The Governmental Process: Political Interests and Public Opinion* (New York: Knopf, 1951), ix. Truman's own work was inspirational to a later generation of political scientists. See e.g. Theodore J. Lowi, *The End of Liberalism: Ideology, Policy, and the Crisis of Public Authority* (New York: Norton, 1969); and also, more generally, Darryl Basken, 'American Pluralism: Theory, Practice, and Ideology', *Jnl. of Politics*, 32 (1970), 71–95.

[237] Truman, *supra* n. 236, 159.

> [T]he 'rules of the game' are interests the serious disturbance of which will result in organized interaction and the assertion of fairly explicit claims for conformity. In the American system the 'rules' would include the value generally attached to the dignity of the individual human being, loosely expressed in terms of 'fair dealing' or more explicitly verbalized in formulations such as the Bill of Rights. . . . Violation of the 'rules of the game' normally will weaken a group's cohesion, reduce its status in the community, and expose it to the claims of other groups.[238]

The prevalence of overlapping membership and general respect for the 'rules of the game' thus requires of interest groups that they share the same standards of restraint and institutional competence. This requirement, furthermore, guarantees a general political consensus. As Truman explains, 'multiple memberships in potential groups based on widely held and accepted interests . . . serve as a balance wheel in a going political system like that of the United States. . . . Without the notion of multiple memberships in potential groups it is literally impossible to account for the existence of a viable polity such as that in the United States or to develop a coherent conception of the political process.'[239] It is in this way that Truman commits himself to the post-war rational consensus perspective. In essence, he argues, the governmental process of the Unites States is comprised of a collection of élites which—because they overlap in membership and share the same broad procedural norms—promote political consensus rather than tension. The assumption is that consensus will be shared by all reasonable people. Bentley's 'soul stuff' is thus reintroduced into American political science:

> [Truman's] argument is based on the tacit assumption that reasonable men agree on what constitute the fundamental procedures of democracy. In the abstract the assumption is tenable, but it is considerably less so when procedure is entangled in substantive issues which are deeply controversial. . . . Consensus on the meaning and scope of freedom of speech . . . is inevitably transformed into sharp disagreement when this right is exercised by the Communist, the bigot, the bookseller of obscene material, the picket, or the employer speaking to a captive labour audience. . . . So it is with most procedural rules; they cannot be extricated from the substantive interests and values with which they interact without being disembodied of their essential meaning.[240]

Since he treats the governmental process as a collection of élites bound together by overlapping membership and by a 'rational' respect for the same procedural norms, Truman is unable to explain how élites themselves might be kept within constitutional bounds. He has no answer, as he puts it, 'to the ancient question: *quis custodiet ipsos custodes?*'[241] It is enough,

[238] Truman, *supra* n. 236, 512–13.

[239] Ibid. 514.

[240] Peter Bachrach, *The Theory of Democratic Elitism: A Critique* (London: University of London Press, 1969; orig. publ. 1967), 52-53.

[241] Truman, *supra* n. 236, 535.

for him, that the consensus which exists among élites upholds the democratic system. Other social theorists of the period were decidedly less sanguine. C. Wright Mills, for example, was of the view that the American élite structure obstructs rather than promotes real democracy.[242] Certainly the 'consensus of élites' perspective on the governmental process was in need of elaboration. That elaboration came in 1956, in the form of Robert Dahl's *A Preface to Democratic Theory*. Building on the insights of Bentley, Schumpeter, and Truman, Dahl contends that power in the United States is held by a plurality of competing interest groups.[243] No one group enjoys a monopoly of control; indeed, the governmental process is characterized by neither majority nor minority rule, but by 'minorities rule'.[244] Competition among a wide variety of interest groups, all of which are in a 'minor'—namely, non-advantaged—position within the governmental process, is the defining characteristic of American democracy. Indeed, the distinction between 'democracy (polyarchy)' and 'dictatorship', according to Dahl, is the distinction 'between government by minority and government by *minorities*. As compared with the political processes of a dictatorship, the characteristics of polyarchy greatly extend the number, size, and diversity of the minorities whose preferences will influence the outcome of governmental decisions.'[245]

By introducing the concept of 'minorities rule' into interest group theory, Dahl highlights the problems which his forebears had failed to solve. Like Schumpeter and Truman, he regards democratic government to be an essentially self-regulatory process, the competition among interest groups serving as a form of internal constraint. The fact that competing groups may find themselves in conflict is accorded no real significance. 'Constitutional rules' may 'help to determine what particular groups are to be given advantages or handicaps in the political struggle,'[246] but 'in so far as there is any general protection in human society against the deprivation by one group of the freedom desired by another, it is probably not to be found in constitutional forms.'[247] More likely, Dahl argues, it is to be found in the American political system itself; for it is 'a political system in which all the active and legitimate groups in the population can make themselves heard at some crucial stage in the process of decision.'[248] Even the Supreme Court reflects and promotes the values of this system. 'To consider the Supreme Court of the United States strictly as a legal institution,' Dahl claimed in 1957, 'is to underestimate its significance in the American political system. For it is also a political institution, an

[242] C. Wright Mills, *The Power Elite* (Oxford: Oxford University Press, 1956).

[243] See Robert A. Dahl, *A Preface to Democratic Theory* (Chicago: University of Chicago Press, 1956), 131. [244] Ibid. 132. [245] Ibid. 133. [246] Ibid. 137.

[247] Ibid. 134. [248] Ibid. 137.

institution, that is to say, for arriving at decisions on controversial questions of national policy.'[249] Law, quite simply, must be seen to be at the service of politics.

In claiming as much, Dahl is not endeavouring to be contentious. For, like Truman, he regards the democratic system to be founded on a consensus of political beliefs. 'Without such a consensus no democratic system would long survive the endless irritations and frustrations of elections and party competition. With such a consensus the disputes over policy alternatives are nearly always disputes over a set of alternatives that have already been winnowed down to those within the broad area of basic agreement.'[250] The foundation of the democratic system in consensus ensures, in other words, that it is able to accommodate and provide solutions for all social problems. Again like Truman, Dahl considers the political consensus on which democracy is founded to be a rational consensus. '[T]he chances are', he observed in 1961, 'that anyone who advocates extensive changes in the prevailing democratic norms is likely to be treated . . . as an outsider, possibly even as a crackpot whose views need not be seriously debated.'[251]

The message which Dahl was promoting—that the United States is blessed with a well-nigh perfect liberal democratic system,[252] a system which political scientists must do their utmost to perpetuate[253]—was by no means unique to him. It was the basic message of post-war consensus theory. '[D]emocracy is vastly more unified in America,'[254] wrote the Harvard historian Louis Hartz, reflecting on the rise of the democratic idea in Europe. 'We have made the Enlightenment work in spite of itself . . . We have implemented popular government, democratic judgement, and the equal state on a scale that is remarkable by any earthly standard. There

[249] Robert A. Dahl, 'Decision-Making in a Democracy: The Supreme Court as a National Policy-Maker', *Jnl. of Public Law*, 6 (1957), 279–95 at 279.

[250] Dahl, *supra* n. 243, 132–33.

[251] Robert A. Dahl, *Who Governs? Democracy and Power in an American City* (New Haven, Conn.: Yale University Press, 1961), 320. More recently, see Robert A. Dahl, *Democracy and Its Critics* (New Haven, Conn.: Yale University Press, 1989), 8–9.

[252] '[T]he common view seems to be that our system is not only democratic but is perhaps the most perfect expression of democracy that exists anywhere.' Dahl, *Who Governs?* 316.

[253] '[E]ven if universal belief in a democratic creed does not guarantee the stability of a democratic system, a substantial decline in the popular consensus would greatly increase the chance of serious instability.' Dahl, ibid. 325.

[254] Louis Hartz, 'The Rise of the Democratic Idea', in Arthur M. Schlesinger, Jr. and Morton White (eds.), *Paths of American Thought* (Boston: Houghton Mifflin, 1963), 37–51, 543–4 at 39. See also John P. Roche, 'American Liberty: An Examination of the "Tradition" of Freedom', in M. R. Konvitz and C. Rossiter (eds.), *Aspects of Liberty: Essays Presented to Robert E. Cushman* (Ithaca, NY: Cornell University Press, 1958), 129–62 at 162. ('American liberty, in short, has become a positive goal of national public policy, rather than a fortuitous consequence of fragmentation, pluralism and social conflict.')

are problems here, but no "crisis", no question of "survival".'[255] The only major problem of American democracy, Hans Morgenthau reflected, concerned its promotion abroad. 'How can the area of equality in freedom be expanded beyond the territorial limits of the United States? How can equality in freedom be offered to the world as a model to emulate? The answer,' he suggested, demands 'the opening of a new cultural frontier' within which American democracy may serve 'as a model of equality for the nations emerging from colonial and semi-colonial status, and as a model of freedom for the nations living under autocratic rule'.[256] 'For if America is the bizarre fulfilment of liberalism, do not people everywhere rely upon it for the retention of what is best in that tradition?'[257]

Just as social theorists were celebrating the maturity and potential universality of the American democratic ethos, so too they were celebrating the exhaustion of 'ideology'. 'The ideologist—Communist, existentialist, religionist—wants to live at some extreme,' wrote Daniel Bell in 1957, 'and criticizes the ordinary man for failing to live at the level of grandeur. One can try to do so if there is the genuine possibility that the next moment could be actually, a "transforming moment" when salvation or revolution or genuine passion could be achieved. But such chiliastic moments are illusions.'[258] By the end of the 1950s, intellectuals in the West had recognized the illusory nature of ideology. 'The point is,' Bell observed, 'that ideologists are "terrible simplifiers". Ideology makes it unnecessary for people to confront individual issues on their individual merits. One simply turns to the ideological vending machine, and out comes the prepared formulae. And when these beliefs are suffused by apocalyptic fervour, ideas become weapons, and with dreadful results.'[259] '[T]he new generation', he concluded, 'finds itself seeking new purposes within a framework of political society that has rejected, intellectually speaking, the old apocalyptic and chiliastic visions.'[260]

Bell refrains from turning his observations on the exhaustion of ideology into an advertisement for American democracy.[261] It is clear, nevertheless, that he attributes the failure of ideology not only to utopianism but also to the resilience of the democratic political framework. Like Truman and

[255] Louis Hartz, 'Democracy: Image and Reality', in W. N. Chambers and R. H. Salisbury (eds.), *Democracy in the Mid-Twentieth Century: Problems and Prospects* (St. Louis: Washington University Press, 1960), 13–29 at 29.

[256] Hans J. Morgenthau, *The Purpose of American Politics* (New York: Knopf, 1960), 300–1.

[257] Louis Hartz, *The Liberal Tradition in America: An Interpretation of American Political Thought Since the Revolution* (New York: Harcourt, Brace & Co., 1955), 308.

[258] Daniel Bell, *The End of Ideology: On the Exhaustion of Political Ideas in the Fifties* (Cambridge, Mass.: Harvard University Press, 1988; orig. publ. 1960), 301–2. The section of the book from which this passage is taken was originally published in 1957: see ibid. 450.

[259] Bell, *The End of Ideology*, 405.

[260] Ibid. 404.

[261] See ibid. 422.

Dahl, he argues that '[d]emocratic politics means bargaining between legitimate groups and the search for consensus',[262] and since democracy is rooted in the notion of consensus, ideology, whether illusory or not, has no useful role to play within the American political system. Ideology appeals to emotion.[263] Democracy, in contrast, being founded in consensus, demands reason. Thus it was that political scientists of the 1950s eschewed ideology and endeavoured instead to demonstrate how American democracy is founded on a rational consensus of political beliefs. As Purcell has remarked, political science became oriented towards 'working out efficient techniques for reaching those values upon which there was a broad consensus. The existing social structure was the criterion of political rationality.'[264]

Post-war political scientists, then, in studying the process of democratic government, regarded American democracy as a rational phenomenon, the product of widespread rational consensus. For these so-called 'process theorists',[265] reason informs political activity in a democracy just as, for process jurists such as Bickel and Wellington, it informs, or certainly ought to inform, judicial activity in a democracy. Although they demonstrated it in different ways, political and legal process theorists of the 1950s shared the same basic faith in reason as the cornerstone of democracy.

Before returning to the matter of how that faith informed jurisprudence, it is worth considering briefly how it found its way also into the philosophy of John Rawls. For the early writings of Rawls demonstrate perhaps better than anything else how the rationalistic orientation of process jurisprudence was but a reflection of broader intellectual concerns. In his article, 'Outline of a Decision Procedure for Ethics', published in 1951, Rawls attempted to describe the essential characteristics of a rational—by which he means a principled—decision-making process. '[I]n ethics,' he asserts, 'we are attempting to find reasonable principles which, when we are given a proposed line of conduct and the situation in which it is to be carried out and the relevant interests which it affects, will enable us to determine whether or not we ought to carry it out and hold it to be just and right.'[266] The determination of whether or not particular principles are reasonable and just demands that they be subjected to what Rawls terms a 'process' of 'explication'.[267] A satisfactory explication of principles will demonstrate that, 'if any competent man were to apply them intelligently and consistently to the same cases under review, his judgements, made systematically nonintuitive by the explicit and conscious use of the principles, would be . . . identical, case by case, with the considered

[262] Bell, *The End of Ideology*, 121.
[263] Ibid. 404.
[264] Purcell, *supra* n. 33, 258.
[265] See Ricci, *supra* n. 234, 262–3.
[266] John Rawls, 'Outline of a Decision Procedure for Ethics', *Philosophical Rev.*, 60 (1951), 177–97 at 178.
[267] Ibid. 184.

judgments of [a] group of competent judges.'[268] In this way, Rawls anticipates the concept of reasoned elaboration. '[A]n explication', he insists, 'must be comprehensive',[269] and 'must be stated in the form of principles'[270] as opposed to rules.[271] The formulation of reasonable principles through the process of explication is essential, furthermore, to the 'integrity'[272] of adjudication: that is 'a judgment in a particular case is evidenced to be rational by showing that, given the facts and the conflicting interests of this case, the judgment is capable of being explicated by a justifiable principle (or set of principles).'[273]

Rawls concludes his article by formulating, in a 'provisionary' manner, 'what are hoped to be satisfactory principles of justice'.[274] By the late 1950s, he was able to formulate these principles in a less tentative fashion.[275] The two principles which he expounds—that each person is to have an equal right to the most extensive liberty, compatible with a similar liberty for others, and that inequalities are to be arranged so that they might reasonably be expected to be to everyone's advantage and attach to positions and offices open to all—were, of course, to become central to modern liberal political philosophy.[276] What concerns us here, however, is not the unfolding of Rawls's theory of justice, but the fact that, in his early work, we can find the same interconnection between reason and principle which we find in process jurisprudence. Rawls too was arguing that official decision-makers must clarify and elaborate the principles on which their decisions are based if they are to uphold the integrity and rationality of the adjudicative process. This is not to claim that process jurisprudence was inspired by Rawlsian philosophy, or vice versa. Rather, it is to reiterate the point that process jurisprudence was but an instance of a more general post-war intellectual tendency. Like Rawls—and indeed, to a lesser extent, like Truman and Dahl—process jurists were attempting to demonstrate that rationality inheres in the particular process being studied. Rationality of process, we might say, was an *idée force* of the post-war period.

THE LEGAL PROCESS

It has been said often, by a variety of legal scholars, that Henry Hart and Albert Sacks's *The Legal Process* is the classic text of post-war process jurisprudence.[277] While such a statement is undoubtedly correct, it is also

268 Ibid. 269 Ibid. 186. 270 Ibid. 271 Ibid. 195.
272 Ibid. 182. 273 Ibid. 187. 274 Ibid. 191.
275 See John Rawls, 'Justice as Fairness', *Philosophical Rev.*, 67 (1958), 164–94 at 165–6.
276 See John Rawls, *A Theory of Justice* (Oxford: Oxford University Press, 1972), 54–117; and see now his *Political Liberalism* (New York: Columbia University Press, 1993), 289–371.
277 See e.g. John Henry Schlegel, 'American Legal Realism and Empirical Social Science: From the Yale Experience', *Buffalo L. Rev.*, 28 (1979), 459–586 at 461 fn. 8; William N.

potentially misleading. For the manuscript is only part of the message: *The Legal Process* is not just a text but a course, a classroom experience. As Hart and Sacks state in the preface to their materials, its contents are intended to serve '[a]s vehicles of class discussion'.[278] The course grew out of a seminar in Legislation which Hart began teaching at Harvard in the late 1930s.[279] Hart's 'approach to the course extended beyond legislation to law-making generally; indeed, his principal early emphasis was on the law-making function of the courts.'[280] In the academic year 1954–5, in collaboration with Sacks, Hart began transforming this course into a much broader second-year elective survey course, initially entitled 'The American Legal System'[281] and eventually retitled 'The Legal Process: Basic Problems in the Making and Application of Law'.[282] The course became the most popular second-year 'perspective' course at the Harvard Law School.[283] '[F]or most Harvard students,' wrote Martin Mayer in 1966, it is 'the centrepiece of their programme.'[284]

The popularity of *The Legal Process* was not confined to Harvard. In 1958, when the last version of the manuscript was compiled, six other American law schools adopted it for use.[285] Ten years later, it was being taught in some twenty-five schools besides Harvard.[286] To this day, there are law professors in the United States who run courses based on the *Legal Process* materials.[287] What makes this remarkable is that fact that,

Eskridge, Jr., 'Metaprocedure', *Yale L.J.*, 98 (1989), 945–74 at 962. The best study of the history, content and impact of *The Legal Process* is, alas, as yet unpublished: William N. Eskridge, Jr. and Philip P. Frickey, 'An Historical and Critical Introduction to "The Legal Process" ' (unpublished mimeograph, Georgetown University Law Center, Washington, DC [on file with author: copy supplied by Professor Eskridge], 26 January 1994), 149 pp.

278 Hart and Sacks, *The Legal Process*, v.

279 Albert M. Sacks, 'Memorandum: To the Committee on Legal Education. Subject: The Course on the Legal Process', mimeograph, n.d. [1959?], Harvard Law School Library [on file with author: copy supplied by Professor Laura Kalman], 7 pp., p. 1. It should be noted that Hart was the 'senior editor' of the *Legal Process* materials (see Hart and Sacks, *The Legal Process,* p. 111 fn. 2).

280 Sacks, Ibid.

281 See Seligman, *supra* n. 172, 82.

282 Precisely when Hart and Sacks's course became the 'Legal Process' course I have been unable to ascertain. I know of one edition of the materials, in the possession of Dr Nigel Simmonds of Corpus Christi College, Cambridge, which is dated 1957 and is some 200 pages shorter than the 1958 edition. What is clear is that Hart and Sacks anticipated producing further editions of the manuscript (see *The Legal Process*, 1037).

283 See Seligman, *supra* n. 172, 82; Kalman, *supra* n. 27, 224.

284 Martin Mayer, *The Lawyers* (New York: Harper & Row, 1966), 88.

285 Sacks, *supra* n. 279, 1.

286 Calvin Woodard, 'The Limits of Legal Realism: An Historical Perspective', *Virginia L. Rev.*, 54 (1968), 689–739 at 725 fn. 74.

287 Peter Teachout [Professor of Law, Vermont Law School], letter to author, 22 July 1992. 'I . . . still offer a course based on the Hart and Sacks materials. It's always interesting to me the extent to which today's students still respond very positively to these materials and to the course. . . . The course seems to offer an education that students find of enduring relevance.'

although Hart and Sacks considered publishing their manuscript,[288] they never did so. Indeed, they were very modest about its scope. 'The essential method [of these materials],' they wrote, 'is nothing more than an application of the method of teaching law first popularized by Christopher Columbus Langdell in the 1870s. The only difference is that Langdell's casebooks had nothing but concrete problems, and left the student to work out the implications for himself. In keeping with the general softness of the age, these materials try to give the student a lift on his job.'[289]

The difference to which Hart and Sacks pointed was, in fact, more significant than they assumed. With the proliferation of so-called 'Cases and Materials' texts in the 1930s, legal instruction in the United States came gradually to centre less on specific cases and more on general legal problems. As Karl Llewellyn wrote in the introduction to his case-book of 1930, 'the focus of law study is the problem situation, not the illustrative case'.[290] By the following decade, American lawyers were distinguishing the traditional Langdellian case-method from the 'problem method'. 'Problems can be assigned in connection with case book study,' wrote David Cavers in 1943. 'Discussion in class can be centred on the problems and the cases introduced as they become relevant to the problems under discussion.'[291] Cavers observed also, however, that although certain realists espoused the problem method, they failed to embrace it. '[T]he Realists have fitted their aspirations into the framework of the casebook system.'[292] Emphasis on cases rather than on problems remained their priority. This is evident from a classic realist text such as Wesley Sturges's *Cases and Materials on the Law of Credit Transactions*, in which specific doctrinal problems are illustrated in the main through the comparison of apparently contradictory judicial decisions.[293] In *The Legal Process*, by contrast, specific cases are used to illustrate general problems concerning law creation and application.[294] Hart and Sacks were attempting to invoke the pedagogic strategy which realism had only promised.

288 Sacks, *supra* n. 279, 1. 'We are now in the course of a revision of these materials that can be sent to the Foundation Press.' Sacks appears to have toyed with the idea of publishing a version of *The Legal Process* almost up until the end of his life. See Norman Dorsen, 'In Memoriam: Albert M. Sacks', *Harvard L. Rev.*, 105 (1991), 11–14 at 13 fn. 12. Publication of the materials is still not an impossibility. Two American law professors, William Eskridge and Philip Frickey, have volunteered to edit the materials with a view to publication. The Foundation Press, the estates of Hart and Sacks and the Harvard Law School are apparently amenable to this idea. William N. Eskridge, Jr., letter to author, 2 November 1992.

289 Hart and Sacks, *The Legal Process*, v–vi.

290 Karl N. Llewellyn, *Cases and Materials on the Law of Sales* (Chicago: Callaghan & Co., 1930), xviii.

291 David F. Cavers, 'In Advocacy of the Problem Method', *Columbia L. Rev.*, 43 (1943), 449–61 at 456.

292 Ibid. 453.

293 See Wesley A. Sturges, *Cases and Materials on the Law of Credit Transactions* (4th edn. St. Paul, Minn.: West Publishing Co., 1955; 1st edn. 1930), esp. 29.

294 See further Seligman, *supra* n. 172, 82.

This is not the only way in which *The Legal Process* constitutes a response to the failures of realist legal thought. Hart and Sacks heard and heeded the basic realist message that law is 'a pervasive aspect of social science'.[295] But they 'reject the teaching of [that] vast body of literature which has accumulated during the last half century seeking to equate the methods of the various social sciences, and in particular of law, with the method of the natural sciences.'[296] Following Fuller, they argue that, in equating social science with natural science, so-called realists 'have tried to construct a science of society and of law based scrupulously upon the "isness" of people's behaviour—of the behaviour of judges, legislators, and other public officials as well as of ordinary private citizens—while at the same time rigorously separating questions of how people ought to behave'.[297] Conceived as a social science, law, they insist, is a normative—or, more precisely, purposive—process.[298]

This assertion rests at the core of Hart and Sacks's jurisprudence. '[T]he ultimate test of the goodness or badness of every institutional procedure and of every arrangement which grows out of such a procedure,' they argue, 'is whether or not it helps to further th[e] purpose' of 'establishing, maintaining and perfecting the conditions necessary for community life to perform its role in the complete development of man.'[299] Since 'societies are made up of human beings striving to satisfy their respective wants under conditions of interdependence,'[300] the basic purpose of legal institutions is 'to maximize the total satisfactions of valid human wants.'[301] The American constitutional framework is fundamental to the realization of this purpose: 'The Constitution of the United States and the various state constitutions commit American society, as a formal matter, to . . . the objective of maximizing the total satisfactions of human wants.'[302] Thus it is that, although Hart and Sacks frame their purposive perspective on law in normative terms—as a matter, that is, of what the primary objective of legal institutions ought to be—they are in fact attempting to explain what law actually is. They are arguing not that American legal institutions ought to, but that they do, pursue the goal of maximization. 'Almost every, if not every, institutional system gives at least lip service to the goal of maximizing valid satisfactions for its members generally.'[303] The desirability of maximizing the satisfaction of valid human wants is considered, accordingly, to be a matter of rational consensus, 'an entirely objective fact'.[304]

[295] Hart and Sacks, *The Legal Process*, 2, and cf. also 198. [296] Ibid. 116.
[297] Ibid. 117. [298] Ibid. iii ('law as an on-going, functioning, purposive process').
[299] Ibid. 110–11. [300] Ibid. 4. [301] Ibid. 114 and cf. 74.
[302] Ibid. 114. [303] Ibid. 115.
[304] Ibid. 111. On the consensus-oriented nature of Hart and Sacks's jurisprudence, see also G. Edward White, 'From Sociological Jurisprudence to Realism: Jurisprudence and Social

The legal process, then, is committed to the goal of maximization. This, for Hart and Sacks, is a matter beyond debate.[305] What is for debate, however, is the question of how the legal process might best pursue this goal.

> For if human life and the forms of social organization are concerned essentially with the purposive pursuit of human ends . . . [m]ust [the decision-maker] not inevitably, at least with problems of any novelty, make a choice among the possible purposes to be pursued and the possible ways of accomplishing them? And how can the observer of decisions understand the actions of the decision-maker unless he takes account of these choices and tries to appraise their soundness?[306]

Thus it is that Hart and Sacks set out their jurisprudential stall. Realist jurisprudence had emphasized the indeterminate, unprincipled nature of judicial decision-making. Fuller and various other process jurists of the 1940s and 1950s regarded adjudication as a peculiar type of institutional activity—an activity which, if it is to command respect, must be based in reason, and which, if it is to be based in reason, must be principled. Between the two jurisprudential traditions, preoccupation with the common law prevailed. Neither legal realism nor process jurisprudence had attempted to grapple with, among other things, legislation and administrative regulation. This is where Hart and Sacks broke decisively from the past. Adjudication, they recognized, is but one form of institutional activity within the legal process. Sometimes, within that process, legislatures, administrative agencies, arbitrators—even private parties themselves—may be better suited than the courts to deal with particular disputes. When considering disputes, the basic question which the lawyer must ask is: 'what kind of settlement will serve best to prevent the recurrence of similar controversies in the future?'[307] One of the central aims of process jurisprudence is to train lawyers to be able satisfactorily to answer this question.[308]

It is to this end that Hart and Sacks develop a variation on the concept of institutional competence which first surfaced in the work of Fuller.[309] '[T]he central idea of law', they contend, is 'the principle of institutional

Change in Early Twentieth-Century America', *Virginia L. Rev.*, 58 (1972), 999–1028 at 1027; 'From Realism to Critical Legal Studies: A Truncated Intellectual History', *Southwestern L.J.*, 40 (1986), 819–43 at 829. There are indications in *The Legal Process* that Hart and Sacks were aware of certain post-war rational consensus theories. See *The Legal Process,* 739 (citing Truman, *The Governmental Process, supra* n. 236) and 746–7 (citing Key, *Politics, Parties and Pressure Groups, supra* n. 228). It is clear, furthermore, that their primary jurisprudential mentor, Lon Fuller, was familiar with the work of Robert Dahl. See Fuller, *supra* n. 120, 480.

305 Hart and Sacks, *The Legal Process*, 111.

306 Ibid. 117–18.

307 Ibid. 16.

308 See Ibid. 869.

309 Often, this concept is attributed mistakenly to Hart and Sacks. See e.g. Patrick Macklem, 'Of Texts and Democratic Narratives', *U. Toronto L.J.*, 41 (1991), 114–45 at 142.

settlement.'[310] 'That principle requires that a decision which is the due result of duly established procedures be accepted whether it is right or wrong—at least for the time being.'[311] The task of legal education is to enable students to recognize which procedures ought to apply to which problems. 'In relation to every one of the concrete problems which are posed [in these materials],' they claim, 'it will be relevant to ask: what is the nature of the knowledge which is useful in solving this problem, and how could more useful knowledge be secured?'[312] Such discernment is the prerequisite of legal expertise, imagination and craft;[313] for '[l]awyers . . . have again and again to consider whether to invoke the procedures of private or of judicial settlement or, often alternatively, of legislative or administrative settlement.'[314] The ability of legal professionals to discern which institutions are suited to which types of settlement is necessary for the maintenance of 'an efficient legal system'[315] and for 'rationalizing the fabric of its law as a whole'.[316]

> The lawyer's business in any given institutional system is to help in seeing that the principle of institutional settlement operates not merely as a principle of necessity but as a principle of justice. This means attention to the constant improvement of all the procedures which depend upon the principle in the effort to assure that they yield decisions which are not merely preferable to the chaos of no decision but are calculated as well as may be affirmatively to advance the larger purposes of the society.[317]

One of the primary institutional distinctions to be highlighted, according to Hart and Sacks, is that which exists between public and private government. '[I]n pursuit of the ultimate goal of maximizing the satisfactions of valid human wants, the law finds many a tool besides force that suits its purpose,'[318] for 'there are other ways than the way of coercion to control a society.'[319] The state may, for example, adopt a 'hands-off' strategy, so that the resolution of particular problems is left to 'the process of private ordering'.[320] Indeed, private ordering—the use of 'self-applying regulation' by private individuals in the government of their own activities—is the principal method of social control in a democratic society.[321] 'Overwhelmingly the greater part of the general body of the law is self-applying, including almost the whole of the law of contracts, torts, property, crimes, and the like. Under such a scheme of control, only the trouble cases come before officials, and these only after the event.'[322] The prevalence of private ordering, for Hart and Sacks, is the sign of an efficient legal system: 'almost every scheme of individualized regulation

[310] Hart and Sacks, *The Legal Process*, 4. [311] Ibid. 119. [312] Ibid. 120.
[313] Ibid. 200. [314] Ibid. iii. [315] Ibid. 230.
[316] Ibid. 105. [317] Ibid. 6. [318] Ibid. 881.
[319] Ibid. 134. [320] Ibid. 870–1. [321] Ibid. 134.
[322] Ibid. 133.

includes some self-applying elements. Again and again, efficient administration suggests the desirability of maximizing these elements.'[323] Public regulation of private activity ought, accordingly, to be permitted only where the processes of private ordering are found wanting.[324] It is in this way that Hart and Sacks commit themselves to a form of utilitarian *laissez-faire* liberalism which they consider to be integral to the American polity.

> Basic in the American system is the assumption that every normal person counts one in determining the objectives of primary control. . . . Basic also, in the structure of this system, is the reflection of this assumption in the equal distribution of personal capacity to be [the] subject of primary liberties, duties, and powers, and to exercise rights of action and defend actions in vindication of them. . . . Given these basic equalities, it follows that every normal member of the society has the same personal capacity to exercise private powers, and thereby to command the backing of society for his own personal arrangements. Every such member has the same personal capacity to be the subject of duties and to exercise liberties. In principle, every such member is supposed to have the same personal capacity in the political processes of the system, both as a potential office holder and as a unit, counting one, in the ultimate institutional procedure of the election.[325]

Individuals, then, enjoy basic equalities and liberties which ought generally to be left unfettered by public control. For it is precisely these equalities and liberties which facilitate the goal of maximizing the satisfaction of valid human wants. Hart and Sacks recognize that, with regard to 'questions of equality of economic opportunity',[326] the freedom of the individual to satisfy his or her wants may suffer 'under the discipline of a market' which is biased towards 'other buyers and sellers potentially able to offer more favourable terms'.[327] They insist, however, that this constraint on personal freedom operates only in the economic domain.[328] Thus it is that one of the major arguments of realist jurisprudence—that the freedom of the individual is a freedom to try to limit the similar freedoms of other individuals[329]—is reduced to a minor academic insight. Realism, very simply, is assumed to reveal remarkably little about the legal world.

This assumption emerges more clearly in Hart and Sacks's analysis of the courts and the legislature as distinct legal institutions. One of the questions which recurs most frequently in *The Legal Process* is that of whether particular legal problems are to be resolved within the common law or the legislative framework.[330] '[A] sound theory of the distribution of institutional responsibility as between the courts and the legislature'[331] demands

[323] Ibid. 872.
[324] See ibid. 184, 213, 289, 300, 406, 533, 833.
[325] Ibid. 309.
[326] Ibid.
[327] Ibid. 207.
[328] Ibid. 309.
[329] See, in particular, Robert L. Hale, 'Coercion and Distribution in a Supposedly Non-coercive State', *Political Science Quarterly*, 38 (1923), 470–94.
[330] See e.g. Hart and Sacks, *The Legal Process,* iv, 10, 105, 407, 487, 515, 535, 603.
[331] Ibid. 515.

the recognition that each must refrain from trying to perform functions for which it is not competent.[332] 'Sound legislation'—or 'wise legislation', as Hart and Sacks sometimes call it[333]—must be 'the product of a sound process of enactment'.[334] This process 'ought to be an *informed process*, in the sense that key decisions are not made until relevant information has been acquired. It ought to be a *deliberative process*, in the sense that key decisions are not made until there has been a full interchange of views and arguments among those making the decisions. And it ought to be an *efficient process*, in the sense that all legislative proposals ought to be disposed of in the time available, with the more significant ones receiving proportionately more time.'[335] Since, however, the interpretation of legislation is a primary function of the courts,[336] it is there that the test of soundness becomes especially important.

Hart and Sacks purport to favour neither common law nor legislation. '[T]he determination of whether legislatively-developed law in the form of an enactment is to be preferred to judicially-developed law in the form of reasoned grounds of decision is inherently discretionary.'[337] Yet they seem to display a peculiar preference for the judicial decision. Whereas courts create law, they assert at one point, legislatures create policy.[338] If the courts function properly, furthermore, a good deal of policy need not be enacted.[339] Indeed, courts are to be criticized when they 'pass the buck to the legislature and avoid taking an open and honest responsibility for their own growth of the law'.[340] But what does it mean to say that a court is not functioning properly or is shirking its responsibility to maintain the growth of the law? What is the appropriate test here? Over and over again, Hart and Sacks propose the test unequivocally. When considering a judicial opinion or the decision of a court, the question to be asked is: 'Is it sound?'[341] This test is not one of procedural soundness, as it is with legislation. Rather, it concerns 'soundness of reasoning'.[342] '[S]ound

332 See ibid. 386, 403, 670, 858.
333 Ibid. 834.
334 Ibid. 715.
335 Ibid. 715–16.
336 Ibid. 140.
337 Ibid. 536.
338 Ibid. iv, and cf. 707.
339 See ibid. 817.
340 Ibid. 488.
341 Ibid. 72, 73, 240, 289, 325, 436, 485, 488, 489, 565. The criterion of soundness features prominently not only in Hart and Sacks's *Legal Process* materials, but also in their examination questions. As examples, consider: 'The American Legal System: Processes of Law Making (a) and (b)' (Professors H. M. Hart and Sacks), Law School of Harvard University, Examinations, First Semester, 1956–7, 29–36 at 35 (Problem III: 'Comment on the soundness of the result reached and the interpretive technique employed by the majority'); 'The Legal Process (a) and (b)' (Professors Hart and Sacks), Law School of Harvard University, Examinations, First Semester, 1958–9, 35–41 at 39 (Problem IV: 'Comment on the soundness of the interpretive techniques employed in the following decision'); 'The Legal Process (a) and (b)' (Professors Hart and Sacks), Law School of Harvard University, Examinations, First Semester, 1959–60, 31–8 at 33, 38; 'The Legal Process (A)' (Professor Sacks), Law School of Harvard University, Examination, 11 January 1972, 275–80 at 280 (Problem III: 'Discuss the soundness of the Court's holding and reasoning').
342 Hart and Sacks, *The Legal Process,* 585, 247.

grounds'[343] of decision are 'reasoned grounds of decision.'[344] Such grounds are essential to 'the integrity . . . of the judicial function in the legal system',[345] for it is only through the development of sound reasoning that a decision might turn out to be '*the* right answer'[346] to a particular legal problem.

So, what makes a judicial decision sound? In answering this question, Hart and Sacks develop certain of the basic themes of process jurisprudence which had already been put into play by Fuller and other process writers of the 1940s and 1950s. They begin by observing that rules are but one form of legal directive. 'Many legal arrangements cannot feasibly be cast in the form of a rule, however inchoate. And often another form is deliberately chosen as preferable. . . . This provision is of the type commonly known as a *standard*.'[347] Standards are legal directives which entail a qualitative or moral appraisal of human behaviour by reference to supposedly ideal behaviour in a comparable situation. Accordingly, within a legal system, there exist general standards of recklessness, due care and the like. Such standards may be rendered more specific—for example, due care may be defined as 'that care which a reasonably prudent person, with opportunities for observation of the actor, would have exercised in a like situation'—so as to give them 'the form and precision of a rule'.[348] Even taken together, however, rules and standards do not constitute 'the whole framework of legal arrangements in an organized society. Notably to be contrasted with rules and standards are principles and policies.'[349]

> Principles and policies are closely related, and for many purposes need not be distinguished from each other. A *policy* is simply a statement of objective. *E.g.*, full employment, the promotion of the practice or procedure of collective bargaining, national security, conservation of natural resources, etc., etc., etc. A *principle* also describes a result to be achieved. But it differs in that it asserts that the result *ought* to be achieved and includes, either expressly or by reference to well understood bodies of thought, a statement of *the reasons why* it should be achieved. *E.g.*, *pacta sunt servanda*—agreements should be observed; no person should be unjustly enriched; etc., etc.[350]

'Primarily, principles and policies are used and useful as guides to the exercise of a trained and responsible discretion.'[351] The judicial use of principles, however—given their normative nature and their foundation in reason—demands more than just discretion; it demands also 'the power of reasoned elaboration'.[352] This means, first of all, that the judge 'is obliged

343 Ibid. 606.
344 Ibid. 871.
345 Ibid. 617.
346 Ibid. 168. Italics in original.
347 Ibid. 157.
348 Ibid. 157–8.
349 Ibid. 159.
350 Ibid.
351 Ibid. 160.
352 Ibid. 161.

to resolve the issue before him on the assumption that the answer will be the same in all like cases' and, secondly, that, where statutory interpretation is necessary, he must 'relate his decision in some reasoned fashion to the . . . statute out of which the question arises. He is not to think of himself as in the same position as a legislator taking part in the enactment of the statute in the first place.'[353] Reasoned elaboration thus determines 'the permitted scope of discretion'.[354] While policy may influence judge-made law and statute law alike, the former, unlike the latter, is guided by the rationalizing force of principle.[355]

Reasoned elaboration, then, is integral to sound adjudication.[356] It is in this way that adjudication may be distinguished not only from legislation, but also from other institutional activities within the legal process. '[A]n arbitrator's award or an administrative order', for example, 'is unexplained by any articulate findings or reasons.'[357] Similarly, apart from in the area of Restitution, the reporters of the first Restatements failed satisfactorily to articulate reasons for their various proposals.[358] In claiming as much, however, Hart and Sacks are not implying that reasoned elaboration is the hallmark of all judicial decision-making. While 'the reasoned elaboration of decisional law'[359] may be essential to the pursuit of substantive justice,[360] while it is inevitably a general feature of the common law process[361]—while, indeed, '[a] reasoned answer' to a legal problem 'will always be possible'[362]—the courts are remarkably prone to producing 'intellectual nonsense'[363] and making 'a lamentable botch'[364] of the task. That a 'court's obligation is to decide . . . on reasoned grounds'[365] does not mean that it always does so. Often—and especially when confronted with a 'hard case'[366]—a court will struggle to articulate a 'statement of general principle'[367] which is 'rationally defensible'.[368] This is why Hart and Sacks urge the study of 'processes of reasoning'.[369] It is important, they insist, to look 'not only to the rightness or wrongness of the particular result but to the validity of the process by which the court arrived at it.'[370] In short, the presence or absence of reasoned elaboration in a judicial decision is the primary indication of whether or not it is sound.

Reasoned elaboration is not, however, the only indicator of judicial soundness. For a different criterion of soundness applies with regard to the

353 Hart and Sacks, *The Legal Process*, 161 and cf. 379.
354 Ibid. 164, and cf. also 398.
355 Ibid. 177–8, and cf. also 1240 (on 'judicially developed principles' and 'statutory policies').
356 Ibid. 665.
357 Ibid. 361.
358 Ibid. 761–2.
359 Ibid. 594.
360 See ibid. 70, 166, 648.
361 Ibid. 588–9.
362 Ibid. 669.
363 Ibid. 488.
364 Ibid. 286. See, in particular, Hart and Sacks's excoriating critique of the Vinson Court's decision in *Youngstown Sheet & Tube Co.* v. *Sawyer* (1952) 343 U.S. 579.
365 Hart and Sacks, *The Legal Process*, 138.
336 Ibid. 397, and cf. also 386.
367 Ibid. 100.
368 Ibid. 101.
369 Ibid. 104, and cf. also 67.
370 Ibid. 1148.

judicial interpretation of statutes. 'The principle of institutional settlement . . . forbids a court to substitute its own ideas for what the legislature has duly enacted.'[371] It is nevertheless naive and indeed irrational for courts to assume that statutes in general can be read literally, as if their wording admits of but one meaning.[372] If 'the integrity of language, as a healthy functioning social institution'[373] is to be maintained in the courts, judges must appreciate that 'meaning depends upon context'.[374] 'An essential part of the context of every statute is its purpose. Every statute must be conclusively presumed to be a purposive act. The idea of a statute without an intelligible purpose is foreign to the idea of law and inadmissible.'[375]

A statute is not only a purposive act. It is commonly a rational purposive act. 'The statute ought always to be presumed to be the work of reasonable men pursuing reasoning purposes reasonably, unless the contrary is made unmistakably to appear.'[376] If the courts are to develop a 'sound method of statutory interpretation',[377] they must be committed to ascertaining such purposes. This requires that they consider—'with [the] mind in neutral',[378] as it were—'the history and general scheme of the statute'.[379] Furthermore, '[t]he purpose of the statute must always be treated as including not only an immediate purpose or group of related purposes but a larger and subtler purpose as to how the particular statute is to be fitted into the legal system as a whole.'[380] Only by 'striv[ing] to develop a coherent and reasoned pattern of applications intelligibly related to the general purpose' of a statute,[381] and by endeavouring to demonstrate how this purpose is 'calculated to serve the ultimate purposes of law', might the courts 'formulate a sound and workable theory' of statutory interpretation.[382]

For Hart and Sacks, accordingly, 'soundness'—meaning both reasoned elaboration and the purposive interpretation of statutes—is the key to demonstrating the essential rationality of the legal process. Although the legislature, administrative agencies and other legal institutions may demand their own criteria of soundness, it is within the common law framework that one discovers the concept at its most refined. For in its pursuit of soundness, Hart and Sacks suggest, borrowing an image used by Lon Fuller, the common law system is able 'to work itself pure'.[383] That is, judicial activity motivated by personal instinct or by considerations of

[371] Ibid. 1225, and cf. also 165.
[372] See Ibid. 1156, 1173–4, 1369–71.
[373] Ibid. 1226.
[374] Ibid. 1412.
[375] Ibid. 1156.
[376] Ibid. 1157.
[377] Ibid. 1203.
[378] Ibid. 1275.
[379] Ibid. 169.
[380] Ibid. 1414.
[381] Ibid. 1417.
[382] Ibid. 1201.
[383] Ibid. 100; and cp. Fuller, *supra* n. 93, 140. This image was used as early as the eighteenth century by Lord Mansfield. According to Mansfield: 'A statute can seldom take in all cases, therefore the common law that works itself pure by rules drawn from the fountain of justice is for this reason superior to an Act of Parliament'. *Omychund* v. *Barker* (1744) 1 Atk. 21 at 33. Jurists associated with the process tradition continue to be attracted to the image. See, in particular, Ronald Dworkin, *Law's Empire* (London: Fontana, 1986), 400–3.

policy is purged from the system and replaced by judicial activity founded on reason. By turning away from discretion and emphasizing reason, Hart and Sacks effectively bid farewell to the realist legal tradition. Commenting on legal realism in 1931, Morris Cohen observed that '[i]t has become a fashion nowadays to belittle the reasons people give for their conduct.'[384] By the 1950s, such reasons were, once again, all the rage.[385]

Although faith in reason had become fashionable, it was nevertheless difficult to preach convincingly. For the concept of 'soundness' is itself unsound. The pursuit of soundness, Hart and Sacks insist, is essential to the development of law as a purposive enterprise. That is, both reasoned elaboration and purposive statutory interpretation are supposed to facilitate the basic goal of maximizing the satisfactions of valid human wants. Yet such a goal does not exist. Reasoned elaboration may yield principles, applicable to the same legal problem, which, though they conflict, appear to be equally persuasive when judged by the basic criterion of maximization. As Duncan Kennedy explains, the principle that ' "A man should pay damages when he has been at fault" cannot be "weighed" against [the principle that] "Damages should be allocated among actors so as to maximize deterrence" unless we are willing to ascend simultaneously two distinct hierarchies of purpose.'[386] The choice of principle, very simply, depends on how the goal of maximization is defined.[387] Indeterminacy similarly infects the purposive interpretation thesis. As Richard Posner has argued, Hart and Sacks's insistence that legislation be treated generally as the product of rational purposive activity—'of reasonable men pursuing reasonable purposes reasonably'—is unrealistic for the reason that, since the 1950s, 'the spectrum of respectable opinion on political questions has widened so enormously that even if we could assume that legislators intended to bring about reasonable results in all cases, the assumption would not generate specific legal concepts.'[388] Furthermore, as Posner and

[384] Morris R. Cohen, 'Justice Holmes and the Nature of Law', *Columbia L. Rev.*, 31 (1931), 352–67 at 366.

[385] See White, *The American Judicial Tradition*, *supra* n. 3, 293.

[386] Duncan Kennedy, 'Utopian Rationalism in American Legal Thought' (unpublished mimeograph [on file with author: copy supplied by Professor Kennedy], June 1970), iii, 44.

[387] Ibid. iii. 46. ('[I]t should be clear that the judge making a good faith effort to reach the correct decision through reasoned elaboration can perfectly consistently mount the two hierarchies of values implied in two different results until he reaches the choice between ideologies, and that he can then make the choice according to which system will, in his earnest opinion, serve to maximize valid human satisfactions. This choice once made, one or the other of the resolutions of the specific problem will in all probability appear quite distinctly "correct".')

[388] Richard A. Posner, 'Legal Formalism, Legal Realism and the Interpretation of Statutes and the Constitution', *Case Western Reserve L. Rev.*, 37 (1986), 179–217 at 193. In the same vein, see also his *The Problems of Jurisprudence* (Cambridge, Mass.: Harvard University Press, 1990), 294. For some reflections on how Posner's jurisprudence is indebted to the process tradition, see Neil Duxbury, 'Pragmatism Without Politics', *Mod. L. Rev.*, 55 (1992), 594–610.

various proponents of public choice theory have demonstrated,[389] many statutes represent not a general public interest, but the particular goals of private interest groups: to interpret such statutes as rational purposive acts embodying Hart and Sacks's general goal of maximization would, if anything, be to overlook their purpose. In short, Hart and Sacks developed an inadequate model of the legislative process.[390]

The assumption that there exists a general goal of maximization which is to be realized through the development of a set of legal institutions with their own areas of competence and criteria of soundness is indicative of the consensus orientation of Hart and Sacks's jurisprudence. Their perspective, according to one commentator, 'rested on the complacent, simplistic assumption that American society [of the 1950s and 1960s] consisted of happy, private actors maximizing their valid human wants while sharing their profound belief in institutional competencies'.[391] Arguments such as this are not uncommon. *The Legal Process* materials, it has been claimed, were 'perfectly attuned to the end-of-ideology politics of the Cold War'.[392] The principle of institutional settlement which is so central to those materials has been conceived as an attempt to rationalize the existing American power structure, as if that structure were inevitable.[393] By invoking the principle of institutional settlement, it has been said, Hart and Sacks introduced 'institutional formalism'[394] into American jurisprudence. The essential premiss of this formalism is the idea that legal institutions have their own specialist areas of competence beyond which they ought not to stray;[395] and the most notable consequence of accepting this premiss is a

389 See Posner, 'Legal Formalism,' ibid. 193. The relevant public choice literature is voluminous. For a selection, see Daniel A. Farber and Philip P. Frickey, 'Legislative Intent and Public Choice', *Virginia L. Rev.*, 74 (1988), 423–69; Steven Kelman, ' "Public Choice" and Public Spirit', *The Public Interest*, 87 (1987), 80–94; Peter L. Kahn, 'The Politics of Unregulation: Public Choice and Limits on Government', *Cornell L. Rev.*, 75 (1990), 280–312; Donald C. Langevoort, 'The SEC as a Bureaucracy: Public Choice, Institutional Rhetoric, and the Process of Policy Formulation', *Washington and Lee L. Rev.*, 47 (1990), 527–40. For a critique of public choice, cf. Mark Kelman, 'On Democracy-Bashing: A Skeptical Look at the Theoretical and "Empirical" Practice of the Public Choice Movement', *Virginia L. Rev.*, 74 (1988), 199–273.

390 See Bruce A. Ackerman, *Reconstructing American Law* (Cambridge, Mass.: Harvard University Press, 1983), 39–40.

391 Elizabeth Mensch, 'The History of Mainstream Legal Thought', in D. Kairys (ed.), *The Politics of Law: A Progressive Critique* (New York: Pantheon, 1982), 18–39 at 30.

392 Auerbach, *supra* n. 174, 260.

393 See Gary Peller, 'The Metaphysics of American Law', *California L. Rev.*, 73 (1985), 1151–290 at 1183–7.

394 See Morton J. Horwitz, *The Transformation of American Law, 1870–1960: The Crisis of Legal Orthodoxy* (New York: Oxford University Press, 1992), 254.

395 See Joseph William Singer, 'Legal Realism Now', *California L. Rev.*, 76 (1988), 465–544 at 518–19; Harold A. McDougall, 'Social Movements, Law, and Implementation: A Clinical Dimension for the New Legal Process', *Cornell L. Rev.*, 75 (1989), 83–122 at 90–1.

commitment to judicial restraint.[396] That is, while the articulation of policy is regarded to be the function of the democratically elected branches of government, the executive and the legislature, the courts are expected to defer to that policy through purposive statutory interpretation while engaging in their own creative function of developing sound common law principles through the process of reasoned elaboration.

These arguments are significant and, for the most part, well founded. Yet, to some extent, they are also exaggerated. For they underplay the critical thrust of the *The Legal Process* materials. Hart and Sacks may have been complacent in assuming the adequacy of the existing American institutional framework, and they were certainly wrong to assume a general social consensus concerning the goal of maximization. But it was not their claim that all is well with the legal world. We have already seen that reasoned elaboration was, for them, a legal ideal rather than a reality—an ideal, indeed, of which the courts often fell short. Furthermore, the argument that their jurisprudence promotes judicial restraint is only partially correct. The notion of institutional competence without doubt denotes restraint. Hart and Sacks were arguing, after all, that the courts ought to restrain themselves from performing those functions for which they are not competent. But there is also a sense in which this argument denotes activism. For it is Hart and Sacks's belief that, so long as judges respect the principle of institutional competence, they ought to engage in the reasoned elaboration of principles as actively as possible in order to achieve substantive justice for the parties to any particular dispute.[397] Process jurisprudence is not entirely antithetical to judicial activism.[398] And although other proponents of the process perspective, as we shall see, were far more committed to promoting judicial restraint, Hart and Sacks themselves remained ambivalent.

In depicting the jurisprudence of Hart and Sacks as somehow 'conservative',[399] critics have tended to underestimate its intellectual significance. '[B]y the end of the 1960s', one commentator has observed, *The Legal Process* 'seemed oddly out of touch with reality'.[400] Yet, to this day, it remains inspirational. '[M]ost legal scholars,' it has been suggested, 'consciously or not, have followed its path.'[401] Certainly public law

[396] See Ackerman, *supra* n. 3, 123–4.

[397] Duncan Kennedy, 'Legal Formality', *Jnl. of Legal Studies*, 2 (1973), 351–98 at 396 fn. 64.

[398] The classic example of process-oriented judicial activism is Justice Harlan Fiske Stone's infamous *Carolene Products* footnote: see *United States* v. *Carolene Products Co.* (1939) 304 U.S. 144, 152–3 fn. 4. See further Ackerman, *supra* n. 3, 124; and, more generally, J. M. Balkin, 'The Footnote', *Northwestern Univ. L. Rev.*, 83 (1989), 275–320.

[399] The depiction appears throughout the literature dealing with *The Legal Process*. See e.g. Seligman, *supra* n. 172, 79.

[400] Mensch, *supra* n. 391, 30.

[401] Guido Calabresi, *A Common Law for the Age of Statutes* (Cambridge, Mass.: Harvard University Press, 1982), 249 n.20, and cf. also 38.

scholarship in the United States remains heavily indebted to Hart and Sacks.[402] Indeed, some contemporary public lawyers, endeavouring to refine classic *Legal Process* themes such as purposive statutory interpretation and institutional specialization, purport to be developing a 'new legal process' perspective on public law.[403] However one may regard this, it is clear that *The Legal Process*, whatever criticisms may be levelled at it, continues significantly to influence American legal thought.

Why, then, has there been a tendency for critics to dismiss *The Legal Process* as an anachronism? The reason for this is very specific. In attempting to uncover institutional integrity and rationality at the heart of the legal process, Hart and Sacks seemed to be restoring order to the legal world in the aftermath of realism.[404] So-called realists had posed, but of course had not solved, the problem of the limits of judicial power. If judges could not rely on determinate principles and processes of reasoning, as certain realists claimed, what institutional or structural mechanisms existed to check the scope of their discretion? If this discretion was unfettered, what, if anything, was there to prevent an unelected federal judge from using the judicial forum to promote his or her own policy preferences at the expense of the policies of Congress and the legislature?[405] In advocating institutional competence, reasoned elaboration and purposive interpretation, Hart and Sacks were offering an answer to these questions. Their answer was that if the courts accept and respect these criteria, then the problem of how to limit judicial power disappears, for the courts will limit themselves. The burning question, of course, was: did the courts abide by Hart and Sacks's criteria?

402 See William N. Eskridge, Jr. and Gary Peller, 'The New Public Law Movement: Moderation as a Postmodern Cultural Form', *Michigan L. Rev.*, 89 (1991), 707–91 at 708, 725–6.

403 See e.g. Robert Weisberg, 'The Calabresian Judicial Artist: Statutes and the New Legal Process', *Stanford L. Rev.*, 35 (1983), 213–57 at 239–49; William N. Eskridge, Jr. and Philip P. Frickey, 'Legislation Scholarship and Pedagogy in the Post-Legal Process Era', *U. Pittsburgh L. Rev.*, 48 (1987), 691–731; *Cases and Materials on Legislation: Statutes and the Creation of Public Policy* (St. Paul, Minn.: West Publishing Co. 1988), chs. 3 and 7; and, for an overview, A. Michael Froomkin, 'Climbing the Most Dangerous Branch: Legisprudence and the New Legal Process', *Texas L. Rev.*, 66 (1988), 1071–95. Certain proponents of this 'new' legal process perspective have been criticized for building on a distinctly narrow conception of the 'old' legal process perspective. See Daniel B. Rodriguez, 'The Substance of the New Legal Process', *California L. Rev.*, 77 (1989), 919–53 at 923.

404 See Jan Vetter, 'Postwar Legal Scholarship on Judicial Decision Making', *Jnl. Leg. Educ.*, 33 (1983), 412–23 at 416. ('One way to describe the considerable achievement of *The Legal Process* is to see it as repairing the damage inflicted by legal realism.')

405 See Akhil Reed Amar, 'Law Story', *Harvard L. Rev.*, 102 (1989), 688–720 at 694; and also Paul Brest, 'Who Decides?', *Southern California L. Rev.*, 58 (1985), 661–71 at 663–4; Frank I. Michelman, 'Justification (and Justifiability) of Law in a Contradictory World', *Nomos*, 28 (1986), 71–99 at 82–3.

In the 1950s and 1960s, even Hart and Sacks would have hesitated to answer this question affirmatively. Certainly some judges, however unselfconsciously, were aspiring towards the ideals of soundness.[406] In the eyes of most process writers, however, this aspiration had eluded the Supreme Court under Chief Justice Warren. The Warren Court demonstrated a basic commitment to broadening the scope of the rights which attach to American citizenship.[407] It was a commitment which process jurists by and large considered admirable. The problem was that the Court seemed to be concerned primarily with securing results. What the Court appeared not sufficiently to be concerned with was the reasoned elaboration of principles supporting those results. Yet this, for process jurists, was the prerequisite of sound adjudication.

Thus it was that process jurists found themselves on the horns of a dilemma. Warren Court decisions tended to be morally correct yet jurisprudentially unsatisfactory. What was to be done? In the *Legal Process* manuscript, Hart and Sacks evaded the problem. The Warren Court's commitment to liberalism without rationalism was not considered to be an issue for concern. In *Brown* v. *Board of Education,* decided in 1954,[408] the Court, distinguishing the principle of 'separate-but-equal',[409] held that racial segregation in public schools—even where black schools are not demonstrably inferior to white schools—denies black children the equal protection of the laws guaranteed by Clause 1 of the Fourteenth Amendment. By declaring state-supported discrimination against racial minorities to be unconstitutional, the Court secured a victory for 'simple justice'.[410] But was *Brown* a 'sound' decision? Hart and Sacks offered no enlightenment. In *The Legal Process*, they failed so much as to mention the case.[411] This omission is significant, for it highlights a fundamental problem of process jurisprudence which Hart and Sacks had neglected to confront: namely, if a court is able to produce laudable results without elaborating its reasons for those results, why treat the requirement of soundness seriously? If those working within the process tradition could not offer a plausible answer to this question, their faith in reason would prove ill-founded. The survival of process jurisprudence demanded that someone grasp the nettle.

[406] See, in particular, White, *The American Judicial Tradition, supra* n. 3, 293–316.

[407] See Charles L. Black, Jr., 'The Unfinished Business of the Warren Court', *Washington L. Rev.*, 46 (1970), 3–45 at 8, 12.

[408] *Brown* v. *Board of Education* (1954) 347 U.S. 483.

[409] See *Plessy* v. *Ferguson* (1896) 163 U.S. 537.

[410] See Richard Kluger, *Simple Justice: The History of Brown v. Board of Education and Black America's Struggle for Equality* (London: Deutsch, 1977; orig. publ. 1975).

[411] On this point, see Eskridge, *supra*, n. 277, 965.

THE APOGEE OF PRINCIPLE

In his Supreme Court Foreword of 1954, Albert Sacks, commenting on *Brown,* observed that '[t]he outstanding feature of the decision lies in the triumph of a principle—a principle which the court must have found to be so fundamental, so insistent, that it could be neither denied nor compromised'—namely, the principle that 'the Constitution requires equal treatment, regardless of race.'[412] The problem with this 'principle' is that it no more justifies the decision in *Brown* than it does the 'separate-but-equal' formula which had been adopted in *Plessy* v. *Ferguson*. The principle behind *Brown*, it may be assumed, not only upholds racial equality but also denies the legitimacy of state-imposed racial segregation. The Warren Court failed, in *Brown*, to articulate any such principle.

In his famous Holmes Lectures, delivered at the Harvard Law School in 1958–9, Herbert Wechsler used this failure on the part of the Court as an opportunity to argue the case for developing 'neutral principles of constitutional law'.[413] The decision in *Brown* was not, however, his initial point of focus. In his Holmes Lectures of the previous year, Learned Hand had argued that the Supreme Court's power to review the constitutionality of acts undertaken by other branches of national and state government can neither be found in, nor inferred from, the words of the Constitution. '[T]his power', he argued, 'is not a logical deduction from the structure of the Constitution but only a practical condition upon its successful operation.'[414] If the Court had not assumed the power to keep legislators and administrators within their prescribed limits, the American system of government 'would have collapsed'.[415]

> The courts were undoubtedly the best 'Department' in which to vest such a power, since by the independence of their tenure they were least likely to be influenced by diverting pressure. It was not a lawless act to import into the Constitution such a grant of power. On the contrary, in construing written documents it has always been thought proper to engraft upon the text such provisions as are necessary to prevent the failure of the undertaking. That is no doubt a dangerous liberty, not lightly to be resorted to; but it was justified in this instance, for the need was compelling.[416]

This was a distinctly-qualified endorsement of the Supreme Court's power of judicial review as established by Chief Justice John Marshall in *Marbury*

[412] Sacks, *supra* n. 187, 96.

[413] Herbert Wechsler, 'Toward Neutral Principles of Constitutional Law', *Harvard L. Rev.*, 73 (1959), 1–35.

[414] Learned Hand, *The Bill of Rights* (Cambridge, Mass.: Harvard University Press, 1958), 15.

[415] Ibid. 29.

[416] Ibid.

v. *Madison*.[417] There is no judicial power to review the actions of government officials, Hand argued, but only to intervene in those cases where the language of the Constitution shows that the official has transcended his or her authority. In those instances where the Supreme Court does assume the power to review legislative and administrative action—and especially in those instances where it assesses the constitutionality of federal and state laws in relation to the broad strictures of the Fifth and Fourteenth amendments—it adopts the undemocratic role of 'a third legislative chamber'.[418]

Wechsler takes issue with Hand's attempt to qualify *Marbury* v. *Madison*. 'I have not the slightest doubt,' he begins, 'respecting the legitimacy of judicial review.'[419] For the judicial power to review the constitutionality of official actions is grounded in the Constitution itself. Indeed, Article VI of the Constitution—the Supremacy clause[420]—makes such review a matter not of judicial discretion but of 'duty'.[421] The Supreme Court is considered to be obliged, in other words, to scrutinize official actions which appear to offend against constitutional limitations. But if this is so, what is to prevent the Court from assuming the role of a 'third legislative chamber'? Wechsler's answer is that the Court is not vested with a complete discretion to read policy preferences into the Constitution, for its constitutional interpretations are 'to be made and judged by standards that should govern the interpretive process generally'.[422] These standards must be 'framed in neutral terms. . . . Only the maintenance and the improvement of such standards and, of course, their faithful application can . . . protect the Court against the danger of the imputation of a bias favouring claims of one kind or another in the granting or denial of review.'[423]

So, what are these standards? According to Wechsler, they are 'criteria that can be framed and tested as an exercise of reason and not merely as an act of wilfulness or will'.[424] The elaboration of such standards demands the recognition that a court is not 'free to function as a naked power organ',[425] but that it must decide cases with regard for genuine principles of law.

I put it to you that the main constituent of the judicial process is precisely that it must be genuinely principled, resting with respect to every step that is involved in reaching judgement on analysis and reasons quite transcending the immediate

[417] *Marbury* v. *Madison* (1803) 5 U.S. (1 Cranch) 137, 177. See, generally, Sylvia Snowiss, *Judicial Review and the Law of the Constitution* (New Haven, Conn.: Yale University Press, 1990).

[418] Hand, *supra* n. 414, 55.

[419] Wechsler, *supra* n. 413, 2.

[420] U.S. Constitution, article VI, s. 2: 'This Constitution, and the Laws of the United States which shall be made in Pursuance thereof; and all Treaties made, or which shall be made, under the Authority of the United States, shall be the supreme Law of the Land; and the Judges in every State shall be bound thereby, any Thing in the Constitution or Laws of any State to the Contrary notwithstanding.'

[421] Wechsler, *supra* n. 413, 6.

[422] Ibid. 9.

[423] Ibid. 9–10.

[424] Ibid. 11.

[425] Ibid. 12.

result that is achieved. To be sure, the courts decide, or should decide, only the case they have before them. But must they not decide on grounds of adequate neutrality and generality, tested not only by the instant application but by others that the principles imply? Is it not the very essence of judicial method to insist upon attending to such other cases, preferably those involving an opposing interest, in evaluating any principle avowed?[426]

Thus it is that the 'reasoned explanation' of neutral principles is considered by Wechsler to be 'intrinsic to judicial action'.[427] More than this, such explanation is exclusively 'the province of the courts'.[428] As the sole forum of principle, '[t]he courts have both the title and the duty . . . to review the actions of the other branches in the light of constitutional provisions, even though the action involves value choices, as invariably action does.'[429] Courts may be entrusted with this duty precisely because 'they are—or are obliged to be—entirely principled'.[430] In deciding a case in a principled fashion, a court must provide 'reasons with respect to all the issues in the case, reasons that in their generality and neutrality transcend any immediate result that is involved'.[431] Principles prevent the court from functioning as a naked power organ.

Presented in outline, Wechsler's thesis—premissed, as it is, on the belief that the reasoned elaboration of principles is a task to which the courts alone are institutionally competent—seems hardly to be an advance on the jurisprudence of Hart and Sacks. Like Hart and Sacks, Wechsler is preoccupied with processes of reasoning. 'The virtue or demerit of a judgement turns', he claims, 'entirely on the reasons that support it.'[432] Apart from his insistence that principles are general and capable of neutral application,[433] he seems simply to recite the established process faith. In professing this faith, furthermore, Wechsler tends, as with Hart and Sacks, to veer between the descriptive and the normative: sometimes principled decision-making is treated as fact, other times as desideratum. But whereas, for Hart and Sacks, this mixing of the normative and the descriptive suggests genuine ambivalence, with Wechsler it is deliberate. For his argument is that courts sometimes do decide cases in a genuinely principled fashion, while at other times, though they ought to, they do not. All too often, in matters of constitutional adjudication, the Supreme Court did not.[434] It was in making this latter claim—a claim which Hart and Sacks

426 Ibid. 15. 427 Ibid. 15–16. 428 Ibid. 16. 429 Ibid. 19.
430 Ibid. 431 Ibid. 432 Ibid. 19–20.
433 A meaning which, as Wechsler himself recognized, is not entirely captured by the phrase 'neutral principles'. See Herbert Wechsler, *Principles, Politics and Fundamental Law* (Cambridge, Mass.: Harvard University Press, 1961), xiii; Norman Silber and Geoffrey Miller, 'Toward "Neutral Principles" in the Law: Selections from the Oral History of Herbert Wechsler', *Columbia L. Rev.*, 93 (1993), 854–931 at 923–31; Ernest J. Brown, review of Wechsler, *Columbia L. Rev.*, 62 (1962), 386–92 at 387.
434 Wechsler, *supra* n. 413, 20.

had been reluctant to advance—that Wechsler added a critical and indeed controversial dimension to process jurisprudence.

During the first half of this century, and especially during the New Deal era, the Supreme Court, Wechsler argues, paid little attention to principles. In so far as it did consider principles, 'some of the principles the court affirmed were strikingly deficient in neutrality, sustaining, for example, national authority when it impinged adversely upon labour . . . but not when it was sought to be employed in labour's aid.'[435] Many of the great early twentieth-century dissenting opinions—Holmes in *Lochner* is the classic example—were powerful precisely because they demonstrated the inability of the Court to 'present an adequate analysis, in terms of neutral principles, to support the value choices it decreed'.[436] 'The poverty of principled articulation' on the part of the Court, especially during the 1930s, also explained its lamentable lack of self-restraint.[437] However, Wechsler's primary concern is not with the past. The failure to articulate principles when considering constitutional matters was as much a sin of the Court in the 1950s as it had been in the 1930s.

To demonstrate this point, Wechsler considers various decisions in which, during the 1940s and 1950s, the Supreme Court held racial discrimination to be unconstitutional under the equal protection clause of the Fourteenth Amendment. *Brown* is the most famous of these decisions, although the others—upholding the right of black voters to vote in primary elections[438] and outlawing the state imposition of racially restrictive covenants[439]—are anything but unimportant. In Wechsler's opinion, all of the decisions had 'the best chance of making an enduring contribution to the quality of our society of any that I know in recent years'.[440] Yet not one of them, he insisted, was genuinely principled.

Brown was especially problematic. The problem, for Wechsler, rests not in the result but in 'the reasoning of the opinion'.[441] The Supreme Court had reached its decision 'on the ground that segregated schools are "inherently unequal",' having 'deleterious effects upon the coloured children in implying their inferiority, effects which retard their educational and mental development'.[442] It was far from obvious, however, that there existed evidence which validated this ground. In reality, Wechsler argued, an integrated school may be a racially hostile school, a school in which blacks suffer by being made to feel inferior. Where segregation exists, on

[435] Wechsler, *supra* n. 413, 23. [436] Ibid. 24. [437] Ibid. 24–5.
[438] *Smith* v. *Allwright* (1944) 321 U.S. 649.
[439] *Shelley* v. *Kraemer* (1948) 334 U.S. 1; *Barrows* v. *Jackson* (1953) 346 U.S. 249.
[440] Wechsler, *supra* n. 413, 27.
[441] Ibid. 32 and cf. Richard A. Givens, 'The Impartial Constitutional Principles Supporting *Brown* v. *Board of Education*', *Howard L.J.*, 6 (1960), 179–85 at 180.
[442] Wechsler, *supra* n. 413, 32.

the other hand, such hostility may be absent and blacks may enjoy a 'sense of security'.[443] 'Suppose that', in such circumstances, 'more Negroes in a community preferred separation than opposed it? Would that be relevant to whether they were hurt or aided by segregation as opposed to integration?'[444] In offering this argument, Wechsler was not attempting to justify segregation. His argument, rather, is that the reasoning in *Brown* fails to explain why segregation is wrong in principle. It was an expedient rather than a principled decision, as were the segregation decisions which followed in its wake.[445]

Basically, the Supreme Court had known how it wanted to tackle the issue of segregation, but, for want of a principle, had failed to do so sincerely. But what principle might it have invoked? For Wechsler, the fundamental issue was not equal facilities. The 'human and constitutional dimensions' of state-enforced segregation 'lie entirely elsewhere, in the denial by the state of freedom to associate.'[446] The denial of this freedom, he argues, disadvantages both blacks and whites. 'I think, and I hope not without foundation, that the Southern white also pays heavily for segregation, not only in the sense of guilt he must carry but also in the benefits he is denied.'[447] When, Wechsler recounts, he himself was joined in litigation by a black lawyer, 'he did not suffer more that I' in knowing that segregation restricted the choice of places at which they could lunch together.[448] Since the removal of segregation is for the benefit of blacks and whites alike, the principle of free association appears—though Wechsler is extremely hesitant on this matter—to be a truly neutral one:

> Given a situation where the state must practically choose between denying the association to those individuals who wish it or imposing it on those who would avoid it, is there a basis in neutral principles for holding that the Constitution demands that the claims for association should prevail? I should like to think there is, but I confess that I have not yet written the opinion. To write it is for me the challenge of the school-segregation cases.[449]

Wechsler's essay on neutral principles begins with a polite criticism of Hand and ends with a polite criticism of *Brown*. It was the latter criticism which attracted controversy. The principle of free association was presented in a rather perfunctory and ham-fisted fashion. That whites may lose out from segregation hardly means that they 'suffer' from it as much as do blacks. In failing to recognize as much, Wechsler seemed somewhat naive and complacent. 'Professor Wechsler's whole argument', one

443 Ibid. 33.
444 Ibid.
445 See e.g. *Baltimore* v. *Dawson* (1955) 350 U.S. 877; *Holmes* v. *Atlanta* (1955) 350 U.S. 879; *Gayle* v. *Browder* (1956) 352 U.S. 903; *New Orleans Park Association* v. *Detiege* (1958) 358 U.S. 54.
446 Wechsler, *supra* n. 413, 34.
447 Ibid.
448 Ibid.
449 Ibid.

commentator has observed, 'depends on his refusal to consider that the Court might have based its decision on a determination that Negroes are intentionally made to feel inferior through the mechanism of segregation.'[450] This does not mean, however, that he was 'defending the legality of racial domination'.[451] He applauded the result in *Brown*, but questioned its lack of reasoning.

While recognition of this fact is crucial if one is properly to understand Wechsler's thesis,[452] many critics have failed to do so. 'If the cases outlawing segregation were wrongly decided,' wrote Charles Black apropos of Wechsler in 1960, 'then they ought to be overruled.'[453] It was never Wechsler's claim that an unprincipled decision is a wrong decision—only that such a decision is insufficiently reasoned. Other critics took issue with his thesis by arguing that there ought to be more rather than less unprincipled decision-making. 'We need the unprincipled decision', insisted Charles Clark, 'to mark judicial progress, of the kind in fact which has been a glorious heritage of the Court's history.'[454] Yet Clark noted also that, in the law school at least, the neutral principles thesis was gaining in popularity. Even Karl Llewellyn, he lamented, seemed by the 1960s to have been taken in by this 'new mythology of the judicial process'.[455] Certainly, many scholars were—and indeed still are—swayed by Wechsler's thesis.[456] However, Llewellyn—although he had suggested as early as 1940 that principles are important for the promotion of judicial 'soundness'[457]—was not one of them.[458] The call for neutral principles, he insisted, was

[450] Ira Michael Heyman, 'The Chief Justice, Racial Segregation, and the Friendly Critics', *California L. Rev.*, 49 (1961), 104–25 at 112. See further, in this context, Cass R. Sunstein, *The Partial Constitution* (Cambridge, Mass.: Harvard University Press, 1993), 76–7.

[451] Gary Peller, 'Neutral Principles in the 1950s', *U. Michigan Jnl. of Law Reform*, 21 (1988), 561–622 at 565.

[452] See Louis H. Pollack, 'Racial Discrimination and Judicial Integrity: A Reply to Professor Wechsler', *U. Pennsylvania L. Rev.*, 108 (1959), 1–34 at 30–3.

[453] Charles L. Black, Jr., 'The Unlawfulness of the Segregation Decisions', *Yale L.J.*, 69 (1960), 421–30 at 421.

[454] Charles E. Clark, 'A Plea for the Unprincipled Decision', *Virginia L. Rev.*, 49 (1963), 660–5 at 665.

[455] Charles E. Clark and David M. Trubek, 'The Creative Role of the Judge: Restraint and Freedom in the Common Law Tradition', *Yale L.J.*, 71 (1961), 255–76 at 268.

[456] See e.g. Robert G. McCloskey, 'The Supreme Court, 1961 Term—Foreword: The Reapportionment Case', *Harvard L. Rev.*, 76 (1962), 54–74 at 66–7; Stephen B. Presser, *The Original Misunderstanding: The English, the Americans and the Dialectic of Federalist Jurisprudence* (Durham, NC: Carolina Academic Press, 1991), 38; Cass R. Sunstein, 'Neutrality in Constitutional Law (With Special Reference to Pornography, Abortion, and Surrogacy)', *Columbia L. Rev.*, 92 (1992) 1–52.

[457] Karl N. Llewellyn, 'On Reading and Using the Newer Jurisprudence', *Columbia L. Rev.*, 40 (1940), 581–614 at 589, and cf. also 586, 592, 594–5.

[458] See Karl N. Llewellyn, *The Common Law Tradition: Deciding Appeals* (Boston: Little, Brown & Co., 1960), 388.

nothing more than a jurisprudential objection to 'a Warrenish type of broad generalization'.[459]

In regarding the neutral principles thesis as somehow in opposition to the initiatives of the Warren Court, Llewellyn was basically echoing Clark and others. To embrace neutral principles, Clark insisted, is to eschew judicial creativity.[460] Others were even more forthright in offering this criticism. 'Professor Wechsler's argument', Eugene Rostow proclaimed, 'is an attack on the integrity of the Supreme Court.'[461] Judicial review, he argued, must be exercised vigorously if constitutional law is to reflect and support democratic values.[462] This, of course, is precisely what the Warren Court was attempting to do. For Justice Black, the duty of the Court was not only to enforce the Constitution but also to ensure its evolution by investing it with new meanings in new settings.[463] Yet, he hesitated to call himself a judicial activist.

> [I]f it is judicial activism to decide a constitutional question which is actually involved in a case when it is in the public interest and in the interest of a sound judicial system as a whole to decide it, then I am an 'activist' in that kind of case and shall, in all probability, remain one. . . . When I get to the other meaning of 'judicial activism,' however, namely, one who believes he should interpret the Constitution and statutes according to his own belief of what they ought to prescribe instead of what they do, I tell you at once I am not in that group.[464]

Black was reluctant to embrace judicial activism because he knew that it could be put to both good and ill purposes.[465] The Supreme Court of the 1930s had adopted the very type of activism from which he distanced himself—the importation of policy preferences into the Constitution—when it struck down major New Deal enactments. Earlier in the century, in *Lochner* v. *New York*, the Supreme Court had practised precisely such activism when it interpreted the Constitution as a Social-Darwinist document.[466] During the early decades of this century, in short, judicial activism had meant 'anti-progressivism'. It was precisely such activism against which Holmes and Brandeis so often dissented.

[459] Ibid. 389.

[460] Clark, *supra* n. 454, 661; Clark and Trubek, *supra* n. 455, 270.

[461] Eugene V. Rostow, 'American Legal Realism and the Sense of the Profession', *Rocky Mountain L. Rev.*, 34 (1962), 123–49 and 139.

[462] See Eugene V. Rostow, 'The Democratic Character of Judicial Review', *Harvard L. Rev.*, 66 (1952), 193–224.

[463] See Hugo LaFayette Black, *A Constitutional Faith* (New York: Knopf, 1969), xvi; Charles A. Reich, 'Mr. Justice Black and the Living Constitution', *Harvard L. Rev.*, 76 (1963), 673–754 at 703.

[464] Black, *supra* n. 463, 20.

[465] On this point, see Howard Ball and Philip J. Cooper, *Of Power and Right: Hugo Black, William O. Douglas, and America's Constitutional Revolution* (New York: Oxford University Press, 1992), 79, 283.

[466] See *Lochner* v. *New York* (1905) 198 U.S. 45, 75–6 (Holmes J. dissenting).

Wechsler and other process jurists regarded judicial activism in just this light. In *Lochner*, they found a judicial decision devoid of reason and principle, a decision based purely on policy preference.[467] In *Brown*, they found a different policy preference—a preference for racial integration rather than for *laissez-faire* and natural selection. While the preference voiced in *Brown* was, for Wechsler and others, far more favourable than that voiced in *Lochner*, it was a prefence all the same. Where a politically appointed judiciary decides cases on the basis of policy preference, there is always the possibility that preferences will change with the political climate, and where such change occurs, judicial activism will come to serve different political ends. That is why Wechsler appealed for neutral principles of constitutional law. Having clerked for Justice Stone in the early 1930s, he had witnessed first hand the Supreme Court's activism in its exercise of constitutional review.[468] Although, by the Warren era, judicial activism was being employed to serve different, more laudable ends, there was no reason that it should always stay that way. Activism could just as easily be used to curb rather than to promote civil liberties.[469]

The appeal for neutral principles of constitutional law was thus an appeal for institutional competence and judicial restraint.[470] The peculiar task of the judge, in matters of constitutional adjudication, is not simply to promote a particular value or reach a specific result but to produce a decision founded on articulated neutral principles. Without doubt—indeed, as *Brown* proved—a decision may be just without being founded on such principles; but so long as a court eschews principles when engaging in judicial review, it risks assuming the role of a naked power organ. That the Supreme Court of the Warren era happened to be pursuing admirable policies did not mean that it would always do so.

Policies may be good or bad; but principles of constitutional law ought to be neutral. In arguing as much, Wechsler was certainly urging judicial restraint in constitutional adjudication; but this does not mean that he was necessarily arguing for judicial conservatism. Just as the outcome of

[467] See e.g. Louis Henkin, 'Some Reflections on Current Constitutional Controversy', *U. Pennsylvania L. Rev.*, 109 (1961), 637–62 at 658; McCloskey, *supra* n. 456, 68.

[468] See 'Resolution of the Faculty', *Columbia L. Rev.*, 78 (1978), 947–50 at 947.

[469] See Morton J. Horwitz, 'The Jurisprudence of *Brown* and the Dilemmas of Liberalism', *Harvard Civil Rights-Civil Liberties L. Rev.*, 14 (1979), 599–613 at 602. ('In some sense, all American constitutional law for the past twenty-five years has revolved around trying to justify the judicial role in *Brown* while trying simultaneously to show that such a course will not lead to another *Lochner* era.')

[470] See Henkin, *supra* n. 467, 656; Herman Belz, 'Changing Conceptions of Constitutionalism in the Era of World War II and the Cold War', *Jnl. of American History*, 59 (1972), 640–69 at 658–59; and, for a general analysis of the ways in which principles constitute a form of binding or restraint in the process of decision-making, see Robert Nozick, *The Nature of Rationality* (Princeton, NJ: Princeton University Press, 1993), 3–40.

judicial activism may, as in *Lochner*, be the promotion of conservative policies, the outcome of judicial restraint—fostered by the demand for neutral principles—may be progressive, enlightened decision-making. Wechsler's view of *Brown*, after all, is that the Supreme Court could have reached the result that it did—indeed, ought to have reached the result that it did—by developing a neutral principle. Neutral principles are not necessarily conservative principles.[471] In advocating neutrality, Wechsler was not urging judicial anti-progressivism but rebelling against the tradition of activism epitomized by *Lochner*.

In another, rather more problematic sense, however, Wechsler was in fact developing the tradition of *Lochner*. For *Lochner* itself not only exemplified judicial activism but also embodied a peculiar constitutional requirement of neutrality. As Cass Sunstein explains, in *Lochner*:

> the Court's concern was that maximum hour legislation was partisan rather than neutral—selfish rather than public-regarding. It was neutrality that the due process clause commanded, and neutrality was served only by the general or 'public' purposes comprehended by the police power. If the statute could be justified as a labour or health law, it would be sufficiently public to qualify as neutral. Since no such justification was available, it was invalidated as impermissibly partisan. . . . The legislative result was thus unprincipled.[472]

The primary legacy of *Lochner*, according to Sunstein, is the peculiar conception of constitutional neutrality which it bequeathed to modern legal thought. If the case is viewed in this light—that is, in terms of its neutrality as opposed to its activism—then Wechsler's neutral principles thesis may be regarded as part of this legacy. For it is a thesis which, in Sunstein's view, 'has a powerful *Lochner*-like dimension'.[473] This is, for Wechsler, '[t]he existing distribution of power and resources as between blacks and whites should be taken by courts as simply "there"; neutrality lies in inaction; it is threatened when the Court "takes sides" by preferring those disadvantaged.'[474] It is by tracing neutrality from *Lochner* to Wechsler that Sunstein is able to demonstrate that the latter represents a continuation of as well as a reaction against the jurisprudence of the former.

Given this jurisprudential connection, it is perhaps unsurprising to find that, as with the Supreme Court in *Lochner*,[475] Wechsler developed a conception of neutrality which was regarded generally to be inadequate for the purposes of constitutional analysis. Even certain of those who applauded his call for neutral principles felt that he had 'not carried the

[471] See John Hart Ely, *Democracy and Distrust: A Theory of Judicial Review* (Cambridge, Mass.: Harvard University Press, 1980), 55.
[472] Cass R. Sunstein, 'Lochner's Legacy', *Columbia L. Rev.*, 87 (1987), 873–919 at 878–9.
[473] Ibid. 895. [474] Ibid. [475] See ibid. 903.

idea of neutrality far enough'.[476] Some critics feared that if courts were to become preoccupied with the development and application of such principles, they might lose sight of the primary purpose of adjudication: the securing of just outcomes.[477] Yet Wechsler himself was careful not to suggest that a principled decision is somehow a 'right' decision.

> I have never thought the principle of neutral principles offers a court a guide to exercising its authority, in the sense of a formula that indicates how cases ought to be decided. . . . That an adjudication be supported or at least supportable in general and neutral terms is no more than a negative requirement. A decision is not sound unless it satisfies this minimal criterion. If it does, but only if it does, the other and the harder questions of its rightness and its wisdom must be faced.[478]

A principled decision, in other words, is a sound, though not necessarily a correct, decision. But if neutral principles do not of necessity lead to correct results, why should a court try to abide by them? Wechsler's answer is that even if a judicial opinion seems wrong, if it is principled it will command respect.[479] This claim—premissed, as it is, on the idea that faith in reason is somehow more significant than faith in justice—cut no ice with those who welcomed Warren Court activism. The problem was not simply that Wechsler demonstrated a misplaced conception of judicial priorities, but that he failed to elaborate what those priorities were. It seems not insignificant to note here that, in *The End of Ideology*, Daniel Bell acknowledges Wechsler 'for many suggestions'.[480] For Wechsler implicitly subscribes to the very notion of consensus which lies at the heart of that book. As various critics have noted, precisely what Wechsler means by 'neutral principles'—or even 'general principles of neutral application'—is far from clear, not least because he fails to define either neutrality or generality for the purposes of constitutional adjudication.[481] 'Neutrality' and 'generality' are assumed by Wechsler to have meanings which might be

[476] Robert H. Bork, 'Neutral Principles and Some First Amendment Problems', *Indiana L.J.*, 47 (1971), 1–35 at 7.

[477] See Charles E. Clark, 'The Limits of Judicial Objectivity', *American Univ. L. Rev.*, 12 (1963), 1–13 at 7; Black, *supra* n. 407, 14–15, 24.

[478] Herbert Wechsler, 'The Nature of Judicial Reasoning', in S. Hock (ed.), *Law and Philosophy: A Symposium* (New York: New York University Press, 1964), 290–300 at 299.

[479] See Wechsler, *supra* n. 413, 26. Others have argued that neutral principles are a necessary condition of 'legitimacy' in constitutional adjudication. See e.g. Michael J. Perry, 'Why the Supreme Court Was Plainly Wrong in the Hyde Amendment Case: A Brief Comment on *Harris* v. *McRae*', *Stanford L. Rev.*, 32 (1980), 1113–28 at 1127.

[480] Bell, *supra* n. 258, 450. Both, at that time, were professors at Columbia.

[481] See e.g. Benjamin F. Wright, 'The Supreme Court Cannot be Neutral', *Texas L. Rev.*, 40 (1962), 599–618 at 600; Jan G. Deutsch, 'Neutrality, Legitimacy, and the Supreme Court: Some Intersections Between Law and Political Science', *Stanford L. Rev.*, 20 (1968), 169–261 at 187–8; David A. J. Richards, 'Rules, Policies, and Neutral Principles: The Search for Legitimacy in Common Law and Constitutional Adjudication', *Georgia L. Rev.*, 11 (1977), 1069–114 at 1084–5.

shared by all reasonable people.[482] Thus it is that courts are considered able to resolve constitutional issues on grounds of 'adequate neutrality and generality'.[483] The concept of adequacy is simply taken to be unproblematic.

Many critics of Wechsler have taken him to task for making this assumption.[484] Others, however, have attempted to make light of the assumption by arguing that it is not Wechsler's claim that there exist principles of constitutional law which are inherently and uncontroversially neutral, but only that courts, in engaging in constitutional adjudication, may and indeed ought to develop general principles which can be applied in a logical and consistent fashion.[485] This interpretation of Wechsler is certainly faithful to his thesis, but it by no means renders the notion of neutral principles unproblematic. For it is still possible that principles may conflict. That is, there may exist two general principles of constitutional adjudication which can be applied by a court with equal consistency to the same issue in order to produce equally sound decisions. In such circumstances, which principle is the court to choose? Wechsler himself implicity acknowledged this difficulty when he confessed that he was unable adequately to explain why, with regard to segregation, freedom to associate is constitutionally more important than freedom not to associate.[486] To the answer that freedom not to associate exists only in the private domain, that 'in public, we have to associate with anybody who has a right to be there',[487] there is the reply that freedom to associate appears in fact not to exist as a constitutionally protected right.[488] The point illustrates a fundamental problem with Wechsler's thesis: namely, that the notion of constitutional adjudication according to neutral principles is found wanting when, to use Wechsler's own words, 'some ordering of social values is essential'—for example, where 'there is an inescapable conflict between claims to free press and a fair trial'.[489] To emphasize, as Wechsler himself does, 'the role of reason and of principle in the judicial . . . appraisal of conflicting values'[490] is to fail to confront this problem.

[482] See Addison Mueller and Murray L. Schwartz, 'The Principle of Neutral Principles', *UCLA L. Rev.*, 7 (1960), 571–88 at 584; Martin Shapiro, 'The Supreme Court and Constitutional Adjudication: Of Politics and Neutral Principles', *George Washington L. Rev.*, 31 (1963), 587–606 at 594; Mark V. Tushnet, 'Following the Rules Laid Down: A Critique of Interpretivism and Neutral Principles', *Harvard L. Rev.*, 96 (1983), 781–827 at 785.

[483] Wechsler, *supra* n. 413, 15.

[484] See e.g. Arthur S. Miller and Ronald F. Howell, 'The Myth of Neutrality in Constitutional Adjudication', *U. Chicago L. Rev.*, 27 (1960), 661–95 esp. 665, 677; Ray D. Henson, 'A Criticism of Criticism: In Re Meaning', *Fordham L. Rev.*, 29 (1961), 553–60 at 559.

[485] See, in particular, Henkin, *supra* n. 467, 653; Deutsch, *supra* n. 481, 188.

[486] Wechsler, *supra* n. 413, 34.

[487] Black, *supra* n. 453, 429.

[488] See Martin P. Golding, 'Principled Decision-Making and the Supreme Court', *Columbia L. Rev.*, 63 (1963), 35–58 at 58.

[489] Wechsler, *supra* n. 413, 25.

[490] Ibid. 16.

For where there exists a conflict of values, it is possible that there will also exist conflicting yet equally 'neutral' principles. To choose one principle over another in such a situation is to prefer one value over another. 'The virtue or demerit of a judgement turns', Wechsler contends, 'entirely on the reasons that support it and their adequacy to maintain any choice of values it decrees.'[491] In the case, however, where there exist competing values which may be upheld through the reasoned explanation of equally valid competing principles, how is one to determine adequacy?[492] Again, Wechsler takes the concept to be unproblematic.

The neutral principles thesis, then, is not a comprehensive guide to correct constitutional adjudication.[493] Even a court dedicated to the application of neutral principles may sometimes be faced with a hard case which, for all the reasoning in the world, can be decided only by preferring one value or policy over another. Respect for neutral principles, very simply, does not preclude judicial activism. 'Of course,' Wechsler argued, 'the courts ought to be cautious to impose a choice of values on the other branches or a state, based upon the Constitution, only when they are persuaded, on an adequate and principled analysis, that the choice is clear.'[494] The problem which the neutral principles thesis left untouched, however, concerned what the courts are supposed to do when the choice is not clear. The implication was that, in such circumstances, a Wechsler Court would be forced to assume the role of the Warren Court. Yet if this was so, process jurisprudence had proved to be a traitor to the notion of judicial integrity. Wechsler, it seemed, had attempted, but had failed, to grasp the nettle of Warren Court activism. If it was persuasively to demonstrate the undesirability of such activism within a democratic system, the process perspective on constitutional adjudication would require further fine tuning.

THE JURISPRUDENCE OF PRUDENCE

What sort of fine tuning was required? In his Foreword to the 1960 Term, Alexander Bickel suggested that the development of process jurisprudence demanded the refinement of the principle of institutional settlement. It was all very well insisting that, unlike the legislative and executive branches, the courts ought to be guided by principle. But precisely 'when and in what

[491] Wechsler, *supra* n. 413, 19–20.

[492] For a development of this point, see Golding, *supra* n. 488, 48–9.

[493] For a different slant on this argument, see Kent Greenawalt, 'The Enduring Significance of Neutral Principles', *Columbia L. Rev.*, 78 (1978), 982–1021 at 1013, 1021.

[494] Wechsler, *supra* n. 413, 25.

circumstances'[495] ought they to be so guided? The neutral principles thesis, Bickel observed, 'is tied to the conviction . . . that there is no escape from the exercise of jurisdiction which is given'.[496] Such a conviction, he suggests, is misplaced.

'No good society can be unprincipled,' Bickel observes, 'and no viable society can be principle-ridden.'[497] There exists no neat dividing line between principle and expediency, and many constitutional issues—racial segregation, for example—entail both. Although we may often believe that the courts ought to deal with such issues in a principled fashion, it may be that these issues resist a principled solution.[498] Certainly, 'it is for legislatures, not courts, to impose what are merely solutions of expediency. Courts must act on true principles, capable of unremitting application. When they cannot find such a principle, they are bound to declare the legislative choice valid.'[499] But what is to happen when the resolution of a constitutional problem 'require[s] principle and expediency at once'?[500] With regard specifically to constitutional adjudication, 'how does the [Supreme] Court, charged with the function of enunciating principle, produce or permit the necessary compromises?'[501] According to Bickel, the Court has three courses of action open to it: it may strike down legislation as inconsistent with principle; it may legitimate it; or—and this is where he departs from Wechsler—it may do neither.[502]

Thus it is that Bickel refines the neutral principles thesis. Whereas Wechsler failed to explain what a court ought to do when faced with a hard case in which the making of a policy choice seems inevitable, Bickel offered an unequivocal solution: the court ought to do nothing. In cases which raise political questions, for example, the Supreme Court may decline to adjudicate on the ground that the particular issue is 'not ripe' for judicial solution.[503] By staying its hand, the Court avoids 'sap[ping] the quality of the political process'[504] and yet is able also to 'guard its integrity'.[505] That is, 'in withholding constitutional judgement, the Court does not necessarily forsake an educational function, nor does it abandon principle. It seeks merely to elicit the correct answers to certain prudential questions that . . . lie in the path of ultimate issues of principle.'[506] In short, by adopting a passive stance towards certain constitutional issues,

[495] Alexander M. Bickel, 'The Supreme Court, 1960 Term—Foreword: The Passive Virtues', *Harvard L. Rev.*, 75 (1961), 40–79 at 41.
[496] Ibid. 48.
[497] Ibid. 49.
[498] See Alexander M. Bickel, *The Least Dangerous Branch: The Supreme Court at the Bar of Politics* (2nd edn. New Haven, Conn.: Yale University Press, 1986; 1st edn. 1962), 64–5.
[499] Ibid. 58.
[500] Ibid. 69.
[501] Ibid.
[502] Ibid. and also Bickel, *supra* n. 495, 50.
[503] Bickel, *supra* n. 495, 74.
[504] Ibid.
[505] Ibid. 77.
[506] Bickel, *supra* n. 498, 70.

the Court neither favours expediency nor stands in the way in principle. Rather, it exercises prudence.[507]

The Supreme Court, then, ought 'to evolve, to defend, and to protect principle'.[508] But it must not do so indiscriminately. If a constitutional issue appears not to be ripe for principled decision, then the Court, as the forum of principle, ought not to sacrifice its integrity by producing a decision.[509] There may be virtue, in other words, in judicial passivity. But it is a strange kind of virtue. It is unlikely, in the wake of *Brown* and the other racial segregation cases, that the American public would have appreciated the tactics of the Supreme Court had it adopted Bickel's strategy and stayed its hand when faced with 'unripe' constitutional issues. 'A Court "staying its hand" is, after all, failing to invalidate.'[510] It is improbable that the public would be sufficiently sophisticated in matters of law and government 'to perceive that "staying its hand" falls short of "legitimation" '.[511] Furthermore, if, as Bickel suggests it ought to have done,[512] the Court had stayed its hand over the matter of racial segregation, if it had neither legitimated nor declared unconstitutional statutes prohibiting integration, then it would effectively have upheld the status quo in the South.[513] Passivity would have been not so much a virtue as a vice, an insidious strategy of avoidance.[514]

For all this, however, Bickel's refinement of Wechsler found favour with many of those jurists who insisted that good judicial decision-making is distinguished not by results but by sound processes of reasoning. Certain of those who had been calling for a 'principled' Supreme court began to appeal instead for a 'prudent court'.[515] By suggesting that the Court may justifiably pass over hard cases, Bickel appeared to have removed the chink in the armour of process jurisprudence. A Bickel Court, unlike a Wechsler Court, would adjudicate only those constitutional matters which permit the reasoned elaboration of principles. If the task of the Supreme

[507] Bickel, *supra* n. 495, 51.

[508] Ibid. 77.

[509] For a more general discussion, see Anthony T. Kronman, 'Alexander Bickel's Philosophy of Prudence', *Yale L.J.*, 94 (1985), 1567–616 at 1569–99.

[510] Gerald Gunther, 'The Subtle Vices of the "Passive Virtues"—A Comment on Principle and Expediency in Judicial Review', *Columbia L. Rev.*, 64 (1964), 1–25 at 7.

[511] Ibid.

[512] Bickel, *supra* n. 498, 194, and cf. also 256. See further Alexander M. Bickel, 'A Communication: Paths to Desegregation', *The New Republic*, 4 November 1957, 3, 22–3.

[513] See Gunther, *supra* n. 510, 24.

[514] On this theme, see further Martin Shapiro, *Freedom of Speech: The Supreme Court and Judicial Review* (Englewood Cliffs, NJ: Prentice-Hall, 1966), 144–5.

[515] McCloskey, *supra* n. 456, 70; and see also Robert G. McCloskey, *The Modern Supreme Court* (Cambridge, Mass.: Harvard University Press, 1972), 283; Walter F. Murphy, *Congress and the Court: A Case Study in the American Political Process* (Chicago: University of Chicago Press, 1962), 256–68; Philip B. Kurland, 'The Supreme Court, 1963 Term—Foreword: "Equal in Origin and Equal in Title to the Legislative and Executive Branches of the Government" ', *Harvard L. Rev.*, 78 (1964), 143–76 esp. 175–6.

Court was conceived in this manner, then the work of the Warren Court appeared to be even more lamentable than process jurists had already suggested. For the Court was not only unprincipled but imprudent.

While the neutral principles thesis embodies a rejection of legal realism and judicial activism, Wechsler himself—always a hesitant rather than a forthright critic[516]—would have considered it distinctly unscholarly and infra dig to attack either realism or the Warren Court directly. Not so Bickel. Fred Rodell, for whom realism and judicial activism—and in particular the activism of the Warren Court—represented all that is good about the law,[517] filled many a newspaper column denouncing Bickel as the arch-defender of 'judicial inertia'.[518] Yet Bickel himself was not averse to producing his own fair share of journalistic polemic.[519] He excoriated those lawyers who supported Warren Court activism because they agreed with the results which were being reached. What, he wondered, would these pro-activists do when—as inevitably it would—the outlook of the Supreme Court changed?[520] Justices Black and Douglas, he observed, had lamented the unprincipled activism of the 'Roosevelt' Court in the 1930s, and yet, by the 1950s, they were subscribing to that very activism.[521] Quite simply, judicial activism appeared to be a philosophy for good times.[522] Supporters of that philosophy would soon cry foul if the policies of the Supreme Court were to change for the worse.[523]

Thus it is that, for Bickel, support for judicial activism is a sure route to inconsistency and even hypocrisy. Proponents of activism want to have their cake and eat it. The folly of legal realism reveals as much. So-called realists, he argued, demonstrate 'a complete lack of interest in the process

[516] Most of the critical points to be found in 'Toward Neutral Principles of Constitutional Law,' *supra* n. 413, are phrased as rhetorical questions. On Wechsler's style of scholarship, see further Warren E. Burger, 'Herbert Wechsler', *Columbia L. Rev.*, 78 (1978), 951.

[517] See Fred Rodell, 'Judicial Activists, Judicial Self-Deniers, Judicial Review and the First Amendment—Or, How to Hide the Melody of What You Mean Behind the Words of What You Say', *Georgetown L.J.*, 47 (1959), 483–90; 'For Every Justice, Judicial Deference is a Sometime Thing', *Georgetown L.J.*, 50 (1962), 700–8.

[518] See Fred Rodell, 'Alexander Bickel and the Harvard–Frankfurter School of Judicial Inertia', *Scanlan's*, May 1970, 76–7; 'The Warren Court', *Yale Daily News,* 2 March 1970, 2–3; 'The Supreme Court and the Idea of Progress', *New York Times Book Review,* 26 April 1970, 3.

[519] Bickel was a regular contributor to *Commentary* and a contributing editor of *The New Republic*.

[520] See Alexander M. Bickel, 'Law and Reason', *The New Republic,* 3 November 1958, 18–19 at 19.

[521] See Bickel, *supra* n. 498, 90–1.

[522] See Alexander M. Bickel, *The Morality of Consent* (New Haven, Conn.: Yale University Press, 1975), 26–7.

[523] Bickel was not, of course, the only process jurist of the 1960s to find fault with activism. For further examples, see Louis Henkin, 'The Supreme Court, 1967 Term—Foreword: On Drawing Lines', *Harvard L. Rev.*, 82 (1968), 63–92; Louis L. Jaffe, *English and American Judges as Lawmakers* (Oxford: Clarendon Press, 1969).

by which the work [of the Supreme Court] is achieved, or in the proper role of that process in a democratic society. . . . They consider only the outcome of a case.'[524] Realists thereby ignore the broader picture, the problem of achieving and maintaining integrity and rational consistency throughout the judicial process as a whole. It was lack of faith in reason which especially irked Bickel. 'The court is to reason, not feel,' he insisted, 'to explain and justify principles it pronounces to the last possible rational decimal point.'[525] '[H]is real disapproval was not for any opposing principle but for lack of principle: for humbug, hypocrisy, unthinking subservience to power.'[526] As early as 1949, only one year out of law school, he suggested that it is the duty of federal courts, in resorting to admiralty jurisdiction, to articulate their reasons for doing so.[527] Throughout his writings on judicial review there runs more or less constantly the idea 'that the process of constitutional adjudication, though one of subtle human and institutional demands, nevertheless could be and often [is] a process of disinterested and open-minded rational analysis guided by evidence and existing legal rules.'[528] In extolling reason, Bickel, like other process jurists of his generation,[529] was keeping faith with what he regarded to be a tradition of judicial candour and integrity typified by Brandeis and Frankfurter.[530] The erosion of that tradition had begun with the advent of the Warren Court.

Indeed, the tradition came to an end, for Bickel, with Frankfurter's retirement from the Court in 1962. 'Since October, 1962,' he observed, 'there has been a new Supreme Court in Washington. . . . Such a retirement as that of Justice Frankfurter does more than merely change a vote; it alters the entire judicial landscape.'[531] The Court without Frankfurter would be even more activist, more innovative, more sweeping in its decision. It would become 'Hugo Black writ large'.[532]

[524] Bickel, *supra* n. 498, 81–2.

[525] Bickel, *supra* n. 522, 26.

[526] Anthony Lewis, 'Foreword', in Alexander M. Bickel, *The Supreme Court and the Idea of Progress* (New Haven, Conn.: Yale University Press, 1978), vii–xiii at xi.

[527] Alexander M. Bickel, 'The Doctrine of *Forum non Conveniens* as Applied in the Federal Courts in Matters of Admiralty: An Object Lesson in Uncontrolled Discretion', *Cornell Law Quarterly*, 35 (1949), 12–47 at 20.

[528] Purcell, *supra* n. 201, 529–30.

[529] See e.g. Paul A. Freund, *On Law and Justice* (Cambridge, Mass.: Harvard University Press, 1968), 63–162.

[530] See Bickel, *supra* n. 526, 23–5; and also Purcell, *supra* n. 201, 527–32. On the Brandeis–Frankfurter 'tradition', see generally Bruce Allen Murphy, *The Brandeis/Frankfurter Connection: The Secret Political Activities of Two Supreme Court Justices* (New York: Oxford University Press, 1982); Leonard Baker, *Brandeis and Frankfurter: A Dual Biography* (New York: Harper & Row, 1984). And for a critique of candour and integrity as adjudicative criteria, cf. Nicholas S. Zeppos, 'Judicial Candor and Statutory Interpretation', *Georgetown L.J.*, 78 (1989), 353–413 at 404–6.

[531] Alexander M. Bickel, *Politics and the Warren Court* (New York: Da Capo, 1973; orig. publ. 1965), 162.

[532] Bickel, *supra* n. 522, 9.

From the early 1960s onwards, Bickel's opposition to Supreme Court activism gradually intensified. In his Holmes Lectures of 1969, the year in which Warren Burger was appointed as Chief Justice, he wrote that '[i]t would be intellectual megalomania not to concede that the Warren Court, like Marshall's, may for a time have been an institution seized of a great vision, that it may have glimpsed the future, and gained it.'[533] Dominated by 'the Hugo Black majority',[534] however, the Court had been increasingly at fault 'for erratic subjectivity of judgement, for analytical laxness, for what amounts to intellectual incoherence in many opinions, and for imagining too much history'.[535] The Burger Court, in Bickel's opinion, was not quick to cure itself of these ills: the decision in *Roe* v. *Wade*[536] in 1973, for example, was proof that the Court remained just as guilty of expediency, just as unprincipled, as it had been in *Brown* two decades earlier.[537]

By remaining committed to activism, furthermore, the Court was at least partially responsible for Watergate. Those implicated in the scandal:

> had been led into their error by the toleration that much liberal opinion had shown for the zealotry of the Left, for draft-dodgers and demonstrators of all sorts . . . Watergate . . . was . . . a reproach to that large body of liberal opinion which had tolerated lawlessness, and ended by infecting even the righteous with it.[538]

The blame for Watergate, in other words, was to be laid not at the feet of the perpetrators, but at the feet of a mis-managed legal system. For it was that system which, manipulated by liberals, had turned good men into bad men. 'Watergate is evidence of a weakened capacity of our legal order to serve as a self-executing safeguard against this sort of abuse of power.'[539] Indeed, 'much of what happened to the legal and social order in the fifteen years or so before Watergate was prologue.'[540] Very simply, Watergate was the price to be paid for abandoning the tradition of judicial candour and integrity.[541] Advocates of judicial activism were unpersuaded by this argument. Not only was it premissed on a distrust of liberals; it was premissed also on the viability of neutral principles. Yet, in truth, as Bickel

[533] Bickel, *supra* n. 526, 100.
[534] Bickel, *supra* n. 531, 172.
[535] Bickel, *supra* n. 526, 45.
[536] *Roe* v. *Wade* (1973) 410 U.S. 113.
[537] See Bickel, *supra* n. 522, 28. For an excellent study of the subtle jurisprudential differences between the Warren and Burger Courts, cf. Gerald Gunther, 'The Supreme Court, 1971 Term—Foreword: In Search of Evolving Doctrine on a Changing Court: A Model for a Newer Equal Protection', *Harvard L. Rev.*, 86 (1972), 1–48.
[538] Alexander M. Bickel, 'Watergate and the Legal Order', *Commentary*, 57 (1974), 19–25 at 19.
[539] Ibid. 20.
[540] Ibid.
[541] See ibid. 25; and also Auerbach, *supra* n. 174, 302–3. For Bickel's views on Watergate, see further Alexander M. Bickel, 'The Tapes, Cox, Nixon', *The New Republic*, 29 September 1973, 13–14; 'What Now?', *The New Republic*, 3 November 1973, 13–14; 'Impeachment', *The New Republic*, 10 November 1973, 9–10; 'How Might Mr. Nixon Defend Himself?', *The New Republic,* 1 June 1974, 11–13; and *supra* n. 522, 91–3.

himself conceded, it seemed to be impossible to ascertain if in fact the Supreme Court had ever been more genuinely principled, in the Wechslerian sense, than it had been throughout the Warren era.[542] 'If past Courts have also systematically failed to meet the requirements of principled decisionmaking,' one critic observed, 'does this not suggest that the requirements themselves . . . are fatally unrealistic?'[543] Furthermore, if a genuinely principled Court has never existed, there is no reason to believe that such a Court could have prevented the occurrence of Watergate.

In his commitment to 'the utility of the principle of the neutral principles',[544] Bickel, like Wechsler, demonstrates a faith in rational consensus.[545] Neutral principles, he insists, are prerequisite to the 'elaboration of any general justification of judicial review as a process for the injection into representative government of a system of enduring basic values'.[546] Since 'the good society . . . will strive to support and maintain' such values, the reasoned elaboration of neutral principles by the courts in matters of constitutional adjudication will, in such a society, 'surely' find favour with 'most of the profession and of informed laity'.[547] By developing and applying neutral principles, and by demonstrating also where it intends to stay its hand, a court may contribute to the evolving morality of our tradition'.[548] The genuinely principled court, that is, will 'enforce as law only the most widely shared values'.[549] Engaged in 'a continuing colloquy with the political institutions and with society at large',[550] it will serve as both a leader and as a register of public opinion, 'declar[ing] as law only such principles as will . . . gain general assent'.[551]

When, accordingly, a court engages in the reasoned elaboration of principles—or when it refuses to undertake such elaboration because it considers a constitutional issue to be 'unripe'—it reinforces basic, shared democratic values. Bickel's insistence, however, that rationalism may serve the interests of democracy did not, by his own estimation, make him a 'liberal'. His reflections on Watergate alone indicate that liberalism, for him, was something of a cause for disenchantment. Near the end of his life, he attempted to express this disenchantment in philosophical terms. The tradition of 'liberal' constitutional interpretation in the Supreme

[542] Bickel, *supra* n. 526, 45.

[543] J. Skelly Wright, 'Professor Bickel, the Scholarly Tradition, and the Supreme Court', *Harvard L. Rev.*, 84 (1971), 769–805 at 778.

[544] Bickel, *supra* n. 498, 55.

[545] Bickel, it should be noted, was familiar with the writings of Truman and Dahl: see *supra* n. 498, 18–19.

[546] Ibid. 51.

[547] Ibid. 27.

[548] Ibid. 236.

[549] Ibid. 239.

[550] Ibid. 240; and cf. also John Moeller, 'Alexander M. Bickel: Toward a Theory of Politics', *Jnl. of Politics*, 47 (1985), 113–39 at 131–5.

[551] Bickel, *supra* n. 498, 239.

Court, which Bickel identifies primarily with Hugo Black, has its intellectual origins, he argues, in the broader tradition of liberal contractarianism as epitomized by Locke, Rousseau and, in more recent times, Rawls. The contractarian model 'rests on a vision of individual rights that have a clearly defined, independent existence predating society and are derived from nature and from a natural, if imagined, contract'.[552] 'Society', according to the liberal contractarian, 'must bend to these rights'.[553] Thus it is that contractarianism 'is committed not to law alone but to a parochial faith in a closely calibrated scale of values. It is moral, principled, legalistic, ultimately authoritarian. It is weak on pragmatism, strong on theory.'[554]

The primary problem with contractarianism, from Bickel's point of view, is that it is antithetical to the values of process jurisprudence. 'For the contractarian liberal is a moralist, and the moralist will find it difficult to sacrifice his aims in favour of structure and process, to sacrifice substance for form. Yet process and form, which is the embodiment of process, are the essence of the theory and practice of constitutionalism.'[555] Liberals are content to dispense with principle and procedural consistency in order to secure what they consider to be morally-desirable results. But without regard for principle and consistency, a constitutional system is open to abuse.[556] It is for this reason, Bickel argues, that constitutional adjudication ought to be founded on a different philosophy, the philosophy of Burkean conservatism.[557]

Bickel finds in the writings of Edmund Burke the respect for process values which he considers to be absent from liberal contractarian thought. Like Bickel and other process jurists, Burke acknowledged the principle of institutional settlement. 'The constituent parts of a state', he claimed, 'are obliged to hold their public faith with each other, and with all those who derive any serious interest under their engagements, as much as the whole state is bound to keep its faith with separate communities. Otherwise competence and power would soon be confounded, and no law be left but the will of a prevailing force.'[558] It is not in the capacity of 'men of theory'[559] to prevent law from dissolving into force; for no theory of law

[552] Bickel, *supra* n. 522, 4. [553] Ibid. [554] Ibid. 5. [555] Ibid. 30.

[556] See ibid. 11; and also, more generally, Robert K. Faulkner, 'Bickel's Constitution: The Problem of Moderate Liberalism', *American Political Science Rev.*, 72 (1978), 925–40 esp. 934.

[557] For a discussion of Bickel as a Burkean conservative, see Robert H. Bork, 'Alexander M. Bickel, Political Philosopher', *Supreme Court Rev.*, [1975], 419–21; Nelson W. Polsby, 'In Praise of Alexander M. Bickel', *Commentary,* January 1976, 50–4; Maurice J. Holland, 'American Liberals and Judicial Activism: Alexander Bickel's Appeal from the New to the Old', *Indiana L.J.*, 51 (1976), 1025–50.

[558] Edmund Burke, in C. C. O'Brien (ed.), *Reflections on the Revolution in France, And on Proceedings in Certain Societies in London Relative to That Event* (Harmondsworth: Penguin, 1968; orig. publ. 1790), 105.

[559] Ibid. 128.

can accommodate all human prejudices and desires. 'The nature of man is intricate . . . and therefore no simple disposition or direction of power can be suitable to man's nature, or to the quality of his affairs.'[560] This insight, according to Bickel, illustrates the poverty of liberal-contractarian theories. Premissed, as they are, on the notion that it is possible to determine in the abstract the nature and scope of human rights, such theories 'always clash with men's needs and their natures . . . and any attempt to impose them . . . breed[s] conflict, not responsive government enjoying the consent of the governed'.[561] Burke elaborates the point:

> The pretended rights of these theories are all extremes. . . . The rights of men are in a sort of *middle*, incapable of definition, but not impossible to be discerned. The rights of men in governments are their advantages; and these are often in balances between differences of good; in compromises sometimes between good and evil, and sometimes, between evil and evil. Political reason is a computing principle; adding, subtracting, multiplying, and dividing, morally and not metaphysically or mathematically, true moral denominations.[562]

Computation, then, not theory, prevents the dissolution of law into force. Bickel argued this point as passionately as did Burke. We can neither live nor govern, he insisted, 'in submission to the dictates of abstract theories'.[563] For government demands pragmatism, and pragmatism in constitutional affairs requires that the courts endeavour to elaborate and balance principles. 'The computing principle is still all we can resort to, and we always return to it following some luxuriant outburst of theory in the Supreme Court, whether the theory is of an absolute right to contract, or to speak, or to stand mute, or to be private.'[564] Burke's philosophy revealed to Bickel that the fundamental problem of constitutionalism is not judicial activism, but the liberal-contractarian theory on which such activism is invariably founded. Eschewing principle and process, such theory inevitably encourages ideological relativism.[565] It allows for either the rejection or the promotion of judicial activism depending on the political climate of the time. In short, liberalism breeds jurisprudential inconsistency.

THE PERSISTENCE OF PROCESS

Although, in recent times, various American legal theorists of differing ideological persuasions have argued that process jurisprudence encourages

[560] Burke, *supra* n. 558, 152–3.
[561] Bickel, *supra* n. 522, 23.
[562] Burke, *supra* n. 558, 153. For a discussion of Burke's conception of rights, see Jeremy Waldron (ed.), *Nonsense upon Stilts: Bentham, Burke and Marx on the Rights of Man* (London: Methuen, 1987), 77–95.
[563] Bickel, *supra* n. 522, 25.
[564] Ibid. 24.
[565] Ibid. 11.

'conservative' as opposed to 'liberal' legal scholarship,[566] only Bickel, of all the major process jurists, attempted actually to develop a conservative philosophy of law. In fact, few constitutional theorists have followed Bickel's path to Burke,[567] and even Bickel himself insisted that Burkean conservatism 'belongs to the liberal tradition'.[568] For all that his legal philosophy has remained unfashionable, nevertheless, Bickel's basic perspective on judicial review has been inspirational. In developing his theory of constitutional adjudication, he sharpened the focus of process jurisprudence. His argument that the courts ought to practise passivity as well as principled restraint reanimated the Wechslerian ideal of determining apolitical criteria according to which the Supreme Court may decide constitutional cases. In criticizing the activism of both the Warren and Burger Courts, he emphasized more forcefully than any of his intellectual predecessors the basic process belief that to practise or to advocate political as opposed to principled adjudication is to promote a form of jurisprudential dishonesty. Judicial activism, Bickel insisted, can only ever be as good or as welcome as the policies which it implements. Those who liked such activism when the result was the outlawing of state-imposed segregation but disliked it when the outcome was the invalidation of legislation imposing a maximum working day had failed to develop a rational philosophy of constitutional adjudication. Thus it was that Bickel railed against legal realists, judicial activists, liberals—all, he insisted, lacked a coherent, guiding philosophy. The Supreme Court was following, and indeed was being applauded for following, the whim of politics. Product was being elevated above process. Integrity in adjudication was being sacrificed in the pursuit of expedient results. Resisting the politicization of law demanded faith in reason and principle. Bickel exemplified and promoted that faith.

The manner in which Bickel promoted process jurisprudence is significant. While other lawyers within the process tradition applied the tenets of their faith to specific legal issues,[569] Bickel, inspired by Wechsler, developed process jurisprudence into a general philosophy of judicial review. In doing so, he offered a new approach to the question of what role, if any, judicial review ought to play in a representative democracy. 'The very essence of democratic government', Tocqueville observed, 'consists in the absolute sovereignty of the majority; for there is nothing in

[566] See e.g. Mark Kelman, *A Guide to Critical Legal Studies* (Cambridge, Mass.: Harvard University Press, 1987), 186–212; Paul M. Bator, 'Legal Methodology and the Academy', *Harvard Jnl. of Law and Public Policy*, 8 (1985), 335–9 at 338–9.

[567] Though see Robert H. Bork, *The Tempting of America: The Political Seduction of the Law* (London: Sinclair-Stevenson, 1990), 187–93, 342–3, 353–5.

[568] Bickel, *supra* n. 522, 25.

[569] Consider, for example, Harry Wellington on collective bargaining: Harry H. Wellington, *Labor and the Legal Process* (New Haven, Conn.: Yale University Press, 1968).

democratic states that is capable of resisting it.'[570] Judicial review, however, is, in essence, a counter-majoritarian institution: that is, whenever a judge declares a statute to be unconstitutional, an unelected official is invalidating a policy adopted by elected representatives of the people. What, then, justifies the existence of judicial review? For Bickel, judicial review is a necessary bulwark against the potential tyranny of majority rule. 'Of all political institutions,' Tocqueville claimed, 'the legislature is the one that is most easily swayed by the will of the majority.'[571] 'In America,' furthermore, 'the authority exercised by the legislatures is supreme; nothing prevents them from accomplishing their wishes with celerity and irresistible power.'[572] Nothing, that is, apart from the judiciary. Only by maintaining an apolitical judiciary, independent of the legislative and executive branches, Tocqueville argued, might American government sustain a representative democracy without incurring the risk of tyrannical majority rule.[573] Bickel refines this argument. Such a judiciary, he insists, if it is to constrain the potential tyranny of majoritarianism, must be entrusted with the power to review the constitutionality of legislative action. In exercising its power of review, however, the judiciary must practise prudence—that is, it must be prepared to elaborate and to apply neutral principles of constitutional adjudication when appropriate, and be willing to stay its hand when not. When judges disregard prudence, they adjudicate politically. To adjudicate politically is to sacrifice judicial independence. Judicial review guided by prudence, accordingly, is essential to the maintenance of democratic government.

In recent times, many American constitutional theorists have followed Bickel's lead in attempting to define and justify the role of the courts in protecting minority interests within a democracy.[574] For example, in endeavouring 'to advance a principled, functional, and desirable role for judicial review in our democratic system,' Jesse Choper argues that 'the Court must exercise this power in order to protect individual rights, which are not adequately represented in the political processes. When judicial review is unnecessary for the effective preservation of our constitutional

[570] Tocqueville, *supra* n. 219, I, 254. [571] Ibid. [572] Ibid. I, 257

[573] Ibid. I, 261.

[574] See Terrance Sandalow, 'Judicial Protection of Minorities', *Michigan L. Rev.*, 75 (1977), 1162–95; Hans A. Linde, 'Due Process of Lawmaking', *Nebraska L. Rev.*, 55 (1976), 197–255 esp. 206–7, 254–55; Frank I. Michelman, 'Politics and Values or What's Really Wrong With Rationality Review?', *Creighton L. Rev.*, 13 (1979), 487–511; Owen M. Fiss, 'The Supreme Court, 1978 Term—Foreword: The Forms of Justice', *Harvard L. Rev.*, 93 (1979), 1–58 esp. 5–17; and cf. also, more generally, Mark Tushnet, 'Truth, Justice and the American Way: An Interpretation of Public Law Scholarship in the Seventies', *Texas L. Rev.*, 57 (1979), 1307–59; and Lawrence G. Sager, 'Rights Skepticism and Process-Based Responses', *New York Univ. L. Rev.*, 56 (1981), 417–45.

scheme, however, the Court should decline to exercise its authority.'[575] This is, of course, classic Bickel. But it is important here to appreciate the precise nature of his influence. The originality of Bickel's jurisprudence lies not in his recognition that the judicial protection of minority interests is consistent with the preservation of democratic government, but in his thesis that, within a democracy, such protection demands a prudent judiciary. The notion that the courts may legitimately protect minority interests was sounded as early as 1938 in footnote 4 of *United States* v. *Carolene Products*.[576] In that footnote, Justice Stone suggested that 'there may be narrower scope for operation of the presumption of constitutionality' where the courts are called upon to determine the validity 'of statutes directed at particular religious . . . or national . . . or racial minorities'.[577] In such instances, he explained, 'prejudice against discrete and insular minorities may be a special condition, which tends seriously to curtail the operation of those political processes ordinarily to be relied upon to protect minorities, and which may call for correspondingly more searching judicial inquiry'.[578] The problem with such a claim, in terms of Bickel's jurisprudence, is that it appears to be a call for judicial activism. On the basis of what principle, after all, might a court determine that one statute affecting the interests of a 'discrete and insular minority'—whatever that might be taken to mean[579]—be subject to more exacting judicial scrutiny than another? *Carolene Products* thus posed a fundamental difficulty for constitutional scholars writing after Bickel: namely, how might the judicial protection of minorities be justified in a principled fashion? The problem is basically the same as that which Wechsler had raised with regard to *Brown*. If process jurisprudence was to persist in the post-Bickel era, proponents of the faith would have to develop a theory of judicial review founded on principle and yet able to accommodate the type of activist, minority-protecting constitutional adjudication epitomized by *Carolene Products*.

Credit for the development of such a theory belongs principally to John Hart Ely. According to Ely, the duty of the Supreme Court in protecting the interests of minorities 'lies at the core of our system'.[580] As 'comparative outsiders in our governmental system,' appointed judges are 'in a position objectively to assess claims . . . that either by clogging the channels of [political] change or by acting as accessories to majority

575 Jesse H. Choper, *Judicial Review and the National Political Process: A Functional Reconsideration of the Role of the Supreme Court* (Chicago: University of Chicago Press, 1980), 2.

576 See *United States* v. *Carolene Products Co.*, *supra* n. 398, 152–53 fn. 4.

577 Ibid. 152. fn. 4.

578 Ibid.

579 See Lawrence H. Tribe, 'The Puzzling Persistence of Process-Based Constitutional Theories', *Yale L.J.*, 89 (1980), 1063–80 at 1072–7.

580 Ely, *supra* n. 471, 135.

tyranny, our elected representatives in fact are not representing the interests of those whom the system presupposes they are'.[581] Judicial review exists, accordingly, both to eradicate 'stoppages in the democratic process'[582]—for example, by invalidating legislation which restricts voting rights—and to ensure the representation of minority interests. A minority which 'keeps finding itself on the wrong end of the legislature's classifications, for reasons that in some sense are discreditable',[583] is likely to require the protection of the courts. Indeed, it would be a discredit to the democratic process if such legislative classifications were impervious to constitutional review, that is, if the courts were precluded from protecting 'those who can't protect themselves politically'.[584]

Judicial review, then, is regarded by Ely to be an integral feature of 'an open and effective democratic process'.[585] In engaging in such review, the role of the courts is not to enforce particular political values, but to guarantee the integrity of that process. That is, it is for the courts, guided by 'the general contours of the Constitution',[586] to 'keep the machinery of democratic government running as it should' by ensuring that 'the channels of political participation and communication are kept open' and that majority rule does not result in minority oppression.[587] In this way, Ely radically reorients process jurisprudence. Previous process jurists had conceived integrity to be a legal or, more narrowly, an adjudicative quality. For Ely, in contrast, integrity is a political quality which constitutional adjudication serves, or ought to serve, to promote. Conceived thus, integrity is no longer something which judicial activism undermines. Indeed, judicial activism may epitomize integrity. The Supreme Court often protects the integrity of the political process, for example, when it invalidates legislation on the basis of open-textured provisions of the Constitution such as the equal protection clause.[588] The Warren Court exemplified the judicial protection of political integrity when it outlawed state-imposed segregation. For, in doing so, it was, in Ely's terms, attempting to remedy a malfunction in the democratic process whereby 'representatives beholden to a representative majority [were] systematically disadvantaging some minority out of simple hostility or a prejudiced refusal to recognize commonalities of interest, and thereby denying that minority the protection afforded other groups by a representative system'.[589]

Thus it is that Ely squares process jurisprudence with judicial activism. The courts demonstrate integrity in constitutional adjudication, he insists, when they strike down statutes which cut off the channels of political change and when they facilitate the representation of minority interests.

[581] Ely, *supra* n. 471, 103.
[582] Ibid. 117.
[583] Ibid. 152.
[584] Ibid.
[585] Ibid. 105.
[586] Ibid. 101.
[587] Ibid. 76.
[588] See ibid. 30–2.
[589] Ibid. 103.

Such adjudication, he argues, is consonant with the premisses of American representative democracy. While the scope of process jurisprudence is accordingly extended, however, it is by no means rendered indiscriminate. In fact, Ely's theory offers an answer to the great constitutional problem of modern times: namely, how 'to find a way of approving *Brown* while disapproving *Lochner*'.[590] Unlike *Brown*, Ely argues, *Lochner* contributed nothing to the maintenance of the democratic process: that is, the decision served neither to unblock closed channels of political participation nor to combat minority oppression. The fact, however, that Ely is able to distinguish *Brown* from *Lochner* in this way reveals a basic flaw in his thesis. For, in arguing that the function of judicial review is to remove political blocks and imbalances from the democratic process, he commits himself to a markedly narrow conception of representative democracy.

The Constitution, Ely argues, is for the most part unconcerned with substantive values—indeed, the choice of such values 'is left almost entirely to the political process'.[591] Rather, the Constitution 'is overwhelmingly concerned . . . with procedural fairness in the resolution of individual disputes . . . and . . . with ensuring broad participation in the processes and distributions of government'.[592] Judicial review, as Ely conceives it, serves to protect these 'process' rights: it upholds the constitutionally guaranteed rights of participation in the political process and fair representation. But how are courts to uphold such rights if not by making substantive value choices? With regard to the right of political participation, for example, '[d]eciding what *kind* of participation the Constitution demands requires analysis . . . of the character and importance of the interest at stake—its role in the life of the individual as an individual.'[593] Such analysis demands precisely the type of judgement call[594] which Ely regards to be the job of the political process.[595] Accordingly, for all that his theory is an attempt to demonstrate precisely the opposite, judicial review appears invariably to involve the importation of substantive value preferences into the Constitution.[596]

The preferences towards which Ely's own theory tilts are discernible from his analysis of minority representation. Although he finds problems with Justice Stone's image of a 'discrete and insular minority', he retains

590 Ibid. 65.

591 Ibid. 87.

592 Ibid.

593 Tribe, *supra* n. 579, 1069.

594 To take a term from Ely: see *supra* n. 471, 103.

595 See Richard Davies Parker, 'The Past of Constitutional Theory—And Its Future', *Ohio State L.J.*, 42 (1981), 223–59 at 234–5.

596 On this point, see further Paul Brest, 'The Substance of Process', *Ohio State L.J.*, 42 (1981), 131–42; Mark V. Tushnet, 'Darkness on the Edge of Town: The Contributions of John Hart Ely to Constitutional Theory', *Yale L.J.*, 89 (1980), 1037–62; P. P. Craig, *Public Law and Democracy in the United Kingdom and the United States of America* (Oxford: Clarendon Press, 1990), 91–116.

the concept for the reason that hostility and stereotyping in general 'social intercourse' often grow out of the perception of a particular minority as discrete and insular.[597] The use of judicial review to invalidate legislative classifications which discriminate against such minorities is essential 'to the amelioration of cooperation-blocking prejudice'.[598] But what of minorities—victims of poverty, for example—that are neither discrete nor insular? Are they also to be protected?[599] Not according to Ely. Although 'a law need not necessarily discriminate explicitly against a disfavoured group' in order to attract judicial scrutiny, he argues, 'failures to provide the poor with one or another good or service . . . generally result . . . from a reluctance to raise the taxes needed to support such expenditures. . . . A theory of suspicious classification will thus be of only occasional assistance to the poor, since their problems are not often problems of classification to begin with.'[600] For Ely, then, the judicial protection of minorities is classification-bound. The fact that specific legislation may disadvantage the poor, for example, ought not to be a valid reason for judicial review, since 'the poor' do not constitute a discrete and insular minority. The problem with Ely's position on the scope of constitutional adjudication is not that he excludes the poor in particular, but that he feels compelled to draw a line. For this in itself demonstrates the value-laden nature of judicial review. Precisely what ought and ought not to qualify as a minority deserving of special protection within the representative system is a matter of choice. That choice may depend upon whether or not eligible minorities must be discrete and insular. It may depend on what the words 'discrete and insular' are taken to mean. Even once the courts have determined what constitutes a minority deserving of special protection, the actual protection of any such minority entails not only the invalidation of a law which appears to offend against the integrity of the democratic process, but also the affirmation of the particular minority right. 'The crux of any determination that a law unjustly discriminates against a group', as Laurence Tribe explains, 'is not that the law emerges from a flawed process, or that the burden it imposes affects an independently fundamental right, but that the law is part of a pattern that denies those subject to it a meaningful opportunity to realize their humanity. Necessarily, such an approach must look beyond process to identify and proclaim fundamental substantive rights.'[601]

So it is that Ely's theory fails to remain faithful to its own premisses. If there is a basic reason for this, it is that Ely wants, as it were, the best of

[597] Ely, *supra* n. 471, 161.
[598] Ibid.
[599] On this point, see generally Bruce A. Ackerman, 'Beyond *Carolene Products*', *Harvard L. Rev.*, 98 (1985), 713–46 and esp. 742.
[600] Ely, *supra* n. 471, 162.
[601] Tribe, *supra* n. 579, 1077.

both worlds. He attempts to develop a process-based theory of judicial review which embraces activism while remaining faithful to the classic Wechslerian ideal of keeping constitutional adjudication distinct from politics. The way in which Ely endeavours to get the best of both worlds is by redefining process. By his definition, 'process' is no longer the process of judicial reasoning or the institutions which make up the legal process, but the democratic process, the integrity of which judicial review must serve to protect. Ultimately, his theory fails because he is incapable of explaining how the institution of judicial review might maintain the integrity of that process without promoting value-preferences. Sustaining integrity *à la* Ely means abandoning integrity *à la* Wechsler and Bickel. Even the democratic process itself turns out to be a peculiar value-construct. That is, for all that Ely eschews consensus-oriented theories of constitutional adjudication,[602] he treats as uncontroversial his own assumption that judicial review is limited to protecting the constitutional rights of political participation and fair representation.[603] In fact, judicial review within a democracy operates to protect a distinctly broader framework of rights.

Such an insight might properly be termed 'Dworkinian'. Ely's theory of judicial review, according to Ronald Dworkin, proves unpersuasive for three primary reasons. First, Ely assumes that his own narrow conception of the democratic process 'is the right conception—right as a matter of "objective" political morality—and that the job of the Court is to identify and protect this right conception'.[604] Secondly, he mistakenly supposes that judges might adopt his theory 'without facing issues that are by any account substantive issues of political morality'.[605] Thirdly, he fails to explain how 'a "process" theory of judicial review will sharply limit the scope of that review'.[606] Criticisms along these lines have been outlined above. For his own part, Dworkin not only elaborates these criticisms but argues that they uncover a basic fact about judicial review: namely, that '[i]f we want judicial review at all—if we do not want to repeal *Marbury* v. *Madison*—then we must accept that the Supreme Court must make important political decisions.'[607] The fundamental question facing American constitutional theorists, in other words, is not whether to retain the power of judicial review, but—given that it has been retained—precisely how the Court ought to exercise the power. More simply—indeed, as Dworkin puts it—the problem at the heart of constitutional jurisprudence is: what reasons will constitute 'good reasons' for the exercise of judicial review?[608]

Dworkin's own answer to this question is well known. The Supreme

[602] See Ely, *supra* n. 471, 63–9.
[603] See Parker, *supra* n. 395, 235.
[604] Ronald Dworkin, *A Matter of Principle* (Oxford: Clarendon Press, 1986), 59.
[605] Ibid. 66.
[606] Ibid. 67.
[607] Ibid. 69.
[608] Ibid.

Court, in exercising the power of judicial review, ought to reach decisions based on principle rather than on policy. Decisions based on arguments of principle are decisions concerned not with the question of how the general welfare of the community is best to be promoted, but with the question of what rights people have under the constitutional system. 'Arguments of principle justify a political decision by showing that the decision respects or secures some individual or group right.'[609] In reaching principled decisions, a court ought to protect not only constitutional but also moral rights, for '[t]he nerve of a claim of right' is not that it is embodied in the Constitution, but 'that an individual is entitled to protection against the majority even at the cost of the general interest'.[610] Where no constitutional right exists, for example, a person still has the right 'to be treated with the same respect and concern as anyone else'.[611] Indeed, for Dworkin, the root principle of government is that people must be treated with equal concern and respect.[612] As a political ideal, 'integrity'—his key jurisprudential theme in recent years—requires 'that government pursue some coherent conception of what treating people as equal means'.[613] In the context of adjudication, furthermore, 'integrity requires our judges, so far as this is possible, to treat our present system of public standards as expressing and respecting a coherent set of principles.'[614] 'The adjudicative principle instructs judges to identify legal rights and duties, so far as possible, on the assumption that they were all created by a single author—the community personified—expressing a coherent conception of justice and fairness.'[615]

Outlined thus, Dworkin's jurisprudence prompts a definite sense of *déjà vu*. The distinction between principle and policy, the notion of adjudication as a principled activity, the concern with integrity, the presumption of a rational consensus—these, as we have seen, are the hallmarks of process jurisprudence. Even Hercules, Dworkin's superhuman judge, fits the role of the supreme, reasoned elaborationist.[616] It would be wrong, however, to align Dworkin squarely with the process tradition. To some extent—certainly in his earlier writings—he implicitly distances himself from that tradition. Pound's vague characterization of principles as starting points for legal reasoning, for example, seemed to exasperate him. '[I]t is not enough', he argued, simply 'to call attention to these principles and to show how they have grown from ancient times.'[617] Having merely

[609] Dworkin, *supra* n. 67, 82.

[610] Ibid. 146. See also Ronald Dworkin, 'The Jurisprudence of Richard Nixon', *New York Review of Books*, 17 (1972), 27–35 at 30–1.

[611] Dworkin, *supra* n. 67, 227.

[612] Ibid. 272.

[613] Dworkin, *supra* n. 383, 223.

[614] Ibid. 217.

[615] Ibid. 225.

[616] See Dworkin, *supra* n. 67, 116–17; and *supra* n. 383, 400.

[617] Ronald Dworkin, 'The Case for Law—A Critique', *Valparaiso Univ. L. Rev.*, 1 (1967), 215–17 at 217; and cf. Roscoe Pound, 'The Case for Law', *Valparaiso Univ. L. Rev.*, 1 (1967), 201–14 at 202.

identified and charted the emergence of certain foundational legal principles, Pound had 'stopped at the beginning . . . he did not put to himself the challenge of setting out clearly the views he opposed, and of studying what he had to show to oppose them'.[618] In his early work, Dworkin was no less critical of Fuller.[619] 'Professor Fuller', he claimed, 'faces a dilemma. He wants to show that making even bad law requires some compliance with principles of morality. When he produces principles compliance with which is indeed necessary to law, they turn out to be strategic or criterial rather than moral principles. When he insists on considering them moral principles (or substitutes for them principles which are moral) he is no longer able to show that compliance with them is necessary to law.'[620] By the early 1960s, Dworkin was developing his own conception of principles. It is by the application of principles, as distinct from both policies and rules, he began to argue—principles such as that 'No man shall profit by his own wrong'—that judges are able to decide hard cases.[621]

Some commentators discern in Dworkin's discussion of principles—and particularly in the distinction that he makes between principles and policies[622]—more than a hint of Hart and Sacks.[623] According to Vincent Wellman, 'Dworkin's view on law and judging are fundamentally the same as those outlined' in *The Legal Process*.[624] Yet, having made this claim, he proceeds to argue that 'Dworkin's distinction between principles and policies is more elegant than that offered by Hart and Sacks.'[625] In fact, he uncovers as many differences as similarities between their respective jurisprudential models. Other commentators regard as significant the fact that 'Dworkin graduated from the Harvard Law School in 1957, at the apogee of legal process' formative period.'[626] Yet Dworkin never took the *Legal Process* course.[627] By his own account, his only experience of Hart and Sacks's process perspective was vicarious, derived mainly from

618 Dworkin, *supra* n. 617, 217. Dworkin appears to hold in much higher estimation the work of Pound's student, John Dickinson: see ibid. 215; and also Stephen Guest, *Ronald Dworkin* (Edinburgh: Edinburgh University Press, 1992), 5.

619 It is interesting to note that, as a student at Harvard in the 1950s, Dworkin did not take any of Fuller's courses. See Guest, *supra* n. 618, 5.

620 Ronald M. Dworkin, 'The Elusive Morality of Law', *Villanova L. Rev.*, 10 (1965), 631–9 at 638. In the same vein, see also Ronald Dworkin, 'Philosophy, Morality, and Law—Observations Prompted by Professor Fuller's Novel Claim', *U. Pennsylvania L. Rev*, 113 (1965), 668–90.

621 See Ronald Dworkin, 'Judicial Discretion', *Jnl. of Philosophy*, 60 (1963), 624–38 at 634–5.

622 See Dworkin, *supra* n. 67, 22.

623 See Eskridge and Peller, *supra* n. 402, 731.

624 Vincent A. Wellman, 'Dworkin and the Legal Process Tradition: The Legacy of Hart and Sacks', *Arizona L. Rev.*, 29 (1987), 413–74 at 414.

625 Ibid. 425.

626 Eskridge and Peller, *supra* n. 402, 731 fn. 72.

627 Professor Ronald Dworkin, letter to author, 12 June 1992.

conversations with his former colleague at the Yale Law School, Harry Wellington.[628]

Wellington began teaching the *Legal Process* materials after he had audited Albert Sacks's course in the early 1960s, while they were both visiting professors at Stanford.[629] 'What especially interested me in *The Legal Process*,' he recollects, 'was the way in which the material addressed the limits of law and the allocation of responsibilities among legal institutions.'[630] Wellington also regarded as important Hart and Sacks's treatment of principles and policies as distinct types of legal criteria.[631] In an essay 'dedicated to the memory of Henry M. Hart, Jr.,' published in 1973,[632] he lamented that '[l]awyers are not especially concerned . . . to distinguish principles from policies.'[633] The distinction, he insists, is crucial, for it is the key to keeping adjudication separate from politics. A judicial institution charged with the task 'of finding the society's set of moral principles and determining how they bear in concrete situations . . . would be sharply different from [an institution] charged with proposing policies'.[634] Whereas '[t]he latter institution would be constructed with the understanding that it was to respond to the people's exercise of political power . . . [t]he former would be insulated from such pressure. It would provide an environment conducive to rumination, reflection, and analysis. "Reason, not power" would be the motto over its door.'[635] Wellington thus not only dedicated his essay to Hart but also echoed him: the courts ought to be the forum of principle, and the articulation of principle is the pathway to reason.[636]

This echo of Hart and Sacks certainly emanates from the writings of Dworkin as well as from those of Wellington. With Dworkin, however, it is very much one echo among many. Whereas the connection which Wellington makes between reason and principle is clearly derived from *The Legal Process*, for example, Dworkin finds the connection at the heart of modern liberal philosophy.[637] Rawls's theory of justice, he observes, entails 'choice conditions . . . constructed so as to reflect . . . principles of

[628] Dworkin, ibid.: 'We talked a great deal about legal theory, and I might well have imbibed some of the legal process mystique from him'.

[629] Dean Harry H. Wellington, letter to author, 7 July 1992.

[630] Ibid.

[631] Ibid.

[632] Harry H. Wellington, 'Common Law Rules and Constitutional Double Standards: Some Notes on Adjudication', *Yale L.J.*, 83 (1973), 221–311 at 221 n.*

[633] Ibid. 222.

[634] Ibid. 246.

[635] Ibid. 246–7.

[636] On Wellington's use of the policy–principle distinction, see further Laurence E. Wiseman, 'The New Supreme Court Commentators: The Principled, the Political, and the Philosophical', *Hastings Constitutional Law Quarterly*, 10 (1983), 315–431 at 381–4.

[637] On rationalism and liberal philosophy, see generally William A. Galston, *Liberal Purposes: Goods, Virtues, and Diversity in the Liberal State* (Cambridge: Cambridge University Press, 1991), esp. 28–32.

reasonableness suited to the political culture of Western liberal democracies'.[638] In identifying the connection of reason and principle in Rawls's work—a connection upon which we remarked earlier—Dworkin in effect highlights the intellectual overlap between the liberal philosophical tradition and the process tradition. Preoccupation with 'neutrality' is another example of this overlap.[639] Owing to its foundation in each of these traditions, Dworkin's legal philosophy is illustrative of the fact that process jurisprudence is wrapped up in a more general intellectual culture. Far from being an exclusive characteristic of process jurisprudence, faith in reason—and the 'principled' articulation of that faith—has motivated the endeavours of many jurists, philosophers and political scientists alike. It is for precisely this reason that process jurisprudence cannot be conceived in a straightforwardly 'causal' fashion. Certainly some process jurists influenced or were influenced by others. But there is much more to the process tradition than merely a network of influences. The tradition must be understood primarily as the embodiment of an attitude concerning the importance of rationality within a democracy. Process jurisprudence is the principal effort of American lawyers to try to make something of that attitude, to give it energy, focus and direction. It is, in essence, an attempt by academic lawyers to turn into theory a faith which they hold in common with other American intellectuals.

CONCLUSION

Many American lawyers appear nowadays to have abandoned this faith. Process jurisprudence has been dismissed by some as little more than a vision of a legal utopia, of a system in which all official action is rational action, identifiable as such by virtue of the fact that it reflects democratic values rooted in consensus.[640] Certainly the rationalistic premisses of process jurisprudence invest it at times with an other-worldy quality. Hart and Sacks, for example, developed a wholly benign image of the legal process. Their vision is one of judges, legislators, administrators and other legal officials as essentially honest, rational agents, compelled to act reasonably because that is what the principle of institutional settlement demands.[641] Even if their vision of law as procedure grounded in reason were a reality, it would by no means be welcomed by all. Many proponents of critical legal studies, for example, take the view that law cannot and,

[638] Ronald Dworkin, 'What is Equality? Part 3: The Place of Liberty', *Iowa L. Rev.*, 73 (1987), 1–54 at 14.

[639] See Sunstein, *supra* n. 456, 48–52.

[640] See e.g. Kelman, *supra* n. 566, 186–212.

[641] This criticism of Hart and Sacks is developed specifically with regard to legislative activity by William N. Eskridge, Jr., 'Spinning Legislative Supremacy', *Georgetown L.J.*, 78 (1989), 319–52.

indeed, even if it could, should not be rational, neutral and detached from politics.[642] For many critical legal theorists, this is the primary lesson of legal realism.

Yet legal realism failed. '[D]espite its liberating virtues,' Thurman Arnold wrote in 1957, realism was 'not a sustaining food for a stable civilization'.[643] Whereas realism was seen to be weak in opposition to tyranny, process jurisprudence was premissed on the rationality of democracy. Inevitably, the latter prospered as the former fell from grace. As I have tried to show, however, process jurisprudence did not emerge in response to legal realism. The process tradition in fact evolved alongside realism rather than in reaction to it. Without doubt, the process perspective was at its most vital during the years following the Second World War. It was during this period that the rationalistic premisses of process thinking—in law as in political science and philosophy—served to legitimate and promote the very democratic ideals which, on the European continent, had been undermined by fascism and communism. In the post-war years, we might say, process jurisprudence found its forte. But process thinking had been around in American jurisprudence at least since the time of Langdell.

My aim in this chapter has been to trace the evolution of process thinking in American jurisprudence. In tracing this evolution, I have sought to demonstrate how the theme of reason has acquired near-paradigmatic status in American legal thought. The emergence of faith in reason has, I believe, been a rather more subtle development than has commonly been assumed. To attribute the growth of this faith exclusively to the challenge of legal realism is far too simplistic. Rather, faith in reason lies at the heart of American jurisprudential culture. The history of process jurisprudence is a history of American lawyers endeavouring to uphold and protect this faith. It is a history of lawyers attempting to uncover reason immanent in law. From the process perspective, the integrity of the legal system depends on its foundation in reason. When the integrity of the legal system is apparently threatened—for example, where a court faced with a hard case appears to be compelled to reach a political rather than a principled decision—process theorists attempt to bolster integrity by modifying the meaning of 'process'. Thus it is that we find successive proponents of the process perspective refining the basic process framework in the effort to preserve the image of adjudication as an apolitical activity.[644] Process jurisprudence transpires in this way to be the very

[642] See Rodriguez, *supra* n. 403, 944.

[643] Thurman Arnold, 'Judge Jerome Frank', *U. Chicago L. Rev.*, 24 (1957), 633–42 at 635.

[644] See further Kent Greenawalt, 'Discretion and Judicial Decision: The Elusive Quest for the Fetters that Bind Judges', *Columbia L. Rev.*, 75 (1975), 359–99; also Michael Wells, 'French and American Judicial Opinions', *Yale Jnl. Int. Law*, 19 (1994), 811–133 at 85–92.

antithesis of legal realism. If so-called realists were concerned with telling it—'law'—as it is, process jurists are concerned primarily with explaining how it ought to be. For, regardless of how it might appear to work in reality, law, from the process perspective, must always be understood in the light of the faith: that is, as an institutionally autonomous activity founded in reason.

5

Economics in Law

It is almost a century since Oliver Wendell Holmes urged American lawyers to turn, for enlightenment, to the discipline of economics.[1] During the first half of this century, this exhortation—in common with many other classic Holmesian proclamations—came to be absorbed into realist legal thought. 'Some of the more progressive schools of law', the Yale lawyer-psychologist Edward Robinson observed in 1934, 'are already turning out graduates whose fundamental attack upon social problems is that of the economist rather than that of the jurist.'[2] Yet he conceded that '[e]ven in such schools we still find prevailing the idea that economics, psychiatry, and the rest are merely techniques that up-to-date lawyers must learn to use. . . . The man who has secured an economic or psychological grasp upon a legal problem is not quite willing to go clear through along that line of thought.'[3] Robinson's concession rather suggests why legal realism in fact left unfulfilled the Holmesian dream of turning *homo juridicus* into *homo oeconomicus*: not only were realist efforts to introduce inter-disciplinary sensibilities into the American law schools highly tentative and underdeveloped; they were also indiscriminate. In the literature of legal realism, more or less any social science—economics, psychiatry, psychology, whatever—was deemed to be somehow useful. Economics was but one tool among many. It was accorded no special status.

American legal theorists have hardly been hesitant to discern some sort of relationship between legal realism and the emergence of economic analysis as a distinctive form of interdisciplinary legal study. Yet the nature of this relationship remains unclear. For some, the realist pedigree of economic analysis is undisputable. 'In the law schools,' Edmund Kitch has observed, 'law and economics evolved out of the agenda of legal realism.

[1] See Oliver Wendell Holmes, 'The Path of the Law', *Harvard L. Rev.*, 10 (1897), 457–78 at 469 ('For the rational study of law the black-letter man may be the man of the present, but the man of the future is the man of statistics and the master of economics') and also 474 ('I look forward to a time when the part played by history in the explanation of dogma will be small, and instead of ingenious research we shall spend our energy on a study of the ends sought to be attained and the reasons for desiring them. As a step toward that ideal it seems to me that every lawyer ought to seek an understanding of economics'). For further legal–economic analysis of these passages, cf. Cento Veljanovski, *The Economics of Law: An Introductory Text* (London: Institute of Economic Affairs, 1990), 12, 88–9.

[2] Edward S. Robinson, 'Law—An Unscientific Science', *Yale L.J.*, 34 (1943), 235–67 at 266.

[3] Ibid.

Legal realism taught that legal scholars should study the law as it works in practice by making use of the social sciences, and economics was one of the social sciences to which academic lawyers turned.'[4] It has also been suggested that proponents of economic analysis embrace the realist tradition by accepting implicitly the politically-malleable and instrumental nature of law.[5] Yet there are others who regard economic analysis as 'an attempt to get over, or at least to get by, the complexity thrust upon us by the Realists'[6]—who perceive it to be 'the contemporary restructuring of formal jurisprudence after the incursion of legal realism'.[7] In modern American jurisprudence, it appears, law and economics simultaneously represents realism fulfilled and realism thwarted.

Detractors from economic analysis have exploited both of these images. Consider, first of all, the image of law and economics as an intellectual tendency at odds with the realist legal tradition. Given that certain lawyer–economists advocate the laboratory experiment as a useful form of legal–economic inquiry[8]—given also that one of the primary virtues of economic

[4] Edmund W. Kitch, 'The Intellectual Foundations of "Law and Economics" ', *Jnl. Leg. Educ.*, 33 (1983), 184–96 at 184. In the same vein, see also Donald H. Gjerdingen, 'The Politics of the Coase Theorem and Its Relationship to Modern Legal Thought', *Buffalo L. Rev.*, 35 (1986), 871–935 at 907. ('At first, the [Coase] theorem was treated as merely a special application of economics to common-law thought. From this perspective, the theorem was merely a continuation of the Realist plea to refine legal thought by using the insights of other disciplines into human behaviour.') For a general attempt to chart an intellectual path from legal realism to law and economics, see Erich Schanze, 'Ökonomische Analyse des Rechts in den U.S.A.—Verbindungslinien zur realistischen Tradition', in Heinz-Dieter Assmann, Christian Kirchner and Erich Schanze (eds.), *Ökonomische Analyse des Rechts* (Kronberg: Athenäum, 1978), 3–19.

[5] Jules L. Coleman, 'Economics and the Law: A Critical Review of the Foundations of the Economic Approach to Law', *Ethics*, 94 (1984), 649–79 at 677. ('[T]he economic analysis of law is apparently committed to legal realism as a jurisprudential thesis. For it is essential to the enterprise that judges be free to decide cases in accordance with the dictates of efficiency rather than in accordance with any set of preexisting claims litigants might have against one another. In addition, the economic analysis is an instrumentalist theory of law since it views litigation in terms of opportunities claimants give courts to promote global or collective aims.') See also Jeffrie G. Murphy and Jules L. Coleman, *Philosophy of Law: An Introduction to Jurisprudence* (rev. edn. Boulder, Colo.: Westview, 1990), 227–8.

[6] Arthur Allen Leff, 'Economic Analysis of Law: Some Realism about Nominalism', *Virginia L. Rev.*, 60 (1974), 451–82 at 459. In essentially the same vein, see also Mark Tushnet, 'Post-Realist Legal Scholarship', *Jnl. of the Society of Public Teachers of Law*, 15 (1980), 20–32 at 24.

[7] Thomas C. Heller, 'Is the Charitable Exemption from Property Taxation an Easy Case? General Concerns about Legal Economics and Jurisprudence', in Daniel L. Rubinfeld (ed.), *Essays on the Law and Economics of Local Governments* (Washington, DC: The Urban Institute, 1979), 183–251 at 185.

[8] See, generally, Elizabeth Hoffman and Matthew L. Spitzer, 'Experimental Law and Economics: An Introduction', *Columbia L. Rev.*, 85 (1985), 991–1036. For a critique of this particular methodology, cf. Mark Kelman, 'Comment on Hoffman and Spitzer's *Experimental Law and Economics*', *Columbia L. Rev.*, 85 (1985), 1037–47.

analysis, according to its most vigorous proponent, rests in the fact that it renders superficial '[m]uch of the doctrinal luxuriance of common law'[9]—characterizations of modern law and economics as anti-realist, 'neo-Langdellian' jurisprudence, although superficial,[10] seem almost inevitable. 'Contemporary normative Law and Economics', in the eyes of one commentator, 'is an almost perfect mirror of Langdellian conceptualism: when an outcome is inefficient, just as when a case did not fit a principle, it is rejected as "wrong".'[11] A 'refined and polished version of the Langdellian idea that law consists of a rational and universal system of scientifically discoverable principles or doctrines,'[12] modern law and economics, '[l]ike the old-fashioned formalism . . . reestablishes the lawyer as the scientist with a norm-free calculus'.[13] Throughout the literature of modern American jurisprudence, observations such as these abound.[14] Yet they fail to capture contemporary critical concerns about economic analysis of law. Indeed, if anything, such observations represent the consternation of a bygone generation: a generation which witnessed modern law and economics emerge just as it had witnessed legal realism decline;[15] which believed that modern economic analysis marked the dawning of a new 'Conceptualist' legal faith;[16] and which disliked this new faith precisely because it appreciated, and indeed could not entirely resist, its powers of seduction.[17]

[9] Richard A. Posner, *The Problems of Jurisprudence* (Cambridge, Mass.: Harvard University Press, 1990), 361.

[10] There is, for example, much more to modern economic analysis than deductivism. The superficiality of the characterization of modern economic analysis of law as neo-Langdellian is analysed more generally by Richard A. Posner, *Overcoming Law* (unpublished mimeograph [on file with author: copy supplied by Judge Posner], 17 January 1994, forthcoming, Cambridge, Mass.: Harvard University Press, 1995), 16–22.

[11] G. Edward White, 'From Realism to Critical Legal Studies: A Truncated Intellectual History', *Southwestern L.J.*, 40 (1986), 819–43 at 840.

[12] Gary Minda, 'The Lawyer–Economist at Chicago: Richard A. Posner and the *Economic Analysis of Law*', *Ohio State L.J.*, 39 (1978), 439–75 at 440.

[13] David Gray Carlson, 'Reforming the Efficiency Criterion: Comments on Some Recent Suggestions', *Cardozo L. Rev.*, 8 (1986), 39–73 at 39.

[14] I am as guilty as is anyone of making such observations. See Neil Duxbury, 'Pragmatism Without Politics', *Mod. L. Rev.*, 55 (1992), 594–610 at 596.

[15] See Robert Stevens, *Law School: Legal Education in America from the 1850s to the 1980s* (Chapel Hill: University of North Carolina Press, 1983), 272.

[16] See Grant Gilmore, *The Ages of American Law* (New Haven, Conn.: Yale University Press 1977), 107–8, 146–7 n. 11. In 1983, in an introduction to a symposium on the role of economics in legal education, the editor of the *Journal of Legal Education* remarked that '[t]he "law and economics movement" is a major development of the '70s. Intellectual trends in the twentieth century, characterized in the law schools by the gradual triumph of legal realism, have tended to result in scepticism about generalizations and unifying ideas. The aftermath of the corrosive acid of legal realism is a search for explanation and prediction that will provide some order for the chaos that otherwise prevails.' Roger C. Cramton, 'The Place of Economics in Legal Education: Introduction', *Jnl. Leg. Educ.*, 33 (1983), 183.

[17] See Leff, *supra* n. 6, 452–53. ('[N]ot only do almost all recent "law and" law review articles and law school courses turn out to be "law and economics," but even people like me,

Nowadays, American academic lawyers appear generally to recognize that economic analysis is not simply re-hashed Langdellianism. This recognition, however, signals not that perceptions of economic analysis have become more sophisticated, but that they have become more ambivalent. If there is a primary source and cause of this ambivalence, it is, I would argue, critical legal studies.

Few American academic lawyers seem to dissent from the proposition that, in recent years, law and economics and critical legal studies have been 'the best-organized, most ambitious voices in the law schools'.[18] Some commentators have argued that, at a very superficial level, the two are not really distinguishable: albeit in different ways, both treat law as a political phenomenon;[19] and both undermine the image of law as an autonomous discipline.[20] Yet anyone professing faith in one of these tendencies is likely to denounce the other. 'It seems a plain fact', according to one observer, 'that people who like law and economics are somewhat inclined to belittle "critical legal studies".'[21] Were they so capable, flies on the walls of faculty lounges in many an American law school would doubtless attest to this fact. Proponents of law and economics, however, appear generally to have been reluctant to attempt such belittlement in print.[22] Law and economics

with no formal background in and little natural taste or aptitude for economic analysis, seem to be drawn to reading it and, in primitive fashion, even writing it.') For an illustration of Leff attempting actually to produce economic analysis, cf. Arthur Allen Leff, 'Injury, Ignorance and Spite—The Dynamics of Coercive Collection', *Yale L.J.*, 80 (1970), 1–46.

[18] George P. Fletcher, 'Why Kant', *Columbia L. Rev.*, 87 (1987), 421–32 at 424.

[19] See Owen M. Fiss, 'The Death of the Law?', *Cornell L. Rev.*, 72 (1986), 1–16 esp. 14 (summarizing his argument that law and economics and critical legal studies 'both start from a rejection of law as an embodiment of a public morality and thus have a common base line'). Less than three years after writing this article, Fiss revised his line of argument, claiming that law and economics had run out of steam, that critical legal studies had been displaced by a feminist jurisprudential project more positively oriented towards justice, equality and ethics and that, in consequence, the threat which these two tendencies had posed to the integrity of the legal process never materialized. See Owen M. Fiss, 'The Law Regained', *Cornell L. Rev.*, 74 (1989), 245–55.

[20] See Charles Fried, 'The Artificial Reason of the Law or: What Lawyers Know', *Texas L. Rev.*, 60 (1981), 35–58 at 48–9 (on law and economics); 'Jurisprudential Responses to Legal Realism', *Cornell L. Rev.*, 73 (1988), 331–4 (on critical legal studies); and Anthony Kronman, 'Jurisprudential Responses to Legal Realism', *Cornell L. Rev.*, 73 (1988), 335–40 at 339 (on both).

[21] Frank I. Michelman, 'Reflections on Professional Education, Legal Scholarship, and the Law-and-Economics Movement', *Jnl. Leg. Educ.*, 33 (1983), 197–209 at 206. According to Mark Tushnet, 'if people interested in law and economics spent one tenth of the time understanding critical legal studies that cls people spend understanding law and economics, we would all be better off.' Mark Tushnet, 'Critical Legal Studies: A Political History', *Yale L.J.*, 100 (1991), 1515–44 at 1519 fn. 17. Quite what 'better off' means in this context seems to me to be far from obvious.

[22] Inevitably, there are exceptions. Consider, e.g. Posner, *supra* n. 9, 441 (though, to be fair, Posner does endeavour to subject critical legal studies to serious scrutiny); Bruce A.

is securely established in American jurisprudential culture. Its proponents have little, if anything, to gain from denouncing critical legal studies. Yet critical legal studies feeds on its own sense of alienation: its proponents make much of the fact that even certain aficionados of law and economics scholarship regard such scholarship to be a safe route to tenure and promotion,[23] whereas critical legal scholarship has at times met with a frosty reception—and has even been turned away—from many law schools.[24] Critical legal studies is also largely oppositional: that is, its identity derives in large measure from the manner in which it opposes other jurisprudential tendencies. Thus it is that a good deal of critical legal literature conveys the impression that to know what is critical legal studies is basically to know what it is not. For all the similarities, critical legal studies is not legal realism.[25] It is not process jurisprudence.[26] It is not public choice theory.[27] And it is certainly not law and economics. It is this last dissociation which has generated much of the ambivalence with which I am concerned in this chapter.

The first point to note about the dissociation of critical legal studies from law and economics is that it is not at all straightforward. It is not simply a case of one group of legal theorists professing their antipathy towards another group. Although certain proponents of critical legal studies appear to dismiss economic analysis summarily, adjudging it to be 'profoundly

Ackerman, *Reconstructing American Law* (Cambridge, Mass.: Harvard University Press, 1984), 42–5 (dismissing critical legal studies as 'pseudocritical posturing'). Elsewhere, Ackerman has characterized himself as 'a weak lawyer-economist'. See Bruce A. Ackerman, 'Law, Economics, and the Problem of Legal Culture', *Duke L.J.*, [1986], 929–47 at 930.

[23] See e.g. Guido Calabresi, 'The New Economic Analysis of Law: Scholarship, Sophistry, or Self-Indulgence?', *Proceedings of the British Academy*, 68 (1982), 85–108 at 85. ('In the United States, where it is said to have been born, [the new economic analysis of law] has been taken up with enthusiasm by young scholars in any number of law and economic faculties, and has been described (rather ruefully) by many an older academic as the only sure route to promotion and tenure.'); Donald N. McCloskey, 'The Rhetoric of Law and Economics', *Michigan L. Rev.*, 86 (1988), 752–67 at 765.

[24] See the special feature, 'The New McCarthyism', *Newsletter of the Conference on Critical Legal Studies*, July 1988, 2–19 (statements of support and letters of protest in respect of critical legal theorists who have been denied tenure); and also Jerry Frug, 'McCarthyism and Critical Legal Studies', *Harvard Civil Rights-Civil Liberties L. Rev.*, 22 (1987), 665–701; Richard D. Kahlenberg, *Broken Contract: A Memoir of Harvard Law School* (Boston: Faber and Faber, 1992), 7–8. For the classic statement which fuelled the critical legal theorists' fire, cf. Paul D. Carrington, 'Of Law and the River', *Jnl. Leg. Educ.*, 34 (1984), 222–8 esp. 227.

[25] See e.g. David M. Trubek, 'Where the Action Is: Critical Legal Studies and Empiricism', *Stanford L. Rev.*, 36 (1984), 575–622 at 584–5; James Boyle, 'The Politics of Reason: Critical Legal Theory and Local Social Thought', *U. Pennsylvania L. Rev.*, 133 (1985), 685–780 at 691–7; and, more generally, G. Edward White, 'The Inevitability of Critical Legal Studies', *Stanford L. Rev.*, 36 (1984), 649–72 at 651–7.

[26] See e.g. Gary Peller, 'Neutral Principles in the 1950s', *U. Michigan Jnl. of Law Reform*, 21 (1988), 561–622.

[27] See Mark Kelman, 'On Democracy-Bashing: A Skeptical Look at the Theoretical and "Empirical" Practice of the Public Choice Movement', *Virginia L. Rev.*, 74 (1988), 199–273.

(almost embarrassingly) inadequate' as a theory of legal politics,[28] or even treating it as a joke,[29] there are others who attempt to argue that the relationship between the two perspectives 'is in fact quite intimate'.[30] Yet arguments stressing intimacy between law and economics and critical legal studies tend to be marked by profound ambivalence. This ambivalence stems from the fact that the supposed intimacy between the two theoretical tendencies is explained in terms of their common connection with, and reaction to, the realist legal tradition. Although they are joined by the 'intellectual bond' of legal realism,[31] one critical legal theorist has claimed, 'law and economics and critical legal studies . . . offer a theoretical approach that goes beyond the approach of the legal realists in establishing a systematic or totalistic critique and analysis of the structure of American law.'[32] 'Practitioners of each movement argue for a new realism that takes into account the deep conflict and tension existing in a world comprised of sharp political and economic differences.'[33] While this may pass as a highly-generalized description of critical legal studies, it is a remarkably unfamiliar depiction of law and economics.[34] As we shall see in due course, a common criticism of the most prevalent form of economic analysis in the United States—a criticism which features prominently in the critical legal literature[35]—is that such analysis is markedly unrealistic because it fails adequately to take into account existing distributions of wealth. Yet even one of the most economically articulate American critical legal theorists, while fully accepting this criticism,[36] insists that law and economics and critical legal studies share a common, realist-inspired vision, that together they constitute 'an attempt to respond to an ongoing

[28] John Stick, 'Charting the Development of Critical Legal Studies', *Columbia L. Rev.*, 88 (1988), 407–32 at 416.

[29] See Clare Dalton, 'An Essay in the Deconstruction of Contract Doctrine', *Yale L.J.*, 94 (1985), 997–1114 at 1035 fn. 131. Many of the best jokes about law and economics are told by lawyer–economists. See, for example, A. Mitchell Polinsky, *An Introduction to Law and Economics* (2nd edn. Boston: Little, Brown & Co., 1989), 1.

[30] Mark Kelman, *A Guide to Critical Legal Studies* (Cambridge, Mass.: Harvard University Press, 1987), 114. There is also the argument that, even if the relationship between law and economics and critical studies is not marked by intimacy, proponents of each intellectual tendency ought nevertheless to aspire to such intimacy, or at least to a greater level of mutual tolerance. See, in particular, Linz Audain, 'Critical Legal Studies, Feminism, Law and Economics, and the Veil of Intellectual Tolerance: A Tentative Case for Cross-Jurisprudential Dialogue', *Hofstra L. Rev.*, 20 (1992), 1017–104.

[31] Gary Minda, 'The Law and Economics and Critical Legal Studies Movements in American Law', in Nicholas Mercuro (ed.), *Law and Economics* (Dordrecht: Kluwer, 1989), 87–122 at 95.

[32] Ibid. 102.

[33] Ibid.

[34] See, generally, Neil Duxbury, 'Is There a Dissenting Tradition in Law and Economics?', *Mod. L. Rev.*, 54 (1991), 300–11 at 306–8.

[35] See e.g Duncan Kennedy, 'Form and Substance in Private Law Adjudication', *Harvard L. Rev.*, 89 (1976), 1685–778 at 1763.

[36] See Kelman, *supra* n. 30, 176–85.

internal legal academic crisis, the difficulty of justifying the separation of law and politics that has beset post-Realist legal academics who have been taught that legal rules are nothing but policy-oriented decisions'.[37]

The purported intimacy between law and economics and critical legal studies thus transpires to be superficial. Intimacy, here, amounts to nothing more than the apparent fact that both theoretical tendencies have sprung from the same well. Even this assertion ought to be contested. According to one critical legal scholar, '[l]aw and economics theory', like critical legal studies, 'is very much an exercise in legal realism,' since many lawyer–economists 'believe that . . . the only reasonable way to judge the efficacy of the legal system is through use of any social scientific methods at our disposal.'[38] '[L]ike the realists', he concludes, lawyer–economists 'attempt to unify law and the social sciences.'[39] Yet this same author, in the very same article, insists also that 'law and economics is very much an exercise in formalism,'[40] that 'law and economics scholars . . . assume, without argument, the existing distribution of wealth,'[41] that they 'base their assertions on hunches or assumptions about the extent to which individuals value entitlements . . . without the empirical work necessary to back up their assertions,'[42] that they 'assume[] a noncontroversial market structure within which [economic] analysis can proceed,'[43] and that at least one of their number 'blithely assum[es] . . . that efficiency is a pretty good proxy for social utility'.[44] This is not the point at which to contest these specific objections. Rather, I am concerned here with the more general belief—implicit in the above and in writings of all those who detect a point of commonality between law and economics and critical legal studies—that, whether economic analysis represents a continuation of or a rebellion against the realist tradition, it is to this tradition that it owes its existence. This is a belief which ought seriously to be questioned.

At least one critical legal scholar has argued likewise. In his second book on the transformation of American law, Morton Horwitz purports to snatch legal realism from the clutches of law and economics and claim it for critical legal studies. Law and economics may only be regarded as 'the legitimate methodological successor to Legal Realism,' he argues, so long as one considers the primary legacy of realism to be the bringing together of law and the social sciences.[45] But he insists that to understand the realist legacy in this fashion is to conceive of it too narrowly. '[T]here was an

[37] Ibid. 125.

[38] Joseph William Singer, 'Legal Realism Now', *California L. Rev.*, 76 (1988), 465–544 at 515.

[39] Ibid.

[40] Ibid. 522.

[41] Ibid. 526.

[42] Ibid. 522.

[43] Ibid. 525–6.

[44] Ibid. 528.

[45] Morton J. Horwitz, *The Transformation of American Law, 1870-1960: The Crisis of Legal Orthodoxy* (New York: Oxford University Press, 1992), 270.

entire body of Legal Realist work that explicitly rejected both ethical positivism and the alliance between Legal Realism and value-free social science.'[46] The primary legacy of the realist tradition, for Horwitz, was its demonstration 'of the complex interrelationship between law and politics'.[47] If legal realism is conceived thus, then critical legal studies, rather than law and economics, can be seen to be its rightful heir.

The credibility of Horwitz's argument depends on the assumption that proponents of law and economics and critical legal studies are somehow battling for the mantle of legal realism. Yet such an assumption seems nothing short of ludicrous. There is no such battle, for lawyer–economists have displayed little interest in legal realism.[48] Moreover, apparent similarities between realist and economic perspectives on law, in so far as they exist, are generally treated by lawyer–economists as wholly fortuitous.[49] Of course, the fact that lawyer–economists consider the debate over the realist credentials of economic analysis to be a non-starter does not mean that this is necessarily the case, but it does raise the question as to why so much effort has been devoted to contextualizing economic analysis in a fashion which most of its proponents would consider irrelevant. Whence comes this desire to see law and economics through the lens of legal realism?

The answer to this question, I believe, is to be found in what seems to be the conventional historiography of American jurisprudence. It was suggested in the introduction to this book that there prevails among American legal theorists a fairly general assumption that, since the Langdellian era, American jurisprudence has been constituted by certain movements and responses to movements—which often themselves become movements—and that, as one movement builds upon another, some of the legal perceptions and beliefs of the past are either rejected or revised. Langdellianism, conceptualism, formalism, or whatever we want to call it was replaced by realism, functionalism, pragmatism, or whatever we want to call that, which in turn was superseded by something else—the process tradition, certainly, but perhaps also law and economics.[50] This is the episodic conception of the past which seems to permeate American

[46] Horwitz, ibid. 270.

[47] Ibid. 271.

[48] See Henry G. Manne, *The Economics of Legal Relationships: Readings in the Theory of Property Rights* (St. Paul: West Publishing Co., 1975), vii–viii; and also Posner, *supra* n. 10, 2: 'The "crits" worry that the practitioners of law and economics will contest with them the mantle of legal realism. But we won't; they're welcome to it.'

[49] See e.g. Jason Scott Johnston, 'Law, Economics, and Post-Realist Explanation', *Law and Society Rev.*, 24 (1990), 1217–54 at 1218–19; also Posner, *supra* n. 9, 441–2.

[50] I say 'perhaps' for the simple reason that some would argue that it is too early to tell precisely how, or even if, economic analysis has superseded the realist tradition. See e.g. Horwitz, *supra* n. 45, 269.

jurisprudential discourse: first there was X, which was displaced by Y, which was then replaced by Z—pre-realism makes way for realism, and realism makes way for post-realism. It is within this rigidly chronological, realist-oriented framework that economic analysis has generally been situated. Thus: 'law-and-economics proffers a solution to a variety of difficulties which have tormented thinking about law since the legal realist attack on formalism in the 1920s . . . legal economic theory is able to pull back and reassert a formal vision of a positivist legal system consistent with the general structure of liberal thought.'[51] Similarly: 'the legal realists . . . ended up in an orgy of law and social science in which not very good sociology was particularly dominant. . . . That petered out in the great flowering of that most extraordinary school, the Harvard Legal Process School, which dominated until the late fifties. . . . Then law and economics, the current law and economics, took over.'[52] Conceived within such a framework, economic analysis comes almost invariably to be represented either as the rejection of realism, the return to some sort of scientism, conceptualism, formalism or whatever, or the revision of realism, the point at which American academic lawyers made another concerted attempt at embracing social science. It is in this way that the dominant—in my view highly inaccurate—perception of post-Langdellian American jurisprudential history has produced an equally dominant, equally inaccurate perception of law and economics.

But what, it might fairly be asked, is actually wrong with this view of law and economics? Why is it misleading to regard economic analysis as at least an indirect response, whether positive or negative, to the realist legal tradition? For surely legal realism introduced into the American law schools a peculiar social-scientific culture without which economic analysis could never have flourished. My argument is not categorically that there is no connection between the realist legal tradition and modern law and economics. Rather, it is that, if we are to understand why American lawyers turned to economic analysis, we must appreciate the degree to which law and economics is profoundly distinct from, rather than how it bears superficial affinities to, realist legal thought. Understanding the law and economics tradition requires more than anything else that we appreciate its peculiar jurisprudential characteristics.

In attempting to justify this contention, I offer three general observations, all of which will be developed more or less thematically. The first is that, even before the realist era—indeed, even before Holmes had urged them to do so—certain American lawyers were beginning to look to

[51] Heller, *supra* n. 7, 205.

[52] Guido Calabresi, 'Thoughts on the Future of Economics in Legal Education', *Jnl. Leg. Educ.*, 33 (1983), 359–64 at 360.

economics for legal enlightenment. This is not to deny that economic analysis of law developed as a distinctive jurisprudential phenomenon in the post-realist era. In terms of methodology and theoretical vision, late nineteenth and early twentieth-century law and economics was light years away from the style of economic analysis which evolved in the United States in the post-realist period. My point, however, is that, as a type of jurisprudence, law and economics possesses its own distinctive—if by no means seamless—history, beginning with the writings of certain early institutionalists, developing through the New Deal period—especially as economics began to feature prominently in the field of antitrust—and culminating in the early 1960s with the extension of economic analysis into areas of ostensibly non-market legal activity. Understanding the emergence and the achievements of law and economics as a distinctive form of jurisprudence requires that we take account of this history.

My second observation is that, when certain post-realist American lawyers turned to economic analysis, they were not so much embracing the social sciences as placing their faith in a specific social scientific methodology. This point, for all its obviousness, deserves to be stressed. For the turn to economics implied a rejection of more general social-scientific inquiry. Indeed, in the literature of law and economics, such rejection is occasionally made quite explicit. In justifying his own economic approach to law, for example, Richard Posner, writing in the mid-1970s, argued that:

> [w]hatever its deficiencies, the economic theory of law seems, to this biased observer anyway, the best positive theory of law extant. It is true that anthropologists, sociologists, psychologists, political scientists, and other social scientists besides economists also do positive analysis of the legal system. But their work is thus far insufficiently rich in theoretical and empirical content to afford serious competition to economists . . . [M]y impression, for what it is worth, is that these fields have produced neither systematic, empirical research on the legal system nor plausible, coherent, and empirically verifiable theories of the system.[53]

The turn to economics implies, accordingly, something different from the general realist belief that lawyers may somehow profit from the social sciences. Economics is considered by its jurisprudential advocates to be not just any old social science, but the queen of the social sciences, the only social science capable of providing analytical models which facilitate the discovery of precise, verifiable answers to many difficult questions about legal policy and decision-making.[54] As one commentator on economic

[53] Richard A. Posner, 'The Economic Approach to Law', *Texas L. Rev.*, 53 (1975), 757–82 at 774–5.

[54] See Michael W. McConnell, 'The Counter-Revolution in Legal Thought', *Policy Review*, 48 (1987), 18–25 at 23. On economics as the queen of the social sciences, see Paul A. Samuelson, *Economics* (9th edn. New York: McGraw-Hill, 1973), 6.

analysis has observed, '[e]conomics appeals to law professors because there is a body of rational, coherent information and theory which can be drawn upon, not, as is largely true of other social sciences, unassociated clusters of ideas which may or may not be relevant to particular legal issues.'[55] Faith in economics can be seen, then, to be distinct from the social-scientific faith which characterized a good deal of realist legal thought.

My final observation on the distinctiveness of law and economics is that the jurisprudential agenda of modern economic analysis appears hardly, if at all, to have been inspired by the realist legal tradition. Many lawyer–economists, for example, conceptualize adjudication in a decidedly non-realist fashion. They tend to be concerned principally with judicial decisions in themselves rather than with the processes of reasoning—or, as certain realists would have had it, non-reasoning—by which decisions are reached.[56] On the question of 'By what principles or practices of reasoning do judges in fact decide cases?', Lewis Kornhauser has remarked, 'economic analysts of law have remained silent'.[57] That body of legal–economic thought which emphasizes the ethic of wealth-maximization, for example, 'does not and cannot give a unique determinate solution to the question of the choice of rights' to be protected in the process of adjudication,[58] for the criterion of wealth-maximization 'cannot provide a determinate answer for the judge's dilemma as to what law to make'.[59] Others eschew economic analysis because it fails adequately to highlight the role of reason and principle in the adjudicative process, because '[t]here appear to be more important types of reasons for legal decisions—'rightness reasons'—that are not obviously collapsible into future-regarding consequentialist reasons of the kind that appeal so strongly to economists'.[60] In essence, the criticism is that economic analysis is a severely limited form of jurisprudence because it fails to confront, let alone solve, the problem of political adjudication.[61]

[55] Murray L. Schwartz, 'Economics in Legal Education', *Jnl. Leg. Educ.*, 33 (1983), 365–8 at 367.

[56] See e.g. William M. Landes and Richard A. Posner, 'The Positive Economic Theory of Tort Law', *Georgia L. Rev.*, 15 (1981), 851–921 at 863; and cf. also A. I. Ogus, 'Social Costs in a Private Law Setting', *Int. Rev. Law & Econ.*, 3 (1983), 27–44 at 28.

[57] Lewis A. Kornhauser, 'An Economic Perspective on Stare Decisis', *Chicago-Kent L. Rev.*, 65 (1989), 63–92 at 63.

[58] Warren J. Samuels and Nicholas Mercuro, 'Posnerian Law and Economics on the Bench', *Int. Rev. Law & Econ.*, 4 (1984), 107–30 at 123.

[59] Duncan Kennedy, 'Form and Substance in Private Law Adjudication', *Harvard L. Rev.*, 89 (1976), 1685–778 at 1763.

[60] Robert S. Summers, 'The Future of Economics in Legal Education: Limits and Constraints', *Jnl. Leg. Educ.*, 33 (1983), 337–58 at 339, and cf. also 348 ('the ways in which law is concerned with values differ importantly from the ways in which economics is concerned with values').

[61] See further James M. Buchanan, 'Good Economics—Bad Law', *Virginia L. Rev.*, 60 (1974), 483–92 at 490–2.

The difficulty with such a criticism is that it is premissed on the assumption that there does in fact exist some competing legal theory which uncovers demonstrably right answers to even the most controversial legal problems. American law professors have tended to display great faith in such a theory, but they have had relatively little success in presenting that theory in a convincing light.[62] The law and economics tradition is very clearly uncommitted to such a faith. Its advocates make no pretence that there exist principles which provide objectively correct solutions to adjudicative controversies. But this is not a return to realism. Just as lawyer–economists are specific in their choice of social science, they tend to be equally specific on the matter of common law policy. For most lawyer–economists find not just any policy at the heart of the common law. Rather, as we shall see, they find economic policy of a very distinctive type.

Some legal theorists have attempted to draw parallels between law and economics and the process tradition in American jurisprudence. As with the comparison with legal realism, however, I would argue that, in order to understand the emergence and endurance of economic analysis, it is important to highlight its distinctness from, rather than its affinities with, the process tradition. According to Mark Kelman, there are at least three perspectives common to proponents of law and economics and process jurisprudence: they support judicial restraint; they treat with scepticism the assumption that legislation is invariably democratically conceived and public-spirited; and they consider private ordering rather than public regulation to be the most desirable form of legal arrangement.[63] To my mind, none of these claims is convincing. First, process jurisprudence is by no means wholly antithetical to judicial activism;[64] law and economics still less so. Indeed, certain of the more insistent proponents of normative economic analysis suggest that the judiciary has a duty to invalidate any legislation which interferes with basic economic liberties such as the right to own and use property.[65] In arguing as much, these lawyer–economists go some way to substantiating Kelman's second claim. Yet to suggest, without any qualification, that a similar degree of scepticism towards legislative activity permeates the process tradition seems quite bizarre. Few American legal theorists can have been more unworldly about the legislature than two of the greatest representatives of the process tradition, Henry Hart and Albert Sacks. Their distinctly 1950s, public interest-based

[62] On this matter, see generally ch. 4.

[63] See Kelman, *supra* n. 27, 199.

[64] On this point, see Duncan Kennedy, 'Legal Formality', *Jnl. Leg. Studs.*, 2 (1973), 351–98 at 396 fn. 64; and also the discussion of Hart and Sacks in ch. 4.

[65] See Richard A. Epstein, 'The Active Virtues', *Regulation*, (1985), 14–18; and also Bernard H. Siegan, 'Rehabilitating *Lochner*', *San Diego L. Rev.*, 22 (1985), 453–97.

conception of legislation—legislation, that is, conceived as 'the work of reasonable men pursuing reasonable purposes reasonably'[66]—has often been criticized by lawyer–economists and others on the basis that it entails an image of statutes emerging out of and embodying a political consensus which, in reality, rarely existed.[67] Contrary to Kelman's assertion, Hart and Sacks romanticized rather than criticized the legislative universe.

Kelman's third claim—that economic analysis and process jurisprudence share a preference for private ordering—in fact points to a fundamental difference rather than a similarity between the two traditions. For each tradition entails its own unique approach to the question of how properly to adjudicate disputes arising out of attempts at private ordering. Consider, for example, breach of contract. Hart and Sacks would argue that instances of breach ought to be adjudicated according to the principle that agreements ought to be observed—*pacta sunt servanda*.[68] In the literature of law and economics, however, a wholly different tack is adopted.[69] Breaches of contract ought to be permitted, certain economic analysts argue, so long as they meet with a peculiar standard of efficiency. If A reneges on his or her contract to supply goods to B in order to sell the same goods to C at a higher price, and if A is able and willing to compensate B fully with damages for injuries caused by his or her action or for loss of expectation, then B is left no worse off by the breach while A and C will be better off. Although the breach may have been wilful, it has nevertheless generated an improvement in the overall economic position of the parties.[70] It is an efficient breach, and, as such, it ought not to be discouraged by the courts.[71]

66 Henry M. Hart, Jr. and Albert M. Sacks, *The Legal Process: Basic Problems in the Making and Application of Law* (tentative edn. Cambridge, Mass.: unpublished mimeograph, 1958), 1157.

67 See e.g. Richard A. Posner, 'The Decline of Law as an Autonomous Discipline: 1962–1987', *Harvard L. Rev.*, 100 (1987), 761–80 at 773–4. ('Writing in the wake of the New Deal, of which they heartily approved, Hart and Sacks implicitly treated the legislature (including the original constitutional convention and the ratifying state legislatures) as a single mind, an intelligent and far-seeing mind, and moreover a mind that both was dedicated to serving the public interest and had a conception of the public interest identical to that of the judges who would be called on to interpret the legislation.') On the discrediting of the public interest theory of regulatory statute-making, see Stephen Breyer, *Regulation and Its Reform* (Cambridge, Mass.: Harvard University Press, 1982), 10.

68 See Hart and Sacks, *supra* n. 66, 159.

69 See, in particular, Richard A. Posner, *Economic Analysis of Law* (4th edn. Boston: Little, Brown & Co., 1992), 89–137. More generally, on the concept of private ordering in law and economics, see Michael J. Trebilcock, *The Limits of Freedom of Contract* (Cambridge, Mass.: Harvard University Press, 1993), 1–22.

70 See, generally, Robert L. Birmingham, 'Breach of Contract, Damage Measures, and Economic Efficiency', *Rutgers L. Rev.*, 24 (1970), 273–92.

71 See Richard A. Posner, 'The Strangest Attack Yet on Law and Economics', *Hofstra L. Rev.*, 20 (1992), 933–40 at 935–7.

The legal–economic concept of efficient breach has been the subject of much criticism. Even where compensation is paid to the party which has suffered the breach, it is argued, efficiency will rarely be the outcome.[72] Such criticism is not, however, of concern here. The point is, rather, that the doctrine of efficient breach highlights a fundamental difference between the law and economics and process traditions in American jurisprudence. Within the process tradition, breach of contract is adjudged to be impermissible because, as an issue of principle, promises ought to be kept. Within the law and economics tradition, however, this principle may be overridden by the dictates of efficiency. That a contract is a promise, that it creates an expectation in the mind of the promisee, that it might be considered morally binding '[b]y virtue of the basic Kantian principles of trust and respect'[73]—such claims cut little ice within the tradition of economic analysis. For efficiency is considered to cut much deeper than principle. The fundamental characteristic of a contract, from a legal–economic perspective, is not that it entails a promise but that it involves an exchange or a bargain. Thus it is that, with the flourishing of law and economics, a distinctive mind-set emerges in American jurisprudence. It is not the ghost of Langdellianism, or a return to or rejection of legal realism, or an offshoot of the process tradition, but a markedly different jurisprudential ethic. My primary aim here is to try to explain the evolution and the appeal of that ethic.

Today, law and economics is a subject over which controversy and confusion reign. Defining the subject is like trying to eat spaghetti with a spoon. Law and economics can be positive, normative, neo-classical, institutional, Austrian—quite simply, the subject is weighed down by a multitude of competing methodologies and perspectives which are not always easily distinguishable. However one conceives it, one finds that, between promoters and detractors, misunderstandings abound.[74] There is

[72] Critical literature on the doctrine of efficient breach is voluminious. Consider, for example, Ian R. Macneil, 'Efficient Breach of Contract: Circles in the Sky', *Virginia L. Rev.*, 68 (1982), 947–69; and also Leonard R. Jaffe, 'The Troubles with Law and Economics', *Hofstra L. Rev.*, 20 (1992), 777–932 at 782–851.

[73] Charles Fried, *Contract as Promise: A Theory of Contractual Obligation* (Cambridge, Mass.: Harvard University Press, 1981), 17.

[74] For a rather extreme illustration of misunderstanding in this context, see Robin Paul Malloy, 'Invisible Hand or Sleight of Hand? Adam Smith, Richard Posner and the Philosophy of Law and Economics', *U. Kansas L. Rev.*, 36 (1988), 209–59; Richard A. Posner, 'The Ethics of Wealth Maximization: Reply to Malloy', *U. Kansas L. Rev.*, 36 (1988), 261–65; Robin Paul Malloy, 'The Merits of the Smithian Critique: A Final Word on Smith and Posner', *U. Kansas L. Rev.*, 36 (1988), 267–74; 'Is Law and Economics Moral?—Humanistic Economics and a Classical Liberal Critique of Posner's Economic Analysis', *Valparaiso Univ. L. Rev.*, 24 (1990), 147–61; Richard A. Posner, 'Law and Economics *is* Moral', *Valparaiso Univ. L. Rev.*, 24 (1990), 163–73; Robin Paul Malloy, 'The Limits of Science in Legal Discourse—A Reply to Posner', *Valparaiso Univ. L. Rev.*, 24 (1990), 175–81.

even debate over whether or not the subject is coming or going. For some, law and economics has reached the peak of its popularity.[75] For others, it continues to grow from strength to strength.[76] Literature criticizing the subject proliferates as rapidly as the literature expounding it. For anyone coming fresh to law and economics, disorientation is a state quickly achieved.

Yet, throughout all of the American law and economics literature, critical and expositional alike, there seems to be something important missing. It is as if economic analysis is something that is simply there to be done or to be denounced. There is little indication as to why law and economics is actually there, rooted in the American jurisprudential tradition, in the first place. Indeed, rarely, if ever, in the legal–economic literature is any sort of attempt made to step back from the subject. American academic lawyers are by and large content simply to assume that, originally, the turn to economics represented an effort either to fulfil or to thwart the realist legal tradition. Yet such an assumption, we have seen, seems misconceived. Modern law and economics did not develop,

[75] See Fiss, 'The Law Regained', *supra* n. 19, 245. ('[L]aw and economics . . . seems to have peaked. None of the excitement and commitment generated by the early work of Richard Posner exists today. There is little interest in the efficiency hypothesis, and its invocation is met with an increasing sense of incredulity'); and also Morton J. Horwitz, 'Law and Economics: Science or Politics?', *Hofstra L. Rev.*, 8 (1980), 905–12 at 905. ('I have the strong feeling that the economic analysis of law has "peaked out" as the latest fad in legal scholarship and that it will soon be treated by the historians of legal thought like the writings of Lasswell and McDougal. Future legal historians will need to exercise their imaginations to figure out why so many people could have taken most of this stuff so seriously.') These observations seem to be implicitly comparative in nature—though it is far from clear as to what is being compared. Perhaps the basis of Fiss's and Horwitz's claims is that, comparatively speaking, the growth of law and economics had settled by the 1980s after the flurry of legal–economic activity in the law schools during the 1970s. On the growth of law and economics in the 1970s, see William A. Lovett, 'Economic Analysis and its Role in Legal Education', *Jnl. Leg. Educ.*, 26 (1974), 385–421. Fairly recently, Robert Ellickson has argued that 'law and economics is no longer growing as a scholarly or curricular force within the leading American law schools. Instead, it is simply holding previously won ground.' Robert C. Ellickson, 'Bringing Culture and Human Frailty to Rational Actors: A Critique of Classical Law and Economics', *Chicago-Kent L. Rev.*, 65 (1989), 23–55 at 26. He suggests also, however, that '[m]uch of the most rigorous L[aw and] E[conomics] work is now being done by faculty in economics departments and business schools,' and that, 'while LE may have plateaued at US law schools,' it is 'on the rise in US universities as a whole.' Robert C. Ellickson, letter to author, 30 June 1993.

[76] William Landes and Richard Posner have suggested 'that the influence of economics upon law was growing at least through the 1980s (it is too early to speak about the 1990s), though the rate of growth may have slowed beginning in the mid-1980s; that the growth in the influence of economics on law exceeded that of any other interdisciplinary or untraditional approach to law; and that the traditional approach . . . was in decline over this period relative to interdisciplinary approaches in general and the economic approach in particular.' William M. Landes and Richard A. Posner, 'The Influence of Economics on Law: A Quantitative Study', *Jnl. Law & Econ.*, 36 (1993), 385–424 at 424. It should be noted also that an American Law and Economics Association, which holds annual meetings, was founded in 1991.

nor did it rebel, under the wing of legal realism. But if we accept this argument, where does it leave us? How are we to explain the evolution of a distinctive North American legal–economic culture? How are we to account, furthermore, for the massive impact of that culture on American legal thought?

While American law professors may occasionally allude to questions such as these,[77] answers seem not to be forthcoming. Those with an interest in law and economics are generally too busy either expounding or denouncing the subject. Although I am certainly not uninterested in the many different approaches to and critical estimations of law and economics, my primary objective here is to engage in a more basic and unsophisticated form of inquiry. I want to try to cast light on the culture of economic analysis in American legal thought and to provide some insight into the history and the appeal of that culture. It is in the nature of this project that a good deal of attention be paid to the emergence of law and economics at the University of Chicago. However, it ought to be stressed immediately that Chicago was responsible only for the development of one distinctive type of economic analysis. Before Chicago, American law and economics possessed a rather different identity—to the extent, that is, that it possessed an identity at all.

FUMBLING IN THE DARK

Quite recently, the American legal historian, Herbert Hovenkamp, has studied the evolution of what he terms the first great law and economics movement.[78] This movement, he argues, began in the 1880s and developed throughout the Progressive era. Oriented originally towards regulatory issues—in particular, 'the creation and administration of an interstate railroad system'—the movement 'quickly moved into the law of trade restraints, and then into more general legislative and common law subjects such as criminal law, corporation law, tax, property and contract'.[79] Unlike modern, Chicago-inspired law and economics, Hovenkamp claims, 'the first great law & economics movement grew out of a reaction against emergent neoclassicism and a search for alternatives,' and was dominated

[77] See e.g. Donald H. Gjerdingen, 'The Coase Theorem and the Psychology of Common-law Thought', *Southern California L. Rev.*, 56 (1983), 711–60 at 759 (posing the question as to '*why* the Coase Theorem began to gain acceptance in the legal culture when it did'); and also James Boyd White, 'Economics and Law: Two Cultures in Tension', *Tennessee L. Rev.*, 54 (1986), 161–202 at 163 (suggesting that 'neoclassical microeconomics rests upon a broad base in our culture, to which it owes much of its intelligibility and appeal').

[78] Herbert Hovenkamp, 'The First Great Law & Economics Movement', *Stanford L. Rev.*, 42 (1990), 993–1058.

[79] Ibid. 994.

by 'more liberal American economists,' most of whom 'were interested in the relationship between law and the distribution of wealth in American society.'[80] While, however, this movement was ideologically distinct from its modern variant, it in fact prefigured a good deal of contemporary legal–economic debate. According to Hovenkamp, modern law and economics has, in certain ways, simply re-trodden ground already covered by the old law and economics;[81] in other ways, it has failed to reach the same level of economic sophistication. Whereas Chicago-dominated law and economics of the modern era 'has made a great deal of rapid progress by assuming away certain fundamental issues for which there is substantial consensus within the modern neoclassical economics community', the 'Progressive Era economists, particularly those writing about law & economics, argued strenuously over the basic ground rules of economics.'[82] Although their 'influence on American lawmakers has been surprisingly under-estimated',[83] these representatives of the first great law and economics movement were 'engaged in identifying fundamental assumptions, such as the principle of self-interest, and in determining basic economic concepts, such as the theory of value, the effect of involuntary redistribution, and the scope and meaning of marginalism. For these reasons their work was much more "fundamental" than most of law & economics today.'[84]

Hovenkamp's argument seems, in essence, to be that, so far as economic analysis is concerned, American lawyers have missed the boat. Law and economics was once a fairly sophisticated affair. Now, however, it is stuck in the rut of neo-classicism. This is winner's history with an unhappy ending: the least deserving economic movement becomes the toast of many an American law school, while the better, more theoretically-cultivated movement is condemned to obscurity. There are at least two basic problems with this position. First of all, in various ways, law and economics of the Progressive era was clearly theoretically less refined than its more modern incarnation. For example, certain economists of the Progressive era supported industrial monopoly,[85] and argued for minimum wage laws,[86] in ways which many contemporary economists, lawyer–economists

[80] Ibid. 994–5. In discussing 'the first great law & economics movement,' Hovenkamp employs the ampersand 'to suggest a single area of activity that is neither wholly law nor wholly economics' (ibid. 993 fn. 1).

[81] See e.g. Hovenkamp, *supra* n. 78, 1053–4.

[82] Ibid. 996–7.

[83] Ibid. 994.

[84] Ibid. 1058.

[85] See e.g. Henry Carter Adams, 'The Relation of the State to Industrial Action', *Publications of the American Economic Association*, 1 (1887), 6–64; and, more generally, Hovenkamp, *supra* n. 78, 999–1000.

[86] See e.g. George Gorham Groat, 'Economic Wage and Legal Wage', *Yale L.J.*, 33 (1924), 489–500 (criticizing the Supreme Court for its policy of *laissez-faire* in relation to wages); and, more generally, Hovenkamp, *supra* n. 78, 1009–13.

included, would consider naive.[87] Secondly, and in my opinion more importantly, it is far from clear that the first great law and economics movement of which Hovenkamp writes was either great, or even a movement. What Hovenkamp in fact identifies is a number of distinct economic perspectives—German historicism,[88] material welfarism,[89] institutionalism[90]—which were all, to a greater or lesser degree, applied to legal problems, and which all, in one way or another, appeared to challenge the basic assumption of classical political economy 'that the best state is the one that governs least'.[91] It is not at all obvious why these various perspectives should be considered to constitute a discrete movement, 'a single area of activity'.[92] Indeed, I would suggest that 'the first great law and economics movement' never actually existed.

So, what did exist? Without doubt, around the turn of this century, there emerged a good deal of literature which, without any stretch of the imagination, could be classified as law and economics literature.[93] But to search this literature for grand themes and theses is to search in vain. The vague notion that the law should somehow promote 'efficiency' clearly preoccupied some early lawyer–economists.[94] Yet one could argue that this preoccupation featured fairly prominently in late nineteenth and early twentieth-century American jurisprudence generally.[95] If there was a theme more or less exclusive to the law and economics literature of this period, it was, ironically, that there existed very little legal–economic

[87] On monopoly, for example, consider George S. Stigler, *The Economist as Preacher and Other Essays* (Chicago: University of Chicago Press, 1982), 38–54; and Richard A. Posner, 'The Social Costs of Monopoly and Regulation', *Jn. Pol. Econ.*, 83 (1975), 807–27.

[88] Hovenkamp, *supra* n. 78, 995. [89] Ibid. 1000. [90] Ibid. 1013.

[91] Ibid. 1009. [92] Ibid. 993 fn. 1.

[93] For an indication of just how much legal–economic literature did emerge around this period, see Warren J. Samuels, 'Legal–Economic Policy: A Bibliographical Survey', *Law Library Jnl.*, 58 (1965), 230–52 at 236–8. This body of literature would be all the more formidable if one were to look beyond the United States. See e.g. Michael Hutter, 'Early Contributions to Law and Economics—Adolf Wagner's *Grundlegung*', *Journal of Economic Issues*, 16 (1982), 131–47.

[94] See e.g. Henry Carter Adams, 'Economics and Jurisprudence', *Science*, 8 (1886), 15–19 at 17 (on the need 'for law to establish uniformity of action' in order to secure 'the efficiency of law in matters pertaining to industrial organization'). More generally, see M.W. Littleton, *Law and Economics* (Philadelphia: Law Academy of Philadelphia, 1911). In modern law and economics, as we shall see in due course, the term 'efficiency' acquired a conceptual specificity which it lacked in the early legal–economic literature—although one occasionally encounters early efforts at economic analysis of law which employ recognizably 'modern' conceptions of efficiency. See, for example, Giorgio Del Vecchio, 'Law and Economics', *Jnl. Soc. Philos.*, 1 (1936), 341–363 (vaguely-conceived argument to the effect that laws may be assessed in terms of Pareto efficiency).

[95] Consider, for example, Wesley Newcomb Hohfeld, 'A Vital School of Jurisprudence and Law: Have American Universities Awakened to the Enlarged Opportunities and Responsibities of the Present Day?', *Proceedings of the Association of American Law Schools*, (1914), 76–139 at 109 (on the need to develop a 'functional, or dynamic, jurisprudence' for the purpose, among other things, of promoting 'maximum efficiency' in the courts).

literature and that the relationship between law and economics needed to be explored and cultivated. Writing in 1886, Henry Carter Adams, an economist of the German historical school, insisted that 'one cannot disregard the close relation that exists between economics and jurisprudence. Both branches of thought are part of the larger study of society, and neither can be satisfactorily pursued to the exclusion of the other.'[96] Yet, generally speaking, this close relationship was indeed being disregarded. In his presidential address to the American Economic Association in 1904, Edwin Seligman, another economist influenced by German historicism, lamented that '[w]e think that we appreciate the social basis of economic law, but in reality our appreciation is fragmentary.'[97] In particular, Seligman argued, those swayed by the classical model of political economy were mistaken in their belief that wealth-distributional, 'economic' law—particularly taxation law—undermined the freedom of the individual. 'The subordination of the individual to the social element in economic life and law,' he claimed, 'does not imply any depreciation of the individual as such, nor does it mean that the ideal polity of the future must resemble the crude socialism that is so loudly proclaimed by some.'[98] For laws created to serve the interests of society do not necessarily compromise the desires and aspirations of individual citizens. Indeed, while '[m]oral development means self-development, and progress can only come through freedom . . . [w]e must not . . . forget that the individual has become what he is largely through society . . . that individual ethics is the result of social ethics, and that individual progress is largely the consequence of social progress.'[99] In essence, Seligman was arguing that American economists in general were jurisprudentially naive, that they had no appreciation of how law functioned and that, in consequence, they assumed that, while economic law could serve either the interests of the individual or of the state, it could not simultaneously serve both. So long as economics and law were treated as wholly distinct bodies of knowledge, it seemed, the development of economics as a discipline would be substantially impeded.

Although the legal–economic perspective which Seligman presented was very much his own, his feeling that the two disciplines were not really connecting was more widely shared. 'The relations between these two professions', H. W. Humble concluded in 1908, 'cannot be considered close. The present condition is one of isolation and, apparently, of unconcern.'[100] Eugene Gilmore, a professor of law at the University of

[96] Adams, *supra* n. 94, 15–16.

[97] Edwin R. A. Seligman, 'Social Aspects of Economic Law', *Publications of the American Economic Association*, 18 (1904), 49–73 at 50.

[98] Ibid. 72.

[99] Ibid. 73.

[100] H. W. Humble, 'Economics From a Legal Standpoint', *American L. Rev.*, 42 (1908), 379–86 at 379.

Wisconsin, observed similarly in 1916 that '[t]he relation between law and economics seems either not to be perceived, or, if perceived, not to be regarded as a relationship desirable or feasible of much cultivation.'[101] Blame for this state of affairs was laid principally at the door of the American law school. '[D]uring his period of academic training,' Humble argued, 'the law student studies economics, only to find on entering law school that he is forced to discard . . . many of the principles so earnestly contended for by his professor of economics . . . He learns that, in the eyes of the law, employees and employers are on a perfect equality, protected alike in their freedom of contract and with the same right to appeal to the Courts for assistance.'[102] The economic theory on which such learning is premissed, Roscoe Pound insisted in 1909, is 'at variance with the common knowledge of mankind'.[103] If economists seemed unable to understand law, lawyers were hardly faring better with economics.

Legal education was generally perceived to be the root of the problem. In 1917, James Parker Hall of the University of Chicago Law School suggested that it is 'more important that lawyers should have some training in economics than that economists should know much about law, desirable as both may be; because experience has demonstrated that the impact of novel economic ideas upon well-established rules of law is quite innocuous, while the economic notions of lawyers and judges are very likely to be translated into the decisions of courts'.[104] For Hall's colleague, Herman Oliphant, the best means of introducing such training was for law schools to develop courses in business law, a subject, he argued, in which legal and economic methods clearly combined.[105] Others envisaged a rather more formidable task. In his address to the American Economic Association in 1924, William Draper Lewis, then Director of the American Law Institute, argued that only with the development of a more social-scientific legal education would the economic sensibilities of American lawyers begin to improve.[106] What was gradually becoming clear was that, however the introduction of economic methods into legal education was to be achieved, an increasing number of American lawyers felt that such an achievement was highly desirable.

It seems instructive in this regard to note that, in the late 1920s and 1930s, certain British lawyers, particularly at the London School of

[101] Eugene Allen Gilmore, 'The Relation of Law and Economics', *Jnl. Pol. Econ.*, 25 (1917), 69–79 at 71.

[102] Humble, *supra* n. 100, 379–80.

[103] Roscoe Pound, 'Liberty of Contract', *Yale L.J.*, 18 (1909), 454–87 at 454.

[104] James Parker Hall, 'Discussion', *Jnl. Pol. Econ.*, 25 (1917), 80–82 at 80.

[105] Herman Oliphant, 'Discussion', *Jnl. Pol. Econ.*, 25 (1917), 82–3.

[106] William Draper Lewis, 'Adaptation of the Law to Changing Economic Conditions', *Am. Bar Assoc. Jnl.*, 12 (1925), 11–15 at 14–15.

Economics, exhibited a sense of anxiety not unlike that of their American colleagues over the matter of how best to develop hitherto neglected connections between the disciplines of law and economics.[107] Yet, in Britain, little if anything was born of this anxiety. British law and economics of the 1930s appears to have gone nowhere fast. Properly to explain this would probably require that one look to the state of British economic as well as legal research during this period. Certainly it seems quite remarkable that Cambridge, with its strong tradition of marginal utility theory and welfare economics, appears around this time to have produced nothing in the way of economic analysis of law. But at least part of the explanation for the differences between the early twentieth-century American and British receptions of law and economics must rest on the fact that profound differences existed—and indeed still exist—between the British and American systems of legal education. To summarize—indeed, to skim over—a great deal in a few words, the American legal education system was, and perhaps still is, characterized by a peculiar style and an intensity of self-analysis and introspection which has never really surfaced, or certainly has never surfaced at the same level, in British law faculties. Traditionally, American academic lawyers have been far less reluctant than have their British counterparts to raise questions about what it is that

[107] See, in particular, William A. Robson, 'Legal Conceptions of Capital and Income', in T. E. Gregory and Hugh Dalton (eds.), *London Essays in Economics: In Honour of Edwin Cannan* (London: George Routledge & Sons, 1927), 249–79 esp. 251, 279; D. Hughes Parry, 'Economic Theories in English Case Law', *Law Q. Rev.*, 47 (1931), 183–202 esp. 190 (arguing that the courts only produce 'economic' decisions when they give effect to economic policies embodied in legislation) and 195 (claiming that '[o]f all doctrines it is the political and economic doctrine of *laissez-faire* that has made the deepest and most enduring marks upon our judge-made law' and that '[f]or a century and a half the doctrine of *laissez-faire* has determined the general attitude of the Bench towards the law'); and H. W. Robinson, 'Law and Economics', *Mod. L. Rev.*, 2 (1939), 257–65 esp. 257 (observing that 'the relationship between law and economics has never been given the consideration it deserves') and 260. ('The economic system must be adapted to changing conditions and must incorporate new ideas if it is to attain the highest possible efficiency. It follows that its institutions must play an important part in this adaptation and that new laws must be made or old laws must be modified in the light of new developments.')

Around this period, Colin Cooke at University College, Oxford, was attempting to steer law and economics in a rather different direction. Whereas the LSE writers, in so far as they exhibited a distinct theoretical perspective, seemed to be swayed by broadly-institutionalist economic sentiments (see e.g. Robson, ibid. 251–2), Cooke was more of a neo-classicist. See, in particular, C. A. Cooke, 'Adam Smith and Jurisprudence', *Law Q. Rev.*, 61 (1935), 326–32 esp. 332 ('[E]conomics and law . . . have a common bearing on the social order in that their rational purpose is to supply the criteria of increasing social advantage. . . . And it is becoming more important that there should be some meeting of the formal theories of economics and law in this application'); 'Legal Rule and Economic Function', *Economic Jnl.*, 46 (1936), 21–43 (commenting on the fact that laws forbidding contracts in restraint of trade themselves offend against the principle of freedom of contract); and 'The Legal Content of the Profit Concept', *Yale L.J.*, 46 (1937), 436–46 esp. 437. ('The few economic studies of conceptions common to law and economics indicate to what an extent the economic ideas used in law are inconsistent and even incoherent.')

they do, about what constitutes their reason for being. Viewed against this backdrop, those American lawyers who first turned to economic analysis appear in retrospect to have been engaging in the distinctive style of academic soul-searching which seems almost to run in their blood.

But what came of this soul-searching? Did anything emerge from the early law and economics literature? Or was it all fumbling in the dark? The answer seems to be that while, in the early part of this century, certain themes were identified which would come to feature prominently in the development of law and economics, these themes were merely sketched or suggested rather than explored. Long before the development, in the 1960s, of a distinctively economic approach to accident and nuisance law, for example, there had emerged various isolated and generally neglected studies in the law of tort which at least hinted at such an approach.[108] Furthermore, like their modern successors, early proponents of economic analysis disagreed over the matter of how, exactly, law might be said to be 'economic'. Certainly some celebrated what they considered to be the implicit economic function of the common law tradition. '[T]he glory of the common law', wrote Harold Healy of the Denver Bar in 1928, rests largely in its natural capacity for distributing economic surplus:

> [I]t might appear from the start of the common law down through the ages, that when some new economic force, combination or business system and condition begins to be felt that the person with the economic surplus gets the first break and imposes a rule of law designed to hold his own property—so with entails, restraints, uses, perpetuities, ultra vires as a corporate defence, lack of warranty and the like. Then comes the urge of the dividers and the pendulum reverses itself. And as the industry grows older and more settled, and the law of supply and demand evens up what was once surplus, the pendulum comes back to centre, and legal rules come more nearly to logical principles. Consciously and unconsciously judges as well as juries consider economic surplus in deciding cases and making law.[109]

Others, while equally enamoured of what they considered to be the economic logic implicit in the common law tradition, interpreted that logic rather differently. The stability of the American common law, insisted Homer Hoyt of Beloit College in 1918, 'aids the present competitive

[108] See e.g. Francis Bohlen, *The Basis of Affirmative Obligations in the Law of Tort* (Philadelphia: Department of Law of the University of Pennsylvania, 1905); Henry T. Terry, 'Negligence', *Harvard L. Rev.*, 29 (1915), 40–54; Roscoe Pound, 'The Economic Interpretation and the Law of Torts', *Harvard L. Rev.*, 53 (1940), 365–85; and, more generally, William M. Landes and Richard A. Posner, *The Economic Structure of Tort Law* (Cambridge, Mass.: Harvard University Press, 1987), 4–5. The literature on this point expands considerably if one looks outside of the American jurisprudential tradition. See e.g. Izhak Englard, 'Victor Mataja's *Liability for Damages From an Economic Viewpoint:* A Centennial to an Ignored Economic Analysis of Tort', *Int. Rev. Law & Econ.*, 10 (1990), 173–191.

[109] Harold H. Healy, 'Economic Surplus and the Law', *Dicta*, 6 (1928), 15–23 at 17, 21.

organization of society' and 'has enormously increased the efficiency of production'.[110] For when the system of common law rules is generally characterized by certainty and stability, entrepreneurs have little reason to fear the judiciary precipitating radical legal change which might adversely influence the market. All they need fear, in fact, are the initiatives of meddlesome legislators intent on disrupting the natural economic efficiency of the common law system:

> The statutory law is more likely to be swayed by the caprice of the moment, to be controlled by narrow interests for personal gain, to enact every fad and fashion into law, and to allow a swapping of personal favours at the expense of the general welfare. . . . The common law is more likely to follow a formal rule after the reasons for its adoption have passed, to allow vested interests to reap a social income after their function has disappeared, to repudiate new movements as transient because they conflict with fundamental principles, and to enforce a standard of morality from which this age has departed. . . . If changes in law are confined to the limits established by the experience table of the common law, modified by the more fundamental changes that occur from time to time, vested rights of property will not be confiscated by the operation of the legal system to any appreciable extent, and the fundamental bases of economic relationships will not be unnecessarily jolted. Although such development may be slow, it will not be followed by the back-sliding that succeeds more rapid progress.[111]

This view—that the economic virtue of the common law system rests in its innate conservatism—was by no means popular among early advocates of the economic analysis of law. Indeed, it was very much a minority view. Most early proponents of law and economics were insistent that the legislature alone was the appropriate forum for formulating and implementing economic policy. 'That the courts ought to be removed from political influences,' the President of the American Economic Association wrote in 1915, 'all right-minded men admit.'[112] Given, some commentators argued, that the courts, and particularly the Supreme Court, had tended to fall back all too predictably on the doctrine of *laissez-faire* when confronted with disputes which were economic in nature, it seemed only right to urge judicial restraint over matters economic and to push for more economic policy-formulation by the legislature. After all, Mark Lichtman argued in 1927, statutes grow out of struggles among economic interest groups competing within the democratic framework; more often than not,

[110] Homer Hoyt, 'The Economic Function of the Common Law', *Jnl. Pol. Econ.*, 26 (1918), 167–99 at 179. For a similar, Social Darwinist perspective, see Robert von Moschzisker, 'The Citizen, the State, and Our Economic System', *Dickinson L. Rev.*, 27 (1922), 1–20 at 8–9.

[111] Hoyt, *supra*, n. 110, 198–9.

[112] John H. Gray, 'Economics and the Law', *Papers and Proceedings of the American Economic Association*, 5 (1915), 3–23 at 13.

they 'are enacted by legislatures in response to direct and immediate economic demands'.[113] Judge-made law, by contrast, lacks this explicitly economic dimension.[114] Viewed in the light of modern political theory, especially public choice theory, [115] this argument—blind, as it is, to the possibility that legislation may sometimes reflect not healthy economic competition but the desire of a powerful industry for the absence of such—seems distinctly naive. Yet it is an argument which rests at the heart of a good deal of the early law and economics literature. That is, in much of this literature we encounter a deep distrust of the perceived economic perspective of the courts, and a gargantuan faith in the economic good sense of the legislature.

The distrust of the courts was perhaps easy to understand. For this was law and economics emerging in the *Lochner* era. Much of the legal–economic analysis of this period started out from the premiss that there could be no economic jurisprudence more unacceptable than the Supreme Court's fusion of free exchange and natural selection.[116] Lawyers such as Robert Hale, Karl Llewellyn, John Dawson and John Dalzell endeavoured to show that the economic freedom by which the Supreme Court swore was not really freedom at all, that it was merely freedom to engage in economic coercion.[117] The Court's mistake, these writers argued, was to assume the existence of a formal equality of bargaining rights among economic agents and, on that basis, to declare constitutionally invalid state legislation which attempted to redress real inequalities of bargaining power. Such legislation—guaranteeing, for example, maximum work-hours and minimum wages for employees—was seen to facilitate rather than to impede economic freedom; for the eradication of inequalities of bargaining power would mean the elimination of economic agents capable of using their wealth to coerce others into accepting their contractual terms. Thus it was that legislation was considered to be the tonic necessary to cure the ills of the common law: legislation would replace *Lochner*-style *laissez-faire*

[113] Mark M. Lichtman, 'Economics, the Basis of Law', *American L. Rev.*, 61 (1927), 357–87 at 361; and, for a comparativist perspective which offers much the same argument, see also Calvin B. Hoover, 'Economic Forces in the Evolution of Civil and Canon Law', *Southwestern Political and Social Science Quarterly*, 10 (1929), 42–55.

[114] Lichtman, *supra* n. 113, 379.

[115] See, in this context, Daniel A. Farber and Philip P. Frickey, *Law and Public Choice: A Critical Introduction* (Chicago: University of Chicago Press, 1991), 21–33.

[116] See e.g. *Lochner* v. *New York* (1905) 198 U.S. 45; *Coppage* v. *Kansas* (1915) 236 U.S. 1.

[117] See Robert L. Hale, 'Coercion and Distribution in a Supposedly Non-coercive State', *Political Science Quarterly*, 38 (1923), 470–94; Karl N. Llewellyn, 'What Price Contract?—An Essay in Perspective', *Yale L.J.*, 40 (1931), 704–51; John P. Dawson, 'Economic Duress—An Essay in Perspective', *Michigan L. Rev.*, 45 (1947), 253–90; John Dalzell, 'Duress by Economic Pressure', *North Carolina L. Rev.*, 20 (1942), 237–77, 341–86.

with a real economic freedom—a freedom based on widespread equality of bargaining power as opposed to a notional equality of bargaining rights.[118]

This was basically institutionalist economics applied to law. Hale and others were, in essence, insisting that economic freedom is determined not by natural laws of the market but by the manner in which legal institutions function. As Karl Llewellyn explained, 'legal institutions fix and guarantee the presuppositions on which the economic order rests.'[119] Ironically, while lawyers were using institutionalist economics in an effort to undermine the classical concept of free exchange in a very specific fashion, those institutionalist economists who turned their attention to law seemed all at sea with the subject. John Commons, for example, wrote vaguely about how the disciplines of law and economics were similarly preoccupied with the concept of scarcity. '[T]he science of economics,' he claimed, 'which is a science of the good and bad habits and common practices of farmers, landlords, business men, workingmen and others in their mutual adjustments to scarcity of resources and in their competitions and conflicts imposed upon them by that scarcity, is a science of the fundamental concepts on which the science of law is also grounded.'[120] Other writers, apparently impressed by this claim, seemed incapable of expanding upon it. 'Economics,' one institutionalist observed in 1932, 'is the science which deals with the proportioning of limited means for purposes assumed to be constant. The juridical science, as far as it is concerned with group forms, is the science which studies the transforming of the order of proportioning.'[121] In the same year, another Commons-inspired lawyer–economist suggested that '[f]unctional jurisprudence, in the economic field, takes various scarcity conditions and observes the effect of various kinds of group behaviour with regard to scarcity consequences in reference to a purpose to produce certain scarcity consequences.'[122] Observations such as these served only to give weight to Ronald Coase's remark that early twentieth-century institutionalism was simply 'a mass of descriptive detail waiting for a theory, or a fire.'[123]

Yet surely these attempts to outline an institutionalist approach to law

[118] See e.g. Llewellyn, *supra* n. 117, 734. On Hale's faith in legislation, See Neil Duxbury, 'Robert Hale and the Economy of Legal Force', *Mod. L. Rev.*, 53 (1990), 421–44 at 442.

[119] Karl N. Llewellyn, 'The Effect of Legal Institutions Upon Economics', *Am. Econ. Rev.*, 15 (1925), 665–83 at 678.

[120] John R. Commons, 'Law and Economics', *Yale L.J.*, 34 (1925), 371–82 at 374.

[121] Josef Solterer, 'Relations Between Economics and Juridical Science', *Georgetown L.J.*, 21 (1932), 9–20 at 20.

[122] Raymond J. Heilman, 'The Correlation Between the Sciences of Law and Economics', *California L. Rev.*, 20 (1932), 379–95 at 387. For a less muddled and more critical attempt from this period to explain Commons's institutionalism, see Ralph F. Fuchs, 'The Newer Social Scientists Look at Law', *St. Louis L. Rev.*, 13 (1927), 33–55 at 47–52.

[123] Ronald H. Coase, 'The New Institutional Economics', *Jnl. of Institutional and Theoretical Economics*, 140 (1984), 229–32 at 230.

and economics could not have been utterly devoid of a perceptible point—surely there was something going on. But what? Why, to be more specific, were Commons and his followers so preoccupied with the concept of scarcity? The answer seems to be that scarcity was regarded as the key to resolving one of the major problems of late nineteenth and early twentieth-century American law—the problem, that is, of how to determine fair property values. 'That which in law is named property arises from the principle of scarcity in economics,' Commons argued.[124] The American courts, when they attempt to determine reasonable property values, are implicitly relying on the economic concept of scarcity: the greater the scarcity of property, the higher its value.[125] This was a fact which, according to Commons and other institutionalists, the courts had generally ignored. In determining property valuations, Donald Richberg observed in 1933, the judiciary tended to be under the illusion 'that, although market prices may rise and fall, at least those things which are commonly bought and sold always have a certain definite and ascertainable "value" '.[126] Indeed, it was by insisting that property must have an inherent market value that the courts had succeeded in defining it in a circular fashion.[127] In the field of rate regulation, for example, the courts were ascertaining the rateable value of property by attempting to establish a proxy for market value, which itself was discovered by looking to its current rateable value. 'We can thus find what rates are reasonable', Robert Hale observed, 'by first ascertaining the value of the property, and we can ascertain the value of the property only by first finding what rates are reasonable.'[128] In their quest to discover fair market values for property, Commons concluded, judges were 'reasoning in a circle'.[129]

This critique of property valuation reveals further how early lawyer–economists were by and large profoundly sceptical of the ability of the American courts to grapple satisfactorily with essentially economic issues. Not that these lawyer–economists were of one mind when it came to the economic sensibilities of legislators. Certainly in the field of taxation law, for example, there was some feeling that legislation was founded in large measure on bad economics. The American government would do well to

[124] John R. Commons, 'The Problem of Correlating Law, Economics and Ethics', *Wisconsin L. Rev.*, 8 (1932), 3–26 at 26.

[125] Commons, *supra* n. 120, 377, 381–2.

[126] Donald R. Richberg, 'Economic Illusions Underlying Law', *U. Chicago L. Rev.*, 1 (1933), 96–101 at 97.

[127] See, generally, Horwitz, *supra* n. 45, 160–7.

[128] Robert Lee Hale, 'The "Fair Value" Merry-go-Round, 1898–1938: A Forty-year Journey from Rates-Based-on-Value to Value-Based-on-Rates', *Illinois L. Rev.*, 33 (1939), 517–31 at 517.

[129] John R. Commons, *Legal Foundations of Capitalism* (New York: Macmillan, 1924), 196.

heed Adam Smith, Charles Haglund argued in 1933, and treat income rather than property as the measure of ability to pay taxes; for not only is income a more reliable measure of wealth, but property, especially when intangible, is often impossible to tax.[130] Generally, however, there seems to run throughout the greater proportion of the early law and economics literature the feeling that, while the American courts had tended to fare poorly when dealing with economic problems, the capacity of the legislature to resolve such problems had yet to be properly tested.

The Depression and the New Deal served to intensify this feeling. The economic collapse of the late 1920s had tarnished the image of American big business and had prompted questions about the government's role in regulating enterprise. Legislation, it was believed, would surely succeed where the courts had failed in correcting market failures and advancing economic productivity in the public interest. The sense that business activity was often economically unsound, and that there was a need for more comprehensive public regulation of such activity, featured prominently in the economic theorizing of this period. In 1933, Edward Chamberlin, then assistant professor of economics at Harvard University, lamented the failure of price theorists and economists in general to appreciate that, 'in real life,' there exists no 'complete theoretical distinction between competition and monopoly'.[131] The endeavour to explain actual competition by reference to a theory of pure competition, he contended, 'has not only led to false conclusions about the facts; it has obscured the theory as well'.[132] Since, in reality, it is 'rarely free of monopoly elements', actual competition needs to be explained by reference to a theory of imperfect rather than pure competition.[133] Whereas, under a system of pure competition, '[t]he utilities offered by all sellers to all buyers must be identical,'[134] the dominant feature of real,

[130] Charles G. Haglund, 'Fundamental Economic and Legal Difficulties with Taxation and Some Suggested Remedies', *Kentucky L.J.*, 21 (1933), 260–307. The Chicago lawyer–economist of this period, Henry Simons, argued for taxation of income and property, though his primary point was that American government underestimated the potential of income taxation. See Henry C. Simons, *Personal Income Taxation: The Definition of Income as a Problem of Fiscal Policy* (Chicago: University of Chicago Press, 1938), 29, 72, 151–3, 205.

[131] Edward Chamberlin, *The Theory of Monopolistic Competition* (Cambridge, Mass.: Harvard University Press, 1933), 3. By coincidence, in England in the same year, there appeared a book by the Cambridge economist, Joan Robinson, offering an argument similar to that presented by Chamberlin. See Joan V. Robinson, *The Economics of Imperfect Competition* (London: Macmillan, 1933). Whereas, however, Chamberlin was concerned primarily with market advantages generated by product differentiation, Robinson was concerned more generally with the problem of oligopoly or tacit collusion between firms—a problem which can occur even when colluding firms produce identical goods. See James A. Clifton, 'Competition and the Evolution of the Capitalist Mode of Production', *Cambridge Jnl. of Economics*, 1 (1977), 137–51 at 149; and, on the similarities and differences between Chamberlin's and Robinson's arguments, Ben B. Seligman, *Main Currents in Modern Economics: Economic Thought Since 1870* (New York: Free Press, 1962), 716–29.

[132] Chamberlin, *supra* n. 131. [133] Ibid. [134] Ibid. 8.

imperfect competition is product differentiation. Sellers, Chamberlin argued, would develop frivolous innovations or engage in excessive advertising in the effort to demonstrate the difference between their product and that of their competitors.[135] Yet such initiatives were but an indication of an undercompetitive market. The effort and expenditure devoted to marketing strategies meant that output tended to be lower and prices higher than they would have been under a less imperfect system of competition. In their quest for product differentiation, firms were serving neither the interests of the consumer nor of the economy. In short, Chamberlin implied, they were acting irresponsibly.

Chamberlin was not the first to make such a suggestion. In *The Modern Corporation and Private Property*, first published in 1932, the lawyer Adolf Berle and the economist Gardiner Means observed that an inherent characteristic of the modern business corporation was the separation of ownership and control.[136] Although they may own the majority of a corporation's shares, shareholders will have little or no say in its management. Since, furthermore, they are likely to be a highly diffuse group, shareholders will usually be incapable of articulating collectively their shared economic concerns—assuming such shared concerns exist—about the management of the corporation. Managers, accordingly, are left free to pursue their own economic interests. The fundamental problem with the modern corporation, Berle and Means argued, is that managerial interests tend to be at variance not only with shareholder interests but also with the interests of the public at large. Corporate management pursues size for its own sake, maximizing output rather than profits; and while profits remain relatively low, managerial salaries soar ever higher.[137] The modern corporation turns out, accordingly, to be a highly inefficient entity, serving neither the shareholder nor the American economy. If a clear message emerged from the studies of Berle and Means and Chamberlin alike, it was that American enterprise was in dire need of legal regulation.

Certainly in the 1930s, this message was heard and heeded. In 1933, *Time* magazine hailed *The Modern Corporation and Private Property* as 'the economic bible of the Roosevelt administration'.[138] While their book, even in the early 1930s, was not without its critics,[139] Berle and Means's observations on the inefficiency of large corporations did indeed seem to

[135] See ibid. 71–4.

[136] Adolf A. Berle and Gardiner C. Means, *The Modern Corporation and Private Property* (New York: Macmillan, 1932).

[137] Ibid. 10–46.

[138] *Time*, 24 April 1993, 14, quoted in Herbert Hovenkamp, *Enterprise and American Law, 1836–1937* (Cambridge, Mass.: Harvard University Press, 1991), 360. On Berle and Means's work in historical context, see more generally Robert Kuttner, 'The Corporation in America: Is it Socially Redeemable?', *Dissent*, Winter 1993, 35–49.

[139] See e.g. Theodore M. Ave-Lallemant, 'Critique of a Revision of Some Fundamental Economic Concepts', *Marquette L. Rev.*, 18 (1933), 20–43.

have influenced government policy. New Deal deconcentration statutes such as the Glass–Steagall Banking Act of 1933[140] and the Public Utility Holding Company Act of 1935[141] were enacted in order to facilitate the breaking up of larger corporate structures into smaller commercial entities. This policy of deconcentration was extended still further in the late 1930s and 1940s as the Antitrust Division, initially under the leadership of Thurman Arnold, made extensive use of its power under Section 2 of the Sherman Act to prosecute firms engaging in monopolistic activity.[142] With Berle and Means, it seemed, the correlation of legal and economic inquiry had at last amounted to something. Here was a legal–economic perspective which justified the use of legislation to regulate economic affairs. According to one legal historian, Berle and Means, along with Chamberlin, had succeeded in demonstrating that only economic inefficiency can come of entrusting the development of enterprise to the invisible hand of the market.[143] Together, these authors had discredited the classical theory of business enterprise and had demonstrated that corporate activity required close scrutiny and careful regulation. 'By the end of the New Deal little was left of the classical corporation. . . . The invisible hand of the market had been struck aside by the very visible hand of the state.'[144]

For all that this conclusion is rich in rhetorical appeal, it seems overstated.[145] Rather than wither away in the 1930s, the classical theory of economic competition began very gradually to develop afresh. In certain quarters, faith in the efficacy of unregulated markets had remained intact. And it was out of this faith, rather than out of the tradition of Berle and Means, that modern law and economics emerged. While their work may have represented the crowning glory of early legal–economic analysis, Berle and Means implicitly accepted a theory of regulation which could hardly have been further divorced from the neo-classical economic world-view on which a good deal of modern law and economics scholarship is

140 48 Stat. 162 (1933) (codified as amended at 12 USC ss. 377–8 (1982)).

141 49 Stat. 803 (1935) (codified as amended at 15 USC ss. 79a–z (1982)).

142 See Frederick M. Rowe, 'The Decline of Antitrust and the Delusions of Models: The Faustian Pact of Law and Economics', *Georgetown L.J.*, 72 (1984), 1511–70 at 1520–4; William E. Kovacic, 'Failed Expectations: The Troubled Past and Uncertain Future of the Sherman Act as a Tool for Deconcentration', *Iowa L. Rev.*, (1989), 1105–50 at 1116–19.

143 See Hovenkamp, *supra* n. 138, 349–62; and also his 'The Classical Corporation in American Legal Thought', *Georgetown L.J.*, 76 (1988), 1593–689 at 1672–88. It ought to be stressed, however, that Berle and Means were arguing not, principally, for increased corporate regulation, but for increased shareholder power. On Berle in particular as an advocate of corporatism, see Roberta Romano, 'Metapolitics and Corporate Law Reform', *Stanford L. Rev.*, 36 (1984), 923–1016 esp. at 936–8.

144 Hovenkamp, *supra* n. 138, 362.

145 See Geoffrey P. Miller, 'The Rise and Fall of the Classical Corporation', *U. Chicago L. Rev.*, 59 (1992), 1677–87 at 1687.

founded. Much of the early law and economics literature had emerged from the premiss that America could legislate its way out of economic trouble. In the post-New Deal era, however, American lawyer–economists began gradually to embrace a very different premiss.

CHICAGO BEFORE CHICAGO

The change which was under way was largely attributable to intellectual developments in the faculties of law and economics at the University of Chicago. Histories of early twentieth-century American legal thought have tended to pay little attention to the Chicago Law School. Harvard had the Langdellian tradition. Columbia and Yale were the great centres of realist legal thought. But a veil has tended to be drawn over what was going on elsewhere. Edmund Kitch speculates that when, in 1929, Robert Maynard Hutchins resigned as Dean of the Yale Law School to become President of the University of Chicago, this may have 'led to a receptiveness to the social sciences in the law school at Chicago'.[146] For two reasons, however, such speculation ought to be doubted. First of all, it appears that when Hutchins left New Haven, he omitted to take his realist sentiments with him (see Chapter 4). Once at Chicago, he began to doubt that the realist appeal to the social sciences had ever amounted to anything: legal realists, he suggested, saluted the social sciences but did not know how to utilize them.[147] Secondly, and perhaps more significantly, interdisciplinary study at the Chicago Law School long predated the arrival of Hutchins. Indeed, a modest tradition of such study can be traced back to the turn of this century.[148] Hutchins certainly did nothing to discourage the development of this tradition.[149] However, the main impetus for the cultivation of interdisciplinary research appears to have come from within the Law School itself. In the 1930s, under the deanship of Wilber Katz, the faculty developed, and for a number of years implemented, a plan for a four-year curriculum embracing both professional and interdisciplinary legal

[146] Edmund W. Kitch (ed.), 'The Fire of Truth: A Remembrance of Law and Economics at Chicago, 1932–1970', *Jnl. Law & Econ.*, 26 (1983), 163–234 at 165 (comment by Kitch).

[147] See Robert M. Hutchins, 'The Autobiography of an Ex-Law Student', *U. Chicago L. Rev.*, 1 (1934), 511–18 at 512–13.

[148] See Frank L. Ellsworth, *Law on the Midway: The Founding of the University of Chicago Law School* (Chicago: The Law School of the University of Chicago, 1977), 98–9.

[149] See Mortimer J. Adler, 'Reflections on the Law School in the '30s', *U. Chicago Law Alumni Jnl.*, 3 (1977), 37–40 at 37–9. ('When President Hutchins invited me to come to the University of Chicago in the Fall of 1930, he . . . proposed that I divide my teaching at Chicago three ways—one quarter in the philosophy department, one quarter in the psychology department and one quarter in the law school—and that, in addition, I conduct with him as co-moderator a great books seminar for a selected group of entering freshmen.')

study.[150] 'It was that new plan', Edward Levi recalls, 'which expanded the horizons of the School to include such radical subjects as economics and accounting.'[151]

In 1939, the Chicago Law School appointed its first professor of economics, Henry Simons. The appointment was hardly path-breaking. Over a decade earlier, Yale Law School, under the deanship of Hutchins, had appointed Walton Hale Hamilton, an institutionalist from the economics department. While Hamilton was by no means entirely uninspirational on the Yale law faculty—Thurman Arnold, for example, came under his spell—his interests generally did not accord with those of his colleagues.[152] Indeed, it is questionable whether, by the time he joined the faculty, he was still particularly interested in economics—certainly much of his work of the early 1930s could have come from the pen of an anthropologist or a psychologist rather than an economist.[153] Possibly this explains why Hamilton failed to give economic analysis any sort of profile at Yale. Simons was, in this regard, somewhat different. Like Hamilton, he had crossed from one department in his University to another. Unlike Hamilton, however, in making this transition, he brought a fair deal of intellectual baggage with him.

Simons's first appointment at the University of Chicago had been as a lecturer in the economics department in 1927. 'The Economics Department of the University of Chicago was regarded as the best in the country,' one his colleagues from that period recollects, 'with the possible exception of its Harvard rival.'[154] Whatever its status happened to be, what is certainly clear is that Chicago economics of that era was characterized by a degree of intellectual diversity which would to a large extent evaporate in later decades. Mathematical economists, Keynesians, socialists, institutionalists and neo-classicists worked side by side—and by no means wholly harmoniously.[155] To understand how the Chicago Law School came to

[150] See Wilber G. Katz, 'A Four-Year Program for Legal Education', *U. Chicago L. Rev.*, 4 (1937), 527–36.

[151] Edward H. Levi, 'Reminiscences', *U. Chicago Law Alumni Jnl.*, 3 (1977), 23–7 at 26; and cf. also Katz, *supra* n. 150, 527. ('Perhaps the most striking feature of our plan is the incorporation of subjects such as economics, political theory, and psychology.')

[152] See John Henry Schlegel, 'American Legal Realism and Empirical Social Science: From the Yale Experience', *Buffalo L. Rev.*, 28 (1979), 459–586 at 494.

[153] See e.g. Walton Hale Hamilton, 'Institution', *Encyclopaedia of the Social Sciences*, 8 (1932), 84–9.

[154] John U. Nef, *Search for Meaning: The Autobiography of a Nonconformist* (Washington, DC: Public Affairs Press, 1973), 109. On the history of the economics department at Chicago, see A. W. Coats, 'The Origins of the "Chicago School(s)?" ', *Jnl. Pol. Econ.*, 71 (1963), 487–93.

[155] For an indication of the intellectual diversity, and hostility, which existed in the Chicago economics department at this time, see Melvin W. Reder, 'Chicago Economics: Permanence and Change', *Jnl. of Economic Literature*, 20 (1982), 1–38 at 2–9.

appoint its first economist, it is important to appreciate how Simons had become entangled in the mêlée of the economics department.

While there existed many general intellectual differences among members of that department, a particularly deep rift had emerged between Paul Douglas, one of the most strident proponents of economic interventionism on the Chicago faculty, and Frank Knight, the most important precursor to the modern neo-classical tradition of Chicago economics. Simons found himself caught in their cross-fire. In common with other colleagues, such as Jacob Viner, Douglas devoted a good deal of his energies to the matter of how to remedy economic depression.[156] The *laissez-faire* approach to business depressions, he believed, could only exacerbate unemployment. 'Without vigorous constructive action,' he asserted in 1935, 'even ultimate recovery is by no means certain, while it is, in any event, likely to be long-delayed.'[157]

Although there were other members of the Chicago economics department—Oskar Lange, for example—who were much more visibly captured by the writings of John Maynard Keynes, Douglas's studies of unemployment were very clearly in a Keynesian vein.[158] In his classic book, *The General Theory of Employment, Interest and Money*, first published in 1936, Keynes argued that with the advent of the Great Depression, American business confidence was so badly shaken that only vigourous governmental action could succeed in stimulating effective demand. In treating price adjustments as a powerful stabilizing force, he claimed, neo-classical economic theorists had assumed the existence of full employment, had assumed that employment levels would rise if wages were cut, had assumed that supply creates its own demand and had neglected to take account of the fact that demand and supply curves in one market will be shifted by disturbances in other markets.[159] Whereas Douglas accepted the basic Keynesian argument that government intervention was the only viable solution to the Depression, Knight found in Keynes's economics only confusion and unsubstantiated conclusions. '[T]he labour I have spent on *The General Theory of Employment, Interest, and Money*,' Knight wrote in 1937, 'leaves me with a feeling of keen disappointment.'[160] Keynes's 'procedure is typically that of replacing conventional assumptions which do not tell the whole story, and were

[156] On this matter, with regard to both Douglas and Viner, see J. Ronnie Davis, *The New Economics and the Old Economists* (Ames: Iowa State University Press, 1971), 38–63.

[157] Paul H. Douglas, *Controlling Depressions* (New York: Norton, 1935), 95.

[158] See Davis, *supra* n. 156, 47.

[159] John Maynard Keynes, *The General Theory of Employment, Interest and Money* (London: Macmillan, 1936).

[160] F. H. Knight, 'Unemployment: And Mr. Keynes's Revolution in Economic Theory', *Canadian Jnl. of Economics and Political Science*, 3 (1937), 100–23 at 123.

never represented as doing so, with some antithetical proposition, or familiar qualification, which is then treated as quite general, though the context of the book itself makes it clear enough that the argument cannot be taken as meaning what it says.'[161] The essential problem with the book, Knight concluded, 'is that it is inordinately difficult to tell what the author means'.[162] Clearly, on the subject of Keynesian economics, Knight and Douglas found little about which to agree.[163]

Knight was very much a reactionary, railing against what he considered to be the misguided economic fashions of his day. Keynes had 'succeeded in carrying economic thinking well back into the dark age';[164] the institutionalists had engaged in 'romantic prejudice and screwy thinking'.[165] In truth, Knight insisted, economics had made little real progress since the time of Adam Smith. Freedom, for Knight, lay at the core of Smith's economic philosophy; and he considered 'entirely sound' the basic Smithian proposition that 'a freely competitive organization of society tends to place every productive resource in that position in the productive system where it can make the greatest possible addition to the total social dividend as measured in price terms.'[166] Smith had shown that individual freedom of choice, the greatest characteristic of human nature, is embodied in the market. It is for this reason, Knight claimed, that economics can do no better than to teach that principles of freedom are of

[161] Ibid. 101. [162] Ibid. 121.

[163] In his autobiography, Douglas suggests that he instigated the Keynesian revolution in the United States before Keynes. See Paul H. Douglas, *In the Fullness of Time: The Memoirs of Paul H. Douglas* (New York: Harcourt, Brace Jovanovich, 1971), 453. He also states that Joan Robinson's *The Economics of Imperfect Competition* (*supra* n. 131) influenced him more than did Keynes's work. See Douglas, ibid. 351.

[164] Frank H. Knight, 'The Role of Principles in Economics and Politics' [1950], in his *On the History and Method of Economics: Selected Essays* (Chicago: University of Chicago Press, 1956), 251–81 at 252.

[165] Ibid. 280. On Knight and institutionalism, see generally Dorothy Ross, *The Origins of American Social Science* (Cambridge: Cambridge University Press, 1991), 420–27. Ross notes that, in some ways, Knight's own economic position was not entirely antithetical to institutionalism, a theme which is developed by David B. Schweikhardt, 'The Role of Values in Economic Theory and Policy: A Comparison of Frank Knight and John R. Commons', *Jnl. of Economic Issues*, 22 (1988), 407–14.

[166] Frank Hyneman Knight, 'The Ethics of Competition' [1923], in his *The Ethics of Competition and Other Essays* (London: Allen & Unwin, 1935), 41–75 at 48; and see also his *Intelligence and Democratic Action* (Cambridge, Mass.: Harvard University Press, 1960), 99: 'I still think Adam Smith is largely right; if the government would keep its hands clean of encouraging monopolies, much of the problem would largely take care of itself.' More generally, see George J. Stigler, 'Perfect Competition, Historically Contemplated', *Jnl. Pol. Econ.*, 65 (1957), 1–17 at 11–14; James M. Buchanan, *Cost and Choice: An Inquiry in Economic Theory* (Chicago: University of Chicago Press, 1969), 12–15; John McKinney, 'Frank H. Knight and Chicago Libertarianism', in Warren J. Samuels (ed.), *The Chicago School of Political Economy* (East Lansing: Association for Evolutionary Economics and Graduate School of Business Administration, Michigan State University, 1976), 191–213.

fundamental ethical and interpretative significance.[167] 'Assuming that men have a right to want and strive to get whatever they do want . . . so long as their conduct does not infringe the equal rights of others, the business of the economics of principles, of utility, productivity, and price, is to explain that, and how, the organization through buying and selling enables everyone to do whatever he tries to do . . . many times more effectively than would be possible if each used his own means in a self-sufficient economic life.'[168] 'Certainly,' Knight conceded, such 'economic principles are subject to sweeping limitations as to their explanatory value. They tell us nothing about concrete economic facts, what wants people have, what goods are produced and exchanged, what resources and techniques are employed, what distribution takes place.'[169] Yet they 'are useful for interpretation even if they do not accurately picture the conscious motives. It suffices that men behave largely "as if" they were trying to conform to the principles. These have great value in the prediction of effects of changes, changes both on and through price movements, changes that happen or are contrived.'[170]

By championing the tradition of Adam Smith in this way, Knight was outlining the "Chicago" style of neo-classical economic analysis before a distinctive Chicago school of economics had actually come into being. His support, for example, for the employment of "as if" reasoning in economic theorizing would later be echoed and popularized by Milton Friedman.[171] Indeed, it was as a teacher of Friedman and other Chicago neo-classicists—such as Aaron Director, George Stigler, Allen Wallis and Gary Becker—that Knight proved most influential.[172] Returning from leave in the mid-1940s, Paul Douglas 'was disconcerted to find that the economic and

[167] See Frank H. Knight, 'Methodology in Economics', *Southern Econ. Jnl.*, 27 (1961), 185–93, 273–82 at 185, 276; and, more generally, R. A. Gonce, 'Frank H. Knight on Social Control and the Scope and Method of Economics', *Southern Econ. Jnl.*, 38 (1972), 547–58.

[168] Knight, *supra* n. 164, 263.

[169] Ibid. 260.

[170] Ibid.

[171] See Milton Friedman, 'The Methodology of Positive Economics' in his *Essays in Positive Economics* (Chicago: University of Chicago Press, 1953), 3–43 at 18, 21. For a more general comparison of the economic methodologies of Knight and Friedman, see Eva Hirsch and Abraham Hirsch, 'The Heterodox Methodology of Two Chicago Economists', in Samuels (ed.), *supra* n. 166, 59–77.

[172] See Don Patinkin, 'Frank Knight as Teacher', in his *Essays on and in the Chicago Tradition* (Durham, NC: Duke University Press, 1981), 23–51. Melvin Reder notes, however, that '[a]lthough they admired Knight, and were devoted to him, the intellectual style of Friedman, Stigler, et al. was very different from Knight's. They were thoroughgoing empiricists with a distinct bias towards application of quantitative techniques to the testing of theoretical propositions.' Knight, in contrast, was decidedly sceptical about the value of empirical social science. See M. W. Reder, 'Chicago School', in John Eatwell, Murray Milgate and Peter Newman (eds.), *The New Palgrave: The World of Economics* (London: Macmillan, 1991), 40–50 at 43.

political conservatives had acquired an almost complete dominance over my department and taught that market decisions were always right and profit values the supreme ones . . . Knight was now openly hostile, and his disciples seemed to be everywhere.'[173] In fact, Knight's powerful influence over the intellectual development of the Chicago economics department can be traced back to the middle of the previous decade,[174] and his feud with Douglas still earlier. It was a feud which, in large measure, had emerged owing to the presence on the economics faculty of Henry Simons.

In his first four years in the economics department, Simons had published a sum total of two book reviews and had proved himself to be an uninspiring and unpopular teacher.[175] Feeling that higher intellectual standards ought to be met by Chicago economists, Douglas proposed at the beginning of 1932 that his contract ought not to be renewed. Prior to his appointment at Chicago, Simons had studied under and worked with Frank Knight at the University of Iowa. The two men had joined the Chicago faculty together in 1927. A notoriously irascible and contrary figure, Knight considered any criticism of Simons to be an attack on himself. Unsupported by the rest of the faculty, he defended Simons against Douglas's criticisms with a passion bordering on the maniacal. Relations between Douglas and Knight had already been rendered rather frosty owing to their very different economic perspectives. But the disagreement over Simons ensured that, by the mid-1930s, communication between them was purely epistolary.[176] In 1932, Knight was successful in his endeavours and Simons was retained. But Douglas renewed his attack in 1934 when Simons came up for tenure. By this stage, Simons was beginning to publish. Yet he still had few allies in the economics department. Doubts about his academic ability persisted even though Douglas gave up his crusade against Simons in 1935.

Simons never moved beyond the level of assistant professor in the economics department. In 1939, Hutchins, who had previously co-authored a report on economic reconstruction with Simons, arranged that he be appointed to teach a course on 'Economic Analysis and Public Policy' in the law school.[177] While there appears to have been no strong desire among the law faculty to have an economist among their ranks,

[173] Douglas, *supra* n. 163, 127–8.

[174] See Reder, *supra* n. 155, 6–7.

[175] See Stigler, *supra* n. 87, 166; Kitch (ed.), *supra* n. 146, 177 (comment by George Stigler). Both of Simons's book reviews appeared in the University of Chicago-based *Journal of Political Economy—Jnl. Pol. Econ.*, 37 (1929), 373–75; *Jnl. Pol. Econ.*, 39 (1931), 263–66—a journal which, at this time, was very much a platform for its editors, Knight and Jacob Viner, and their disciples. See John P. Henderson, 'The History of Thought in the Development of the Chicago Paradigm', in Samuels (ed.), *supra* n. 166, 341–61 at 355.

[176] For the relevant letters and commentary, see George J. Stigler, *Memoirs of an Unregulated Economist* (New York: Basic Books, 1988), 180–90.

[177] See Kitch (ed.), *supra* n. 146, 176–7.

there seems to have been no strong resentment either; and indeed it was there that Simons was promoted to associate professor in 1942 and eventually to full professor in 1945. Disagreement in the economics department had given the Chicago Law School their first economist.

Simons's achievements in the law school were quite modest. '[T]here was no visible impact of his law school association upon his own work, although he became an extremely popular teacher and had a substantial influence upon several of the law faculty.'[178] His appointment to the law school nevertheless marked the beginning of the Chicago law and economics tradition; for his writings provide a fairly clear indication of how that tradition would develop. Not that his work straightforwardly exemplified the Chicago tradition. While he argued for *laissez-faire* as vigorously as did any other Chicago economist, Simons was not an unswerving advocate of the minimal state. And while he criticized Keynes,[179] many of his ideas were markedly Keynesian.[180]

In 1926, Keynes had produced a short monograph entitled *The End of Laissez-Faire*, in which he argued that the survival and the furtherance of capitalism demanded a style of public interest regulation which would at once accommodate state interventionism and also facilitate individual economic freedom.[181] In 1934, Simons wrote *A Positive Program for Laissez Faire*, a similarly short pamphlet which, despite its title, offered an argument not wholly dissimilar to that which Keynes had developed in the previous decade. 'Competition and laissez faire have not brought us to heaven,'[182] Simons observes, and 'there is now imperative need for a sound, positive programme of economic legislation.'[183] At first blush, these could easily be taken to be the words of a New Dealer. Indeed,

[178] Stigler, *supra* n. 87, 168.

[179] See Henry C. Simons, 'Keynes Comments on Money', *The Christian Century*, 22 July 1936, 1016–17; and cf. more generally, Don Patinkin, 'Keynes and Chicago', in his *Essays on and in the Chicago Tradition*, *supra* n. 172, 289–308 at 301–3.

[180] See Milton Friedman, 'The Monetary Theory and Policy of Henry Simons', *Jnl. Law & Econ.*, 10 (1967), 1–13 at 7–9.

[181] 'I believe that in many cases the ideal size for the unit of control and organization lies somewhere between the individual and the modern State. I suggest, therefore, that progress lies in the growth and the recogntion of semi-autonomous bodies within the State—bodies whose criterion of action within their own field is solely the public good as they understand it, and from whose deliberations motives of private advantage are excluded. . . . There is nothing in [these reflections] which is seriously incompatible with what seems to me to be the essential characteristic of Capitalism, namely the dependence upon an intense appeal to the money-making and money-loving instincts of individuals as the main motive force of the economic machine.' John Maynard Keynes, *The End of Laissez-Faire* (London: Hogarth Press, 1926), 39, 50.

[182] Henry C. Simons, 'A Positive Program for Laissez Faire: Some Proposals for a Liberal Economic Policy', in Harry D. Gideonse (ed.), *Public Policy Pamphlet No. 15* (Chicago: University of Chicago Press, 1934), 6.

[183] Ibid. 2.

Simons goes further in fostering this impression. Bemoaning the prevalence of 'the gigantic corporation',[184] he echoes Berle and Means in proclaiming that '[a]ll corporations should be held to a Spartan simplicity in their capital structures.'[185] For all that Simons considered *A Positive Program* to be a 'propagandist tract',[186] however, he was by no means attempting to justify the policies of the New Deal. Government regulation of business, he argued, had tended to exacerbate rather than alleviate the allocative inefficiencies caused by monopoly.[187] 'The major responsibility for the severity of industrial fluctuations . . . falls directly upon the state . . . '[T]he state has forced the free-enterprise system . . . to live with a monetary system as bad as could well be devised.'[188] 'No diabolical ingenuity could have devised a more effective agency for retarding recovery . . . than the National Recovery Act and its codes.'[189] Nationalization, not regulation, Simons insisted, was the best way to revive industry; for only through a policy of nationalization might there be established a general standard of economic freedom conducive to burgeoning business competition.[190] Nationalization would bring true *laissez-faire*.

> The representation of laissez faire as a merely do-nothing policy is unfortunate and misleading. It is an obvious responsibility of the state under this policy to maintain the kind of legal and institutional framework within which competition can function effectively as an agency of control. . . . Laissez faire . . . implies a division of tasks between competitive and political controls; and the failure of the system, if it has failed, is properly to be regarded as a result of failure of the state, especially with respect to money, to do its part.[191]

The economic philosophy which Simons offers in *A Positive Program* seems hardly remarkable in retrospect. Here was a man arguing—as Keynes had insisted and as many have contended since[192]—that sensitive economic regulation facilitates, rather than frustrates, market freedom. This was certainly not the neo-classical economics of Frank Knight and his Chicago disciples.[193] Yet, in the context of the mid-1930s, Simons's distrust of government intervention and his basic faith in the free market system ran very much against the grain of popular economic wisdom.[194] In many

[184] Ibid. 12, 19. [185] Ibid. 21. [186] Ibid. 1. [187] Ibid. 7–12.
[188] Ibid. 14–16 [189] Ibid. 35. [190] Ibid. 11–12. [191] Ibid. 3, 15.

[192] Even at the Chicago Law School. See, in particular, Cass R. Sunstein, *After the Rights Revolution: Reconceiving the Regulatory State* (Cambridge, Mass.: Harvard University Press, 1990), 11–73 esp. 38–46, 51–5 (on how social and economic regulation can facilitate freedom).

[193] Though the temptation to locate him straightforwardly within this tradition appears to have been great. See Stigler, *supra* n. 87, 168–9; Warren S. Gramm, 'Chicago Economics: From Individualism True to Individualism False', in Samuels (ed.), *supra* n. 166, 167–89 at 173; Aaron Director, 'Prefatory Note', in Henry C. Simons, *Economic Policy for a Free Society* (Chicago: University of Chicago Press, 1948), v–vii at vi.

[194] See Kitch (ed.), *supra* n. 146, 178–9 (comments of George Stigler and Milton Friedman).

of his other writings, Simons demonstrated a markedly less equivocal affinity with the Chicago neo-classical tradition. As early as 1936, for example, he had sketched what was to become a distinctively 'Chicago' line of reasoning regarding the tendency of economists, lawyers and other policy-makers to exaggerate the prevalence of private monopoly. 'I am', he proclaimed, 'not much distressed about private monopoly power', for government interference poses a much greater threat to an enterprise economy than does cartelization.[195]

> Unregulated, extra-legal monopolies are tolerable evils; but private monopolies with the blessing of regulation and the support of law are malignant cancers in the system. . . . For every suppression of competition gives rise to an apparent need for regulation; and every venture in regulation creates the necessity of more regulation; and every interference by government on behalf of one group necessitates, in the orderly routine of democratic corruption, additional interference on behalf of others. The outcome along these lines is . . . an enterprise economy paralysed by political control.[196]

There is perhaps irony in the fact that Simons's writings came more clearly to epitomize modern Chicago economic philosophy after he had joined the law school. From the beginning of the 1940s up until his death in the summer of 1946, we find Simons becoming ever more outspoken about what he considered to be the dangers of regulatory legislation and governmental intervention in economic affairs.[197] 'American conservatives and libertarians', he claimed in 1944, 'still hold all the cards.'[198] By the following year, he was proclaiming economic libertarianism as his own political credo.[199] It was around this time also that he expressed an intense antipathy towards trade unionism. 'Unionists are much like our Communist friends,' he insisted; they:

> are essentially occupational armies, born and reared amidst violence, led by fighters. . . . Organized economic warfare is like organized economic banditry and, if allowed to spread, must lead to total revolution. . . . The public interest demands free exchange and free movement of workers among occupations . . . Unionism implies ability of established workers in high-wage areas and occupations to insulate themselves from competition. . . . There is little hope that mass

[195] Hency C. Simons, 'The Requisites of Free Competition' [1936], in his *Economic Policy for a Free Society*, *supra* n. 193, 78–89 at 87–8.

[196] Simons, ibid. 86–8.

[197] See e.g. Henry C. Simons, 'For a Free-Market Liberalism' [1941], in his *Economic Policy for a Free Society*, *supra* n. 193, 90–106 at 102; 'Economic Stability and Antitrust Policy' [1944], in ibid. 107–20 at 119.

[198] Henry C. Simons, 'Money, Tariffs, and the Peace' [1944], in his *Economic Policy for a Free Society*, *supra* n. 193, 260–76 at 273.

[199] Henry C. Simons, 'Introduction: A Political Credo', in his *Economic Policy for a Free Society*, *supra* n. 193, 1–39 at 38–9.

organizations with monopoly power will submit to competitive prices for their services while they retain their organization and power. No one and no group can be trusted with much power; and it is merely silly to complain because groups exercise power selfishly. The mistake lies simply in permitting them to have it.[200]

By the time of his death, Aaron Director recalls, Simons, through his teaching and his writing, 'was slowly establishing himself as the head of a "school" ' of economic thought at Chicago.[201] Having been moved out of the economics department in the 1930s, he was, by the outset of the next decade, beginning to exert a considerable intellectual influence on that department. Along with the occasional member of the law faculty—Walter Blum being the most notable[202]—those Chicago economists who had earlier been inspired by Knight began increasingly to identify also with the ideas of Simons.[203] Yet the primary historical significance of Simons—certainly as regards the development of law and economics at Chicago—rests not in how he came to influence others, but in how his ideas changed. For the transformation of his economic thought—from the semi-interventionist perspective of *A Positive Program for Laissez Faire* to the self-styled libertarian credo embodied in his later works—epitomizes the unfolding of the distinctive philosophy upon which Chicago law and economics came to be founded. Henry Simons did not invent law and economics at the University of Chicago. But his work exemplifies how economic analysis there became distanced from the legislation-oriented, regulated-enterprise perspective which typified legal–economic inquiry and policy in the New Deal era. When, in the mid-1940s, Simons was succeeded at the law school by Aaron Director, the difference between the style of economic analysis which was evolving at Chicago and the economic philosophy behind the New Deal was not only brought into still sharper focus, but was accorded special legal as well as economic significance.

CHICAGO MYTHOLOGY AND THE SEEDS OF A SCHOOL

By the middle of the 1940s, law and economics outside Chicago appeared to be all washed up. The Depression and the New Deal had stimulated a

[200] Henry C. Simons, 'Some Reflections on Syndicalism' [1944], in his *Economic Policy for a Free Society*, *supra* n. 193, 121–59 at 150, 152, 127, 138, 129.

[201] Director, *supra* n. 193, v; and cf. also Clara Ann Bowler, 'The Papers of Henry C. Simons', *Jnl. Law & Econ.*, 17 (1974), 7–11 at 9; and H. H. Liebhafsky, 'Price Theory as Jurisprudence: Law and Economics, Chicago Style', in Samuels (ed.), *supra* n. 166, 237–57 at 240.

[202] See Kitch (ed.), *supra* n. 146, 179.

[203] See ibid. 178–9. It appears that certain of those who had been influenced by Knight in the 1930s gradually became rather exasperated with his temperament. See Leonard Silk, *The Economists* (New York: Basic Books, 1976), 52.

good deal of legal–economic inquiry in the previous decade. But that stimulus had now gone. Academic lawyers and economists would occasionally appeal for more bridge-building between their disciplines. But there seemed to be little purpose to such appeals. '[T]he controlling system of law should reflect adequately the economic environment in which its rules and standards and policies are applicable,' I. L. Sharfman wrote in his Presidential Address to the American Economic Association at the beginning of 1946. 'If law is to serve as a living instrument for the guidance of human relationships in the economic sphere, it must necessarily embrace a process of reasonable adjustment to social change; and, in point of fact, the relative stability of our institutions is attributable in large measure to the actual recognition of this principle of growth in our legal system.'[204] Law, in other words, should—and generally will—reflect economic policy. Beyond this, lawyer–economists appeared to have little else to say.

Chicago, however, was a different story. It is at the University of Chicago in the 1940s that law and economics as a discipline began to develop. Accounts of this development, however, have tended to be rather simplistic. Periodization has been the most prevalent problem in this context. Usually, periodization has meant conceiving of an 'old' law and economics—that is, the economic analyses of antitrust law, corporate law, public utility regulation and federal taxation which emerged during the 1940s and 1950s—and a 'new' law and economics—that is, the application of economics to core legal doctrines and subjects such as contract, property, tort and criminal law, which began in the 1960s. Not every effort at periodization follows this dichotomy.[205] Nevertheless, the distinction between old and new law and economics is fairly commonplace. The problem with such periodization is that it encourages historical reductionism. In particular, it entails the belief that, some time around 1960, there was a definite break in legal–economic thinking: whereas, it is assumed, up until the end of the 1950s, economic analysis was applied only in explicitly economic legal fields such as antitrust, from the 1960s onwards it was used to explain and criticize legal rules which possess no obvious economic dimension.[206] Such an assumption is not wholly inaccurate. The face of law and economics did indeed begin to change significantly in the 1960s. However, the cut-off point between old and new law and economics

[204] I. L. Sharfman, 'Law and Economics', *Am. Econ. Rev.*, 36 (1946), 1–19 at 9.

[205] See e.g. Ejan Mackaay, 'La règle juridique observée par le prisme de l'économiste: Une histoire stylisée du mouvement de l'analyse économique du droit', *Revue internationale de droit économique*, [1986], 43–88 at 47 (distinguishing three phases of legal–economic analysis in the United States: the initial take-off (*décollage*) of the subject (1957–72); 'le paradigme accepté' (1972–80); and 'le grand débat et la recherche d'un nouveau fondement' (1980 onwards)).

[206] See e.g. Calabresi, *supra* n. 23, 86–7.

is by no means as distinct as is commonly believed.[207] In fact, at Chicago during the mid-1940s, when the 'old' law and economics was just about beginning to unfold, the seeds of the 'new' law and economics were also being planted.

It seems that no one was more responsible for getting law and economics off the ground at Chicago than Aaron Director. Precisely how he did this, however, is far from clear. At the beginning of the 1930s, while an instructor in the economics department at Chicago, he had collaborated with Paul Douglas in writing *The Problem of Unemployment*, a study which proposed the introduction in the United States of public unemployment insurance legislation.[208] Yet he studied under and was very much a disciple of Frank Knight.[209] While *The Problem of Unemployment* focused on what was basically Douglas's hobby-horse—the question of how to remedy unemployment caused by the Depression—Director himself seemed more concerned with demonstrating that fears about escalating unemployment were exaggerated. In 1933, he criticized those economists of the period who argued that the employment levels of the pre-Depression years could never be restored owing to the increase in technological innovations which made certain sectors of the work-force ever more obsolete. The scare-mongering of these technocrats, he insisted, grew out of ignorance of the fact that, as technology evolves, markets change rather than decline. Technological advance requires new equipment and machinery, which has to be invented, manufactured and operated. Even where such advance does make the production of a particular commodity less labour-intensive, furthermore, this will by no means result in increased unemployment, for 'consumers get their product for a smaller total expenditure, and they will therefore have some purchasing power left with which to buy more of the other commodities they previously consumed, or entirely new commodities or services they previously could not afford to buy. It is in this way that the workers displaced in any one industry can find employment in other occupations.'[210] On the basis of this reasoning, Director dismissed the argument of the technocrats that employment should be protected by extending the powers of trade unions. '[H]owever effective trade-union organizations may be in preventing a fall in the wage-rate, they cannot dictate the volume of employment; and however powerful employers may

[207] The distinction between old and new law and economics is also misleading in that it implies that the former made way for the latter. This is not the case. Influential mainly in the field of antitrust, 'old' law and economics, as we shall see in due course, continues to make its mark on that field to this day. 'Old', in this context, by no means denotes extinct.

[208] Paul H. Douglas and Aaron Director, *The Problem of Unemployment* (New York: The Macmillan Co., 1931).

[209] See Reder, *supra* n. 155, 6–7.

[210] Aaron Director, 'The Economics of Technocracy' in Harry D. Gideonse (ed.), *Public Policy Pamphlet No. 2* (Chicago: University of Chicago Press, 1933), 18.

be, they cannot compel people to buy as much at high prices as they would buy at lower prices.'[211] The ebb and flow of employment levels would be dictated by neither technological innovations nor trade unions, but by the invisible hand of the market. 'Adam Smith', Director concluded, 'said all that needs to be said on this point.'[212] Yet this was more than just Adam Smith re-worked. This was Chicago-style, neo-classical price theory two decades ahead of its time.

What is most puzzling—and, from an historical point of view, most frustrating—about Director is that his writings on employment of the early 1930s represent at least half of his published output. He had more or less stopped publishing before his academic career had taken off. Even more oddly, he published next to nothing in the field in which he was most inspirational. Yet his ability to influence the thinking of others was profound. Director was instrumental in persuading the University of Chicago to appoint Friedrich von Hayek in 1950;[213] and a few years later, after a number of other American publishers had rejected the book, he successfully urged the University of Chicago Press to publish Hayek's *The Road to Serfdom*.[214] In part, it seems, Director's support of Hayek at Chicago was repayment of an earlier debt. At the end of 1945, after having spent time both in a variety of government posts and as a visiting professor at Howard University in Washington, DC, Director accepted an offer to return to the economics department at Chicago. His return the following year coincided with Hayek's securing of a substantial amount of funding for the establishment of a centre at Chicago dedicated to the promotion of private enterprise.[215] The centre was to be affiliated with the law school rather than the economics department. Henry Simons suggested to Hayek that the centre should be headed by Director. The dean of the law school was happy to accommodate this suggestion so long as Director was prepared to teach at least one law school course. Simons, who died in the summer of 1946, had declared himself tired of teaching his course on Economic Analysis and Public Policy. Director stepped straight into his shoes.[216]

[211] Director, ibid. 24.

[212] Ibid. and cf. Adam Smith, *The Theory of Moral Sentiments* (orig. publ. 1759, D. D. Raphael and A. L. Macfie (eds.), Indianapolis: Liberty Press, 1982), 184–5; *An Inquiry into the Nature and Causes of the Wealth of Nations* (two vols. orig. publ. 1776, R.H. Campbell and A.S. Skinner (eds.), Indianapolis: Liberty Press, 1981), I, 456.

[213] See Kitch (ed.), *supra* n. 146, 187–9.

[214] See Stigler, *supra* n. 176, 140. *The Road to Serfdom* was published by the University of Chicago Press in 1956; it was published in Britain by Routledge & Kegan Paul in 1944.

[215] Hayek's connection with the University of Chicago at this time appears to have come about through his founding of the Mont Pelerin Society, an organization for social scientists dedicated to defending the principles of the free market, at the end of the Second World War. Director attended the first meeting of the Society in 1947.

[216] See further Kitch (ed.), *supra* n. 146, 180–1; and also R. H. Coase, 'Law and Economics at Chicago', *Jnl. Law & Econ.*, 36 (1993), 239–54 at 244–6.

Mythology shrouds Director's achievements as Professor of Economics and general *éminence grise* at the University of Chicago Law School. Living up to his name, he invested law and economics with a sense of direction which had been wholly absent during Simons's era. Director established the first law and economics programme in the United States. In 1958, he founded the *Journal of Law and Economics*. More generally, he was responsible for promoting a distinctively post-New Deal style of law and economics, the fundamental premiss of which was that regulation is the proper function of markets rather than governments. At a conference on the regulation of military defence and mobilization, which he organized under the auspices of the Chicago Law School in 1951, Director proclaimed that '[a]t Chicago the advantages of the market as a method of organizing economic affairs are valued too highly to be laid aside during so-called emergency periods.'[217] The Chicago economist Jacob Viner, in attendance at the conference, was startled by the degree to which the free market ethos dominated the proceedings: 'everything about the conference except the unscheduled statements and protests from individual participants were [*sic*] so patently rigidly structured. . . . Even the source of financing of the Conference, as I found out later, was ideologically loaded. . . . From then on, I was willing to consider the existence of a "Chicago School" (but one not confined to the economics department and not embracing all of the department).'[218] Within the law school, there were certainly some members of faculty—Karl Llewellyn, for example—who, like Viner, rather disapproved of the type of legal–economic analysis which Director was encouraging.[219] Others, however, especially among the student body, were coming gradually to see sense in his economic vision.[220] Director was winning converts.

In virtually all cases, the reason for conversion was the same: Director's economic explanation of the law of antitrust. In December 1946, his colleague at the Chicago Law School, Edward Levi, proclaimed that widespread deconcentration of industrial power in the United States could be achieved only through more effective regulation. 'It is doubtful if a free

217 Aaron Director (ed.), *Defense, Controls, and Inflation: A Conference Sponsored by the University of Chicago Law School* (Chicago: University of Chicago Press, 1952), 158 (comment by Director).

218 Jacob Viner, letter to Don Patinkin, 21 December 1969, quoted in Don Patinkin, 'The Chicago Tradition, the Quantity Theory, and Friedman', in his *Essays on and in the Chicago Tradition*, *supra* n. 172, 241–74 at 266.

219 See Kitch (ed.), *supra* n. 146, 184–7. Director himself apparently insisted that price theory is a scientific, politically neutral technique, and would usually refuse to discuss the normative consequences of accepting micro-economic assumptions. William Twining, letter to author, n. d.

220 See Kitch, *supra* n. 146, 183–5; and also, more generally, Edward H. Levi, 'Aaron Director and the Study of Law and Economics', *Jnl. Law & Econ.*, 9 (1966), 3–4; Bernard D. Meltzer, 'Aaron Director: A Personal Appreciation', *Jnl. Law & Econ.*, 9 (1966), 5–6.

and competitive society can be maintained if the direction of concentration is to continue,' he concluded. 'It is surely doubtful whether the antitrust method of regulation will remain if it is not to be more effective.'[221] By the following decade, writing in collaboration with Director, Levi appeared to have undergone a complete volte-face: 'We believe the conclusions of economics do not justify the application of the antitrust laws in many situations in which the laws are now being applied.'[222] Since economic theory demonstrates that the presence of monopoly is much more often alleged than confirmed, they argued, less rather than more regulation ought to be prescribed.[223]

What had changed Levi's mind so? Soon after joining the Chicago Law School, Director had begun to teach on Levi's antitrust course. According to law school folklore,[224] Levi would spend the first four classes of each week attempting to demonstrate how seemingly inconsistent antitrust decisions were, in fact, rationally interconnected. In the last class, Director would use economic analysis to show that everything that Levi had said was wrong. It was in the classroom that Director won his converts, Levi included. 'A lot of us who took the antitrust course,' Robert Bork has reminisced, 'underwent what can only be called a religious conversion. It changed our view of the entire world. . . . One of the pleasures of that course was to watch Ed [Levi] agonizing as these cases he had always believed in and worked on were systematically turned into incoherent statements. Ed fought brilliantly for years before he finally gave way.'[225] Director was responsible for ensuring that at Chicago, in the field of antitrust, legal reasoning lost out to economic analysis.

But why should this have happened? Why should Director's economic perspective have proved so persuasive? Part of the reason was that it presented academic lawyers of the 1950s with a message which was at once unfamiliar and yet quite understandable. Reflecting on law and economics at the Chicago Law School between 1950 and 1962, the years during which he served as Dean, Levi has quipped that '[t]he economics of today . . . is not quite the way it was then. For one thing, some of it was still in English at that time.'[226] Director's central message was really quite simple to grasp.

[221] Edward H. Levi, 'The Antitrust Laws and Monopoly', *U. Chicago L. Rev.*, 14 (1947), 153–83 at 183. Levi's paper was originally presented as a talk at the Practising Law Institute in New York City, December 1946.

[222] Aaron Director and Edward H. Levi, 'Law and the Future: Trade Regulation', *Northwestern Univ. L. Rev.*, 51 (1956), 281–96 at 282.

[223] See Ibid. 290–1, 294–6.

[224] See Kitch (ed.), *supra* n. 146, 183; Coase, *supra* n. 216, 247; Richard A. Posner and Frank H. Easterbrook, *Antitrust: Cases, Economic Notes, and Other Materials* (2nd edn. St. Paul, Minn.: West Publishing Co., 1981), xvi; Cass R. Sunstein, 'On Analogical Reasoning', *Harvard L. Rev.*, 106 (1993), 741–91 at 747 fn. 25.

[225] Kitch (ed.), *supra* n. 224, 183–4 (comment by Robert Bork).

[226] Levi, *supra* n. 151, 26.

Since it is virtually impossible to eliminate competition from economic life, he argued, monopolies are essentially unstable: if a firm buys up all of its rivals, new competitors will emerge; if it secures a lucrative patent on a product, rivals will compete for its profits by developing similar alternative products; if the state offers particular monopoly privileges, there will be strong competition among bidders for those privileges. Monopoly is not simply something to be exercised. It is, rather, something to be obtained, defended, shared and ultimately eliminated. For monopoly is always threatened by efficiency—by the basic economic desire, that is, to produce and sell goods at the lowest possible cost (and therefore the largest possible profit). Thus it is that many commercial practices which are prima facie monopolistic or exclusionary turn out to be underscored by competition.

Director used the example of the United States government's suit against John D. Rockefeller's Standard Oil Trust in 1911[227] to demonstrate this argument. Standard Oil, the government alleged, had acquired its position of commercial dominance through discriminatory tactics such as the sabotaging of rival companies and, most commonly, predatory pricing. By lowering oil prices below costs in particular regions, Standard Oil—so the allegation went—was able to price smaller competitors in those regions out of the market and then buy them up. Its pricing practices, in other words, were seen to be dictated by the urge to monopolize. Director rejected this line of argument. Price wars, he pointed out, invariably prove most costly to the victor, whose output and losses are likely to exceed those of the smaller rival. Furthermore, competition is a Hydra: assuming a policy of predatory pricing was indeed adopted by a company, new competitors would emerge as soon as that company restored its normal prices—which inevitably it would be compelled to do if prices had been reduced below cost. Thus, Director concluded, the prevalence of predatory pricing is highly unlikely. Prices are generally lowered owing to competitive rather than monopolistic instinct. Just as he had employed neo-classical price theory in the 1930s to refute the claims of the technocrats, so too Director used it in the 1950s to dismiss the fears of those lawyers who perceived a steady growth in monopolistic trade arrangements.

In a report on the state of research into antitrust law, published in 1963, Herbert Packer remarked that Director's collaboration with Levi in the 1950s was the clearest indication of an emerging 'School' of antitrust law and economics at Chicago. Yet he also observed that the Chicago project was a rather 'nebulous affair'.[228] Such a comment is hardly surprising. For the antitrust tradition over which Director presided at Chicago was

[227] *Standard Oil Co. of New Jersey* v. *United States* (1911) 221 U.S. 1.

[228] Herbert L. Packer, *The State of Research in Antitrust Law* (New Haven, Conn.: Walter E. Meyer Research Institute of Law, 1963), 55.

primarily an oral one.[229] Director introduced to the Chicago Law School the 'workshop' ethos which was already dominant in the economics department.[230] Vigorous debate about the current research projects of colleagues and visitors became—and indeed remains—a primary faculty activity.[231] Director himself thrived within this dialogic tradition—to the extent, indeed, that he seemed content to leave the writing up of his ideas to those whom he influenced.[232] By the 1970s, Chicago-trained lawyer–economists had begun to publish books on antitrust which were inspired explicitly by, and which derived much of their substance from, Director's teachings in the 1950s.[233]

It would in fact be very convenient, in examining the history of law and economics in America, to skip straight from Director's Chicago of the 1950s to the Director-inspired antitrust scholarship of the 1970s. By doing this, a definite sense of historical continuity could be achieved: the intellectual history of law and economics could be portrayed as an exercise in baton-passing among the major protagonists. It is unlikely, however, that such a portrayal could capture the complex evolution of American legal–economic thought. There is, first of all, much more to antitrust law and economics than the Chicago tradition and, secondly, there is much more to the Chicago tradition than antitrust law and economics. These two claims will be elaborated in due course. Before we turn to the first claim,

[229] See Stigler, *supra* n. 87, 51.

[230] The economist Karl Brunner, on joining the economics department at Chicago from Harvard in the late 1940s, felt that he had entered 'a somewhat different world. I became exposed to a group around Aaron Director, Frank Knight, and Milton Friedman. . . . The group met with some regularity for discussions ranging over a wide array of problems . . . They emphatically advanced the relevance of economic analysis as an important means of understanding the world, in a manner that I had never encountered before.' Karl Brunner, 'My Quest for Economic Knowledge', in Michael Szenberg (ed.), *Eminent Economists: Their Life Philosophies* (Cambridge: Cambridge University Press, 1992), 84–97 at 88. More generally on the workshop ethos in the Chicago economics department, see Reder, *supra* n. 155, 2.

[231] See William H. Page, 'The Chicago School and the Evolution of Antitrust: Characterization, Antitrust Injury, and Evidentiary Sufficiency', *Virginia L. Rev.*, 75 (1989), 1221–308 at 1229–30.

[232] See e.g. John S. McGee, 'Predatory Price Cutting: The Standard Oil (N.J.) Case', *Jnl. Law & Econ.*, 1 (1958), 137–69; 'Predatory Pricing Revisited', *Jnl. Law & Econ.*, 23 (1980), 289–330; George J. Stigler, 'Director's Law of Public Income Redistribution', *Jnl. Law & Econ.*, 13 (1970), 1–10; Lester G. Telser, 'Abusive Trade Practices: An Economic Analysis', *Law and Contemporary Problems*, 30 (1965), 488–505.

[233] See Robert H. Bork, *The Antitrust Paradox: A Policy at War with Itself* (New York: Basic Books, 1978) esp. ix ('Much of what is said here derives from the work of Aaron Director, who has long seemed to me, as he has to many others, the seminal thinker in antitrust economics and industrial organization. . . . I had the good fortune to be his student in 1953 and 1954, the latter year as a graduate research associate, and our discussions permanently and substantially altered my ways of thinking about much more than antitrust'); Ward S. Bowman, Jr., *Patent and Antitrust Law: A Legal and Economic Appraisal* (Chicago: University of Chicago Press, 1973), 57–60; Richard A. Posner, *Antitrust Law: An Economic Perspective* (Chicago: University of Chicago Press, 1976), x.

however, we might consider briefly how the second connects very specifically to our earlier observation that the so-called 'old' and 'new' law and economics overlap.

The work and the influence of Aaron Director proves again to be of fundamental significance here. The only paper which Director cared to publish during the 1960s concerned not the economic analysis of antitrust law, but the manner in which legal systems often embrace ambivalent criteria regarding what constitutes market behaviour. In 'The Parity of the Economic Market Place', he highlighted the manner in which the modern American legal system has departed from the liberal tradition of the nineteenth century by treating the freedom of political, artistic and religious speech as somehow more important than the freedom of commercial speech. In truth, he argued, 'the bulk of mankind will for the foreseeable future have to devote a considerable fraction of their active lives to economic activity. For these people freedom of choice as owners of resources . . . in . . . areas of employment, investment, and consumption is fully as important as freedom of discussion and participation in government.'[234] Yet freedom in the market for ideas is commonly accorded much greater protection than freedom in the market for 'ordinary' goods and services.[235]

In offering this analysis, Director had sketched an argument which would, in due course, be elaborated by many other lawyers and economists.[236] The significance of the argument rested in its suggestiveness: markets, Director implied, not only pervade the legal framework much more than American lawyers have commonly recognized but, more importantly—owing to this general failure to appreciate the pervasive functioning of markets—the legal system deals with different types of market activity in an inconsistent fashion. Thus it is that *laissez-faire* is upheld with much greater vigilance in the realm of ideas than it is in the realm of commerce. Director had indicated, in short, that there exists an

234 Aaron Director, 'The Parity of the Economic Market Place', *Jnl. Law & Econ.*, 7 (1964), 1–10 at 6. This paper was originally contributed to the proceedings of a conference in 1953 (see ibid. p. 1 n. *). To suggest that, in the 1960s, Director made the effort to publish it is in a sense misleading, for it was not Director but the then editor of the *Journal of Law and Economics*, Ronald Coase, who decided to reprint it. Ronald H. Coase, letter to author, 15 November 1993.

235 The 'market of ideas' notion of free speech comes from Holmes. See *Abrams* v. *United States* (1919) 250 U.S. 616, 630 (Holmes J. dissenting). ('The best test of truth is the power of the thought to get itself accepted in the competition of the market.')

236 See e.g. Ronald H. Coase, 'The Market for Goods and the Market for Ideas', *Papers and Proceedings of the American Economic Review*, 64 (1974), 384–91; Milton Friedman, 'Free Markets and Free Speech', *Harvard Jnl. of Law & Public Policy*, 10 (1987), 1–9; Richard A. Posner, 'Free Speech in an Economic Perspective', *Suffolk Univ. L. Rev.*, 20 (1986), 1–54; Nicholas Wolfson, *Corporate First Amendment Rights and the SEC* (New York: Quorum, 1990), ch. 4; Alex Kozinski and Stuart Banner, 'Who's Afraid of Commercial Speech?', *Virginia L. Rev.*, 76 (1990), 627–53 esp. 652.

intimate though by no means straightforward relationship between law and markets—a relationship which lawyers and economists alike had generally neglected. Analysis of this relationship would gradually become one of the central features of modern economic analysis of law. Director may well have pioneered the so-called 'old' law and economics at Chicago, but this does not mean that the 'new' economic analysis was none of his doing.

To dwell on the so-called 'new' law and economics at this stage would be to advance too far too quickly. At the University of Chicago during the 1950s and 1960s, neo-classical economic analysis was substantially refined; and understanding how certain developments in modern law and economics came about requires, first of all, an examination of how, during this period, neo-classical economics itself changed. Before undertaking this task, however, it is important to consider briefly how, throughout this same period, the 'old' law and economics—the economic analysis of antitrust—evolved in such a way as to substantiate Director's thesis that monopolies are essentially unstable. For gradually, from the late 1950s onwards, there began to emerge theoretical perspectives on antitrust which, in different ways, challenged the particular style of legal–economic analysis which had evolved under Director's tutelage at Chicago. Just how valuable Chicago law and economics would prove to be in the field of antitrust would depend on the quality of the theoretical alternatives offered by its competitors.

STRUGGLING FOR THE SOUL OF ANTITRUST

'Antitrust policy', Robert Bork has observed, 'cannot be made rational until we are able to give a firm answer to one question: What is the point of the law—what are its goals? Everything else follows from the answer we give.'[237] It is not uncommon to find American academic lawyers describing the primary goal of antitrust law as one of 'assuring a competitive economy', or some such words.[238] Yet assertions along these lines serve only to compound rather than to resolve the problem which Bork poses.[239] How much competition do we want? Where, exactly, do we want it? Assuming these questions can be answered, how is competition to be

[237] Bork, *supra* n. 233, 50.

[238] See e.g. Ernest Gellhorn, 'An Introduction to Antitrust Economics', *Duke L.J.*, [1975], 1–43 at 1–2. ('The objective of antitrust law is to assure a competitive economy. . . . The antitrust laws are a legislative acknowledgement of an imperfect system—in reality competitive markets often do not exist. Their purpose is to make certain that the gap between the ideal of competition and the reality of private rule does not become dangerously wide.')

[239] See Frank H. Easterbrook, 'The Limits of Antitrust', *Texas L. Rev.*, 63 (1984), 1–40 esp. 1–3, 39.

promoted? And assuming we know how competition is to be promoted, why should we want to promote it?

American lawyers and economists have been endeavouring to provide answers to these sorts of questions since the late nineteenth century.[240] Today, it is commonly recognized that a distinctive and—in the eyes of many—highly-persuasive collection of answers to such questions has emerged from the Chicago tradition of economic analysis. Even those not predisposed to that tradition generally acknowledge the massive influence of Chicago law and economics on the development of modern antitrust policy.[241] Indeed, there exists very little in the way of contemporary antitrust theory which has not been inspired to some degree by Chicago economic analysis.

To a large extent, inspiration has taken the form of rebellion. Antitrust theorists working within the Chicago tradition have been variously accused of ignoring the complexities and practicalities of modern antitrust policy and of misinterpreting legislative history.[242] In particular, certain critics of that tradition have argued that the basic objective of the major American antitrust statutes—the Sherman Act 1890 and the Clayton and Federal Trade Commission Acts of 1914[243]—is not to promote an efficient allocation of resources but to prevent firms abusing their market power in order to acquire consumer wealth unfairly.[244] Distributive justice rather than allocative efficiency, in other words, is seen to be the *raison d'être* of antitrust law. Other critics of the Chicago tradition have argued that, even if the original intent behind the antitrust legislation was indeed to promote

[240] See James May, 'Antitrust in the Formative Era: Political and Economic Theory in Constitutional and Antitrust Analysis, 1880–1918', *Ohio State L.J.*, 50 (1989), 257–395 esp. 391–5; F. M. Scherer, 'Efficiency, Fairness, and the Early Contributions of Economists to the Antitrust Debate', *Washburn L.J.*, 29 (1990), 243–55; Thomas J. DiLorenzo, 'The Origins of Antitrust: An Interest-Group Perspective', *Int. Rev. Law & Econ.*, 5 (1985), 73–90.

[241] See e.g. Herbert Hovenkamp, 'Chicago and its Alternatives', *Duke L.J.*, [1986], 1014–29 at 1020. ('The Chicago School has done more for antitrust policy than any coherent economic theory since the New Deal. No one . . . can escape its influence on antitrust analysis.')

[242] See Peter C. Carstensen, 'How to Assess the Impact of Antitrust on the American Economy: Examining History or Theorizing?', *Iowa L. Rev.*, 74 (1989), 1175–217 esp. 1192, 1214–17; Victor P. Goldberg, 'The Law and Economics of Vertical Restrictions: A Relational Perspective', *Texas L. Rev.*, 58 (1979), 91–129.

[243] For the main provisions of these statutes, see Posner and Easterbrook, *supra* n. 224, 18–35.

[244] See Robert H. Lande, 'Wealth Transfers as the Original and Primary Concern of Antitrust: The Efficiency Interpretation Challenged', *Hastings L.J.*, 34 (1982), 65–151; Herbert Hovenkamp, 'Distributive Justice and the Antitrust Laws', *George Washington L. Rev.*, 51 (1982), 1–31; 'The Sherman Act and the Classical Theory of Competition', *Iowa L. Rev.*, 74 (1989), 1019–65; Gregory J. Werden, 'A Closer Analysis of Antitrust Markets', *Washington Univ. L.Q.*, 62 (1985), 647–69; Fred S. McChesney, 'On the Economics of Antitrust Enforcement', *Georgetown L.J.*, 68 (1980), 1103–11.

allocative efficiency, there is no reason that such a goal should dominate antitrust policy today.[245]

Yet it seems that for every critic there is a counter-critic. Antitrust law, these counter-critics argue, cannot be founded on populist or distributive goals; for such goals are simply too open-ended and ambivalent to sustain a rational economic philosophy. When detractors from the Chicago tradition argue that the primary goal of antitrust law should be to protect consumer welfare through distributivist measures, for example, they omit to explain what courts ought to do when such a goal can only be pursued by neglecting the commercial interests of small businesses.[246] Economic efficiency, the counter-critics insist, can be the only significant goal of antitrust policy.[247] More than this, with the pursuit of efficiency will come greater distributive justice, for a policy which promotes the efficient allocation of resources in a free, competitive market will serve the economic interests of producers and consumers alike.

Thus it is that there has emerged what one commentator has termed a 'battle for the soul of antitrust'.[248] Between efficiency theorists and distributivists, there exists a basic difference of opinion regarding what the point of antitrust law happens to be. Increasingly, this difference of opinion has become polarized: it has become a difference, that is, between those who subscribe to 'the Chicago school' of antitrust theory and those who do not.[249] In due course, we shall see just how pervasive the influence

[245] See Eleanor M. Fox, 'The Modernization of Antitrust: A New Equilibrium', *Cornell L. Rev.*, 66 (1981), 1140–92; 'Consumer Beware Chicago', *Michigan L. Rev.*, 84 (1986), 1714–20; Eleanor M. Fox and Lawrence A. Sullivan, 'Antitrust: Retrospective and Prospective, Where are We Coming From? Where are We Going?', *New York Univ. L. Rev.*, 62 (1987), 937–88; Kenneth G. Elzinga, 'The Goals of Antitrust: Other than Competition and Efficiency, What Else Counts?', *U. Pennsylvania L. Rev.*, 125 (1977), 1191–213; William J. Curran III, 'Beyond Economic Concepts and Categories: A Democratic Refiguration of Antitrust Law', *St. Louis Univ. L.J.*, 31 (1987), 349–78; David W. Barnes, 'Nonefficiency Goals in the Antitrust Law of Mergers', *William & Mary L. Rev.*, 30 (1989), 787–866.

[246] See Michael DeBow, 'The Social Costs of Populist Antitrust: A Public Choice Perspective', *Harvard Jnl. of Law & Public Policy*, 14 (1991), 205–23 at 211–12; and also, from an earlier era, Robert H. Bork and Ward S. Bowman, 'The Goals of Antitrust: A Dialogue on Policy', *Columbia L. Rev.*, 65 (1965), 363–76 at 370.

[247] See e.g. Wesley J. Liebeler, 'Resale Price Maintenance and Consumer Welfare: *Business Electronics Corp.* v. *Sharp Electronics Corp.*', *UCLA L. Rev.*, 36 (1989), 889–913; Paul C. Rogers, 'The Limited Case for an Efficiency Defense in Horizontal Mergers', *Tulane L. Rev.*, 58 (1983), 503–42; John Shepard Wiley, Jr., 'Antitrust and Core Theory', *U. Chicago L. Rev.*, 54 (1987), 556–89; Warren F. Schwartz, 'An Overview of the Economics of Antitrust Enforcement', *Georgetown L.J.*, 68 (1980), 1075–102.

[248] Eleanor M. Fox, 'The Battle for the Soul of Antitrust', *California L. Rev.*, 75 (1987), 917–23.

[249] See, generally, Herbert Hovenkamp, 'Antitrust Policy after Chicago', *Michigan L. Rev.*, 84 (1985), 213–84; John Shepard Wiley, Jr., ' "After Chicago": An Exaggerated Demise?', *Duke L.J.*, [1986], 1003–13; Hovenkamp, *supra* n. 241, *passim*; Wesley J. Liebeler, 'What Are the Alternatives to Chicago?', *Duke L.J.*, [1987], 879–96; Herbert Hovenkamp, 'Fact, Value and Theory in Antitrust Adjudication', *Duke L.J.*, [1987], 897–914; Willard F.

of Chicago economic analysis in the field of antitrust has been. Given its influence, it is hardly surprising that modern theoretical debate about antitrust policy should have become ever more centred on the question of whether or not there exist viable alternatives to the Chicago tradition. The problem with such debate, however, is that it tends to posit 'Chicago' as a monolith. As Oliver Williamson has noted, Chicago lawyer–economists do not speak as one on antitrust issues.[250] Theoretical differences exist among them.[251] Furthermore, many modern antitrust theorists appear to have lost sight of the fact that not everyone who regards economic efficiency to be the primary goal of antitrust policy necessarily belongs to the Chicago tradition of economic analysis. 'Chicago', it seems, has come to mean more than just Chicago.

It is notable that one of the few critical studies of American antitrust theory to have been produced outside of the United States rather downplays the significance of Chicago economic analysis. In their study of antitrust scholarship in the Chicago tradition, Schmidt and Rittaler argue that Chicago lawyer–economists not only make unrealistic assumptions regarding the manner in which competitive markets operate, but also engage in 'selective empiricism' in order to substantiate their assumptions.[252] In the United States, credit for the development of a sophisticated efficiency-based antitrust theory, they argue, properly belongs not to Chicago but to Harvard.[253] Such an argument relies heavily on exaggeration—on the image, as one commentator puts it, of 'a full-fledged battle between two faculties—Chicago and Harvard—and their hangers-on'.[254] Harvard Law School never really developed a tradition of antitrust scholarship as distinctive as that which evolved at Chicago.[255] Nevertheless, in so far as Harvard did develop such a tradition, it did so

Mueller, 'A New Attack on Antitrust: The Chicago Case', *Antitrust Law & Econ. Rev.*, 18 (1986), 29–66; Gordon B. Spivack, 'The Chicago School Approach to Single Firm Exercises of Monopoly Power: A Response', *Antitrust L.J.*, 52 (1983), 651–74.

250 Oliver E. Williamson, 'Intellectual Foundations: The Need for a Broader View', *Jnl. Leg. Educ.*, 33 (1983), 210–16 at 212.

251 For example, over the issue of predatory pricing: see Page, *supra* n. 231, 1247–8.

252 Ingo Schmidt and Jan B. Rittaler, *Die Chicago School of Antitrust Analysis: Wettbewerbstheoretische und -politische Analyse eines Credos* (Baden-Baden: Nomos, 1986), 97, 109 (on how Chicago antitrust theory attracts the 'reproach of selective empiricism' [*Vorwurf des selektiven Empirismus*]).

253 See ibid. 56–7, 79–80, 103.

254 George Bittlingmayer, 'Chicago Credo', *Jnl. of Institutional and Theoretical Economics*, 143 (1987), 658–67 at 659.

255 See, generally, Richard A. Posner, 'The Chicago School of Antitrust Analysis', *U. Pennsylvania L. Rev.*, 127 (1979), 925–52. Both Posner and Bittlingmayer (*supra* n. 254, 665) note that the primary difference between the Harvard and Chicago traditions of antitrust theory rests in the fact that Harvard theorists are more prone to identifying monopolistic practices and less willing to apply price theory in order demonstrate the possibility of genuine efficiency justifications for those practices than are their Chicago counterparts.

independently of Chicago. What many American legal theorists and historians fail to appreciate—unlike Schmidt and Rittaler—is that, for all the similarities between the Harvard and Chicago traditions of antitrust scholarship, they are not all of a piece.

The Chicago and Harvard antitrust traditions began to emerge around the same time. In the early 1950s, the Harvard law professor, Edward Mason, obtained funding from the Merrill Foundation to undertake a study of monopoly and competition in American industry. Mason had been arguing since the 1930s that monopoly is both a legal and an economic problem, the tackling of which demands collaboration between lawyers and economists.[256] With the Merrill sponsorship, he organized a discussion group, comprised of various Harvard lawyers and economists, to address the problem of monopoly in American industry.[257] The group met regularly over several years and produced a number of studies, one of the most important of which was Carl Kaysen and Donald Turner's inquiry into the economics of antitrust policy.[258] Kaysen and Turner's central thesis was that there was a need, by the end of the 1950s, for new legislation in the United States facilitating the restructuring of concentrated industries. Existing legislation, they argued, was simply incapable of combating the erosion of the competitive market structure. It was a problem which could be traced back to the Sherman Act. In passing that Act, Kaysen and Turner suggest, the legislators were well aware of 'the power of monopolists to hurt the public by raising price, deteriorating product, and restricting production. At the same time, there was at least equal concern with the fate of small producers driven out of business, or deprived of the opportunity to enter it, by "all-powerful aggregations of capital" '.[259] The intention behind the Act, nevertheless, was not the wholesale prohibition of monopoly. Where a firm is able to dominate a particular market because there exists no one else with the necessary intelligence and skill to compete at the same level, then the Act ought not to apply. '[P]ower obtained or maintained by the kind of behaviour that competition is thought to foster if not compel, was immune,' Kaysen and Turner argue, 'even though business and business opportunities were destroyed in the process. In short, in the event of conflict in goals, protection of incentives to competitive behaviour would prevail over dispersion of market power.'[260]

[256] See Edward S. Mason, 'Monopoly in Law and Economics', *Yale L.J.*, 47 (1937), 34–49.

[257] See Packer, *supra* n. 228, 54–5, 164 n. 38.

[258] Carl Kaysen and Donald F. Turner, *Antitrust Policy: An Economic and Legal Analysis* (Cambridge, Mass.: Harvard University Press, 1959). Kaysen was a professor of industrial organization on the Harvard economics faculty. Turner held a law degree and a doctorate in economics and was a professor at the Harvard Law School. Between 1965 and 1968, he headed the Antitrust Division of the Justice Department.

[259] Ibid. 19.

[260] Ibid. 19–20.

The antitrust policy embodied in the Sherman Act was, accordingly, ambivalent. Monopoly would be permitted so long as it was monopoly acquired through competitive merit; and the courts would be entrusted with the somewhat ill-defined task of balancing 'the economic interests of those possessing legitimately acquired power, and the economic interests of others'.[261] It was owing to this ambivalence, Kaysen and Turner claimed, that, by the 1950s, American antitrust law was unable satisfactorily to deal with the growth of oligopoly—with the fact, that is, that, in many markets, the supply of product was controlled by a small number of producers. Since the Sherman Act in fact sanctioned a particular type of monopoly, concentration of market power in the hands of a few large firms was by no means necessarily illegal. 'The principal defect of the present antitrust law is its inability to cope with market power created by jointly acting oligopolists', Kaysen and Turner observed. '[W]e believe it is safe to say that a considerable number of industrial markets exist in which oligopolists, acting jointly, possess substantial degrees of market power, which they exercise without engaging in conduct violating the Sherman Act.'[262]

Hence the call for new legislation. '[C]hanging a tight oligopoly market into a looser one, or a market dominated by a single seller into one in which several large firms operate by reorganizing the larger firms in the market, will in fact change the market sufficiently so that the degree of market power exercised by the (still) relatively few large firms will be greatly reduced.'[263] Eradicating oligopoly and monopoly in this way requires that 'an unreasonable degree of market power as such must be made illegal. . . . This change in the law is sufficiently far-reaching so that it would be necessary to embody it in new legislation.'[264] Kaysen and Turner's call for deconcentration through legislation seems, on the face of it, hardly to differ from the antitrust jurisprudence of the New Deal era. Conceived in historical context, however, their ideas seem timely rather than dated. In the 1950s, they were hardly alone in offering proposals for the deconcentration of American industry. Many economists and public policy-makers alike during this period were convinced that only through a greater degree of market regulation could the trend towards oligopoly and monopoly be reversed.[265] By the following decade, the deconcentration

[261] Ibid. 22. [262] Ibid. 110. [263] Ibid. 114–15. [264] Ibid. 111.

[265] See Joe S. Bain, *Barriers to New Competition: Their Character and Consequences in Manufacturing Industries* (Cambridge, Mass.: Harvard University Press, 1956); *Attorney General's National Committee to Study the Antitrust Laws* (Washington, DC: United States Department of Justice Report, 1955); Derek C. Bok, 'Section 7 of the Clayton Act and the Merging of Law and Economics', *Harvard L. Rev.*, 74 (1960), 226–355. More generally, see Herbert Hovenkamp, 'Derek Bok and the Merger of Law and Economics', *U. Michigan Jnl. of Law Reform*, 21 (1988), 515–39, an article which deals with much more than just Bok.

initiative had intensified. The White House Task Force on Antitrust Policy, appointed in 1968 by President Lyndon Johnson and chaired by Phil Neal, then Dean of the Chicago Law School, recommended the adoption of a Concentrated Industries Act, designed to reduce concentration in any industry in which four or fewer firms possessed at least 70 per cent of the aggregate market share.[266] Considered in the light of such developments, Kaysen and Turner's call for legislation enabling the restructuring of concentrated industries can be seen to embody the antitrust orthodoxy of the period. Indeed, their perspective influenced significantly the thinking of antitrust enforcement officials in the post-war era.[267] 'Their proposals are important', Robert Bork wrote as late as 1978, 'because they are representative of the trend of thinking about problems of monopoly and oligopoly. The prospect that such proposals may one day be enacted should not be dismissed as fanciful.'[268]

Given that Kaysen and Turner had so clearly articulated post-war concerns about antitrust policy, one might be forgiven for wondering why so much attention has been devoted to the economic analysis of antitrust at Chicago. One of the principal representatives of Chicago antitrust analysis, Richard Posner, studied law at Harvard between 1959 and 1962 and has acknowledged his own intellectual debt to Kaysen and Turner.[269] Turner in particular, he has suggested, did more than anyone else to introduce economic analysis into the antitrust field.[270] Yet Posner also notes that Turner—like Phil Neal, who had headed the White House Task Force on deconcentration initiatives—eventually came under the spell of the Chicago tradition.[271] By the mid-1970s, Turner was arguing—in classic Chicago fashion—that the primary objective of the antitrust laws is to maximize consumer welfare through the efficient allocation of resources. Any attempt to accommodate non-efficiency goals within the antitrust framework was considered likely to subvert this basic objective.[272]

[266] White House Task Force on Antitrust Policy, 'Report of the White House Task Force on Antitrust Policy', *Antitrust Law & Econ. Rev.*, 2 (1968–9), 11–52.

[267] See Kovacic, *supra* n. 142, 1136.

[268] Bork, *supra* n. 233, 177.

[269] Richard A. Posner, letter to author, 12 November 1991. ('[A]mong the jurists and scholars from whom I derived my scholarly agenda—Stigler, Becker, Coase, Director, Kaysen and Turner, Calabresi—none is or was a legal realist.')

[270] Kitch (ed.), *supra* n. 146, 198 (comment by Posner): '[I]f you wanted to pick a single individual whose economic writings have been most influential on the legal profession in the antitrust area, it would be Turner.'

[271] Ibid. (comment by Posner): 'Don Turner has been an enormously influential factor in the economic analysis of law. It is interesting to me that his own ideas have been influenced by Aaron [Director] and his students and by George [Stigler] and his students, and today his ideas are not easily distinguishable from those of the Chicago school.' On Neal, see Posner and Easterbrook, *supra* n. 224, 913. In the 1960s, Neal taught the antitrust course at the Chicago Law School with Aaron Director.

[272] See Phillip Areeda and Donald F. Turner, *Antitrust Law* (3 vols. Boston: Little, Brown & Co., 1978), I, paras. 103–4.

Furthermore, the existence of predatory pricing strategies within markets, Turner insisted, is rarely ever confirmed.[273] It is precisely such arguments which have caused many modern legal theorists to treat the Chicago and Harvard traditions of antitrust scholarship as barely distinguishable.[274] By the 1970s, Chicago-inspired economic analysis was beginning clearly to dominate debate about antitrust policy in the United States. Why should this have happened?

There is no simple answer to this question. One reason is that, as an area of law, antitrust is peculiarly open to the influence of economic ideas; and since economic analysis at Chicago evolved largely in response to certain prevalent assumptions about the objectives of antitrust policy, it has a direct applicability to antitrust problems which is often lacking in other economic theories.[275] As regards antitrust law, according to Robert Bork, '[o]ne does not have to be a real economist to benefit' from the teachings of Chicago neo-classical economics, for this is a field 'in which the simple ideas are the most powerful ideas'.[276] Indeed, Bork's own antitrust scholarship exemplifies this claim. In passing the Sherman Act 1890, Bork argues, Congress intended no goal other than the attainment of economic efficiency.[277] In fact, '[t]he whole task of antitrust', he asserts, 'can be summed up as the effort to improve allocative efficiency without impairing productive efficiency so greatly as to produce either no gain or a net loss in consumer welfare. That task must be guided by basic economic analysis, otherwise the law acts blindly upon forces it does not understand and produces results it does not intend.'[278] Although, by the early 1970s, the Supreme Court appeared to be modifying its approach to antitrust, in the previous decade, Bork argued, it had generally paid little attention to economic analysis, and in consequence had tended to treat the antitrust legislation as embracing non-efficiency goals.[279]

Bork's thesis illustrates how Chicago economic analysis, as applied to antitrust, is prescriptive as well as descriptive. He describes what he considers to be the basic goal of antitrust, and he argues that the enforcement agencies, if they are to remain faithful to that goal, ought to

[273] See Phillip Areeda and Donald F. Turner, 'Predatory Pricing and Related Practices Under Section 2 of the Sherman Act', *Harvard L. Rev.*, 88 (1975), 697–733; and also Wesley J. Liebeler, 'Whither Predatory Pricing? From Areeda and Turner to *Matsushita*', *Notre Dame L. Rev.*, 61 (1986), 1052–98.

[274] See Hovenkamp, 'Distributive Justice and the Antitrust Laws', *supra* n. 244, 4; Lande, *supra* n. 244, 86–7 fn. 89; Fox, 'The Modernization of Antitrust', *supra* n. 245, 1177.

[275] See William E. Kovacic, 'The Influence of Economics on Antitrust Law', *Economic Inquiry*, 30 (1992), 294–306 at 299.

[276] Robert H. Bork, 'The Role of the Courts in Applying Economics', *Antitrust L.J.*, 54 (1985), 21–26 at 22.

[277] Bork, *supra* n. 233, 20–1.

[278] Ibid. 91.

[279] See ibid. 210–16. On Bork's influence on antitrust policy in the United States, see William E. Kovacic, '*The Antitrust Paradox* Revisited: Robert Bork and the Transformation of Modern Antitrust Policy', *Wayne L. Rev.*, 36 (1990), 1413–71.

learn some elementary economics. Writing in the mid-1970s, Richard Posner observed similarly that:

> As a result of neglect of economic principles, the judges, lawyers, and enforcement personnel who are responsible for giving meaning to the vague language of antitrust statutes have fashioned a body of substantive doctrine and a system of sanctions and procedures that are poorly suited to carrying out the fundamental objectives of antitrust policy—the promotion of competition and efficiency. The per se rule against price fixing, the merger rules, the rules governing competition in the distribution of goods, the tie-in rule, the use of structural remedies, the trial of antitrust cases according to methods of proof developed hundreds of years ago—these . . . reflect above all an endeavour, sometimes ingenious and sometimes pathetic, to set antitrust free from any dependence on economic principles. The endeavour has failed; the system is in disarray. The time has come to rethink antitrust with the aid of economics.[280]

The degree to which Chicago economic analysis has become entrenched in modern American antitrust culture seems to be attributable in large measure to its explicitly normative dimension. Antitrust policy, it is argued, ought to develop in a very specific direction. That is, if it is properly to promote allocative efficiency, it must accept certain basic postulates: for example, that there will often exist non-monopolistic explanations for ostensibly monopolistic practices such as dominant firm pricing;[281] that, where concentration exists, it is likely eventually to be dissolved by the market itself if it produces inefficiency;[282] and that, in dealing with market concentration, the courts have limited fact-finding and remedial capabilities and are unlikely to be able to envisage the costs of implementing a particular deconcentrative policy.[283] These are the basic lessons of the Chicago tradition of antitrust analysis as inspired by Aaron Director.[284] The principal message behind these lessons is that the capacity of the legislature, the courts and other enforcement agencies in combating industrial concentration is very limited and that, since economic enterprise depends upon and flourishes with free competition, concerted efforts to eliminate such competition are likely to meet with market resistance. It is

[280] Posner, *supra* n. 233, 236.

[281] See Lester G. Telser, 'Why Should Manufacturers Want Fair Trade?', *Jnl. Law & Econ.*, 3 (1960), 86–105; 'Why Should Manufacturers Want Fair Trade II?', *Jnl. Law & Econ.*, 33 (1990), 409–17; 'Cooperation, Competition, and Efficiency', *Jnl. Law & Econ.*, 28 (1985), 271–95; Harold Demsetz, *Efficiency, Competition, and Policy: The Organization of Economic Activity, Volume II* (Oxford: Blackwell, 1989), 208–24.

[282] See Frank H. Easterbrook, 'Breaking Up is Hard To Do', *Regulation*, 5 (1981), 25–31.

[283] See Frank H. Easterbrook, 'Allocating Antitrust Decisionmaking Tasks', *Georgetown L.J.*, 76 (1987), 305–20; Richard A. Posner, 'Information and Antitrust: Reflections on the *Gypsum* and *Engineers* Decisions', *Georgetown L.J.*, 67 (1979), 1187–203.

[284] See, generally, Page, *supra* n. 231, 1237–57.

on the basis of such reasoning that some lawyer–economists have argued that there is really no need for legislation in this domain, that markets should be left to rely on their own capacity for self-correction[285]—an argument, in other words, not for an antitrust policy, but for an anti-antitrust policy.

While the image of Chicago economic analysis embodying an 'anti-antitrust' perspective is somewhat exaggerated—most lawyer–economists in the Chicago tradition wish to see the legal regulation of monopoly limited and exercised realistically rather than abolished[286]—it is by no means insignificant. According to certain of its critics, the primary characteristics of Chicago antitrust jurisprudence—the sanctification of efficiency and the distrust of intervention—ensured that it was perfectly suited to the economic outlook of the Reagan administration.[287] Certainly it would be wrong to assume that the appeal of Chicago antitrust analysis has grown solely out of the fact that it reflected the economic sensibilities of one particular political party in government. What does seem to be of significance, however, is the fact that lawyer–economists in the Chicago tradition were primarily responsible for providing the theoretical justification for the antitrust programme of that party. Equally importantly, it was owing to both academic and political initiatives that this programme became fairly well established—although not quite firmly entrenched—in American law.

[285] See e.g. Dominick T. Armentano, 'Time to Repeal Antitrust Legislation?', *Antitrust Bulletin*, 35 (1990), 311–28; William F. Shugart II, 'Don't Revise the Clayton Act, Scrap It!', *Cato Jnl.*, 6 (1987), 925–32; Craig M. Newmark, 'Is Antitrust Enforcement Effective?', *Jnl. Pol. Econ.*, 96 (1988), 1315–28; Lester C. Thurow, 'Let's Abolish the Antitrust Laws', *New York Times* 19 October 1980 at 2 F. col. 3.

[286] See e.g. Posner, *supra* n. 233, 212–17 (arguing for the repeal of all antitrust legislation other than Section 1 of the Sherman Act).

[287] See John J. Flynn, ' "Reaganomics" and Antitrust Enforcement: A Jurisprudential Critique', *Utah L. Rev.*, [1983], 269–312 esp. at 271–2. ('According to the Chicago school, we should pretend that the economy is governed by consumers equal in all respects, that consumers behave rationally in all circumstances, that power and wealth distribution are equal, that large institutions either do not exist or behave like individuals and that the task of the law is to rid rational economic man of government interference in the free competitive economy. . . . These policies have been implemented for the past three years by the Reagan Administration. . . . [T]he leaders of the enforcement agencies have bluntly stated that they intend to apply the Chicago school theology of microeconomics to all aspects of antitrust enforcement.') In this context, see also David R. Bickel, 'The Antitrust Division's Adaptation of a Chicago School Economic Policy Calls for Some Reorganization: But is the Division's New Policy Here to Stay?', *Houston L. Rev.*, 20 (1983), 1083–127; Thomas J. Campbell, 'The Antitrust Record of the First Reagan Administration', *Texas L. Rev.*, 64 (1985), 353–69; John J. Flynn, 'The Reagan Administration's Antitrust Policy: "Original Intent" and the Legislative History of the Sherman Act', *Antitrust Bulletin*, 33 (1988), 259–307; and Ira M. Millstein and Jeffrey L. Kessler, 'The Antitrust Legacy of the Reagan Administration', *Antitrust Bulletin*, 33 (1988), 505–41. More generally, on the influence on the Reagan administration of pro-market economic theory, see Ann M. Reilly, 'Reagan's Think Tank', *Dun's Review*, April 1981, 110–14.

In assessing the influence of Chicago economic analysis on the evolution of modern American antitrust law, two distinct developments deserve consideration. First of all, there is the matter of how economic analysis has found its way into the courts. Between 1981 and 1988, besides selecting three new members for and appointing a new Chief Justice of the Supreme Court, the Reagan administration was responsible for the appointment of 47 per cent of all judges sitting on the federal district courts and courts of appeals.[288] While the use of judicial appointments to promote policy objectives is nothing new in the American political arena, the general initiative of the Reagan administration—and the continuation of that initiative by President George Bush[289]—stands nonpareil. The Reagan administration made a concerted effort to alter the ideological perspective of the federal judiciary by selecting individuals who, among other things, tended to doubt the wisdom of government intervention into the affairs of business.

This effort is perhaps epitomized by appointment to the federal courts of appeals of Richard Posner, Robert Bork—whose nomination to the Supreme Court was rejected by Senate—and Frank Easterbrook: all representatives of the Chicago tradition of antitrust analysis. By appointing to the bench lawyer–economists and other individuals with distinctive pro-market, anti-interventionist views, the Reagan administration was able to influence strongly the evolution of antitrust in the courts.[290] Antitrust adjudication by no means became totally dominated by Chicago economic analysis—many judges, including certain of those with roots in the Chicago tradition,[291] resisted such a development[292]—but the impact of the

[288] See Sheldon Goldman, 'Reagan's Judicial Legacy: Completing the Puzzle and Summing Up', *Judicature*, 72 (1989), 318–38 at 318–19. During his presidency, Reagan also appointed two lawyer–economists—first, William Baxter of Stanford, then Douglas Gibsburg of Harvard (now a judge on the United States Court of Appeals for the District of Columbia Circuit)—to head the Antitrust Division of the Justice Department.

[289] On Bush's continuation of the Reagan judicial appointment programme, see Bill Clinton, 'Judiciary Suffers Racial, Sexual Lack of Balance', *National L.J.*, 2 November 1992, 15–16. On the prospects of Clinton stamping his own mark on the federal judiciary, see William E. Kovacic, 'Judicial Appointments and the Future of Antitrust Policy', *Antitrust,* Spring 1993, 8–13 at 8.

[290] See William E. Kovacic, 'Public Choice and the Public Interest: Federal Trade Commission Antitrust Enforcement During the Reagan Administration', *Antitrust Bulletin*, 33 (1988), 467–504 at 495–7; Comment, 'Changing Configurations of Antitrust Law: Judge Posner's Applications of His Economic Analysis to Antitrust Doctrine', *De Paul L. Rev.*, 32 (1983), 839–71.

[291] See e.g. Antonin Scalia, 'On the Merits of the Frying Pan', *Regulation*, [1985], 10–14; Richard A. Posner, *The Federal Courts: Crisis and Reform* (Cambridge, Mass.: Harvard University Press, 1985), 152 (arguing that one of the problems with the establishment of a specialized antitrust appeals court is that it would most likely become dominated by judges affiliated to a particular economic 'camp').

[292] See Ian Shapiro, 'Richard Posner's Praxis', *Ohio State L.J.*, 48 (1987), 999–1046 at 1036–45 (arguing that, although Posner's antitrust opinions on the Seventh Circuit reflect the

Reagan–Bush judicial appointment strategy on the economic orientation of antitrust was well-nigh impossible to ignore. According to William Kovacic, 'President Reagan's selection of distinguished academics to sit on the courts of appeals yielded jurists with the necessary reservoir of ideas to make the process of opinion-writing an important vehicle for adjusting the boundaries of legal doctrine. The intellectual capital of these appointees supplies a significant tool for shaping the thinking of other members of the same court.'[293] Also important in this context is the work of law clerks, to whom the task of judicial opinion-writing is often delegated.[294] 'Since the mid-1970s,' Kovacic has noted, 'law school graduates have absorbed large doses of Chicago School learning,'[295] and it is partially a consequence of their efforts as clerks that neo-classical economic analysis appears at times to underscore antitrust adjudication. To put the matter very straightforwardly, in one way or another, Chicago economic analysis has made its mark on judicial decision-making in the field of antitrust.

Also significant in this context have been the efforts of certain lawyer–economists to educate federal judges in the principles of neo-classical economics. In the mid-1970s, at the University of Miami, Henry Manne established a Law and Economics Centre offering a two-week intensive training programme in economic analysis for federal judges.[296] In 1980, Manne moved the programme to Emory University, Atlanta; and in 1986 he moved it again, to Virginia, when he assumed his present position as Dean of the George Mason University School of Law. A graduate of the University of Chicago Law School and a disciple of Aaron Director,[297] Manne had established a reputation in the 1960s as a critic of the Securities and Exchange Commission and a vigorous advocate of corporate *laissez-faire*.[298] Although the original objective of Manne's law and economics

minimalist view of antitrust law which he has developed in his academic writings, certain of his colleagues have attempted to distance themselves from his style of economic analysis). For Posner's reply to Shapiro, see Richard A. Posner, 'On Theory and Practice: Reply to "Richard Posner's Praxis" ', *Ohio State L.J.*, 49 (1989), 1077–84.

293 William E. Kovacic, 'Reagan's Judicial Appointees and Antitrust in the 1990s', *Fordham L. Rev.*, 60 (1991), 49–124 at 114.

294 On the delegation of judicial tasks to law clerks, see Robert A. Carp and Ronald Stidham, *The Federal Courts* (Washington, DC: Congressional Quarterly Press, 1991), 75–9.

295 Kovacic, *supra* n. 275, 302.

296 For the historical details, see Editors, 'Foreword: Antitrust Law and Economics at the University of Miami', *Antitrust Law & Econ. Rev.*, 14 (1982), 1–8 at 2–3.

297 See Kitch (ed.), *supra* n. 146, 184 (comments of Henry Manne).

298 See e.g. Henry G. Manne, 'Our Two Corporate Systems: Law and Economics', *Virginia L. Rev.*, 53 (1967), 259–84; 'The Higher Criticism of the Modern Corporation', *Columbia L. Rev.*, 62 (1962), 399–432; 'Mergers and the Market for Corporate Control', *Jnl. Pol. Econ.*, 73 (1965), 110–20; *Insider Trading and the Stock Market* (New York: Free Press, 1966); 'In Defense of Insider Trading', *Harvard Business Rev.*, 44 (1966), 113–22; and also Romano, *supra* n. 143, 977–8.

programme was to provide judges with some basic economic training, it has been widely criticized for embodying a distinctively Chicago-inspired, pro-corporate, anti-antitrust agenda[299]—'Henry Manne's summer indoctrination session', as Arthur Leff once labelled it.[300] Critics have also alleged that a substantial amount of the funding for the programme has come from corporate donors.[301] In the past, according to one critic, certain of these corporations have even had cases 'before the very judges attending the Centre'.[302] Thus it is that a rather murky image emerges—an image, that is, of corporations funding the Law and Economics Centre to persuade federal judges that legal regulation of corporate activity is foolhardy and unnecessary.

While lawyers and economists involved with Manne's programme have denied the charge of pro-corporate bias, what nobody would dispute is the actual success of the initiative. Almost since its inception, the programme—which judges attend all expenses paid—has been over-subscribed;[303] and by 1983, over one third of the federal judiciary had attended it at least once.[304] The suggestion that the law and economics programme is a free-market indoctrination session, that it brainwashes federal judges, seems distinctly far-fetched. Surely even a judge cannot be brainwashed within a fortnight. Nevertheless, the Manne initiative has clearly proved successful in exposing a significant proportion of the federal judiciary to a particular style of legal–economic inquiry; and there indeed appears to be at least some evidence that certain judges, after having attended the programme, have begun to apply the principles of Chicago neo-classical analysis in the

[299] See Roger E. Meiners (interview), 'No Antitrust "Bias" at the Law and Economics Center: Federal Judges Can't be "Brainwashed" ', *Antitrust Law & Econ. Rev.*, 14 (1982), 71–86; Robert J. Staaf (interview), 'Roots of Our Antitrust Doubt: From Jefferson to Chicago', *Antitrust Law & Econ. Rev.*, 14 (1982), 87–94; Louis De Alessi (interview), 'Antitrust, "Bias", and the Special Vision of Henry Manne: A Merger of Law and Science', *Antitrust Law & Econ. Rev.*, 14 (1982), 95–110; William J. Guzzardi, Jr., 'Judges Discover the World of Economics', *Fortune,* 21 May 1979, 58, 66.

[300] Leff, *supra* n. 6, 452.

[301] See Gregory C. Staple, 'Free-Market Cram Course for Judges', *The Nation*, 26 January 1980, 78–81 at 79; Steven Barbash, 'Big Corporations Bankroll Seminars for US Judges', *The Washington Post,* 20 January 1980, A–1, col. 1.

[302] Willard F. Mueller, 'The Anti-Antitrust Movement and the Case of Lester Thurow', *Antitrust Law & Econ. Rev.*, 13 (1981), 59–91 at 71.

[303] See Editors, 'Foreword: Chicago Economics, the FTC, and the Education of the Federal Judiciary', *Antitrust Law & Econ. Rev.*, 15 (1983), 1–8 at 6–7.

[304] Ibid. 7. See also Henry G. Manne, *An Intellectual History of the School of Law, George Mason University* (Arlington, Va.: Law and Economics Center, 1993), 12. ('From its beginning this programme has proved enormously popular and useful to the federal judiciary. At the present time more than 400 federal judges have completed at least the basic course, and most of them have returned for one or more of the five advanced courses the LEC offers. In recent years the Centre has also branched out by offering a course in basic science and scientific method to federal judges as well.')

resolution of antitrust cases.[305] Estimating the influence of Manne's law and economics programme is clearly very difficult; but there can be little doubt that the impact of Chicago antitrust analysis on federal judicial thinking would have been less significant without it.

The second development to consider in assessing the influence of Chicago economic analysis is the changing outlook of the courts themselves. For, irrespective of the particular political and academic initiatives that have been undertaken to shape judicial approaches to antitrust, the courts appear at times to have embraced neo-classical economic principles of their own accord. This is especially evident in the modern antitrust jurisprudence of the Supreme Court. In *Continental T.V., Inc.* v. *GTE Sylvania, Inc.*, decided in 1977, the Court held that non-price restrictions on commercial distribution, such as attempts by manufacturers to map out exclusive territories for their retail outlets, should not be treated as *per se* illegal but ought to be governed by the so-called 'Rule of Reason'—that is, they should be judged by reference to their actual effect on competition.[306] The decision marked a significant move away from previous antitrust adjudication. Before *Sylvania*, territorial restraints imposed by manufacturers had been considered by the Court to constitute a form of vertical monopoly, reducing competition among dealers.[307] *Sylvania* did not quite overturn this previous position—it provided, after all, not that distributional restraints are always lawful, but that they should be judged by the Rule of Reason[308]—but it showed the Court to be focusing less on the market share and the internal structure of companies and more on the actual effect of their activities in the market-place. An essential lesson of Chicago antitrust analysis—that the existence of market concentration does not necessarily denote a diminution in competition—had been judicially absorbed.[309] Mergers which increased the market share of firms,

[305] See Staple, *supra* n. 301, 80–1.

[306] *Continental T.V., Inc.* v. *GTE Sylvania, Inc.* (1977) 433 U.S. 36. On the notoriously vague 'Rule of Reason'—first formulated in the *Standard Oil* case (*supra* n. 227)—see Tony Freyer, 'The Sherman Antitrust Act, Comparative Business Structure, and the Rule of Reason: America and Great Britain, 1880–1920', *Iowa L. Rev.*, [1989], 991–1017 at 1004–16; Ernest Gellhorn and Theresa Tatham, 'Making Sense Out of the Rule of Reason', *Case Western Reserve L. Rev.*, 35 (1985), 155–82; Posner and Easterbrook, *supra* n. 224, 258–62. For a discussion of why the effect of antitrust regulation on economic competition is often different from what regulators intended, see Michael H. Best, *The New Competition: Institutions of Industrial Restructuring* (Cambridge: Polity, 1990), 88–96.

[307] See e.g. *United States* v. *Sealy, Inc.* (1967) 388 U.S. 350; *United States* v. *Topco Assocs.* (1972) 405 U.S. 596; *United States* v. *Arnold Schwinn & Co.* (1967) 388 U.S. 365.

[308] In this context, see Richard A. Posner, 'The Rule of Reason and the Economic Approach: Reflections on the *Sylvania* Decision', *U. Chicago L. Rev.*, 45 (1977), 1–20; 'The Next Step in the Antitrust Treatment of Restricted Distribution: *Per Se* Legality', *U. Chicago L. Rev.*, 48 (1981), 6–26.

[309] See Bork, *supra* n. 233, 86–7. ('*Sylvania*. . .. adopt[ed] a mode of reasoning that will prove enormously beneficial if employed throughout antitrust. . . . The great virtue of

it was now recognized, could often be justified on efficiency grounds. Concentration was no longer quite the dirty word that it had once been.

Throughout the 1970s and 1980s, the Supreme Court—with the exception of the odd retrogressive decision[310]—drew itself ever closer to the basic Chicago line on purportedly monopolistic activity. With increasing frequency, the Court declined to treat predatory strategies such as price-fixing and restraint of trade as necessarily anti-competitive.[311] Endorsement of Chicago antitrust analysis was made most explicit in the *Matsushita* case of 1986, in which the Court, taking into account scholarly literature on the subject, declared that allegations of predatory pricing are rarely ever plausible.[312] Firms would only invest in sustained predatory pricing strategies, the Court emphasized, so long as they could reasonably expect that their competitors would be 'neutralized'; for only thus would such firms be able to acquire market control and thereby recoup their losses through monopoly profits. If one were to believe in the prevalence of predatory pricing, the Court insisted, then one would be compelled to conclude that firms such as Matsushita—which had, for some twenty years, been setting low prices in the American consumer electronics market without ever coming near to monopolizing it—were operating in an economically irrational fashion. In truth, the Court concluded, firms would not spend twenty years attempting to monopolize a market through price predation when such a strategy patently did not work. Thus it is that, in *Matsushita*, the Supreme Court demonstrated writ large its faith in Chicago antitrust analysis.

Detractors from the Chicago tradition insist, however, that it is easy to overemphasize the influence of that tradition on modern antitrust adjudication. In spite of *Matsushita*, critics observe, the lower courts

Sylvania is not so much that it preserves a method of distribution valuable to consumers, though that is certainly a welcome development, but that it displays a far higher degree of economic sophistication than we have become accustomed to, and introduces an approach that, generally applied, is capable of making antitrust a rational, proconsumer policy once more.')

[310] See, in particular, *Arizona* v. *Maricopa County Medical Society* (1982) 102 S. Ct. 2466; and, more generally, Peter M. Gerhart, 'The Supreme Court and Antitrust Analysis: the (Near) Triumph of the Chicago School', *Sup. Ct. Rev.*, [1982], 319–49 esp. 344. ('Had the Supreme Court recognized the substantial doctrinal synthesis it achieved in its pre-*Maricopa* cases, it would have written a much different opinion in *Maricopa*. Its *Maricopa* opinion is retrogressive: it champions a wooden, mechanical view of the *per se* rules and fails to recognize the full range of circumstances in which trade restraints may promote competition.')

[311] See e.g. *National Society of Professional Engineers* v. *United States* (1978) 435 U.S. 679; *Broadcast Music, Inc.* v. *Columbia Broadcasting System, Inc.* (1979) 441 U.S. 1; *Reiter* v. *Sonotone Corp.* (1979) 442 U.S. 330; *Catalano, Inc.* v. *Target Sales, Inc.* (1980) 446 U.S. 643.

[312] *Matsushita Electric Industrial Co.* v. *Zenith Radio Corp.* (1986) 475 U.S. 574.

continue to entertain predatory pricing suits;[313] and, in many respects, the Supreme Court itself appears simply to have refused to embrace Chicago ideas. By repeatedly reaffirming the Rule of Reason treatment of territorial restrictions, the Court has demonstrated a clear unwillingness to move beyond the *Sylvania* decision; furthermore, despite *Matsushita*, it has not accepted outright the proposition that predatory pricing is *per se* legal. In these and other respects, the antitrust jurisprudence of the Supreme Court falls noticeably short of Chicago ideals.[314] Most significantly, according to William Page, 'despite the assertions of Chicagoans to the contrary, the Court has never expressly adopted the standard of economic efficiency as the sole goal of antitrust. The various references the Court has made to "economic efficiency" and "consumer welfare" as goals are too ambiguous in their lexical meaning and in their content to justify the conclusion that the Court has adopted the Chicago conception of efficiency as its sole standard in antitrust cases.'[315] It is owing to the fact that neo-classical economic analysis has been only partially, rather than wholly, embraced by the Supreme Court that opponents of the Chicago tradition continue vigorously to promote competing theories of antitrust, theories which assume to at least some degree the rationality and the anti-competitive effects of predatory pricing, which emphasize non-efficiency antitrust goals and which advocate a policy of legislative activism.[316] While Chicago may have dominated the struggle for the soul of antitrust, it is a struggle which seems destined to continue.[317]

Antitrust, however, is only one aspect of law and economics. Compared with other developments in the subject, furthermore, it is for the most part rather unsophisticated. The reason for this, ironically, is that antitrust has an obvious economic dimension. The cutting-edge of modern legal–economic inquiry has tended to evolve around areas of law which lack such a dimension—areas, that is, in which the demonstration of the explanatory and critical powers of economic analysis has proved generally to be more challenging. It is only by considering how law and economics has branched out in this way that we might begin properly to appreciate its appeal and its

[313] See e.g. *U.S. Philips Corp.* v. *Windmere Corp.* (Fed. Cir. 1988) 861 F.2d 695 (reversing directed verdict); *McGahee* v. *Northern Propane Gas Co.* (11th Cir. 1988) 858 F.2d 1487; and, more generally, Susan S. DeSanti and William E. Kovacic, '*Matsushita:* Its Construction and Application by the Lower Courts', *Antitrust L.J.*, 59 (1991), 609–53 at 618–35.

[314] See further Page, *supra* n. 231, 1254.

[315] Ibid.

[316] See Louis Kaplow, 'Antitrust, Law and Economics, and the Courts', *Law and Contemporary Problems*, 50 (1987), 181–216; Jonathan B. Baker, 'Recent Developments in Economics that Challenge the Chicago School Views', *Antitrust L.J.*, 58 (1989), 645–55 esp. 648–9 (on the rationality, in certain circumstances, of predatory pricing); Robert H. Lande, 'The Rise and (Coming) Fall of Efficiency as the Ruler of Antitrust', *Antitrust Bulletin*, 33 (1988), 429–66; and Kovacic, *supra* n. 142, 1143–50.

[317] See, generally, Robert Pitofsky, 'Does Antitrust Have a Future?', *Georgetown L.J.*, 76 (1987), 321–7; 'Antitrust in the Next 100 Years', *California L. Rev.*, 75 (1987), 817–33.

influence within American legal thought. In the most simplistic of terms, this requires that we turn from the 'old' to the 'new' law and economics. Yet—and this demonstrates the very imprecision of these labels—doing this demands first of all that we step backwards to consider further the development of neo-classical economics at the University of Chicago in the post-war years. For it is only through an appreciation of the economic analysis of this period that we might begin to make sense of much of the legal–economic analysis which followed in its wake.

TOURING HYDE PARK WITH THE RATIONAL ECONOMIC MAN

'A few people', George Stigler wrote in 1972, 'believe that almost all regulation is bad, and by a singular coincidence a significant fraction of the academic part of this group resides within a radius of one mile of my university.'[318] For all its apparent flippancy, the observation is a fairly significant one. In the early 1950s, while a professor at Columbia University, Stigler had argued *à la* Berle and Means for corporate deconcentration through a more effective system of antitrust regulation. 'The proper way to deal with monopolistic practices', he had insisted, 'is to replace the general prohibitions of the Sherman Act by a specific list of prohibited practices, so businessmen may know in advance and avoid committing monopolistic practices.'[319] By the following decade—having returned to the Chicago economics department (from where he had received his doctorate under Frank Knight in 1938)—Stigler was professing his loss of faith in such regulatory initiatives.[320] In due course, he would demonstrate also how this loss of faith led him to doubt the conclusions of Berle and Means.[321] Stigler, in returning to Chicago, had found a new faith—the faith which, in his eyes, was being practised most devoutly within a one mile radius of his university.

Since the Second World War, the Hyde Park district of Chicago, in which the University is situated, has become home to many of America's most eminent neo-classical economists. The great advantage of universities

[318] George J. Stigler, 'Regulation: The Confusion of Means and Ends' [1972], in his *The Citizen and the State: Essays in Regulation* (Chicago: University of Chicago Press, 1975), 167–77 at 167.

[319] George J. Stigler, 'The Case Against Big Business', *Fortune*, May 1952, 123, 158, 162, 164, 167 at 162, 164; and see further Stigler, *supra* n. 176, 97.

[320] See e.g George J. Stigler (in collaboration with Claire Friedland), 'What Can Regulators Regulate?: The Case of Electricity' [1962], in his *The Citizen and the State*, *supra* n. 318, 61–77; Stigler, 'The Economic Effects of the Antitrust Laws', *Jnl. Law & Econ.*, 9 (1966), 225–8.

[321] See George J. Stigler and Claire Friedland, 'The Literature of Economics: The Case of Berle and Means', *Jnl. Law & Econ.*, 26 (1983), 237–68.

based in big cities, Stigler has observed, is that they tend to lack the homogeneity and insularity of provincial colleges.[322] Yet the University of Chicago does not entirely lend weight to this observation. Hyde Park is a highly affluent and very beautiful district situated between downtown Chicago and the south-side of the city. While to stray a few blocks too far north or south is to enter into other worlds, Hyde Park itself is a wonderful academic environment—by no means in splendid isolation, but certainly quite different from the city which surrounds it. The neo-classical economic tradition 'was able to flourish and to be successful at the University of Chicago', Milton Friedman has claimed, 'largely because of our geographic location. Had the University been established in or near New York under precisely the same auspices and the same initial personnel, I believe that the results would have been very different.'[323]

One must, of course, be wary of reading too much into geographical location. While economics at Chicago has evolved within a fairly close-knit intellectual environment, it would be wrong to imagine that the economics department there is simply a neo-classical enclave.[324] Hyde Park, furthermore, is not quite the home of *Das Glasperlenspiel* and the University of Chicago is by no means a totally unworldly place. Indeed, Chicago economists in particular have been especially critical of what they consider to be the economic folly of the intellectual.[325] The lower classes, Stigler argues, generally have a taste for *laissez-faire*; they tend to oppose economic regulation much more than they approve of it. 'These classes', after all, 'have little to gain from regulatory policies that reduce the income of society.'[326] The intellectual, on the other hand, being comparably immune from the ill-effects of economic regulation, will promote its virtues most vigorously. '[M]aterialism is hostile to the ethical values cherished by the intellectual classes',[327] so it is hardly surprising that they should be unconcerned with the promotion of economic productivity through free competition. Yet '[o]nly economies that are highly productive by historical standards can send their populations to schools for twelve to eighteen years, thus providing employment to a large class of educators.'[328] The economic naiveté of the intellectual, Stigler argues, is surpassed only by

[322] Stigler, *supra* n. 176, 41–2.

[323] Milton Friedman, 'Schools at Chicago', *University of Chicago Magazine*, Autumn 1974, 11–16 at 16.

[324] Ibid. 15. It ought at least to be noted that the economics department at Chicago was not solely responsible for the development of neo-classical theory. Responsibility for this development must also be attributed to the business school, and especially to the Center for the Study of the Economy and the State, which was founded in the business school by George Stigler for the purpose of conducting studies into the effects of government regulation.

[325] See Milton Friedman, *Capitalism and Freedom* (Chicago: University of Chicago Press, 1982; orig. publ. 1962), 8.

[326] Stigler, *supra* n. 87, 31.

[327] Ibid. 32.

[328] Ibid.

those professional advocates of regulation—epitomized, during Stigler's era, by Ralph Nader and his followers[329]—who, although they are indignant about the failure of regulatory initiatives in the past, remain irrationally optimistic that such initiatives can be made to work better in the future. 'The professor is an easy burden: if he is responsible and competent, we can be certain that his audience will be at most in the hundreds, not in the hundreds of thousands or millions. The Nader type of reformer is more fearsome, because he is armed with passion, and any irresponsibility and slovenliness in his accusations seems to have little cost to him.'[330]

It seems, accordingly, that the insular intellectual environment of Hyde Park has produced neither total homogeneity nor thorough unworldliness in the Chicago economics tradition. What it does appear to have generated is an intense degree of like-mindedness among a substantial proportion of Chicago economists. 'To economists the world over,' Friedman has claimed, ' "Chicago" designates not a city, not even a University, but a "school". . . . In discussions of economic policy, "Chicago" stands for belief in the efficacy of the free market as a means of organizing resources, for scepticism about government intervention into economic affairs, and for emphasis on the quantity of money as a key factor in producing inflation.'[331] Chicago neo-classical economists, according to another commentator, 'form an interconnected group with a set of common attitudes and interests which distinguishes them from the rest of the economics profession'.[332] Rarely has a school of economic thought been identified so positively.[333]

For all this, however, the constitution of this school is a matter for debate. Certain economic historians trace the beginnings of the school

[329] On the pro-regulatory recommendations of the Nader Study Group, see e.g. Edward F. Cox, Robert C. Fellmeth and John E. Schultz, *The Nader Report on the Federal Trade Commission* (New York: Grove Press, 1969).

[330] Stigler, *supra* n. 318, 173–4.

[331] Friedman, *supra* n. 323, 11.

[332] H. Laurence Miller, Jr., 'On the "Chicago School of Economics" ', *Jnl. Pol. Econ.*, 70 (1962), 64–9 at 64. As a native and resident of the city of Manchester, I cannot resist quoting George Stigler's response to Miller on this point. George J. Stigler, 'Comment', *Jnl. Pol. Econ.*, 70 (1962), 70–1 at 70. ('There obviously are economists who have a strong preference for a private competitive organization of economic activity (and, for that matter, accept the relevance of price theory to substantive problems). Whether this group deserves the name "Chicago"—it once carried the name of an English town—is hardly for a literal Chicagoan to say.')

[333] For one of the earliest attacks on the Chicago school, see G. C. Archibald, 'Chamberlin versus Chicago', *Rev. Econ. Studs.*, 29 (1962), 2–28. Archibald considers as representatives of the school only Friedman and Stigler, both of whom took him to task for his presentation of Chicago price theory: see George J. Stigler, 'Archibald versus Chicago', *Rev. Econ. Studs.*, 30 (1963), 63–4; Milton Friedman, 'More on Archibald versus Chicago', *Rev. Econ. Studs.*, 30 (1963), 65–7; and see also G. C. Archibald, 'Reply to Chicago', *Rev. Econ. Studs.*, 30 (1963), 68–71.

back to the era of Knight and Simons.[334] More commonly, however—and this, to me, seems the more acceptable view—Chicago economics of that era is considered to be methodologically quite distinct from Chicago economics of the post-war era. 'There are not one but two Chicago Schools', wrote the Chicago economics graduate, Martin Bronfenbrenner, in 1962.[335] 'A considerable difference exists between the present generation of Chicagoans and the earlier generation.'[336] As compared with their successors, for example, Chicago neo-classical economists of the 1930s and 1940s were little concerned with, and indeed tended to doubt the validity of, empirical research as a method of testing hypotheses. More importantly, the later generation of Chicago neo-classicists developed a philosophical basis for their economic analysis which had been generally absent from the work of their predecessors.

Knight, Director and other early Chicago economists assumed, but did not explain the proposition, that competition is intrinsic to economic life in a liberal democracy. The rationality of economic self-interest was simply taken as a given, as something which Adam Smith had demonstrated conclusively and that required no further elaboration. Certainly Smith had attempted to demonstrate as much,[337] as many post-war Chicago economists readily acknowledged.[338] But these post-war Chicagoans also regarded Smith's work as a starting rather than as a concluding point for economic analysis. In consequence, their arguments occasionally diverged from those of their mentor. Smith, Stigler observed, was not quite the out-and-out anti-interventionist which many social and political scientists had assumed him to be. 'Where the individual does not know, or does not have the power to advance, his own interests, Smith feels remarkably free to have the state intervene.'[339] Furthermore, in so far as Smith did argue for individual economic liberty, he omitted to explain 'exactly why he wishe[d] most economic life to be free of state regulation'.[340] Modern Chicago neo-classical economists endeavoured, among other things, to fill in the gaps which they believed had been left open by Adam Smith. This demanded, most importantly of all, that they explain more precisely than had Smith

[334] See e.g. Charles K. Wilber and Jon D. Wisman, 'The Chicago School: Positivism or Ideal Type', in Samuels (ed.), *supra* n. 166, 79–93 at 86.

[335] Martin Bronfenbrenner, 'Observations on the "Chicago School(s)" ', *Jnl. Pol. Econ.*, 70 (1962), 72–5 at 72.

[336] Miller, *supra* n. 332, 65.

[337] See Smith, *The Theory of Moral Sentiments*, *supra* n. 212, 82–3; *An Inquiry into the Nature and Causes of the Wealth of Nations*, *supra* n. 212, I, 26–7. More generally, cf. Samuel Hollander, 'Adam Smith and the Self-Interest Axiom', *Jnl. Law & Econ.*, 202 (1977), 133–52.

[338] See George J. Stigler, 'The Economist and the State' [1964], in his *The Citizen and the State*, *supra* n. 318, 38–57 at 38 (on Adam Smith as 'our venerable master'); and cf. more generally Ronald H. Coase, 'Adam Smith's View of Man', *Jnl. Law & Econ.*, 19 (1976), 529–46.

[339] Stigler, *supra* n. 338, 40.

[340] Ibid.

the rationality of economic self-interest; for, without such an explanation, the conclusion that the public regulation of private economic affairs ought to be kept to a bare minimum would seem inevitably, to those not naturally inclined to such a conclusion, to lack foundation. Earlier Chicago neo-classicists had grasped and applied certain of the basic economic insights of Adam Smith. Post-war Chicagoans were more intent on elaborating and extending those insights.

'The cult of efficiency', Daniel Bell observed in 1956, dominated American industry in the post-war era.[341] 'Contemporary America', he claimed, 'is, above all, the machine civilization';[342] and neo-classical economic theory is ill-equipped to explain or assess this phenomenon. 'The economic theory that developed in the West in the last 200 years . . . has been ahistorical and abstractly analytical.'[343] By and large, it 'is based on the model of classical mechanics and operates in the image of the natural sciences. The model leads to the idea of an "equilibrium" in which the "natural" forces seek to reassert themselves and restore economic relations to a balance, the fulcrum of which is 'perfect competition"'.[344] Such a model belongs, Bell argued, to an era and a culture very much distanced from modern America. Adam Smith had written at a time when the industrial class was seeking to rise against the resistance of powerful feudal authority. In contemporary America, in contrast, industry occupied a position of social dominance. Indeed, industry was largely responsible for the cult of efficiency. Explaining and evaluating this cult, Bell insisted, required the development of a new, 'political' economic theory.[345]

While Bell may have hit the target in identifying a post-war cult of efficiency in the United States, he was thoroughly wide of the mark in assuming that the emergence of this cult marked the withering away of neo-classical economics. For it was in the post-war era that neo-classical analysis began to dominate economic discourse.[346] The cult of efficiency could hardly confound Chicago neo-classical economists, for the concept of efficiency was—and indeed still is—at the heart of the neo-classical economic vision. Chicago neo-classicists argue for less government intervention and fewer wealth-distribution policies and for the promotion of more private enterprise—which in turn is assumed to facilitate a more efficient allocation of resources. Intrinsic to this argument is a defence of

[341] Daniel Bell, 'Work and Its Discontents: The Cult of Efficiency in America' [1956], in his *The End of Ideology: On the Exhaustion of Political Ideas in the Fifties* (Cambridge, Mass.: Harvard University Press, 1988), 227–72.

[342] Ibid. 229–30.

[343] Daniel Bell, 'Models and Reality in Economic Discourse', in Daniel Bell and Irving Kristol (eds.), *The Crisis in Economic Theory* (New York: Basic Books, 1981), 46–80 at 76–7.

[344] Ibid. 77.

[345] Ibid. 78–80.

[346] See, generally, Homa Katouzian, *Ideology and Method in Economics* (London: Macmillan, 1980), 45–84.

voluntary exchange as the most efficient method of organizing resources, extending individual choice and preserving political freedoms.[347] In the absence of government intervention, so the argument goes, the free market will function at least as well as, and most likely better than, any other type of economic arrangement. Not that there are never grounds for state paternalism in economic affairs. Children and the insane, for example, will clearly deserve protection.[348] Yet public intervention into the affairs of the market ought to be limited, for with less interference with private enterprise comes a greater degree of individual choice and overall dispersal of market power.[349] It was in endeavouring to justify this argument—that the key to promoting allocative efficiency is to allow, to the greatest extent possible, the flourishing of free competition within the market—that modern Chicago economists began to develop a theoretical foundation for neo-classical analysis which was not borrowed wholly from the writings of Adam Smith.

The theoretical foundation which Chicago neo-classicists developed was by no means one-dimensional. In fact, Chicago neo-classical analysis splits roughly into two types—positive and normative—and within each of these categories it is possible to identify different approaches and arguments. 'The common intellectual framework' of the Chicago school, according to one of their number, 'is derived from three beliefs: first, that theory is of fundamental importance; second, that theory is irrelevant unless set in a definite empirical context; and third, that in the absence of evidence to the contrary, the market works.'[350] Each of these beliefs is exhibited in different ways by different representatives of the Chicago tradition. In short, the quest to justify the premisses of neo-classical analysis has resulted in a variety of 'Chicago' economic perspectives.

Perhaps the most basic of these perspectives is that which can be summarized by the proposition that human beings, since they generally maximize their own self-interests, must be adjudged to be rational economic creatures.[351] It is owing to the fact that individuals are essentially self-interested that they thrive best in a competitive market economy, for such an economy is able to accommodate this intrinsic feature of human nature. This perspective was elaborated as early as 1950 by Armen

[347] See Friedman, *supra* n. 325, 15.

[348] See Friedman, ibid. 33. ('Freedom is a tenable objective only for responsible individuals. We do not believe in freedom for madmen or children.')

[349] On this point, see Ezra J. Mishan, 'The Folklore of the Market: An Inquiry into the Economic Doctrines of the Chicago School', in Samuels (ed.), *supra* n. 166, 95–165 at 142–3.

[350] David Wall, 'Introduction', in David Wall (ed.), *Chicago Essays in Economic Development* (Chicago: University of Chicago Press, 1972), vii–xvi at vii.

[351] See George J. Stigler, 'Economists and Public Policy', *Regulation*, 13 (1982), 13–17 at 16–17.

Alchian, who contended that economic competition resembles a Darwinian process in that the survival of businesses will depend on their ability in the long run to achieve lower costs and greater profits than their competitors.[352] While businesses may not strive at all times to maximize profits, and while they may have other goals, it is not unreasonable to assume that the pursuit of profit maximization is essential to their survival in the market-place.[353] The implication of such an argument is not that economic agents are lightning calculators of costs and benefits, capable in all instances of acting in a perfectly rational fashion. So to act, such agents would require the impossible—complete information regarding every transaction into which they contemplate entering. Nevertheless, Chicago neo-classical economists do contend that economic agents have the capacity to approximate economic rationality.

In arguing as much, representatives of the Chicago tradition basically make light of what Herbert Simon has termed 'bounded rationality'. Economic action, according to Simon, is 'bounded' by the costs of obtaining information about alternative opportunities and by uncertainty about what the future holds. Economic actors, rather like chess-players, are faced with a plethora of alternative possibilities when deciding on their next move: they cannot consider all of these possibilities—that is, they cannot acquire 'perfect' information—even if they so wish. Therefore, rather than adopt a strategy of maximization, economic actors endeavour to 'satisfice' their position by setting certain aspiration levels and, depending on whether their initiatives exceed or fall short of their original target, adjusting these levels upwards or downwards.[354] Chicago economic theorists certainly acknowledge the bounded nature of economic rationality. Indeed, it was George Stigler who first suggested that information can be conceived as an economic commodity. According to Stigler, the standard economic theorem that, in a competitive market, buyers and sellers will seek out and eliminate all differences in prices fails to take account of information costs. Conventional economic wisdom teaches that, so long as there exists a single seller who is willing to accept a price lower than that which the buyer was about to pay, the buyer will seek him out. Yet such a claim, Stigler argues, ignores the fact that buyers must bear the costs of time and travel in gathering information about comparative prices

[352] See Armen A. Alchian, 'Uncertainty, Evolution, and Economic Theory', *Jnl. Pol. Econ.*, 58 (1950), 211–21.

[353] Much the same argument was developed by Stigler in his study of the distribution of firm sizes. See George J. Stigler, *The Organization of Industry* (Homewood, Ill: Irwin, 1968).

[354] See, generally, Herbert A. Simon, *Models of Bounded Rationality and Other Topics in Economic Theory* (two vols. Cambridge, Mass.: MIT Press, 1982); and, for a summary of bounded rationality, Herbert A. Simon, 'Bounded Rationality', in John Eatwell, Murray Milgate and Peter Newman (eds.), *The New Palgrave: A Dictionary of Economics* (four vols. London: Macmillan, 1987), I, 266–8.

and services. For all this, however, Stigler does not regard information costs as necessarily an obstacle to rational economic action. 'Ignorance', he asserts, 'is like subzero weather: by a sufficient expenditure its effects upon people can be kept within tolerable or even comfortable bounds,' even though 'it would be wholly uneconomic entirely to eliminate all its effects.'[355] In other words, despite the fact that individuals contemplating a transaction can never possess perfect information, they will nevertheless acquire and act with due regard for all the available information which they ought, in their own economic interests, to acquire.[356] Thus it is that economic agents approximate rationality.

A rather different slant on this argument is developed by Milton Friedman. Despite the bounded nature of economic rationality, he suggests, it is reasonable to assume that business firms behave as if they are seeking rationally to maximize their profits and as if they are fully aware of the information necessary to succeed in this endeavour. Friedman attempts to demonstrate his proposition by offering the analogy of the expert billiard player:

> It seems not at all unreasonable that excellent predictions would be yielded by the hypothesis that the billiard player made his shots *as if* he knew the complicated mathematical formulas that would give the optimum directions of travel, could estimate accurately by eye the angles, etc., describing the location of the balls, could make lightning calculations from the formulas, and could then make the balls travel in the directions indicated by the formulas. Our confidence in this hypothesis is not based on the belief that billiard players, even expert ones, can or do go through the process described; it derives rather from the belief that, unless in some way or other they were capable of reaching essentially the same result, they would not in fact be *expert* billiard players.[357]

As for expert billiard players, so too for businesses. Following Alchian, Friedman contends that it is reasonable to assume that businesses act as if pursuing a strategy of maximization since, 'unless the behaviour of businessmen in some way or other approximated behaviour consistent with the maximization of returns, it seems unlikely that they would remain in business for long'.[358] Businesses are as unlikely consciously to pursue a strategy of profit-maximization as they are to be run by expert economists; but this does not detract from the fact that businesses, if they are to survive, must approximate rational economic action.

Not only is the maximization of economic self-interest inevitable within a

[355] George J. Stigler, 'The Economics of Information', *Jnl. Pol. Econ.*, 69 (1961), 213–25 at 224.

[356] See Stigler, *supra* n. 351, 16. ('The [Chicago] credo does assert . . . that economic agents learn all the presently knowable things it pays them to know—always on average—and act with due regard for this knowledge.')

[357] Friedman, *supra* n. 171, 21.

[358] Ibid. 22.

competitive economy. It is also, according to certain Chicago neo-classicists, a peculiarly ethical form of behaviour. Such an argument is hinted at in Adam Smith's *Lectures on Jurisprudence*,[359] but within the Chicago neo-classical tradition it is developed in a much more forthright fashion. '[T]he free enterprise economy,' writes Harold Demsetz, professor of economics at the University of Chicago from 1963 to 1971, 'impose[s] a predetermined moral framework within which to work, for it implies that the good society limits the use of legal sanctions, expands the opportunities for choice by individuals, and, therefore, places the responsibility for behaving ethically on its citizens.'[360] Much the same conclusion—albeit accompanied by a different line of argument—is offered by George Stigler. 'Market transactions', he asserts, 'are voluntary and repetitive.'[361] Since they are voluntary, 'they must benefit at least one party and not injure the other. Because they are repetitive, they (usually) make deceit and non-fulfilment of promises unprofitable.'[362] A reputation for commercial probity and goodwill is likely to be an asset to any economic competitor, just as a reputation for dishonesty is likely to work against one's economic self-interest. Accordingly, a competitive economic system characterized by individual utility-maximizing behaviour is by no means a totally selfish and unethical system. For the pursuit of rational self-interest requires often that economic agents take into account the interests and expectations of others.

The rational self-interest thesis as presented thus far has come in for its fair share of criticism. One of the most powerful criticisms of the thesis is commonly formulated in terms of the so-called 'prisoner's dilemma'. Two prisoners are suspected of a crime, placed in separate cells, interrogated individually and offered the same deal by the interrogator. Each prisoner is told that if he confesses to the crime, and if the other prisoner does not confess, he will be a witness for the prosecution and freed without charge;

[359] Adam Smith, *Lectures on Jurisprudence* (orig. publ. 1896, written 1762–66, R. L. Meek, D. D. Raphael and P. G. Stein (eds.), Indianapolis: Liberty Press, 1982), 538–9. ('Whenever commerce is introduced into any country, probity and punctuality always accompany it. These virtues in a rude and barbarous country are almost unknown. . . . This is not at all to be imputed to national character, as some pretend. There is no natural reason why an Englishman or a Scotchman should not be as punctual in performing agreements as a Dutchman. It is far more reduceable to self interest, that general principle which regulates the actions of every man, and which leads men to act in a certain manner from views of advantage, and is as deeply implanted in an Englishman as a Dutchman. A dealer is afraid of losing his character, and is scrupulous in observing every engagement. When a person makes perhaps 20 contracts in a day, he cannot gain so much by endeavouring to impose on his neighbours, as the very appearance of a cheat would make him lose. Where people seldom deal with one another, we find that they are somewhat disposed to cheat, because they can gain more by a smart trick than they can lose by the injury which it does to their character.')

[360] Harold Demsetz, 'Social Responsibility in the Enterprise Economy', *Southwestern Univ. L. Rev.*, 10 (1978), 1–11 at 1.

[361] Stigler, *supra* n. 87, 22.

[362] Ibid.

if he does not confess, and the other prisoner does, he will receive the maximum sentence of ten years; if both prisoners confess, each will be convicted of the crime and receive a five year sentence; and if neither confess, each will be convicted of a lesser crime carrying a one-year sentence. Deciding independently, the best strategy for each prisoner is to confess. Yet if both prisoners adopt that strategy, the outcome is worse than if neither were to confess. Co-operative behaviour would be necessary to ensure the best result for both prisoners. Yet, even assuming that co-operation was permitted, that the prisoners were allowed to speak to one another, their dilemma would remain, for each prisoner would recognize that, by duping the other and deciding to confess after all, he could—so long as the other prisoner had not hit on the same plan—walk free. To act out of pure self-interest in these circumstances is by no means to act rationally. For if both prisoners confess—and neither of them can be sure that this is not going to happen—the result will be worse than if neither were to confess. The prisoner's dilemma demonstrates, accordingly, that rational choice cannot be perceived simply as a matter of maximizing self-interest, that wholly self-interested decision-making does not necessarily ensure individual utility-maximization.[363]

A further common criticism of the rational self-interest thesis is that it is clearly contradicted by reality. 'Even if the characterization of rational behaviour in standard economics were accepted as just right,' Amartya Sen observes, 'it might not necessarily make sense to assume that people would *actually* behave in the rational way characterized. There are many obvious difficulties with this route, especially since it is quite clear that we all do make mistakes, we often experiment, we get confused, and so forth. The world certainly has its share of Hamlets, Macbeths, Lears and Othellos. The coolly rational types may fill our textbooks, but the world is richer.'[364] For all that this seems fair comment, it is not a criticism which can be easily levelled at the Chicago tradition of neo-classical economics, for the simple reason that certain representatives of that tradition argue that realism is not the appropriate criterion by which to evaluate economic assumptions. The classic formulation of this argument is to be found in Milton Friedman's essay, 'The Methodology of Positive Economics', first published in 1953. The purpose of positive economics, Friedman asserts in that essay, 'is to provide a system of generalizations that can be used to make correct predictions about the consequences of any change in circumstances'.[365]

363 See further Amartya K. Sen, 'Rational Fools: A Critique of the Behavioral Foundations of Economic Theory', *Philosophy and Public Affairs*, 6 (1977), 317–44 at 340–1.

364 Amartya Sen, *On Ethics and Economics* (Oxford: Blackwell, 1987), 11.

365 Friedman, *supra* n. 171, 4. On the history of positivism in economic thought, see generally Ben B. Seligman, 'The Impact of Positivism on Economic Thought', *History of Political Economy*, 1 (1969), 256–78.

Properly to assess such generalizations, economists must ask 'not whether they are descriptively "realistic", for they never are, but whether they are sufficiently good approximations for the purpose in hand'.[366] Accordingly, the claim that neo-classical theorists, in assuming economic actors to be rationally self-interested, rely on an outmoded psychology of human motivation 'is largely beside the point unless supplemented by evidence that a hypothesis differing in one or another of these respects from the theory being criticized yields better predictions for as wide a range of phenomena'.[367] It is on the basis of this argument that Friedman is able to support his claim regarding the profit-seeking initiatives of businesses: for all that detractors from the neo-classical perspective may find fault with the concept of rational economic self-interest, he insists, they appear to be incapable of developing economic hypotheses which facilitate more accurate predictions of business strategy.

According to various of its advocates, the peculiar merit of positive economics in the Chicago neo-classical mould, as compared with other economic models, is that it generates predictions of economic behaviour the general accuracy of which can be demonstrated by empirical testing.[368] George Stigler argues, for example, that markets are normally best left to their own devices because neo-classical theory leads us to predict that any attempt at economic regulation is likely to yield unintended and unwelcome consequences. Such a prediction, he insists, is demonstrable as a matter of fact.[369] Yet one of the most common criticisms of Chicago neo-classical economics is that the assumptions on which it is premissed are remarkably difficult to test empirically. Friedman's claim that economic models ought to be judged by their predictive power rather than by the realism of their assumptions has, in this context, come in for particular attention.[370] Critics and supporters of the thesis alike argue that its internal logic makes it untestable and therefore non-falsifiable.[371] How, for

[366] Friedman, *supra* n. 171, 15. [367] Ibid. 31.

[368] On this point, see Karl-Heinz Paqué, 'How Far is Vienna from Chicago? An Essay on the Methodology of Two Schools of Dogmatic Liberalism', *Kyklos*, 38 (1985), 412–34 at 417–18.

[369] See Stigler, *supra* n. 338, 39, 50, 52, 55–7; and cf. also Sam Peltzman, 'Toward a More General Theory of Regulation', *Jnl. Law & Econ.*, 19 (1976), 211–40; Alfred E. Kahn, 'I Would Do It Again', *Regulation*, 12 (1988), 22–8.

[370] See e.g. Ernest Nagel, 'Assumptions in Economic Theory', *Papers and Proceedings of the American Economic Association*, 53 (1963), 211–19; 'Discussion', *Papers and Proceedings of the American Economic Association*, 53 (1963), 227–36; and Jack Melitz, 'Friedman and Machlup on the Significance of Testing Economic Assumptions', *Jnl. Pol. Econ.*, 73 (1965), 37–60; though compare Gary S. Becker, 'Irrational Behavior and Economic Theory', *Jnl. Pol. Econ.*, 70 (1962), 1–13; and Israel M. Kirzner, 'Rational Action and Economic Theory', *Jnl. Pol. Econ.*, 70 (1962), 380–5.

[371] See Sen, *supra* n. 363, 322–3; Katouzian, *supra* n. 346, 66–7; Wilber and Wisman, *supra* n. 334, 85; Mark Blaug, *The Methodology of Economics: Or How Economists Explain* (2nd edn., Cambridge: Cambridge University Press, 1992), 91–7; Daniel Hausman, *The Inexact*

example, are we to test the proposition that businesses act as if guided by the primary goal of profit-maximization? By interrogating those involved in business as to their motivations? What would we make of their answers? Precisely who, furthermore, would qualify as 'those involved in business'? And what sort of sample would we compile? Even Friedman concedes that 'questionnaire studies of businessmen's or other's motives or beliefs about the forces affecting their behaviour are . . . almost entirely useless as a means of *testing* the validity of economic hypotheses'—although he adds that '[t]hey may be extremely valuable in suggesting leads to follow in accounting for divergencies between predicted and observed results'.[372] Still more importantly, what if the empirical data amassed fails to tally with the prediction generated by the economic hypothesis? The discrepancy, in such an instance, could be attributable to the hypothesis, the formulation of the prediction or the method of empirical testing. Yet determining precisely where the source of discrepancy lies would be impossible.[373]

For all that the neo-classical appeal to empiricism has been considered by critics to be highly problematic, many Chicago economists appear to regard receptiveness to empirical testing as one of the strongest features of neo-classical economic theory. For it is owing to their grounding in empiricism, Chicagoans argue, that positive neo-classical hypotheses are able to justify normative economic proposals. If an economic theory provides an hypothesis which enables us to predict how individuals will act under given economic circumstances, and if empirical study shows the prediction generated by that hypothesis to be generally accurate, then account ought to be taken of that hypothesis in the process of economic

and Separate Science of Economics (Cambridge: Cambridge University Press, 1992); Lawrence A. Boland, 'On the Futility of Criticizing the Neoclassical Maximization Hypothesis', *Am. Econ. Rev.*, 71 (1981), 1031–6; Bruce J. Caldwell, 'The Neoclassical Maximization Hypothesis: Comment', *Am. Econ. Rev.*, 73 (1983), 824–7; Lawrence A. Boland, 'The Neoclassical Maximization Hypothesis: Reply', *Am. Econ. Rev.*, 73 (1983), 828–30.

372 Friedman, *supra* n. 171, 31 fn. 22.

373 For a particularly forceful formulation of this argument, see Martin Hollis and Edward J. Nell, *Rational Economic Man: A Philosophical Critique of Neo-classical Economics* (Cambridge: Cambridge University Press, 1975), 42. ('Positive economists and positivists in general are committed to holding that the test of a scientist's model is whether its predictions fit the facts. This does not call for a simple comparison of prediction with raw fact, since that would mean wrongly discarding many sound theories. So tests of predictions are decisive only when *ceteris paribus* conditions are satisfied and only after observed variables have been adjusted to their true values. But . . . the only way for a Positive economist to discover whether *ceteris* are *paribus* and to decide what adjustments to make to the observed values of variables, is to measure the degree to which the facts fail to fit the model. Tests are thus decisive only when the facts fit the model, which is like saying that verdicts are just only when they are favourable. Since irrefutable "hypotheses" are, according to Positivism, not hypotheses at all, economic models turn out analytic and devoid of all factual content. The predictive science of Positive economics is thus reduced to absurdity.')

policy formulation. More specifically, if neo-classical theory does indeed demonstrate that public regulation generally undermines rather than facilitates economic efficiency as generated by a system of voluntary exchange, then there exists a normative rationale for an economic policy of anti-interventionism.[374]

Within the Chicago tradition, no one has been more vigorous in elaborating and promoting the normative implications of positive neo-classical economics than Milton Friedman. After returning to the Chicago economics department in 1948—he had acquired an MA from the department in 1933—Friedman gradually became established as the dominant Chicago neo-classicist in the post-Knight era. From the late 1940s through to his retirement at the end of the 1970s, Friedman not only produced a prodigious amount of technical economic research; more importantly still, by developing the normative dimension of neo-classical analysis, he was able to spread the economic faith of the Chicago school not only beyond Hyde Park, but beyond the American universities generally. On the basis of neo-classical analysis, Friedman argued, it is possible to demonstrate the superiority of *laissez-faire* over government control and planning in a variety of domains.

In one of his earliest normative studies, in collaboration with George Stigler, Friedman attempted to expose the economic inefficiency of statutory rent control.[375] Where rents are determined by legislation rather than by markets, Stigler and Friedman indicated, there will be little incentive for property-owners to make premises available to prospective tenants. Accordingly, the market for private-sector rented accommodation will remain constricted. By contrast, if landlords are allowed to set their own rent levels, there will be a greater incentive for property owners to provide leasehold accommodation. Owing to this greater incentive, more tenancies will be available in a free market than in a rent-controlled one. And in consequence, there will be a greater degree of competition, which will be reflected in prices for and standards of rented accommodation. This line of normative economic reasoning rests at the heart of modern Chicago legal–economic analysis of rent control.[376] It is a line of reasoning which entails a very clear logic—that the absence of regulation facilitates free market pricing, that free market pricing engenders competition, and that

[374] See Reder, *supra* n. 155, 31–32.

[375] See Milton Friedman and George Stigler, *Roofs or Ceilings? The Current Housing Problem* (Irvington-on-Hudson, NY: Foundation for Economic Education, 1946).

[376] See, in particular, Richard A. Epstein, 'Rent Control and the Theory of Efficient Regulation', *Brooklyn L. Rev.*, 54 (1988), 741–74; and also 'Rent Control Revisited: One Reply to Seven Critics', *Brooklyn L. Rev.*, 54 (1989), 1281–304. Epstein, it ought to be noted, objects to statutory rent control not only on economic but also on constitutional grounds. Legislative initiatives designed to control or stabilize rents, he argues, are *per se* unconstitutional takings of private property.

competition generates allocative efficiency—and it is from this logic that the normative economic proposal, that rents ought not to be regulated, is deduced.

In developing normative neo-classicism, Friedman applied this logic relentlessly, opposing government subsidies and the public regulation of industry and arguing generally—and often successfully—for the expansion of free choice. A highly influential teacher and a brilliant debater and promoter of ideas, Friedman, more than anyone else, was responsible for ensuring that the normative dimension of Chicago neo-classicism made as profound an impact on American government as did Chicago law and economics on antitrust adjudication. According to one estimation, around 80 per cent of the economists in the Reagan administrations studied under him.[377] Friedman proposed and campaigned vigorously for a 'negative income tax'—a sliding scale of benefits for people willing to work—as an alternative to welfare payment and other social benefits such as public housing and food stamps. He opposed tax breaks for industries, social security programmes and foreign economic aid, on the basis that all such government initiatives—with the odd exception, such as maintaining law and order and overseeing currency—are better entrusted to the system of competitive capitalism. He argued for a volunteer army, and for the introduction of an educational voucher system which would permit students to attend the public school of their choice. Quite simply, in promoting the normative dimension of neo-classicism, he extended the scope of economic inquiry far beyond its conventional market domain.

At Chicago, Friedman was not solely or even principally responsible for extending the ambit of economic inquiry in this way. In his Chicago doctoral dissertation of 1955, *Discrimination in the Market Place*,[378] Gary Becker addressed the problem of pay differentials between blacks and whites in the labour market. Racial discrimination, he argued, is likely to reduce the income of discriminators and discriminated alike; and, since majority groups enjoy a more balanced distribution of labour and capital, retaliatory discrimination by minorities tends to cause more economic harm to themselves than to those against whom they discriminate. Although, initially, Becker's study was received with indifference and hostility by many economists, it came gradually to be seen as a work of some significance within the modern Chicago tradition.[379] For it exemplified how neo-classical economic analysis could be employed to explain ostensibly non-market behaviour. '[I]t is not a caricature,' wrote one commentator on the Chicago school of economics in 1962, 'to imagine

[377] See John Lichfield, 'Freedom's Demon King', *Independent on Sunday*, 26 July 1992, 23.

[378] Published as Gary S. Becker, *The Economics of Discrimination* (2nd edn. Chicago: University of Chicago Press, 1971; 1st edn. 1957).

[379] See Stigler, *supra* n. 176, 195.

some modern-day Chicagoans hard at work on the problem of introducing the price system into the family organization.'[380] By 1965, Becker was doing just that.[381] The decision to marry, to have children, the division of labour within the household, inter-generational transfers among family members—all such phenomena, Becker argued, can be explained by neo-classical economic theory.

Consider, for example, the decision to marry. '[S]ince men and women compete as they seek mates,' Becker contends, 'a *market* in marriages can be presumed to exist. Each person tries to find the best mate, subject to the restrictions imposed by market conditions.'[382] Defining income broadly so as to include children, domestic comfort, a desirable social life and the like, Becker claims that males and females endeavour to maximize their income when they choose their mates. Thus it is that a person decides to marry 'when the utility expected from marriage exceeds that from remaining single or from additional search for a more suitable mate. . . . Similarly, a married person terminates his (or her) marriage when the utility anticipated from becoming single or marrying someone else exceeds the loss in utility from separation, including losses due to physical separation from one's children, division of joint assets, legal fees, and so forth.'[383]

It hardly needs to be stated that Becker's use of neo-classical logic to explain the motivation to marry and divorce has attracted much criticism.[384] Since many economists insist that neo-classical theory fails adequately to explain conventional market behaviour, it is not surprising that economists and other social scientists have generally balked at the suggestion that rational self-interest rests at the heart of something so other-regarding as entering into marriage.[385] Undeterred, Becker himself has attempted to extend rather than modify his basic thesis. 'The heart of my argument,' he has stated, 'is that . . . all human behaviour can be viewed as involving participants who maximize their utility from a stable set of preferences and accumulate an optimal amount of information and other inputs in a variety of markets.'[386] Altruism, fertility, love, drug-taking—all these things and more, Becker has attempted to show, are susceptible to neo-classical economic explanation. For many detractors,

[380] Miller, *supra* n. 332, 66.

[381] See Gary S. Becker, 'A Theory of the Allocation of Time', *Economic Jnl.*, 75 (1965), 493–517.

[382] Gary S. Becker, *The Economic Approach to Human Behaviour* (Chicago: University of Chicago Press, 1976), 206.

[383] Ibid. 10.

[384] See, in particular, Blaug, *supra* n. 371, 220–8.

[385] This should not, however, be taken to suggest that no one has followed Becker's lead. Some economists—particularly at Chicago—clearly have. See, for example, Ray C. Fair, 'A Theory of Extramarital Affairs', *Jnl. Pol. Econ.*, 86 (1978), 45–62.

[386] Becker, *supra* n. 382, 14.

such a claim inspires only derision.[387] For others, Becker's effort to extend neo-classical inquiry into domains traditionally dominated by other social scientific disciplines smacks of economic imperialism.[388] In making this effort, still others have claimed, he has risked eradicating the disciplinary distinctiveness of economics itself.[389]

For the purposes of this chapter, however, a rather less negative perspective on Becker's efforts needs to be stressed. Whatever the disagreements over their application and limitations, basic economic concepts such as scarcity, cost, preferences and opportunities, Becker has demonstrated, possess explanatory power outside the conventional market domain. No longer is economics just economics; it has been expanded to cover the entire social and political universe.[390] Becker's basic thesis—that human beings are rational utility maximizers throughout a broad, if not the whole, spectrum of social interactions—has, among other things, definite jurisprudential implications. For if one accepts this thesis, one is compelled to conclude that neo-classical economic analysis may profitably be applied to areas of law lacking any apparent market dimension. Thus it is that the expansion of neo-classical economic theory at Chicago prepared the ground for what is often termed the 'new' law and economics—the economics, that is, of crime, tort, family and constitutional law and the like.[391]

While the extension of Chicago neo-classical analysis into ostensibly non-market domains certainly accounts to a large degree for the flourishing of law and economics in the United States, it is, as we shall see, by no means the whole story. Although the initiatives of Friedman and Becker may well have set the scene for the growth of the so-called 'new' law and economics, the economic analysis of apparently non-market legal activities in fact developed very much independently of their initiatives. Indeed, it would be wrong to assume that such analysis developed wholly within the Chicago neo-classical tradition.

In so far as modern legal–economic analysis has evolved within that

387 See e.g. Alan S. Blinder, 'The Economics of Brushing Teeth', *Jnl. Pol. Econ.*, 82 (1974), 887–91; T. C. Bergstrom, 'Towards a Deeper Economics of Sleeping', *Jnl. Pol. Econ.*, 84 (1976), 411–12.

388 See R. Swedberg, *Economics and Sociology. Redefining Their Boundaries: Conversations with Economists and Sociologists* (Princeton, NJ: Princeton University Press, 1990), 325–7.

389 See Alexander Rosenberg, 'Can Economic Theory Explain Everything?', *Philosophy of the Social Sciences*, 9 (1979), 509–29.

390 See Jack Hirschleifer, 'The Expanding Domain of Economics', *Am. Econ. Rev.*, 75 (1985), 53–68; and also, for a collection of essays which illustrates this claim, George J. Stigler (ed.), *Chicago Studies in Political Economy* (Chicago: University of Chicago Press, 1988).

391 For an elaboration of this point, see generally Richard A. Posner, 'The Law and Economics Movement', *Papers and Proceedings of the American Economic Review*, 77 (1987), 1–13.

tradition, it has struggled against one particular obstacle which appears to stand in the way of most efforts to introduce economics into the study of supposedly non-market activity. The obstacle is not jargon, as one might expect—many, if not most, American academic lawyers seem to possess at least a basic grasp of core economic concepts, and most scholarship within the Chicago law and economics tradition is clear and readable. Rather, the obstacle is one of counter-intuitiveness. The Chicago law and economics tradition adopts essentially the same methodology and set of assumptions as does the modern Chicago economics tradition—and, in consequence, as will become clear, the criticisms of the former more or less mirror those which we found above to have been directed at the latter. Many lawyers and economists alike have been left cold by claims such as that—on the basis that demand curves slope negatively (that people will partake of something less the more expensive it gets)—the execution of murderers may be justified on deterrence grounds, given especially that a policy of non-execution, by failing to deter, indirectly sentences many anonymous individuals to death;[392] or that crime is simply an occupation which some people, having considered the attendant costs, benefits and risks, engage in as a matter of rational choice.[393] It would be wrong to assume, however, that economists and lawyers unsympathetic to neo-classical economic insights share exactly the same reaction. Economists, even when not inclined towards neo-classical theory, tend to be familiar with it, or at least with the ideas of Adam Smith. However, when, in the 1960s, Chicago neo-classical economics began to penetrate areas of legal study lacking an explicit market dimension, many American academic lawyers seemed thoroughly puzzled as to how to respond. Their conceptual universe had been invaded by something which bore absolutely no connection with their own intellectual tradition. For some time, Chicago law and economics was treated as something of a 'lunatic fringe' in American academic legal circles.[394] And for all that nowadays it tends to be treated less dismissively, there still runs throughout the literature of American jurisprudence a good deal of bewilderment and even, at times, resentment concerning the impact that neo-classical economic theory has made on the study of law. The expansion of economic analysis into purportedly non-market areas of

[392] See Isaac Ehrlich, 'The Deterrent Effect of Capital Punishment: A Question of Life and Death', *Am. Econ. Rev.*, 65 (1975), 397–417.

[393] See Gary S. Becker, 'Crime and Punishment: An Economic Approach', *Jnl. Pol. Econ.*, 76 (1968), 169–217.

[394] Richard A. Posner, letter to author, 15 June 1993; Theodore P. Roth, 'Law & Economics', *University of Chicago Magazine*, August 1991, 28–32 at 28. ('Twenty years ago, Law and Economics—the application of market-oriented economics to the law—was still considered a crackpot theory espoused by neo-reactionaries in Hyde Park.') Paul M. Barrett, 'A Movement Called "Law and Economics" Sways Legal Circles', *Wall Street Journal*, 4 August 1986, 1, 16 at 16 col. 3.

legal activity represented a revolution in American legal thought, a revolution with which many academic lawyers have never quite come to terms.

THE REVOLUTION

So, what was the nature of this revolution? How did it unfold? The subject of property rights appears to have been the first so-called non-market legal theme to be subjected to economic scrutiny. By the late 1950s, Armen Alchian had begun to develop a conception of property rights as exchangeable economic goods. A system of voluntary exchange, he argued, depends on the capacity of its citizens to possess secure—that is, capable of enforcement at low cost—alienable private property rights; and if such a system is unencumbered by excessive regulatory intervention, the free and competitive exchange of such rights within the market-place should ensure increased availability and decreasing costs of valued commodities.[395] Expanding on Alchian's effort to demonstrate how clearly-specified property rights are a pre-condition for the functioning of free markets, Harold Demsetz attempted, during the following decade, to show that the satisfactory allocation of property rights within such markets often proves to be difficult, if not impossible, given the costs of obtaining information.[396] Alchian and Demsetz attempted together to illustrate this observation by highlighting the difficulties involved in monitoring industrial production.[397] While team-work often turns out to be the most efficient form of productive activity, they argue, the allocation of rewards for such work proves invariably to be problematic, given the difficulty of ascertaining the different productivity levels of individual team members. Generally, rewards will be geared to the average productivity of the team, even though this is likely to undercompensate the hard workers and overcompensate the slackers; and since team members are paid an average amount rather than according to their own productivity, there will exist an incentive to shirk which is likely to reduce overall productivity. Maximizing productive efficiency, Alchian and Demsetz conclude, requires some cost-efficient means of organizing productivity. But how could this be achieved?

An answer to this question had been formulated as early as the 1930s by the British economist, Ronald Coase. In one of his earliest papers, 'The

[395] See Armen A. Alchian, *Some Economics of Property Rights* (Rand Paper No. 2316, Santa Monica: Rand Corporation, 1961); reprinted in *Il Politico*, 30 (1965), 816–29. It appears that Alchian had already written a version of this paper by the late 1950s: see Kitch (ed.), *supra* n. 146, 228 (comment by Henry Manne).

[396] See Harold Demsetz, 'Toward a Theory of Property Rights', *Papers and Proceedings of the American Economic Review*, 57 (1967), 347–59.

[397] See Armen A. Alchian and Harold Demsetz, 'Production, Information Costs, and Economic Organization', *Am. Econ. Rev.*, 62 (1971), 777–95.

Nature of the Firm', Coase argued that the reason for the existence of firms is that they provide an efficient means of organizing productivity.[398] Where the organization of production is, as it were, decentralized—that is, where every contract between employer and employee is individually negotiated—the costs of entering into individual transactions will impede productive efficiency. Firms are thus established to minimize the 'costs of the exchange transaction on the open market'.[399]

> The main reason why it is profitable to establish a firm would seem to be that there is a cost of using the price mechanism. The most obvious cost of 'organizing' production through the price mechanism is that of discovering what the relevant prices are. This cost may be reduced but it will not be eliminated by the emergence of specialists who will sell this information. The costs of negotiating and concluding a separate contract for each exchange transaction on a market must also be taken into account. . . . It is true that contracts are not eliminated when there is a firm, but they are greatly reduced. A factor of production (or the owner thereof) does not have to make a series of contracts with the factors with whom he is co-operating within the firm, as would be necessary, of course, if this co-operation were a direct result of the working of the price mechanism.[400]

Coase's lesson was simple: 'the operation of a market costs something'.[401] With the establishment of a firm, such costs may be largely eradicated since, 'in place of the complicated market structure with exchange transactions is substituted the entrepreneur-co-ordinator, who directs production'.[402] 'The entrepreneur has to carry out this function at less cost, taking into account the fact that he may get factors of production at a lower price than the market transactions which he supersedes, because it is always possible to revert to the open market if he fails to do this.'[403] The costs of transacting within the market, Coase had demonstrated, impede the efficiency of the market itself. By cutting out such costs, firms restore efficiency. The concept of transaction costs thus turns out to be essential to a proper understanding of the working of the economic system and for the purposes of determining policy.

In offering this thesis, Coase was peculiarly ahead of his time. Although generally ignored in the 1930s, his study anticipated—and, indeed, was

[398] Ronald H. Coase, 'The Nature of the Firm', *Economica*, n.s. 4 (1937), 386–405; reprinted in R. H. Coase, *The Firm, the Market and the Law* (Chicago: University of Chicago Press, 1988), 33–55. Citations follow the pagination in the book. Coase had in fact formulated the main ideas which appear in 'The Nature of the Firm' as early as 1932. See R. H. Coase, 'The Nature of the Firm: Origin', *Jnl. of Law, Economics, and Organization*, 4 (1988), 13–17 esp. 3–5; 'The Institutional Structure of Production', *Les Prix Nobel*, [1991], 193–202 at 197. He recounts that '[t]he delay in publishing my ideas was partly due to a reluctance to rush into print and partly to the fact that I was heavily engaged in teaching and research on other projects.' Ronald H. Coase, 'Ronald H. Coase', *Les Prix Nobel*, [1991], 189–192 at 191.

[399] Coase, 'The Nature of the Firm', *supra* n. 398, 43.

[400] Ibid. 38–9.

[401] Ibid. 40.

[402] Ibid. 35–6.

[403] Ibid. 40.

more sophisticated than—a good deal of research into the nature of the firm which emerged out of the Chicago neo-classical tradition from the 1960s onwards.[404] It would be wrong, however, to regard Coase's article as some sort of freak occurrence, as the work of an isolated British economist which just happened to foreshadow by around twenty years the theoretical inquiries of various modern Chicago neo-classicists. Coase had begun his research into the nature of the firm in the early 1930s while travelling in the United States as a Cassel scholar. In 1932, he had attended certain of Frank Knight's lectures at the University of Chicago.[405] While Knight made little intellectual impression upon Coase, he had nonetheless, in the 1920s, formulated an idea which would become central to Coase's economic thinking—the idea, that is, that a system of free enterprise is never perfect, since the process of making transactions in a market economy entails inevitably what Knight called 'social costs'.[406] During the 1930s, Coase was by no means uninterested in British economics scholarship. But it was in the United States that he discovered among economists a greater concern with business regulation. In Britain, owing to the fact that there existed no distinct tradition of antitrust, economic regulatory theory was comparably slow to develop.[407] Coase himself had studied various law subjects as a commerce student at the London School of Economics in the late 1920s. After completing his degree, he stayed on for an extra year to acquire a D.Sc. in industrial law. He had almost become a lawyer, and, as a member of the economics department at the LSE, was disappointed by the general failure of his colleagues to develop legally-oriented research.[408] In 1951, he migrated to the United States.

As a professor first at Buffalo and then at Virginia in the 1950s, Coase began to develop his own legally-inspired approach to specific economic problems. It was in developing this approach that he came to revolutionize the Chicago law and economics tradition. By the end of the 1950s, he had produced a study of the Federal Communications Commission, in which he argued that radio frequencies ought to be awarded to the highest bidders rather than according to regulatory discretion. By awarding radio

[404] On this point, see William W. Bratton, Jr., 'The New Economic Theory of the Firm: Critical Perspectives From History', *Stanford L. Rev.*, 41 (1989), 1471–527 at 1477–8. See also, more generally, R. H. Coase, 'The Nature of the Firm: Influence', *Jnl. of Law, Economics, and Organization*, 4 (1988), 33–47.

[405] See Kitch (ed.), *supra* n. 146, 212–13 (comments of Ronald Coase); R. H. Coase, 'The Nature of the Firm: Meaning', *Jnl. of Law, Economics, and Organization*, 4 (1988), 19–32 at 20. ('It can, I think, be said with some confidence that Knight played no part in the development of my ideas on the firm, a point I emphasize because some have thought the contrary.')

[406] See Kitch (ed.), *supra* n. 146, 215 (comment by Ronald Coase); and also Frank H. Knight, 'Fallacies in the Interpretation of Social Cost' [1924], in Knight, *supra* n. 166, 217–36.

[407] See Kitch (ed.), *supra* n. 146, 214 (comment by Ronald Coase).

[408] See ibid. 215–18 (comment by Ronald Coase).

frequencies without charging for their scarcity value, the government was failing to prevent the mis-allocation of such frequencies away from their most valued use. This conclusion was, in itself, not especially remarkable. Coase proceeded, however, to consider the type of rights which would be acquired by those highest bidders. While economists, he suggested, had traditionally conceived of that which is bought and sold in terms of physical units—acres of land, tons of coal and the like—lawyers thought in terms of bundles of rights to perform certain actions. Since one cannot regard radio frequencies as physical units, Coase argued, economists must adopt a perspective more akin to that of the lawyer. This requires, in this context, that economists consider rights in terms of what use is being made of the particular radio frequency spectrum. It would be impossible to think concretely about what might be paid for the use of a particular frequency, Coase insisted, without some specification of the rights possessed by all those who use this and adjacent frequencies or who might use them.

Coase's study of the Federal Communications Commission appeared in *The Journal of Law and Economics* in October 1959.[409] Various Chicago economists involved with the journal, though they were prepared to see the piece published as it stood, were unconvinced by his position on rights. Coase, however, was adamant that it was they who were wrong. In the following year, he accepted an invitation to the Chicago economics faculty to present a workshop defending and elaborating his position. The visit and its aftermath hold pride of place in Chicago folklore. On the evening before his workshop, Coase met with various Chicago economists at Aaron Director's home to discuss his position. At the beginning of the discussion, he apparently had no supporters among those gathered. By the end of the discussion, he had no detractors. Coase was duly urged to write up his seminar for publication in *The Journal of Law and Economics*, and in September 1964 he joined Director as a professor of economics at the University of Chicago Law School.[410] Early in 1961, the ideas which he had expounded that evening appeared in print under the title, 'The Problem of Social Cost'.[411]

[409] Ronald H. Coase, 'The Federal Communications Commission', *Jnl. Law & Econ.*, 2 (1959), 1–40.

[410] The details which make up this paragraph are taken from Kitch (ed.), *supra* n. 146, 220–2.

[411] Ronald H. Coase, 'The Problem of Social Cost', *Jnl. Law & Econ.*, 3 (1960), 1–44; reprinted in Coase, *The Firm, the Market and the Law*, *supra* n. 398, 95–156. Citations follow the pagination in the book. Although 'The Problem of Social Cost' is dated 1960, *The Journal of Law and Economics* was, at that time, somewhat behind publication schedule. Coase himself has pointed out that the article eventually appeared in print in 1961 (see Kitch (ed.), *supra* n. 146, 221). The claim, by Richard Posner, that it did not appear until 1962 (see, for example, Posner, *supra* n. 53, 759 fn. 9) has now been retracted. Richard A. Posner, letter to author, 4 October 1993. ('I believe 1961 is the correct date.'); Coase, *supra* n. 234. ('Posner now agrees with me.')

Modern lawyer–economists appear almost unanimously to agree that 'The Problem of Social Cost' is the most important legal–economic study ever to have been produced. It was on the strength of both this article and 'The Nature of the Firm' that, in 1991, Coase was awarded the Alfred Nobel Memorial Prize in Economic Sciences.[412] 'The Problem of Social Cost' offers insights which overturned conventional thinking in both economics and law. Coase's principal aim in this article was to demonstrate certain inadequacies implicit in Pigovian welfare economics. In *The Economics of Welfare*, Arthur Pigou attempted 'to bring into clearer light some of the ways in which it now is, or eventually may become, feasible for governments to control the play of economic forces in such wise as to promote the economic welfare, and, through that, the total welfare, of their citizens as a whole'.[413] According to Coase, the fallacy of this proposition—that economic welfare ought to be improved through government action—is especially clear from Pigou's treatment of nuisance law. Pigou had argued that externalities—that is, the by-products of engaging in an activity which affects adversely the levels of production or the well-being of other individuals[414]—ought to be dealt with through government action such as taxation or, less commonly, regulation. Where, for example, 'costs are thrown upon people not directly concerned, through . . . uncompensated damage done to surrounding woods by sparks from railway engines,' the government ought to intervene to remedy this situation, by requiring railways to compensate those whose woods are burnt.[415] By imposing this form of taxation, the state is able to ensure that the social costs of any externality will be 'internalized' by the party who is seen to cause the nuisance. State intervention thus promotes economic welfare by ensuring that costs generated by externalities are borne only by those responsible for such externalities.

In 'The Problem of Social Cost', Coase strikes at the very heart of Pigou's thesis. Where the smoke from a factory has harmful effects on those occupying neighbouring properties, he observes, Pigou considers it desirable 'to make the owner of the factory liable for the damage caused to those injured by the smoke; or to place a tax on the factory owner varying with the amount of smoke produced and equivalent in money terms to the damage it would cause; or, finally, to exclude the factory from residential

[412] See Geoffrey R. Stone, 'Ronald's Nobel', *U. Chicago Law School Record*, 38 (Spring 1992), 2–3.

[413] A. C. Pigou, *The Economics of Welfare* (4th edn. London: Macmillan and Co., 1932; 1st edn. 1920), 129–30.

[414] On externalities, see generally Ezra J. Mishan, 'The Post-war Literature on Externalities: An Interpretative Essay', *Jnl. Econ. Lit.*, 1 (1971), 1–28.

[415] See Pigou *supra* n. 413, 134–5.

districts'.[416] Such courses of action, Coase argues, 'lead to results which are not necessarily, or even usually, desirable'.[417]

In developing this argument, he begins by observing that externalities are not simply produced by polluters and suffered by victims. Rather, they emerge out of the circumstances of both parties. The cost of pollution, for example, is attributable not only to the actions of the polluter but also to the fact that the victim is in a position to be affected by the polluter. It may be that the victim has less to lose in avoiding pollution than does the polluter in preventing it. In such a case, Coase insists, the appropriate question is not that of how to restrain the polluter, but how to maximize the net social benefit.[418] Imagine a situation in which pollution from a factory causes £100,000 worth of damage to neighbouring land each year. The elimination of pollution, let us say, would cost £80,000 per year, whereas the cost of changing the use of the land so that it is no longer affected by the pollution would be £50,000 per year. The Pigovian solution in such a scenario would be to impose an emission fee on the factory. Yet the more efficient solution would be for the owner of the neighbouring land—the party who is capable of remedying the problem at the lowest cost—to decide on a different use.

In offering this argument, Coase was not merely undermining Pigovian economic analysis. He was also casting doubt on the common law notion of causality as a means of assigning responsibility. That someone 'causes' a nuisance, as determined by common law principles, does not, for Coase, imply the efficiency of holding that person liable. If sparks from the railroad engine start a fire in the woods, one ought not simply to conclude that the railway has caused the fire; rather, in determining with whom responsibility for preventing such accidents ought to rest, one might, among other things, ask whether the social cost of cutting down trees near the railway tracks would be less than the cost of installing new safety devices in railroad engines.

Coase pushed this analysis still further. So long as the parties to a dispute possess clearly defined rights and duties and are able to make and enforce contracts in their mutual interest, no form of regulation or taxation will be necessary in order to secure an efficient outcome. For the parties will simply negotiate around those rights and duties in order to achieve the allocation of resources which they desire. It may be, for example, that the neighbours of a polluting factory possess a right not to have their land polluted. Yet, rather than enforce this right, the parties may contract around it if it fails to produce an efficient result. The factory may find that it costs less to compensate their neighbours than it does to eliminate pollution; just as the neighbours may benefit more from accepting

[416] Coase, *supra* n. 411, 95. [417] Ibid. 96. [418] Ibid.

compensation than from enforcing their strict legal rights. Market forces, in other words, internalize costs irrespective of rules imposing liability.

For Coase, then, externalities are not really a problem. Markets are able to find their way around them. But what will be a problem are transaction costs. For while it is all very well to claim that initial assignments of legal entitlements will have no bearing on the efficient allocation of resources, the fact is that there are invariably costs involved in the process of bargaining between parties—costs which may even be so high as to deter the parties from attempting to negotiate their way around initial assignments of entitlements.[419] 'If these arrangements are the result of market transactions,' Coase himself explains, 'they will tend to lead to the rights being used in the way which is most valued, but only after deducting the costs involved in making these transactions. Transaction costs therefore play a crucial role in determining how rights will be used.'[420]

The concept of transaction costs is thus every bit as central in 'The Problem of Social Cost' as it had been in 'The Nature of the Firm'.[421] But whereas, in the latter article, Coase had done no more than emphasize the importance of taking account of transaction costs when analysing the operation of a market, in 'The Problem of Social Cost' he raised the question of what sorts of arrangement would evolve in a world in which there were no costs involved in carrying out market transactions. Coase's conclusion—the so-called 'Coase theorem'[422]—is that, assuming the absence of transaction costs, the legal assignment of property rights to parties involved in negotiation would have no effect on the eventual allocation of resources between them. '[T]he ultimate result', as Coase puts it, 'is independent of the legal position if the pricing system is assumed to work without cost.'[423]

Since the appearance of 'The Problem of Social Cost', the Coase theorem has been tugged in all sorts of different directions. It has been advocated as a method of judicial reasoning[424]; it has been subjected to experimental testing[425]; it has been criticized by some for its implicit anti-

[419] On this point, see generally Herbert Hovenkamp, 'Marginal Utility and the Coase Theorem', *Cornell L. Rev.*, 75 (1990), 783-810.

[420] Ronald H. Coase, 'The Firm, the Market, and the Law', in Coase, *The Firm, the Market and the Law*, *supra* n. 398, 1–31 at 12–13.

[421] On the thematic unity of the two articles, see Guido Calabresi, 'The Pointlessness of Pareto: Carrying Coase Further', *Yale L.J.*, 100 (1991), 1211–37 at 1211–15.

[422] So labelled by George Stigler. See George J. Stigler, *The Theory of Price* (3rd edn. New York: Macmillan, 1966), 113. ('The Coase theorem . . . asserts that under perfect competition private and social costs will be equal.')

[423] Coase, *supra* n. 411, 104.

[424] See Barbara White, 'Coase and the Courts: Economics for the Common Man', *Iowa L. Rev.*, 72 (1987), 577–635.

[425] See e.g. Elizabeth Hoffman and Matthew L. Spitzer, 'The Coase Theorem: Some Experimental Tests', *Jnl. Law & Econ.*, 25 (1982), 73–98; Glenn W. Harrison and Michael

statism,[426] and by others for its excessive legal centralism;[427] it has been both appropriated and criticized by proponents of critical legal studies;[428] very generally, it has been the subject of diverse refutations,[429] defences,[430] tributes,[431] applications,[432] reassessments[433] and attempts at modification.[434] One of the most common criticisms of the Coase theorem is that, owing to the fact that it entails the assumption of zero transaction costs, it is wholly unrealistic.[435] Yet this is not a valid criticism. It was never

McKee, 'Experimental Evaluation of the Coase Theorem', *Jnl. Law & Econ.*, 28 (1985), 653–70; Stewart J. Schwab, 'A Coasean Experiment on Contract Presumptions', *Jnl. Leg. Studs.*, 17 (1988), 237–68.

[426] See e.g. Mark Kelman, 'Consumption Theory, Production Theory, and Ideology in the Coase Theorem', *Southern California L. Rev.*, 52 (1979), 669–98 at 697–8.

[427] See, in particular, Robert C. Ellickson, *Order Without Law: How Neighbors Settle Disputes* (Cambridge, Mass.: Harvard University Press, 1991), 2–3, 138–9, 280–1.

[428] The most obvious example of appropriation is Pierre Schlag, 'An Appreciative Comment on Coase's *The Problem of Social Cost:* A View From the Left', *Wisconsin L. Rev.*, [1986], 919–62. See also Pierre Schlag, 'The Problem of Transaction Costs', *Southern California L. Rev.*, 62 (1989), 1661–99 (attempting to turn the Coase theorem against neo-classical economics); and also Gjerdingen, *supra* n. 4, 874 ('the [Coase] theorem is controversial because it has an end-state or distributive justice political structure'). Examples of criticism in this context are voluminous. See, for but one example, Kelman, *supra* n. 426, *passim*.

[429] See, in particular, Donald H. Regan, 'The Problem of Social Cost Revisited', *Jnl. Law & Econ.*, 15 (1972), 427–37.

[430] See Steven N.S. Cheung, 'The Fable of the Bees: An Economic Investigation', *Jnl. Law & Econ.*, 16 (1973), 11–33; David B. Johnson, 'Meade, Bees, and Externalities', *Jnl. Law & Econ.*, 16 (1973), 35–52; and J. R. Gould, 'Meade on External Economies: Should the Beneficiaries Be Taxed?', *Jnl. Law & Econ.*, 16 (1973), 53–66.

[431] See e.g. David B. Friedman, 'The World According to Coase', *U. Chicago Law School Record*, 37 (Spring 1992), 4–9.

[432] See e.g. Yehoshua Lieberman, 'The Coase Theorem in Jewish Law', *Jnl. Leg. Studs.*, 10 (1981), 293–303.

[433] See e.g. Ronald H. Coase, 'The 1987 McCorkle Lecture: Blackmail', *Virginia L. Rev.*, 74 (1988), 655–76; 'Notes on the Problem of Social Cost' in Coase, *The Firm, the Market and the Law*, *supra* n. 398, 157–85; James Lindgren, 'Blackmail: On Waste, Morals and Ronald Coase', *UCLA L. Rev.*, 36 (1989), 587–608; Robert D. Cooter, 'The Cost of Coase', *Jnl. Leg. Studs.*, 11 (1982), 1–33; Harold H. Liebhafsky, 'The Problem of Social Cost: An Alternative Approach', *Natural Resources Jnl.*, 13 (1973), 615–76; Warren J. Samuels, 'The Coase Theorem and the Study of Law and Economics', *Natural Resources Jnl.*, 14 (1974), 1–33; Alfred Endres, 'Die Coase-Kontroverse', *Zeitschrift für die gesamte Staatswissenschaft*, 133 (1977), 637–51; Cento G. Veljanovski, 'The Coase Theorems and the Economic Theory of Markets and Law', *Kyklos*, 35 (1982), 53–74.

[434] See George A. Mumey, 'The Coase Theorem: A Re-examination', *Quarterly Journal of Economics*, 85 (1971), 718–23; Jeffrey F. Jaffee, 'The "Coase Theorem": A Re-examination and Comment', *Quarterly Journal of Economics*, 89 (1975), 660–7; Richard O. Zerbe, Jr., 'The Problem of Social Cost: Fifteen Years Later', in Lin Say (ed.), *Theory and Measurement of Economic Externalities* (New York: Academia Press, 1976), 29–36.

[435] See e.g. Ackerman, *Reconstructing American Law*, *supra* n. 22, 65 (arguing that Coase constructs 'a frictionless world inhabited by hyperrational actors capable of understanding all the implications of their organizational activities' and that 'the Chicagoans . . . would like lawyers to talk torts as if they lived in a world very close to Coase's never-never land'); Daniel A. Farber, 'The Case Against Brilliance', *Minnesota L. Rev.*, 70 (1986), 917–30 at 918–24

Coase's argument that transaction costs will be absent from market exchanges. Rather, his intention, in assuming their absence, was to try to impress upon economists in particular just how significant transaction costs actually are in the fashioning of economic arrangements.[436] Where transaction costs are not especially prohibitive, Coase indicated, externalities represented by nuisances might best be remedied through private bargaining between disputing parties rather than by formal recourse to the law. The manner in which disputes over rights and entitlements are resolved, in other words, will depend on the nature and size of the relevant transaction costs.

In developing this line of argument, Coase was principally urging economists to question the Pigovian assumption that efficient solutions to such disputes may be generated through government action. As regards the development of modern law and economics, however, the fundamental insight which he offers is somewhat different. In identifying a relationship between transaction costs and dispute resolution, Coase demonstrates compelling reasons for engaging in the economic analysis of common law rules. For not only does he implicitly cast doubt on the common law concept of causality, but he shows also that the utility of common law rules for the purpose of remedying disputes regarding rights and entitlements—even where those disputes appear to be of a non-market type—will in effect be eradicated if transaction costs are not so high as to deter disputing parties from negotiating for themselves an efficient allocation of resources. From the perspective of the lawyer–economist, 'The Problem of Social Cost' illustrates *par excellence* how economic analysis may force lawyers to question and revise certain of the assumptions and concepts on which, traditionally, they have been happy to rely. The Coase theorem embodies the revolution in legal–economic thinking with which modern American lawyers have been forced to contend. That they have attempted to tug the theorem in so many different directions is very much an indication of the difficulties and the bewilderment which they have experienced in attempting to come to terms with it.

To a large degree, post-Coasean law and economics has evolved as an effort to clarify and resolve certain problems which were either left unaddressed or treated ambiguously in 'The Problem of Social Cost'. Two points in particular required elaboration. First of all, there was the question of how the law ought to operate if transaction costs were so

(although compare Daniel A. Farber, 'Brilliance Revisited', *Minnesota L. Rev.*, 72 (1987), 367–82 at 379–80); Kelman, *supra* n. 426, *passim*; and cf. also Matthew Spitzer and Elizabeth Hoffman, 'A Reply to *Consumption Theory, Production Theory, and Ideology in the Coase Theorem*', *Southern California L. Rev.*, 53 (1980), 1187–214; and Mark Kelman, 'Spitzer and Hoffman on Coase: A Brief Rejoinder', *Southern California L. Rev.*, 53 (1980), 1215–23.

[436] See Coase, *supra* n. 420, 13.

prohibitive as to prevent the parties to a dispute from determining an efficient allocation of resources. In the first edition of his *Economic Analysis of Law*, Richard Posner argued that, where legal intervention is necessary because an efficient outcome cannot be obtained through negotiation between the parties, the relevant entitlements ought to be assigned so as to produce the result which would have prevailed in an efficient market: that is, legal rights ought to be conferred on the highest bidders.[437]

Secondly, there was the more basic question of what, precisely, is meant by efficiency in this context. Lawyer–economists have tended to assume—though the assumption is not explicitly affirmed in 'The Problem of Social Cost'—that Coase, in referring to allocative and allocational efficiency, is conceiving of efficiency in Paretian terms.[438] An allocation of resources, whether through market transaction or government intervention, is said to be Pareto optimal if, and only if, any further reallocation of those resources can make one person better off only at the expense of another. While an allocation of resources may not be Pareto optimal, it may still be efficient if it is Pareto superior, that is, if it makes at least one person better off and no one worse off. By yet another definition—the so-called Kaldor–Hicks definition—even if an allocation of resources makes some people worse off, it will still be deemed efficient if those made better off by the allocation are able (though not compelled) to compensate those who have suffered from it.[439] Coase's own conception of efficiency appears most closely to approximate Pareto optimality: that is, in the absence of transaction costs, negotiating parties will allocate resources under their control in such a way that there will be no alternative allocation which enables any one party to improve his or her utility without a reduction occurring in the utility of at least one other party. But not all lawyer–economists subscribe to this conception of efficiency. In arguing that the law should mimic the market where transaction costs prohibit an efficient allocation of resources through negotiation, for example, Posner appears to move away from the implicit Coasean conception of efficiency as Pareto

[437] See Richard A. Posner, *Economic Analysis of Law* (Boston: Little, Brown & Co., 1973), 18.

[438] See Calabresi *supra* n. 420, 1212–17; Jules L. Coleman, *Markets, Morals and the Law* (Cambridge: Cambridge University Press, 1988), 76; E. J. Mishan, 'Pareto Optimality and the Law', *Oxford Economic Papers*, 19 (1967), 255–87 at 279–80.

[439] See Nicholas Kaldor, 'Welfare Propositions of Economics and Inter-personal Comparisons of Utility', *Economic Jnl.*, 49 (1939), 549–52 esp. 550; J. R. Hicks, 'The Foundations of Welfare Economics', *Economic Jnl.*, 696–712. For an excellent analysis of these different conceptions of efficiency, see Jules L. Coleman, 'The Economic Analysis of Law', in J. Roland Pennock and John W. Chapman (eds.), *Nomos XXIV: Ethics, Economics, and the Law* (New York: New York University Press, 1982), 83–103 at 83–9.

optimality in favour of the Kaldor–Hicks criterion. [440] The general tendency of American lawyer–economists to juggle different conceptions of efficiency—to shift between utilitarianism and Paretianism, between Paretianism and Kaldor–Hicks, and so on[441]—has been a notable feature of law and economics since the appearance of 'The Problem of Social Cost'; and, since such shifts often alter significantly the analytical and normative implications of particular efforts at legal–economic analysis, they tend to invoke the criticisms of proponents of and detractors from law and economics alike. Indeed, as will become clearer in the next section, the manipulability of efficiency and the potential import of the term for the purposes of legal inquiry and policy formulation has caused American lawyers to be both attracted to and unnerved by the economic analysis of law.

Even in the early 1960s, at the time that Coase was writing 'The Problem of Social Cost', a distinctive strand of legal–economic inquiry was beginning to emerge which emphasized the limited analytical utility of efficiency criteria. In 1961, Guido Calabresi, then an associate professor at the Yale Law School, attempted to sketch an economic analysis of the relationship between rules of liability and the spreading of loss in tort law.[442] Calabresi's work differed from that of Coase in that he demonstrated a greater interest in distinguishing forms of entitlements and was less preoccupied with the assumption of zero transaction costs. Unlike Coase, furthermore, Calabresi emphasized the importance of distributional concerns in economic analysis. In his classic article on entitlements, written in collaboration with Douglas Melamed, Calabresi observed that '[t]he state not only has to decide whom to entitle' but must also decide on 'the manner in which entitlements are protected and . . . whether an individual is allowed to sell or trade the entitlement.'[443] The determination of entitlements in such a way as to ensure an efficient allocation of resources

[440] For an elaboration of this point, see Coleman, *supra* n. 439, 95–100. This is not to imply confusion on Posner's part. Posner himself argues that the Kaldor–Hicks standard may function as a practical approximation of Pareto efficiency. See Richard A. Posner, 'The Ethical and Political Basis of the Efficiency Norm in Common Law Adjudication', *Hofstra L. Rev.*, 8 (1980), 487–507 at 495.

[441] A tendency which is perhaps as common in economics as it is in law and economics. See Robert D. Cooter, 'Law and the Imperialism of Economics: An Introduction to the Economic Analysis of Law and a Review of the Major Books', *UCLA L. Rev.*, 29 (1982), 1260–9 at 1263. ('Economists draw on many different forms of [efficiency], such as efficient production, efficient exchange, Pareto efficiency, national income maximization, wealth maximization, and utilitarian efficiency. Most economists move easily from one form to another, but the subtle shifts in significance are lost upon noneconomists.')

[442] Guido Calabresi, 'Some Thoughts on Risk Distribution and the Law of Torts', *Yale L.J.*, 70 (1961), 499–553.

[443] Guido Calabresi and A. Douglas Melamed, 'Property Rules, Liability Rules, and Inalienability: One View of the Cathedral', *Harvard L. Rev.*, 85 (1972), 1089–128 at 1092.

is only desirable, according to Calabresi, if it is consistent with socially-prevalent distributional objectives.[444]

At the heart of this argument rests the belief that the influence of efficiency criteria on the formulation and application of legal rules ought to be kept in check. This belief is elaborated and defended by Calabresi in his famous study of accident law, *The Costs of Accidents*, first published in 1970. Bemoaning the failure of American academic lawyers to devise a general theory of accident law, Calabresi argues that an important—though, as we shall see, not the primary—goal of such law 'is to reduce the sum of the costs of accidents and the costs of avoiding accidents'.[445] Determining such costs—let alone the appropriate strategies for their reduction—is no easy feat. Certain activities—the driving of motor vehicles, for example—may clearly be regarded generally to provide benefits which outweigh their costs. Balancing the costs and benefits of many other activities, however, is likely to be far less straightforward. 'Every decision we make regarding what we do, how we do it, what goods we use, how and by whom they should be made, involves a choice between a safer and a more accident prone way.'[446] Such 'dramatic choices'[447] cannot be left purely to guesswork and intuition; and so we need a general theory of accident law.[448] But what sort of theory?

The significance of Calabresi's answer to this question, given our concern here with the concept of efficiency, rests not in the theory which he favours but in the one which he eschews. By focusing on cost reduction, certain commentators have suggested, Calabresi—like Coase and other representatives of the Chicago neo-classical tradition—in effect emphasizes efficiency as the primary goal of tort law.[449] Yet, as Calabresi himself

[444] For an analysis of Calabresi's distributivist philosophy, see John B. Attanasio, 'The Principle of Aggregate Autonomy and the Calabresian Approach to Products Liability', *Virginia L. Rev.*, 74 (1988), 677–750 at 723–34.

[455] Guido Calabresi, *The Costs of Accidents: A Legal and Economic Analysis* (New Haven, Conn.: Yale University Press, 1970), 26.

[446] Ibid. 108.

[447] Ibid. The difficulty of choice—e.g. where scarcity of resources ensures that, whatever choice is made, the outcome will be 'tragic'—is a dominant theme in Calabresi's work. See, in particular, Guido Calabresi and Philip Bobbitt, *Tragic Choices* (New York: Norton & Co., 1978).

[448] See Calabresi, *supra* n. 445, 157–8.

[449] See Ronald M. Dworkin, 'Is Wealth a Value?', *Jnl. Leg. Studs.*, 9 (1980), 191–226 at 201–5; and also Mark G. Kelman, 'Misunderstanding Social Life: A Critique of the Core Premises of "Law and Economics" ' *Jnl. Leg. Educ.*, 33 (1983), 274–84. Kelman seems to regard Calabresi as a sort of closet Chicago neo-classicist who is 'acutely aware that the social role of the story of efficient tort rules is to preserve the ideological vitality of the liberal state from collectivist attacks in a world in which transaction costs prevent a fully voluntarist, liberal social organization'. Ibid. 281–2). Kelman appears to base this assertion on little more than the observation that Calabresi shares with representatives of the Chicago neo-classical tradition the feeling that regulation frequently fails to achieve its desired ends. For Calabresi's scepticism regarding the efficacy of collectivist regulatory strategies, see Guido Calabresi, 'Torts—The Law of the Mixed Society', *Texas L. Rev.*, 56 (1978), 519–34 at 518–19.

insists,[450] this is not the case. '[E]conomic theory', he claims, 'cannot tell us how far we want to go to save lives and reduce accident costs. Economic theory can suggest one approach—the market—for making the decision. But decisions balancing lives against money or convenience cannot be purely monetary ones, so the market method is never the only one used.'[451] Sometimes, decisions to allow or to deter an activity will clearly fall outside the realm of the market. While, for example, certain activities may be sustainable in market terms, they may be prohibited for the simple reason that 'there are some things we do not want in our society regardless of costs. Prostitution and murder should be barred even if they can pay their way a thousandfold because—and the answer is self-evident as well as self-serving—they are immoral'.[452]

The difference between Calabresian and Chicago-inspired law and economics is considerable. For Calabresi, legal arrangements are not always susceptible to market explanations; and consequently, the utility of neo-classical economic analysis for the purpose of determining the costs of accidents is significantly limited. Neo-classical analysis may well work in theory; but economic theory is not situated in the real world.[453] 'The classical economist will show *ad nauseam* that those who were made better off by moving to a free market choice system based on full costs could more than compensate those who were made worse off. The problem is that such hypothetical compensation rarely comes about. . . . In all such cases, the theoretical desirability of the totally free market approach has little significance in practice.'[454]

Even if the argument for cost reduction as a goal of accident law could be conceived purely as a proposal for greater economic efficiency, Calabresian and Chicago law and economics would still be worlds apart. For, as intimated above, reducing costs, according to Calabresi, ought not to be the principal function of accident law. First and foremost, he argues, a system of accident law 'must be just or fair'.[455] 'No system of accident law can operate unless it takes into account which acts are deemed good, which deemed evil, and which deemed neutral. Any system of accident law that encourages evil acts will seem unjust to critic and community even if economically it is very efficient indeed.'[456] Although, in *The Costs of Accidents*, Calabresi never seems to get to grips with justice—while it is

[450] See Guido Calabresi, 'About Law and Economics: A Letter to Ronald Dworkin', *Hofstra L. Rev.*, 8 (1980), 553–62 at 556–9; and cf. Ronald Dworkin, 'Why Efficiency? A Response to Professors Calabresi and Posner', *Hofstra L. Rev.*, 8 (1980), 563–90 at 563–4.

[451] Calabresi, *supra* n. 445, 18.

[452] Calabresi, *supra* n. 445, 100.

[453] See ibid. 170–2.

[454] Ibid. 79.

[455] Ibid. 24.

[456] Ibid. 294.

never really clear what he takes the word to mean[457]—he is nevertheless adamant that justice must be regarded 'as a veto or constraint on what can be done to achieve cost reduction', as 'a final test which any system of accident law must pass'.[458] Whatever 'the demands of economic efficiency,'[459] quite simply, '[j]ustice must ultimately have its due'.[460]

Calabresi's legal–economic studies of the 1960s and 1970s stand apart from the bulk of the law and economics literature of that period. On the whole, post-Coasean lawyer–economists accepted, and continue to accept, the criterion of efficiency as the starting-point for economic analysis, even if disagreements persist about the concept of efficiency itself. To express the same point in a rather different fashion, the dominant—albeit not exclusive—theoretical inspiration behind the economic analysis of law in the United States continues to be modern Chicago neo-classical analysis. The theoretical assumptions embodied in modern Chicago neo-classicism are effectively replicated within the Chicago law and economics tradition. Not only do modern Chicago lawyer–economists accept the basic insights of neo-classical economic theory—the rationality and ethical attractiveness of economic self-interest, the belief that free market competitive pricing secures the most efficient allocation of resources, the general distrust of government regulation and the like—but, equally, like many economists within the Chicago neo-classical tradition, they have endeavoured to apply these insights to an ever-expanding variety of human affairs. Both the fascination with, and the distrust of, Chicago law and economics in the United States stems largely from the fact that, as with Chicago neo-classical economics itself, its proponents have demonstrated a general eagerness to use economic analysis in just about any domain of inquiry. Thus it is that, in the modern American law school, few subjects have failed to come under the scrutiny of law and economics.

EFFICIENCY AND DEMONOLOGY

From the mid-1960s onwards—in the aftermath of 'The Problem of Social Cost'—legal–economic research, especially in the Chicago mould, began to

[457] Quite early on in the book, he asserts that, 'if the elusiveness of justice cannot justify ignoring the concept, it at least justifies delaying the discussion of it' (*supra* n. 455, 26). When he does eventually address the concept, his discussion is, perhaps inevitably, highly generalized. For example, 'We must always remember that the community's sense of justice is not, and never can be, simply a rational reaction, and that it must be reckoned with whether or not it is sensible. The critic can only hope that over time rational considerations will overcome irrational ones.' (Ibid. 294.)

[458] Ibid. 24 fn. 1.

[459] Ibid. 296.

[460] Ibid. 26.

proliferate.[461] The impact of such research on American jurisprudence in the late 1960s and 1970s is especially clear from the reactions of certain of its earliest critics. 'Economic jurisprudence is becoming the new core doctrine of liberal legal thought,' Thomas Heller observed in 1976, 'because . . . it affords a more complete explanation of the contemporary role of the modern state than did pre-existing legal philosophy, and [because] it appears to offer a value free or procedural theory of social justice.'[462] For '[t]hose who come to identify law with economics,' Frank Michelman suggested around the same time, '[n]ormative economics is a far more polished, a far better articulated, a far more accessible and presentable, a far better systematized body of analytical and critical material, commanding far more internal disciplinary consensus than the rest of moral and political theory.'[463] No matter how much they disparaged the subject, critics of law and economics could not help but recognize and acknowledge its appeal and impact. Even H. L. A. Hart, writing from the other side of the Atlantic in 1977, noted the degree to which 'the contemporary Chicago-bred school of the economic analysis of law . . . now has a great hold upon American teaching of the law of torts.'[464] To borrow a metaphor from another jurisprudential context,[465] law and economics appeared to have fallen like a bomb on the academic legal world.

If any one person is to be credited—or blamed—for the impact of neo-classical economic analysis on American academic legal thought around this period, it is Richard Posner. On joining the Stanford Law School in 1968, Posner began researching into the fields of antitrust and the regulation of public utilities and common carriers[466]—areas in which he had specialized since 1962 while in government service.[467] A self-educated

[461] For bibliographical evidence, see Warren J. Samuels, 'Law and Economics: A Bibliographical Survey, 1965–1972', *Law Library Jnl.*, 66 (1973), 96–110, though it should be noted that, in deciding what constitutes legal–economic research, Samuels casts his net extremely wide.

[462] Thomas C. Heller, 'The Importance of Normative Decision-Making: The Limitations of Legal Economics as a Basis for a Liberal Jurisprudence—As Illustrated by the Regulation of Vacation Home Development', *Wisconsin L. Rev.*, [1976], 385–502 at 468.

[463] Frank I. Michelman, 'Norms and Normativity in the Economic Theory of Law', *Minnesota L. Rev.*, 62 (1978), 1015–48 at 1030.

[464] H. L. A. Hart, 'American Jurisprudence through English Eyes: The Nightmare and the Noble Dream', *Georgia L. Rev.*, 11 (1977), 969–89 at 987–8.

[465] See Charles E. Clark, 'Jerome N. Frank', *Yale L.J.*, 66 (1957), 817–8 at 817 (suggesting that Frank's *Law and the Modern Mind* 'fell like a bomb on the legal world').

[466] See Richard A. Posner, 'Natural Monopoly and Its Regulation', *Stanford L. Rev.*, 21 (1969), 548–643; 'Oligopoly and the Antitrust Laws: A Suggested Approach', *Stanford L. Rev.*, 21 (1969), 1562–75.

[467] Posner, *supra* n. 10, 437. For further biographical details, see Mark Blaug, *Great Economists Since Keynes: An Introduction to the Lives and Works of One Hundred Modern Economists* (Brighton: Harvester, 1985), 202–3.

neo-classicist,[468] Posner was already familiar with Aaron Director's ideas on antitrust before he moved to the University of Chicago Law School in 1969.[469] On moving to Chicago—he holds a post as a senior lecturer at the Law School to this day, although since 1981 he has been a Judge on the United States Court of Appeals for the Seventh Circuit—Posner began to follow the lead of other neo-classicists by developing the application of economics in so-called non-market areas of law. Whereas '[f]ormerly law and economics intersected only in the fields of antitrust and public utility regulation,' he observed in the first edition of his *Economic Analysis of Law*, 'today the diligent reader of scholarly journals can also find economic analyses of crime control, accident law, contract damages, race relations, judicial administration, corporations and securities regulation, environmental problems, and other areas of central concern in the contemporary legal system.'[470] No one has been more responsible for introducing economic analysis into these various areas than has Posner himself. The most recent edition of the *Economic Analysis of Law* opens with the observation that the book now covers '*almost* the whole legal system . . . not only the familiar examples [of the legal regulation of nonmarket behaviour] such as crimes and accidents and lawsuits, but also the less familiar examples such as drug addiction, sexual acts, surrogate motherhood, rescues at sea, and religious observances'.[471] What Gary Becker has done for economics, Posner has done for law and economics.[472]

Posner's seemingly tireless initiatives in expanding the domain of legal–economic analysis have earned him a good deal of praise. Maintaining a remarkable level of academic productivity from the bench (leaving aside the fact that he is apparently the most prolific federal appeals judge in the United States[473]), Posner has been lauded as 'not only the premier legal scholar of our time, but, indeed, [as] one of the extraordinary intellectuals of the late Twentieth Century'.[474] For others, however, Posner's achievements ought to be regarded with suspicion. While his assiduousness in

[468] See ARIC Press with Ann McDaniel, 'Free Market Jurist: Can Richard Posner Go From Judge to Justice?', *Newsweek*, 10 June 1985, 93–4 at 93 col. 2. ('[F]irst briefly at Stanford and then at the University of Chicago, Posner taught himself free-market economics . . . and applied his learning to the law.')

[469] See Kitch (ed.), *supra* n. 146, 207–8 (comment by Richard Posner); Coase, *supra* n. 216, 251.

[470] Posner, *supra* n. 437, ix.

[471] Posner, *supra* n. 69, xix.

[472] According to Posner, Becker's work is of especial significance to the development of the economic analysis of law. See e.g. Posner, *supra* n. 53, 760–1; 'Gary Becker's Contributions to Law and Economics', *Jnl. Leg. Studs.*, 22 (1993), 211–15; *Economic Analysis of Law* (2nd edn. Boston: Little, Brown & Co., 1977), 17. ('Becker's insistence on the relevance of economics to a surprising range of nonmarket behaviour . . . opened up to economic analysis large areas of the legal system not reached by Calabresi's and Coase's studies of property rights and liability rules.')

[473] See ARIC and McDaniel, *supra* n. 468, 93 col. 1.

[474] Ellickson, 'Bringing Culture and Human Frailty to Rational Actors', *supra* n. 75, 26. Not everyone, however, is impressed by Posner's output. See e.g. Anthony D'Amato, 'As

raising the profile and expanding the domain of law and economics is beyond doubt, his efforts, critics often argue, have served primarily to confer academic respectability on a theory of law which, sharing the neo-classical faith in rational self-interest, offers an essentially cold, hard and, in consequence, inordinately narrow vision of human nature.[475] One cannot help but notice, according to one commentator, the 'temperamental affinity' between Posner and Holmes—'their shared tough-minded antisentimentalism, the bleak Malthusian wisdom that there is no free lunch and that well-intentioned efforts to redistribute wealth are usually self-defeating, the ultimate grounding of law—and indeed all social life—in the brute facts of self-preference, territorial defence, revenge instincts, and the struggle for survival'.[476] Just as Holmesian jurisprudence has provoked a good deal of exaggerated moral outrage,[477] so too Posnerian economic analysis has been portrayed as an illiberal, elitist, exploitative and potentially tyrannical legal theory.[478] Not that all, or even many, criticisms of Posner's ideas are underscored by such moral fury; but for all this, as should gradually become clearer, the temptation to demonize him has, for many American academic lawyers, proved irresistible.

So, what is all the fuss about? Posnerian jurisprudence is essentially law seen through the eyes of the Chicago neo-classical economist. Starting out from 'the assumption that man is a rational maximizer of his ends in life',[479] Posner observes that, where rational self-interest is allowed to flourish—that is, where there exists a system of voluntary exchange—resources tend to gravitate towards their highest valued uses. 'When resources are being used where their value is greatest, we say that they are being employed efficiently.'[480] According to Posner, efficiency 'means exploiting economic resources in such a way that human satisfaction as measured by aggregate consumer willingness to pay for goods and services is maximized'.[481]

Gregor Samsa Awoke One Morning From Uneasy Dreams He Found Himself Transformed Into An Economic Analyst of Law', *Northwestern Univ. L. Rev.*, 83 (1989), 1012–21 (suggesting that quantity of product may disguise paucity of original thought and that, '[b]y writing replies,' Posner is 'able to avoid some of the mental costs associated with original thinking' (p. 1018)). For Posner's reply (!), see 'Gregor Samsa Replies', *Northwestern Univ. L. Rev.*, 83 (1989), 1022–5.

475 See e.g. Robin West, 'Authority, Autonomy, and Choice: The Role of Consent in the Moral and Political Visions of Franz Kafka and Richard Posner', *Harvard L. Rev.*, 99 (1985), 384–428; and also Richard A. Posner, 'The Ethical Significance of Free Choice: A Reply to Professor West', *Harvard L. Rev.*, 99 (1986), 1431–48; and Robin West, 'Submission, Choice, and Ethics: A Rejoinder to Judge Posner', *Harvard L. Rev.*, 99 (1986), 1449–56.

476 Robert W. Gordon, 'Introduction: Holmes's Shadow', in R. W. Gordon (ed.), *The Legacy of Oliver Wendell Holmes, Jr.* (Edinburgh: Edinburgh University Press, 1992), 1–15 at 6.

477 See Neil Duxbury, 'The Reinvention of American Legal Realism', *Legal Studies*, 12 (1992), 137–77 at 159–64.

478 See Malloy, 'Invisible Hand or Sleight of Hand?', *supra* n. 74, 240–54; and also White, *supra* n. 77, 183, 191.

479 Posner, *supra* n. 437, 1.

480 Ibid. 4.

481 Ibid.

Efficiency, in other words, is to be equated with wealth-maximization—wealth, in this context, being conceived broadly to include not only money but any form of utility which is increased through exchange.

At first glance, the emphasis on maximization puts one in mind of utilitarianism. Indeed, 'Bentham's utilitarianism,' Posner states in the first edition of the *Economic Analysis of Law*, 'is another name for economic theory.'[482] For example, 'Bentham's point that the unnecessary infliction of punishment creates avoidable and therefore wasteful costs' is but a forerunner to the neo-classical claim, endorsed by Posner himself, that, '[i]f the value of the criminal conduct to the criminal exceeds all relevant costs to society, including those of allocation by legal rather than market transactions, the criminal conduct is value maximizing and should be tolerated.'[483] The utilitarian implications of Posner's theory have attracted much criticism. While he assumes that the individual's willingness to pay for what he or she values demonstrates rational self-interest, it has been argued, there 'exists no evidence to indicate that people's existing orientations are the most conducive to their greatest happiness or greatest satisfaction'.[484] Posner seems simply to believe that 'what people do is good, and [that] its goodness can be determined by looking at what it is they do'.[485]

By the time of the appearance of the second edition of the *Economic Analysis of Law*, Posner was beginning to dissociate his theory from what he had previously taken to be its utilitarian underpinnings.[486] This dissociation, it transpired, was crucial for the development of his own legal–economic position. 'Bentham's major weaknesses as a thinker,' he suggested in 1976, 'were the sponginess of the utility principle as a guide to policy, his lack of interest in positive or empirical analysis, and his excessive, if characteristically modern, belief in the plasticity of human nature and social institutions.'[487] While utilitarianism emphasizes happiness and its maximization as the basis of just legal policy-making, it offers no reliable method of determining whose happiness should be deemed to count for the purpose of designing policy,[488] or how the impact of changes in policy is to be measured in terms of its effect on levels of satisfaction.[489]

[482] Ibid. 357. H. L. A. Hart assumed that Posnerian law and economics was 'designed to establish the utilitarian underpinnings of the law'. Hart, *supra* n. 464, 988.

[483] Posner, *supra* n. 437, 358–9; and see, more generally, Becker, *supra* n. 393, *passim.*

[484] C. Edwin Baker, 'The Ideology of the Economic Analysis of Law', *Philosophy and Public Affairs*, 5 (1975), 3–48 at 34.

[485] Leff, *supra* n. 6, 458.

[486] See Posner, *supra* n. 472, 12; and also, more generally, C. Edwin Baker, 'Starting Points in Economic Analysis of Law', *Hofstra L. Rev.*, 8 (1980), 939–72 at 948–9.

[487] Richard A. Posner, 'Blackstone and Bentham' [1976], in his *The Economics of Justice* (Cambridge, Mass.: Harvard University Press, 1981), 13–47 at 42.

[488] Richard A. Posner, 'Utilitarianism, Economics, and Social Theory' [1979], in his *The Economics of Justice*, 48–87 at 52.

[489] Ibid. 55.

Furthermore, utilitarianism justifies immoral action. If I spend my leisure time pulling wings off flies, while you spend yours feeding pigeons, and I derive greater pleasure from my pastime than do you from yours, then, in utilitarian terms, I must be judged to engage in the activity which adds more to the sum total of human happiness.[490] Within a utilitarian system, the formulation of legal policy and the content of legal rights are, like human activities generally, to be judged not in terms of their morality but according to whether or not they lead to an increase in overall happiness.

As compared with the concept of utility, wealth-maximization, according to Posner, provides a more solid foundation for ethical theory and legal policy-making. For 'the pursuit of wealth . . . involves greater respect for individual choice than in classical utilitarianism.'[491] Wealth-maximization requires that individuals be able to make choices regarding how they wish to maximize their wealth; and this requires that they are accorded distinct rights which facilitate such choices. 'Sometimes, to be sure, these rights have to be qualified because of the costs of protecting them. . . . Nonetheless, the commitment of the economic approach to the principle of rights is stronger than that of most utilitarians.'[492] With wealth-maximization, furthermore, comes honesty and self-improvement, for 'the wealth-maximization principle encourages and rewards the traditional "Calvinist" or "Protestant" virtues and capacities associated with economic progress.'[493] 'Most of the conventional pieties—keeping promises, telling the truth, and the like—can', Posner insists, 'be derived from the wealth-maximization principle. Adherence to these virtues facilitates transactions and so promotes trade and hence wealth by reducing the costs of policing markets through self-protection, detailed contracts, litigation, and so on.'[494]

The ethical attractiveness of the wealth-maximization principle derives also, Posner argues, from the fact that it is premissed on social consensus. In elaborating this argument, he contrasts his own position with that of John Rawls. In the original position, Rawls argues, individuals, given their lack of knowledge, will agree that inequalities ought to be arranged so that they might reasonably be expected to be to the advantage of everyone.[495] Individuals will agree to this proposition because, until the so-called veil of ignorance is lifted, they are likely to fear the worst regarding their own position in society. People in the original position would not argue in favour of the principle of wealth-maximization because, while in that

[490] See ibid. 56–7. [491] Ibid. 66. [492] Ibid. 69.

[493] Ibid. 68. For a highly sympathetic analysis of Posner's 'Calvinism', see Annalise E. Acorn, 'Valuing Virtue: Morality and Productivity in Posner's Theory of Wealth Maximization', *Valparaiso Univ. L. Rev.*, 28 (1993), 167–210.

[494] Posner, *supra* n. 488, 67.

[495] See John Rawls, *A Theory of Justice* (Oxford: Oxford University Press, 1972), 155–8.

position, they could not be sure that they would be the beneficiaries of such a principle. Risk aversion will thus determine the type of justice which they choose. Posner highlights the artificiality of the Rawlsian position.[496] In the real world, he argues, people are more likely to agree on the principle of wealth-maximization than on the Rawlsian principle of maximin, for in the real world people are forced to rely on their energy, skill and character, and to make choices under uncertainty.[497] Wealth-maximization is the principle which is most likely, accordingly, to command social consensus when people are forced to contend with natural as opposed to artificial, Rawlsian ignorance.

In Posner's words, his defence of wealth-maximization has met with 'a barrage of criticism'.[498] Along with other neo-classical economists, he has been taken to task for failing to acknowledge the fact that economic behaviour may not always be founded on self-interest—even when self-interest is understood to include self-serving regard for others[499]—and for failing to appreciate that self-interested action is not necessarily rational action.[500] In so far as economic action is rational, it has been argued, Posner and other neo-classicists fail to take account of the peculiarly bounded nature of rationality.[501] In neo-classical legal–economic literature, contracts are treated as essentially uncomplicated, discrete and predictable transactions between rational actors whose dealings with one another are confined purely to the contract at hand. Little, if any, account is taken of the planning which goes into the formation of contracts, of the fact that

[496] See Posner, *supra* n. 440, 498, citing Kenneth J. Arrow, 'Some Ordinalist-Utilitarian Notes on Rawls's Theory of Justice', *Jnl. of Philosophy*, 70 (1973), 245–263 at 250–1.

[497] Posner, *supra* n. 440, 498–9.

[498] Richard A. Posner, 'The Justice of Economics', *Economia delle scelte pubbliche*, 1 (1987), 15–25 at 15.

[499] See e.g. Mark Kelman, 'Choice and Utility', *Wisconsin L. Rev.*, [1979], 769–97 (arguing that neo-classicists such as Posner pay insufficient attention to the fact that factors such as mistake, regret and coercion are likely to influence consumer choices); David W. Carroll, 'Two Games that Illustrate Some Problems Concerning Economic Analysis of Legal Problems', *Southern California L. Rev.*, 53 (1980), 1371–422 esp. 1403–17 (using game theory—particularly the 'prisoner's dilemma'—to criticize the rational self-interest assumption as embodied in the work of Posner and other Chicago neo-classical lawyer–economists); and, with regard to law and economics generally, Jeffrey L. Harrison, 'Egoism, Altruism, and Market Illusions: The Limits of Law and Economics', *UCLA L. Rev.*, 33 (1986), 1309–63.

[500] See e.g. Pierre Schlag, 'Cannibal Moves: An Essay on the Metamorphoses of the Legal Distinction', *Stanford L. Rev.*, 40 (1988), 929–72 at 967–70; John Finnis, 'Allocating Risks and Suffering: Some Hidden Traps', *Cleveland State L. Rev.*, 38 (1990), 193–207 at 200–6; and, with regard to law and economics generally, Thomas S. Ulen, 'Cognitive Imperfections and the Economic Analysis of Law', *Hamline L. Rev.*, 12 (1989), 385–410; and, with regard to economics generally, Bernard M. S. van Praag, 'Linking Economics with Psychology: An Economist's View', *Jnl. of Economic Psychology*, 6 (1985), 289–311.

[501] See e.g. Ian R. Macneil, 'Economic Analysis of Contractual Relations: Its Shortfalls and the Need for a "Rich Classificatory Apparatus" ', *Northwestern Univ. L. Rev.*, 75 (1981), 1018–63 at 1024, 1043 and (on Posner specifically) 1056–62.

current contractual relations may be affected by future economic developments, or of the fact that people, and more particularly firms, will often be involved in a variety of contractual relations and that these relations may impinge upon one another.[502] Many critics are unpersuaded, furthermore, by Posner's efforts to present his wealth-maximization thesis as somehow an improvement upon utilitarianism. Wealth, they argue, is hardly less spongy a criterion than happiness or utility.[503]

The maximization of wealth, moreover, may sometimes turn out to be no more—and possibly even less—ethically attractive than the maximization of utility. Wealth-maximization, for Posner, is to be equated with Kaldor–Hicks efficiency.[504] A transaction will be efficient, in other words, when those whom it affects detrimentally are capable, in theory, of being compensated fully by those whose wealth is increased. But the Kaldor–Hicks criterion demands only hypothetical, not real, compensation. This raises a fundamental question: 'how does one ethically justify losers going uncompensated when the gainers by definition reap gains more than sufficient to compensate them?'[505] Posner's answer appears to be that efficiency may be justified on consensual grounds: that is, transactions

[502] The so-called relational contracts literature is vast. For examples of how relational contract theorists have attempted to criticize Posner and other neo-classical lawyer–economists, see Ian R. Macneil, 'Restatement (Second) of Contracts and Presentation', *Virginia L. Rev.*, 60 (1974), 589–610; 'The Many Futures of Contracts', *Southern California L. Rev.*, 47 (1974), 691–816; 'A Primer of Contract Planning', *Southern California L. Rev.*, 48 (1975), 627–704; 'Contracts: Adjustment of Long-Term Economic Relations Under Classical, Neoclassical, and Relational Contract Law', *Northwestern Univ. L. Rev.*, 72 (1978), 854–905; *The New Social Contract: An Inquiry Into Modern Contractual Relations* (New Haven, Conn.: Yale University Press, 1980), 72–7; 'Reflections on Relational Contract', *Zeitschrift für die gesamte Staatswissenschaft*, 141 (1985), 541–6; Victor P. Goldberg, 'Relational Exchange: Economics and Complex Contracts', *American Behavioral Scientist*, 23 (1980), 337–52; Charles J. Goetz and Robert E. Scott, 'Principles of Relational Contracts', *Virginia L. Rev.*, 67 (1981), 1089–150; Daniel A. Farber, 'Contract Law and Modern Economics Theory', *Northwestern Univ. L. Rev.*, 78 (1983), 303–39.

[503] See M. Neil Browne, John H. Hoag and S. M. Ashiquzzaman, review of Posner, *The Economics of Justice*, *Georgia L. Rev.*, 16 (1982), 767–74 esp. 769; Lewis A. Kornhauser, 'A Guide to the Perplexed Claims of Efficiency in the Law', *Hofstra L. Rev.*, 8 (1980), 591–639 at 592, 597–604; Robin F. Grant, 'Judge Richard Posner's Wealth Maximization Principle: Another Form of Utilitarianism?', *Cardozo L. Rev.*, 10 (1989), 815–45 esp. 832; and, more generally, Ernest J. Weinrib, 'Utilitarianism, Economics and Legal Theory', *U. Toronto L.J.*, 30 (1980), 307–32; Stephen F. D. Guest, 'Utilitarianism, Economics and the Common Law', *Otago L. Rev.*, 5 (1984), 656–63; and Alain Strowel, 'Utilitarisme et approche économique dans la théorie du droit: Autour de Bentham et de Posner', *Revue interdisciplinaire d'études juridiques*, 18 (1987), 1–45 (on 'the ambiguous relationship between Benthamite utilitarianism and Posner's economic approach to law' (p. 44).

[504] See Posner, *supra* n. 440, 491. For a critique of Posner's application of Kaldor–Hicks efficiency, see Herbert Hovenkamp, 'Positivism in Law & Economics', *California L. Rev.*, 78 (1990), 815–52.

[505] Cento G. Veljanovski, 'Wealth Maximization, Law and Ethics—On the Limits of Economic Efficiency', *Int. Rev. Law & Econ.*, 1 (1981), 5–28 at 14.

which are wealth-maximizing will be legitimate if individuals, in exercising their economic liberty, are prepared to consent to them.[506] Yet 'why would a possible loser consent to a system that made him worse off[?]'[507] People engage in transactions in the belief that they have something to gain from them; and if it turns out that they in fact lose rather than benefit from the transaction, it is surely not the case that they have consented to the loss, but only to the risk of loss. If I buy a lottery ticket and lose, my loss may well be legitimate owing to the fact that I clearly consented to a particular risk. But it does not follow that I have consented to the loss.[508] Nor can the acceptance of compensation be taken to imply consent to an activity which causes a loss.[509] There seems to be a serious flaw in the proposition that wealth-maximizing transactions may be justified on the basis of consent.[510]

Critics of the wealth-maximization thesis go still further in disputing its superiority over utilitarianism. Wealth-maximization often fares no better than utilitarianism, it is claimed, in determining what ought to be protected and prohibited as a matter of legal right.[511] Indeed, if anything, rights affect wealth-maximization rather than vice versa, for there can be no such

[506] Posner, *supra* n. 440, 492.

[507] Jules L. Coleman, 'Efficiency, Utility, and Wealth Maximization', *Hofstra L. Rev.*, 8 (1980), 509–51 at 534.

[508] See Coleman, ibid. 534–5; Dworkin, *supra* n. 450, 574–9. For further criticisms of Posner on consent to loss, see Lawrence G. Sager, 'Pareto Superiority, Consent, and Justice', *Hofstra L. Rev.*, 8 (1980), 913–37 at 930–7; Richard S. Markovits, 'Legal Analysis and the Economic Analysis of Allocative Efficiency', *Hofstra L. Rev.*, 8 (1980), 811–903 at 863.

[509] If it could, 'the only way traffic victims . . . could refuse to consent to being run over would be to refuse to accept compensation.' (Coleman, *supra* n. 507, 536). Coleman seems, however, to push this analogy too far, suggesting that one could hardly assert that the person who chooses to live in an area with a high incidence of crime is consenting to burglary by accepting compensation in the form of a comparably reduced housing price. (Ibid. 536–7 fn. 45.) My own suspicion is that Posner would not make such a claim. What he probably would claim, however, is that, in choosing to live in an area which suffers a high crime rate, one implicitly consents to a higher risk of burglary. For another critique which seems to stretch Posner's consent argument too far, see Gary T. Schwartz, 'Economics, Wealth Distribution, and Justice', *Wisconsin L. Rev.*, [1979], 799–813 at 804–7 (using the example of rape).

[510] See, generally, Veljanovski, *supra* n. 505, 16–18; Eric Rakowski, *Equal Justice* (Oxford: Clarendon Press, 1991), 218–26.

[511] See Charles Fried, 'Difficulties in the Economic Analysis of Rights', in Gerald Dworkin, Gordon Bermant and Peter G. Brown (eds.), *Markets and Morals* (Washington: Hemisphere, 1977), 175–95 esp. at 181. ('[A]lthough economic analysis can tell us what might be the effect on allocation of recognizing . . . rights, it cannot pretend to provide the means for deriving these rights from economic premises'); and also, similarly, Bruce Chapman, 'Raising Johnny to be Good: A Problematic Case for Economic Analysis of Law', *U. Toronto L.J.*, 34 (1984), 358–76 (on the inability of Posnerian economic analysis to determine children's rights); Warren J. Samuels, 'Maximization of Wealth as Justice: An Essay on Posnerian Law and Economics as Policy Analysis', *Texas L. Rev.*, 60 (1981), 147–72 at 154; Mario J. Rizzo, 'The Mirage of Efficiency', *Hofstra L. Rev.*, 8 (1980), 641–58 at 647. More generally, see Anthony T. Kronman, 'Wealth Maximization as a Normative Principle', *Jnl. Leg. Studs.*, 9 (1980), 227–42; Yew Kwang Ng, 'Economic Efficiency versus Egalitarian Rights', *Kyklos*, 41 (1988), 215–37; Richard A. Posner, 'The Value of Wealth: A Comment on Dworkin and Kronman', *Jnl. Leg. Studs.*, 9 (1980), 243–52.

thing as a uniquely wealth-maximizing result, but only one which maximizes wealth on the basis of an existing distribution of entitlements.[512] The meaning of wealth itself depends on this initial distribution. 'Wealth in any society depends on tastes, on what people want, on what they value. But what they value depends on what they have to begin with.'[513] One of the most common criticisms of the wealth-maximization thesis is that it demands that one simply accepts the existing distribution of entitlements in society, thereby favouring the economic *status quo* and, by extension, those who have already amassed considerable wealth.[514] Hence the common charge that the ideology of Posner's brand of law and economics is essentially conservative.[515] And for some critics, conservatism cannot be equated with justice.

> The normative idea of free choice central to economic analysis of law fails to recognize that economic rationality and market incentives may mask an unequal distribution of economic power. For those who lack economic power or interest, the system of wealth maximization can be just as coercive as an arbitrary master. The victims of poverty, the homeless, and the economically disadvantaged are in some ways no more free to choose under wealth maximization than a person living under the rule of an arbitrary master. . . . What is needed for the development of a more just economics of justice is the internal perspective or consciousness of those human beings who are either the subject of the analysis or those affected by its outcome. . . . The problem with Posner's concept of economic justice is that it lacks an appreciation that people can be dominated, coerced, and constituted by a market plagued by distributional inequalities based on factors such as race, class, gender, religion, and sexual preference.[516]

[512] See Lucian A. Bebchuk, 'The Pursuit of a Bigger Pie: Can Everyone Expect a Bigger Slice?', *Hofstra L. Rev.*, 8 (1980), 671–709 at 686–7.

[513] Calabresi, *supra* n. 23, 90.

[514] For the classic presentation of this argument, see Baker, *supra* n. 484, *passim*.

[515] For illustrations from a vast literature, see Kelman, *supra* n. 30, 151–185; Robin Paul Malloy, *Law and Economics: A Comparative Approach to Theory and Practice* (St. Paul, Minn.: West, 1990), 48–58, 60–8; Kurt A. Strasser, Robert L. Bard and H. Thomas Arthur, 'A Reader's Guide to the Uses and Limits of Economic Analysis with Emphasis on Corporation Law', *Mercer L. Rev.*, 33 (1982), 571–93 (arguing that to emphasize the importance of wealth-maximization is effectively to smuggle conservative ideology into legal analysis); Grant, *supra* n. 503, 844. On ideology in economics generally, see Robert M. Solow, 'Science and Ideology in Economics', *The Public Interest*, 21 (1970), 94–107. For an argument to the effect that Posner and other lawyer–economists would do well to follow the example of Marxist theorists by acknowledging the major part that ideology plays in economic analysis, see A. I. Ogus, 'The Parameters of Law and Economics: From Pashukanis to Posner', in Robert N. Moles (ed.), *Law and Economics* (Stuttgart: Steiner, 1988), 14–27. For the opposite argument—that law and economics must shake off its ideological baggage if it is to continue to flourish—see John J. Donohue III, 'Law and Economics: The Road Not Taken', *Law and Society Rev.*, 22 (1988), 903–26.

[516] Gary Minda, 'Towards a More "Just" Economics of Justice—A Review Essay', *Cardozo L. Rev.*, 10 (1989), 1855–77 at 1864–5.

In the critical literature on law and economics, statements such as this are to be found ten-a-penny. The free markets within which wealth is maximized are not really free; rather, they are markets within which the economically powerful are able to dominate the economically weak.[517] To express a preference for such markets is arbitrarily to uphold the legitimacy of existing power relations.[518] Given this conservatism inherent in the principle of wealth-maximization, the courts would do well not to try to promote such a principle.[519] Indeed, the securing of justice in the settlement of disputes will rarely be achieved by resorting to a particular principle of economic efficiency;[520] for such principles are by nature reductionist—they effectively strip the common law of its complexity.[521]

These are but a handful of the criticisms which have been levelled at the

[517] See Duncan Kennedy and Frank Michelman, 'Are Property and Contract Efficient?', *Hofstra L. Rev.*, 8 (1980), 711–70; Duncan Kennedy, 'Distributive and Paternalist Motives in Contract and Tort Law, With Special Reference to Compulsory Terms and Unequal Bargaining Power', *Maryland L. Rev.*, 41 (1982), 563–649; 'The Role of Law in Economic Thought: Essays on the Fetishism of Commodities', *American Univ. L. Rev.*, 34 (1985), 939–1001 at 958–67.

[518] See Nancy K. Kubasek, 'The Artificiality of Economic Models as a Guide for Legal Evolution', *Cleveland State L. Rev.*, 33 (1984–5), 505–12 (arguing that the pro-market assumptions of neo-classical economics are wholly arbitrary and that lawyers would do better to rely on economic models embodying assumptions which tend to justify rather than repudiate regulatory strategies); and Belinda Bennett, 'The Economics of Wifing Services: Law and Economics on the Family', *Jnl. Law & Soc.*, 18 (1991), 206–18 esp. 208. ('The effect of the Law and Economics analysis of family law is one of closure toward the experiences of the marginalized members of society. The logic of the market assumes that individuals interact on an equal footing. Differential power relations are not taken into account. The closing off of differential power relations from the economic discourses on the family operates as the effective utilization of a universalized white male standard; the very purported neutrality of the economic model masks its bias.')

[519] See Calabresi, *supra* n. 450, 561; Kornhauser, *supra* n. 503, 606; also Patricia M. Wald, 'Limits on the Use of Economic Analysis in Judicial Decisionmaking', *Law and Contemporary Problems*, 50 (4) (1988), 225–43; Jerome Culp, 'Judex Economicus', *Law and Contemporary Problems*, 50 (4) (1988), 95–140. Assessments of the impact of the wealth-maximization principle on judicial decision-making have ranged from the critical to the sympathetic. For the critical, see Shapiro, *supra* n. 292, *passim*; George M. Cohen, 'Posnerian Jurisprudence and Economic Analysis of Law: The View From the Bench', *U. Pennsylvania L. Rev.*, 133 (1985), 1117–66 esp. 1151 (arguing that, during his first three years on the bench, Posner used the wealth-maximization principle selectively in order to promote his own conservative ideology); and, for the more sympathetic, see Samuels and Mercuro, *supra* n. 58, *passim*; Izhak Englard, 'Law and Economics in American Tort Cases: A Critical Assessment of the Theory's Impact on Courts', *U. Toronto L.J.*, 41 (1991), 359–430. See also Richard A. Posner, 'Wealth Maximization and Judicial Decision-Making', *Int. Rev. Law & Econ.*, 4 (1984), 131–5 (responding to Samuels and Mercuro).

[520] See Michelman, *supra* n. 463, 1024–5; 'Ethics, Economics, and the Law of Property', in Pennock and Chapman (eds.), *supra* n. 439, 3–40; J. M. Steiner, 'Economics, Morality and the Law of Torts', *U. Toronto L.J.*, 26 (1976), 227–52.

[521] See Arthur Allen Leff, 'Law and', *Yale L.J.*, 87 (1978), 989–1011 at 1005–8; Laurence H. Tribe, 'Technology Assessment and the Fourth Discontinuity: The Limits of Instrumental Rationality', *Southern California L. Rev.*, 46 (1973), 617–60 at 628–30; Thomas C. Grey, 'Langdell's Orthodoxy', *U. Pittsburgh L. Rev.*, 45 (1983), 1–53 at 51.

wealth-maximization principle. To certain of these criticisms Posner has conceded some ground. 'There is', he admits, 'nothing in the ethic of wealth maximization which says that society has a duty to help the needy. It has a duty not to hurt them, to leave them alone; but it has no duty, and in a strict ethic of wealth maximization no right, to force the productive people to support the unproductive. . . . In this regard, wealth maximization is . . . out of phase with powerful currents of contemporary moral feeling,' and therefore 'an incomplete guide to social decision-making.'[522] On the whole, however, he continues to defend his position against its critics, arguing that wealth-maximization, despite its limitations, is the best ethic available for the purpose of guiding public policy generally, and that it is the only ethic which the courts in particular can do much to promote.[523]

To the most sustained criticism of the wealth-maximization principle—that it cannot guide social or legal policy because it ignores inequalities of wealth distribution—Posner appears to have conceded no ground at all. Even if an unequal distribution of resources does restrict the level of economic freedom which some people may enjoy, he argues, it by no means necessarily prevents them from maximizing their wealth. For '[e]ven choices within an extremely restricted feasible set may make the chooser better off and thereby make society wealthier.'[524] That the parties to a transaction may possess unequal bargaining power should not conceal the fact that they enter into that transaction for their own benefit, that they hope to be better off after the transaction than they were before.[525] It is possible to detect here a clear distinction between the legal–economic thinking of the New Deal era and the modern Chicago tradition. Whereas earlier lawyer–economists, particularly institutionalists, regarded inequality of wealth as an obstacle in the path of economic freedom, modern Chicagoans, and Posner in particular, insist that such inequality cannot diminish the pursuit of rational economic self-interest.[526] Between the

[522] Richard A. Posner, 'Wealth Maximization Revisited', *Notre Dame Jnl. of Law, Ethics and Public Policy*, 2 (1985), 85–105 at 101. For further concessions, see Posner, *supra* n. 9, 376–7, 391–2; *supra* n. 498, 23.

[523] See Posner, 'Wealth Maximization Revisited', *supra*, *passim*; *supra* n. 519, 133.

[524] Posner, *supra* n. 498, 23.

[525] As Richard Epstein states, why worry about inequality of bargaining power 'as long as somebody can sense, no matter what his original wealth, that he is going to be better off after the agreement than he was before'? 'Discussion: The Classical Theory of Law', *Cornell L. Rev.*, 73 (1988), 310–25 at 312 (comment by Epstein).

[526] Indeed it seems that, for Posner, such inequality is irrelevant for the purposes of economic analysis. See Richard A. Posner, 'Reflections on Consumerism', *U. Chicago Law School Record*, 20 (1973), 19–25 at 24–5. ('[T]here are economic grounds for questioning whether a completely free market will bring about an optimum level either of product information or product safety. (The argument of "exploitation" based on "unequal bargaining

1920s and the 1970s, law and economics in America had acquired a wholly new philosophical foundation.

While the wealth-maximization thesis has attracted criticism in abundance, it has not been without its defenders. Even detractors from law and economics occasionally profess astonishment at the degree to which the subject has been misrepresented, and it is perhaps no surprise that certain lawyer–economists have come to Posner's aid by attempting to demonstrate that wealth-maximization is neither as ethically problematic nor as ideologically biased as many critics have maintained.[527] For all that the wealth-maximization thesis has been subjected to intense criticism, furthermore, there is little doubt that Posner's work has inspired a good deal of modern legal–economic analysis. Indeed, of late, American lawyers and economists have been concerned increasingly with the development of legal–economic theories which either extend or stand methodologically distinct from the Chicago neo-classical, and particularly the Posnerian, perspective. Thus it is that we find contemporary American lawyer–economists heralding the arrival of 'post-Chicago' and 'non-Posnerian' law and economics.[528] Chicago neo-classical methodology, it is argued, may be supplanted or enriched by a whole host of different perspectives—game theory,[529] public choice theory,[530] neo-institutionalism,[531] cost-benefit

power", however, lacks, so far as I can see, any economic basis.) But that the free market is unlikely to work perfectly is not a sufficient condition for government intervention, since government, too, is invariably imperfect in actual operation . . . [W]e may well prefer to rely on a highly imperfect market.')

527 See e.g. John L. Hanks, 'On a Just Measure of the Efficiency of Law and Government Policies', *Cardozo L. Rev.*, 8 (1986), 1–38 (attempting to show that Posner's efficiency criterion may be refined and thereby rendered ethically more attractive); Gordon Tullock, 'Two Kinds of Legal Efficiency', *Hofstra L. Rev.*, 8 (1980), 659–69 at 669 (suggesting that, '[i]n most cases where efficiency considerations dictate a change in the law, moral principles are either irrelevant or unimportant'); Murphy and Coleman, *supra* n. 5, 213–15 (arguing that Posnerian law and economics is not inherently ideological); and, similarly, Robert D. Cooter, 'The Best Right Laws: Value Foundations of the Economic Analysis of Law', *Notre Dame L. Rev.*, 64 (1989), 817–37 at 831–3.

528 See generally the *Symposium on Post-Chicago Law and Economics*, *Chicago-Kent L. Rev.*, 65 (1989), 1–191 and the *Non-Posnerian Law and Economics Symposium*, *Hamline L. Rev.*, 12 (1989), 193–419.

529 See, for example, Carroll, *supra* n. 499, *passim*; Jules L. Coleman, 'Afterword: The Rational Choice Approach to Legal Rules', *Chicago-Kent L. Rev.*, 65 (1989), 177–91.

530 See, for an overview, Charles K. Rowley, 'Public Choice and the Economic Analysis of Law', in Mercuro (ed.), *supra* n. 31, 123–73.

531 See generally Warren J. Samuels and A. Allan Schmid (eds.), *Law and Economics: An Institutional Perspective* (Boston: Kluwer, 1981); and also Warren J. Samuels, 'Law and Economics: An Introduction', *Jnl. Econ. Issues*, 7 (1973), 535–41; Nicholas Mercuro, 'Toward a Comparative Institutional Approach to the Study of Law and Economics', in Mercuro (ed.), *supra* n. 31, 1–26; A. Allan Schmid, 'Law and Economics: An Institutional Perspective', in Mercuro (ed.), *supra* n. 31, 57–85; Charles K. Rowley, 'The Law of Property in Virginia School Perspective', *Washington Univ. L.Q.*, 64 (1986), 759–74.

critique,[532] Austrian economics,[533] and much more.[534]

Many of these efforts to develop new perspectives have generated only marginal enthusiasm among lawyer–economists generally. Precisely how economic analysis of law will be enriched or improved or whatever by turning away from Chicago and embracing the teachings of, say, the Austrian school or of modern institutionalism is not always clear.[535] Such alternatives, advocates invariably insist, offer lawyer–economists theoretical perspectives which account for those dimensions of socio-economic life which are generally neglected by Chicago neo-classicists. But

[532] Cost-benefit analysis is often equated with Chicago-style analysis of allocative efficiency. See e.g. Duncan Kennedy, 'Cost-Benefit Analysis of Entitlement Problems: A Critique', *Stanford L. Rev.*, 3 (1981), 387–445; Richard S. Markovits, 'Duncan's Do Nots: Cost-Benefit Analysis and the Determination of Legal Entitlements', *Stanford L. Rev.*, 36 (1984), 1169–98. Since the early 1980s, there has emerged in American public law scholarship a debate concerning the degree to which the implementation of regulatory statutes ought to be guided by cost-benefit analysis (although in this context, it ought to be noted, the term 'cost-benefit analysis' is not always used to denote analysis based on the principle of wealth-maximization). For various expressions of concern over the use of cost-benefit analysis for the purpose of regulatory decision-making, see Michael S. Baram, 'Cost-Benefit Analysis: An Inadequate Basis for Health, Safety, and Environmental Regulatory Decisionmaking', *Ecology L.Q.*, 8 (1980), 473–531; Cass R. Sunstein, 'Cost-Benefit Analysis and the Separation of Powers', *Arizona L. Rev.*, 23 (1981), 1267–82; Mark Sagoff, 'At the Shrine of Our Lady of Fatima or Why Political Questions Are Not All Economic', *Arizona L. Rev.*, 23 (1981), 1283–98; Bill Shaw and Art Wolfe, 'A Legal and Ethical Critique of Using Cost-Benefit Analysis in Public Law', *Houston L. Rev.*, 19 (1982), 899–927.

[533] Most of the studies in the *Non-Posnerian Law and Economics Symposium*, *supra* n. 528, draw on economic literature in the Austrian tradition. See also Christopher T. Wonnell, 'Contract Law and the Austrian School of Economics', *Fordham L. Rev.*, 54 (1986), 507–43. The principal legal–economic study in the Austrian tradition is the work of an Italian: Bruno Leoni, *Freedom and the Law* (3rd edn. Indianapolis: Liberty Press, 1991; 1st edn. 1961); and see further Peter H. Aranson, 'Bruno Leoni in Retrospect', *Harvard Jnl. of Law and Public Policy*, 11 (1988), 661–711; Leonard P. Liggio and Tom G. Palmer, '*Freedom and the Law:* A Comment on Professor Aranson's Article', *Harvard Jnl. of Law and Public Policy*, 11 (1988), 713–25.

[534] For further discussion of legal–economic research which is intended either to complement or to supersede the Chicago tradition, see Mackaay, *supra* n. 205, 74–85; Gary Minda, 'The Jurisprudential Movements of the 1980s', *Ohio State L.J.*, 50 (1989), 599–662 at 604–14; Cento G. Veljanovski, 'The Economic Approach to Law: A Critical Introduction', *British Jnl. of Law & Society*, 7 (1980), 158–93 at 187–92; Susan Rose-Ackerman, 'Progressive Law and Economics—And the New Administrative Law', *Yale L.J.*, 98 (1988), 341–68; 'Law and Economics: Paradigm, Politics, or Philosophy', in Mercuro (ed.), *supra* n. 31, 233–58.

[535] For a development of this point in relation to neo-institutionalism, see Richard A. Posner, 'The New Institutional Economics Meets Law and Economics', *Jnl. Institutional and Theoretical Economics*, 149 (1993), 73–87; and, for the critical response which this article provoked, cf. Wernhard Möschel, 'The New Institutional Economics Meets Law and Economics', *Jnl. Institutional and Theoretical Economics*, 149 (1993), 88–91; Kenneth E. Scott, 'The New Institutional Economics Meets Law and Economics', *Jnl. Institutional and Theoretical Economics*, 149 (1993), 92–5; Ronald H. Coase, 'Coase on Posner on Coase', *Jnl. Institutional and Theoretical Economics*, 149 (1993), 96–8; Oliver E. Williamson, 'Transaction Cost Economics Meets Posnerian Law and Economics', *Jnl. Institutional and Theoretical Economics*, 149 (1993), 99–118; and Richard A. Posner, 'Reply', *Jnl. Institutional and Theoretical Economics*, 149 (1993), 119–21.

the very appeal of Chicago neo-classical perspectives such as that developed by Posner rests in their lack of complexity.[536] A word which crops up constantly in the critical literature on Posnerian law and economics is 'hard': there is, it seems, a hardness about Posner's methodology and conclusions which critics generally find unpalatable.[537] At a most basic level, this hardness is demonstrated by the matter-of-fact, uncompromising manner in which he presents his arguments: 'man is a rational maximizer of his ends in life'—no questions. Furthermore, the conclusions which he reaches on the basis of his arguments, as we shall see in a moment, are often considered to be just as hard, just as ideologically loaded or morally dubious, as the arguments themselves. Legal–economic theories which purport to be more sensitive and sophisticated tend, by comparison, to be more equivocal and mushy. American lawyer–economists are often unsure as to what to make of them.[538] With the Posnerian perspective, in contrast, they tend to know where they stand.

This is not to suggest that all legal–economic theories which have emerged outside Chicago have fallen on deaf ears. Yet those theories which have influenced American academic legal thought have tended to share rather than to contradict the basic assumptions of Chicago neo-classicism. The increasing interest demonstrated by modern American academic lawyers in the application of economic reasoning to governmental policies and processes, for example, can more often than not be traced to an economic theory of public choice which treats political activity as a form of market activity.[539] Self-interest dominates governmental behaviour, according to public choice theorists, just as it determines economic behaviour.[540] Given that this is so, it is implausible for courts—or anyone else, for that matter—to try to justify regulatory strategies on the assumption that imperfect and greedy markets ought to be subject to controls imposed by detached and virtuous governments. For governments

[536] See Leff, *supra* n. 6, 456–9.

[537] For a meditation on this theme, see Peter R. Teachout, 'Chicago Exposition: The New Jurisprudential Writing As a Cultural Literature', *Mercer L. Rev.*, 39 (1988), 767–849 at 773, 788–803.

[538] See e.g. Gary Lawson, 'Efficiency and Individualism', *Duke L.J.*, 42 (1992), 53–98 at 96–7 (on the woolliness of economic analysis in the Austrian tradition).

[539] The American legal literature on public choice is now voluminous. See, generally, Farber and Frickey, *supra* n. 115, *passim.*

[540] The classic study in this field is James M. Buchanan and Gordon Tullock, *The Calculus of Consent: Logical Foundations of Constitutional Democracy* (Ann Arbor: University of Michigan Press, 1962). On the neo-classical foundations of public choice theory, see James M. Buchanan, *What Should Economists Do?* (Indianapolis: Liberty Press, 1979), 17–37; and on the intersections between public choice and Chicago neo-classicism, see Stigler, *supra* n. 176, 115. On the history of public choice generally, see W. C. Mitchell, 'Virginia, Rochester, and Bloomington: Twenty-five Years of Public Choice and Political Science', *Public Choice*, 56 (1988), 101–19.

often indulge in vices not dissimilar to those exhibited by markets themselves: regulation purportedly in the public interest turns out frequently to serve special interests. Although many American academic lawyers question certain of the assumptions inherent in public choice theory—while, generally, they argue that regulatory activity is rarely as preference-driven as public choice theorists like to claim[541]—it is primarily because of that theory that interest in the economic analysis of statute law, a subject which appeared to have reached its apogee in the New Deal era, has been revitalized.[542]

By and large, however, modern law and economics remains rooted in the common law tradition. It has often been observed,[543] and indeed we saw earlier, that the distinction between positive and normative analysis in Chicago neo-classical economics is by no means clear cut. Positive and normative analysis often go hand in hand, the latter evolving out of the former. In the first edition of the *Economic Analysis of Law*, Posner suggests that positive and normative analysis are of equal importance for the development of law and economics.[544] Within a few years, however, his opinion had changed. 'It is a general, and in my opinion deplorable, characteristic of legal scholarship', he commented in 1975, 'that normative analysis vastly preponderates over positive. . . . The result of the preference for normative analysis is that our knowledge of the legal system is remarkably meagre, incomplete, and unsystematic—a situation which, ironically, makes it very difficult to propose sound reforms of the system.'[545] It was around this time that Posner began to take issue with those critics who had failed to appreciate that he was far more interested in positive rather than normative economic analysis.[546] In the second edition

[541] See Daniel A. Farber and Philip P. Frickey, 'The Jurisprudence of Public Choice', *Texas L. Rev.*, 65 (1987), 873–927; also Michael DeBow and Dwight R. Lee, 'Understanding (and Misunderstanding) Public Choice: A Response to Farber and Frickey', *Texas L. Rev.*, 66 (1988), 993–1012; Daniel A. Farber and Philip P. Frickey, 'Integrating Public Choice and Public Law: A Reply to DeBow and Lee', *Texas L. Rev.*, 66 (1988), 1013–19.

[542] An indication of just how recently American jurisprudence in the public choice tradition has begun to emerge is evident from Richard Posner's observation in 1975 that the 'effort to explain . . . in economic terms . . . the behaviour of political institutions . . . is not a well developed area of law and economics'. Posner, *supra* n. 53, 765.

[543] See e.g. Reder, *supra* n. 155, 31–2.

[544] Posner, *supra* n. 437, 6. ('Economics turns out to be a powerful tool of normative analysis of law and legal institutions—a source of criticism and reform. . . . The positive role [of economic analysis]—that of explaining the rules and outcomes in the legal system as they are—is less obvious, but not less important.')

[545] Posner, *supra* n. 53, 768.

[546] See, in particular, Richard A. Posner, 'Some Uses and Abuses of Economics in Law', *U. Chicago L. Rev.*, 46 (1979), 281–306 at 287–95; and, for a sceptical response, Frank I. Michelman, 'A Comment on *Some Uses and Abuses of Economics in Law*', *U. Chicago L. Rev.*, 46 (1979), 307–15. More generally, for an excellent study of the positive-normative distinction in Posnerian legal–economic analysis, see Herbert Hovenkamp, 'The Economics of Legal History', *Minnesota L. Rev.*, 67 (1983), 645–97 at 647–61.

of the *Economic Analysis of Law*, positive and normative analysis were no longer placed on a level pegging. 'While the normative role of economic analysis in the law is . . . an important one, the positive role—that of explaining the rules and outcomes in the legal system as they are—is . . . even more important.'[547] For positive analysis reveals that 'many areas of the law, especially—but by no means only—the great common law fields of property, torts, crimes, and contracts, bear the stamp of economic reasoning.'[548]

In purporting to favour positive over normative economic analysis, Posner had pulled something of a master stroke. In short, he had revised Lord Mansfield's famous dictum that the common law works itself pure.[549] What the common law in fact does, Posner was claiming, is work itself efficient. By the time of the publication of the third edition of the *Economic Analysis of Law*, he had a very carefully worked out thesis. Owing to the fact that judicial opinions are frequently suffused with rhetoric, it is invariably very difficult to figure out what types of concerns lead judges to reach the decisions that they do. 'It would not be surprising', Posner asserted, 'to find that legal doctrines rest on inarticulate gropings towards efficiency, especially when we bear in mind that many of those doctrines date back to the late eighteenth and nineteenth century, when a *laissez-faire* ideology based on classical economics was the dominant ideology of the educated classes in society.'[550]

This is, of course, precisely what Posner finds. While statute law is often likely to reflect political concerns about wealth redistribution, judge-made rules tend to promote economic efficiency.[551] This is not a normative proposition that the common law ought to be concerned solely with the promotion of efficiency—Posner has no doubt that efficiency must sometimes be sacrificed in favour of other social values[552]—nor is it to suggest that every common law doctrine and decision is in fact efficient. It is simply to observe, rather, that, on the whole, the common law comprises a system of rules 'for inducing people to behave efficiently, not only in explicit markets but across the whole range of social interactions. In settings in which the cost of voluntary transactions is low, common law doctrines create incentives for people to channel their transactions through

[547] Posner, *supra* n. 472, 18. [548] Ibid.

[549] See *Omychund* v. *Barker* (1744) 1 Atk. 21 at 33.

[550] Richard A. Posner, *Economic Analysis of Law* (3rd edn. Boston: Little, Brown & Co., 1986), 21.

[551] Ibid. 495–6. Posner also claims (ibid. 21) that constitutional law, like legislation, tends not to be efficiency-promoting. For all this, however, he has tended increasingly to regard the Constitution as an economic text. See generally Posner, *supra* n. 69, 615–86; 'The Constitution as an Economic Document', *George Washington L. Rev.*, 56 (1987), 4–38.

[552] See Posner, *supra* n. 53, 772–4.

the market. . . . In settings in which the cost of allocating resources by voluntary transactions is prohibitively high, making the market an infeasible method of allocating resources, the common law prices behaviour in such a way as to mimic the market.'[553] The common law system is best, if not perfectly, explained as a system which works so as to maximize the wealth of society.

Many a criticism has been directed at Posner's positive economic analysis of the common law. First of all, there is the question of whether or not his thesis is empirically plausible. For all that Posner insists that it is, plenty of studies have been produced which purport to show that common law doctrines rarely promote efficiency.[554] While efficiency concerns may sometimes dominate adjudication regarding private law matters, moreover, this will seldom be the case in public law adjudication.[555] Even when common law doctrines do promote efficiency, it has been argued, we should not necessarily applaud that fact, for the common law ought to provide more than just a framework which facilitates the maximization of wealth, however broadly one conceives that term.[556]

Precisely how, furthermore, is efficiency supposed to be promoted? How can a collection of decisions or doctrines be conceived to be essentially wealth-maximizing when those responsible for these decisions and doctrines tend neither to resort explicitly to wealth-maximization theory nor even to give the impression that they think in economic terms? Posner's answer to this question is pure Friedman: in developing the common law, judges—like everyone else—may be assumed to act 'as if' they are attempting explicitly to facilitate an efficient allocation of resources.[557] Why might we be justified, however, in making this assumption? Friedman argued that it is reasonable to assume that businesses act as if consciously pursuing a strategy of profit-maximization since, if businesses fail to act in this way, they are unlikely to survive. But

[553] Posner, *supra* n. 69, 252.

[554] See e.g. Neal A. Roberts, 'Beaches: The Efficiency of the Common Law and Other Fairy Tales', *UCLA L. Rev.*, 28 (1980), 169–96 (arguing that common law property doctrines cannot be explained in terms of efficiency); C. Edwin Baker, 'Posner's Privacy Mystery and the Failure of Economic Analysis of Law', *Georgia L. Rev.*, 12 (1978), 475–95; Kim Lane Scheppele, *Legal Secrets: Equality and Efficiency in the Common Law* (Chicago: University of Chicago Press, 1988), 91–105, 308. Though there are studies which lend support to Posner's thesis, too. See e.g. William Bishop, 'Negligent Misrepresentation Through Economists' Eyes', *Law Q. Rev.*, 96 (1980), 360–79.

[555] See Frank I. Michelman, 'Political Markets and Community Self-Determination: Competing Judicial Models of Local Government Legitimacy', *Indiana L.J.*, 53 (1977), 145–206.

[556] See Izhak Englard, 'The Failure of Economic Justice', *Harvard L. Rev.*, 45 (1982), 1162–78; A. I. Ogus, 'Economics, Liberty and the Common Law', *Jnl. of the Society of Public Teachers of Law*, 15 (1980), 42–57 at 50–4, 57.

[557] See Posner, *supra* n. 53, 763; 'A Reply to Some Recent Criticisms of the Efficiency Theory of the Common Law', *Hofstra L. Rev.*, 9 (1981), 775–94 at 775.

judges are not business people; and courts are not profit-making enterprises. Why, then, should we assume that they act as if driven by the desire to maximize?

The answer which Posner offers to this question seems to me to be far from satisfactory. Judges may be assumed to act as if endeavouring to promote economic efficiency when formulating common law rules because they themselves are wealth-maximizers: 'judges, like other people, seek to maximize a utility function that includes both monetary and nonmonetary elements.'[558] Rather than seek to maximize profits in a conventional sense, they will concern themselves with other kinds of wealth—popularity, reputation, prestige, power, and the like. But it is not at all clear why this broad concern with wealth should cause judges to act as if promoting efficiency when developing the common law. Friedman's presentation of 'as if' methodology demonstrates a clear necessity for the assumption of rational maximizing behaviour, for he uses to illustrate his argument examples of people engaged in competition—businessmen, expert billiard players—people, that is, who must act as self-interested utility maximizers if they are to survive and prosper in their particular fields of activity. Judges, however, seem not to fall into this class. While, like everyone else, they may be driven by a basic desire to maximize their own wealth, it is far from obvious why this should impact on the job that they do, that is, why it should lead them to act as if endeavouring to formulate rules and doctrines which promote an efficient allocation of resources.

If Posner has failed satisfactorily to explain why judicial decision-making might be assumed to promote allocative efficiency, does this mean that he is entirely wrong, that the common law does not in fact generate such efficiency? In the late 1970s, an economist, Paul Rubin, attempted to demonstrate that Posner's faith in the efficiency of the common law process was not misplaced but that, in attempting to justify his faith, he had been barking up the wrong tree.[559] According to Rubin, litigation rather than judicial activity is the key to explaining the efficiency of the common law. The rational self-interest of disputants, particularly firms, he argues, will lead them to litigate inefficient rules, whereas efficient rules are likely to lead to out-of-court settlements: 'if rules are inefficient, parties will use the courts until the rules are changed; conversely, if rules are efficient, the courts will not be used and the efficient rule will remain in force.'[560] Thus it is that the stock of efficient common law rules accumulates over time.

[558] Posner, *supra* n. 69, 534. For a more elaborate discussion of the utility function which judges supposedly maximize, see Posner's chapter, 'What Do Judges Maximize? (The Same Thing Everybody Else Does)' in Posner, *supra* n. 10, 117–56.

[559] See Paul H. Rubin, 'Why is the Common Law Efficient?', *Jnl. Leg. Studs.*, 6 (1977), 51–63; reprinted in Paul H. Rubin, *Business, Firms and the Common Law: The Evolution of Efficient Rules* (New York: Praeger, 1983), 3–15. Citations are to the pagination in the book.

[560] Ibid. 7.

'[E]fficiency occurs because of an evolutionary process, not because of any particular wisdom on the part of judges. . . . Intelligent judges may speed up the process of attaining efficiency but they do not drive the process.'[561]

Although Rubin's argument modified Posner's efficiency thesis, it demonstrated also that there may in fact be a grain of truth in it. For while judges cannot determine which disputes are taken to court, it is ultimately for them, not for disputants, to replace inefficient rules with efficient ones. The degree to which the common law evolves in an efficient manner will ultimately depend on what judges do.[562] Quite how disputants decide on whether or not to challenge inefficient rules, furthermore, is not entirely clear. For Rubin, disputing parties must be affected by a particular rule to such a degree that they are willing to invest in litigation in the hope that the courts will use their case to replace that rule with a comparably efficient one. Commenting on Rubin's paper, the Yale law professor, George Priest, argued that the evolution of efficient rules does not in fact depend on the degree to which disputing parties have an interest in the outcome of litigation; for inefficient rules are likely to be replaced for the simple reason that, as compared with efficient rules, they impose greater costs on disputing parties.[563] Furthermore, it has been argued, disputants will often be prepared to increase their expenditure on litigation if it increases the probability of the court overturning an inefficient rule.[564] Since Posner first propounded the efficiency thesis, various lawyer–economists have endeavoured to revise it, so that there now exists a fairly vast literature devoted to the positive economic analysis of the common law.[565] With one or two exceptions,[566] the basic message to be discerned from this literature

[561] Ibid.

[562] For a critique of the thesis that the common law can evolve in an efficient manner without the help of judges, see Robert D. Cooter and Lewis A. Kornhauser, 'Can Litigation Improve the Law Without the Help of Judges?', *Jnl. Leg. Studs.*, 9 (1980), 139–63.

[563] George L. Priest, 'The Common Law Process and the Selection of Efficient Rules', *Jnl. Leg. Studs.*, 6 (1977), 65–82.

[564] See John C. Goodman, 'An Economic Theory of the Evolution of Common Law', *Jnl. Leg. Studs.*, 7 (1978), 393–406.

[565] For further examples, see Peter R. Terrebone, 'A Strictly Evolutionary Model of Common Law', *Jnl. Leg. Studs.*, 10 (1981), 397–407; William M. Landes and Richard A. Posner, 'Adjudication as a Private Good', *Jnl. Leg. Studs.*, 8 (1979), 235–84; and, for an overview, Jack Hirschleifer, 'Evolutionary Models in Economics and Law: Cooperation versus Conflict Strategies', *Research in Law and Economics*, 4 (1982), 1–60. For critique of the efficiency thesis, see Roger D. Blair and Carolyn Schafer, 'Antitrust Law and Evolutionary Models of Legal Change', *U. Florida L. Rev.*, 40 (1988), 379–409; Note [Wes Parsons], 'The Inefficient Common Law', *Yale L.J.*, 92 (1983), 863–87; and Nicholas Mercuro and Timothy P. Ryan, *Law, Economics and Public Policy* (Greenwich, Conn.: JAI Press, 1984), 119–23.

[566] Since the early 1980s, for example, George Priest has been arguing that indeterminacy rather than efficiency characterizes the influence of settlement decisions on the common law. See, for example, George L. Priest, 'Selective Characteristics of Litigation', *Jnl. Leg. Studs.*, 9 (1980), 399–421 at 410, 421.

is that, in one way or another, the common law system promotes allocative efficiency.

The positive economic analysis of the common law turns out, accordingly, not only to fit within, but significantly to build upon, the Chicago neo-classical economic tradition. Whereas economists and lawyers in the Chicago mould have typically been concerned with uncovering the shortcomings of regulatory legislation, Posner and other post-Coasean lawyer–economists complement that line of analysis by endeavouring to demonstrate that efficiency is to be discovered in the fabric of the common law. By demonstrating as much, modern Chicago and Chicago-inspired lawyer–economists reveal a clear preference for the common law over statute law as a system for the ordering of private affairs. It is a preference which is justified in terms of positive economic analysis: that is, one prefers the common law as a system of private ordering because it is a matter of fact that, unlike statute law, it tends to be driven by the ethic of wealth-maximization.

When this preference is expressed in such a stark fashion, it is possible to see very clearly that the line between positive and normative legal–economic analysis is very fine indeed. From the observation that the wealth-maximizing tendencies of common law rules make them preferable to legislation it is only a short step to the proposition that, given what we know about the common law, existing legal rules ought sometimes to be altered in order to promote still greater allocative efficiency. One of the grievances commonly voiced by Chicago lawyer–economists—and by Posner in particular—is that critics habitually fail to appreciate that, while the distinction between positive and normative analysis may seem subtle and even fuzzy, it exists and is important all the same.

Certainly detractors from, and proponents of, the Chicago tradition generally do not hold the same perceptions of neo-classical economic methodology, as is especially clear from many of the reactions to Landes and Posner's famous study of the adoptions market.[567] The economic analysis of adoptions which they offered was widely interpreted as normative rather than positive, and Posner in particular was accused of advocating 'baby selling'.[568] Posner himself has since insisted that the phenomenon of baby selling—or rather, parental right selling[569]—was

[567] Elisabeth M. Landes and Richard A. Posner, 'The Economics of the Baby Shortage', *Jnl. Leg. Studs.*, 7 (1978), 323–48.

[568] See e.g. West, 'Submission, Choice, and Ethics', *supra* n. 475, 1449; and also Kelman, *supra* n. 426, 688 fn. 51. (Posner's proposals for 'perfecting a market for babies' condemned as 'both irrational and immoral'.) For further references, see Richard A. Posner, 'The Regulation of the Market in Adoptions', *Boston Univ. L. Rev.*, 67 (1987), 59–72 at 59 fn. 1.

[569] See Richard A. Posner, *Sex and Reason* (Cambridge, Mass.: Harvard University Press, 1992), 410. ('The term *baby selling*, while inevitable, is misleading. A mother who surrenders

something which he and Landes wished only to explain, not advocate; that they were engaging in pure positive analysis.[570] This, however, was not quite the case. Landes and Posner used neo-classical economic analysis to support a very specific normative proposal—not the proposal which many of their critics believed them to be making, but a normative proposal all the same. There exists, they observed, a clear imbalance between the demand for and supply of babies for adoption, an imbalance which might be remedied through partial—not total—deregulation of the adoptions market. To this end, they proposed that certain adoption agencies should, on an experimental basis, be permitted to use part of their adoption fees to pay women contemplating abortion to have the baby instead and to put it up for adoption through the agency.[571] If implemented, such an experiment might maximize wealth at various different levels. In particular, in cases of unwanted pregnancy, women will be provided with an extra option, that is, with an incentive neither to abort nor to raise the baby in burdensome circumstances; and, since the existence of such an incentive should ensure an increase in the number of children available for adoption, the range of choice available to prospective adoptive parents will also be increased. Posner and Landes do not suggest that laws forbidding the sale of babies for adoption should, accordingly, be abolished forthwith, but only that changes in the current legal rules might make the existing adoptions market more efficient and equitable. Their argument is not merely positive economic analysis; but neither is it a strident normative argument to the effect that there should be a free market in adoptions.

The real problem with Landes and Posner's argument is not what some commentators perceive to be its ethical unattractiveness—that a comparably deregulated market may fail, for example, to discriminate between *bona fide* adoptive parents and child abusers[572]—but its unswerving rationality. Babies for adoption are treated as commodities to which there attach price tags. By decreasing the level of market regulation, the price of these commodities is likely to drop. Landes and Posner thus apply to the market

her parental rights for a fee is not selling her baby. . . . She is selling her parental rights . . . I hereby rename "baby selling" "parental right selling".')

570 Richard A. Posner, 'The Ethics and Economics of Enforcing Contracts of Surrogate Motherhood', *Journal of Contemporary Health Law and Policy*, 5 (1989), 21–31 at 22 ('"baby selling" [is] a practice that, contrary to the impression fostered by the media and others, I have not advocated but have merely tried to explain').

571 See Landes and Posner, *supra* n. 567, 347–8.

572 See William L. Pierce, Correspondence, in *Wall Street Journal*, 22 August 1986, 16 col. 1. ('If I am a child pornographer, may I purchase a baby so that I will have a "model" or "rentable object" that can be reared to be compliant with my wishes?'). In fact, Posner and Landes make clear in their article that, if their proposal were to be implemented, laws forbidding child abuse and neglect 'would continue to be fully applicable to adoptive patents'. Landes and Posner, *supra* n. 567, 34.

for adoptions the same neo-classical economic logic which Stigler and Friedman applied to the market for private-sector rented accommodation.

For many critics, the fundamental problem with Landes and Posner's position rests not in its underlying logic—indeed, generally, the logic is considered to be sound[573]—but in the fact that logic is being used to support normative proposals in areas of law where its utility is considered to be decidedly limited.[574] Given his belief that neo-classical analysis may generate novel insights into just about any area of the law, it is inevitable that Posner himself should reject such a criticism. But what is more interesting than his own reaction is the continuing reaction of critics themselves. Posner's economic logic generally leaves them cold, and his efforts to expand the domain of economic analysis—to introduce his logic into areas such as adoption, surrogacy and sex—result in the frequent accusations that his work is hard, sterile, immoral, conservative, élitist and the like. More often than not, in Posner's writings, the critics of law and economics find Swift without the satire—the deification of efficiency with scant regard for justice.[575] As he continues to develop and promote his faith in the principle of wealth-maximization, those who stand resolutely opposed to that principle continue, with equal vigour, to demonize him.

CONCLUSION

Economic analysis of law has generally evolved independently of modern American jurisprudential concerns. In recent years, the subject has generated novel insights in a variety of legal fields. Corporate law, bankruptcy, commercial law, international trade law—these are but some of the fields which, owing to the development of economic analysis, have been subjected to radical reassessment in the past twenty years or so. During this period, furthermore, law and economics has become ever more dominated by the highly technical, invariably model-based research of

[573] See e.g. Ronald A. Cass, 'Coping with Life, Law, and Markets: A Comment on Posner and the Law-and-Economics Debate', *Boston Univ. L. Rev.*, 67 (1987), 73–97 at 85–90.

[574] See J. Robert S. Prichard, 'A Market for Babies?', *U. Toronto L.J.*, 34 (1984), 341–57; Tamar Frankel and Francis H. Miller, 'The Inapplicability of Market Theory to Adoptions', *Boston Univ. L. Rev.*, 67 (1987), 99–103; Jane Maslow Cohen, 'Posnerism, Pluralism, Pessimism', *Boston Univ. L. Rev.*, 67 (1987), 105–75.

[575] See e.g. Cohen, *supra* n. 574, 154 fn. 190; Kelman, *supra* n. 426, 688 fn. 51; cf. also Jonathan Swift, 'A Modest Proposal for Preventing the Children of Poor People From Being a Burthen to Their Parents or the Country, and for Making Them Beneficial to the Public', in Angus Ross and David Woolley (eds.), *Jonathan Swift: A Critical Edition of the Major Works* (Oxford: Oxford University Press, 1984), 492–9.

economists.[576] Even to the degree that it has been shaped by lawyers, economic analysis has remained remarkably distinct from the realist legal tradition. Understanding the history and the culture of law and economics requires that we set it apart from that tradition, that we resist treating it as either an extension of, or a rebellion against, realist legal thought.

Yet although economic analysis of law has remained essentially separate from other jurisprudential concerns, it would be incorrect to deduce from this that it is somehow defined by methodological homogeneity. In the early part of this century, law and economics was comprised of little more than a mixed bag of lawyers and economists attempting to demonstrate that, to the pressing economic problems of the day, there existed definite legal solutions. Modern legal–economic analysis, in contrast, is concerned primarily with demonstrating that there may exist convincing economic solutions to particular legal problems. While early legal–economic inquiry tended to be influenced by broad political concerns and generally urged a greater role for government in the organization of economic affairs, furthermore, the free market, anti-interventionist ideology which dominates neo-classical law and economics is to be traced not to the wider political arena but principally to the initiatives of academics. Early efforts at legal–economic analysis petered out when the economic problems which had initially inspired such analysis no longer seemed especially troublesome. Neo-classical analysis, on the other hand, emerged and has endured within the universities. As compared with other social-scientific perspectives, neo-classical economics offered academic lawyers not only determinacy—that is, a theoretical model embodying a distinctive logic which could be employed to yield both positive and normative insights—but also, as the domain of neo-classical inquiry was subjected to ever greater expansion, an opportunity to extend the frontiers of interdisciplinary legal research to a degree which previously had been no more than contemplated.

This must not be taken to suggest that modern law and economics has evolved within a vacuum. Economic analysis of law will inevitably be shaped by political and legal institutions and arrangements, and by social norms, conventions and common beliefs regarding the rights and obligations of citizens and the state.[577] The significance of Chicago law and economics in particular is that—notwithstanding the fact that the conclusions of certain of its proponents seem often to be too counter-intuitive for

[576] For an early prediction of the highly technical contribution of economists to the development of law and economics, see Alvin K. Klevorick, 'Law and Economic Theory: An Economist's View', *Papers and Proceedings of the American Economic Association*, 65 (1975), 237–43.

[577] See Alvin K. Klevorick, 'Legal Theory and the Economic Analysis of Torts and Crimes', *Columbia L. Rev.*, 85 (1985), 905–20.

common acceptance, and despite all the criticisms to which it has been subjected—it is peculiarly suited to the 'non-economic', cultural context in which it is situated. Indeed, the defining traits of Chicago neo-classical economics—the suspicion of government and the insistence that markets protect rational individual choice and self-determination—reflect a distinctively American style of individualist ideology.[578] Even critics of Chicago law and economics tend to concede this fact. In spite of his sanctification of economic efficiency, Arthur Leff observed, there is at least one value which 'directs and informs Posner's whole analysis. God (and history) knows it's one that does him credit: individual human freedom.'[579]

Besides embodying individualism, Chicago law and economics also epitomizes a distinctively modern form of rationalism. We saw, in the previous chapter, that there rests at the heart of the process tradition in American jurisprudence the belief that judges ought to strive to cultivate reason in adjudication through the principled elaboration of grounds for decisions. Within the Chicago law and economics tradition, however, reason raises its head in a rather different fashion. Neo-classical lawyer–economists focus specifically on instrumental reason, on the type of reasoning upon which people rely when they calculate the most efficient application of specific means to a given end. The dominance of such reason in modern culture, according to Charles Taylor, is partially responsible for the spiritual and political impoverishment which characterizes western liberalism at the end of the twentieth century.[580] For lawyer–economists within the Chicago tradition, however, the primacy of instrumental reason is something to be celebrated rather than lamented. Such reasoning is considered to be immanent in the common law system: judges intuitively, if rarely consciously, invest common law doctrines and decisions with economic rationality. While academic lawyers and neo-classical economists may use different styles of rhetoric,[581] in instrumental reason they have discovered a common language.[582] In the late 1940s, Aaron Director began

[578] For an account of this ideology, see Seymour Martin Lipset, 'American Exceptionalism Reaffirmed', in Byron E. Shafer (ed.), *Is America Different? A New Look at American Exceptionalism* (Oxford: Clarendon Press, 1991), 1–45 esp. 16–25; and for an identification of this ideology in relation to the Chicago law and economics tradition (specifically with regard to Posner), see Kelman, *supra* n. 30, 117–8.

[579] Leff, *supra* n. 6, 477. For a suggestion, however, that the promotion of wealth-maximization and the pursuit of liberty may prove to be incompatible, see Robert D. Cooter, 'Liberty, Efficiency, and Law', *Law and Contemporary Problems*, 50 (4) (1988), 141–63 at 158–63.

[580] See Charles Taylor, *The Malaise of Modernity* (Concord, Ont.: Anansi, 1991), 4–8, 97.

[581] See McCloskey, *supra* n. 23, *passim*.

[582] See Bruce A. Ackerman, 'Foreword: Talking and Trading', *Columbia L. Rev.*, 85 (1985), 899–904 at 900; and also Robert W. Gordon, 'Critical Legal Studies as a Teaching Method, Against the Background of the Intellectual Politics of Modern Legal Education in

to introduce this language into American legal thought when he successfully urged his colleagues at the Chicago Law School to discard conventional wisdoms regarding the legal control of monopoly. Since then, this language has become an almost elementary feature of modern American legal education;[583] and, in learning it, American lawyers of tomorrow are forced to contemplate the possibility that, when a law is created or applied, it demonstrates, first and foremost, not the desire to do justice or to accord weight to popular morality, but the necessity of imposing a price.

the United States', *Legal Educ. Rev.*, 1 (1989), 59–83 at 74–5. ('For all the well-known weaknesses of the law-and-economics school . . . it has greatly improved the conduct of legal discourse . . . I remember the excitement that I and many other people in my cohort felt when we started reading the early work in this field . . . Some of it seemed dazzling, some perverse, wrong-headed, oppressive and reactionary; but even the worst stuff was at least about something real and important and had some graspable intellectual content. Unlike the maddeningly elusive post-War games of doctrinal analysis and ad hoc armchair policy invention, it was something you could sink your teeth into.')

583 The power of law and economics in the classroom is often acknowledged even by those who display no taste at all for economic analysis. See e.g. James Boyle, 'The Anatomy of a Torts Class', *American Univ. L. Rev.*, 34 (1985), 1003–63 at 1012. More generally, see Mark Cooney, 'Why is Economic Analysis so Appealing to Law Professors?' *Stanford L. Rev.*, 45 (1993), 2211–30.

6
Uses of Critique

> Let us face it, they do not write well, and their stylistic failings spring from these very features—careless neologism, a slapdash indifference to precision and rigour in exposition, an eager willingness to say more and to say it again rather than refining what one had already said, and so forth—which have been noticeable in the sociological world from which they sprang long before their own particular twist was ever heard of.[1]

The task of the critic is very often an invigorating one. In the quotation above, one senses Gellner's relish in attempting to make ethnomethodologists look ludicrous. When debunking is done well, it is frequently impossible for the spectator—unless the target—not to experience *Schadenfreude*. To be responsible for generating such experience must be exhilarating. For most critics, it is enough that they are able to attract a readership. That they might also cause their readers to smile, that they might be able to bring a little bit of plain old-fashioned pleasure into their lives—that is surely something else entirely.

It seems that the critical legal studies movement in the United States was dedicated to the generation of pleasure from its very inception. In the late 1960s, Duncan Kennedy—who, in due course, would become one of the principal representatives of the movement—wrote an article exposing the hostility, insecurity and cynicism which pervaded the law school at which he was then a student. Articles on law are rarely more iconoclastic. Asked about his experiences at the Yale Law School in the late 1970s, one of the characters in Tom Wolfe's *The Bonfire of the Vanities* remembers its selective tolerance. 'Yale is terrific for anything you wanna do, so long as it don't involve people with sneakers, guns, dope, lust, or sloth.'[2] In denouncing authoritarianism at Yale, Kennedy went much further. The war in Vietnam, he asserted, 'has made young people . . . more reluctant than in the past to commit a part of themselves which they know to be fragile to a [legal] process which they know to be brutal'.[3] Law school, for

[1] Ernest Gellner, 'Ethnomethodology: The re-enchantment Industry or the Californian way of Subjectivity', in his *Spectacles and Predicaments: Essays in Social Theory* (Cambridge: Cambridge University Press, 1979), 41–64 at 46.

[2] Tom Wolfe, *The Bonfire of the Vanities* (London: Picador, 1988), 417.

[3] Duncan Kennedy, 'How the Law School Fails: A Polemic', *Yale Review of Law and Social Action*, 1 (1970), 71–90 at 80.

many prospective students, was no longer the attractive option that it once was;[4] and those who did choose to study law often found themselves stranded in an environment where professorial aggression dulled the desire for intellectual self-improvement. Subjected to the case method of instruction, Kennedy claimed, 'students see professors as people who want to hurt them; professors' actions often do hurt them, deeply.'[5] While the law school may purport to be intellectually stimulating, 'when you have been competing in deadly earnest since the age of ten, submitting constantly to your own fear of the teacher's disapproval, accepting your own status as a non-person, there is a point at which *no* amount of intellectual interest will overcome your fear and revulsion at the spectacle of the professor smiling quietly to himself as he prepares to lay your guts out on the floor yet once again, paternally.'[6]

For all that it was written *avant la lettre*, Kennedy's attack on the Yale Law School is critical legal studies at its best, a *cri de cœur* against the repressiveness of an institution which purports to epitomize freedom and tolerance. But the critical legal studies movement has failed to capitalize on the sense of disenchantment out of which it was born. Like the legal realists before them, proponents of critical legal studies have proved to be better debunkers than reformers. Indeed, the reforms which they have advocated have tended to be thoroughly utopian, prompting the popular criticism that critical legal studies is all bark and no bite, that it is a style of critique which, for all its pretensions to radicalism, suggests no viable alternative to existing legal arrangements.[7]

During the past decade or so, criticism of this type has proliferated. Even legal commentators not directly concerned with critical legal studies often cannot resist taking a dig at it.[8] The rise and decline of legal realism—so the criticism goes—is being re-enacted. Vaguely left-wing legal radicalism has proved yet again to inspire little apart from hypocrisy and posturing.[9] Very often, this criticism conceals both a sense of alarm and a desire to deride. In attacking the rule of law and the entrenchment of institutional hierarchy, for example, critical legal theorists have been accused of biting the very hands that feed them. If these theorists feel genuinely disaffected with the teaching, the practice and the institutions of

[4] See Guyora Binder, 'On Critical Legal Studies As Guerrilla Warfare', *Georgetown L.J.*, 76 (1987), 1–36 at 24. ('Going to law school in the late sixties was like having to go to summer school while your friends were all out playing ball.')

[5] Kennedy, *supra* n. 3, 73.

[6] Ibid. 80.

[7] For good illustrations of this criticism, see Phillip E. Johnson, 'Do You Sincerely Want To Be Radical?', *Stanford L. Rev.*, 36 (1984), 247–91; Michael A. Foley, 'Critical Legal Studies: New Wave Utopian Socialism', *Dickinson L. Rev.*, 91 (1986), 467–96.

[8] See Neil Duxbury, 'Some Radicalism about Realism? Thurman Arnold and the Politics of Modern Jurisprudence', *Oxford Journal of Legal Studies*, 10 (1990), 11–41.

[9] See Bruce A. Ackerman, *Reconstructing American Law* (Cambridge, Mass.: Harvard University Press, 1984), 42–5.

the law, it has been suggested, then perhaps they ought not to be working in law schools.[10] Still others have professed their inability to take this sense of disaffection seriously, given that critical legal theorists are manifestly privileged beneficiaries of the very system of liberal legalism which they attack.[11] In short, detractors, whatever their angle, have found very little difficulty in presenting critical legal studies as, in one way or another, phoney. Exposing the myriad vices of 'the crits'—the fuzzy reasoning, the abstruse jargon, the moral impoverishment, the double standards, the political naiveté, the unworldly ideals, the legal incompetence, and so on—has become a popular pastime among clever-dicks, reactionaries and attention-seekers. There would be no easier, more enjoyable or up-beat way to conclude this book than to get in on the act, to do to the crits what Gellner did to the ethnomethodologists.

It is certainly not my intention to leave critical legal studies uncriticized. Indeed, it would no doubt seem odd to many readers if no account were taken here of the fairly vast body of literature opposing critical legal studies which has emerged since the early 1980s. It is precisely because this body of literature is so vast and so detailed, however, that there seems to be little point in trying to put yet another nail in the coffin of critical legal studies. Critique, in this context, has been rather overdone. A more interesting issue to address is that of why critical legal studies has inspired so much opposition: just how did it touch a nerve in the American law schools? The intensity with which critical legal studies has been criticized perhaps tells us as much about American jurisprudential culture as does critical legal studies itself.

Perhaps the most basic lesson to be learned from the previous two chapters is that, since the middle part of this century, American jurisprudence has been dominated by a quest for consensus. Both process jurisprudence and neo-classical law and economics are founded, albeit in very different ways, on the belief that it is possible to demonstrate the existence of certain theoretical premisses which, if properly articulated, may prove acceptable to all reasonable people. In process jurisprudence, this belief manifests itself most obviously in the quest for neutral principles of constitutional adjudication. In the literature of neo-classical law and economics, we encounter the very different belief that rational human behaviour is founded on self-interest. Not only do the law and economics and process traditions assume, in their different ways, the possibility of

[10] See Paul D. Carrington, 'Of Law and the River', *Jnl. Leg. Educ.*, 34 (1984), 222–8 at 227. For further development by Carrington of the argument that law, as a disciplinary domain, is essentially the preserve of lawyers, see Paul D. Carrington, 'Afterword: Why Deans Quit', *Duke L. J.*, [1987], 342–60.

[11] See e.g. Louis Menand, 'Radicalism For Yuppies', *The New Republic*, 17 March 1986, 20–1, 23.

consensus; they also take it for granted that the American legal system protects individual liberty, and that the basic purpose of legal theory is to demonstrate how that system might serve the cause of liberty still better. Accordingly, we find neo-classical lawyer-economists—whether engaging in positive or normative analysis—endeavouring to demonstrate that the maximization of wealth is best achieved within an essentially non-paternalistic, pro-competitive legal framework. Similarly, we find process theorists insisting that private ordering is the most desirable form of legal regulation. At the heart of both process jurisprudence and law and economics rests not only a faith in consensus but also a belief that the liberty of the individual is something which legal theory ought to affirm and promote.

Critical legal studies emerged out of this environment. It evolved as a reaction against the individualism and consensus-orientation which has dominated American jurisprudence at least since Lasswell and McDougal put forward their blueprint for the post-realist law school. For the proponent of critical legal studies, post-realist jurisprudence has been characterized by complacency and closure, by a belief that controversial legal questions—regarding, for example, the relationship between law and reason, the values embodied in the legal process, and the meaning of individual freedom—have been answered satisfactorily and definitively. In reacting against this perceived complacency and closure, critical legal scholars have re-invoked the realist tradition of challenging accepted jurisprudential wisdom.[12] Like legal realism, critical legal studies represents an attempt to shatter a particular sense of consensus.

One has to tread carefully in drawing analogies between legal realism and critical legal studies. Such analogies are certainly popular,[13] and critical legal scholars occasionally go some way to conceding their validity.[14] By and large, however, critical legal scholars are more intent on

[12] See Richard Davies Parker, 'The Past of Constitutional Theory—And Its Future', *Ohio State L. J.*, 42 (1981), 223–59 at 224.

[13] See e.g. J. Stuart Russell, 'The Critical Legal Studies Challenge to Contemporary Mainstream Legal Philosophy', *Ottawa L. Rev.*, 18 (1986), 1–24 at 5 (claiming that critical legal studies has 'a very pronounced ancestral relationship with Legal Realism'); Neil Duxbury, 'Jerome Frank and the Legacy of Legal Realism', *Jnl. Law & Soc.*, 18 (1991), 175–205 at 198 (suggesting that critical legal studies has reached the same impasse as did legal realism); 'Discussion: Jurisprudential Responses to Legal Realism', *Cornell L. Rev.*, 73 (1988), 341–9 at 345 (comment by Charles Fried). ('The whole difficulty which the pseudo-philosophy of critical legal studies and legal realism raise [*sic*], is the difficulty about explaining right down to the bottom of the earth and out the other side, how it is that you can follow rules, the rules about following rules, and so on. And that is a mug's game. What I am suggesting is that it is a mug's game we do not need to play.')

[14] See e.g. Sanford Levinson, 'Writing About Realism', *American Bar Foundation Research Journal*, [1985], 899–908 at 908; Mark Tushnet, 'Critical Legal Studies: An Introduction to its Origins and Underpinnings', *Jnl. Leg. Educ.*, 36 (1986), 505–17 at 505–6; 'Critical Legal Studies: A Political History', *Yale L.J.*, 100 (1991), 1515–44 at 1524.

stressing product differentiation.[15] For all the similarities, they argue, critical legal studies and legal realism constitute very different jurisprudential projects: the former offers a more advanced, more sophisticated form of legal critique than did the latter.[16] If the discussion which follows demonstrates anything, it should be that critical legal studies—for all that it may have progressed little further than did legal realism in grappling with law as a political phenomenon—is not simply realism repeated. While I insisted in Chapter 2, furthermore, that legal realism was intellectually too amorphous to be described as anything other than a mood, the development of critical legal studies has in comparison been more co-ordinated, institutionalized and clearly self-identified.[17] There were, to my knowledge, no realist conferences and mailing-lists; and while so-called realists rarely labelled themselves as such, proponents of critical legal studies have generally shown little reluctance to march under that banner. In short, while realism was a mood, critical legal studies has evolved very much as a movement.

For anyone studying the history of American jurisprudence, there is one sense in which legal realism and critical legal studies seem to be more or less identical: in terms of impact, they are equally difficult to assess.

[15] If there is a basic similarity between realism and critical legal studies, one critical legal scholar has argued, it is that they have been subjected to the same sorts of misinterpretation. See Pierre Schlag, 'Missing Pieces: A Cognitive Approach to Law', *Texas L. Rev.*, 67 (1989), 1195–250 at 1198–200.

[16] See Charles M. Yablon, 'The Indeterminacy of the Law: Critical Legal Studies and the Problem of Legal Explanation', *Cardozo L. Rev.*, 6 (1985), 917–45 at 934–5; Gerald E. Frug, 'A Critical Theory of Law', *Leg. Educ. Rev.*, 1 (1989), 43–57 at 52; John Henry Schlegel, 'Critical Legal Studies for the Intelligent Lawyer', *New York State Bar Jnl.*, January 1988, 10–15, 64 at 13–14; Robert W. Gordon, 'Critical Legal Histories', *Stanford L. Rev.*, 36 (1984), 57–125 at 114 (on critical legal and realist notions of indeterminacy); Morton J. Horowitz, *The Transformation of American Law, 1870–1960: The Crisis of Legal Orthodoxy* (New York: Oxford University Press, 1992), 270–1. For further efforts to distinguish the critical legal and realist projects, see Note [Debra Livingston], ' 'Round and 'Round the Bramble Bush: From Legal Realism to Critical Legal Scholarship', *Harvard L. Rev.*, 95 (1982), 1669–90 at 1677. ('The work of the critical legal scholars can be understood as the maturation of . . . realist methodologies—a maturation in which critical scholars explore incoherences at the level of social or political theory and critical scholarship is linked, not to reformist policy programmes, but to a radical political agenda.'); Frank I. Michelman, 'Justification (and Justifiability) of Law in a Contradictory World', in J. Roland Pennock and John W. Chapman (eds.), *Nomos XXVIII: Justification* (New York: New York University Press, 1986), 71–99 at 84; G. Edward White, 'The Inevitability of Critical Legal Studies', *Stanford L. Rev.*, 36 (1984), 649–72 at 652 ('CLS has substantially enlarged and reoriented the Realists' concern with values'); and Menand, *supra* n. 11, 21 (claiming that, unlike critical legal scholars, 'the legal realists never challenged the *aspiration* of law to serve justice'). For the argument that critical legal studies and legal realism are wholly-different jurisprudential projects, see Jeffrey A. Standen, 'Critical Legal Studies as an Anti-Positivist Phenomenon', *Virginia L. Rev.*, 72 (1986), 983–98.

[17] See William Twining, 'Talk about Realism', *New York Univ. L. Rev.*, 60 (1985), 329–84 at 356–7 fn. 87.

Realism, according to its many obituarists, was variously social-scientific,[18] political,[19] polemical,[20] an enlightening failure,[21] an unenlightening failure[22]—whom is one to believe? The sheer variety of conclusions on the legacy of legal realism make the subject seem almost impossible to fathom. With critical legal studies, retrospective appraisal is not quite so abundant. In that statement, however, lies the rub. Just what is the status of American critical legal studies today? How is one to speak of it? American academic lawyers—even certain of those who have affiliated themselves with the critical legal studies movement[23]—nowadays tend to refer to it as something which, if not entirely dead, certainly has little life left in it.[24] In various ways, modern American jurisprudence appears to have moved beyond critical legal studies. While developments in post-modern, pragmatist and feminist jurisprudence and critical race theory are certainly not unrelated to the general critical legal initiative, they possess sufficient independence and self-identity to suggest that the time for critical legal studies has passed. Except for a handful of stragglers and resisters, those who express disenchantment with the process and law and economics traditions in the law schools appear now to have moved on to pastures fresh.

One gets a sense, even from across the Atlantic, that critical legal studies peaked in the American law schools in the middle of the 1980s and has been losing momentum ever since. Given, however, that critical legal studies is very much the jurisprudence of modern times—given that it is

[18] John Henry Schlegel, 'American Legal Realism and Empirical Social Science: From the Yale Experience', *Buffalo L. Rev.*, 28 (1979), 459–586; 'American Legal Realism and Empirical Social Science: The Singular Case of Underhill Moore', *Buffalo L. Rev.*, 29 (1980), 195–323.

[19] Horwitz, *supra* n. 16, viii, 182 and *passim*.

[20] Edward A. Purcell, Jr., 'American Jurisprudence Between the Wars: Legal Realism and the Crisis of Democratic Theory', *American Historical Rev.*, 75 (1969), 424–46.

[21] Neil Duxbury, 'In the Twilight of Legal Realism: Fred Rodell and the Limits of Legal Critique', *Oxford Journal of Legal Studies*, 11 (1991), 354–95.

[22] Richard A. Posner, *The Problems of Jurisprudence* (Cambridge, Mass.: Harvard University Press, 1990), 19–20.

[23] Consider the effort at resuscitating critical legal studies which is made by Richard Michael Fischl, 'The Question That Killed Critical Legal Studies', *Law and Social Inquiry*, 17 (1992), 779–820.

[24] This is my impression from discussing critical legal studies with many American legal academics. There seems to be little in print to substantiate the point. (Fischl, ibid. *passim* is an exception, as is John Henry Schlegel, 'A Certain Narcissism; A Slight Unseemliness', *U. Colorado L. Rev.*, 63 (1992), 595–614 at 610–11.) Indeed, I can offer little apart from epistolary evidence: e.g. Robert C. Ellickson (Professor, Yale Law School), letter to author, 1 October 1993 (critical legal studies issues 'were vigorously debated in the US 5 or 10 years ago but, given the faddishness of the academy, are now distinctly passé. Although it might be hard to detect from afar, the CLS movement is in rapid retreat in the US. Scholars on the Left have moved into deconstructionism, Post-Modernism, feminism, Critical Race Theory, and so on; most now pay little heed to CLS work').

impossible, as yet, to establish any degree of historical or critical distance from the subject—it might sensibly be concluded that, at this point in time, there is little to be gained from trying to write up critical legal studies as a chapter in the history of American jurisprudence.[25] For two interrelated reasons, I have concluded otherwise. First, I do not believe that we ought to divorce the jurisprudential concerns of the present from those of the past. While it is probably the case that contemporary assessments of critical legal studies, if they do not seem ill-informed now, will most certainly seem so in a decade or two, this hardly warrants the conclusion that there is nothing to be learned from subjecting our current jurisprudential problems to historical scrutiny. Within any generation, the development of knowledge requires invariably that account be taken of past mistakes. Given that this is so, historians of jurisprudence ought not to be reluctant to risk making mistakes by tackling subjects from which they lack distance. If we commit our mistakes to paper, they may serve to enlighten our successors.

Secondly, critical legal studies may illustrate how the present might improve our understanding of the past. The story of realist jurisprudence is a story without a conclusion. There was no great *coup de grâce* which brought realism to an end; it just faded away. The problems to which it had pointed, furthermore, remained unresolved. For all that legal realists had declared political adjudication to be an inevitability, process jurists seemed committed to the belief that they could encourage the Supreme Court to become a forum of principle. While neo-classical lawyer-economists argued for less regulation and more *laissez-faire*, they paid no attention at all to the realist insight that behind economic freedom lurks coercion. Critical legal studies embodies a recognition of the fact that important realist lessons have been conveniently ignored, and it endeavours to teach these lessons to American academic lawyers yet again. A study such as this one, in which the realist legal tradition features so prominently, would be very obviously incomplete if no account were taken of the endeavour by modern American legal theorists to conclude that tradition.

As I intimated above, I consider especially interesting the ways in which critical legal studies, like legal realism itself, has been dismissed as a jurisprudence without a conclusion. Critical legal studies has been written off for failing to supply answers to the problems which realism merely posed: adjudication is still a political affair; economic freedom still conceals coercion. Yet if there is one fundamental lesson which critical legal studies teaches, it is that there are no right answers to the problems which realism posed. The basic conclusion of critical legal studies is that

[25] This is the conclusion of Horwitz, *supra* n. 16, 269. See also Ronald Dworkin, *Law's Empire* (London: Fontana, 1986), 272. ('[C]ritical legal studies resembles the older movement of American legal realism, and it is too early to decide whether it is more than an anachronistic attempt to make that dated movement reflower.')

lawyers must constantly be reminded of these problems. That is more or less as far as critical legal studies goes. It is, I shall conclude, in the outgrowths from critical legal studies—particularly in feminist jurisprudential literature and in critical race theory—that we discover American legal theorists at last moving beyond realist and critical legal thought in ways which do not entail the basic appeal to consensus which is evident in the law and economics and process traditions.

THE POLITICAL BACKDROP

America, Tocqueville insisted, is unique. 'The position of the Americans is . . . quite exceptional, and it may be believed that no democratic people will ever be placed in a similar one.'[26] Until very recently, American exceptionalism was considered to be primarily economic in nature.[27] As early as 1851, Friedrich Engels wrote of 'the special American conditions: the ease with which the surplus population is drained off to the farms, the necessarily rapid and rapidly growing prosperity of the country, which makes bourgeois conditions look like a beau ideal to them'.[28] America confounded marxian logic: if capitalism was the penultimate stage in history, why was it that the country with the most developed capitalist economy in the world showed no signs of completing the historical cycle? Why, in short, was socialism not flourishing in the United States?

In the early years of this century, the German sociologist, Werner Sombart, attempted to answer this question. In *Why is There No Socialism in the United States?* Sombart argued that socialism is incompatible with the culture and aspirations of the American working class. 'All Socialist utopias', he proclaimed, 'came to nothing on roast beef and apple pie.'[29] The truth of the matter is that 'the American worker . . . is not on the whole dissatisfied with the present condition of things.'[30] Indeed, 'emotionally the American worker has a share in capitalism . . . he loves

[26] Alexis de Tocqueville, *Democracy in America* (two vols. New York: Vintage, 1945; orig. publ. 1835–40), II, 36.

[27] See Peter Temin, 'Free Land and Federalism: American Economic Exceptionalism', in Byron E. Shafer (ed.), *Is America Different? A New Look at American Exceptionalism* (Oxford: Clarendon Press, 1991), 71–93. According to Temin, 'American business no longer appears as distinctive as it did thirty or forty years ago. . . . The United States economy is losing its exceptional character as it adapts to growing international competition. And other economies are recasting themselves in a more American mould through privatization and *perestroika*.' (p. 93)

[28] Friedrich Engels, letter to Joseph Weydemeyer, 7 August 1851, in Karl Marx and Friedrich Engels, *Letters to Americans* (New York: International Publishers Co., 1953), 26.

[29] Werner Sombart, *Why Is There No Socialism in the United States?* (Eng. trans. P. M. Hocking and C. T. Husbands, London: Macmillan, 1976; orig. German publ. 1906), 106.

[30] Ibid. 18.

it'[31]—he appreciates and enjoys the opportunities for self-improvement and the material rewards which capitalism provides.

If a prize were to be awarded for the book with the weakest ever conclusion, Sombart's would surely be a contender. Having argued that socialist ideas are anathema to the American worker, he concludes by suggesting that the United States is about to witness the growth of indigenous socialism.[32] Why this might happen is left totally unexplained. The merit of Sombart's book, however, rests not in its conclusion but in its identification of the fact that the United States is a highly developed industrialized country which, uniquely, does not have a significant socialist movement or labour party.[33] Sombart had demonstrated, in effect, that exceptionalism in the United States is largely attributable to the fact that American capitalist culture prevented socialism from taking root.[34]

This is not to suggest that efforts to secure a political foothold for socialism in the United States have never been undertaken. The early decades of this century witnessed the emergence of various strands of American socialism. But these different strands were extremely limited in terms of their appeal and success. The socialist movement proved generally to be unattractive to Americans because of its parochialism, factionalism, utopianism, militancy and political and economic naiveté.[35] In so far as it supposedly represented the interests of a specific sector of the American public, furthermore, it turned out to be 'a movement not of but on behalf of the working class'.[36] By attempting to further the cause of the working class, early twentieth-century American socialists served basically to further the cause of capitalism. That is, to the limited extent that socialists did accelerate the growth of trade unionism and regulatory legislation, they ensured, in effect, that workers felt more at ease with the capitalist system.[37] Their initiatives, in short, bolstered rather than undermined the dominant political and economic values of American society.

[31] Ibid. 20.

[32] See ibid. 119.

[33] See Seymour Martin Lipset, 'American Exceptionalism Reaffirmed', in Shafer (ed.), *supra* n. 27, 1–45 at 2.

[34] While Sombart successfully identifies American economic exceptionalism, he is less successful in explaining it. The primary problem with his explanation of exceptionalism is that he exaggerates the degree to which the American working class enjoys material abundance. Regarding the late nineteenth-century worker, for example, he claims that he enjoys material comforts to such a degree that 'he does not even outwardly become aware of the gap that separates him from the ruling class'. Sombart, *supra* n. 29, 105. For criticism of Sombart on this point, see Irving Howe, *Socialism and America* (San Diego: Harcourt, Brace Jovanovich, 1985), 117–23. More generally, cf. Mark F. Kann, *The American Left: Failures and Fortunes* (New York: Praeger, 1982), 13–40 (on 'a politics without a country').

[35] See, generally, John Patrick Diggins, *The Rise and Fall of the American Left* (New York: Norton & Co., 1992), 62–90; Milton Cantor, *The Divided Left: American Radicalism, 1900–1975* (New York: Hill and Wang, 1978), 17–128.

[36] Diggins, *supra* n. 35, 90.

[37] See Cantor, *supra* n. 35, 39–40.

Given that, for most Americans, socialism proved generally to be unappealing—and given that the American working class tended only to find socialism attractive when it helped them to enjoy the fruits of capitalism—it is hardly surprising that, during the early decades of this century, it should have made very little impression on American political life. Certainly the Depression served to reaffirm to American socialists the precariousness of capitalist prosperity. But the rise of fascism in Europe demonstrated to them also that socialism itself is precarious, that, in practice, it does not always turn out to be democratic.[38] This fact became all the more apparent as the horrors of Stalinism began to unfold. By the mid-1950s, in a United States gripped by the fear of internal as well as external communist threat, the political left was all but dead.[39]

No sooner had the left reached its nadir, however, than it was revived. Out of the politically silent generation of the 1950s emerged the so-called 'New Left'. Primarily a student movement, the New Left was inspired by a basic sense of alienation.[40] Disillusioned with the shallowness, the sterility and the conformity which seemed to typify suburban, middle-class affluence, many of those who grew up in the Eisenhower years began to search for fulfilment of a kind different from the material comfort which had so preoccupied their parents. While many young political activists considered John F. Kennedy to have been reckless in his handling of the Cuban missile crisis in 1962, certain of them nonetheless hoped that his administration would put an end to the poverty and racism which were all but invisible from the middle-class suburbs. With the assassination of Kennedy in November of the following year, such hope was, in the eyes of most of those who had kept faith with his administration, effectively snuffed out. Young American radicals were left politically homeless.

It was against this background that they set about establishing a political location of their own. While the New Left was not especially structured or politically co-ordinated, it discovered its natural habitat on the American university campus. Between 1946 and 1970, attendance at colleges and universities in the United States increased fourfold.[41] By the 1960s, enrolments had expanded much faster than had the supply of qualified instructors. The sheer volume of undergraduates, compared with the relative paucity of faculty, ensured that teaching was largely remote and uninspiring. Professors were invariably either unavailable or unapproachable; untenured faculty and the graduate students who graded papers

[38] See Diggins, *supra* n. 35, 155.

[39] See Maurice Isserman, *If I Had a Hammer . . . The Death of the Old Left and the Birth of the New Left* (New York: Basic Books, 1987), 3–34.

[40] See Christopher Lasch, *The Agony of the American Left* (New York: Knopf, 1969), 180.

[41] See John Morton Blum, *Years of Discord: American Politics and Society, 1961–1974* (New York: Norton & Co., 1991), 96–7.

tended to have little time for undergraduate matters because of the pressure on them to complete their own research. The shortcomings of the American universities seemed to student radicals to be indicative of a deeper American malaise. 'In our free speech fight at the University of California,' one student at Berkeley wrote in 1964, 'we have come up against what may emerge as the greatest problem of our nation—depersonalized, unresponsive bureaucracy.'[42]

It was on the college campus that the New Left made its greatest impression. The establishment, in 1962, of Students for a Democratic Society (SDS)—a movement which would become virtually synonymous with the New Left—marked the beginning of concerted campus radicalism in the United States. In its inaugural manifesto, issued at its 1962 national convention at Port Huron, Michigan, the SDS spelled out its agenda.[43] The universities, the Port Huron statement proclaimed, supported American militarism and racism. By undertaking classified research for defence agencies, university faculties effectively earned income by sacrificing their basic intellectual commitment to freedom of information. In the southern colleges in particular, so few blacks and other minorities gained admission that there could only be active bias against them on the part of admissions officers, administrators and trustees. Yet the SDS was not about to give up on the university. On the contrary, the university was regarded as a springboard for social change. From the college campus, the Port Huron statement urged, students 'must consciously build a base for their assault upon the loci of power'.[44]

This required more than merely the drugs, dress, music and casual attitude towards sex which are commonly identified with the 1960s. It required both a theory and a style of practice. The New Left found its master-theoretician in the unlikely figure of Herbert Marcuse. Convinced that 'exactness and clarity in philosophy cannot be attained within the universe of ordinary discourse',[45] Marcuse employed a highly technical and abstruse prose style which must surely have been lost on many a student radical. Yet, with the publication of his *One-Dimensional Man* in 1964, he became something of an unwilling hero of the New Left.[46]

The modern liberal society, Marcuse argued, is a repressive society:

[42] Mario Savio, 'An End to History' [1964], in Mitchell Cohen and Dennis Hale (eds.), *The New Student Left: An Anthology* (Boston: Beacon Press, 1966), 253–7 at 254.

[43] For the text of the Port Huron statement, see James Miller, *'Democracy is in the Streets': From Port Huron to the Siege of Chicago* (New York: Simon & Schuster, 1987), 329–74.

[44] Cited in Diggins, *supra* n. 35, 228.

[45] Herbert Marcuse, *One-Dimensional Man: Studies in the Ideology of Advanced Industrial Society* (London: Ark, 1986; orig. publ. 1964), 179.

[46] On Marcuse's ambivalent relationship to the New Left, see Peter Clecak, *Radical Paradoxes: Dilemmas of the American Left, 1945–1970* (New York: Harper & Row, 1973), 175–229 esp. 212–13.

'domination—in the guise of affluence and liberty—extends to all spheres of private and public existence, integrates all authentic opposition, absorbs all alternatives.'[47] Whereas there had existed in pre-industrial societies a necessity to defer immediate gratification and sublimate drives into productive work owing to the economic reality of scarcity, with the advent of material abundance this necessity disappeared. Yet the one-dimensionality of modern liberal societies rests in the fact that they continue to adhere strictly and unnecessarily to the pre-industrial division of work and play. Citizens in these societies are slaves to an ethic of production and consumption from which they ought, by now, to be emancipated. And yet, paradoxically, these citizens remain repressed precisely because of the type of liberty which liberalism grants them; for, within the modern liberal society, liberty operates as 'a powerful instrument of domination',[48] whereby citizens are deceived into believing that their aspirations are accommodated by virtue of their freedom to produce and consume. Liberty, in the advanced industrial society, is essentially repressive. It ensures that '[t]he people recognize themselves in their commodities; they find their soul in their automobile, hi-fi set, split-level home, kitchen equipment.'[49] It offers not real liberation—liberation from the ethic of production and consumption—but 'free choice between brands and gadgets.'[50]

Marcuse's message—that liberalism breeds false-consciousness, that the freedom which it promotes merely perpetuates capitalist domination—gave the New Left a greater sense of purpose. *One-Dimensional Man* had identified what it was that student radicals were attempting to rebel against—namely, the repressiveness of liberty, conventionally understood. In putting rebellion into practice, students challenged liberal conventions in the place that they knew best: the university. For the best part of the 1960s—certainly from 1964 onwards—American university life was severely disrupted by student activism. Bolstered by developments elsewhere—the war in Vietnam, the worldwide student revolts of 1968 and, to a lesser degree, the growing militancy of the black civil rights movement—student discontent and activism became ever more intense as the decade progressed.[51] 'In the early sixties,' John Diggins observes, 'students demonstrated outside administration buildings; by the late sixties they were inside the president's office, rifling his files, smoking his cigars, and, with feet up on his desk, placing long-distance calls to Paris announcing that the "revolution" had begun.'[52]

[47] Marcuse, *supra* n. 45, 18. [48] Ibid. 7. [49] Ibid. 9. [50] Ibid. 7.

[51] See, generally, Diggins, *supra* n. 35, 248–60; and also Jerry Rubin, *Do It! Scenarios of the Revolution* (New York: Simon and Schuster, 1970).

[52] Diggins, *supra* n. 51, 249.

But of course, the revolution had not begun. And there was no possibility that it could begin. For revolution needed to be precipitated—something which the New Left simply could not do. The impotence of the New Left was attributable primarily to its evolution within, and obsession with the ills of, the university. 'Student radicalism,' Christopher Lasch wrote in 1969, 'being university-based, suffers from the . . . disadvantage of identifying the university as the major enemy.'[53] Outside of the campus, the political concerns of the New Left were likely to seem parochial. Furthermore, there was an ambivalence about the relationship between the New Left and the university which suggested that student radicalism was generally more superficial than sincere. 'Within the university,' Irving Howe observed in 1965, 'the New Left students engage with more or less liberal faculties, and behind these engagements there is often the assumption that, finally, the university will behave like a middle-class parent.'[54] On the occasions that universities failed so to behave—when they demonstrated the insensitivity of which they were being accused—students were quick to cry foul. The implication behind this reaction was that universities may well be repressive and corrupt, but they ought nevertheless to demonstrate tolerance and good faith in their dealings with student radicals. That there existed such an expectation suggested that the agenda of the New Left was defined more by posturing than by genuine commitment to political change.

The preoccupation of the New Left with the university was not the only reason for its failure as a political movement. Student radicalism in the United States emerged at a time when the country lacked an organized political left.[55] Whereas the students regarded those who comprised the working class as victims of false consciousness, workers themselves tended to be indifferent if not hostile to the initiatives of the New Left. Radicals on the left were thus 'deprived of what was always thought the essential revolutionary base. America's union bureaucrats enjoyed the sun at Miami Beach, and making capitalism work more efficiently governed their strategic vision. . . . Labour was not even nominally socialist.'[56] More generally, the New Left was anything but a structured political movement. Indeed, by definition, it lacked coherence. 'Opposing bureaucracy, it relied upon spontaneous activity, and its suspicion of the hierarchical tendencies of organizational structures precluded the possibility that a sense of leadership could emerge with a single voice.'[57] Accordingly, 'the

[53] Lasch, *supra* n. 40, 202.

[54] Irving Howe, ' "Confrontation Politics" is a Dangerous Game', in Irving Howe (ed.), *Beyond the New Left* (New York: McCall, 1965), 40–54 at 45.

[55] See James Weinstein, *Ambiguous Legacy: The Left in American Politics* (New York: New Viewpoints, 1975), 130–1.

[56] Cantor, *supra* n. 35, 221–2.

[57] Diggins, *supra* n. 35, 265.

new radicals who contributed in important ways to the emergence of anticapitalist modes of consciousness in the sixties were unable to organize the energies they helped to unleash.'[58] '[D]espite the rapid spread of radical consciousness among students and a growing awareness that it was the system as a whole and not just particular issues that were at stake, the new left did not develop a strategy that posed the existing social structure against a new one.'[59]

That the New Left failed as a political movement does not mean, however, that it failed totally. '[M]any radicals of the sixties', by the end of that decade, 'were settling in for a long season of theorizing and teaching, using criticism both as a lengthy prelude to more muscular sorts of action and as a substitute for more direct varieties of political action.'[60] Having failed to dismantle the university system, many of those who had affiliated themselves with the New Left proceeded to join it. The transition was not always an easy one. Some New Left academics were considered to be too radical for the universities, and tenure denials were not uncommon.[61] The majority of their number, however, took to academic life like ducks to water. 'When they entered the universities', Russell Jacoby remarks:

> New Left intellectuals became professors who neither looked backward nor sideways; they kept their eyes on professional journals, monographs, and conferences. Perhaps because their lives had unfolded almost entirely on campuses they were unable or unwilling to challenge academic imperatives. . . . By establishing a credible body of radical, feminist, Marxist, or neo-Marxist scholarship, they assailed the venerable, sometimes almost official, interpretations dominant in their fields. The extent of this literature, the outpouring of left academics, is extraordinary, without precedent in American letters. . . . Yet it is also extraordinary for another reason; it is largely technical, unreadable and—except by specialists—unread. . . . Their scholarship looks more and more like the work it sought to subvert.[62]

From the end of the 1960s onwards, the university became the life-support system of the New Left. 'No one who had watched campus demonstrations in the sixties could have anticipated the eagerness with which former protesting graduate students later accepted positions at the very institutions they said were responsible for racism, imperialism, fascism, sexism, and other evils of "liberalism".'[63] Appointed at a time of expansion, New Left academics found posts at most universities; and, having acquired tenure by

[58] Clecak, *supra* n. 46, 270.

[59] Weinstein, *supra* n. 55, 140.

[60] Peter Clecak, *America's Quest for the Ideal Self: Dissent and Fulfillment in the 60s and 70s* (New York: Oxford University Press, 1983), 49.

[61] See Russell Jacoby, *The Last Intellectuals: American Culture in the Age of Academe* (New York: Basic Books, 1987), 119–39.

[62] Ibid. 140–1.

[63] Diggins, *supra* n. 35, 289.

the time of the budget-cutting contractions of the early Reagan years, they remain a significant ideological presence in those universities to this day. Lacking an American proletariat on behalf of whom to speak, the remnants of the New Left in the universities, Robert Hughes has argued, have been responsible for promoting a 'culture of complaint', a culture in which freedom of expression is generally stymied owing to the fanatical pursuit of political correctness.[64] Increasingly, this culture 'has taken over the campus and is bringing free thought to a stop'; so that, while 'the ideology of totalitarianism has collapsed in Europe and Russia, it survives in China, Cuba—and American universities.'[65]

Although Hughes obviously exaggerates, his basic point is a serious one: unable to affect American politics generally, leftist academics have attempted to exert greater influence over the university. In highlighting their own feelings of victimization, furthermore, these academics have tended to underplay the fact that, in university life, they remain a dominant force. In the latter half of the 1980s, many of those on the left pointed to the rise of neo-classical economics, particularly at the University of Chicago, and the funding of neo-conservative think-tanks by various wealthy foundations as indicative of a move rightwards in academic life.[66] Yet the growth of activity on the academic right did not signal the demise of the academic left. Publications, book-stores, courses and conferences devoted to the issues of the left continued, and continue, to proliferate.[67] While the New Left failed as a political movement, it has enjoyed success as an academic enterprise.

THE EMERGENCE OF CRITICAL LEGAL STUDIES

It is against the backdrop of the New Left that the critical legal studies movement ought initially to be considered. For critical legal studies grew out of the New Left tradition. 'It's really a rag-tag band of left over '60s people and people with nostalgia for the great events of 15 years ago,' Duncan Kennedy observed in 1985.[68] The roots of critical legal studies,

[64] Robert Hughes, *Culture of Complaint: The Fraying of America* (New York: Oxford University Press, 1993).

[65] Ibid. 55. More generally, see Paul Berman (ed.), *Debating P.C.: The Controversy Over Political Correctness on College Campuses* (New York: Dell, 1992); and also James Boyle, 'The PC Harangue', *Stanford L. Rev.*, 45 (1993), 1457–84.

[66] See David A. Bell, 'Ghosts of Leftists Past', in *The New Republic*, 11–18 August 1986, 17.

[67] See Diggins, *supra* n. 35, 290–1.

[68] Robert Clark, Duncan Kennedy, Paul Bator, Abram Chayes and Ralph Winter, *A Discussion on Critical Legal Studies at the Harvard Law School* (Cambridge, Mass.: The Harvard Society for Law and Public Policy and the Federalist Society for Law and Public Policy Studies, Occasional Paper No. 1, 1985), 8–9 (comment by Duncan Kennedy).

commentators tend to claim, can be traced to the political movements and events of the late 1960s and 1970s:[69] in critical legal studies, that is, we find the New Left acted out in the law school.[70] But what might this mean? To pose the question in the most general terms: if, as Mark Tushnet believes, 'critical legal studies is a political location for a group of people on the Left who share the project of supporting and extending the domain of the Left in the legal academy,'[71] how, in this context, are we to conceive of 'the Left'? The proposition that critical legal studies grew out of the New Left tradition simply raises the question of how that tradition came to be reflected in critical legal studies.

In order to identify how critical legal studies relates to the New Left, it is important to consider the context in which it emerged. Political controversy rarely impinged on the American law schools of the 1960s. Both the tactics and the anti-intellectualism of student radicals must have seemed thoroughly unappealing to law professors. Law students themselves, furthermore, were generally disinclined towards political activism. 'The students I knew at the Law School in the late fifties and early sixties,' the Harvard graduate Calvin Trillin has noted, 'tended to think of themselves as nonpolitical. Both they and their professors took it for granted that the American system—particularly the American legal system—was a basically good system, with some flaws that could eventually be cleared up by precisely the sort of principled, tough-minded people Harvard Law School was producing.'[72] By the end of the 1960s, however, many law students were becoming increasingly disillusioned with what they considered to be a glaring disparity between the presentation of law in the case-books and the classroom and the actual use of law as an instrument of social control.[73] The sterility of legal rules and doctrines imparted via the case method contrasted sharply with the legal problems which were vividly posed by the civil rights struggles and the anti-war demonstrations.[74] 'Critical legal

[69] See Robert W. Gordon, 'Critical Legal Studies as a Teaching Method, Against the Background of the Intellectual Politics of Modern Legal Education in the United States', *Leg. Educ. Rev.*, 1 (1989), 59–83 at 71–2; Binder, *supra* n. 4, 13–25; White, *supra* n. 16, 658–60.

[70] Catherine G. Cahan, 'Rebels Without a Pause', *Student Lawyer*, October 1984, 43–51 at 44 col. 2; and see Ben Gerson, 'Professors for The Revolution', *National Law Journal*, 23 August 1982, 1, 10–11, 25 at 10 col. 1 (on critical legal theorists 'trying to incorporate into law the ideals of the counterculture of the 1960s').

[71] Tushnet, 'Critical Legal Studies: A Political History', *supra* n. 14, 1516.

[72] Calvin Trillin, 'A Reporter at Large: Harvard Law', *New Yorker (Magazine)*, 26 March 1984, 53–83 at 65.

[73] See Robert Stevens, *Law School: Legal Education in America from the 1850s to the 1980s* (Chapel Hill: University of North Carolina Press, 1983), 234–47.

[74] See Ellen K. Coughlin, 'The Crits v. the Legal Academy: Arguing a Case Against the Law', *The Chronicle of Higher Education*, 17 July 1985, 5–6 at 6 col. 3. ('Influenced by the political tumult of the '60s, they [radical law students who went on to become proponents of critical legal studies] were united at first by a thoroughgoing dissatisfaction with the increasingly conservative bent of many of their senior professors, and by an acute awareness

studies was born of this dissonance between the student political experience of the sixties and the law school curriculum of the sixties and seventies.'[75]

The path from student radicalism to critical legal studies turns out, however, to be not quite so straightforward. For it is not the case that critical legal studies emerged directly out of this radicalism. By no means should it be assumed that, during the 1960s and early 1970s, there were no American law schools running courses which held at least some appeal for the politically disaffected law student. Throughout this period, Harvard, Stanford, Wisconsin and Yale established 'law and development' research programmes.[76] The purpose of such programmes, David Trubek observed in 1972, was 'to formulate valid generalizations about the relationships between law and the major economic, social, and political transformations associated with industrialization'[77] and to suggest how developing countries might establish legal frameworks which will ensure that they are able both to promote and to benefit from such industrialization. The law and development initiative was part of a more general response to pressure, put on American universities by development agencies, to assist Third World nations in the process of 'modernization'. As the United States increased bilateral aid to the Third World, foundations and agencies committed to the promotion of modernization looked increasingly to academic lawyers for help. And it was precisely here, in the field of law and development, that certain of those who would eventually come to be identified with critical legal studies discovered an approach to law which gave them a sense that they were not politically impotent.

This sense proved, however, to be only fleeting. During the 1960s, among the critical legal scholars to be, nobody became more committed to the law and development project than did David Trubek. On graduating from the Yale Law School in 1961, Trubek accepted a post as an attorney advisor with the Agency for International Development (AID). The AID endeavoured to export American capitalism, technology and government

of how miserably the conception of law being imparted to students failed to jibe with "real life," especially as it was lived in the era of civil-rights riots and anti-war demonstrations.')

[75] Binder, *supra* n. 4, 23. In a similar vein, see also Cahan, *supra* n. 70, 44 col. 1. The best study of this dissonance and its relationship to the emergence of critical legal studies is, as yet, unpublished: Gary Minda, *Postmodern Legal Movements: Law and Jurisprudence at Century's End* (unpublished mimeograph [on file with author: copy supplied by Professor Minda], 1994, forthcoming, New York: New York University Press, 1995), 109–15.

[76] See David M. Trubek and Marc Galanter, 'Scholars in Self-Estrangement: Some Reflections on the Crisis in Law and Development Studies in the United States', *Wisconsin L. Rev.*, [1974], 1062–102 at 1090.

[77] David M. Trubek, 'Toward a Social Theory of Law: An Essay on the Study of Law and Development', *Yale L. J.*, 82 (1972), 1–50 at 21.

to developing countries. Its lawyers, Trubek remembers, were charged with expediting this task:

> As lawyers, our job was to expedite the operation of America's civilizing mission: we were hard-headed pragmatists dedicated to getting things done in a cumbersome bureaucratic maze. We helped arrange the financing and construction of dams and steel mills, we created legal structures for transmissions of American knowhow. With our help, experts from America's universities came to Latin America to teach Brazilians, Colombians, Bolivians how to produce better eggs and more butter. Many AID lawyers of that day thought of themselves as an élite: we were smarter than the development experts whose work we facilitated, more pragmatic than the foreign officials and lawyers we worked with, more committed to liberal values than the governments we were assisting.[78]

The AID eventually failed in its efforts to export American-style social engineering to developing countries: some Third World nations accepted its money but rejected its lessons; others embraced the idea that their legal systems should be modernized, but not the proposition that they should be more liberal.[79] By 1966, Trubek was back at the Yale Law School, teaching law and development rather than putting it into practice. While a student at Yale, he had co-authored, with Charles Clark, an article which basically accused Karl Llewellyn of being traitor to the realist legal tradition. Llewellyn's book, *The Common Law Tradition*, Clark and Trubek argued, was very much an exercise in apostasy, an abandonment of realism in favour of process jurisprudence.[80] Their article represented, in effect, a last ditch plea for the revitalization of realist legal thought. Although, in returning to Yale, Trubek was abandoning the idealistic plans of the AID, he was not turning his back on the general law and development project. For in law and development, he saw the opportunity to revive realist sensibilities: here was a project which cried out for insights from the social sciences, an idea in need of a theory. '[W]hen law's solutions to social problems fail to satisfy,' he argued in 1972, 'it becomes necessary to examine the basic theory from which they derive.'[81] The fundamental problem with the law and development initiative was that it lacked any such theory. 'What is needed', accordingly, is 'a social theory capable of formulating and verifying propositions about the relationship between legal and social variables. It should start from the assumption that there are

[78] David M. Trubek, *Back to the Future: The Short, Happy Life of the Law and Society Movement* (Madison, WI: Institute for Legal Studies Working Papers, No. 4–7, University of Wisconsin Law School, 1990), 36.

[79] For a general account of this failure, see James A. Gardner, *Legal Imperialism: American Lawyers and Foreign Aid in Latin America* (Madison: University of Wisconsin Press, 1980), esp. 239–81.

[80] See Charles E. Clark and David M. Trubek, 'The Creative Role of the Judge: Restraint and Freedom in the Common Law Tradition', *Yale L.J.*, 71 (1961), 255–76.

[81] Trubek, *supra* n. 77, 1.

systematic and universal relations between such variables and address itself to the task of uncovering them. So the question becomes: How may law and development be studied in a more systematic way?'[82]

Trubek believed, at this time, that the theory which was required was to be found in the work of Max Weber.[83] By adopting the Weberian method of ideal-type construction, he claimed, '[w]e can . . . employ a methodology of comparative research to isolate the underlying relationships between legal and social variables.'[84] By isolating these variables, it should be possible at the very least to determine the problems and the obstacles involved in attempting to use law as an instrument of modernization in developing countries. Law and development in theory, in other words, might highlight the difficulties of putting law and development into practice. Trubek was not alone in offering such an argument. At the time that Trubek returned to Yale, Marc Galanter was attempting to formulate a theory of self-perpetuating legal development. Since societies never stop developing, he argued, the modernization of law in any particular society can never be said definitively to have been achieved. 'As society becomes modernized in all spheres, new kinds of diversity and complexity are generated. . . . So the very factors that encourage modernization of law and are encouraged by it finally impede and undermine it.'[85] Like Trubek, Galanter was using theory to demonstrate that, in the field of law and development, there can be no room for idealism.

Neither Trubek nor Galanter stopped there. By 1974, they were together professing their loss of faith in the law and development project. The fundamental problem with the project, they argued, was that it was founded on the 'paradigm' of 'liberal legalism'.[86] 'Liberal legalism was . . . a clear reflection of the basic ideas about the relationship between law and society and between the United States and the Third World that prevailed in the United States universities in the late 1950s and 1960s.'[87] Embodied in the liberal legal paradigm is a collection of beliefs: that 'society is made up of individuals'; that 'the state exercises its control over the individual through law'; that 'rules are consciously designed to achieve social purposes or effectuate basic social principles'; that rules 'are enforced equally for all citizens'; that 'the behaviour of social actors tends to conform to the rules'; and that the interpretation, application and changing of these rules accords with the separation of powers.[88] Proponents of law and development, Trubek and Galanter argued, had mistakenly assumed

[82] Ibid. 22.

[83] See, generally, David M. Trubek, 'Max Weber on Law and the Rise of Capitalism', *Wisconsin L. Rev.*, [1972], 720–53.

[84] Trubek, *supra* n. 77, 22–3.

[85] Marc Galanter, 'The Modernization of Law', in Myron Weiner (ed.), *Modernization: The Dynamics of Growth* (New York: Basic Books, 1966), 153–65 at 164.

[86] Trubek and Galanter, *supra* n. 76, 1070.

[87] Ibid. 1088.

[88] Ibid. 1071–2.

that this liberal legal model could be established fairly unproblematically in developing countries.[89] Such an assumption, while 'not insincere',[90] was 'ethnocentric and naive'.[91] By the mid-1970s, the primary lesson to be learned from the law and development project was 'that legal change may have little or no effect on social economic conditions in Third World societies and, conversely, that many legal "reforms" can deepen inequality, curb participation, restrict individual freedom, and hamper efforts to increase material well-being'.[92]

Disaffection with what Trubek and Galanter call the paradigm of liberal legalism would, in due course, become a principal characteristic of critical legal studies. At this stage, however, those on the left in the law schools were still searching for a legal channel through which to vent their political concerns. Law and development had failed them.[93] Its liberal legalist foundations had led its academic proponents 'to question the moral worth of some or all legal development assistance activities, and thus, necessarily to question their own scholarship itself'.[94] Suffering from self-estrangement, these academics embarked on 'a search for a new research agenda',[95] for 'a new paradigm'[96] which would stimulate a different type of politicized legal study. This new paradigm, Trubek and Galanter believed, was to be discovered in yet another field of 'law and' scholarship: law and society.

The law and development project was, in a sense, a training ground for the law and society movement. '[T]he atmosphere of the law and development centres made them more conscious than most legal academics of the need for empirical study, and gave them increased access to the burgeoning domestic law and society field.'[97] However, while many of those involved in the law and society movement—Trubek, Galanter, Stewart Macaulay, Lawrence Friedman, to name but some—had participated in one way or another in law and development initiatives,[98] it would be wrong to assume that the former grew out of the latter. Established by academic lawyers and sociologists in 1964, the Law and Society Association—its journal, the *Law and Society Review*, was founded two years later—began as an attempt to promote greater collaboration and understanding between academic lawyers and sociologists. Bolstered by financial support from funding agencies—particularly the Russell Sage Foundation and the Walter E. Meyer Research Institute of Law—law and society research programmes were established during the 1960s and 1970s at Berkeley, Denver and Wisconsin. It was at this last institution that the law and society movement became entrenched.

[89] See ibid. 1074–8. [90] Ibid. 1088. [91] Ibid. 1080. [92] Ibid.
[93] See Gardner, *supra* n. 79, 211–30.
[94] Trubek and Galanter *supra* n. 76, 1064. [95] Ibid. 1080. [96] Ibid. 1093.
[97] Ibid. 1091.
[98] For further detail, see Trubek, *supra* n. 78, 61–2 fn. 71.

At the University of Wisconsin during the early 1960s, there already existed a well established tradition of interdisciplinary research.[99] It was at that university, furthermore, that the seeds of the New Left were originally sown. *Studies on the Left*, the first forum for New Left intellectual debate, was established by students at Wisconsin in 1959.[100] By the late 1960s, Wisconsin had attracted a sizeable group of academics—Stewart Macaulay, Robert Rabin, Jack Ladinsky and Lawrence Friedman were among its number—professing an especial interest in the relationship of law to other disciplines. There was also Willard Hurst. Of a different generation to the law and society people—he joined the law faculty at Wisconsin (where he remains to this day) in 1937—Hurst is one of the most respected and neglected American legal historians of modern times.[101] While historians have tended to chart the development of American law by focusing on the role of the courts and activities related to litigation, Hurst argues, they have placed far too little emphasis on the social functions of law. 'This popular focus on courts and lawsuits fitted our deeply ingrained middle-class belief in constitutionalism.'[102] Yet, throughout the twentieth century, American law has evolved into a complex network of not only courts but also legislatures,[103] administrative agencies,[104] private groups[105] and other 'legal elements'.[106] In elaborating this thesis throughout a series of historical studies, Hurst was more or less solely responsible for developing what might be termed an alternative process tradition in American jurisprudence.[107] Unlike those who represented the Harvard-dominated

[99] See G. Edward White, 'From Realism to Critical Legal Studies: A Truncated Intellectual History', *Southwestern L. J.*, 40 (1986), 819–43 at 832.

[100] See Diggins, *supra* n. 35, 222.

[101] Various studies of Hurst and his work depict him as a generally overlooked genius who, during his prime, produced a number of brilliant—if often laborious and repetitive—historical studies which went largely unread. See, in particular, Earl Finbar Murphy, 'The Jurisprudence of Legal History: Willard Hurst as a Legal Historian', *New York Univ. L. Rev.*, 39 (1964), 900–43; Russell E. Brooks, 'The Jurisprudence of Willard Hurst', *Jnl. Leg. Educ.*, 18 (1966), 257–73; David H. Flaherty, 'An Approach to American History: Willard Hurst as Legal Historian', *Am. J. Leg. Hist.*, 14 (1970), 222–34; and, for a more measured assessment, Harry N. Scheiber, 'At the Borderland of Law and Economic History: The Contributions of Willard Hurst', *Am. Hist. Rev.*, 75 (1969), 744–56.

[102] Willard Hurst, 'Changing Popular Views About Law and Lawyers', *Annals of the American Academy of Political and Social Science*, 287 (1953), 1–7 at 1.

[103] See James Willard Hurst, *Law and Markets in United States History: Different Modes of Bargaining Among Interests* (Madison: University of Wisconsin Press, 1982), 119–31.

[104] See James Willard Hurst, *Law and Social Process in United States History* (Buffalo: William S. Hein & Co., 1987; orig. publ. 1960), 71–3, 326–8.

[105] See James Willard Hurst, *Law and the Conditions of Freedom in the Nineteenth-Century United States* (Madison: University of Wisconsin Press, 1956), 3–32.

[106] See, generally, James Willard Hurst, 'Legal Elements in United States History', *Perspectives in American History*, 5 (1971), 1–92; *The Growth of American Law: The Law Makers* (Boston: Little, Brown & Co., 1950).

[107] In this context, see esp. James Willard Hurst and Lloyd K. Garrison (eds.), *The Legal Process: An Introduction to Decision-making by Judicial, Legislative, Executive, and*

process tradition, he emphasized the pragmatic lessons of realist legal thought.[108] Not for him the sanctity of reasoned elaboration and neutral principles of constitutional adjudication.[109] But he also departed from the realist jurisprudential tradition by attempting to highlight the very legal complexity with which realists had failed to grapple. 'Legal history', Hurst insisted:

> should deal with the organization and functions of a wide range of legal agencies, simply because there has been a substantial division of labour among them—in large part they have done different jobs—and they have developed different ways of doing even similar jobs, with different consequences. To ask attention to a wide range of legal agents might seem to worry an obvious point, were it not that scholarship has exaggerated the judicial process at the expense of other principal forms of law-making. Apart from neglecting key areas of legal process because courts figure little in them, as in the spending power of legislatures, this bias has distorted estimates of the role of the courts themselves. . . . Legal historians need, first, to direct their studies more outside the courts, and, second, when they focus on courts to measure what courts do more closely against related work of other agencies.[110]

Legal historians, in other words, must learn from the lessons of both realist and process jurisprudence. To understand how law really works—to comprehend the multi-faceted character of law-making in American society—demands an appreciation of institutional competence; of the fact, that is, that different legal agencies do different jobs and that the courts are but one feature within this overall picture. Such understanding requires, in short, an appreciation of the complexity of the relationship between law and society.[111]

Many of those affiliated with the law and society movement appeared to take heed of Hurst's message. During the 1960s, empirical studies focusing on the law-making functions of private groups in their interactions with courts and legislatures became staple law and society scholarship.[112] In his

Administrative Agencies (Madison, WI: Capital Press, 1941); James Willard Hurst, Lloyd K. Garrison, Carl A. Auerbach and Samuel Mermin (eds.), *The Legal Process: An Introduction to Decision-making by Judicial, Legislative, Executive, and Administrative Agencies* (San Francisco: Chandler Publishing, 1961).

[108] See Hurst, *supra* n. 104, 14–15, 241–2; *Justice Holmes on Legal History* (New York: Macmillan, 1964), 44; also Murphy, *supra* n. 101, 921–22; Robert W. Gordon, 'Introduction: J. Willard Hurst and the Common Law Tradition in American Legal Historiography', *Law and Society Review*, 10 (1975), 9–55 at 45. ('[I]n Hurst's work pragmatic legal theory reached full flowering, probably unexcelled anywhere else in American legal scholarship.')

[109] See Murphy, *supra* n. 101, 942.

[110] Hurst, 'Legal Elements in United States History', *supra* n. 106, 68–9.

[111] See Willard Hurst, 'Consensus and Conflict in Twentieth-Century Public Policy', *Daedalus*, 105 (1976), 89–101; also Gordon, *supra* n. 108, 53.

[112] See, for example, Stewart Macaulay, *Law and the Balance of Power: The Automobile Manufacturers and their Dealers* (New York: Russell Sage Foundation, 1966); Lawrence M.

massive study, *A History of American Law*, which appeared in 1973, Lawrence Friedman remarked that the reader would find the influence of Hurst 'on every page'.[113] For David Trubek—who in that same year had joined the Wisconsin law faculty after having failed in his efforts both to establish a law and society centre and to obtain tenure at Yale[114]—the future advancement of the law and society movement would depend on the extent to which its representatives followed the example set by Hurst. 'Looking back on Hurst's critical history of the growth of American law,' he observed in 1977, 'we can realize how long the programme of critical social thought about law has been with us, and how little we have done to develop it. That is the task that is now before us.'[115] By building upon the lessons taught by Hurst, Trubek believed, the law and society movement might introduce 'a new realism'[116] into the law schools. The plea for the revitalization of realist legal thought—which he and Charles Clark had sent out at the beginning of the 1960s—might, after all, turn out not to be in vain:

> The outlines of the agenda of critical social inquiry on law seem clear. Our programme must be concerned with an analysis of the tension between ideals and reality in the legal order, and of the relations between law and society. It will have to admit the normative character of social research, while avoiding the temptation to rely on the subjective preferences of individual researchers as the source of normative guidance. It will have to be empirical and historical without becoming detached or technocratic. It must be concerned with the gap between the ideals of the law and its reality, between law in books and law in action, without falling into the belief either that all such gaps are inevitable or that any is merely accidental.[117]

While others marching under the banner of law and society have presented it similarly as the effort to fulfil realist promise,[118] there existed, even in the 1970s, a sense among certain leftist legal academics that this was not quite the case. In 1972, Mark Tushnet, fresh out of the Yale Law School and serving as law clerk to Judge George Edwards of the United States Court of Appeals for the Sixth Circuit, suggested that Hurst's conception of legal history, for all its sophistication, belonged much more to the process than to the realist tradition of American jurisprudence. Hurst, after all, believed in the concept of institutional competence: he assumed

Friedman, 'Legal Rules and the Process of Social Change', *Stanford L. Rev.*, 19 (1967), 786–840.

[113] Lawrence M. Friedman, *A History of American Law* (1st edn. New York: Simon & Schuster, 1973), 11.

[114] See Trubek, *supra* n. 78, 50.

[115] David M. Trubek, 'Complexity and Contradiction in the Legal Order: Balbus and the Challenge of Critical Social Thought about Law', *Law and Society Review*, 11 (1977), 529–69 at 566.

[116] Ibid. 540.

[117] Ibid. 566–7.

[118] See, in particular, Lawrence M. Friedman, 'The Law and Society Movement', *Stanford L. Rev.*, 38 (1986), 763–80 at 775–7.

that the legal process is comprised of a variety of agencies performing more or less distinct tasks, and that the role of the legal historian is, among other things, to demonstrate which tasks are best suited, and which are not suited, to which agencies. The very notion that a legal system might function properly owing to the fact that tasks have been allocated appropriately among legal agencies is unrealistic, Tushnet argued, since it is premissed on the impossible—namely, on the idea that a consensus may be reached concerning the most appropriate allocation of tasks among agencies. 'Hurst's explanation of the development of the law begins by assuming just that sort of consensus.'[119] It is for this reason, according to Tushnet, that, '[e]ven in 1965, Hurst had an outmoded air. In his view, a properly working legal system can resolve social conflict and promote the creation of a just society. This optimism seems naive.'[120]

If Hurst's work suffered from an outmoded air, law and society scholarship, in Tushnet's view, fared little better. Four years after the publication of Friedman's *A History of American Law*, Tushnet, by now an associate professor at Wisconsin, used the book as an opportunity for analysing the failures of the law and society movement. Friedman's book, Tushnet claimed, 'is best treated as the last great work of the 1950s, not as the first work of the 1970s or 1980s.'[121] The basic objective behind the law and society movement—to develop realist legal thought in a more systematic fashion[122]—is one with which Tushnet found himself in sympathy.[123] But systematization, he believed, could be taken too far. In doing just this,[124] Friedman had failed to recognize 'the autonomous internal dynamics of the legal process'[125] and, in consequence, had 'ignore[d] the ideological functions of law.'[126] His book exemplified the fashion in which law and society scholarship by and large dismissed out of hand the notion that a legal system may in some important sense remain autonomous from the political and economic systems within any particular society.[127] It is owing to his refusal 'to conceive of the legal order as

[119] Mark Tushnet, 'Lumber and the Legal Process', *Wisconsin L. Rev.*, [1972], 114–32 at 115.
[120] Ibid.
[121] Mark V. Tushnet, 'Perspectives on the Development of American Law: A Critical Review of Friedman's "A History of American Law" ', *Wisconsin L. Rev.*, [1977], 81–109 at 82.
[122] See Friedman, *supra* n. 118, 763–64 ('What makes the law and society movement different, perhaps, is that its scholars try to be systematic about their subject; they try to achieve rigour in method or theory, and they attempt to separate normative from descriptive issues'); Trubek, *supra* n. 78, 45 (claiming that '[s]ystemicity' is one of the basic elements 'of the law and society idea').
[123] See Tushnet, 'Critical Legal Studies: A Political History', *supra* n. 14, 1524. ('The law and society tradition, with which Trubek and I were particularly sympathetic, had attempted to provide a more systematic basis for the realists' informal sociology of law.')
[124] See Tushnet, *supra* n. 121, 90.
[125] Ibid. 83.
[126] Ibid. 94.
[127] Ibid. 83.

relatively autonomous',[128] Tushnet argues, that Friedman fails to appreciate just how law-makers, by failing to address or respond to particular social and economic problems, may serve actually to perpetuate those problems. The legal process is political because it is 'responsive directly to social or economic needs at some times with respect to some matters, responsive indirectly at other times on other matters, and not responsive at all in still other instances'.[129] In short, law and society scholarship, as exemplified by Friedman, failed to account for 'the development and importance of an ideology of legal autonomy'.[130]

Law and society scholarship never really caught on in the American law schools. The empirical research which such scholarship often demands is considered by many law professors to be both unappealing and unrewarding.[131] Yet, for certain of those who identified with the tradition of left politics in the American universities, the empiricism of the law and society movement was its saving grace; if critical legal studies was to take anything from the law and society tradition, these people argued, it should be its empirical thrust.[132] The principal objection levelled at law and society scholarship was not that it is rooted in empiricism but that it fails to reveal how ideology underpins the manner in which law both relates to and remains autonomous from society. The law and society tradition demands that law be studied as part of a broader social system rather than as an ideology in its own right.[133] It was owing to the fact that law and society scholarship tends to be inordinately system-oriented as opposed to ideology-oriented that, in the early 1970s, Tushnet and various other leftist American law professors began to develop a new jurisprudential platform from which they could articulate their political concerns about law. Like law and development, law and society had failed to offer them the style of politicized legal study after which they sought.[134] Something new was needed.

It is not the case, however, that the relationship between the law and society and critical legal studies traditions resembles that of caterpillar and butterfly. The law and society movement did not simply transmogrify into something else. Many law and society scholars retained faith in what they were doing and kept their distance from the critical legal studies

[128] Ibid. 84. [129] Ibid. [130] Ibid. 91.

[131] See Friedman, *supra* n. 118, 774.

[132] See, in particular, David M. Trubek, 'Where the Action Is: Critical Legal Studies and Empiricism', *Stanford L. Rev.*, 36 (1984), 575–622; David M. Trubek and John Esser, ' "Critical Empiricism" in American Legal Studies: Paradox, Program, or Pandora's Box?', *Law and Social Inquiry*, 14 (1989), 3–52.

[133] For further discussion on this point, see Hendrik Hartog, 'The End(s) of Critical Empiricism', *Law and Social Inquiry*, 14 (1989), 53–9; and William C. Whitford, 'Critical Empiricism', *Law and Social Inquiry*, 14 (1989), 61–7 esp. 65–7.

[134] For further development of this point, see White, *supra* n. 99, 830–6.

movement.[135] Others, while attracted to critical legal studies, were reluctant to abandon entirely their law and society roots.[136] Accordingly, while the emergence of critical legal studies marked the beginning of a search for something new in American jurisprudence, it by no means represented a total break from the past. The law and society movement, though it was fast 'becoming an intellectual backwater',[137] was no Langdellian bugbear. To most of those on the left in the law schools of the 1970s, it represented an ally rather than an enemy. Generally it was recognized, however, that even allies can seem misguided. And critical legal studies emerged out of disagreement over just how misguided the law and society tradition was.

By 1977, there existed in the American law schools a small but significant group of tenured professors who identified with the political left but who did not align themselves with the law and society tradition. Tushnet was among their number; and there were three others at the Harvard Law School—Morton Horwitz, Roberto Unger and Duncan Kennedy. Earlier in that decade, there had been a similar size group of vaguely 'leftist' law professors at Yale, all of whom had been denied tenure.[138] Trubek had belonged to this group—he would later be rejected for tenure at Harvard as well—and it has been suggested that Kennedy, who had studied property law and participated in the Law and Modernization programme with Trubek,[139] was precluded from so much as seeking a post at Yale because of his notorious 'polemic' against the law school system.[140] Although the situation would appear rather different by the following decade, it seemed, by the late 1970s, that prospects were actually improving for those on the left in the American law schools. Wisconsin was

[135] See, in this context, Trubek and Esser, *supra* n. 132, 31–4. Consider also Willard Hurst, 'Hurst Story', *New Mexico L. Rev.*, 16 (1986), 585–86 (arguing, in response to a critical legal studies teaching proposal, that law ought not to be taught as if it were simply an instrument of class oppression).

[136] See e.g. William C. Whitford, 'Lowered Horizons: Implementation Research in a Post-CLS World', *Wisconsin L. Rev.*, [1986], 755–79.

[137] Trubek and Esser, *supra* n. 132, 5.

[138] See Mark Tushnet, 'Legal Scholarship: Its Causes and Cure', *Yale L. J.*, 90 (1981), 1205–3 at 1221; *supra* n. 14, 1530–4.

[139] See John Henry Schlegel, 'Notes Toward an Intimate, Opinionated, and Affectionate History of the Conference on Critical Legal Studies', *Stanford L. Rev.*, 36 (1984), 391–411 at 393.

[140] See Kennedy, *supra* n. 3, *passim*; and also Schlegel, ibid. 393. ('Debarred, it is said, from seeking a job at Yale because of the *Polemic*, Kennedy returned to Cambridge.') It appears, in fact, that in the early 1970s, Yale attempted to appoint Kennedy. Robert Stevens, letter to author, 29 October [1991]. ('Yale did try to appoint Duncan Kennedy. I was on the appointments committee at the time.') Kennedy himself, however, was reluctant to join the Yale faculty. Mark Tushnet, letter to author, 9 February 1994. ('Duncan has said to me that he decided not to pursue an appointment at Yale (which he was confident he could have gotten) because he thought that the struggle against the people who taught him would have been too difficult.')

the home of the law and society tradition, Harvard appeared to be demonstrating a measure of intellectual openness which had eluded Yale, and there was a fair number of legal academics, affiliated with the left in one way or another, scattered throughout various law schools. Clearly there was an initiative to be seized. This growing leftist presence in the law schools would surely have more of an impact and be taken more seriously if it could somehow be made to seem less disparate and casual, if some sort of alliance could be forged among the law and society people, the tenured radicals at Harvard and any other academics or groups of academics who identified themselves with the left. The time had come to invent critical legal studies.

So, who was to invent it? As early as 1976, David Trubek and Duncan Kennedy had remarked on the growing presence of left-oriented academics in the American law schools and had decided that there might be some value in organizing a conference which would bring these people together so as determine what, if anything, they shared in common.[141] In order to get the conference off the ground, Trubek and Kennedy established an organizing committee comprised of various Harvard, Wisconsin and former Yale people.[142] One of the first tasks of this committee was to draw up a list of invitees to the conference. Various law and society scholars,[143] professors with leftist leanings of one sort or another,[144] and former students of those on the committee[145] were targeted. Tushnet—who, as Associate Dean at Wisconsin at that time, possessed 'a certain amount of excess energy'[146]—was appointed as secretary to the committee; and, in January 1977, he issued the first critical legal studies communiqué. Written

[141] See Tushnet, *supra* n. 14, 1523; Schlegel, *supra* n. 139, 394.

[142] Besides themselves, the committee was constituted by Richard Abel (one of those who, along with Trubek, had been denied tenure at Yale in the early 1970s), Tom Heller (a former participant, with Trubek, in the Yale law and development programme), Morton Horwitz (Kennedy's colleague at Harvard), Stewart Macaulay (one of Trubek's law and society colleagues at Wisconsin), Rand Rosenblatt (who, with Kennedy, had studied and worked on the law review at Yale), Mark Tushnet (another contemporary of Kennedy's at Yale, also on the law review, and a colleague of Trubek at Wisconsin) and Roberto Unger (Kennedy's colleague at Harvard).

[143] For example, Lawrence Friedman, Philip Selznick and Philippe Nonet, 'List of Invitees (In addition to the Organizing Committee and members of the U[niversity of] W[isconsin] Law School).' (n.d., on file with author: copy supplied by Professor J. H. Schlegel).

[144] The list included, among others, Isaac Balbus, Arthur Leff and George Fletcher ('List of Invitees', *supra*). All three would have identified with the left in very different ways.

[145] Most of whom were crits-in-waiting: for example, Peter Gabel, Robert Gordon, Mark Kelman and Karl Klare. 'List of Invitees', *supra*.

[146] Tushnet, *supra* n. 14, 1523. According to Schlegel, 'Tushnet was included on the organizing committee in large measure because, at the time, he was the Associate Dean at Wisconsin and, as such, had a secretary and easy access to duplicating facilities and other amenities without which organizing a large meeting is impossible.' Schlegel, *supra* n. 139, 396.

on behalf of the Organizing Committee of the Conference on Critical Legal Studies, it proposed:

> a gathering of colleagues who are pursuing a critical approach towards the study of law in society. Our notion is that we are already a substantial group. But we are scattered around the country, many of us work in one or another degree of isolation, and we have not had, up to now, an opportunity for the kind of intellectual exchange that would help us become a critical community.[147]

Critical legal studies emerged, then, as an effort to establish an identifiable intellectual community.[148] The intention of the organizing committee was not to define critical legal studies but merely to identify the sorts of work which, and individuals who, might be considered 'critical'. At this stage, the word 'critical' appeared to denote little more than the disaffection which those on the left expressed with regard to traditional law teaching and scholarship. In seeking to co-ordinate disaffection—by forging out of it a distinctive jurisprudential and political perspective—the organizing committee 'sought something akin to New Leftists'.[149] This was the New Left being played out in the law schools. Tushnet suggested in his original communiqué that there were two lines of disaffection out of which critical legal studies could grow. First of all, there was the disaffection of the law and society scholars. Stressing the difference between law in action and law in books, these people, Tushnet observed, 'have emphasized the ways in which the real [legal] system violates the ideals professed by the formal one' and 'have tended to explain these deviations in part by reference to the political and economic interests of those who control the working system'.[150] However, their 'dominant mode of explanation is not overtly "political". It refers rather to the functional necessities of any economically advanced Western society, such as the maintenance of bureaucratic discipline and morale, the facilitation of standardized mass transactions, the adjustment of institutional conflict, and the preservation of order.'[151] The second line of disaffection which Tushnet identified was of a more recent pedigree. 'Many of those who carry it on', he suggested, 'are intellectually indebted in one way or another to those in the first group, yet

[147] Mark Tushnet, letter to Dear Colleague, 17 January 1977 (on file with author: copy supplied by Professor J. H. Schlegel). Tushnet apparently had 'very little to do with the drafting' of this letter. Most of it, he recalls, was drafted by Trubek and Kennedy. Tushnet, *supra* n. 140.

[148] Tushnet, *supra* n. 147. ('Our goal is the creation of a loose, expanding critical community rather than a formal organization.') Tushnet was in fact one of the first to try to identify this community as a collection of individuals, themes and academic writings. See Mark Tushnet, 'A Marxist Analysis of American Law', *Marxist Perspectives*, (Spring 1978), 96–116.

[149] Mark Kelman, *A Guide to Critical Legal Studies* (Cambridge, Mass.: Harvard University Press, 1987), 1.

[150] Tushnet, *supra* n. 147.

[151] Ibid.

have chosen a path quite different from that of their teachers.'[152] Tushnet himself epitomized the concerns of this second group. These were people who emphasized 'the ideological character of legal doctrine,' who believed 'that law is an instrument of social, economic and political domination' and 'that modern liberal theorizing about society is beset by contradictions that are fundamental and inescapable'.[153] While there are, without doubt, tensions and conflicts between these two groups, Tushnet concluded, if brought together they might form 'a critical enterprise whose members learn from each other'.[154]

Bringing these two groups together was the basic purpose of the first Conference on Critical Legal Studies, held at the University of Wisconsin Law School at the end of May 1977. In a sense, the Conference was a great success—some classic critical legal scholarship was presented at it.[155] Yet, after the Conference, certain of those involved in the event looked back on it with mixed feelings. 'The conference was clearly an act of hope', David Trubek remarked. 'It expressed a feeling of dissatisfaction with studies of law and society in this country, and a belief that new directions could be found that would end these dissatisfactions.'[156] But the Conference had left him 'with confused feelings. . . . Below the surface of the debates and forgotten momentarily as we searched for common ground, there were subtle attacks on positions held by many.'[157] Although 'there was more consensus in the conference than might have appeared',[158] he felt, there was no denying that the proceedings were dominated by 'sectarianism'[159] and 'name-calling'.[160] Other participants more or less shared Trubek's feelings.[161] For Rick Abel, part of the problem was a perceived cliquishness. 'We need to avoid domination, or the sense of domination, by those who are, or are perceived to be, the inner circle.'[162] Yet this sense

[152] Ibid. [153] Ibid. [154] Ibid.

[155] For example, Karl E. Klare, 'Judicial Deradicalization of the Wagner Act and the Origins of Modern Legal Consciousness, 1937–1941', *Minnesota L. Rev.*, 62 (1978), 265–339; Peter Gabel, 'Intention and Structure in Contractual Conditions: Outline of a Method for Critical Legal Theory', *Minnesota L. Rev.*, 61 (1977), 601–43; and the already published Duncan Kennedy, 'Form and Substance in Private Law Adjudication', *Harvard L. Rev.*, 89 (1976), 1685–778. 'Conference on Critical Legal Studies: Schedule', (n.d., on file with author: copy supplied by Professor J. H. Schlegel).

[156] David M. Trubek, 'Slaying Dragons or Creating Them? Preliminary Reactions to the First Conference on Critical Legal Studies', *Conference on Critical Legal Studies Newsletter*, no. 1, 6 June 1977, 1–8 at 1. [157] Ibid. [158] Ibid. 3.

[159] Ibid. 1. [160] Ibid. 3.

[161] See Warren Samuels, letter to David Trubek and Mark Tushnet, 30 June 1977, *Conference on Critical Legal Studies Newsletter*, no. 2, n.d.. 3–4 at 3 (on Trubek's comments as 'a most perceptive diagnosis of what transpired at the meeting'); John H. Schlegel, letter to David Trubek, 5 June 1977, *supra* n. 156, 5–9 at 5 (confessing to 'intellectual disquiet with what I heard at the Conference') and 8 (noting 'the grumping in the corridors').

[162] Comments of Rick Abel, in *Conference on Critical Legal Studies Newsletter*, *supra* n. 161, 1–2 at 1.

that there existed a critical legal cabal endured. In due course, critical legal studies would become 'divided between an inner circle of old timers who dominate the organization and whose ideas and interests set its tone and direction, and a great unwashed whose presence is tolerated, but little more, unless introduced by the right people'.[163]

In the early days of critical legal studies, cliquishness served a purpose. Even at the first Conference, Abel noted, there was something of a split between a younger generation of leftist academics and an 'old guard' which provided, in the eyes of the former group, 'a convenient target for attack'.[164] This old guard was made up of established law and society people, old-fashioned marxists and traditional liberals. Duncan Kennedy, it seems, was especially energetic in ensuring that the old guard was increasingly alienated from the critical legal studies movement.[165] By the time of the second conference—billed as the first 'regional', as opposed to national, conference and held at Northeastern University in February 1978—many of the old guard had basically given up on critical legal studies.[166] At the plenary session of the second national conference, at Wisconsin the following November, the organizing committee effectively assumed control of the movement—and, in the process, flabbergasted many of its rank and file—by introducing a set of membership by-laws and establishing a 'board of directors'.[167] Critical legal studies had, in effect, been appropriated. Those who had previously failed to find a home on the left in the American law schools, who had felt either disillusioned with or ambivalent about law and development and law and society, had at last acquired a jurisprudence which they could call their own.

THE EARLY DAYS

But what was this jurisprudence? Certainly it seems possible to identify the emergence of critical legal studies by demonstrating how the Conference came into being, who the prime movers and shakers behind the movement were, and how it came to be distinguished from other types of leftist legal study. But this would reveal very little about the intellectual substance of critical legal studies. Apart from setting up their own support group, what were these so-called critical legal scholars actually doing?

Given that the critical legal studies movement began life as a miscellany of leftist academics curious to discover whether or not they shared common ground, it is not surprising that many of the earliest representatives of that movement should have found themselves doing different things. This lack

163 Schlegel, *supra* n. 139, 401.
164 Abel, *supra* n. 162, 2.
165 See Schlegel, *supra* n. 139, 399–400.
166 Ibid. 400.
167 Ibid.

of intellectual homogeneity among early critical legal scholars is especially evident from the manner in which the movement was represented in the late 1970s at the Harvard Law School. By the early 1980s, Harvard was perceived to be something of a critical legal stronghold. Before it had acquired much of an identity, however, critical legal studies at Harvard was associated with three professors—Horwitz, Unger and Kennedy[168]—all of whom were affiliated with the Conference, all of whom had obtained tenure, and all of whom, in one way or another, aligned themselves with the left. Despite these similarities, however, it would be an exaggeration to assert that Horwitz, Unger and Kennedy were engaged in a common intellectual enterprise.

During the late 1970s, all three produced studies which were neither legal theory nor legal history but path-breaking combinations of both. Horwitz—who had obtained a doctorate from the Government Department at Harvard before he entered the LL.B programme in the Law School—had begun, by the early 1970s, to document the emergence in the late eighteenth century of what he terms an 'instrumental' conception of the American common law.[169] By the early nineteenth century, he claimed in 1971, the American courts were no longer treating the common law 'as an eternal set of principles expressed in custom and derived from natural law. . . . Instead, judges ha[d] come to think of the common law as equally responsible with legislation for governing society and promoting socially desirable conduct.'[170] This thesis is elaborated by Horwitz in his *magnum opus*, *The Transformation of American Law, 1780–1860*, published in 1977. In that book, Horwitz endeavours to demonstrate that American judges, from the late eighteenth century onwards, began to mould common law doctrine so that it favoured mercantile as opposed to other group interests within society. In tort law, for example, there existed '[a]t the beginning of the nineteenth century . . . a general private law presumption in favour of compensation, expressed by the oft-cited common law maxim *sic utere*. . . . By the time of the Civil War, however, many types of injuries had been reclassified under a "negligence" heading,

[168] There is also Richard Parker. A tenured professor at Harvard Law School since 1979 (he initially joined the faculty in 1974), Parker appears on the list of invitees to the first Conference on Critical Legal Studies (*supra* n. 143), though he is not named in the 'List of Conference Participants' (n.d., on file with author: copy supplied by Professor J. H. Schlegel). In the early 1980s, Parker produced a critique of post-Bickelian process jurisprudence in which he aligned himself squarely with the critical legal studies tradition. See Parker, *supra* n. 12, 223–4. Though Parker has associated himself with critical legal studies, it seems that he has always been very much on the margins of the movement.

[169] See Morton J. Horwitz, 'The Emergence of an Instrumental Conception of American Law, 1780–1820', *Perspectives in American History*, 5 (1971), 285–326.

[170] Ibid. 326.

which had the effect of substantially reducing entrepreneurial liability.'[171] The turn towards instrumentalism thus marked the birth of political adjudication in the United States. In outlining the growth of instrumentalism, Horwitz was attempting to demonstrate precisely how 'a major transformation of the legal system took place'.[172]

Horwitz's efforts to substantiate so bold a thesis have been subjected to a fair deal of criticism. It is a thesis, certain detractors have argued, which depends for its credibility on the manipulation and neglect of relevant historical data.[173] Similar criticisms have been levelled at the work of Roberto Unger.[174] Yet the affinity between Unger's historical project and Horwitz's—for all that both are commonly treated as classic examples of early critical legal scholarship—more or less ends there. Unger studied law in Brazil. The Harvard human rights lawyer, Henry Steiner, apparently encountered Unger in the academic year 1968–9 while serving as a visiting professor in Rio de Janeiro, and suggested that he move to Massachusetts to pursue post-graduate study.[175] Graduating from the LL.M programme in 1970, Unger began teaching contracts at the Law School in the following year while studying for his S.J.D. For a student to step straight out of the LL.M course and into a teaching post at Harvard was remarkable. At this time, Unger was attempting to produce a study of the nature and limits of legal reasoning.[176] In fact, the study unfolded into something rather more ambitious. His first book, *Knowledge and Politics*, published in 1975, opens with the confession that it constitutes 'an act of hope', that it 'points towards a kind of thought and society that does not yet and may never exist'.[177] The reconstitution of legal and social relations, Unger argues, demands total criticism of classical liberal thought.[178] Liberal beliefs turn out to be fundamentally flawed because they cannot provide us with 'a criterion of value that goes beyond individual will'[179]—with a notion of 'the good', in other words, which is both particular and universal.[180] Since

[171] Morton J. Horwitz, *The Transformation of American Law, 1780–1860* (Cambridge, Mass.: Harvard University Press, 1977), 85.

[172] Ibid. xvi.

[173] See, for example, A. W. B. Simpson, 'The Horwitz Thesis and the History of Contracts', *U. Chicago L. Rev.*, 46 (1979), 533–601; R. Randall Bridwell, 'Theme v. Reality in American Legal History: A Commentary on Horwitz, *The Transformation of American Law, 1780–1860*, and on the Common Law in America', *Indiana L. J.*, 52 (1978), 449–96.

[174] See e.g. William P. Alford, 'The Inscrutable Occidental? Implications of Roberto Unger's Uses and Abuses of the Chinese Past', *Texas L. Rev.*, 64 (1986), 915–72.

[175] Steiner, it should be noted, was also one of those who was on the margins of critical legal studies in its formative period. He appears on both the list of invitees for the first Conference (*supra* n. 143) and also on the list of first participants (*supra* n. 168). It seems likely that Steiner would have become involved with the Conference through Trubek, with whom he worked at the Yale Law School between 1972 and 1973.

[176] For a sketch of the proposed study, see Roberto Mangabeira Unger, 'Isonomy and Justice', *Archiv für Rechts- und Sozialphilosophie*, 56 (1970), 181–7.

[177] Roberto Mangabeira Unger, *Knowledge and Politics* (New York: Free Press, 1975), v.

[178] Ibid. 1–3.

[179] Ibid. 238.

[180] Ibid. 239–40.

liberal thought fails in this manner, it 'leaves us at a loss about what we ought to do' and 'makes it impossible to justify any exercise of power at all'.[181] Accordingly:

> a shift of focus is needed. Instead of asking what people want, we should ask first under what conditions their choices might inform us more fully about what is distinctive to each of them and to mankind as a whole. Our first concern should be to determine the circumstances in which we are entitled to give greater or lesser weight to consensus, taking agreed-upon values as better or worse indications of our common humanity. It may be that such an inquiry will show that one cannot hope to discover universal and permanent moral laws, and that the very striving for such laws betrays a misconception of what man and his good are like.[182]

Uncertainty lies at the heart of this appeal for total critique. While liberal thought may disclose no universally shared values, there is no guarantee that by transcending such thought—assuming this to be possible—we will be left any the wiser. 'Shared values', Unger observes, 'carry weight only in the measure to which they are not simply products of dominance.'[183] But what is dominance? 'To be dominated by another is to be subject to his unjustified power. Thus, to define domination one must be able to distinguish the justified and the unjustified forms of power, and to trace the true limits of autonomy. This requires judgements that have to rely to a greater or lesser extent on our established moral intuitions and practices.'[184] In order to distinguish between justified and unjustified power, in other words, we must assume, even if we cannot prove, the existence of shared moral values. Yet it is Unger's claim that the fundamental problem with liberal consciousness rests in the fact that it demands this assumption. Moving beyond liberalism—to a form of consciousness which enables us to distinguish between arbitrary and legitimate exercise of power—entails exactly the same assumption. There exists, therefore, no convincing reason to abandon liberalism.[185]

In *Knowledge and Politics*, Unger suggests that beyond liberalism there lies the politics and ethics of the community. 'Community begins with sympathy. Sympathy means that people encounter each other in such a way that their sense of separateness from one another varies in direct rather than inverse proportion to their sense of social union.'[186] Unger does not deny that the move towards a communitarian form of life would entail many 'risks and difficulties'.[187] Indeed, simply to believe that such a form of life is possible and achievable demands 'child-like innocence in the anticipation of the future'.[188] This is the act of hope on which *Knowledge*

[181] Ibid. 238. [182] Ibid. 242. [183] Ibid. 243. [184] Ibid.

[185] For the classic formulation of this argument in relation to Unger's work, see Arthur Allen Leff, 'Memorandum', *Stanford L. Rev.*, 29 (1977), 879–89.

[186] Unger, *supra* n. 177, 262. [187] Ibid. 284. [188] Ibid.

and Politics is premissed. That such acts of hope meet with objections and problems, however, does not mean that they are futile. It may simply be that we have failed—owing to the fact that we are rooted in the liberal tradition—to see the path towards a better form of life. That we have failed to see the light does not necessarily mean that there is no light to see.

But where are we to seek enlightenment? In *Law in Modern Society*, published in 1976, Unger sketches an answer to this question. First of all, he suggests, we must look to the problems of modern liberalism. 'In liberal society, there is a constant and overt struggle between what men are led to expect of society and what they in fact receive from it.'[189] With 'its tendency to multiply the number and to diminish the individual importance of the group settings in which each person lives,'[190] furthermore, liberalism debases human individuality. 'Individuals expose only a limited portion of their humanity to their fellows in each of the strips of life on which they meet'; and, since people 'lack the grace of community, they can be held together and kept in place only by their need to use each other as means to the satisfaction of their own desires.'[191] Liberalism also 'increases the possibility of a widening gap between the existence and the felt legitimacy of hierarchy'.[192] That is, since it cannot generate universal consensus regarding social values, liberalism fails satisfactorily to justify the unequal distribution of privilege within society. Efforts to rank human qualities and achievements turn out to be by and large arbitrary; and, in consequence, '[e]very conventional criterion for the allocation of social advantages falls under the suspicion that it, too, is arbitrary.'[193] Over time, as 'every consensus or tradition begins to be tainted in the eyes of its adherents with the failings of the hierarchic social circumstance from which it arose,' citizens 'become increasingly sensitive to the influence of past or present distributions of power on accepted ideas about right conduct. . . . Thus, a vicious (or liberating) circle of demoralization of existing social arrangements starts on its way.'[194]

The parenthesis here is signal. Out of the ashes of liberalism will come enlightenment. By despiritualizing humanity, by thwarting genuine aspiration, and by fostering feelings of insecurity, injustice and resentment, the liberal tradition will ultimately awaken in us a desire for communal solidarity.[195] One of the primary consequences of this will be a change in the function of law. As citizens become increasingly dissatisfied with the arbitrary social hierarchies legitimated by liberalism, legal systems which

[189] Roberto Mangabeira Unger, *Law in Modern Society: Toward a Criticism of Social Theory* (New York: Free Press, 1976), 153–4.
[190] Ibid. 167.
[191] Ibid. 168.
[192] Ibid. 171.
[193] Ibid. 172.
[194] Ibid. 173–4.
[195] See ibid. 206. For a critique of Unger's position here, see Harold J. Berman, *Law and Revolution: The Formation of the Western Legal Tradition* (Cambridge, Mass.: Harvard University Press, 1983), 40–1.

justify 'systematic disparities of power' will be tempered more and more 'by equitable and communal doctrines'.[196] And as 'the attack on structures of domination in the name of substantive justice' intensifies, there will emerge the 'hope that equity and solidarity will become major sources of normative order rather than just residual limitations on formality'.[197]

The nature of the post-liberal, solidaristic society is something about which Unger is able only to speculate.[198] The advent of post-liberalism, he concludes, 'could mean a relapse into the logic of tribalism, which sanctifies the existing order of the group as an irrevocable decree of nature,'[199] or it might 'mean that individual freedom could be rescued from the demise of the rule of law and brought into harmony with the reassertion of communitarian concerns'.[200] Having produced two books within as many years dealing with the question of whether or not modern societies might ever outgrow liberalism, Unger, at the end of the 1970s, returned for a period to Brazil in order to work as a political activist for the democratic left.[201] Not until 1983 did he return in print to the questions of how liberalism might be transcended and what post-liberal social and legal arrangements might look like.[202] Yet Unger's failure, in the 1970s and early 1980s, to flesh out his communitarian vision hardly diminished his influence among proponents of critical legal studies.[203] Inconclusive though they may have been, his first two books could not have been better designed for the critical legal studies movement. For, behind the erudition and the fondness for abstraction lay a powerful message: that liberal consciousness is somehow a false or corrupted consciousness, that there exists within liberal thought—liberal legal thought included—a tension so fundamental, so irresolvable, that it must ultimately implode and make way for radical social transformation.[204] That no critical legal scholar could

[196] Unger, *supra* n. 189, 211. [197] Ibid. 213. [198] See ibid. 220–3.

[199] Ibid. 238–39. [200] Ibid. 239.

[201] On Unger's involvement in Brazilian politics, see Roberto Mangabeira Unger, *Social Theory: Its Situation and Its Task. A Critical Introduction to* Politics, *a Work in Constructive Social Theory* (Cambridge: Cambridge University Press, 1987), 67–79; William H. Simon, 'Social Theory and Political Practice: Unger's Brazilian Journalism', *Northwestern Univ. L. Rev.*, 81 (1987), 832–68; Perry Anderson, *A Zone of Engagement* (London: Verso, 1992), 130.

[202] From the appearance of *Law in Modern Society* up until 1983, the only work which Unger appears to have published, apart from his Brazilian journalism (see Simon, *supra* n. 201, *passim*), is a short piece on the state of modern psychiatry. See Roberto Mangabeira Unger, 'A Program for Late Twentieth-Century Psychiatry', *American Journal of Psychiatry*, 139 (1982), 155–64.

[203] For an extremely powerful critique of Unger which suggests that critical legal scholars have tended to read him in far too rosy a light, see William Ewald, 'Unger's Philosophy: A Critical Legal Study', *Yale L. J.*, 97 (1988), 665–756. And for a far less rigorous analysis of Unger's impact on critical legal studies generally, see Jonathan Turley, 'The Hitchhiker's Guide to CLS, Unger, and Deep Thought', *Northwestern Univ. L. Rev.*, 81 (1987), 593–620.

[204] See further Steven Shiffrin, 'Liberalism, Radicalism, and Legal Scholarship', *UCLA L. Rev.*, 30 (1983), 1103–217 at 1174–92.

say how this transformation might come about or what it might entail—that nobody apart from Unger appeared to be interested in actually confronting such matters[205]—seemed almost unimportant. What mattered was that critical legal studies had been invested with a vision.

Unger himself conceded that his views about how law works within liberal systems were very much shaped by Duncan Kennedy.[206] It would be wrong, however, to assume that, in the early days of critical legal studies, the two men were involved in similar theoretical projects. Unger was concerned essentially with the prospects for radical social transformation. As the impossibility of establishing real consensus under liberalism becomes ever more apparent, as liberal legal systems become increasingly riddled with tensions, he believed, the likelihood of such transformation would increase. Kennedy, unlike Unger, was less concerned with the potential for transformation than he was with the very tensions within liberal legal systems which might ultimately be responsible for transformation. While Unger may have imported a visionary dimension into critical legal studies, Kennedy, more than anyone else, was responsible for investing it with a doctrinal dimension: he attempted to demonstrate how the doctrines, rules, principles, and theoretical premisses on which liberal legal systems are founded turn out to be infected by distinctive tensions. In due course, the endeavour to highlight these tensions inherent in liberal legal systems and thought would become a dominant feature of critical legal studies.

Like Horwitz and Unger, Kennedy himself had embarked on his own particular critical legal project some years before critical legal studies had been dreamed up. In 1970, the year in which he graduated from the Yale Law School, Kennedy produced a manuscript—never published—on 'utopian rationalism' in American jurisprudence. Hart and Sacks's *The Legal Process*, he argued, exemplifies this form of rationalism. 'Like the neo-classical economists who elaborated the concept of "perfect competition," Hart and Sacks base their system on a utopia'[207]—on the ideal, that is, of a perfectly ordered, perfectly functioning legal system in which all officials accept and are careful not to overstep their institutional responsibilities and in which judges in particular, blessed with the gift of reasoned elaboration, are able and willing to find the 'correct'—that is, the most socially acceptable and thoroughly principled—answer to every legal problem they confront. Yet utopian rationalism is pointless. Judges, for example, simply cannot decide cases in accordance with Hart and Sacks's

205 See, in this context, Richard W. Bauman, 'The Communitarian Vision of Critical Legal Studies', *McGill L. J.*, 33 (1988), 295–356 at 325–39.

206 See Unger, *supra* n. 189, 291 n. 44.

207 Duncan Kennedy, 'Utopian Rationalism in American Legal Thought', unpublished mimeograph (on file with author: copy supplied by Professor Kennedy), June 1970, III, 35.

ideal. 'No judge could be expected to do the research necessary to make up his mind about the sociological and psychological questions implied in every jurisdictional question—even supposing that social science offers adequate frameworks for such research in the first place.'[208] Furthermore, the appeal for principled adjudication turns out to be generally futile, for principles tend to stand not in isolation but in conflict with one another. 'In antitrust law,' for instance, 'there coexist two equally long and equally distinguished lines of cases, one based on the notion that the goal of maximization implies that the economy must be made to correspond as closely as possible to the model of perfect competition, the other on the notion that in an imperfectly competitive, regulated economy the law can achieve no more than atomization of economic power.'[209] Since principles conflict, their application by judges will turn out to be 'either largely indeterminate or not appropriate at all'.[210] Utopian rationalism, in short, denies the possibility of tension between principle and counter-principle.

Throughout the 1970s, in a series of quite brilliant studies, Kennedy elaborated still further the tensions inherent in liberal legal thought and doctrine. Legal decision-making and rule-application within liberal systems, he argued in 1973, generate arbitrary compromise rather than rational consensus. Rules 'do not represent an attempt to determine the "right" or "just" solution to conflicts, but rather each is a piece of a larger puzzle accepted not for its own sake but in exchange for benefits or injuries received through other rules.'[211] Equally, '[t]he process of rule application itself has nothing to do with "justice" or "right" ' but 'is merely a *cost*'[212]—the cost, that is, of facilitating 'the compromise of conflicting interests'.[213] By 1975, he had completed what amounted to a book—though again, it remains unpublished[214]—detailing the manner in which classical legal thought had been founded on a basic antinomy. 'Modern theorizing about private law', he claimed, 'has left us with the sense that it is a mass of rules that cannot be understood as the rational working out of consistent general principles. It must rather be understood as the accumulation of the victories and defeats of two conflicting visions of the universe.'[215] From approximately 1850 up until around the late 1930s, legal thought in the United States struggled to embrace both of these visions: that is, '[c]lassical legal thought reflected a state of mind deeply preoccupied with an

[208] Ibid. III, 38. [209] Ibid. III, 45. [210] Ibid. III, 43.

[211] Duncan Kennedy, 'Legal Formality', *Jnl. Leg. Studs.*, 2 (1973), 351–98 at 369.

[212] Ibid. 370. [213] Ibid. 362.

[214] Duncan Kennedy, 'The Rise and Fall of Classical Legal Thought, 1850–1940', unpublished mimeograph (on file with author: copy supplied by Professor Kennedy), 1975. Chapter 1 of this study has in fact been published: Duncan Kennedy, 'Toward an Historical Understanding of Legal Consciousness: The Case of Classical Legal Thought in America, 1850–1940', *Research in Law and Sociology*, 3 (1980), 3–24.

[215] Kennedy, 'The Rise and Fall of Classical Legal Thought', *supra* n. 214, III, 3.

opposition between freedom, conceived as arbitrary and irrational, yet creative and dynamic, and restraint, conceived in similar stark terms, as rigid, principled in an absolutist way, yet necessary as the antidote to freedom.'[216] This conflict between the desire for freedom and the necessity of restraint manifested itself in the efforts of classical lawyers to accommodate within the private law framework a variety of 'conflicting positions'.[217] Those responsible for the creation and application of private law attempted simultaneously to promote self-determination and paternalism, facilitation and regulation, the desire for autonomy and the goals of the community, and legal formality and informality.[218] While each of these perspectives represented an effort 'to describe the world accurately, and to prescribe for it rationally given obviously acceptable common goals'—while, in fact, these perspectives 'cancel and refute each other'—'the [classical] private law system adopt[ed] all of them'.[219]

In his paper to the first Conference on Critical Legal Studies in 1977, 'Form and Substance in Private Law Adjudication', Kennedy returned to the question of how modern, post-classical legal thought is underscored by conflict. Liberal consciousness, he suggested, is torn between individualism and altruism—a fact which is borne out by the form and content of modern American law. 'The individualist attempt at a comprehensive rational theory of the form and content of private law was a failure.'[220] Classical lawyers believed that while common law rules should guarantee citizens a formal equality of bargaining rights, they ought not to interfere with real inequalities of bargaining power, since such inequalities are simply evidence of a properly functioning system of free exchange.[221] The 'altruist attack'[222] on this position—the critique mounted by Robert Hale and other legal realists—demonstrated its incoherence.[223] While the common law rules which guarantee freedom of exchange may appear to be neutral, ensuring an equality of bargaining rights for all, they are of necessity partial, Hale and others argued, because they serve the interests of those citizens who enjoy considerable bargaining power. For when the common law promotes freedom of exchange, it ensures, in effect, that those with greater bargaining power are free to coerce those with less economic advantage to accept their contractual terms. '[B]argaining power', as Kennedy explains, 'is a function of the legal order. All the individualist rules restrain or liberate that power. Changes in the rules alter its pattern.'[224] Accordingly, the more that rules promote freedom of

[216] Kennedy, 'Toward an Historical Understanding', *supra* n. 214, 8.
[217] Kennedy, 'The Rise and Fall of Classical Legal Thought', *supra* III, 17.
[218] Ibid. III, 3–27.
[219] Ibid. III, 3.
[220] Kennedy, *supra* n. 155, 1766.
[221] See ibid. 1745–8.
[222] Ibid. 1748.
[223] Ibid. 1748–51.
[224] Ibid. 1748.

choice, the more likely it is that many individuals will in fact suffer a diminution in such choice, since these rules will enable the economically powerful to coerce the economically disadvantaged.[225]

The use of rules to promote individualism thus transpires to be a double-edged sword. The pursuit of individualism often stymies individualism. Yet, if individualist initiatives are highly problematic in private law adjudication, 'altruism has not emerged as a comprehensive rational counter theory able to accomplish the task which has defeated its adversary'.[226] Whereas 'individualism seems to harmonize with an insistence on rigid rules rigidly applied,' Kennedy contends, 'altruist views on substantive private law issues lead to willingness to resort to standards in administration.'[227] 'Standards refer directly to the substantive values or purposes of the community. They involve "value judgements".'[228] Consequently, they are subject to arbitrary judicial enforcement. Since judges are incapable of formulating or interpreting standards in such a way as to reflect accurately the values and goals of the community—whatever that might be taken to mean—'[t]he direct application of moral norms through judicial standards . . . leaves us far from anything worthy of the name of altruistic order.'[229] As with rules, then, standards cannot be applied in a determinate fashion.

Despite their flaws, however, the individualistic and altruistic perspectives continue to 'live on and even flourish'[230] in the private law domain. Indeed, there exists at the heart of private law adjudication a basic contradiction between the individualistic preference for following rules and the altruistic preference for applying standards. Indeterminacy infects the legal system, Kennedy argues, largely because 'there are no available metaprinciples'[231] which might enable judges to determine correctly whether or not to enforce a rule or apply a standard in settling a particular dispute.[232]

This argument—the so-called 'indeterminacy thesis'—has a distinctively realist ring about it. Yet it represents more than merely a return to the lessons of legal realism. So-called realists pointed to the existence of uncertainty in law.[233] Now and again, they raised the question of why

[225] See, generally, Duncan Kennedy, 'Distributive and Paternalist Motives in Contract and Tort Law, With Special Reference to Compulsory Terms and Unequal Bargaining Power', *Maryland L. Rev.*, 41 (1982), 563–649.

[226] Kennedy, *supra* n. 155, 1766. See also Kelman, *supra* n. 148, 40–5.

[227] Kennedy, *supra* n. 155, 1685. [228] Ibid. 1752. [229] Ibid. 1771.

[230] Ibid. 1766. [231] Ibid. 1724.

[232] See further Kelman, *supra* n. 148, 54; and William W. Bratton, Jr., 'Manners, Metaprinciples, Metapolitics and Kennedy's *Form and Substance*', *Cardozo L. Rev.*, 6 (1985), 871–915 at 884–6.

[233] Sometimes, in doing so, they sounded remarkably like critical legal scholars. Consider, for example, Herman Oliphant and Abram Hewitt, 'Introduction', in Jacques Rueff, *From the Physical to the Social Sciences: Introduction to a Study of Economic and Ethical Theory*

lawyers and ordinary citizens alike insisted on seeing certainty in the law when such certainty was little in evidence.[234] Yet they neglected to consider in detail the question of why there is uncertainty in law. Kennedy moves onwards from the realist jurisprudential tradition by trying to figure out from where it is that legal indeterminacy springs.

In his article, 'The Structure of Blackstone's Commentaries', published in 1979, Kennedy developed the broadly-Hegelian idea that indeterminacy is embedded in human consciousness. The essence of individuality, according to Hegel, 'is awareness of one's existence as a unit in sharp distinction from others'.[235] Yet 'this spirit of individualism'[236] is mediated by the very fact that we live in communities, that we exist for one another.[237] As Marcuse explains, for Hegel, '[t]he individual can become what he is only through another individual; his existence consists in his "being for another".'[238] Inspired by both Hegel and Marcuse (among others[239]) Kennedy attempted to elaborate an idea which he had left underdeveloped in 'Form and Substance in Private Law Adjudication': the idea, that is, that there exists a basic tension between the individual and the community. Liberalism, he argues, denies that individualism conceals a 'fundamental contradiction':

> [T]he goal of individual freedom is at the same time dependent on and incompatible with the communal coercive action that is necessary to achieve it. Others (family, friends, bureaucrats, cultural figures, the state) are necessary if we are to become persons at all—they provide us the stuff of our selves and protect us in crucial ways against destruction. . . . But at the same time that it forms and protects us, the universe of others . . . threatens us with annihilation and urges upon us forms of fusion that are quite plainly bad rather than good. . . . Numberless conformities, large and small abandonments of self to others are the

(Baltimore: The Johns Hopkins Press, 1929), ix–xxxii at xv. ('Upon reflection, it must be clear that, for any case wherein there is a clash of two groups having conflicting interests, two conflicting major premisses can always be formulated, one embodying one set of interests, the other embodying the other.')

[234] See, for example, Jerome Frank, *Law and the Modern Mind* (Gloucester, Mass.: Peter Smith, 1970; orig. publ. 1930).

[235] Georg Wilhelm Friedrich Hegel, *Hegel's Philosophy of Right* (Eng. trans. T. M. Knox, Oxford: Oxford University Press, 1952; orig. German publ. 1821), 208.

[236] Georg Wilhelm Friedrich Hegel, *The Phenomenology of Mind* (Eng. trans. J. B. Baillie, New York: Harper and Row, 1967; orig. German publ. 1807), 497.

[237] See ibid. 218–27.

[238] Herbert Marcuse, *Reason and Revolution: Hegel and the Rise of Social Theory* (2nd edn. London: Routledge & Kegan Paul, 1955; 1st edn. 1941), 114.

[239] See Duncan Kennedy, 'The Structure of Blackstone's Commentaries', *Buffalo L. Rev.*, 28 (1979), 205–382 at 210 fn. 2, where he lists the works of Hegel and Marcuse cited above among those which 'have most influenced me'. This style of footnote, listing 'inspirational' works without any precise indication of their bearing upon the author's ideas, became a common feature in much (though by no means all) of the critical legal studies literature.

price of what freedom we experience in society. . . . Through our existence as members of collectives, we impose on others and have imposed on us hierarchical structures of power, welfare, and access to enlightenment that are illegitimate.[240]

Around the time that Kennedy wrote this, Arthur Allen Leff put the point rather more succinctly and less dramatically: 'What we want', he observed, 'is simultaneously to be perfectly ruled and perfectly free.'[241] Of course—and this was Kennedy's claim—we are neither: liberalism offers a compromise, whereby individualistic aspirations are held in check by forms of collective constraint which sometimes we will welcome, sometimes we will resent. For the individual, in other words, the community is at once a source of liberation and repression. Liberal thought, according to Kennedy, denies this fact.[242] It is for this reason that liberal legal thought has tended to be blind to the sorts of tensions inherent in legal doctrine which Kennedy himself had been highlighting throughout his writings of the 1970s.

What, then, is to be done? Unger, in his work of the late 1970s, had attempted to visualize law in the context of a society freed from the tensions which beset liberal legal thought. Kennedy, however, engages in a rather more modest theoretical enterprise. He has no suggestions regarding how we might transcend the fundamental contradiction. '[I]t would be a delusion', he believes, 'to think that the study of the history and prehistory of our contradictory feelings can resolve the contradiction. . . . Even if we *could* resolve the contradiction at the level of theory, we would still be subject to its influence in practice.'[243] To argue for the transcendence of the contradiction, furthermore, would 'mean proceeding on the basis of faith and hope in humanity, without the assurances of reason'.[244] The basic task of critical legal theory ought, rather, to be the confrontation of contradiction. While 'we cannot resolve the contradiction within legal theory . . . [t]he task of criticism is to demystify our thinking by confronting us with the fact that the contradiction is a historical artifact. It is no more immortal than the society that created and sustains it. Understanding this is not a salvation, but it is a help.'[245]

Although not in the manner that he intended, Kennedy's notion of the fundamental contradiction did indeed become an historical artefact. It has been subjected to an abundance of criticism from both inside and outside

[240] Ibid. 211–12. I confine my attention here to Kennedy's methodology. I pay no regard to his historical interpretation of the *Commentaries*. Suffice it to say that, like his Harvard colleagues, Horwitz and Unger, he has, as a legal historian, been criticized fairly severely. Regarding Blackstone see, for example, John W. Cairns, 'Blackstone, An English Institutist: Legal Literature and the Rise of the Nation State', *Oxf. Jnl. Leg. Studs.*, 4 (1984), 318–60 at 350–2.

[241] Arthur Allen Leff, 'Unspeakable Ethics, Unnatural Law', *Duke L. J.*, [1979], 1229–49 at 1229.

[242] See Kennedy, *supra* n. 239, 217.

[243] Ibid. 221.

[244] Ibid. 213.

[245] Ibid. 221.

the critical legal studies movement,[246] and by the mid-1980s Kennedy himself had renounced the idea.[247] Yet, in terms of the intellectual history of the movement, the idea is very significant. Throughout the best part of the 1980s, other proponents of critical legal studies, as we shall see in due course, tended to follow Kennedy's lead in attempting to uncover contradiction and indeterminacy in liberal legal thought.[248] Of the Harvard trio, he was by far the most significant in influencing the development of the movement.

It is important, however, not to identify critical legal studies with Harvard in the same way that realism tends to be identified with Columbia and Yale. While Harvard features significantly in the history of critical legal studies, it is but part of a much broader picture. In focusing on critical legal studies at Harvard in the late 1970s—in attempting to show that Horwitz, Unger and Kennedy did not engage in anything approximating a uniform style of critical legal scholarship—my intention has been to emphasize that, even in its early years, the movement possessed little in the way of homogeneity or strategy. In doing this, however, I have clearly risked exaggerating the contribution of Harvard to the initial development of critical legal studies.[249]

What is certainly clear is that there were other styles of critical legal scholarship emerging in the late 1970s. Three papers from the first Conference on Critical Legal Studies illustrate as much. Inspired by the existential phenomenology of Jean-Paul Sartre, Peter Gabel, in his paper

[246] For criticism from the inside, see e.g. Kelman, *supra* n. 148, 234–7; and from the outside, see e.g. Johnson, *supra* n. 7, 252–7.

[247] See Peter Gabel and Duncan Kennedy, 'Roll Over Beethoven', *Stanford L. Rev.*, 36 (1984), 1–55 at 15 (comment by Duncan Kennedy). For a critique of this renunciation, see Alan Hunt, 'The Theory of Critical Legal Studies', *Oxford Jnl. Leg. Studs.*, 6 (1986), 1–45 at 20–8.

[248] Kennedy himself, throughout the 1980s and 1990s, has continued to produce detailed analyses of the tensions inherent in liberal legal (and especially neo-classical) thought and reasoning. For examples, see Duncan Kennedy and Frank Michelman, 'Are Property and Contract Efficient?', *Hofstra L. Rev.*, 8 (1980), 711–70; Duncan Kennedy, 'The Role of Law in Economic Thought: Essays on the Fetishism of Commodities', *American Univ. L. Rev.*, 34 (1985), 939–1001; 'The Effect of the Warranty of Habitability on Low Income Housing: "Milking" and Class Violence', *Florida State Univ. L. Rev.*, 15 (1987), 485–519; and 'A Semiotics of Legal Argument', *Syracuse L. Rev.*, 42 (1991), 75–116.

[249] Indeed, it should be noted in this regard that, apart from serving on the Organizing Committee for the Conference on Critical Legal Studies, Roberto Unger's primary and possibly only effort to contribute to the development of the movement came in the form of his address to the sixth Conference, at Harvard in March 1982. Roberto Unger, 'The Critical Legal Studies Movement', *Harvard L. Rev.*, 96 (1982), 563–675. For some (see, for example, Stephen B. Presser, 'Some Realism about Orphism, or The Critical Legal Studies Movement and the New Great Chain of Being: An English Legal Academic's Guide to the Current State of American Law', *Northwestern Univ. L. Rev.*, 79 (1985), 869–99 at 873), he is the master-theoretician of the movement. For others (see e.g. Schlegel, *supra* n. 139, 400), he is wholly peripheral to it.

to the first Conference, criticized the tendency of American legal theorists to reify rules and principles, to abstract them from their concrete reality. 'Legal theory', he argued, 'must avoid producing fiction by transforming its phenomena into facts: that is, its method must incorporate a critical phenomenology.'[250] For Gabel, the jurisprudence of Ronald Dworkin exemplifies this tendency towards reification. If we 'decode' or 'concretiz[e]'[251] Dworkin's rights thesis—if 'we suspend our participation in the normative assumptions that guide [his] reasoning'[252]—it becomes untenable. 'Once Dworkin's theory has been concretized, we are left with the real world. Here in the concrete we do not find a group of abstract "citizens" engaging in lively moral discourse, but rather a group of dispersed and isolated *persons* impotently linked through the cycle of production and consumption that determines their social existence.'[253] Dworkin's failure to situate law in the real world, Gabel concludes, explains why he 'cannot help us to realize in the concrete the values of dignity and mutual respect upon which he places so much emphasis.'[254]

In arguing as much, Gabel was basically developing a form of fancy realism.[255] A rather different effort to build on realist legal thought was offered at the first Conference by Karl Klare in his study of the Supreme Court's reception of the National Labour Relations (Wagner) Act of 1935. Max Lerner has remarked of the Great Depression and its aftermath that 'it made Americans judge-conscious to a degree they had never been before'.[256] To a large degree, realist jurisprudence epitomizes this. When certain so-called realists remarked on the capacity of judges to make rather than to find law, to reach decisions according to instinct rather than in accordance with a rule, they seemed basically to be reporting what they saw when the Supreme Court, paying little regard to the principle that it ought to try to preserve the constitutionality of statutes, invalidated major New Deal legislative initiatives. Yet does this describe accurately what the

[250] Gabel, *supra* n. 155, 602.

[251] Peter Gabel, review of R. Dworkin, *Taking Rights Seriously*, *Harvard L. Rev.*, 91 (1977), 302–15 at 306.

[252] Ibid. 307.

[253] Ibid. 311.

[254] Ibid. 315.

[255] This much is especially clear from the manner in which he argues that judges are no less prone to reificatory reasoning than are legal theorists. 'In precisely the same way that the natural scientist "reifies nature" by treating the physical world as an object,' he claims, 'so the judge as a "legitimation scientist" reifies the social world as if it too were an object, immutably moving according to its own internal dynamic. In his very way of knowing the social world, the judge represents it as natural, and it is precisely his intention to show, in the manner of the natural scientist, that the social world follows certain laws.' By virtue of laws which reify the social world, the process of adjudication in effect 'substitutes an harmonious abstract world for the concrete domination that characterizes . . . lived experience.' See Peter Gabel, 'Reification in Legal Reasoning', *Research in Law and Sociology*, 3 (1980), 25–51 at 32, 26.

[256] Max Lerner, 'Constitution and Court as Symbols', *Yale L. J.*, 46 (1937), 1290–319 at 1313–14.

Supreme Court was doing during this period? Some argue that it does not.[257] Klare, in focusing on the Wagner Act, attempts to demonstrate that although the Supreme Court's approach to statutory interpretation was far more complicated than many so-called realists may have believed, the basic realist assumption that New Deal statutes were politically manipulated by the Court ought not to be discounted. Intended to promote collective bargaining and workplace democracy, The Wagner Act, according to Klare, was 'perhaps the most radical piece of legislation ever enacted by the United States Congress'.[258] Yet the Supreme Court effectively deradicalized the Act by, among other things, adopting a distinctly narrow view of what constitutes legitimate union activity,[259] by 'interpret[ing] the Act as standing against the possibility of emancipatory workplace experiments',[260] and by refusing to treat the Act as an opportunity to attempt to redress the inequalities of industrial bargaining power which emerge within a free market system.[261] In deradicalizing the Act, the Court in effect protected the interests of employers and industrialists, who feared 'that collective bargaining meant the loss of control over the production process, the fatal subversion of the hallowed right of managerial freedom to run the enterprise'.[262]

For Klare, the Supreme Court's reading of the Wagner Act represents a fundamental missed opportunity in the history of American labour law. In his later writings, he has turned his attention increasingly to matters such as how collective bargaining, industrial democracy and workers' rights might be enhanced in the workplace[263]—the very matters which the Wagner Act addressed and the Supreme Court played down. His interpretation of the Act has hardly gone uncriticized.[264] But that need not concern us here. What is especially interesting about his view of the legislation is the manner in which it is informed by theory. According to Klare, his approach to the Supreme Court's interpretation of the Wagner Act is inspired primarily by the writings of Antonio Gramsci.[265] 'It is not suggested that the Supreme

[257] See e.g. David P. Currie, 'The Constitution in the Supreme Court: The New Deal, 1931–1940', *U. Chicago L. Rev.*, 54 (1987), 504–55 at 517–23.

[258] Klare, *supra* n. 155, 265.

[259] Ibid. 321.

[260] Ibid. 325.

[261] Ibid. 330.

[262] Ibid. 287.

[263] See, for example, Karl E. Klare, 'The Quest for Industrial Democracy and the Struggle Against Racism: Perspectives from Labor Law and Civil Rights Law', *Oregon L. Rev.*, 61 (1982), 157–200; 'Workplace Democracy & Market Reconstruction: An Agenda for Legal Reform', *Catholic Univ. L. Rev.*, 38 (1988), 1–68.

[264] See Matthew W. Finkin, 'Revisionism in Labor Law', *Maryland L. Rev.*, 43 (1984), 23–92; Karl Klare, 'Traditional Labor Law Scholarship and the Crisis of Collective Bargaining: A Reply to Professor Finkin', *Maryland L. Rev.*, 44 (1985), 731–840; Matthew W. Finkin, 'Does Karl Klare Protest Too Much?', *Maryland L. Rev.*, 44 (1985), 1100–10; Karl Klare, 'Lost Opportunity: Concluding Thoughts on the Finkin Critique', *Maryland L. Rev.*, 44 (1985), 1111–23.

[265] Klare, *supra* n. 155, 268 fn. 12.

Court engaged in a plot or conspiracy to defeat or co-opt the labour movement,' Klare observes,

> nor do I think that the Court can adequately be understood as an instrument of particular economic interests. I emphatically reject any such reductionism or determinism. That the Court did so much to guide the long-run development of the labour movement into domesticated channels and, indeed, to impede workers' interests is, in fact, ironic precisely because it was so often attacked by contemporaries as overly friendly to labour. Many decisions of the prewar period were intended to be, and were then understood as, tremendous victories for organized labour. But these prolabour victories contained the seeds of long-term defeats, because through them the Court, including its most liberal members, set in motion a distinctive style of legal analysis characteristic of modern American legal consciousness that came to stand, whatever the intentions of the authors, as an ineluctable barrier to worker self-activity.[266]

In other words, for Klare, the Supreme Court undermined the interests of the labour movement even when it supported them. Thus it is that we find in the literature of early critical legal studies yet another formulation of contradiction. In his paper to the first regional meeting of the Conference on Critical Legal Studies in 1978, Klare expressed this contradiction in more general terms: within a system of liberal legalism, liberty conceals repression, and therefore 'it is inevitable that the *form* of liberal legalist justice must be a negation of the human spirit even when the impulse to justice forces its way into the *content* of particular legal decisions'.[267] This is to conceive law in terms of the Gramscian philosophy of praxis. For Gramsci, 'the philosophy of praxis . . . is consciousness full of contradictions, in which the philosopher . . . not only grasps the contradictions, but posits himself as an element of the contradiction.'[268] Klare was not alone among the first critical legal scholars in turning to what Duncan Kennedy called 'fancy theory'[269] for inspiration. As we shall see in due course, Kennedy himself, besides developing an essentially Hegelian critique of individualism, offered a Gramscian diagnosis of the ills of the American law school. With varying degrees of success and sophistication, other critical legal scholars dabbled with, among other things, structuralism, phenomenology and the critical theory of the Frankfurt school.[270] Yet, in

[266] Ibid. 269–70.

[267] Karl Klare, 'Law-Making as Praxis', *Telos*, 40 (1979), 123–35 at 132.

[268] Antonio Gramsci, *Selections from the Prison Notebooks of Antonio Gramsci* (Ed. and Eng. trans. Q. Hoare and G. N. Smith, London: Lawrence and Wishart, 1971), 404–5.

[269] Kennedy, *supra* n. 225, 564.

[270] See Kennedy, ibid. 564 fn. 3; Mark Tushnet, 'Post-Realist Legal Scholarship', *Jnl. of the Society of Public Teachers of Law*, 15 (1980), 20–32 at 31; Trubek, *supra* n. 132, 597–8; and also Schlegel, *supra* n. 139, 403. ('I would hazard a guess that the reference to the Frankfurt School of Critical Marxism in the title of the organization was probably lost on many, if not most, of the participants at the first meeting.') On the relationship of critical legal

reading early critical legal studies literature, one is likely to be struck not by the actual use of theories, but by the basic desire to use theories—all sorts of theories. Never before in the history of American jurisprudence, it seems, had law professors been so entranced by the very idea of trying to theorize about law.

In the late 1970s, not every proponent of critical legal studies was dressing up his or her arguments in the exotic garb of continental social theory. Indeed, in one of the most inspired and underestimated pieces of early critical legal scholarship, presented at the first Conference, Al Katz eschewed the popular critical legal appeal to such theory and instead constructed a theory of his own.[271] Katz argues that legal consciousness—indeed, consciousness generally—is perpetually confronted by contradiction, and that human reason confronts contradiction by either accommodating or denying some form of compromise. In the context of adjudication, he claims, the manner in which contradiction is confronted is often likely to be of considerable political significance. Katz's study of contradiction in legal consciousness appeared in the second issue of the *Buffalo Law Review* in 1979, alongside Kennedy's analysis of Blackstone's *Commentaries*.[272] Both articles were described in the introduction to that issue as exemplifying a general 'critical jurisprudence' which had grown out of 'a belief that law is relative to social practice and social theory; that contemporary jurisprudence is an obfuscating apologetic; that legal analysis that gets relevant by gesturing outside law towards a pseudo-consensus morality or the technical abstraction of efficiency has already lost its own battle for autonomy and is madly searching for allies who have

studies to critical social theory and structuralist theory, see David Kennedy, 'Critical Theory, Structuralism and Contemporary Legal Scholarship', *New England L. Rev.*, 21 (1985–6), 209–89. For a superb analysis of the relationship between critical legal studies and critical social theory in particular, see Donald F. Brosnan, 'Serious But Not Critical', *Southern California L. Rev.*, 60 (1980), 259–396 esp. 271–87, 300–16, 332–43, 360–76. And on the failure of critical legal studies to develop either a definitive methodology or a distinct theoretical framework, see Frank Munger and Carroll Seron, 'Critical Legal Studies versus Critical Legal Theory: A Comment on Method', *Law & Policy*, 6 (1984), 257–97 (on how critical legal scholars have struggled unsuccessfully to develop a methodology); and Jennifer C. Jaff, 'Radical Pluralism: A Proposed Theoretical Framework for the Conference on Critical Legal Studies', *Georgetown L. J.*, 72 (1984), 1143–54 (criticizing critical legal scholars for their over-reliance on marxist theory and their underestimation of radical pluralism). Suggestions for a way forward are offered by Rosemary J. Coombe, 'Room for Manoeuver: Toward a Theory of Practice in Critical Legal Studies', *Law & Social Inquiry*, 14 (1989), 69–121.

[271] See Al Katz, 'Studies in Boundary Theory: Three Essays in Adjudication and Politics', *Buffalo L. Rev.*, 28 (1979), 383–435. Katz's theory is not entirely home-grown. He does concede that his notion of human experience is influenced by the work of Jean Piaget (see ibid. 384).

[272] Kennedy's study was apparently very much influenced by Katz's. See Kennedy, *supra* n. 239, 210.

seemingly secured their own autonomous turf; that there can be no plausible legal theory without a social theory; and that the notion of legal autonomy is a lie'.[273] By the end of the 1970s, it seems, critical legal studies had developed an identity of its own. The highlighting of tensions, contradictory impulses and indeterminacy, the belief that legal liberalism is in crisis, that it might even be transcended, the faith in just about any type of 'radical' social theory, the revivification of realist sensibilities—these are the themes which mark out the early days of critical legal studies. In the following decade, the movement would become still more thematically variegated. It would also be subjected to a good deal more criticism.

THE JURISPRUDENCE OF THE 1980s

'If the original CLS membership was hard to generalize about,' Robert Gordon wrote in 1988, 'the expanded new one is so exotically varied and internally divided as to defy characterization almost entirely.'[274] It is not uncommon to find commentators suggesting that the first generation of critical legal scholars was superseded by a second generation which both built upon and undermined the ideas of their mentors.[275] The image of old

[273] John Henry Schlegel, 'Introduction', *Buffalo L. Rev.*, 28 (1979), 203. According to Schlegel, all of this passage apart from the final clause was in fact written by Al Katz. John Henry Schlegel, note to author, n.d.

[274] Robert W. Gordon, 'Law and Ideology', *Tikkun*, 3 (1988), 14–18, 83–6 at 15. The Canadian philosopher, Jerome Bickenbach, appeared to overstate the case when he observed in 1984 that '[t]he sheer variety [of themes] is daunting: there are critical and polemical CLS pieces, filled with blistering attacks and purposefully incautious language, catch-words and slogans, guaranteed to entertain, if not edify. There are calls to arms—praxis pieces. There are dissections of the "grand theories" of American Constitutional law and liberal theory. And there are also historically careful and factually dense works of patient scholarship, yielding conclusions about the character of the ideology underlying the law. There are also Marxist, Austro-Marxist, Neo-Marxist, Horkheimerian, Weberian, Marcusian, Gramscian, Habermasian, Gadamerian, Durkheimian, Heideggerian, Kuhnian, Foucaultian, Sartrian, Althusserian, Levi-Straussian, Husserlian, Merleau-Pontean and (most frequently) Ungerian inspired analyses of law. There are technical pieces, and there is whimsy. Critiques of legal education, of lawyers, of legal academics abound. There are articles which employ structuralist, historicist, phenomenological, transformational, ethno-anthropological, psycho-analytical, sociological, feminist, contextualist, destabilizational, and other, innominate analyses. Some pieces are examples of liberal "trashing"; others are examples of chutzpa. (So far, to my knowledge, the current Derridean fad has not been picked up; but there can be little doubt that the law must soon face the fate of being "deconstructed".)' Jerome E. Bickenbach, 'CLS and CLS-ers', *Queen's L.J.*, 2 (1984), 263–72 at 266–8. As a description of critical legal studies, this is fairly slapdash. It is ironic, nevertheless, that the one thing which Bickenbach left out of his picture, Derridean deconstruction, was, by 1984, already finding its way into critical legal studies literature. See, for example, David Fraser, 'Truth and Hierarchy: Will the Circle Be Unbroken?', *Buffalo L. Rev.*, 33 (1984), 729–75 (deconstructive critique of liberal theories of constitutional adjudication).

[275] See, for example, Duncan Kennedy, 'Psycho-Social CLS: A Comment Upon the Cardozo Symposium', *Cardozo L. Rev.*, 6 (1985), 1013–31 at 1016–19.

timers making way for youngsters is by no means inappropriate when discussing the intellectual history of critical legal studies. Perhaps inevitably, many of those involved with the movement in the early years did indeed appear to become noticeably less passionate about it as time passed; and with this decline in interest among many of the early protagonists, new figures and themes began to dominate the critical legal scene. I do not believe, however, that the history of critical legal studies is best explained in terms of generational progression. Critical legal studies was not marked by a changing of the guard: the second generation did not suddenly take the place of the first. Rather, the first generation lingered—and to some degree continues still to linger—while the second generation tried to take the movement down a variety of paths.

Although critical legal studies grew out of the New Left-inspired academic disaffection of the 1970s, it will probably be remembered as the jurisprudence of the 1980s. By the end of that decade, critical legal studies seemed rather moribund. American academic lawyers—nothing if not slaves to faddishness and product differentiation—had developed new platforms for radical scholarship: in particular, feminism, post-modernism and critical race theory. These new tendencies had been emerging throughout the late 1970s and 1980s, and to some degree the critical legal studies movement had managed to co-opt them.[276] As these tendencies became ever more identifiable in their own right, however, their relationship to critical legal studies became increasingly fragile. By the beginning of the 1990s, one critical legal scholar, who only five years earlier had been introducing the subject to newcomers, was writing its history.[277] Critical legal studies was already being consigned to the past tense.

For a period, however, it blossomed.[278] Throughout the best part of the

[276] This is especially clear from the history of the Conference on Critical Legal Studies. The ninth annual conference, which took place at Pine Manor College, Massachusetts, in May–June 1985, was billed as a 'CLS Feminist Conference' and was organized by the 'critical feminists' within the critical legal studies movement. One of the purposes of this particular conference, according to the organizers, was to explore '[t]he links between feminism, critical legal studies and people of colour'. Martha Minow, Mary Joe Frug, Judi Greenberg and Clare Dalton, letter to Dear Critical Community, 10 October 1984 (on file with author: copy supplied by Professor J. H. Schlegel). The tenth national conference, held at the University of California at Los Angeles Law School, was titled 'The Sounds of Silence: Racism and the Law'. Since the second national conference in 1978, panel discussions on race, gender and class have been a regular feature at critical legal studies meetings. For an indication of the types of problems which critical legal scholars have been forced to confront by engaging in such discussions, see Joseph William Singer, 'Should Lawyers Care About Philosophy?', *Duke L.J.*, [1989], 1752–83 at 1773–6.

[277] See the articles by Tushnet, *supra* n. 14.

[278] For an indication of the degree to which it blossomed, see Duncan Kennedy and Karl Klare, 'A Bibliography of Critical Legal Studies', *Yale L.J.*, 94 (1984), 461–90, though it should be noted that Kennedy and Klare, in categorizing work as critical legal scholarship, cast their net extremely wide.

1980s, it contrasted starkly with the politics and values of the Reagan administration. While Chicago lawyer-economists were, at Reagan's behest, finding their way into the highest courts in the land, the critical legal studies movement was being excoriated on a variety of fronts. Journalists and law professors alike took their stand against 'the crits'. For the movement, things could hardly have worked out better. Academics in the United States seem perpetually to be troubled by the relationship between American individual and society. The pressures and frustrations of modern American life—so the argument goes—produce a consciousness which is somehow corrupted or despiritualized. Studies purporting to demonstrate as much constitute something of a tradition in American social theory.[279] In focusing on the tensions inherent in modern liberal consciousness and legal thought, critical legal scholars were basically bringing this tradition—and with it, a little drama—into the law schools. If only for a short time, critical legal studies represented the spectre of the radical left which periodically re-emerges to haunt the American psyche. Its representatives were certainly being attacked. But they were being attacked because they were ruffling feathers; because they were claiming that the problems inherent in American law were the consequence of an impoverished American consciousness. Critical legal studies was more than just a critique of the legal system.

Ultimately, the critical legal studies movement was to a large degree debilitated by external criticism. To an equally large degree, however, it was strengthened by it, in so far as much of this criticism served simply to confirm that the movement caused considerable consternation. If anything, internal tensions rather than external criticisms would prove to be the ultimate undoing of critical legal studies. But this is to risk jumping too far ahead. There are other matters to address before turning to the question of how critical legal studies fell on its own sword. First of all, it is important to consider just how critical legal studies evolved in the 1980s. During the first half of that decade, critical legal scholarship broadened out in two distinct

[279] Examples of studies which seem to fit within this tradition are David Reisman (with Nathan Glazer and Reuel Denney), *The Lonely Crowd: A Study of the Changing American Character* (abridged edn. New Haven, Conn.: Yale University Press, 1961; orig. publ. 1950); Philip E. Slater, *The Pursuit of Loneliness: American Culture at the Breaking Point* (Boston: Beacon Press, 1970); Christopher Lasch, *The Culture of Narcissism: American Life in an Age of Diminishing Expectations* (New York: Norton, 1979); Marshall Berman, *All That Is Solid Melts Into Air: The Experience of Modernity* (London: Verso, 1983; orig. publ. 1982); Robert N. Bellah *et al.*, *Habits of the Heart: Individualism and Commitment in American Life* (New York: Harper & Row, 1985). There are also what might be termed emigré studies—the works of academics whose views of modern western consciousness were very clearly influenced by what they found on migrating to the United States. See e.g. Marcuse, *supra* n. 45, *passim*; Theodor Adorno and Max Horkheimer, *Dialectic of Enlightenment* (Eng. trans. J. Cumming, London: Verso, 1979; orig. publ. 1944), 120–67.

ways. Certain proponents of critical legal studies attempted to elaborate some of the ideas which had originally been put forward in the 1970s. Yet it is clear also that the elaboration of those ideas led to the development of some new critical legal themes. In the 1970s, critical legal theorists reflected upon the poverty of liberal legalism, doctrinal indeterminacy and the fundamental contradiction; by the 1980s, they were discussing, among other things, the inadequacy of rights discourse and the viability of nihilism as the basis for a legal theory. Critical legal studies in the 1980s was something different from critical legal studies in the 1970s.

Whereas, in the 1970s, critical legal scholars were concerned largely with developing certain basic realist insights, by the 1980s they were concerned more with consolidating the efforts to develop those insights. Critical legal studies was building upon critical legal studies building upon legal realism. Like realism, it represented, in very crude terms, a reaction against formalist legal thinking.[280] But, as Roberto Unger recognized in his address to the sixth annual Conference in 1982, formalism had come a long way since the realist era.[281] In a sense, the formalism against which the so-called realists had reacted had never disappeared. In their use of the case method of instruction, the laws schools were stil teaching law as science rather than as politics.[282] 'Classical contract theory'[283] not only endured in the courts but, with the advent of modern law and economics, it became a highly valued and respected academic enterprise. By the 1980s, however, the consequences of allowing American law to develop in accordance with the dictates of formalism were much clearer than they had been fifty years earlier. For example, the formalist conception of contractual relations—entailing, as it does, the implicit rejection of the realist argument that inequalities of bargaining power preclude real freedom of contract[284]—demanded that regulation be regarded as a phenomenon which exists almost exclusively in the public sphere.[285] Equally importantly, this conception of contractual relations made its mark on legal thinking not only in the field of contract law as conventionally understood, but also in other spheres of private life. On the basis of classical contract theory, Unger argues, the family came to be conceived as an ideal private community governed by the principle of free negotiation.[286] As legal formalism would have it, since this principle ensures that the family unit is

[280] See Mark V. Tushnet, 'Perspectives on Critical Legal Studies: Introduction', *George Washington L. Rev.*, 52 (1984), 239–42.

[281] See Unger, *supra* n. 249, 570–6. For a critique of Unger's analysis of formalism, see J. M. Finnis, 'On "The Critical Legal Studies Movement" ', in John Eekelaar and John Bell (eds.), *Oxford Essays in Jurisprudence* (3rd series, Oxford: Clarendon Press, 1987), 145–65.

[282] Unger, *supra* n. 249, 668–9.

[283] Ibid. 618.

[284] See ibid. 618–33.

[285] See ibid. 617.

[286] See ibid. 623–5.

able to regulate itself, public intervention into this private domain ought to be kept to a minimum.[287]

In the time which had passed between the demise of legal realism and the emergence of critical legal studies, not only had the implications of formalist legal thought become clearer, but the actual import of the term 'formalism' had changed significantly. Langdellianism in the law schools and Social Darwinism in the courts, I argued in Chapter 1, epitomize legal formalism in the late nineteenth and early twentieth centuries. Realism, I suggested in Chapter 2, represents a fairly hesitant reaction against this conception of formalism. But this only takes us up to the 1930s. Since then, Unger argues, two distinct traditions have emerged in American jurisprudence which constitute 'attempt[s] to deflect the critique of formalism'.[288] The first of these—neo-classical law and economics—reinforces the idea that the law, rather than embody distributivist policies, ought to respect the natural inequalities of wealth and bargaining power which emerge owing to the fact that citizens exploit their formal equality of bargaining rights with differing degrees of success. The second tradition, process jurisprudence, constitutes not an attempt to reinforce an already established formalist perspective, but a totally new formalist perspective. Regarding post-realist efforts to revive formalism, Unger argues that '[t]he single most striking example in twentieth century American legal thought has been the development of a theory of legal process, institutional roles, and purposive legal reasoning as a response to legal realism.'[289] Not only is this new style of formalism deductive in nature—premissed, as it is, on the notion that judges possess the capacity to discover, elaborate and apply principles of adjudication which will yield formally correct solutions to disputes—but it is also institutional, that is, it entails the presupposition that the legal process is comprised of various discrete organs, each with its own formally distinct domain of competence. Together, Unger concludes, law and economics and process jurisprudence have carried the torch for the formalist tradition in the post-realist era.

Whether, in fact, one agrees with Unger's interpretation of the history of post-realist jurisprudence is not especially significant. To my mind—as I hope to have made clear in Chapters 4 and 5—it is a mistake to regard process jurisprudence and law and economics as 'formalist' responses to legal realism. Indeed, I have tried to demonstrate generally that the history of modern American jurisprudence does not resemble a boxing contest—that it is not simply the trading of punches between formalists and anti-formalists. What ought to be stressed, however, is the fact that

[287] For a development of the critical legal perspective on this matter, see Frances E. Olsen, 'The Myth of State Intervention in the Family', *U. Michigan Jnl. of Law Reform*, 18 (1985), 835–64.

[288] Unger, *supra* n. 249, 576.

[289] Ibid.

Unger's account reflects the views and assumptions of critical legal scholars in general. Unger insists that the efforts at reinvigorating formalism basically failed to convince. 'In and outside the law schools, most jurists looked with indifference and even disdain upon the legal theorists who, like the rights and principles or the law and economics schools, had volunteered to salvage and recreate the formalist and objectivist view.'[290] Despite the failure of formalism in the post-realist era, however, there existed no legal world-view to succeed it. Law professors generally resembled 'a priesthood that had lost their faith and kept their jobs. They stood in tedious embarrassment before cold altars.'[291] But critical legal studies 'turned away from those altars'[292] in its effort to discover a new world-view. It offered hope for the future.

In the 1980s, Unger's conception of critical legal studies—as the revolt against the revolt against the revolt against formalism—was affirmed in the relevant literature in a variety of ways. Critical legal scholars, as we saw in the introduction to the previous chapter, opposed the neo-classical tradition in law and economics. With equal vigour, they rejected the process tradition in American jurisprudence, deflating the myth of neutrality in constitutional adjudication.[293] They endorsed activism and denounced passivity in judicial decision-making.[294] They reiterated and extended the Haleian lesson (see Chapter 2) that classical contract doctrine is premissed on a notion of pure freedom which could never

[290] Ibid. 674. [291] Ibid. 675. [292] Ibid.

[293] See Mark Tushnet, *Red, White, and Blue: A Critical Analysis of Constitutional Law* (Cambridge, Mass.: Harvard University Press, 1988), 46–57; 'Truth, Justice, and the American Way: An Interpretation of Public Law Scholarship in the Seventies', *Texas L. Rev.*, 57 (1979), 1307–59; 'Darkness on the Edge of Town: The Contributions of John Hart Ely to Constitutional Theory', *Yale L. J.*, 89 (1980), 1037–62; 'Following the Rules Laid Down—A Critique of Interpretivism and Neutral Principles', *Harvard L. Rev.*, 96 (1983), 781–827; 'Legal Realism, Structural Review, and Prophecy', *U. Dayton L. Rev.*, 8 (1983), 809–31; Parker, *supra* n. 12, *passim*; Gary Peller, 'In Defense of Federal Habeas Corpus Relitigation', *Harvard Civil Rights-Civil Liberties L. Rev.*, 16 (1981), 579–691; 'The Politics of Reconstruction', *Harvard L. Rev.*, 98 (1985), 863–81; 'Neutral Principles in the 1950s', *U. Michigan Jnl. of Law Reform*, 21 (1988), 561–622; David Fraser, 'Laverne and Shirley Meet the Constitution', *Osgoode Hall L. J.*, 22 (1984), 783–7; *supra* n. 274, *passim*; Paul Brest, 'Who Decides?', *Southern California L. Rev.*, 58 (1985), 661–71; and Alan Freeman, 'Introduction', *Buffalo L. Rev.*, 36 (1987), 211–15.

[294] See, in particular, Joseph William Singer, 'Catcher in the Rye Jurisprudence', *Rutgers L. Rev.*, 35 (1983), 275–84. I argued in Chapter 4 that to embrace judicial activism is to accept a Faustian pact of sorts: that is, while activism may serve society well when the politics of the judiciary meet with majority approval, it may serve us less favourably when the political outlook of courts changes. Singer takes no account of this. His failure to do so, however, must not be attributed to all critical legal scholars. Others have recognized the Faustian pact. See, for example, Morton J. Horwitz, 'The Jurisprudence of *Brown* and the Dilemmas of Liberalism', *Harvard Civil Rights-Civil Liberties L. Rev.*, 14 (1979), 599–613 at 602.

exist.[295] They argued that, owing to inequalities of bargaining power, a system of free exchange of necessity imposes its own regulatory regime.[296] And they argued that, in consequence, the depiction by liberal judges and legal theorists of the private domain as a realm of free choice and the public domain as a forum of constraint can be seen to entail a wholly fictitious distinction between public and private in American law and life.[297]

Some proponents of critical legal studies have endeavoured to demonstrate that the process tradition and the classical/neo-classical tradition in modern American jurisprudence are all of a piece—that both may be conceived as efforts to de-politicize legal doctrine.[298] This argument, while it demands that both of these traditions be depicted in ways which their adherents would find misleading, is nevertheless fundamental for the purpose of understanding the peculiarly 'critical' element in critical legal studies. Depending on which particular critical legal scholar is developing it, the argument derives from a mixture of at least three themes. First of all, it rests on the assumption that process theorists are intent on de-politicizing legal doctrine by emphasizing reasoned elaboration as a method according to which judges might come to discover and apply apolitical principles of adjudication.[299] Secondly, it is based on the claim that the classical theory of exchange facilitates the de-politicization of doctrine by glossing over disparities of bargaining power and emphasizing instead the neutrality of the law in relation to bargaining rights. Thirdly, it entails the belief that neo-classical lawyer–economists in effect de-politicize doctrine when they purport to offer positive observations rather than normative assertions in pointing to the efficiency of the common law.

295 See, for example, Gerald E. Frug, 'The City as a Legal Concept', *Harvard L. Rev.*, 93 (1980), 1057–154 at 1134–5; Jay M. Feinman, 'Critical Approaches to Contract Law', *UCLA L. Rev.*, 30 (1983), 829–60; Gary Peller, 'The Classical Theory of Law', *Cornell L. Rev.*, 73 (1988), 300–309.

296 See, for example, Kenneth M. Casebeer, 'Teaching an Old Dog New Tricks: *Coppage* v. *Kansas* and At-will Employment Revisited', *Cardozo L. Rev.*, 6 (1985), 765–97; Carol Dalton, 'An Essay in the Deconstruction of Contract Doctrine', *Yale L.J.*, 94 (1985), 997–1114 esp. at 999–1039.

297 See, for example, Morton J. Horwitz, 'The History of the Public/Private Distinction', *U. Pennsylvania L. Rev.*, 130 (1982), 1423–28; Duncan Kennedy, 'Stages of Decline of the Public/Private Distinction', *U. Pennsylvania L. Rev.*, 130 (1982), 1349–57; Karl E. Klare, 'The Public/Private Distinction in Labor Law', *U. Pennsylvania L. Rev.*, 130 (1982), 1358–422; Kenneth M. Casebeer, 'Toward a Critical Jurisprudence—A First Step by Way of the Public-Private Distinction in Constitutional Law', *U. Miami L. Rev.*, 37 (1983), 379–431; Alan Freeman and Elizabeth Mensch, 'The Public-Private Distinction in American Law and Life', *Buffalo L. Rev.*, 36 (1987), 237–57.

298 For the best example, see Gary Peller, 'The Metaphysics of American Law', *California L. Rev.*, 73 (1985), 1151–290.

299 I have argued elsewhere in relation to critical legal studies that this assumption is too simplistic. See Neil Duxbury, 'The Theory and History of American Law and Politics', *Oxford Jnl. Leg. Studs.*, 13 (1993), 249–70.

Such strategies, critical legal scholars argue, enable liberal legal theorists to present law as somehow neutral and rational. The basic critical task of critical legal studies is to undermine this image of law, to follow the example of realism in casting doubt on conventional jurisprudential wisdom. For critical legal scholars in the 1980s, this entailed many things: it meant emphasizing inconsistencies and conflicts among legal principles;[300] it meant highlighting the fact that, owing to such inconsistencies and conflicts, legal doctrines can never provide totally satisfactory explanations of legal outcomes;[301] it meant demonstrating the impossibility of neutral standpoints;[302] it meant focusing on the manner in which law legitimates existing distributions of wealth and privilege.[303] In short, it entailed the demystification of the legal process.[304] Reasoned elaboration—that grand old phrase of the 1950s—was out of favour.[305] 'Trashing'—a word which evokes memories of New Left radicalism in the 1960s[306]—became, for a short while, the new jurisprudential vogue.[307]

Trashing—sticking pins in the inflated rhetoric of liberal legal theory—was clearly fun to do, and is often enjoyable to read.[308] But where was it supposed to lead? More generally, was there any definite objective or sense of direction behind the critical legal project? By the beginning of the 1980s, there were enough American law professors engaging in critical

[300] See, for example, Gerald E. Frug, 'A Critical Theory of Law', *Leg. Educ. Rev.*, 1 (1989), 43–57 at 52–5; and also, for an excellent analysis of the critical legal perspective in this context, Andrew Altman, 'Legal Realism, Critical Legal Studies, and Dworkin', *Philosophy and Public Affairs*, 15 (1986), 205–35 at 216–34.

[301] See Yablon, *supra* n. 16, *passim*.

[302] See Arthur J. Jacobson, 'Modern American Jurisprudence and the Problem of Power', *Cardozo L. Rev.*, 6 (1985), 713–37 at 732–5.

[303] See Wythe Holt, 'Tilt', *George Washington L. Rev.*, 51 (1984), 280–8; 'Labour Conspiracy Cases in the United States, 1805–1842: Bias and Legitimation in Common Law Adjudication', *Osgoode Hall L.J.*, 22 (1984), 591–663.

[304] See Alan D. Freeman, 'Truth and Mystification in Legal Scholarship', *Yale L.J.*, 90 (1981), 1229–37.

[305] See Kelman, *supra* n. 149, 200. ('The Hart and Sacks model of "reasoned elaboration" of established rules, the process of deciding cases *under* the rules, seems hopeless as a description of an apolitical method.')

[306] On 'trashing' as a 1960s term, see White. *supra* n. 16, 659; Diggins, *supra* n. 35, 264; Richard A. Posner, 'A Manifesto for Legal Renegades', *Wall Street Journal*, 27 January 1988, 23.

[307] According to Robert Gordon, '[t]his sixties-evoking phrase covers a big miscellaneous grab bag of techniques designed to dent the complacent message embedded in legal discourse, that the system has figured out the arrangements that are going to make social life as free, just, and efficient as it can ever be. The trasher tries to show how discourse has turned contingency into necessity and to reveal the repressed alternative interpretations that are perfectly consistent with the discourse's stated premises.' Gordon, *supra* n. 274, 17. See generally Mark Kelman, 'Trashing', *Stanford L. Rev.*, 36 (1984), 293–348.

[308] See, for example, Alan David Freeman and John Henry Schlegel, 'Sex, Power and Silliness: An Essay on Ackerman's *Reconstructing American Law*', *Cardozo L. Rev.*, 6 (1985), 847–64; Allan C. Hutchinson, *Dwelling on the Threshold: Critical Essays on Modern Legal Thought* (Toronto: Carswell, 1988).

legal studies—and, indeed, engaging in more or less the same style of critical legal studies—to create the impression that there was a fair degree of intellectual unity within the movement. Out of the third Conference on Critical Legal Studies, held in Madison in 1979, came a collection of essays, *The Politics of Law*, a joint project of the Conference and the National Lawyers Guild.[309] Many of the essays in *The Politics of Law* demonstrate the various ways in which critical legal scholars stand opposed to liberal legal thought. According to one commentator, the book 'comes close to being a manifesto for the critical legal studies movement'.[310] Yet, by the early 1980s, it was becoming clear that certain of those affiliated with the movement did not identify with the style of scholarship to be found in *The Politics of Law*. Reviewing the book in 1983, Clare Dalton detected in it a fundamental tension between 'reformism' and 'irrationalism'.[311] Generally, she argued, critical legal theorists were attempting, and failing, to be both irrationalists and reformists: while they dismantled the rationalist premisses of liberal legal thought, they appeared generally to have nothing—apart from the occasional Ungerian post-liberal vision—to put in the place of that thought.[312] Certain critical legal scholars reacted similarly when Mark Kelman—the primary advocate of 'trashing'—produced a 'guide' to critical legal studies.[313] By the middle of the 1980s, it had become clear that some law professors associated with critical legal studies were questioning the direction of the movement.

Part of the problem was internal politics. Newer recruits to the movement felt frustrated by the fact that the Conference was still largely in

[309] David Kairys (ed.), *The Politics of Law: A Progressive Critique* (New York: Pantheon, 1982).

[310] Hunt, *supra* n. 247, 2.

[311] Clare Dalton, review of Kairys, *supra* n. 309, *Harvard Women's L.J.*, 6 (1983), 229–48 at 230.

[312] Ibid. 242–7. Dalton was not the only critical legal scholar to profess disappointment with the Kairys collection. See also Sanford Levinson, 'Escaping Liberalism: Easier Said Than Done?', *Harvard L. Rev.*, 96 (1983), 1466–88.

[313] Kelman, *supra* n. 149. See David Gray Carlson, 'Contradiction and Critical Legal Studies', *Cardozo L. Rev.*, 10 (1989), 1833–54; John Stick, 'Charting the Development of Critical Legal Studies', *Columbia L. Rev.*, 88 (1988), 407–32; and cf. Fischl, *supra* n. 23, 781–2. Outside of critical legal studies, consider Eugene D. Genovese, 'Critical Legal Studies as Radical Politics and World View', *Yale Jnl. of Law & the Humanities*, 3 (1991), 131–56; Neil MacCormick, 'Reconstruction after Deconstruction: A Response to CLS', *Oxford Jnl. Leg. Studs.*, 10 (1990), 539–58; Richard L. Barnes, 'Searching for Answers Without the Questions', *South Dakota L. Rev.*, 34 (1989), 220–5 esp. 221. ('Kelman's first failure . . . is his inability to make a positive case for CLS by showing that CLS itself posits something other than destruction of the current legal order.'); Daniel Farber, 'Down By Law', *The New Republic*, 4 and 11 January 1988, 36–40 at 39–40. ('The real message of Kelman's book is finally one of despair. . . . All Kelman can recommend is a shot in the dark.'); William B. Lindsey, 'Well-Plowed Fields', *National Review*, 29 April 1988, 47–8 at 48 (accusing Kelman of producing 'vague and sentimental socialist mush').

the hands of many of those who had set the ball rolling in the 1970s.[314] Commenting, in 1985, on the composition of the movement, Duncan Kennedy noted 'the urge of the second generation to cut the first generation down to size, to place its exaggerated pretensions in perspective, to impress with dazzling new talent and dazzling new sources'.[315] While a fair number of those who turned to the movement in the 1980s produced a stream of exemplary and original critical legal scholarship, many—though by no means all—of those who had been there since the early days retained something of a grip on the movement even while they became intellectually less central to it. Critical legal studies, it seemed, had provided jobs for the boys.

Internal politics alone, however, does not account for the sense of disquiet which had emerged. In the literature of critical legal studies, a question frequently resurfaces: the question of what lies in the future.[316] By the middle of the 1980s, representatives of the movement were suggesting that its peculiarly critical thrust was encapsulated in the critical legal buzz-words of the period—words such as delegitimation, demystification and trashing. But these words simply brought into sharp relief the question of what the future might hold for the movement. After all, once one has carried out the exercise of delegitimation, demystification or trashing, where is one to go?[317]

According to one critical legal scholar, this question—the question of what is to be done once liberal legalism has been dismantled—would ultimately debilitate the movement.[318] In the mid-1980s, however, most critical legal scholars were not about to be overwhelmed by such a question. Indeed, around this period, many of those who were both central to and on the margins of the movement were inspired rather than intimidated by the question. For it was a question which forced them to develop their ideas, to demonstrate that the theory and the agenda behind critical legal studies involved, or ought to involve, more than a mere revival and refinement of realist sentiments. Demonstrating as much demanded not only the further elaboration of key critical legal themes but also, more importantly, the development of certain new ones.

[314] This much is clear from a memo drafted by Toni Pickard, 'To: All Interested Members of the Conference, About: Excavating the Foundations of the Organizing Group Event That was Felt by me as a Personal Crisis and was Being Generally Referred to as a Crisis for the Organization,' which accompanied the advertisement for the 1984 Conference Summer Camp (on file with author: copy supplied by Professor J. H. Schlegel).

[315] Kennedy, *supra* n. 275, 1016.

[316] See, for example, Allan C. Hutchinson, 'Introduction', in A. C. Hutchinson (ed.), *Critical Legal Studies* (Totowa, NJ: Rowman & Littlefield, 1989), 1–11 at 9–10.

[317] 'The new genre of trashing', Duncan Kennedy noted in 1985, 'may be as dismissive and snide as its liberal counterpart.' Kennedy, *supra* n. 275, 1016.

[318] See Fischl, *supra* n. 23, *passim* and esp. 819; also his 'Privileged Positions', *Law and Social Inquiry*, 17 (1992), 831–8.

So, what did this entail? How were key themes elaborated? And what sorts of new themes found their way into the critical legal literature? Perhaps inevitably, there are no simple answers to these questions. The fact is that, in the mid-1980s, critical legal studies developed in a variety of directions. Certain of these developments were not novel. For example, since its very inception, critical legal studies had been an historical enterprise. Some of the classic illustrations of early crtical legal scholarship—Kennedy's analysis of Blackstone's *Commentaries*, for example, or Klare's study of the reception of the Wagner Act—are basically attempts to write legal history in a critical vein. By the mid-1980s—though, in truth, the seeds of this development had been sown at the outset of the decade[319]—one finds proponents of and detractors from critical legal studies reflecting increasingly on the question of what it means to produce critical legal history, and what effect such history might have on legal scholarship generally.[320] A development more distinctive to the mid-1980s and beyond is the effort by certain critical legal scholars to outline the implications of critical legal studies in the classroom. Ironically, Langdell's great innovation, the case method, provided a perfect springboard for critical legal teaching. While critical legal scholars often struggled to demonstrate the reality and the implications of legal indeterminacy in the law journals, in the classroom, it seems, their arguments became more tangible. Comparisons of cases would often reveal to students the manner in which principles stand opposed to one another; and the Socratic style of teaching proved, for some critical legal scholars, to be a useful means by which to demonstrate how every effort at legal reasoning has a flip-side.[321] '[I]n the

[319] See, in particular, Robert W. Gordon, 'Historicism in Legal Scholarship', *Yale L.J.*, 90 (1981), 1017–56 (on the potential of legal history to demonstrate the contingency of legal principles and thereby subvert 'mainstream' legal scholarship); also Morton J. Horwitz, 'The Historical Contingency of the Role of History', *Yale L.J.*, 90 (1981), 1057–9.

[320] See, in particular, Robert W. Gordon, *supra* n. 16, *passim*; also Kelman, *supra* n. 149, 213–41; Morton J. Horwitz, 'Progressive Legal Historiography', *Oregon L. Rev.*, 63 (1984), 679–87; 'Republicanism and Liberalism in American Constitutional Thought', *William & Mary L. Rev.*, 29 (1987), 57–74. Gordon's work—which, in my opinion, is by far the most important in this context—has met with considerable criticism, not least because it is felt by critics that, in setting critical legal history against mainstream legal scholarship, he in effect mounts a figure of straw as his object of critique. See, in particular, Joan C. Williams, 'Culture and Certainty: Legal History and the Reconstructive Project', *Virginia L. Rev.*, 76 (1990), 713–46. For further criticisms of Gordon's work, see Stephen Diamond, 'The Not-So-Critical Legal Studies', *Cardozo L. Rev.*, 6 (1985), 693–711; Stanley Fish, 'Anti-Professionalism', *Cardozo L. Rev.*, 7 (1986), 645–77 at 656–8.

[321] See, generally, James Boyle, 'The Anatomy of a Torts Class', *American Univ. L. Rev.*, 34 (1985), 1003–63. This should not, of course, be read as a claim that all critical legal scholars are good law teachers. It is simply to suggest that critical legal ideas and arguments may be more amenable to classroom exposition than might commonly be assumed. On critical legal scholars as bad law teachers, see Mark Tushnet, 'On Being a Bad Law Teacher', in *Lizard: Newsletter of the Conference on Critical Legal Studies*, May 1987, 22–6; Richard D. Kahlenberg, *Broken Contract: A Memoir of the Harvard Law School* (Boston: Faber & Faber, 1992), 46.

end,' Robert Gordon argues, 'what teaching CLS is all about, or ideally ought to be about, is empowering students to read multiple interpretations, multiple alternative institutions and practices, multiple possible directions, out of a legal order that is too often presented as complacently or tragically frozen into a unitary system and course of development. It is about teaching students to recognize the larger political visions buried in the most technical arguments of doctrine and policy, and to debate these visions openly.'[322] In short, '[c]ritical teaching ought to embody a transformative pedagogy as well as convey a transformative message.'[323]

This idea—that critical legal studies is, in essence, a transformative jurisprudence—was also developed further in the mid-1980s. We saw earlier that it was through the work of Roberto Unger in the late 1970s that the idea first made its mark on critical legal scholarship. Unger, I suggested, invested critical legal studies with a vision—a vision, that is, of a post-liberal society and its legal structure. On completing his meditation on the critical legal studies movement, he set about elaborating what he had so far only sketched: the values and the institutional arrangements of a society which has outgrown liberalism. His first objective was to try to establish that human beings actually possess the capacity to outgrow liberalism. Expanding upon what Kennedy had called the fundamental contradiction in human consciousness, Unger argued in *Passion*, published in 1984, that, within liberal societies, people fear being trusting and yet want be trusted. This simultaneous fear of and desire for trust ensures that individuals are thoroughly incapable of determining satisfactorily to what degree they ought to live detached from or attached to others. Decisions to reach out to or to shun others are always underscored by risk. We can never be sure that we have made the right choice: constantly we mediate 'between the disempowerment of isolation and the disempowerment of submission'.[324] But this uncertainty, Unger argues, ought not to cause us to despair. Rather, we ought to see it for what it is: that is, as an opportunity to experiment with individuality and forms of association. Recognition of the precariousness of human life ought to alert us to the question of what we might become, of how we might 'reinvent ourselves'.[325]

The readiness to experiment with different kinds of encounters, and with their distinctive styles of vulnerability, is akin to central features of the practical, transformative political imagination: its refusal to take any established set of

[322] Gordon, *supra* n. 69, 83; see also Grace Blumberg and Peter Gabel, 'Special Feature: Teaching Techniques', in *Lizard: Newsletter of the Conference on Critical Legal Studies*, November 1989, 86–95.

[323] Jay M. Feinman, 'The Failure of Legal Education and the Promise of Critical Legal Studies', *Cardozo L. Rev.*, 6 (1985), 739–64 at 762.

[324] Roberto Mangabeira Unger, *Passion: An Essay on Personality* (New York: Free Press, 1984), 14.

[325] Ibid. vii.

alliances and antagonisms for granted, its effort to mobilize people in ways that are not predefined by the existing social order, and its capacity to make these essays in mobilization the means for building new varieties of collaboration and community in the practical affairs of society.[326]

For Unger, 'all varieties of self-reflection and communication must come to be seen as having an uncertain, troubled relation to received conventions and established arrangements.'[327] If we fail to challenge that which is conventional and established, '[n]ot only do we fail to make many discoveries about ourselves and about the world . . . but we may find ourselves increasingly reduced to an unconscious servitude.'[328] Only by exploring our collective vulnerability might we come 'to develop practical collective capabilities',[329] to discover '[d]ifferent schemes of human association'[330] and to realize 'that one way or another we do care'.[331] If we refuse to confront this vulnerability, 'we lose our hold upon reality. Our self-satisfied common sense becomes a hallucination, as we congratulate one another upon its mendacious transparency and fixity.'[332]

Stirring words. As in his writings of the late 1970s, however, Unger does little more than propose that no particular form of human association or social organization is necessary or inescapable. For all the portentuous prose, he simply suggests that we have the capacity, and indeed perhaps ought, to re-make ourselves and our societies. But why ought we? That is, why risk surrendering what we have for some hazy vision of a different world? In his most elaborate work so far, the completed volumes of an ongoing project entitled *Politics*,[333] Unger attempts yet again to refine his argument. *Politics*, he begins, embodies 'a programme for social reconstruction'.[334]

The programmatic arguments of *Politics* reinterpret and generalize the liberal and leftist endeavour by freeing it from unjustifiably restrictive assumptions about the practical institutional forms that representative democracies, market economies, and the social control of economic accumulation can and should assume. At the heart of this vision of alternative institutional forms lies an appreciation of the link between the extent to which an institutional and imaginative framework of social life makes itself available to revision in the midst of ordinary social activity and the

[326] Ibid. 110. [327] Ibid. 68. [328] Ibid. [329] Ibid. 265.
[330] Ibid. 256. [331] Ibid. 3. [332] Ibid. 70.
[333] Unger, *supra* n. 201; *False Necessity: Anti-Necessitarian Social Theory in the Service of Radical Democracy. Part I of* Politics, *a Work in Constructive Social Theory* (Cambridge: Cambridge University Press, 1987); *Plasticity into Power: Comparative-Historical Studies on the Institutional Conditions of Economic and Military Success. Variations on Themes of* Politics, *a Work in Constructive Social Theory* (Cambridge: Cambridge University Press, 1987). The project is not yet complete. Unger concludes Part I of the project with the observation that certain of the ideas sketched in that volume are 'to be developed more fully in a future Part II of *Politics*'. Unger, *False Necessity*, 630 n.
[334] Unger, *supra* n. 201, 6.

success with which this framework undermines rigid social roles and hierarchies. *Politics* argues for a particular way of reorganizing governments and economies that promises to realize more effectively both aspects of the radical commitment: the subversion of social division and hierarchy and the assertion of will over custom and compulsion.[335]

Politics, in other words, is Unger's endeavour to take transformative social theory one step further than he had taken it in his earlier works. The vision of post-liberal society is at last fleshed out: it will be an emancipatory society, founded on institutional arrangements which undermine hierarchies, tendencies towards social division, impediments to freedom and social stasis; a society:

> whose formative system of powers and rights is continuously on the line, a system neither invisible nor protected against ordinary conflict; a society in which the collective experience of setting the terms of social life passes increasingly into the tenor of everyday experience; a society that therefore frees itself from the oscillation between modest, aimless bickering and extraordinary revolutionary outbursts; a society where, in some larger measure, people neither treat the conditional as unconditional nor fall to their knees as idolaters of the social world they inhabit.[336]

Transforming this vision into reality demands that existing liberal societies develop institutions and forms of social arrangement which invite rather than resist their own disruption. The post-liberal society, in other words, must embody what Unger calls structure-denying structures, 'designed to prevent any definite institutional order from taking hold in social life'.[337] Elaboration of his thesis is inappropriate and indeed impossible here. Suffice it to say that the post-liberal society would, among other things, guarantee rights which not only 'protect the individual against oppression by concentrations of public or private power'[338] but which would also enable citizens to 'break[] open the large-scale organizations or the extended areas of social practice that remain closed to the destabilizing effects of ordinary conflict,' thereby 'ensuring that all institutions and practices can be criticized and revised to the individual interest in avoiding oppression'.[339] In short, Unger envisions a society in which plasticity is preferred to security, where people are allowed and indeed encouraged to disrupt the formation of social traditions and hierarchies.

Many a critic has taken issue with the Ungerian vision.[340] Unger fails to

[335] Unger, *supra* n. 201, 6.
[336] Ibid. 22.
[337] Unger, *False Necessity*, *supra* n. 333, 572.
[338] Ibid. 524.
[339] Ibid. 530.
[340] See e.g. Anderson, *supra* n. 201, 130–48; Ewald, *supra* n. 203, 733–53; Andrew Fraser, 'Legal Amnesia: Modernism versus the Republican Tradition in American Legal Thought', *Telos*, 60 (1984), 15–52; Bernard Yack, 'Toward a Free Marketplace of Social Institutions: Roberto Unger's "Super-Liberal" Theory of Emancipation', *Harvard L. Rev.*, 101 (1988),

explain at all convincingly why we might desire a form of social life which puts a premium on generating insecurity, which prioritizes contingency, which encourages a 'cultural-revolutionary attack on rigid roles',[341] which makes a nonsense of many conventional rights by ensuring that they may be destabilized, and which apparently provides no mechanism for ensuring that the very process of destabilization can be kept in check. Assuming that the types of institutional revision deemed necessary for the transition from liberalism to post-liberalism could ever be effectuated, why should we wish to commit ourselves to such an upheaval? Yet again, Unger confesses and avoids. The first three volumes of *Politics* 'merely suggest the outline of a vision that needs to be worked out later'.[342] So many books, pages and words, and Unger is still promising to deliver the goods next time. God, it seems, has not yet spoken.[343]

In the mid-1980s, critical legal scholars in general fared no better with the transformative project. Throughout much of the critical literature of this period there runs little more than a vaguely formulated belief that things could be otherwise. 'The critics are confident that when they have succeeded in demystifying legal consciousness, things will get better,' David Trubek wrote in 1984.[344] They 'see capitalist legal consciousness as a complex set of messages which deny immanent possibilities of human action and freedom' and '[t]hey believe that by demonstrating the falseness or incoherence of our dominant legal concepts, critique can lead to change through an imaginative reconstruction of our social reality.'[345] This belief is exemplified by the critical legal scholarship of Robert Gordon. According to Gordon, 'the commonplace legal discourses'—he does not elaborate upon the phrase—'often produce such seriously distorted representations of social life that their categories regularly filter out complexity, variety, irrationality, unpredictability, disorder, cruelty, coercion, violence, suffering, solidarity and self-sacrifice.'[346] These discourses, moreover, tend

1961–77; and, generally, the 'Symposium: Roberto Unger's *Politics: A Work in Constructive Social Theory*', *Northwestern Univ. L. Rev.*, 81 (1987), 589–951. For a sympathetic and comprehensive discussion of Unger's work and its many critics, see Andrew Phang, *Toward Critique and Reconstruction: Roberto Unger on Law, Passion and Politics* (Hull: Hull University Law School Studies in Law, 1993).

341 Unger, *False Necessity*, *supra* n. 333, 563.

342 Ibid. 560.

343 See Unger, *supra* n. 177, 295; and also Stanley Fish, *Doing What Comes Naturally: Change, Rhetoric, and the Practice of Theory in Literary and Legal Studies* (Oxford: Clarendon Press, 1989), 399–435 esp. 435.

344 Trubek, *supra* n. 132, 596.

345 Ibid. 610. To my mind, the least implausible—precisely because it is the least ambitious—critical legal effort at suggesting how critique might prompt legal change is to be found in Richard Abel's early work on tort law. See, in particular, Richard L. Abel, 'Torts', in Kairys (ed.), *supra* n. 309, 185–200; and 'A Socialist Approach to Risk', *Maryland L. Rev.*, 41 (1982), 695–754.

346 Robert W. Gordon, 'Unfreezing Legal Reality: Critical Approaches to Law', *Florida State Univ. L. Rev.*, 15 (1987), 195–220 at 200.

systematically to 'exclude or repress alternative visions of social life'.[347] Critical legal studies may help us 'to dredge up and give content to these suppressed alternative visions'.[348] For one of the purposes of critical legal studies 'as an intellectual enterprise is to try to thaw out, or at least hammer some tiny dents on, the frozen mind sets induced by habitual exposure to legal practices—by trying to show how normal legal discourses contribute to freezing, and to demonstrate how problematic these discourses are'.[349] As lawyers become ever more aware of the problematic nature of conventional legal reasoning, the more likely they are to recognize that 'it *is* possible that altruism, community, democratic participation, equality, and so forth, can be promoted without destroying freedom and economic efficiency.'[350]

Gordon's extremely vague and highly speculative claims typify the transformative faith which is often in evidence in the literature of critical legal studies. While it is frequently the case, G. Edward White observes, that 'the utopian proposals made at the conclusion of Critical articles are deliberately vague, since most Critical theorists concede that their concrete thinking about utopia has not yet crystallized . . . where concrete proposals have been advanced, they appear to have a surrealistic quality.'[351] Yet this surrealism is not to be taken lightly. The fact is that commitment, however vague, to transformative social theory and politics is a fundamental feature of critical legal scholarship. For, without this commitment, such scholarship would add up to little more than a jurisprudence of despair.[352] In the literature of critical legal studies, watered-down Ungerian visions symbolize hope. They represent part of a more general endeavour by critical legal scholars to demonstrate that critique—the demystification, delegitimation or trashing of liberal legal thought—is not an exercise in negativism, but the foundation for legal reconstruction.

Since around the middle of the 1980s, the promotion of critical legal studies as an essentially constructive style of critique has flourished. One of the major developments in this regard has been the turn by critical legal scholars to literary interpretive theories[353] and, ironically, to deconstructive theory in particular. To a large degree, deconstruction has become, for

[347] W. Gordon, ibid. 200.
[348] Ibid.
[349] Ibid. 201.
[350] Ibid. 220.
[351] White, *supra* n. 16, 657. See also Foley, *supra* n. 7, 496; cf. Tushnet, 'Critical Legal Studies: An Introduction to its Origins and Underpinnings', *supra* n. 14, 510–11.
[352] See Philip Mechem, 'The Jurisprudence of Despair', *Iowa L. Rev.*, 21 (1936), 669–92.
[353] See generally David Kennedy, 'The Turn to Interpretation', *Southern California L. Rev.*, 58 (1985), 251–75; Jerry Frug, 'Henry James, Lee Marvin and the Law', in *New York Times (Book Reviews)*, 16 February 1986, 1, 28–9; also Gary Peller, 'Reason and the Mob: The Politics of Representation', *Tikkun*, 2 (1987), 28–31, 92–5 at 30. ('I believe that the rise

critical legal theorists, another buzz-word. During the second half of the 1980s, the critical legal penchant for trashing and demystification was superseded. Increasingly, proponents of critical legal studies purported to 'deconstruct' liberal legal doctrines and reasoning.[354] But these proponents have tended to insist that deconstruction is not tantamount to destruction; rather, they argue, it is a necessary preliminary to legal reconstruction. As one advocate of the deconstructive project explains:

> The deconstruction of legal concepts, or of the social vision that informs them, is not nihilistic. Deconstruction is not a call for us to forget about moral certainty, but to remember aspects of human life that were pushed into the background by the necessities of the dominant legal conception we call into question. Deconstruction is not a denial of the legitimacy of rules and principles; it is an affirmation of human possibilities that have been overlooked or forgotten in the privileging of particular legal ideas. . . . By recalling the elements of human life relegated to the margin in a given social theory, deconstructive readings challenge us to remake the dominant conceptions of our society.[355]

By the early 1990s, there had evolved, in the United States, a voluminous literature purporting to demonstrate the positive ethical thrust of deconstructive theory.[356] While it may be too early to tell, it seems that this

of the new interpretative approaches marks an important movement towards unmasking the politics of intellectual life, and opens up new possibilities for understanding the politics of social life more generally.') In truth, since the mid-1980s, all sorts of interpretive theories have been adopted by American legal (and not only critical legal) scholars. Doing justice to them all would be impossible here. For some generally disparate examples, see Dworkin, *supra* n. 25, *passim*; Gary Minda, 'Phenomenology, Tina Turner and the Law', *New Mexico L. Rev.*, 16 (1986), 479–93; Steven L. Winter, 'Transcendental Nonsense, Metaphoric Reasoning, and the Cognitive Stakes for Law', *U. Pennsylvania L. Rev.*, 137 (1989), 1105–237; William N. Eskridge, Jr., 'The New Textualism', *UCLA L. Rev.*, 37 (1990), 621–91; Pierre Schlag, 'Normativity and the Politics of Form', *U. Pennsylvania L. Rev.*, 139 (1991), 801–932; Sanford Levinson and J.M. Balkin, 'Law, Music, and Other Performing Arts', *U. Pennsylvania L. Rev.*, 139 (1991), 1597–658; and, more generally, the special issue, 'Beyond Critique: Law, Culture, and the Politics of Form', *Texas L. Rev.*, 69 (1991), 1595–2041.

354 See, for example, Dalton, *supra* n. 296, *passim*; Peller, *supra* n. 297, *passim*; and James Boyle, 'The Politics of Reason: Critical Legal Theory and Local Social Thought', *U. Pennsylvania L. Rev.*, 133 (1985), 685–780. For a discussion of how deconstruction has come to feature in critical legal thought, see James Boyle, 'Introduction', in James Boyle (ed.), *Critical Legal Studies* (New York: New York University Press, 1992), xiii–liii esp. xiv–xxi, xxxvi–xxxix.

355 J. M. Balkin, 'Deconstructive Practice and Legal Theory', *Yale L.J.*, 96 (1987), 743–86 at 763. In a similar vein, see Allan C. Hutchinson, 'From Cultural Construction to Historical Deconstruction', *Yale L.J.*, 94 (1984), 209–37 at 230–1; *supra* n. 308, 48; Martin F. Katz, 'After the Deconstruction: Law in the Age of Post-Structuralism', *U. Western Ontario L. Rev.*, 24 (1986), 51–66; and also Neil Duxbury, 'Deconstruction, History and the Uses of Legal Theory', *Northern Ireland Legal Quarterly*, 41 (1990), 167–75 at 169–70.

356 The work of Drucilla Cornell is especially significant in this context. See e.g. Drucilla Cornell, 'Toward a Modern/Postmodern Reconstruction of Ethics', *U. Pennsylvania L. Rev.*, 133 (1985), 291–380; 'The Poststructuralist Challenge to the Ideal of Community', *Cardozo L. Rev.*, 8 (1987), 989–1022; *The Philosophy of the Limit* (New York: Routledge, 1992). In the latter work, Cornell argues that deconstruction demands that we conceive of law in terms

literature has by and large fallen on deaf ears. Part of the problem is that, for those who refuse or find themselves unable to enter into the spirit of deconstruction, who consider it abstruse or self-indulgent, the moral and reconstitutive implications of the theory are, to say the least, elusive.[357] Perhaps more importantly—and despite all the efforts of critical legal scholars to persuade them otherwise—some detractors from the critical legal studies movement regard deconstruction as ultimate confirmation that the movement in fact promotes a wholly relativistic, unprincipled jurisprudence.[358] Deconstruction, so the argument goes, leads to nihilism.

This is a charge which many proponents of critical legal studies have denied.[359] But not every critical legal scholar eschews nihilism. By the mid-1980s, as will become clear in the next section, the critical legal studies movement was facing a barrage of attack from various quarters. It seemed that the gravest accusation which could be levelled at the movement was that it espoused legal nihilism. Yet it was at this very time that one critical legal scholar, Joseph Singer, decided to embrace the label. '[A]ppropriating a label placed on you by your adversaries,' he observed, 'can drive home the difference between your views and the views of others by emphasizing the extent to which you reject their criteria for judging what is and is not praiseworthy. What they consider an insult, you consider a compliment.'[360] By accepting as 'superficially plausible'[361] the nihilist tag, Singer hoped to demonstrate the depth and the nature of the division between critical legal studies and liberal legal thought.

of integrity, that we '[b]e just with Justice'. (*The Philosophy of the Limit*, 153–4). For further efforts to locate the ethics of deconstruction, see e.g. Christine A. Desan Husson, 'Expanding the Legal Vocabulary: The Challenge Posed by the Deconstruction and Defense of Law', *Yale L.J.*, 95 (1986), 969–91; James Boyle, 'Is Subjectivity Possible? The Post-Modern Subject in Legal Theory', *U. Colorado L. Rev.*, 62 (1991), 489–524; J. M. Balkin, 'What is a Postmodern Constitutionalism?', *Michigan L. Rev.*, 90 (1992), 1966–90; and, generally, the symposium, 'Deconstruction and the Possibility of Justice', *Cardozo L. Rev.*, 11 (1990), 919–1726.

[357] For my own sketchy reflections on this matter, see Neil Duxbury, 'Post-Modern Jurisprudence and its Discontents', *Oxford Jnl. Leg. Studs.*, 11 (1991), 589–97; also Kenney Hegland, 'Goodbye to Deconstruction', *Southern California L. Rev.*, 58 (1985), 1203–21.

[358] See, for example, Philip B. Kurland, 'Curia Regis: Some Comments on the Divine Right of Kings and Courts ' "To Say What the Law Is" ', *Arizona L. Rev.*, 23 (1981), 581–97 at 586. ('My own view is that deconstruction makes nonsense of the concept of a written constitution.') More generally, see Alan Hunt, 'The Big Fear: Law Confronts Postmodernism', *McGill L.J.*, 35 (1990), 507–40.

[359] See, for example, Schlag, *supra*. n. 15, 1198; Richard Michael Fischl, 'Some Realism About Critical Legal Studies', *U. Miami L. Rev.*, 41 (1987), 505–32; David Fraser, 'What a Long, Strange Trip it's Been: Deconstructing Law from Legal Realism to Critical Legal Studies', *Australian Jnl. of Law and Society*, 5 (1988–9), 35–43 at 39–40; and also, outside of critical legal studies, Michelman, *supra* n. 16, 83–94.

[360] Joseph William Singer, 'The Player and the Cards: Nihilism and Legal Theory', *Yale L.J.*, 94 (1984), 1–70 at 3–4 fn. 5.

[361] Ibid. 6. Singer himself would 'prefer not to label' his own position but 'for clarity's sake' terms it 'irrationalism'. Ibid. 4 fn. 8.

Singer's core thesis is that we have failed to appreciate the proper purpose of legal theory. Not only do legal theorists overestimate the importance and the attainability of legal certainty, but they tend to engage in an essentially futile endeavour to demonstrate that law is founded on moral values and principles which are capable of commanding the consensus of rational citizens and therefore must be adjudged to be true or objective. Legal theorists have remained committed to this endeavour because they believe that 'both the good life and just government require a rational foundation,' that '[w]ithout a rational method to adjudicate value conflicts . . . everything is up for grabs.'[362] Singer rejects this belief. 'The point is that morality is not a matter of truth or logical demonstration. It is a matter of conviction based on experience, emotion and conversation.'[363] These are the characteristics of legal reasoning—indeed, they are the characteristics of human reasoning generally.

> When people decide whether to get married, to have children, to go to law school, to move to another state, to quit their jobs . . . they do not follow a procedure that generates, by itself, an answer. They do think long and hard about what they want in life; they imagine what their lives would be like if they were to follow one path rather than another; they talk with the people who are most important to them and whose opinions they value; they argue with others and with themselves; and in the end, they make a decision. And later, in looking back at it, they are sometimes pleased with their decisions, sometimes not. . . . Legal decisions are no different: Judging, in whatever context it appears, is just decisionmaking.[364]

There is something fishy about this analogy. By and large, when judges, acting in an official capacity, make decisions, they are not engaging in an activity which may have a significant impact on how their own lives unfold. They lack a personal stake in their decisions: deciding in favour of either plaintiff or defendant in a particular case is hardly the same as deciding whether or not to marry. However, it seems that, for Singer, the purpose of this analogy is to stress that legal reasoning is, in essence, a dialogical rather than a rational activity. 'Legal reasoning . . . consists of conversation.'[365] Acceptance of this proposition 'does not logically require us to become agnostic about all our moral and political values. . . . It does, however, allow us consciously to assume responsibility for what we do.'[366] What, however, connects conversation with responsibility? On this point, Singer seems thoroughly vague. His point appears to be that when, in the process of dialogue, we offer our opinions, we are in a sense demonstrating commitment to others. That is, by offering our opinions, we may indicate the degree to which we do or do not care about something or somebody. Furthermore, in so doing, we may become accountable or responsible to

[362] Singer, *supra* n. 360, 49.
[363] Ibid. 39.
[364] Ibid. 62.
[365] Ibid. 51.
[366] Ibid. 52.

others: that is, we may be required to elaborate our opinions when they seem vague; or we may sense a need to do so when they provoke objection or disagreement. To engage in dialogue, in short, is to eschew human indifference.

And that, for Singer, is all that we can ask of legal reasoning. There is no innate rationality in the exercise; only 'the human assertion of responsibility'.[367] But what if legal officials are able to abandon this responsibility? That is, what '[i]f we let them do just what they like'?[368] According to Singer, there really is nothing to fear. '[P]eople do not want just to be beastly to each other. . . . The evidence is all around us that people are often caring, supporting, loving, and altruistic, both in their family lives and in their relations with strangers.'[369] State officials are no exception; and therefore, we ought not to assume 'that if left to do "just what they like," government officials will necessarily harm or oppress us.'[370] Even should they do so, we must recognize that rationality will not protect us. 'What protects us is outrage.'[371]

The virtue of legal theory, in Singer's view, is that it facilitates the articulation of standpoints. 'Nothing tells us conclusively when to accept and when to reject a particular argument.'[372] But theories may help us to present our arguments more persuasively than we might otherwise have done.[373] What theories cannot do is provide rational foundations for legal systems. There are no such foundations. There is simply dialogue. And where there is dialogue, there is hope.[374]

Detractors from critical legal studies have had a field day with Singer's article. To pick just a handful of criticisms from many, it has been argued that Singer oversimplifies the rationalist tradition in legal theory; that he fails to explain how outrage—an emotion which occurs, as it were, after the event—can protect citizens against state oppression; that he believes in the power of persuasion and yet is unable to see that principles and rationality are often the very qualities which make arguments persuasive; and that he fails to explain how disputes are ever settled, that is, why dialogues do not simply continue *ad infinitum*.[375] These and other criticisms seem perfectly valid. While Singer has proved to be an easy target, however, it has proved

[367] Ibid. 53. [368] Ibid. 54. [369] Ibid.
[370] Ibid. 55. [371] Ibid. [372] Ibid. 16.
[373] See ibid. 60. [374] See ibid. 67–70.
[375] For these criticisms and more, see John Stick, 'Can Nihilism be Pragmatic?', *Harvard L. Rev.*, 100 (1986), 332–401; Daniel C. K. Chow, 'Trashing Nihilism', *Tulane L. Rev.*, 65 (1990), 221–98; Michel Krauss, 'Nihilisme et interprétation des lois', *Revue Juridique Thémis*, 20 (1986), 125–54 (on nihilism in legal theory generally); Peter D. Swan, 'Critical Legal Theory and the Politics of Pragmatism', *Dalhousie L.J.*, 12 (1989), 349–76 at 356–76; and Brosnan, *supra* n. 270, 344–60. For a realist-inspired discussion of Stick's analysis of Singer's thesis, see Steve Fuller, 'Playing Without a Full Deck: Scientific Realism and the Cognitive Limits of Legal Theory', *Yale L.J.*, 97 (1988), 549–80.

equally easy to lose sight of, or to fail to see, what it is that he is trying to do. Singer is not, as some critics have suggested, arguing for total relativism in legal theory.[376] His point is that the various criteria of rationality which have been formulated by liberal philosophers and legal theorists do not and cannot impose any form of constraint upon legal officials.[377] That rationality fails to constrain, however, does not mean that legal officials cannot be held accountable for their actions. They will be accountable by virtue of the fact that legal reasoning is a dialogic, responsibility-inducing activity. While that proposition is extremely woolly, the one thing that is clear—and this is what ought to be stressed—is that Singer does not believe that legal officials are totally unconstrained. His insistence, rather, is that constraint is generated by something other than rationality.

Singer presents a highly flawed argument; but it is not, for all its faults, intended to be an unconstructive argument. That it has been interpreted as such epitomizes the predicament of the critical legal studies movement generally. As compared with Singer's endeavour, the effort by certain of those within the movement to develop a critique of the idea that, under liberalism, individual rights are protected in accordance with the rule of law is underscored by a similar degree of muddled analysis and has provoked an equally unsympathetic critical response. While it gained momentum in the middle of the 1980s, the critique of the rule of law and liberal rights discourse by critical legal scholars can be traced back to the late 1970s.[378] Responding to E. P. Thompson's suggestion that the rule of law embodies principles of equality and universality which may operate independently, and sometimes even run against the grain of the interests of the ruling class,[379] Morton Horwitz argued in 1977 that the virtues of the rule of law ought not to be overestimated. The fact of the matter is, he argued, that the rule of law often constrains benevolent and beneficial as well as oppressive and misguided uses of power:

> [T]he rule of law . . . undoubtedly restrains power, but it also prevents power's benevolent exercise. It creates formal equality—a not inconsiderable virtue—but it *promotes* substantive inequality by creating a consciousness that radically separates law from politics, means from ends, processes from outcomes. By promoting

[376] No one has been more guilty of this misreading than I. See Duxbury, *supra* n. 8, 33–4.

[377] For the criteria, the philosophers and the legal theorists which he has in mind, see Singer, *supra* n. 360, p.10.

[378] See, for example, Alan David Freeman, 'Legitimizing Racial Discrimination Through Anti-discrimination Law: A Critical Review of Supreme Court Doctrine', *Minnesota L. Rev.*, 62 (1978), 1049–119.

[379] See E. P. Thompson, *Whigs and Hunters: The Origin of the Black Act* (Harmondsworth: Penguin, 1975), 261–5.

procedural justice it enables the shrewd, the calculating, and the wealthy to manipulate its forms to their own advantage.[380]

From this critique of the rule of law, it is possible to ascertain why many critical legal scholars are suspicious of liberal rights discourse. Horwitz's point is that individual rights are largely gloss, that, while the rule of law may guarantee a formal equality of rights among citizens, it sanctions general inequalities of economic and other forms of power. Other critical legal scholars have attempted to extend this critique of rights in two distinct ways. First of all, it has been argued that individual rights are a double-edged sword. While such rights may certainly aid the weak and the powerless, the very fact that they are individualistic in nature means that they are likely to facilitate competition and inequality: one's rights, in short, will be as good as one's ability to take advantage of them.[381] The American legal system is clearly capable of protecting rights which are communal in nature.[382] That it tends not to do so, however, demonstrates just how firmly American law is rooted in the individualistic culture of capitalism.[383]

The second strand of the critique of rights entails the assertion that they are straightforwardly and misleadingly assumed to be a good thing. 'The concept of rights was a radical and liberating idea a couple of hundred years ago,' Frances Olsen observes, but '[o]ver time . . . talk of rights became routinized and the pursuit of rights became sometimes an empty scholastic enterprise.'[384] It is owing to the fact that the utility of rights is nowadays generally taken for granted that they are rarely subjected to detailed sceptical scrutiny. Yet, for many critical legal scholars, individual rights are no less incoherent and indeterminate than the body of liberal legal thought and doctrine out of which they emerge. Modern liberal jurisprudence, Joseph Singer has argued, has failed 'to explain why the legal system sometimes allows people to harm each other and sometimes does not'.[385] It appears to be similarly impossible, Mark Tushnet claims, to determine the precise degree to which a particular right ought to be

380 Morton J. Horwitz, 'The Rule of Law: An Unqualified Human Good?', *Yale L.J.*, 86 (1977), 561–6 at 566.

381 See Mark Tushnet, 'Rights: An Essay in Informal Political Theory', *Politics and Society*, 17 (1989), 403–51 at 419–20; Morton J. Horwitz, 'Rights', *Harvard Civil Rights-Civil Liberties L. Rev.*, 23 (1988), 393–406.

382 See, for example, Staughton Lynd, 'Communal Rights', *Texas L. Rev.*, 62 (1984), 1417–40.

383 See Peter Gabel, 'The Phenomenology of Rights-Consciousness and the Pact of the Withdrawn Selves', *Texas L. Rev.*, 62 (1984), 1563–99 at 1576.

384 Frances Olsen, 'Liberal Rights and Critical Legal Theory', in Christian Joerges and David M. Trubek (eds.), *Critical Legal Thought: An American-German Debate* (Baden-Baden: Nomos, 1989), 241–54 at 253.

385 Joseph William Singer, 'The Legal Rights Debate in Analytical Jurisprudence from Bentham to Hohfeld', *Wisconsin L. Rev.*, [1982], 975–1059 at 1058.

protected—at what point, for example, ought freedom of speech and expression to be curbed?—or to formulate criteria by which to choose satisfactorily between equally fundamental but competing rights.[386] In short, rights are unstable—the very fact that they require interpretation guarantees as much.[387]

As with Singer's arguments in favour of anti-rationalist legal theory, the effort by certain critical legal scholars to develop a critique of the rule of law and individual rights has met with some fairly damning criticism.[388] Like Singer, these scholars have been castigated for misinterpreting and caricaturing the liberal jurisprudential project. The rule of law, it has been argued, is conceived by liberal legal philosophers to be a rather more complex phenomenon than proponents of critical legal studies would have us believe.[389] These proponents, furthermore, are frequently criticized for their inordinate distrust of rights.[390] Such distrust—as I shall try to elaborate in due course—is regarded by some as proof that critical legal studies is founded on false radicalism. The essence of this criticism is that members of oppressed and vulnerable minorities appreciate the importance of rights. They have struggled, and continue to struggle, for the recognition and protection of their rights. But critical legal studies is very much divorced from such struggles. Its constituents by and large share the political sensibilities not of a vulnerable minority but of a body of mainly white, male, affluent, tenured law professors—people who fail to recognize the importance of rights for the simple reason that their own rights are rarely threatened.

The tendency of critical legal scholars to question the desirability of something which they take for granted—which they seem to accept, quite ironically, as a matter of right—has led certain of their critics to accuse

[386] See, for much more detailed discussion, Mark Tushnet, 'An Essay on Rights', *Texas L. Rev.*, 62 (1984), 1363–1403 at 1364–84.

[387] More generally, see Anthony Chase, 'The Left on Rights: An Introduction', *Texas L. Rev.*, 62 (1984), 1541–61.

[388] See, for example, the intemperate comments of Don Herzog, 'As Many As Six Impossible Things Before Breakfast', *California L. Rev.*, 75 (1987), 609–30 at 623–30; and John Underwood Lewis, 'Survey of Canadian Law: Jurisprudence', *Ottawa L. Rev.*, 20 (1988), 671–710 at 683–86.

[389] For a stringent but not ungenerous critique of critical legal studies in this regard, see Andrew Altman, *Critical Legal Studies: A Liberal Critique* (Princeton, NJ: Princeton University Press, 1990), 57–103. For a critical analysis along similar lines to, but less impressive than, Altman's, see Raymond A. Belliotti, 'The Rule of Law and the Critical Legal Studies Movement', *U. Western Ontario L. Rev.*, 24 (1986), 67–78. And for a critical legal reply to Altman, see David Gray Carlson, 'Liberal Philosophy's Troubled Relation to the Rule of Law', *U. Toronto L.J.*, 43 (1993), 257–88.

[390] See, for example, Amy Bartholomew and Alan Hunt, 'What's Wrong With Rights?', *Law and Inequality*, 9 (1990), 1–58 at 49.

them of hypocrisy.[391] In a sense, this criticism is unfair. As with Singer's reflections on nihilism in legal theory, the critique of rights represents an essentially sincere if thoroughly muddled effort by critical legal scholars to demonstrate that the conventional wisdoms of liberal legal thought are not unshakable.[392] The struggles waged by oppressed groups to secure rights, Mark Tushnet remarks, are obviously important. 'The critique of rights does not deny the historical achievements of these struggles; it suggests only that success in the future will depend on simultaneously acknowledging the importance of the past and transcending the limitations that the language of rights places on continuing struggles.'[393] The point is a crucial one. Critical legal theorists by and large emphasize not the unimportance but the limited utility and the problematic features of rights.[394] The securing of formal rights, they argue, turns out often to be a limited victory; for what matters most is precisely what cannot be guaranteed—that these rights be interpreted in a consistent and enlightened manner. The argument is not that rights do not matter, but that they are indeterminate.

The reliance by critical legal scholars on the indeterminacy thesis rings hollow with many of their detractors. It is possible, certain of these detractors argue, to exaggerate the degree to which liberal legal systems exhibit indeterminacy. Yet, if indeterminacy is not exaggerated, its revelation hardly represents a major critical breakthrough, since few if any modern lawyers would suggest that legal systems are wholly neutral, systematic and coherent.[395] Along with the claim that critical legal scholars have failed to present the transformative dimension of their project in a convincing light, the assertion that the indeterminacy thesis is inevitably either overblown or uncontroversial represents, to my mind, the most penetrating criticism of the movement. By the middle of the 1980s, however, the movement was increasingly being criticized not so much for the ideas which

[391] See, in particular, David Andrew Price, 'Taking Rights Cynically: A Review of Critical Legal Studies', *Cambridge L.J.*, 48 (1989), 271–301.

[392] See Trubek, *supra* n. 132, 596.

[393] Tushnet, *supra* n. 381, 418.

[394] Consider, however, Gabel and Kennedy, *supra* n. 247, 33. ('Exactly what people don't need is their *rights*. What they need are the actual forms of social life that have to be created through the building of movements that can overcome illusions about the nature of what is political, like the illusion that there is an entity called the state, that people possess rights.')

[395] On the banality of the indeterminacy thesis, see Lawrence B. Solum, 'On the Indeterminacy Crisis: Critiquing Critical Dogma', *U. Chicago L. Rev.*, 54 (1987), 462–503; Ken Kress, 'Legal Indeterminacy', *California L. Rev.*, 77 (1989), 283–337; Brian Langille, 'Revolution Without Foundation: The Grammar of Scepticism and Law', *McGill L.J.*, 33 (1988), 451–505; Calvin R. Massey, 'The Faith Healers', *Law and Social Inquiry*, 17 (1992), 821–9; Joan C. Williams, 'Critical Legal Studies: The Death of Transcendence and the Rise of the New Langdells', *New York Univ. L. Rev.*, 62 (1987), 429–96 at 485–91; Martin Krygier, 'Critical Legal Studies and Social Theory—A Response to Alan Hunt', *Oxford Jnl. Leg. Studs.*, 7 (1987), 26–39 at 34–7; John W. Van Doren and Patrick T. Bergin, 'Critical Legal Studies: A Dialogue', *New England L. Rev.*, 21 (1985–6), 291–304 esp. at 292–3; and Posner, *supra* n. 22, 153–7, 254–9.

it represented, but for the very fact that it existed. Rather than try to grapple seriously with critical legal studies as a set of jurisprudential claims, certain detractors were beginning to attack it as an act of academic treason, as something which not only offended against generally accepted political values and beliefs but which also threatened to undermine the fabric and integrity of the American law school.

MORE DEMONOLOGY

'Legal Education in the United States today,' wrote Roger Cramton in 1981, 'is the healthiest it has ever been.'[396] Out of the critical legal studies movement around this time, however, there emanated a rather different message. At the second national conference on critical legal studies, held at the University of Wisconsin in November 1979, Duncan Kennedy presented a paper in which he argued that first-year law teaching is more or less always ideologically conservative. Law professors, he observed, are overwhelmingly white, male and middle-class; they discourage radicalism and diversity and encourage competition and the cultivation of hierarchy among students; and they invariably insist that passion, unlike reason, has no place in legal discourse.[397] Kennedy's dissatisfaction with the law school experience, as we have already seen, dates back to his own student days in the late 1960s.[398] By the early 1980s, however, he was arguing more than merely that legal education is authoritarian and soul-destroying. '[L]egal education', he insisted, 'contributes to the reproduction of illegitimate hierarchy in the bar and in society.'[399]

This, in essence, was Gramscian analysis applied to the modern American law school. 'Every social group,' Gramsci believed, 'creates . . . one or more strata of intellectuals which give it an awareness of its own function not only in the economic but also in the social and political fields.'[400] Kennedy's point is that law schools are especially adept at

[396] Roger C. Cramton, 'Change and Continuity in Legal Education', *Michigan L. Rev.*, 79 (1981), 460–77 at 470.

[397] Duncan Kennedy, 'First Year Law Teaching as Political Action', listed in the 'Second National Conference on Critical Legal Studies: Program' (n.d. [10–12 November 1979], on file with author: copy supplied by Professor J. H. Schlegel); published at *Law and Social Problems*, 1 (1980), 47–69.

[398] See Kennedy, *supra* n. 3, *passim*.

[399] Duncan Kennedy, *Legal Education and the Reproduction of Hierarchy: A Polemic Against the System* (Cambridge, Mass.: Afar, 1983), i. For an abridged version of this text, see Duncan Kennedy, 'Legal Education as Training for Hierarchy', in Kairys (ed.), *supra* n. 309, 40–61.

[400] Gramsci, *supra* n. 268, 5. It ought to be noted that the notion of the intellectual is used here in an extremely broad fashion. Indeed, according to Gramsci, 'non-intellectuals do not exist. . . . Each man . . . carries on some form of intellectual activity, that is, he is a

stratifying intellectuals. Law schools themselves are stratified. 'Each law school has its arrangement of professors, assistant professors, students and [non-academic] staff. . . . Law schools themselves are ranked' with respect to 'differences in what they teach, how they teach it, how much power they have in the field of legal education, and what rewards their faculties receive.'[401] Out of this hierarchy emerges a further hierarchy of lawyers. 'Legal education structures the pool of prospective lawyers so that their hierarchical organization seems inevitable, and trains them in detail to look and think and act just like all the other lawyers in the system.'[402]

The claim that law schools are founded on and supportive of hierarchy is hardly controversial. But Kennedy went further. This hierarchy, he argued, ought to be eradicated: 'we should go as far as possible towards the total dismantling of the existing system.'[403] This would mean, among other things, doing away with student grading and degree classifications,[404] allowing students to 'pass' when called upon to answer questions in class,[405] encouraging the formation of leftist student reading groups,[406] determining admissions by lottery[407] and, most importantly of all, ensuring that everyone involved in the running of the law school is regarded and rewarded equally. 'Equalize all salaries in the school (including secretaries and janitors)', Kennedy proposed, 'regardless of educational qualifications, "difficulty" of job, or 'social contribution".'[408] 'I don't think we'd lose anything', he added, 'if we abolished the hierarchy of the law schools by equalizing dollars per student and assigning professors to schools at random. Or if we attacked the division of labour and the differentiation of capacities . . . through training and rotation for everyone through all law jobs.'[409] Indeed, in the ideal law school, 'every person should spend one month per year performing a job in a different part of the hierarchy from his or her normal job.'[410]

Kennedy's call for the dismantling of the law schools is perhaps the

"philosopher," an artist, a man of taste, he participates in a particular conception of the world, has a conscious line of moral conduct, and therefore contributes to sustain a conception of the world or to modify it, that is, to bring into being new modes of thought.' Gramsci, ibid. 9.

[401] Kennedy, *Legal Education and the Reproduction of Hierarchy*, *supra* n. 399, 45–6.

[402] Ibid. 71.

[403] Ibid. 105.

[404] Ibid. 27. ('Most of the process of differentiating students into bad, better and good could simply be dispensed with without the slightest detriment to the quality of legal services.')

[405] Ibid. 109 (encouraging 'the refusal to go along with the ritual of the socratic method—for example, by refusing to attack another student's position, or insisting on the right to "pass" when called upon').

[406] Ibid. 109–119.

[407] Ibid. 121–22. ('There should be a test designed to establish minimal skills for legal practice and then a lottery for admission to the school; there should be quotas within the lottery for women, minorities and working class students.')

[408] Ibid. 123.

[409] Ibid. 79.

[410] Ibid. 123.

crudest illustration of how New Left idealism impinged upon American academic legal thought. His proposal reads like a classic piece of campus marxism—strong on exhortation, weak on practicalities. During the 1980s, one would occasionally read reports of students at particular law schools following Kennedy's advice by, for example, setting up 'counter-hegemonic' study groups.[411] But such initiatives hardly impacted on general law school life. Kennedy appeared to expect little else. Knowing full well that there is rarely if ever any likelihood of left-wing radical projects enjoying much success in the United States,[412] he conceded that he had nothing to offer but a 'utopian proposal',[413] that much of what he argued for was merely 'the elaboration of fantasies'.[414] While he linked his proposals for the utopian law school with the critical legal studies movement,[415] other critical legal scholars seemed to be reluctant—the occasional denunciation of hierarchy notwithstanding[416]—to follow his lead. Indeed, if Kennedy had not been a professor at an Ivy League law school, it is unlikely that anyone would have so much as entertained his proposals.

But then this is the crucial point. Kennedy's article in the late 1960s denouncing the authoritarianism of the Yale Law School represented little more than the rantings of a disaffected second-year student. While his writings of the early 1980s may often have read like sophomoric agitprop, however, they could not so easily be swept aside. 'What I am suggesting', he wrote in 1981, 'is the politicization of corporate law practice, which means doing things and not doing things in order to serve left purposes. . . . It means engaging in indirect struggle to control the political tone of the office, say by refusing to laugh at jokes. . . . If you think before you act, if you are subtle, collusive, skilful and tricky, if you use confrontation when confrontation will work, you should be able to do left office politics without being fired, and make partner.'[417] These words appeared not in

411 See, for example, Anon., 'Counter-Hegemonic Front at Harvard Law School', in *Lizard: Newsletter of the Conference on Critical Legal Studies*, December 1986, 4.

412 See Duncan Kennedy, 'Radical Intellectuals in American Culture and Politics, or My Talk at the Gramsci Institute', *Rethinking Marxism*, 1 (1988), 100–29 at 121. ('[I]t was never likely that radical intellectuals in the US could live the European dream. We simply lack the base of traditional authority that has been the hidden underpinning for the influence of thinkers on European radical politics.')

413 Kennedy, *Legal Education and the Reproduction of Hierarchy*, *supra* n. 399, 120.

414 Ibid. 99.

415 See ibid. 84. ('Though I present it in my own subjective, individual manner, this way of seeing things grows out of the collective endeavour of radicals in legal education across the country to find a mode of resistance.'); and also Duncan Kennedy, 'The Political Significance of the Law School Curriculum', *Seton Hall L. Rev.*, 14 (1983), 1–16 at 2.

416 See, for example, Unger, *supra* n. 249, 669 (on how law schools entice their students 'into the absurd attempt to arrange themselves into a hierarchy of smart alecks'). For a British attempt to mimic Kennedy on legal education, see Christopher Stanley, 'Training for the Hierarchy? Reflections on the British Experience of Legal Education', *Law Teacher*, 22 (1988), 78–86.

417 Duncan Kennedy, 'Rebels From Principle: Changing the Corporate Law Firm From Within', *Harvard Law School Bulletin*, 33 (1981), 36–40 at 39–40.

some obscure left-wing pamphlet,[418] but in the Harvard Law School alumni magazine. While Kennedy's claims may have seemed preposterous, they were the claims of a Harvard law professor. This man was responsible for teaching some of the nation's brightest law students, the legal élite of the future. Not since Richard Posner had advocated the partial deregulation of the adoptions market had an American law professor caused such an uproar. Damning profiles of Kennedy, portraying him as a hypocritical pseudo-radical, appeared in the national press. Here was a man, it was alleged, who enjoyed the very privileges which he denounced, who patronized students while purporting to respect them and who eschewed genuine radical causes.[419] When a petition was organized at Harvard to oppose the nomination of Robert Bork to the Supreme Court, one former law student recounts, the liberals on the faculty stood up to be counted. 'The liberals spoke . . . [Lawrence] Tribe and Professor Kathleen Sullivan had gone down to Washington to testify. Where, I wondered, were the hard-core crits? . . . While the liberals were out fighting, Duncan Kennedy was busy writing dense pieces for publications like the *Buffalo Law Review*, pages few people read and even fewer understood.'[420] The fairness or accuracy of such observations is hardly important. What matters is that, certainly in the press, such observations were not uncommon. Duncan Kennedy's proposals for the restructuring of the law school were generally considered to epitomize the basic pretentiousness and insincerity of the critical legal studies movement.

If Duncan Kennedy was to be subjected to such harsh criticism, what was to be said about the law school which employed him? During the 1980s, the Harvard Law School came increasingly to be connected with critical legal studies. Indeed, the manner in which critical legal scholars attempted to exert an influence at Harvard indicates, for many of their

[418] As such works often did. See, for example, Anon., 'Don't Trash the Job Market, Make it Work', in *Lizard: Newsletter of the Conference on Critical Legal Studies*, January 1984, 6. At p. 2 of the same issue, it is stated that '*Lizard* is an emanation of a small faction within the critical legal studies movement, sometimes referred to as the True Left. *Lizard* does not in any way, official or unofficial, represent the views of the Conference on Critical Legal Studies. The contents of *Lizard* have not been discussed within CCLS, and it does not conform to the general attitude of the membership, which is far more responsible and boring than anything we would be interested in printing.' On *Lizard*, see further Johnson, *supra* n. 7, 286 fn. 103; White, *supra* n. 99, 835–6 fn. 80.

[419] See Menand, *supra* n. 11, 20; Cahan, *supra* n. 70, 44–5; Gerson, *supra* n. 70, 10 col. 2; Trillin, *supra* n. 72, 69–70, 83; Marc Granetz, 'Duncan the Doughnut' in *The New Republic*, 17 March 1986, 22; Peter Canellos, 'Overruling Tradition: The Critical Legal Studies Challenge at Harvard Law School', *The Boston Phoenix*, 18 February 1986, sect. 2, 1, 4–5, 8–9, 12; Brian Timmons, 'That's No Okie, That's My Torts Professor', *Wall Street Journal*, 3 April 1990, Part A at 20; and, for a critical response to Timmons, Richard Michael Fischl and Jeremy Paul, Correspondence, *Wall Street Journal*, 7 May 1990, Part A at 15.

[420] Kahlenberg, *supra* n. 321, 78.

detractors, precisely why the movement must be deemed incompatible with law school activity. The issue was presented primarily in terms of academic politics. During the mid-1980s, there appeared in the press numerous articles and reports detailing faculty divisions at Harvard.[421] The divisions—invariably presented as part and parcel of a feud between the political left and the political right on the faculty—were generally perceived to be affecting scholarly standards at the school. In 1985, James Vorenberg, the then Dean of the school, assured the alumni that 'while the divisions are real and sometimes damaging, there is more collaboration among faculty members in teaching and scholarship than I have seen since I joined the faculty in 1962.'[422] Such assurances, however, could hardly paper over the cracks which had emerged. In 1985, Paul Bator—a civil procedure specialist who was generally regarded as representative of the right wing of the faculty—left Harvard to join the University of Chicago Law School. For a tenured professor to leave the Harvard Law School for an academic post elsewhere is an extremely rare event. Bator's resignation was especially disquieting since it was apparently prompted by concern about the activities of critical legal scholars at the school.[423] 'The trouble', he observed, 'is that their programme has led them to subordinate academic ideals and standards to political ideals and standards. . . . Starting from the premiss that Harvard Law School is a wicked participant in an illegitimate and exploitive political system, they feel justified to violate, whenever it serves left purposes, the institutional and constitutional moralities that used to govern us.'[424]

Bator, along with others at Harvard, was especially dismayed by the tendency of critical legal scholars to vote *en bloc* at appointments

[421] See, for example, Trillin, *supra* n. 72, 59–83; Miguel Rodriguez, 'Faculty Divisions Spark Pointed Political Debate', *Harvard Law Record*, 2 March 1984, 1, 6–7; ' "Politicized" Faculty Affects Tenure, Teaching, Research', *Harvard Law Record*, 9 March 1984, 1, 6–7; Adam Eisgrau and Miguel Rodriguez, 'Explanation Found For Faculty Split', *Harvard Law Record*, 1 April 1984, 1, 9; David Margolick, 'Deep Philosophical Fractures Mar a Pillar of Legal Training; Meanwhile, Students Get Mixed Brief on Topic of Social Values', *Los Angeles Daily Journal*, 8 October 1985, 4 col. 6; Richard Lacayo, 'Critical Legal Times at Harvard', *Time*, 18 November 1985, 87; David Margolick, 'The Split at Harvard Law Goes Down to Its Foundation', *New York Times* (late edition), 6 October 1985, Part E, 7; Terry Eastland, 'Radicals in the Law Schools', *Wall Street Journal* 10 January 1986, 16; Anon., 'The Veritas About Harvard [Editorial]', *Wall Street Journal*, 3 September 1986, 26; Peter Mancusi, 'The Harvard Law School Feud', *The Boston Globe*, 27 April 1986, 30.

[422] James Vorenberg to Dear Alumnus/a, 10 December 1985 (on file with author: copy supplied by Professor J. H. Schlegel).

[423] See David Margolick, 'A Professor at Harvard Law Heads to West and to Right', *New York Times* (late edition), 15 September 1985, 58 col.1; David A. Kaplan, 'Goodbye, Harvard', *National Law Journal*, 7 October 1985, 4; Michael Sturm, 'Bator to Take Chicago Post', *Harvard Law Record*, 20 September 1985, 1, 14. It should be noted, however, that Bator did not expressly cite the growth of critical legal studies at Harvard as his reason for leaving. See Margolick, 'Deep Philosophical Fractures', *supra* n. 421, 4 col. 9.

[424] Clark *et al.*, *supra* n. 68, 13 (comment by Paul Bator).

committees in order to prevent the recruitment to the faculty of scholars unsympathetic towards their own project. Despite constituting a minority group, the critical legal faction could usually rely on a sufficient proportion of the liberal majority on the faculty to vote along with them, thereby blocking the appointment of those perceived to be undesirable. In 1985, various commentators noted that, during the past four years, Harvard had failed to recruit anyone from another law school to a tenured post.[425] For Bator, this was simply unacceptable at a school of Harvard's stature. Scholarly excellence, he argued, was being tragically sacrificed to ideology:

> In my opinion, CLS has become an instrument of and force for mediocrity, rather than excellence, at the Harvard Law School. This is so, at the simplest level, because the CLS faction has been successful in blockading our appointments process. Some distinguished appointments have been blocked on political grounds; in the rare case that a non-left lateral appointment does manage to get through, it is not accepted because serious and productive non-left scholars do not want to be at an institution devoted to guerrilla warfare. . . . It is the vitality of intellectual integrity and academic excellence at Harvard Law School that is at stake. On that, there is no right or left, only right and wrong.[426]

The strength of Bator's feelings on this issue is obvious. Yet, the fact of the matter is that, during the 1980s, the critical legal faction at Harvard felt no less aggrieved than did he. They too claimed to suffer casualties owing to faculty in-fighting. In 1986, Daniel K. Tarullo, a proponent of critical legal studies, became the first assistant professor to be denied tenure by the Harvard Law School in seventeen years.[427] In the following year, another assistant professor and critical legal scholar, Clare Dalton, fell only a few votes short of the two thirds faculty majority necessary for a tenure recommendation. David Trubek—also at Harvard during this year as a visiting professor—won faculty approval by a vote of 30 to 8, but his case for tenure was rejected by the president of the University, Derek Bok. Trubek—whose tenure rejection seemed the most glaringly unjust—decided not to pursue his case further.[428] Dalton, however, in fighting her case, became something of a *cause célèbre* among critical legal scholars.

[425] See, for example, Lacayo, *supra* n. 421, 87 col. 1; Margolick, 'The Split at Harvard', *supra* n. 421, 7 col. 3. By 1986, however, the problem appeared to be easing. In that year, the Harvard Law School appointed Mary Ann Glendon from Boston College Law School and Thomas Jackson from Stanford. It also reappointed Derrick Bell (Harvard's first black tenured law professor), granted tenure to Susan Estrich and Martha Minow and appointed David Wilkins, another black lawyer, as an assistant professor.

[426] Clark *et al.*, *supra* n. 68, 14–15 (comment by Paul Bator). See also Paul Bator, 'Legal Methodology and the Academy', *Harvard Jnl. of Law and Public Policy*, 8 (1985), 335–9 (on how conservative legal scholars should oppose critical legal studies).

[427] See Kahlenberg, *supra* n. 321, 47.

[428] See David Trubek, letter to President Derek Bok, 12 August 1987, in *Lizard: Newsletter of the Conference on Critical Legal Studies*, July 1988, 14–17.

Not only did the right wing of the Harvard faculty conspire to vote against her, her supporters argued, but, when her case was reviewed, her scholarship was subjected to a level of critical scrutiny which would not have been applied to the work of less radical academics.[429] Critical legal scholars were not alone, it seemed, in engaging in guerrilla warfare.

The Harvard Law School came eventually to live with its inner tensions. One of the faculty's more recent recruits, when asked if he embraced the critical legal or the neo-classical economic perspective on law, answered that he 'was surprised to discover that one could, after all, be a professor at HLS without espousing one or the other'.[430] 'Things cannot be as bad', he added, 'as some newspapers would have you believe.'[431] By the beginning of the 1990s, divisions and feuds still existed—as was especially clear from the responses at Harvard in 1991 to the murder of Mary Jo Frug, a feminist legal theorist at the New England School of Law and wife of the Harvard critical legal scholar, Gerald Frug[432]—but they appeared now to be more about personalities rather than politics,[433] and the future well-being of the school no longer seemed to hang on them. Increasingly, on the matter of appointments, the left and right wings of the faculty appeared to be less uncooperative.[434] Indeed, the outcry over alleged block-voting on appointments committees was superseded by a somewhat different controversy: namely, the under-representation of women and minorities on the faculty. In 1987—the year in which Clare Dalton was denied tenure—there were, out of a faculty of fifty-five tenured staff, only five women and two blacks.[435] The representation of blacks in particular at Harvard University—both among staff and students—had, for some time, been a

[429] See Bob Kuttner, 'Free Ideas at Harvard Law School Aren't So Free', *The Boston Globe*, 18 May 1987, 19; Jennifer A. Kingson, 'Harvard Tenure Battle Puts "Critical Legal Studies" on Trial', *The Harvard Crimson*, 6 May 1987, 3; Emily M. Bernstein, 'Law Profs Question Dalton Vote', *The Harvard Crimson*, 13 May 1987, 1; Mark M. Colodny, 'Bok Reluctant to Enter Dalton Tenure Dispute', *The Harvard Crimson*, 27 May 1987, 1, 8; also Clare Dalton, 'Discrimination in Academe: The Political is Personal Too', *Lizard: Newsletter of the Conference on Critical Legal Studies*, July 1988, 7–11.

[430] Nancy Waring, 'Coat of Many Colors [Interview with Professor Joseph Weiler]', *Harvard Law Bulletin*, February 1993, 4–7 at 6.

[431] Ibid. 7.

[432] On the relationship between Mary Jo Frug's murder and discontent on the Harvard law faculty, see Peter Collier, 'Blood on the Charles', *Vanity Fair*, October 1992, 58, 60–1, 64–7. On Frug, see the special issue, 'In Memory of Mary Joe Frug', (November 1991) in *Lizard: Newsletter of the Conference on Critical Legal Studies*; and also the material collected in the commentary section of issue no. 5 of the 1992 *Harvard Law Review*: *Harvard L. Rev.*, 105 (1992), 1045–105.

[433] See, in this regard, Ken Emerson, 'When Legal Titans Clash', *New York Times Magazine*, 22 April 1990, sec. 6 at 26, 28, 53, 63, 66, 68–9.

[434] See Collier, *supra* n. 432, 65 cols. 1–2.

[435] See Kuttner, *supra* n. 429, 19.

highly debated and sensitive issue.[436] During the late 1980s, Derrick Bell, one of the black law professors at Harvard, campaigned strenuously in an endeavour to ensure that, in the future, his school would make greater efforts to recruit minorities. The school might start, he proposed, by employing a black woman—eventually he left Harvard because of its failure to do so.[437] The feud between the left and the right at the school appeared to have given way to a somewhat different struggle—a struggle between those who promoted and those who resisted greater ethnic and gender diversity.[438] Critical legal studies at Harvard was no longer front-page news.

However, the plight of the critical legal studies movement was not confined to Harvard. In the 1980s, critical legal scholars protested not infrequently that, owing to their association with the movement, they were being denied appointments, tenure and promotions at other law schools.[439] To proclaim oneself a critical legal scholar, it was felt, was to risk academic rejection or even persecution.[440] There is no doubt that there was some foundation to such fears. '[P]eople often misinterpret the critical position because qualifications and reservations aren't made explicit,' Duncan Kennedy observed in 1981.[441] As the 1980s unfolded, however, it became clear that the style of critique adopted by many critical legal scholars generated not only misinterpretation but also outrage. 'Law professors are used to hearing their colleagues call their arguments *wrong*,' Mark Kelman remarked in 1987, 'but are quite unused to having their arguments *typologized*, *anthropologized*, treated as unself-conscious *instances* of characteristic modes of "liberal" thought.'[442] Critical legal studies outraged because it purported to diagnose the ills of American legal education and scholarship; and because it seemed to lead inevitably to the conclusion that those who failed to recognize these ills were themselves part of the

[436] See, for example, Martin Kilson, 'The Black Experience at Harvard', *New York Times Magazine*, 2 September 1973, 13, 31–2, 34, 37; and also Eddie Williams, Jr., 'A Black Undergraduate Replies', *New York Times Magazine*, 2 September 1973, 34.

[437] See Anon., 'Lawyer Reports Harvard', *The Higher*, 13 March 1992, 9; also, more generally, Derrick Bell, *Reflections of an Ardent Protester* (Boston: Beacon Press, 1994).

[438] See Collier, *supra* n. 432, 61–2; also, more generally, Tushnet, 'Critical Legal Studies: A Political History', *supra* n. 14, 1541–2.

[439] See, for example, Jennifer Jaff, 'An Open Letter to Critical Legal Studies' in *Lizard: Newsletter of the Conference on Critical Legal Studies*, May 1987, 9–10; Editors, 'The New McCarthyism: Introduction', in *Lizard: Newsletter of the Conference on Critical Legal Studies*, July 1988, 2–4; Karl Klare, 'Broad Community Support for the NESL Four', in *Lizard: Newsletterof the Conference on Critical Legal Studies*, July 1988, 6–7.

[440] For a discussion of how critical legal scholars have been persecuted and their work misrepresented, see Jerry Frug, 'McCarthyism and Critical Legal Studies', *Harvard Civil Rights-Civil Liberties L. Rev.*, 22 (1987), 665–701.

[441] Duncan Kennedy, 'Cost-Reduction Theory as Legitimation', *Yale L.J.*, 90 (1981), 1275–83 at 1276.

[442] Kelman, *supra* n. 149, 298 n. 12.

problem. The fundamental difficulty which detractors from critical legal studies faced in attempting to refute this argument was that they found it to be non-falsifiable. How, after all, do you demonstrate that there is no illness when you are told that you are the illness?

It is owing to the fact that the critical legal standpoint is essentially non-falsifiable, I believe, that many detractors simply lashed out at the movement. Robert Gordon noted in 1988 that some of the cruder attacks on critical legal studies 'make up a fascinating collage of what Americans tend to think a left-wing movement must be about. . . . In these bizarre fantasies, Crits are Bolshevik saboteurs who will take over if you allow any in your faculty or firm, dangerous (in the age of Reagan, yet) "nihilist" subverters of the "rule of law," infantile but basically harmless hippie/yippies—or all of these at once.'[443] The fundamental incoherence of these attacks—the depiction, that is, of critical legal studies as simultaneously ineffectual and subversive—indicates the acute sense of frustration suffered by many of those who oppose the critical standpoint. In 1984, the then Dean of Duke University School of Law, Paul Carrington, articulated this sense of frustration in the most dramatic of terms when he declared that the nihilistic lessons of critical legal studies have no place in the law school:

> The nihilist teacher threatens to rob his or her students of the courage to act on such professional judgement as they may have acquired. Teaching cynicism may, and perhaps probably does, result in the learning of the skills of corruption: bribery and intimidation. In an honest effort to proclaim a need for revolution, nihilist teachers are more likely to train crooks than radicals. If this risk is correctly appraised, the nihilist who must profess that legal principle does not matter has an ethical duty to depart the law school, perhaps to seek a place elsewhere in the academy.[444]

Carrington's expression of distaste for critical legal endeavours proved, in a sense, to be counterproductive. This was no journalist accusing the Harvard crits of radical chic. This was the dean of a highly respected law school claiming that critical legal studies in general is inimical to the values of legal education. Carrington had misinterpreted and, to a large extent, had simply ignored the intellectual content and drift of the critical legal studies movement.[445] His assertion that the presence of the movement in the law schools would facilitate the teaching of corrupt practices was vigorously contested: the purpose of questioning the legitimacy of existing

[443] Gordon, *supra* n. 274, 84.

[444] Carrington, 'Of Law and the River', *supra* n. 10, 227.

[445] See the letters of Robert W. Gordon to Paul D. Carrington in ' "Of Law and the River," and of Nihilism and Academic Freedom', *Jnl. Leg. Educ.*, 35 (1985), 1–26 at 1–9, 13–16.

legal arrangements, it was argued, is not to deny the possibility of integrity and justice in law but to suggest that these values might be realized more effectively within a different legal structure.[446] In short, Carrington had failed to see any message of hope emanating from the critical legal studies movement—indeed, he had even gone so far as to single out Roberto Unger, the most obvious visionary within the movement, as the classic legal nihilist.[447]

That Carrington should have misrepresented critical legal studies was, advocates of the movement argued, unfortunate but only to be expected. That he should have encouraged intolerance of the movement, however, was considered to be an offence against academic freedom. On this issue, many liberal law professors—the very figures against whom critical legal scholars railed—jumped to the defence of the movement.[448] Proponents of critical legal studies may well be nihilists, they may indeed see only darkness where others see light, Guido Calabresi contended, but this does not mean that they ought to be censored.[449] By urging that they leave the law schools, Carrington ensured that critical legal scholars attracted liberal sympathy.

Perhaps the most significant dimension of the Carrington affair, however, is that critical legal scholars generally welcomed this sympathy. When the Stanford critical legal scholar, Paul Brest, joined in with the liberal chorus, asserting that Carrington's position 'violate[d] the most fundamental principles of academic freedom,'[450] one opponent of critical legal studies wondered why Brest felt able to uphold such principles. Was not the very purpose of critical legal studies, after all, to demonstrate that there are no fundamental principles—that principles are neither basic nor neutral but indeterminate? Brest's position seemed to be one of 'pure liberalism, so incongruous coming from a prominent member of a movement dedicated to exposing the mystification and reification of liberal legalism'.[451] The manner in which critical legal scholars responded to the

[446] See Sanford Levinson, 'Professing Law: Commitment of Faith or Detached Analysis?', St. Louis Univ. L.J., 31 (1986), 3–26; *Constitutional Faith* Princeton, NJ: Princeton University Press, 1988), 155–79; Gary Minda, 'Of Law, the River and Legal Education', *Nova L.J.*, 10 (1986), 705–21; 'The Politics of Professing Law', *St. Louis Univ. J.L.*, 31 (1986), 61–71.

[447] See Carrington, *supra* n. 10, 287 fn. 21; and cf. Gordon to Carrington, *supra* n. 445, 9, 14–15. For an analysis of Unger's work which suggests that Carrington might not be wrong, see Ewald, *supra* n. 203, 733–53.

[448] See, generally, David A. Kaplan, 'A Scholarly War of Words Over Academic Freedom', *National L.J.*, 7 (22) (1984), 1, 28, 30.

[449] Guido Calabresi to Paul D. Carrington in ' "Of Law and the River," and of Nihilism and Academic Freedom', *supra* n. 445, 23–4.

[450] Paul Brest to Phillip E. Johnson in ' "Of Law and the River," and of Nihilism and Academic Freedom', *supra* n. 445, 16–17 at 17.

[451] Phillip E. Johnson to Paul Brest in ' "Of Law and the River," and of Nihilism and Academic Freedom', *supra* n. 445, 18–19 at 18.

Carrington outburst echoed the New Left objection of the 1960s that the universities against which students demonstrated, despite being authoritarian and corrupt, ought nevertheless to act responsibly and in good faith. 'If CLS is a truly revolutionary movement,' one of its most outspoken adherents claimed, 'if it is to be true to its self proclaimed goal of permanently changing and radically transforming legal education, practise [*sic*] and discourse, then we should expect to be denied tenure, not hired, fired, harassed etc. etc.'[452] Critical legal scholars by and large appeared to expect determinacy from a system which they had labelled indeterminate. When their position in the law school was attacked, when they were made to feel vulnerable, they seemed quite content to cry foul, to object that their assailants were trying to take away their individual rights to academic freedom. For the critical legal studies movement, traditional liberal rights discourse appeared no longer to be quite such a problem.

CONSENSUS AND EXPERIENCE

Thus it is that the critical legal studies movement appeared to fall on its own sword. In fact, as we saw above, critical legal scholars endeavoured generally to demonstrate not that rights are wholly unimportant, but that they are indeterminate and therefore often problematic. The fact that critical legal scholars seemed able to ignore the problematic features of rights when they felt that they needed them, however, simply played into the hands of those detractors eager to demonstrate that critical legal studies was itself indeterminate. Along with other common criticisms of the critical legal studies movement—that, by the early 1980s, it had abandoned its radicalism,[453] that it had never really been radical in the first place,[454] that it was weighed down by theoretical contradictions,[455] that it promoted hypocrisy[456]—the claim that critical legal scholars contradicted themselves on the issue of rights implicitly raised the more general question of whether, in the United States, radical leftist jurisprudential

[452] David Fraser, 'Touch of Gray: Critical Legal Studies and the New McCarthyism', *Macquarie Law Students' Jnl.*, 1 (1989), 44–7 at 45.

[453] See, for example, Diamond, *supra* n. 320, 693. ('What was once angry and aggressive is now more conciliatory, less critical, more troubled.')

[454] See Johnson, *supra* n. 7, *passim*.

[455] See Fish, *supra* n. 320, 655–61; and also, for a reply, Drucilla Cornell, ' "Convention" and Critique', *Cardozo L. Rev.*, 7 (1986), 679–91.

[456] See, for example, James D. Gordon III, 'Law Review and the Modern Mind', *Arizona L. Rev.*, 33 (1991), 265–71 at 269. ('Crits argue that the law is hypocritical, and they deconstruct it to expose the hidden values it refuses to acknowledge. Then, after taking us into the wilderness and leaving us there, they zoom off in their BMWs and Jaguars to continue their class struggle against hierarchy and privilege.')

initiatives could ever be genuinely sustained.[457] All such initiatives seem doomed to suffer the fate of the New Left. If their endeavours are to prove at all successful, proponents of any form of radical jurisprudence will be compelled to rely on the very legal apparatus which they oppose. The necessity of compromise determines the limits of radical legal critique.[458]

Does this mean, then, that critical legal studies has inevitably burnt itself out, that there remains nothing but embers? As yet, I believe, this question cannot be answered. A significant number of American legal theorists have recently turned for inspiration to the pragmatist tradition in American philosophy.[459] The philosophy of pragmatism, it is argued, provides legal theorists with an alternative to the realist and critical legal traditions—an alternative which avoids the major pitfalls of both these traditions and yet which extends the basic realist-cum-critical legal insight that law is political.[460] While those who subscribe to the pragmatist tradition seem eager to distance themselves from the critical legal perspective, others—certain critical legal scholars included—believe that there really is no distance, that pragmatist legal theory is but a particular shade of critical legal theory.[461] Whether or not pragmatist jurisprudence is critical legal theory by another name—I suspect that it is not—is not the issue. My point is that it is far too early to tell one way or the other. The degree to which very recent jurisprudential developments in the United States are either distinct from or part and parcel of the critical legal tradition is impossible to determine.

So, is this not the point at which to draw this book to a close? Not quite. The year 1990 saw the appearance of a 'revised edition' of *The Politics of Law*, one of the classic texts of critical legal studies.[462] As compared with its predecessor, this new edition devoted considerably more space to two

[457] For a discussion of this theme, see Peter Goodrich, 'Sleeping With the Enemy: An Essay on the Politics of Critical Legal Studies in America', *New York Univ. L. Rev.*, 68 (1993), 389–425.

[458] For further development of this theme, see Duxbury, *supra* n. 21, *passim*.

[459] See, generally, 'Symposium on the Renaissance of Pragmatism in American Legal Thought', *Southern California L. Rev.*, 63 (1990), 1569–1853; and also, in a far less serious vein, J. M. Balkin, 'The Top Ten Reasons to be a Legal Pragmatist', *Constitutional Commentary*, 8 (1991), 351.

[460] See, in particular, Posner, *supra* n. 22, *passim*; also Frederic R. Kellogg, 'Legal Scholarship in the Temple of Doom: Pragmatism's Response to Critical Legal Studies', *Tulane L. Rev.*, 65 (1990), 15–56.

[461] See, for example, Sanford Levinson, 'Strolling Down the Path of the Law (and Toward Critical Legal Studies?): The Jurisprudence of Richard Posner', *Columbia L. Rev.*, 91 (1991), 1221–52; also Peter Junger, 'A Fox Interprets the Hedgehog', in *In Brief: Law Alumni News Bulletin of Case Western Reserve University*, January 1987, 5–8 at 5. ('I would not suggest that Posner has revealed himself as a member of the Critical Legal Studies movement: his ideology is clearly not theirs. But could he be doing to the Crits what Marx did to Hegel?—standing their arguments on their heads.')

[462] David Kairys (ed.), *The Politics of Law: A Progressive Critique* (New York: Pantheon, 1990).

themes in particular: gender and race. That it should have done so is hardly surprising. Discussions of gender and race issues had been very much a staple feature of critical legal studies conferences throughout the 1980s.[463] By the end of that decade, feminists and race theorists appeared to represent distinctive enclaves within the critical legal studies movement.[464] The ideas of, and discussions of the ideas of, 'fem-crits' and 'critical race theorists' were increasingly to be encountered in the American law reviews.[465] These two groups, along with the deconstructivist strand of critical legal studies, were considered to offer hope for the future vitality of the movement.[466] Even certain of the white, male law professors who represented the movement's past seemed to recognize as much.[467]

[463] See *supra*, n. 276.

[464] It seems that feminism became established within critical legal studies slightly sooner than did race theory. By 1985, Duncan Kennedy observes, feminists were already engaging in 'the strategy of creating separate enclaves within cls.' Kennedy, *supra* n. 275, 1021. The first critical race theory workshop took place at the University of Wisconsin Institute of Legal Studies in July 1989. See Stephanie Phillips, 'First Critical Race Theory Workshop', in *Lizard: Newsletter of the Conference on Critical Legal Studies*, November 1989, 83; and Angela Harris, 'What Reconstruction Jurisprudence Means to Me (A Report on the First Annual Conference on Critical Race Theory)', in *Lizard: Newsletter of the Conference on Critical Legal Studies*, November 1989, 83–5. For a decent bibliography of critical race theory, see Richard Delgado and Jean Stefancic, 'Critical Race Theory: An Annotated Bibliography', *Virginia L. Rev.*, 79 (1993), 461–516.

[465] Feminist and race theories, it should be noted, are not mutually exclusive. On shared experience between feminists and race theorists, see Kimberlé Crenshaw, 'Demarginalizing the Intersection of Race and Sex: A Black Feminist Critique of Antidiscrimination Doctrine, Feminist Theory and Antiracist Politics', *U. Chicago Legal Forum*, [1989], 139–67; Judy Scales-Trent, 'Black Women and the Constitution: Finding Our Place, Asserting Our Rights', *Harvard Civil Rights-Civil Liberties L. Rev.*, 24 (1989), 9–44; and also, more generally, Toni Morrison (ed.), *Race-ing Justice, En-gendering Power: Essays on Anita Hill, Clarence Thomas and the Construction of Social Reality* (New York: Pantheon, 1992).

[466] See Tushnet, 'Critical Legal Studies: A Political History', *supra* n. 14, 1517–18; Gary Minda, 'The Jurisprudential Movements of the 1980s', *Ohio State L.J.*, 50 (1989), 599–662 at 617; J. M. Balkin, 'Ideology as Constraint', *Stanford L. Rev.*, 43 (1991), 1133–69 at 1134.

[467] See, for example, Duncan Kennedy, 'A Cultural Pluralist Case for Affirmative Action in Legal Academia', *Duke L.J.*, [1990], 705–57; *Sexy Dressing Etc.: Essays on the Power and Politics of Cultural Identity* (Cambridge, Mass.: Harvard University Press, 1993), 34–82, 126–213; Gary Peller, 'Race Consciousness', *Duke L.J.*, [1990], 758–847. In this context, one should note also the remarkable skirmish in the 1992 *Georgetown Law Journal* between two colleagues at that law school, Mark Tushnet and Gary Peller. The skirmish was prompted by an article by Tushnet, in which he suggests that those who use stories to make points about law—critical race theorists, among others—often sacrifice narrative integrity and sound judgement in so doing. Mark Tushnet, 'The Degradation of Constitutional Discourse', *Georgetown L.J.*, 81 (1992), 251–311. Responding to this article, Peller accused Tushnet of opposing 'recent developments in critical discourse and left cultural politics' and of 'almost exclusively target[ing] people of colour'. Gary Peller, 'The Discourse of Constitutional Degradation', *Georgetown L.J.*, 81 (1992), 313–41 at 313–14. In his reply, Tushnet accuses Peller of producing 'a motivated misreading' of his thesis—the misreading, that is, of a second-generation critical legal scholar who is determined to differentiate his views from those of Tushnet and other first-generation critical legal scholars but who is also desperate not to be left behind by an emerging third generation of critical legal scholars, the critical race theorists. Mark Tushnet, 'Reply', *Georgetown L.J.*, 81 (1992), 343–50 at 344, 349–50.

Yet the relationship of feminist and critical race theories to critical legal studies seems extremely ambivalent. The critical legal studies movement has been generally eager to weave feminism and race theory into its tapestry. Many feminists and race theorists, furthermore, seem not to object to being identified with the movement. Nevertheless, it seems that there exists, between critical legal studies on the one hand and feminist and race theories on the other, a basic distinction. Critical legal studies is founded on the idea that liberal legalism is not a necessity, that it may be possible to devise an alternative set of political and legal arrangements which would command social consensus. But feminist and race theories seem to question the very notion of consensus. Legal systems, feminists and race theorists argue, ought to be premissed not on the possibility of consensus but on the reality of difference. Different groups within society tend to have different legal experiences. While the transformative agenda of the critical legal studies movement may be laudable, feminists and race theorists claim, it fails to accommodate their own experiences.[468]

Critical race theorists have emphasized this failure to appreciate differences of experience by focusing on the critical legal assault on rights discourse. While critical legal studies is to a large degree supportive of minority interests, it is argued,[469] the critical legal position on rights is antithetical to such interests. In attacking this position, race theorists have been as severe as has any other critic in portraying the critical legal enterprise as essentially naive, complacent and hypocritical. 'The attack by the Critical Legal Studies movement on rights and entitlement theory,' Robert Williams observes, 'can be seen as a counter crusade to the hard campaigns and long marches of minority peoples in this country. Minority people committed themselves to these struggles not to attain some hegemonically functioning reification leading to false consciousness, but a seat in the front of the bus, repatriation of treaty-guaranteed sacred lands,

[468] See e.g. Patricia J. Williams, *The Alchemy of Race and Rights* (Cambridge, Mass.: Harvard University Press, 1991), 149. ('[W]hile the goals of CLS and of the direct victims of racism may be much the same, what is too often missing is acknowledgment that our experiences of the same circumstances may be very different; that the same symbol may mean different things to each of us.')

[469] See, for example, Robert A. Williams, Jr., 'Taking Rights Aggressively: The Perils and Promise of Critical Legal Theory for Peoples of Color', *Law and Inequality*, 5 (1987), 103–34 at 130. ('Critical legal histories can be used to aid minority scholars in one of their most important scholarly tasks—the decoding of the apocrypha of European-derived colonial and cultural imperialist discourse.'); Richard Delgado, 'The Ethereal Scholar: Does Critical Legal Studies Have What Minorities Want?', *Harvard Civil Rights-Civil Liberties L. Rev.*, 22 (1987), 301–22 at 302–3. ('CLS challenges and decodes "Euromyths" that rule the lives of minorities and consign us to lowly fates.') For a study exploring how critical race theorists and critical legal scholars might learn from one another, see Mari J. Matsuda, 'Looking to the Bottom: Critical Legal Studies and Reparations', *Harvard Civil Rights-Civil Liberties L. Rev.*, 22 (1987), 323–99.

or a union card to carry into the grape vineyards.'[470] According to Richard Delgado, 'the average Crit . . . has little use for rights. . . . Rarely is he the victim of coercion, revilement or contempt. . . . Yet, when Crits are treated insensitively or unfairly, or are coerced into giving up something of value—such as an academic appointment in a tenure battle tinged by anti-Crit bias—they have been as quick as anyone to resort to the language of rights.'[471]

The disenchantment expressed by critical race theorists regarding the perspective of many critical legal scholars on the issue of rights reflects certain broader differences between the two groups. As compared with critical legal scholars in general, critical race theorists argue, minorities tend to experience law—as something which they teach or are taught,[472] or as something which they encounter in their lives[473]—very differently. Vaguely-articulated transformative agendas and post-liberal visions hold little appeal for them.[474] 'While Critical scholars claim that their project is concerned with domination,' furthermore, 'few have made more than a token effort to address racial domination specifically, and their work does not seem grounded in the reality of the racially oppressed.'[475] In short,

[470] Williams, *supra* n. 469, 120; also Patricia J. Williams, 'Alchemical Notes: Reconstructing Ideals From Deconstructed Rights', *Harvard Civil Rights-Civil Liberties L. Rev.*, 22 (1987), 401–33; Williams, *supra* n. 468, 153. ('For the historically disempowered, the conferring of rights is symbolic of all the denied aspects of their humanity: rights imply a respect that places one in the referential range of self and others, that elevates one's status from human body to social being. For blacks, then, the attainment of rights signifies the respectful behaviour, the collective responsibility, properly owed by a society to one of its own.')

[471] Delgado, *supra* n. 469, 305–6. More generally, see Bartholomew and Hunt, *supra* n. 390, 34–49; Price, *supra* n. 391, *passim*.

[472] See Kimberlé Williams Crenshaw, 'Foreword: Toward a Race-Conscious Pedagogy in Legal Education', *National Black L.J.*, 11 (1989), 1–14; Milner S. Ball, 'The Legal Academy and Minority Scholars', *Harvard L. Rev.*, 103 (1990), 1855–63; Robert S. Chang, 'Toward an Asian American Legal Scholarship: Critical Race Theory, Post-Structualism, and Narrative Space', *California L. Rev.*, 81 (1993), 1243–323; Jerome McCristal Culp, Jr., 'Toward a Black Legal Scholarship: Race and Original Understandings', *Duke L.J.*, [1991], 39–105.

[473] See Williams, *supra* n. 468, *passim*; 'Spirit-Murdering the Messenger: The Discourse of Fingerpointing as the Law's Response to Racism', *U. Miami L. Rev.*, 42 (1987), 127–57; Jerome McCristal Culp, Jr., 'Notes from California: Rodney King and the Race Question', *Denver Univ. L. Rev.*, 70 (1993), 199–212.

[474] See Anthony E. Cook, 'Beyond Critical Legal Studies: The Reconstructive Theology of Dr. Martin Luther King, Jr.', *Harvard L. Rev.*, 103 (1990), 985–1044; Gerald Torres, 'Critical Race Theory: The Decline of the Universalist Ideal and the Hope of Plural Justice—Some Observations and Questions of an Emerging Phenomenon', *Minnesota L. Rev.*, 75 (1991), 993–1007; Richard Delgado, 'Critical Legal Studies and the Realities of Race—Does the Fundamental Contradiction Have a Corollary?', *Harvard Civil Rights-Civil Liberties L. Rev.*, 23 (1988), 407–13; and Williams, *supra* n. 469, 122–3.

[475] Kimberlé Williams Crenshaw, 'Race, Reform, and Retrenchment: Transformation and Legitimation in Antidiscrimination Law', in Joerges and Trubek (eds.), *supra* n. 384, 255–95 at 271; and cf. Alan Freeman, 'Racism, Rights and the Quest for Equality of Opportunity: A Critical Legal Essay', *Harvard Civil Rights-Civil Liberties L. Rev.*, 23 (1988), 295–392.

critical legal studies 'seldom speaks to or about black people'.[476] It is for this reason that, in the past, critical race theorists have commented on 'their exclusion from CLS'.[477] While wishing to feature centrally in the critical legal studies movement, one such theorist observes, '[we] have circled around CLS' door in fluctuating numbers for the last ten years, always invited for tea, but rarely invited to stay for supper, lest we use the wrong intellectual fork.'[478] Critical legal scholars want to be seen to be associated with critical race theorists, it seems, but they are not especially eager to prioritize their concerns.

As compared with critical race theory, the relationship of American feminist jurisprudence to critical legal studies is different, but no less ambivalent. At certain superficial levels, feminist legal theory replicates the lessons of critical legal studies.[479] As with their critical legal counterparts, for example, some feminist legal theorists argue that post-modern or deconstructive techniques may facilitate the development of legal ethics.[480] Certain feminists have also joined in the critique of liberal rights discourse.[481] Beneath such similarities of perspective, however, rests a difference in jurisprudential strategy. Whereas, for critical legal theorists, liberal legal thought and doctrine is indeterminate, for feminist legal theorists, the purported neutrality of such thought and doctrine conceals gender bias.[482] Traditional legal case-books, feminists argue, tend

[476] Crenshaw, *supra* n. 475, 271. See also Robin D. Barnes, 'Race Consciousness: The Thematic Content of Racial Distinctiveness in Critical Race Scholarship', *Harvard L. Rev.*, 103 (1990), 1864–71 esp. 1868.

[477] José A. Bracamonte, 'Minority Critiques of the Critical Legal Studies Movement: Foreword', *Harvard Civil Rights-Civil Liberties L. Rev.*, 22 (1987), 297–9 at 299. On alleged racism within the critical legal studies movement, see the 'Statement by José Bracamonte, Richard Delgado and Gerald Torres: Minority Critique Panel, CLS Annual Meeting, Los Angeles, CA, Jan. 1987', in *Lizard: Newsletter of the Conference on Critical Legal Studies*, May 1987, 1–2.

[478] Harlon L. Dalton, 'The Clouded Prism', *Harvard Civil Rights-Civil Liberties L. Rev.*, 22 (1987), 435–47 at 439.

[479] See, in this context, Carrie Menkel-Meadow, 'Feminist Legal Theory, Critical Legal Studies, and Legal Education or "The Fem-Crits Go to Law School" ', *Jnl. Leg. Educ.*, 38 (1988), 61–85.

[480] See, especially, Mary Joe Frug, *Postmodern Legal Feminism* (New York: Routledge, 1992); and also Frances Olsen, 'Feminism, Post-modernism and Critical Legal Studies', in David Hutchinson (ed.), *University College London Working Papers* (no. 5, London: UCL, 1987), 28–34; Dennis Patterson, 'Postmodernism/Feminism/Law', *Cornell L. Rev.*, 77 (1992), 254–317; Joan C. Williams, 'Dissolving the Sameness/Difference Debate: A Post-Modern Path Beyond Essentialism in Feminist and Critical Race Theory', *Duke L.J.*, [1991], 296–323.

[481] See, in particular, Frances Olsen, 'Statutory Rape: A Feminist Critique of Rights Analysis', *Texas L. Rev.*, 63 (1984), 387–432; Martha Minow, *Making All the Difference: Inclusion, Exclusion, and American Law* (Ithaca, NY: Cornell University Press, 1990), 164–72. Compare, however, Sylvia A. Law, ' "Girls Can't be Plumbers"—Affirmative Action for Women in Construction: Beyond Goals and Quotas', *Harvard Civil Rights-Civil Liberties L. Rev.*, 24 (1989), 45–77 (feminist argument in favour of rights discourse).

[482] See, generally, Frances Olsen, 'The Sex of Law', in Kairys (ed.), *supra* n. 462, 453–67.

to be written and compiled in a manner which renders women invisible and silent.[483] The universalistic abstractions of liberal philosophy—Rawls's original position, for example—often turn out to be gender-specific.[484] Even rights themselves, it has been argued, reflect an essentially masculine view of the world. According to the educational psychologist, Carol Gilligan, whereas women tend to conceive of moral problems as problems of care and responsibility in relationships, men tend to conceive of such problems in terms of justice and rights. 'While an ethic of justice proceeds from the premiss of equality—that everyone should be treated the same—an ethic of care rests on the premiss of nonviolence—that no one should be hurt.'[485]

While it has been disputed by psychologists and feminists alike,[486] the jurisprudential significance of Gilligan's thesis rests in the fact that it indicates how liberal rights discourse might be understood in terms of gender.[487] By promoting the idea that rights are crucial for the protection of individual autonomy, Robin West argues, liberal jurisprudence fails adequately to represent more identifiably 'feminine' values such as intimacy and care.[488] Liberal jurisprudence is essentially masculine jurisprudence, in other words, because it prioritizes the distinctively male ethic of justice or rights.[489] Other feminist legal theorists develop an even more candid argument: namely, that liberal jurisprudence is masculine because liberal legal systems are masculine. 'No woman had a voice in the design of the legal institutions that rule the social order under which women, as well as men, live,' Catharine MacKinnon observes, '[n]or was the condition of women taken into account or the interests of women as a sex represented.'[490] Control of the legal system by men is perpetuated, she

[483] See, for example, Mary Joe Frug, 'Re-reading Contracts: A Feminist Analysis of a Contracts Casebook', *American Univ. L. Rev.*, 34 (1985), 1065–140.

[484] See Mari J. Matsuda, 'Liberal Jurisprudence and Abstracted Visions of Human Nature: A Feminist Critique of Rawls' Theory of Justice', *New Mexico L. Rev.*, 16 (1986), 613–30; also Deborah L. Rhode, *Justice and Gender: Sex Discrimination and the Law* (Cambridge, Mass.: Harvard University Press, 1989), 316.

[485] Carol Gilligan, *In a Different Voice: Psychological Theory and Women's Development* (Cambridge, Mass.: Harvard University Press, 1982), 174. See also Carol Gilligan and Jane Attanucci, 'Two Moral Orientations', in Carol Gilligan, Janie Victoria Ward and Jill McLean Taylor (with Betty Bardige) (eds.), *Mapping the Moral Domain: A Contribution of Women's Thinking to Psychological Theory and Education* (Cambridge, Mass.: Harvard University Press, 1988), 73–86.

[486] See, for example, Lawrence Kohlberg, *Essays on Moral Development, Volume 2: The Psychology of Moral Development* (San Francisco: Harper & Row, 1984), 338–70.

[487] For a general discussion of this point, see Isabel Marcus *et al.* 'Feminist Discourse, Moral Values, and the Law—A Conversation', *Buffalo L. Rev.*, 34 (1985), 11–87.

[488] See Robin West, 'Jurisprudence and Gender', *U. Chicago L. Rev.*, 55 (1988), 1–72.

[489] See Carrie Menkel-Meadow, 'Portia in a Different Voice: Speculations on a Women's Lawyering Process', *Berkeley Women's L.J.*, 1 (1985), 39–63 esp. 43–55.

[490] Catharine A. MacKinnon, 'Reflections on Sex Equality Under Law', *Yale L.J.*, 100 (1991), 1281–328 at 1281.

claims, through liberal legal theory and doctrine. 'Liberalism defines equality as sameness'[491]—that is, equality demands that like cases be treated alike. Yet likeness is implicitly defined in terms of maleness. 'Unquestioned is how difference is socially created or defined, who sets the point of reference for sameness. . . . Why should anyone have to be like white men to get what they have, given that white men do not have to be like anyone except each other to have it?'[492] While the liberal definition of equality is supposed to be generally applicable and acceptable, it is in fact inimical to the interests of women, since it fails to account for their values and experiences. 'Liberal legalism,' MacKinnon concludes, since it embraces this definition of equality as sameness, operates as 'a medium for making male dominance both invisible and legitimate.'[493]

So, what of critical legal studies? Feminist legal theorists in the United States clearly recognize that critical legal scholars are similarly disaffected with liberal legalism.[494] Like critical race theorists, however, feminists have tended to be suspicious of critical legal studies. '[N]o matter how much gratitude we might feel towards institutional CLS for the insights it has offered,' Robin West claims, 'it is nevertheless an institution within which we work from a position of relative disempowerment.'[495] For feminist legal theorists, this sense of marginalization is attributable primarily to the fact that critical legal studies, like liberal jurisprudence, fails sufficiently to take into account women's experiences, values and concerns.[496] Echoing critical race theorists, certain feminists argue that the visionary dimension of critical legal studies—the belief that liberalism can be transcended—is particularly problematic. 'Most critical theory that has attempted to construct alternative visions,' Deborah Rhode observes, 'assumes away the problems with which feminists have been most concerned or opens itself to the same challenges of indeterminacy that it

[491] Catharine A. MacKinnon, *Feminism Unmodified: Discourses on Life and Law* (Cambridge, Mass.: Harvard University Press, 1987), 22.

[492] MacKinnon, *supra* n. 490, 1287.

[493] Catharine A. MacKinnon, *Toward a Feminist Theory of the State* (Cambridge, Mass.: Harvard University Press, 1989), 237. On MacKinnon's work generally, see Emily Jackson, 'Catharine MacKinnon and Feminist Jurisprudence: A Critical Appraisal', *Jnl. Law & Soc.*, 19 (1992), 195–213.

[494] See Deborah L. Rhode, 'Feminist Critical Theories', in Patricia Smith (ed.), *Feminist Jurisprudence* (New York: Oxford University Press, 1993), 594–609 at 599–603.

[495] Robin West, 'Deconstructing the CLS-Fem Split', *Wisconsin Women's L.J.*, 2 (1986), 85–92 at 85.

[496] For a discussion, from a legal perspective, of these experiences, values and concerns, see Robin L. West, 'The Difference in Women's Hedonic Lives: A Phenomenological Critique of Feminist Legal Theory', *Wisconsin Women's L.J.*, 3 (1987), 81–145. In West's view, this criticism is just as applicable to neo-classical law and economics as it is to critical legal studies. See Robin West, 'Economic Man and Literary Woman: One Contrast', *Mercer L. Rev.*, (1988), 867–78.

has directed at other work.'[497] According to West, the Ungerian vision of post-liberal society seems not to encompass feminine experience. '[T]he Ungerian ideal', she claims, 'is a world in which contexts are there to be shattered—not understood, appreciated, interpenetrated or infused with an ethic of care'; a world which 'exclude[s] the emotional and subjective root of many women's, and more than a few men's, aspirational and moral lives.'[498]

Feminists and critical race theorists appear, then, to share a similar sense of disquiet regarding the purpose of critical legal studies. While critical legal scholars have attacked the quest for consensus which has dominated post-realist American jurisprudence, their transformative agenda, feminists and critical race theorists argue, betrays their faith in the possibility of a society founded on some sort of alternative consensus. Yet this new society, with its alternative consensus, would not necessarily fare any better than does liberal legalism in accommodating the experiences, values and concerns of women and minority groups. Taken together, feminist jurisprudence and critical race theory may be read as a call for an end to the quest for consensus. But it is not yet clear how, or to what degree, American academic lawyers will respond to this call.[499] The drift and the patterns of American jurisprudence in the future will depend on how the present comes to be interpreted as history.

[497] Rhode, *supra* n. 494, 605.

[498] Robin West, 'Feminism, Critical Social Theory and Law', *U. Chicago Legal Forum*, [1989], 59-97 at 81.

[499] Reflections on what the future might hold are to be found in the forthcoming book by Minda, *supra* n. 75, 333–457.

Index